THE STRENGTH OF THE HILLS

THE STRENGTH
OF THE HILLS

Middlebury College, 1915–1990

━━►◦◄━━

David M. Stameshkin

MIDDLEBURY COLLEGE PRESS

Published by University Press of New England

Hanover and London

Middlebury College Press
Published by University Press of New England, Hanover, NH 03755
© 1996 by the President and Fellows of Middlebury College
Printed in the United States of America
5 4 3 2 1
CIP data appear at the end of the book

Cosponsored by the Middlebury College Bicentennial Commission

Front endpaper: New York Alumni gather in January 1941 as America edges closer to war. *Back endpaper*: First year orientation for the Class of 1994, the final class admitted during Olin Robison's presidency. Photo by Panorama International, West Newton, MA.

To Anne Miriam and Elizabeth Lee

CONTENTS

List of Tables ix

Foreword xi

Acknowledgments xiii

Introduction xv

PART I
The College Endures Wars and a Depression,
1915–1945

CHAPTER 1
John Thomas and the Great War, 1915–1921 5

CHAPTER 2
Paul Moody and College Growth, 1921–1942 22

CHAPTER 3
Coeducation at Middlebury, 1921–1941 36

CHAPTER 4
Culture and Curriculum: Educational Change, 1915–1941 47

CHAPTER 5
The Impact of World War II, 1940–1945 69

PART II
The Growth of the Modern College,
1945–1990

CHAPTER 6
The Stratton Years: Faculty and Curricular Concerns, 1945–1963 85

CHAPTER 7
The Stratton Years: Physical Growth, 1945–1963   103

CHAPTER 8
The Armstrong Years, 1963–1975   118

CHAPTER 9
The Robison Years, 1975–1990   146

PART III
A Social History of Campus Life,
1915–1990

CHAPTER 10
The Student Body   185

CHAPTER 11
Fraternities   215

CHAPTER 12
Social and Extracurricular Life   243

CHAPTER 13
Athletics   270

CHAPTER 14
Student Involvement: College Governance and the World Outside 294

CHAPTER 15
". . . And a Cast of Thousands"   321

Notes   353

Bibliography   423

Index   433

TABLES

1. Student Enrollment, 1908–1921   7
2. Student Enrollment, 1921–1941   29
3. Student Enrollment, 1945–1963   87
4. Student Enrollment, 1963–1975   121
5. Language Schools—Total Enrollment by Session, 1972–1986   154
6. Major Donations to Middlebury College $60-Million Campaign, 1984–1989   173
7. Enrollment, by Gender, 1972–1990   200
8. Home Regions of Middlebury Students, 1915–1985   201
9. Comprehensive Fee Increases, 1979–1990   213

FOREWORD

History, wrote Thucydides, is "philosophy teaching by example." If higher education in the United States has, in the past two hundred years, developed a coherent philosophy, it is the product of such examples as that offered in the pages that follow. The residential liberal arts college can indeed be said to have contributed to, and drawn from, a philosophy that character is shaped and leadership developed where the life of the mind is lived. Graduates of Middlebury College, some twenty-one thousand of whom now carry the mark of their alma mater, offer living testimony to this simple truth.

The first volume of Middlebury's history, which covered the years 1800–1915, bore the appropriate title, *The Town's College*. For much of the college's first century, its fortunes rose and fell with those of the town. As its second century dawned, Middlebury stood poised on the brink of rapid growth and significant change.

The present volume carries the narrative forward through much of the twentieth century. Though still much a part of the town and owing much of its identity to its glorious setting and to those Vermont traits of persistence and tenacity that carried it through many troubled times, the college after 1915 would become more and more an international institution. Indeed, though Middlebury in the year 2000 may not yet be the world's college, it is very much a college whose reach and reputation now extend around the globe.

This increasing worldliness lies, I believe, at the heart of the story that follows and gives that story shape and direction. Drawn inexorably into this "real world" of excitement, risk, and change, the college would see its enrollment grow in numbers and diversity, its faculty increase in size and stature, and its reputation expand into new areas. Always pressed to find resources to meet new challenges and opportunities, the college would find in a succession of remarkable presidents, extraordinarily gifted faculty and staff, and generous alumni and friends a vision raised to more distant horizons and a resolve to match the vision.

Though each reader will find his or her own moments of edification, all who read this story will be impressed by its human elements: the repeated efforts to make long-range plans and the inevitable reconsideration and recasting of those plans, the steady growth of the college and the accompanying stresses and tensions that result from its increased prosperity and complexity, the steadfast loyalty of the college's extended family and the remarkable sensitivity of alumni to the institution's remembered past, the singular resilience of the college in moments of crisis, and the boldness of the college's leadership in promoting adaptation to changing times in the spirit of Gamaliel Painter, Cyrus Hamlin, Ezra Brainerd, and John Thomas.

Middlebury College approaches its third century, then, aware of the responsibilities of global citizenship and prepared to educate its students to those responsibilities. Thanks to David Stameshkin, we are aware, too, of the past that has shaped us and challenges us to teach, by our own example, the philosophy that has made us what we are.

John M. McCardell, Jr.
President

ACKNOWLEDGMENTS

I have been writing a history of Middlebury College for over two decades, and, for the most part, I researched both this book and the first volume simultaneously. Therefore, with a few exceptions, the acknowledgments for the first volume are applicable to this book as well, and, because I do not wish to repeat them all, I urge the reader to consult the earlier volume for a more complete listing. For example, space does not allow me to thank all of the Middlebury faculty, staff, administrators, alumni, and students who have assisted me over the years, but I would like to mention a few.

First, Presidents James Armstrong and Olin Robison allowed me full access to all relevant documents and gave me numerous opportunities to interview them personally. Robert Buckeye and Kay Lauster guided me through the special collections of the Middlebury College Library and always let me know when new materials had been accessioned. Walter Brooker, the late Reginald "Doc" Cook, Nicholas Clifford, and John McCardell reviewed earlier drafts and provided very useful advice.

I had several research assistants, but it was particularly Deborah Clifford, a fine biographer and historian, who, many years ago, assisted me with this second volume.

As with the first volume, my friend and former colleague, Bill Catton, was kind enough to edit the entire manuscript. Once again, he was able to cut down significantly on my excess verbiage and offer numerous suggestions for making the manuscript more coherent, concise, and readable.

Ron Nief and Will Melton have coordinated the publication efforts at Middlebury in fine fashion, and Erik Borg was particularly helpful in selecting the pictures that appear in the book. Mary Crittendon, of the University Press of New England, has been a kind and careful editor, and I am very grateful to her.

Finally, I wish to thank my family, particularly my wife, Colleen, for putting up with this project for the past two decades. The first volume was dedicated to her. This book is dedicated to my teenage daughters, Anne and Elizabeth, who both show promise of becoming writers and have, for many years, expressed their great appreciation of my manuscript with such helpful comments as: "Daddy, is that *still* the same book you were working on when I was a baby?"

December 1995   D.M.S

INTRODUCTION

The College like the individual is the expression of its heredity and its environment. The basic characteristics of an old college are slow to change. The stability of purpose in that group of lawyers, doctors, farmers which met in 1800 as the first Middlebury trustees, the prayer meetings in the 1830's, the harsh Vermont winters and the strength of hills, the resolve of Labaree and the perseverance of Thomas, are in the texture of Middlebury and will remain inextricably there. For long periods the environs have sheltered booms in lumber, wool, and marble industries; the face has changed, but the contours remain essentially the same, imparting to the internal structure as much as mountains and valley can, in strength, soberness, and permanence.

> —W. Storrs Lee '28, *Father Went to College*
> (New York, 1936), 238

I know how thoroughly these granite hills, the hard winters, the sweet days of spring in these parts work their way into your spirits and stay with you for your life. You will miss them, you will be drawn back to them. They will never let you go, not quite. And that is good. There is tough simplicity to this land, which measures the soul and imparts moral strength. Take it with you.

> —David Shipler, "How Will You Answer to
> Your Children?" the 1988 Commencement
> address at Middlebury College, reprinted in
> *Middlebury College Magazine*, 62 (summer
> 1988): 45

> Up here we've had the mountains and the sky
> And all that clear clean rush of mountain air.
> These filled our lives
> And made for nothing but the good . . .
> > —From Esther Spooner's Class Poem of 1925,
> > reprinted in *Middlebury College Magazine*, 63
> > (summer 1989): 58

"The Strength of the Hills is His Also." Most Middlebury alumni remember that those words from the Ninety-fifth Psalm appear on the front of Mead Chapel. It is one of the themes of this book that the mountainous beauty that surrounds and graces Middlebury—the strength of the hills—has also been a major factor in the remarkable success of Middlebury College in the twentieth century.

This volume chronicles the history of Middlebury since 1915—the year in which the mountains truly began to affect the fortunes of the college in a positive way. In 1915, Joseph Battell—eccentric conservationist, lover of Morgan horses, wealthy town philanthropist, amateur scientist, innkeeper, and newspaper editor—died and left the college his Green Mountain kingdom of thirty thousand acres of virgin timber, which he had lovingly bought piece by piece to protect the land from lumber interests. Over the years a few acres of his unique gift were utilized to establish several of the institutions that have distinguished Middlebury from many other private liberal arts colleges in the Northeast: the Bread Loaf School of English, the Bread Loaf Writers' Conference, and the Snow Bowl.

Also in 1915, Fraulein Lilian Stroebe, professor of German at Vassar, decided that the college had the ideal physical plant and summer climate to accommodate her two-year-old German summer school. This school, highly unusual in its emphasis on isolation, advanced training, and intensiveness, has grown over the past eighty years into the famous Middlebury College Foreign Language Schools. When people think of Middlebury, many of them think "languages." Without the mountains, the Middlebury language schools would most likely never have been.

People who visit Middlebury have been strongly affected by the environment of the campus. Indeed, some students, trying to decide which of several good colleges to attend, enrolled at Middlebury in part because of the autumns, the winters, the snow, the beauty of the hills. The story goes that when the trustees were searching for a successor to President Samuel Stratton (1943–1963), they invited their first choice, James I. Armstrong, to visit Middlebury. At the end of the stay, Armstrong was driven on back roads across the mountains to Montpelier in the dead of winter by a trustee. "It was one of those clear, moonlit winter nights," the trustee recalled, and the trip "was sort of a turning point" in persuading Armstrong to take the job. As they crossed the mountains, Armstrong said, "I think I am beginning to see what you mean about this Vermont atmosphere."[1] Armstrong was president from 1963 to 1975.

It was not always that way. Indeed, the hills helped keep Middlebury isolated, poor, small, and unknown during much of the nineteenth century. The winters were difficult and long. And Middlebury was hard to reach—geographically and psychologically—even though the railroad went right through town. The rage for skiing, which grew with a frenzy after World War II, changed much of that. In addition, accelerating urban development surrounded many erstwhile rural institutions; Americans looking for a true country environment discovered Middlebury. The college, isolated and clean, with its mountain skiing just minutes away, now beckoned to people. In short, the strength of the hills set the school apart, gave it unique characteristics, and helped ensure its remarkable progress and success in the twentieth century.

Sounds interesting, right? Now for a confession. This is the second volume, and in many ways—I know I'm not supposed to say this—I enjoyed writing the first volume, *The Town's College: Middlebury College, 1800-1915*, more. Although trained as a historian, I am a frustrated actor and dramatist, and *The Town's College* was consciously written as a dramatic work of nonfiction. It had a hopeful and exciting *beginning* as the townspeople of late-eighteenth-century Middlebury struggled and connived to found a college on the Vermont frontier and then nurtured it through the first four decades of growth and success; a nearly tragic *middle* period in which the school, with few pupils and fewer prospects, nearly disappeared several times between 1840 and 1881; and a Hollywood *ending* in which several key individuals made critical decisions (such as admitting women in 1883) that saved the college and enabled it to develop into a relatively large and successful institution by 1915. Beginning, middle, and end: Aristotle would have approved the form, if not the content.

This second volume, on the other hand, aside from some rather unusual moments during and after both world wars, is more of a linear progression, as Middlebury grows increasingly larger and wealthier and gradually becomes one of the finest educational institutions in the world. I am very happy for the college, but the plot doesn't play particularly well on the feverish stage of my imagination.

I liked the first volume more for other reasons, too. First, I am an early American historian by training. I am used to spending many hours contemplating what various eighteenth-century figures may have thought about a certain subject or why they acted in a certain way or what they meant by certain passages in their letters. I also like visiting graveyards—I can ask questions of the people buried there and develop creative answers without any interference from them. I wrote the first volume primarily from written sources (and accompanying voices from the graveyards), and I allowed myself the usual excitement of reading into them what I thought the sources would bear. To me, that's what history is all about.

But this second volume is very different. Many of the people about whom I wrote are still alive, and as my friends will tell you, I hate to hurt people. Writing about the living is not easy (I guess I never could be a journalist) because the living are available as sources, and I had to learn the art of interviewing them, as well as the more difficult task of how to figure out whether to take what they said at face value. Of course, written sources are also of dubious value, but I am more accustomed to working with them.

Another difficulty I found in the second volume was the sheer number of sources. In fact, I could probably have spent the rest of my life trying to read all of the files, papers, and notes related to the history of Middlebury between 1915 and 1990 and never come close to finishing them. For the first volume there was much less to look at, and I felt that I did a pretty good job of finding whatever there was and analyzing each document thoroughly. I do not have that feeling here. I have read perhaps a hundred times as many documents, letters, newspapers, magazines, alumni notes, files, and reports for this volume as I did for the earlier one (I am not exaggerating), and I feel sometimes that I have not read them with the care they deserve, that I have not done my job well enough, that I was not up to the task. This feeling stems from the fact that most early American historians are accustomed to reading a relatively small quantity of written materials very carefully.

Finally, those who write about the present and the recent past are limited by a lack of perspective. I have this vague uneasiness that almost anything I have written about the period after World War II (and particularly the years since 1975) is flawed in this regard. There are undoubtedly important issues (as defined by the historian who writes about this period in the year 2025) that I am missing or misjudging because not enough time has elapsed to let me see things in the proper light.

Now that I have revealed all the reasons I liked writing and researching the first volume better than the one you have in your hands, perhaps I should describe briefly some of the interesting, even exciting things about this book (before you stop reading it and send it back for a refund). This volume is divided into three parts. The first, consisting of chapters 1-5, is an analysis of the administrative history of the college from 1915 to 1945. In this section I attempt to chronicle the effect of two world wars and the Great Depression. Against that backdrop, I also describe Middlebury's growth and development in the interwar period, some of the fund-raising efforts during the presidencies of John Thomas (1908-1921) and Paul Moody (1921-1942), curricular changes, and the college's somewhat awkward attempts to define its coeducational character.

The second part, chapters 6-9, deals with administrative history from 1945 to 1990. Many of the same issues—fund-raising, curriculum, new buildings—are central to this section. The college continues to grow in wealth, students, faculty, buildings, and acreage. However, the backdrop is different. Increased national interest and investment in higher education, beginning with the GI Bill, give a stronger impetus to the development of excellence, and the college emerges as one of the finest liberal arts colleges in the country. The stormy administration of Samuel Stratton (1943-1963), during which the faculty attempted to force his ouster, is the subject of chapters 6 and 7; the successful presidencies of James I. Armstrong (1963-1975) and Olin C. Robison (1975-1990) are analyzed in chapters 8 and 9.

Part III (chapters 10-15) is my attempt to write a social history of the college (with an emphasis on students): many of the truly revolutionary transformations in campus life between 1915 and 1990 are analyzed. Until 1945, for example, campus social life revolved around the fraternities, and class traditions were a significant part of college life. The women's college, composed of students who were generally superior in academic ability and economic status to the men, was dominated by sororities, circumscribed by tight parietal hours, and characterized by a lack of social and political power in an unequal (and unrealized) coordinate educational system. Still, required daily chapel and intercollegiate athletics helped unify the predominantly white, Protestant, middle-class students (most of whom were from New England and New York) into a tight-knit, rather homogeneous and relatively unsophisticated community.

In the four decades after 1950, the college was fundamentally altered. The changes were gradual at first, but the pace accelerated after 1960, and by 1990 important aspects of college life bore little resemblance to those of forty years earlier. The reasons were varied but often related: an increased enrollment from 800 to 1,900 under Presidents Stratton and Armstrong, a growing emphasis on academic quality and a concomitant increase in costs, a commitment to equal facilities and opportunities for women (particularly under Armstrong and Robison), and the changing social mores and growing privatism of students. All of these factors contributed to the decline of fraternities after 1965, the end of required chapel in the 1950s, a lessening of interest in class traditions, a growing student involvement in college governance, the increasing wealth and continued homogeneity of the student body, the disappearance of sororities and women's parietal hours, and the creation of a more truly coeducational college. In addition, concerted efforts to diversify in the 1980s led to the matriculation of growing numbers of African-American, Hispanic, international, and rural American students. In the final chapter, ". . . And a Cast of Thousands," I analyze some of the changes in the lives of faculty, staff, and administrators; student–faculty relations; the activities of alumni; and, returning to a major theme of the first volume, town–gown relations.

PART I

THE COLLEGE ENDURES WARS AND A DEPRESSION, 1915–1945

⇒•◄⇐

Higher education began to play a prominent role in the development of American society during World War I. Between 1915 and 1940 it experienced unprecedented change and growth. For the first time young people looked primarily to education as the avenue to economic and social mobility, businessmen and professionals looked to the college for its talent and its stamp of legitimacy, and society looked to the university for the benefits of its research. This was a time of skyrocketing enrollments and admissions quotas, of new practical courses of study and selective honors programs, of federal financial assistance and social snobbery, of trend-setting fraternity life and sophisticated scientific research. The developments that education has undergone since World War II could not have taken place in the absence of the emotional debates on mission, curriculum, and admissions which stirred the campuses in the 1920s and 1930s.

> —David O. Levine, *The American College and the Culture of Aspiration, 1915–1940* (Ithaca, N.Y., 1986), 13–14

A considerable part of me is there in Middlebury and always will be. They could take me out of Middlebury, but they could not take Middlebury out of me.

> —Paul D. Moody to W. Storrs Lee, November 21, 1944, in Lee's possession

Every detail of our college life is being focused on the dual but inseparable purpose—of fitting young men and women to give their maximum service in winning this war, and in creating a stable peace thereafter. . . . Some day this war will be over. We must not allow this present generation of students to return to a peace-time world, their life career sabotaged, their real talents untrained, their best service to civilization spoiled by our short-sightedness. So we are saying to them, proceed with your long-run plan for your life, but make a place in your program for doing your duty in the present emergency.
        —Stephen A. Freeman, "As the Year Begins," *MCNL*
    17 (September 1942): 7

The outside world pressed in on Middlebury College between 1915 and 1945 as it never had before, and the effects of these intrusions were, for the most part, unfortunate. Two wars and an economic depression slowed college growth and disrupted college life for much of the thirty-year period. Except for a small endowment drive during World War I, it was only during the relatively prosperous 1920s and a brief period just before American entry into World War II that the college was able to expand its permanent fund or physical plant. At the same time, more young Americans began to attend college after World War I, and Middlebury, along with most other comparable schools, expanded its enrollment significantly. Nonetheless, for most of this period Middlebury was strapped for money; in particular, it could not finance its post-1918 commitment to separate the men and women and establish a coordinate educational system like those at Barnard–Columbia and Radcliffe–Harvard.

Although growth moved forward at a less spectacular pace between 1915 and 1945 than during the early years of President John Thomas (1908–1915), Middlebury did expand gradually, almost in spite of itself. President Paul D. Moody (1921–1942), Thomas's successor, stressed "quality" over "quantity," and repeatedly claimed that the aim of the college was not to expand but to seek excellence. Yet under Thomas and Moody, endowment grew from $561,453 in 1915 to $4,250,000 in 1942; and enrollment more than doubled, from 343 to 785. The larger enrollment placed additional pressure on existing facilities, although five new buildings (along with two new library wings and a new community hospital) helped ease the overcrowding problem. The other major area of growth and change during these years was the founding and development of innovative summer programs in languages, English, and writing.

Although Part I opens with the story of the final years of the Thomas administration and concludes with the description of the first two years of President Samuel Stratton's tenure (1943-1963), the major figure of this period was the urbane and witty Paul D. Moody. No other Middlebury president ever earned the love of his students and faculty as Moody did. His forced resignation in 1942 (due in part to the effects of the Depression and World War II) hurt Moody deeply, angered a number of faculty, and left lingering problems for the next administration. His successor, Samuel Stratton, has been credited with "saving" the school in 1943-1945 by arranging for a V-12 unit to train at the college and take the place of Middlebury's male undergraduates, most of whom had left to fight in the war. Indeed, Middlebury's struggle with two world wars and the Depression provides the central theme for Part I.

CHAPTER 1

JOHN THOMAS AND THE GREAT WAR, 1915-1921

Middlebury College, through the activities of President Thomas, in a new and peculiar sense has been put upon the educational map of New England and has gained wide and enviable recognition as an institution of sound learning, clean morals, and worthy ideals.
> —Middlebury College Board of Trustees,
> Corporation Minutes, vol. 3, pp. 148-49

Without uniforms and armed with sticks they drill around the campus five afternoons a week, and a competent observer told me that in some respects they excel any company of the Vermont National Guard. . . . Of course we cannot keep on permanently without something in the way of equipment.
> —President John Thomas to A. Barton
> Hepburn, April 25, 1917, Thomas Papers, MCA

I am pretty well convinced that the College will be swamped by girls who will utilize all additional facilities that we may be able to obtain. . . . The determination not to admit girls in 1920 would be a drastic step, but it certainly would solve all questions and perhaps most satisfactorily. To continue a coeducational institution will, I fear, by degrees, but eventually, make it a college for women. A compromise might be to organize a college for women with a separate Board of Trustees, like Barnard and Radcliffe, working with Middlebury sharing recitation rooms and other facilities until growth and progress enabled each to stand on its own foundation.
> —A. Barton Hepburn '71 to President John
> Thomas '90, November 6, 1919, Thomas
> Papers, MCA

President John Thomas, class of 1890, set the course of the college for the twentieth century. He improved the quality of the faculty, insisted that they be paid appropriately for their work, founded the summer language program, enlarged the college, and found generous benefactors to help pay for his changes. He stands with the college's first dean, Walter E. Howard, class of 1871, on his right.

In his last six years as president, John Thomas (1908–1921) attempted to build upon the admirable accomplishments of his first seven. In particular, he initiated two fund-raising drives to increase endowment and thereby raise faculty salaries. Unfortunately, American's entrance into World War I in 1917 and the war's aftermath significantly influenced events at Middlebury and often diverted Thomas's energies from his principal goals of upgrading the college's finances and determining its stance toward coeducation.

If presidential success were measured solely on the basis of the growth and improvement of a college's physical facilities, then John Thomas would probably rank as Middlebury's greatest president. His first seven years had witnessed the construction of Pearsons, McCullough, Mead Chapel, Hepburn, and Chemistry, as well as the acquisition of key parcels of land for future expansion. Yet Thomas still desired additional buildings for Middlebury in 1915. An infirmary was needed, with the nearest hospital thirty-five miles away in Burlington; a new recitation hall would ease the overcrowded condition of the humanities departments and allow the growing num-

TABLE I
Student Enrollment, 1908–1921

Year	Men	Women	Total
1908–1909	115	107	222
1909–1910	125	131	256
1910–1911	142	133	275
1911–1912	158	147	305
1912–1913	173	147	320
1913–1914	176	151	327
1914–1915	175	164	339
1915–1916	187	156	343
1916–1917	203	169	372
1917–1918	135	151	286
1918–1919	160[a]	159	319
1919–1920	200	187	387
1920–1921	209	224	433

[a] Ninety-nine of the 160 men in 1918–1919 were in the SATC the first term. All figures are for fall-term enrollment and are based on numbers listed in the original type script, Middlebury Attendance Records, 1800–1951, Middlebury College Archives.

ber of scattered administrative offices to be housed together in Old Chapel; and the increasing student body (see Table 1) required more dormitory facilities.[1]

On the other hand, Thomas reluctantly admitted that an even greater deficiency was the college's paltry endowment and its corollary, low faculty salaries. While Williams, Bowdoin, Amherst, and Wesleyan each had endowments of between $2 million and $3 million and an annual endowment income per student of between $213 and $297, Middlebury's endowment was a mere $566,000, earning only $76 per student. Furthermore, most good New England colleges were paying their full professors $3,000 or more, while Middlebury could afford a maximum salary of only $2,000.[2] Even worse, many faculty members who had served for six years or more as assistant professors were paid only between $1,200 and $1,600, and there was not enough money to promote them. Thomas complained that he could not retain the better teachers under such conditions and somberly predicted that the school was doomed to a mediocre teaching corps without increased faculty compensation.[3] Although most students were thrilled by the growth of the college under Thomas,[4] even they began to complain about the competence of their professors. "On the score of the faculty," J. Glenn Anderson '15 told the trustees, "I feel we are placing emphasis upon building at the expense of an efficient instructing force. The personality of the men is, in the whole, pleasing, but as teachers many of them rank very low." [5]

Between 1913 and 1917, Thomas had failed to win Carnegie Foundation support for proposed fund-raising efforts aimed at increasing the endowment.[6] Finally, A. Barton Hepburn once again lent a munificent hand. Hepburn, the president of the Chase Bank, had attended the college for several years in the late 1860s. A strong supporter, he had given several hundred thousand dollars to Middlebury before World War I, including $115,000 in 1915 to construct the men's residence hall that bears his name. This time he pledged $100,000 in April 1917 if Thomas could raise another $200,000 by July 1, 1918; all $300,000 would be added to the college's endowment. Thomas gratefully accepted the offer. "What Middlebury owes and will owe to you can never be expressed," Thomas wrote. "Whenever kind things are said of my work in connection with the recent progress of the institution, I always feel an inner protest that the recognition should go to you instead of me." [7]

With characteristic energy and dedication, Thomas set out to secure the $300,000. He assigned the popular assistant dean, Edgar "Cap" Wiley '13, to organize campaign committees and traveled himself to the Midwest and to several eastern cities in search of funds.[8] After the United States entered the war in April 1917, Thomas pleaded with alumni and friends of the college, stating that the decrease in male enrollment due to the war made the endowment drive even more important.[9] With many Americans investing their savings in Liberty Bonds to help finance the war effort, at Thomas's urging the Middlebury students subscribed for a $1,000 liberty bond and presented it to the college for the endowment drive. Thomas quickly hit upon the idea of asking other people to buy Liberty Bonds and give them to the Middlebury fund, thus serving both college and country. The idea proved popular, and they named it the Liberty Endowment Drive.[10]

By late January 1918, Thomas had raised only half of the $200,000 he needed to meet Hepburn's conditional demand, and he once again turned to the Carnegie Foundation's General Education Board for help. The board rewarded him for his perseverance by agreeing on March 2 to give $75,000 toward the Liberty Endowment Fund if the goal were increased to $400,000. In other words, Thomas had to raise $225,000 to earn the $175,000 in conditional offers made by

Hepburn and the Board.[11] He accepted the challenge and received several healthy contributions from Vermont residents and alumni in the closing weeks.[12] Although Thomas claimed that the fund was $23,000 short of the goal on June 19, the drive went over the top ten days later, and eventually more than $428,000 was raised.[13] During the next six months, the maximum faculty salary was increased from $2,000 to $2,500, and the impact of wartime inflation on many professors was eased somewhat.[14]

Notwithstanding the success of the Liberty Endowment Drive, World War I did not generally work to Middlebury's advantage. Indeed, during the eighteen months of American participation, male attendance dropped, draft uncertainties negatively affected academic life, and college activities were circumscribed. By the end of the war, the campus resembled less a college than a military camp.

The war fever struck Middlebury on February 16, 1917, when the men of the college met and decided to form a military company under the direction of Professor Raymond McFarland. After the United States declared war on April 6, Middlebury tried to establish a unit of the Federal Officers Reserve Training Corps but was turned down due to a shortage of training officers.[15] Thomas quickly managed to secure a lieutenant from Norwich University (Northfield, Vt.) to act as drillmaster and was pleased with the results: "The interest of the students has been remarkable," he told Hepburn. "Without uniforms and armed with sticks they drill around the campus five afternoons a week, and a competent observer told me that in some respects they excel any company of the Vermont National Guard. . . . Of course we cannot keep on permanently without something in the way of equipment." [16]

Some of the men wanted more than just drills, and when an aggressive group of naval reserve recruiting officers appeared on campus in early April to recruit men for the "mosquito fleet" (the converted private yachts that were to protect American shores from German submarines), they signed up fifty eager Middlebury men.[17] Thomas, who was trying to keep the men in college as long as possible (for the sake of the school and, to some extent, to assist in determining how each individual could contribute most effectively to the war effort), was upset at such recruiting methods.[18] Still, before classes ended in the spring of 1917, nearly one-third of the

Middlebury's battalion of the Vermont Volunteer Militia double-timed in front of the recently completed Chemistry Building.

male students had left college, the largest number of them to work on farms.[19]

Although the campus calmed down later in the term, the military frenzy began again that fall after the students returned from summer vacation. One hundred college men successfully petitioned the governor in November for the establishment at Middlebury of a unit of the Vermont Volunteer Militia, which had taken the place of the federalized Vermont National Guard. A Middlebury battalion was organized on January 30, 1918, with two companies of fifty men each under the direction of Professor McFarland, who was appointed a major. Finally, the men had the uniforms, guns, and official military status they had desired for nearly a year.[20]

While the students were excited over the war and the formation of the battalion, World War I and its aftermath had a generally deleterious effect. Enrollment in the fall of 1917 was down to 292, 80 less than the previous year, and Starr Hall was closed due to the lack of men on campus. Thomas and Professor Frank Cady engaged in an almost frantic campaign to attract more students and to encourage those now in the service to return to Middlebury after the war.[21] Sports teams and some student groups had difficulty finding enough men to perform effectively, school dances and activities were canceled or drastically curtailed, the German Club (Deutscher Verein) was forced "to use its influence against the growing intolerance toward everything German," students had difficulty concentrating on their studies, and the college year ended more than a month early.[22] Understandably, people were preoccupied with the war effort, and some student groups turned their attention in that direction. The YMCA and YWCA helped form a War Service Committee in April 1917, which sent letters, newspapers, comfort kits, and Christmas boxes to Middlebury students in uniform; other groups, such as the Women's Civics Club, performed similar services.[23]

By early summer, since it was clear that few men would be entering American colleges, the government adopted a policy of training men at various colleges for military service. On August 19, 1918, Middlebury College was approved by the War Department's Committee on Education and Special Training for the establishment of a unit of the Students' Army Training Corps (SATC). The government was to pay SATC students $30 a month plus tuition, room, and board.[24] This greatly pleased Thomas, who had feared mass withdrawal of male students. "It is the greatest thing that ever happened for the American college boy," he wrote enthusiastically.[25] The college was quickly transformed into an army base of sorts, and the curriculum changed drastically to include numerous military courses. Returning students and faculty tried to take the changes in stride, but it was obvious that the college had sacrificed much of its educational character to stay alive.[26]

The SATC experience quickly turned into a disaster. The students had barely arrived in the fall of 1918 when a devastating influenza epidemic broke out among the men. Although two hundred were taken ill, only two died, thanks to the untiring work of Dr. Stanton S. Eddy of Middlebury and a group of other doctors and nurses from nearby communities. The epidemic brought military and academic work to a near standstill during October.[27] The war ended on November 11, and the short-lived SATC was slowly demobilized.[28] Since most of the men admitted to the Middlebury unit could not qualify (financially or academically) for regular admission at the beginning of the next term, only 99 of the 294 men who fought "the battle of Middlebury" remained to begin the process of "Reconstruction."[29]

During World War II the college would once again compensate for the loss of male students by serving as a training center for the military. However, the V-12 unit stationed at Middlebury in the 1940s had a longer and much more successful life than the ill-fated SATC.[30]

The postwar period—a brief orgy of right-wing reaction, political conformity, and intolerance throughout the United States (sometimes called "The Big Red Scare")—found Middlebury College embroiled in an unfortunate and disheartening episode that resulted in the resignation of a popular history professor and the dismissal of the campus newspaper's student editor.[31]

In the late fall of 1919, each college trustee received a one-page letter from an anonymous writer.[32] Although at least four trustees were incensed that such a letter should have been written, others apparently wanted Thomas to reassure them that Middlebury professors were not using their classrooms to "propagate radicalism."[33] One trustee, Charles M. Swift, after reading a letter of history professor Henry W. Lawrence to the *Middlebury Register* concerning American labor problems, commented to Thomas: "In my opinion, Professor Lawrence ought to change his views or his habitat."[34] Lawrence, who held three degrees from Yale, including the Ph.D., had come to Middlebury from Dartmouth in 1917. He became a highly regarded and respected instructor, and his religious and moral conduct had been unimpeachable: active in the local Congregational church and the YMCA and a prominent member of several important college committees.[35] Considered a most effective teacher, he called himself a liberal in politics—arguing for instance, that the numerous strikes that beset the United States after the war should not be crushed but rather that capital and labor should work together to develop a reasonable and fair relationship.[36]

In his controversial *Middlebury Register* letter, though, Professor Lawrence may have jeopardized his case somewhat by casually utilizing analogies that placed the French Revolution in a favorable light. Postwar America took a dim view of revolutions. Summoned to Thomas's office in late November, Lawrence was shown Swift's ominous letter and was then reassured that the president could probably persuade the board not to take any action against him.[37] The slight, thirty-eight-year-old professor was understandably upset. He became increasingly concerned after learning during several private meetings in December that, although Thomas supported him completely, the final decision regarding his future rested with the trustees. When Lawrence received an offer to teach at the Roxbury School in Cheshire, Connecticut, for a larger salary than he was earning at Middlebury, he asked if the president could positively guarantee his position. Thomas said no, and Lawrence reluctantly resigned.[38]

Another professor mentioned in the anonymous letter to the trustees, James G. Stevens, an economist on a one-year contract, was informed that his services would not be needed after the 1919–1920 academic year. Unlike Lawrence, Stevens apparently was not a good instructor, held unusual pedagogical ideas, taught suspiciously liberal economic and social theories, and had a cynical attitude that must have grated on people such as Thomas. A faculty meeting voted to support his retention, but they may have acted out of sympathy rather than good judgment. In any event, the trustees dismissed him.[39] One trustee wrote that "the times are such that on such questions the college must be like Caesar's wife, 'above suspicion.'"[40]

The Lawrence and Stevens affairs might have concluded at that point without further notice. However, Lawrence learned that Thomas was claiming he had left Middlebury purely for financial reasons and that his position had been entirely secure. Lawrence wrote Thomas in early 1920 asking it to be made known that he had left because his position had *not* been completely secure. Thomas responded that Lawrence had merely been criticized by a few trustees and that he had not been forced to leave in any way.[41] The two men had obviously perceived the situation much differently. Lawrence, angry at Thomas's refusal to admit that any pressure had been brought upon him, penned a scathing and sarcastic unsigned letter to the *New Republic*. Published in late February 1920, the letter lambasted an unnamed New England liberal arts college for its treatment of several unnamed professors.[42]

The *New Republic* letter caused a mild sensation at Middlebury. Students, thinking that the popular Lawrence had departed completely of his own volition, were stunned by the charges. The editor of the *Campus* called for an explanation and an investigation, and Thomas found it necessary to give a lengthy speech to the student body defending his assertion that Lawrence had not been "kicked out" but only criticized by a few trustees because of Lawrence's letter to the *Register*.[43] The facts of the Lawrence controversy were finally collected and made available by a committee of the Undergraduate Association (the men's student government) headed by Joseph Kasper '20, president of the association.[44] The editor of the *Campus*, Dwight Moody '21, held, however, that the committee report was actually blocked by Thomas, who instead "read a statement of his own concerning the case."[45] Moody, a supporter of Lawrence, wrote an editorial calling for action on the investigation. Professor Charles Baker Wright, using for the first time his power as press chief (which included prior approval of all articles), suppressed the April 7 issue, in which Moody's editorial would have appeared. Several weeks later, the student body voted 254 to 62 in favor of changing the faculty supervision over the *Campus* from supervision with authority to merely advisory.

But the relationship was not changed, and on April 28, Moody wrote an editorial he did not show to Professor Wright before publication (after assuring him that he *had* shown everything that was going to be printed), which included the following: "the editor was informed sometime ago that if he printed anything which the Administration preferred that he should not, such as references to the Lawrence controversy, he would be requested to resign."[46] The faculty voted to dismiss Moody from the college for lying to Professor Wright, and this resulted in more adverse publicity, particularly near Moody's home in western Massachusetts.[47]

The *New Republic* letter also spurred a thorough investigation by the American Association of University Professors (AAUP) of Middlebury's actions toward Lawrence and Stevens. In its final report the AAUP supported Thomas and the college. They argued that if Lawrence had been dismissed because of his letter to the *Register*, "it would have constituted an unwarranted interference with academic freedom." But Lawrence had not been dismissed, and (no matter how frightened he had been by the Swift letter) he could have presented his case before the faculty–trustee conference committee created in 1918 to discuss faculty dismissals and related problems. Instead, Lawrence chose to resign, and since he had not even begun to utilize the existing machinery for dealing with such questions, the AAUP could hardly rule in his favor.[48]

The Lawrence–Stevens controversy, born in the reactionary atmosphere of the early 1920s, was one more affliction visited upon the college by the war and its aftermath. Unlike the Civil War, however, World War I did not reverse a period of prewar growth. Indeed, Middlebury experienced a postwar enrollment boom in the 1920s, and Thomas faced two major problems in his final years: how to increase college income in an inflationary period and whether Middlebury should remain a coeducational institution.

While the Liberty Endowment Fund drive of 1917–1918 had raised faculty salaries, postwar inflation erased those gains in terms of spending power.[49] Thomas had two options to obtain more annual income: increase the endowment or raise tuition. Both proved necessary.

The permanent funds had been enhanced by several recent bequests, aside from the Liberty fund: $65,000 from Hepburn to support an athletic program, for example, and an unrestricted gift of $50,000 from another trustee, Theodore Vail.[50] Even more important was a $100,000 contribution in 1917 from Henry Freeman Walker '60, a wealthy New York physician, to create a fund for sabbaticals and emergency leaves; for the next forty years, income from the Walker Fund provided nearly the only means whereby faculty could take a paid leave of absence.[51] And in 1918, Mrs. Russell Sage, a former pupil of the famous Middlebury female educator Emma Willard, bequeathed $100,000. Twice in the 1890s, Middlebury President Ezra Brainerd had spoken before Mrs. Sage's group—the Emma Willard Foundation of New York City—and had been rewarded once with a $2,000 scholarship for college women. Brainerd had also published a pamphlet describing Emma Willard's life and work in Middlebury and had given a large number of copies to the grateful Mrs. Sage for distribution. When her $100,000 bequest was announced, more than twenty years later, Brainerd was overjoyed that his earlier efforts had not been in vain.[52]

The major contribution in this period—the huge Joseph Battell estate willed to Middlebury in 1915—had proved in some respects a difficult and controversial bequest. Battell's will was laced with critical contradictions on how to handle the 30,000 acres of valuable forest land he had accumulated during the last fifty years of his life and had entrusted to the college. One interpretation of the will indicated that Battell had wanted nearly the entire tract to be left completely untouched forever, with the college also responsible for creating a park on the land that would allow the public to enjoy the unspoiled sight of his mountain domain. In that case, the college would realize little revenue from the estate and would have to incur the expense and responsibility of a public park. Hepburn, for instance, read the will in that manner, and counseled against accepting the Battell Trust.[53]

On the other hand, the will contained numerous statements and assumptions that suggested a different interpretation. Battell obviously assumed that the college would obtain a large financial benefit from the bequest, yet this could come only from selective cutting and lumbering of the forest lands. Furthermore, Thomas and others who had consulted with Battell before his death knew that he had intended to place only a few restrictions on most of the land. With the advice of the respected lawyer and trustee Frank C. Partridge '81, the college rejected the restrictive interpretation and agreed upon a compromise plan that saved some of the lands as a park and earmarked most of the rest as a source of lumber.[54] The difficulty in properly managing the large tract meant that the annual income it yielded at first was small.[55] But by selling or leasing the remainder of Battell's estate—the town newspaper, the Battell Block in downtown Middlebury, and various other properties—the college did obtain some immediate income.[56]

Then there was the Bread Loaf Inn, Battell's unusual mountain home and guest retreat in Ripton. It was from the inn that Battell had looked out over the Green Mountains in the early 1870s and had vowed that he would buy all the mountains and forests he could see to keep them inviolate for posterity. A meeting place for Battell's cultured friends for many years, the inn had a powerful sentimental value for many people. But it had become rather shabby and had been losing money as a hotel since Battell's death in 1915. The trustees therefore decided, in January 1919, to sell the place.[57]

Happily for the future of the college, they then encountered a persuasive argument, advanced by President Thomas and the man in charge of summer programs, Provost Edward Day Collins.[58] Thomas and Collins argued that the inn might make an ideal place for a new summer school, which would be limited to the study of English language and literature. The summer foreign language schools, inaugurated in 1915, had already proved a great success, and there would not be enough space on the main campus to house everybody in the summer if an English school were added. The beautiful location at Bread Loaf, Thomas and Collins claimed, would provide the necessary additional facilities for summer programs, and the English school would soon rival the language schools in popularity.[59] The trustees were convinced. They rescinded their earlier vote to sell the property, and the Bread Loaf School of English has been an important part of Middlebury ever since.[60] Thus, while the Battell bequest created headaches, it also provided some unexpected academic and extracurricular dividends, as thousands of Bread Loaf scholars and Snow Bowl enthusiasts have discovered during the twentieth century.

Even with all these recent additions to income, the endowment did not yield an adequate sum for the needs of the growing college. Thomas once again pleaded with the Carnegie Foundation's General Education Board (GEB) for a conditional grant that might spur another endowment drive. Again, he succeeded. In June 1920 the board announced that it would provide $250,000 toward a fund of $1 million to be raised by 1923.[61] Although a wary board of trustees had doubted Thomas's ability to obtain $75,000 twelve years earlier, this time they confidently agreed to let him raise ten times that amount and accepted the GEB offer.[62] Gifts from Mrs. Fletcher D. Proctor in December 1920 ($60,000) and from Hepburn in June 1921 ($100,000) gave the fund a decisive early push.[63] The remainder was raised during the early 1920s under Thomas's successor.

Thomas also increased the college's annual income by raising student tuition from $100 to $150 in the fall of 1920.[64] Although he knew that the increase meant great sacrifice for some students, Thomas had already embarked Middlebury on a path away from its old image as an inexpensive, poor-man's college. The increase, like the construction of the modern Hepburn dormitory in 1915, was part of a plan to attract more middle-class students. Better faculty could then be retained, and Middlebury would eventually rank with the best colleges in New England.[65] The choice for Thomas had been clear: a small school like Middlebury with a relatively tiny endowment could not become an outstanding institution without raising tuition and courting a different kind of student.

The other important problem during the final years of the Thomas administration was the issue of coeducation.

More and more women were becoming interested in higher education in the twentieth century. Since the doors of many New England schools were closed to them, they applied to Middlebury in large numbers after 1900. As early as 1908, Thomas and the trustees had been concerned that the influx of women might frighten away male applicants, many of whom considered coeducational schools inferior. Indeed, coeducation was under attack at a variety of colleges in these years, and schools such as the University of Chicago and Wesleyan, among others, moved toward segregation of men and women or even the exclusion of women altogether.[66]

At Middlebury, too, several trustees, notably Hepburn and James Gifford '77, urged that women be excluded or that a truly separate college for women be established. The board, at Hepburn's request, agreed in May 1918 that a trustee committee be appointed by Thomas "to look into the matter of the segregation of the Women's College from the Men's College, and present . . . a practical plan, if possible, for a complete separation of the two colleges."[67] Hepburn, one of the members of the committee, arranged for the GEB (which frowned upon coeducation) to investigate and make recommendations concerning the education of women at Middlebury.[68] Hepburn apparently favored exclusion over segregation, but as he implied to Thomas, he was prepared to accept compromise:

> I am pretty well convinced that the College will be swamped by girls who will utilize all additional facilities that we may be able to obtain. . . . The determination not to admit girls in 1920 would be a drastic step, but it certainly would solve all questions and perhaps most satisfactorily. To continue a co-educational institution will, I fear, by degrees, but eventually, make it a college for women. A compromise might be to organize a college for women with a separate Board of Trustees, like Barnard and Radcliffe, working with Middlebury sharing recitation rooms and other facilities until growth and progress enabled each to stand on its own foundation.[69]

Thomas and an apparent majority of the trustees opposed Hepburn's ideas. The president held that two separate institutions could not be established merely "by passing a vote" and that adequate financial resources were needed first. Thomas also worried that a strong affiliated women's college "would soon swamp the old one, would absorb its facilities and energies and destroy its standings and its appeal as a college for men."[70]

The issue came to a head at the meeting of January 23, 1920, and the board reached a compromise. It voted to develop a "semi-detached institution for women." A single board of trustees would retain control over both schools and one faculty, of which "some members would teach only men, some only women, and where possible separate courses for men and women should be maintained at least in the first two or three years." However, the board decided first to negotiate with Vermont to see whether the state would establish a proposed teachers college at Middlebury, in which case the state would take over the women's college and it would "cease to exist." [71] Thus, Thomas and the majority of the board appeared willing to end coeducation, but only if they had adequate funding for both schools or if they could turn the women entirely over to the state.

Hepburn was unhappy with the compromise on segregation and was opposed to establishing a state teachers college at Middlebury. One month after the January meeting, he confided to a surprised James Gifford '77 that he had hoped to endow a women's college in New England. Gifford wrote anxiously to Thomas:

> I think it is on that theory that he [Hepburn] worked out the plan to have the proposed Women's College at Middlebury, separate and distinct from the College, separately incorporated and with a distinct board of trustees. He states, however, that in view of developments at Middlebury he is inclined to think that the College should be founded elsewhere and he wished me to see you as soon as possible and discuss this matter in all its details. . . . I think now is rather a crucial time and as events are shaped the future of the college, the connection of our good friend, Mr. Hepburn, therewith, as well as the disposition made regarding the education of girls in Vermont will be decided.[72]

Hepburn had seriously considered endowing a rigidly segregated women's college at Middlebury, and Gifford wanted Thomas to reassess the entire matter in view of Hepburn's possible actions. Hepburn had $4 million to $6 million available for such a bequest.[73] Thomas organized an advisory committee of six women to consult with the trustees on matters relating to the women's college. "This action was taken unanimously and heartily," Thomas wrote Gifford, "as the next logical step in the development of a co-ordinate institution." [74]

Apparently still dissatisfied with the progress of segregation, Hepburn changed his will, which had provided several million dollars for the endowment of a separate women's college at Middlebury. Although Thomas's successor, Paul D. Moody, was hired in 1921 with instructions from the trustees to segregate the women in an affiliated college as soon as possible, Hepburn died in January 1922 before anything could be changed significantly.[75] The loss of the Hepburn funds and the fear of similar actions by other potential donors helped shift trustee opinion toward a more decided prosegregation stance. Yet as we shall see, Moody could not raise the necessary funds to institute affiliated colleges, and for the most part Middlebury remained a coeducational school, in fact if not in name, during the interwar years.

After thirteen years of service to his alma mater, Thomas tendered his resignation on January 28, 1921, to accept the presidency of the Pennsylvania State College (now the Pennsylvania State University).[76] Although he had politely rebuffed tentative presidential feelers from Dartmouth and Tufts a few years earlier and had not entered into the race for the United States Senate from Vermont, as some had hoped he would, the ambitious fifty-two-year-old Thomas did accept the challenge of transforming the Pennsylvania school into a state university.[77] Still, it was difficult for him to leave Middlebury. He and his family had moved into his wife's childhood home, the Seely residence, in 1919, after the college had bought and renovated it as the official presidential house.[78] The memories of youth and the ties of thirteen busy and productive years were strongly felt. Indeed, when Thomas tried to give a farewell speech to an assembly of students, faculty, and friends in Mead Chapel in April 1921, he could not read the speech and sat down choked with emotion.[79]

The entire college community heralded the success of his administration. Thomas had helped increase (1) the endowment from $415,340 to $1,597,329, (2) the enrollment from 203 to 447 (765 if summer school is included), (3) the annual income from tuition and fees from $1,080 to over $50,000, (4) the physical plant from a 30-acre campus worth $240,000 to a 244-acre plant valued at $771,363, and (5) the faculty from 11 to 41 members.[80] Most important, as the trustees proclaimed, "Middlebury College, through the activities of President Thomas, in a new and peculiar sense has been put upon the educational map of New England and has gained wide and enviable recognition as an institution of sound learning, clean morals, and worthy ideals."[81]

Ironically, one of the areas in which Thomas had experienced the most opposition—his attempt to turn the college into a state-supported school—would also bedevil him at Penn State. He left there in 1925 after a moderately successful and very frustrating tenure to accept the presidency of Rutgers, where he stayed until 1931.[82] Later, he served as vice president of the National Life Insurance Company in Montpelier (1931–1938) and president of Norwich University (1939–1944), before retiring to Mendon, Vermont. Even in retirement (and somewhat crippled by an automobile accident in 1947), Thomas maintained his characteristic level of activity. He was elected several times to the state legislature, helped found Rutland Junior College, studied for and was ordained into the Episcopal ministry, and served on a variety of boards and committees. In 1949, after the death of his wife, Grace Seely Thomas, he married Dean Eleanor Ross, with whom he had worked closely during his last six years at Middlebury. He died three years later in Rutland at the age of eighty-two, mourned by hundreds of grateful alumni, faculty, and friends who remembered his outstanding work for the college.[83]

CHAPTER 2

PAUL MOODY AND COLLEGE GROWTH, 1921–1942

The qualitative must become our standard, rather than the quantitative, not only in students but what we offer them. . . . There are colleges where a much larger variety of courses is offered. We cannot cover everything. We do not intend to try. But we want to do some things as well as they are done in this country.

—Paul Moody, "The Inaugural Address of
President Paul Dwight Moody of Middlebury
College," *Middlebury College Bulletin* 16 (June
1922): 19–36

I think I can say that we all were very fond of President Moody as a person. He was the kind that went to your heart to a very great extent. His managerial style was very personal. He made people, as persons, the focal point of his concern. . . . And he judged people, very largely, by their personal style and by their personality; even perhaps, to some extent more than he should have.

—Dr. Stephen Freeman, quoted in
"Dr. Freeman Recalls 45 Years of College
History and Language Growth at Middlebury,"
MCNL 44 (summer 1970): 39

During the first nine months of 1921, as the trustees searched for a successor to President Thomas, Provost Edward Day Collins watched over the college as acting president. Indeed, Collins might have been selected to succeed Thomas, had it not then been the board's policy to choose a president from the clergy and from outside the faculty.[1] Collins, who had earned his Ph.D. from Yale in 1899, had rapidly become a valuable and effective administrator after his arrival at the college in 1909 as a professor of pedagogy. His earlier experience as treasurer and managing director of the Canadian Carbonate Company of Montreal and as principal of the state normal school at Johnson, Vermont, prepared him well for the variety of positions he would hold at Middlebury. He directed the Middlebury Summer Session in 1910–1911, 1915–1916, and 1919–1923 and served as provost from 1919 to 1921 and as comptroller from 1923 to 1925. Reginald "Doc" Cook '24 remembered Collins as a "man of force and ambition" and a "pragmatic and innovative administrator" who handled his duties with "authority and self-assurance" and was liked by all: "Although a Canadian by birth, the impression he made on me was that of the early New England Yankee. He was reserved in manner, staid in behavior, and conservative in his views. This does not imply that he was in any way either stiff-necked or stuffy. On the contrary, he was both kindly and gentle."[2]

On July 28, 1921, the board unanimously voted to offer the presidency to Reverend Paul Dwight Moody, associate pastor of the Madison Avenue Presbyterian Church in New York City.[3] The forty-two-year-old Moody accepted the offer, took over the reins of power from Collins in the fall, and embarked on a difficult twenty-one-year tenure—one that began with great hope and ended in the personal tragedy of forced resignation for the man who was perhaps Middlebury's most popular president.

Moody was born in Baltimore in 1879, son of the celebrated revivalist Dwight L. Moody. He received a fine classical and religious education at Mt. Hermon School; Yale (A.B., 1901); New College in Edinburgh, Scotland; the Glasgow (Scotland) Free Church College; and Hartford (Connecticut) Theological Seminary. He taught for six years in the Northfield, Vermont, schools and worked from 1909 to 1912 for the George Doran publishing house. Ordained as a Congregational minister in 1912, he served as pastor of South Church in St. Johnsbury, Vermont, from 1912 to 1917. He was an army chaplain during World War I, serving in 1918–1919 as the senior chaplain at General Pershing's headquarters. He was sent on various missions in France and settled numerous problems with the French military and civil authorities. For his outstanding work, he was awarded the Academic Palms and in 1924 was made a chevalier of the Legion of Honor. When he returned to the United States in 1919, Moody accepted a position at New York's Madison Avenue Presbyterian Church, which he held until he went to Middlebury in 1921.[4]

Moody was a tall, portly, handsome man who displayed great dignity and stature in his bearing.[5] Howard Munford '34 recalled sitting at a Middlebury football game with a friend from another school. When Moody entered the stands, the friend blurted out, "That *must* be the president!" But Moody had more than just a presence. Students and faculty remembered him as a deeply cultivated minister and gentleman with a serious commitment to quality. He was neither stuffy nor austere, and he disliked pomposity. Rather, he was a witty, warmhearted, and engaging conversationalist and had an earthiness (for a minister) that endeared him to many: he would not turn down an occasional cigar (despite the disapproval of fellow clergymen) and had a "keen (though entirely innocent) eye for a beautiful woman." A political conservative but a religious liberal, he kept certain radical speakers from appearing on campus yet wrote an innovative marriage service for Howard Munford '34 and Marian Munford '32 in which he struck out "obey" from "love, honor and obey." The short, vibrant readings and scriptural interpretations he delivered in chapel nearly every school day for twenty-one years deeply impressed many students.

Above all, he was the faculty's president, and he cultivated an image of the loving and paternal leader who devotedly guided his flock. He believed in hiring men whom he intuitively judged to be "teachers" and paid little attention to academic or professional credentials. Stephen Freeman, whom Moody hired in 1925 and who worked at the college for over forty years, recalled that while sometimes Moody's appointments were excellent, at other times, his intuitions proved faulty.

> I think I can say that we all were very fond of President Moody as a person. He was the kind that went to your heart to a very great extent. His managerial style was very personal. He made people, as persons, the focal point of his concern. To him they were not numbers or cogs, by any means. And he judged people, very largely, by their personal style and by their personality; even perhaps, to some extent more than he should have. Some people who were not particularly good teachers were successful on the campus because they were warm personalities . . . or interesting personalities.[6]

Robert Pack and Howard Munford '34 talked outside the Little Theater at Bread Loaf during the School of English in 1978.

In any case, Moody took a deep personal interest in his staff, and if he saw that a professor was physically or spiritually exhausted, he would take away the man's office keys and send him home. His paternalism, however, was tempered by respect, and he encouraged dissent and discussion on educational questions (while occasionally curtailing political expression). Moody was a complex man. Sometimes easily bored and prone to make impetuous decisions, on other occasions he was indecisive and procrastinated. Most important, perhaps, he had a difficult time saying no or firing people. He was loved and admired by faculty and students, but several powerful trustees had reservations about him and eventually grew impatient with his inability to deal more forcefully with faculty, finances, and other issues.

In his inaugural address, Moody set the tone for his administration. First, he stressed that Middlebury would seek excellence rather than further growth:

> The qualitative must become our standard, rather than the quantitative, not only in students but what we offer them. . . . There are colleges where a much larger variety of courses is offered. We cannot

cover everything. We do not intend to try. But we want to do some things as well as they are done in this country.[7]

After the tremendous expansion during the Thomas years, Moody planned to concentrate on improving the quality of both the faculty and the student body.

Moody also urged that the college reject a vocational and utilitarian philosophy, arguing that efficiency could not be the sole criterion for good education. Middlebury should emphasize the criteria of culture and character and produce Christian gentlemen (and gentlewomen, presumably) who could think for themselves, tell right from wrong, and serve society. And the study of the arts would facilitate the conversion of crude freshmen into cultivated graduates: "We may in four years time help a man to a better knowledge of the past and so to a right conception of himself in relation to that and to the present. By music, by art, by literature, by acquaintance with great principles and their history, the cave man may become the polished gentlemen."[8] Thomas had emphasized utilitarian educational ideas; Moody would try to move instead toward a more studied commitment to a liberal arts education. Finally, he stated that his eventual aim was to create a separate college for women and that the first steps would be the segregation of students by sex in freshmen classes in the fall of 1922.[9]

Moody's threefold commitment—to quality over quantity, culture over vocation, and segregation over coeducation—was articulated continually for the next twenty years. Ironically, under Moody the student body grew more in absolute numbers than ever before, and his desires to upgrade quality and segregate the sexes were both blunted by the lack of financial resources. He did, however, modify the curriculum and academic program by offering more humanities courses, by allowing more opportunities for independent study and honors, and by introducing comprehensive examinations. And he raised enough money to keep the college plant and endowment abreast of the rising enrollment. Indeed, in order to understand his limited success in improving quality, segregating the sexes, and reforming the curriculum, an examination of fund-raising and plant expansion during his administration is necessary.

Paul Moody, unlike his predecessor, was not an avid fund-raiser. John Thomas was at his best when urging a doubtful board to expand its vision of what Middlebury could become and support an ambitious campaign effort. He even relished the endless speeches and correspondence that accompanied fund-raising. Moody was more comfortable leading a faculty discussion of educational ideals or delivering a moving chapel sermon. Still, during his years the $1 million campaign initiated by Thomas was completed; the endowment was nearly tripled, to $4,250,000; and funds were obtained for the Music Practice Studios, Porter Hospital, two new wings on Starr Library, the Chateau, Munroe Hall, and the Gifford men's residence. The hopes for a separate women's college were dimmed, however, by an inability to raise funds during the Depression; only Forest Hall, a woman's residence built in 1936 with funds obtained from the sale of Battell forest lands to the federal government, was constructed.

The college had until July 1, 1922, to raise $750,000 to receive the General Education Board's $250,000 conditional grant toward the endowment campaign goal of $1 million, a sum earmarked specifically for increased salaries.[10] Moody and the trustees arranged a time extension so that the new president could have a full year "to devote his time to the problems of the College" and settle into his new position before engaging in extensive efforts on the fund drive.[11] After an intensive and well-orchestrated push in the spring of 1923, $790,000 was subscribed by June (including $250,000 by Hepburn), and the goal had been reached.[12] The funds were collected during the rest of Moody's presidency.[13] Since the endowment had been only $1,597,329 in 1920, the new funds were a relatively large addition to permanent funds and allowed salary increases of 20 to 50 percent during the next five years.[14] By selling many of the Hepburn-donated securities in the late 1920s, Middlebury officials earned a handsome $800,000 profit just before the market crashed. Endowment soared to over $4,250,000 during Moody's first ten years in office.[15]

The Great Depression took its toll on every area of American society, including higher education. Colleges and universities were hard hit, as endowments shrank, many students could not find the funds to attend (and part-time college jobs became scarce), and faculty members faced pay cuts or even layoffs.[16] At Middlebury, the Depression halted the growth of the endowment and sharply reduced the income from the securities and western farm mortgages in which the college had invested heavily.[17] In addition, Vermont had decided in 1923 to cut its annual $31,200 appropriation to Middlebury by 10 percent each year until it reached $7,200, which would continue to be set aside for senatorial scholarships.[18] All this reduction in income accelerated the college's growing dependence on tuition receipts. Even before the Depression, the percentage of total income received from students had risen from 9 percent in 1900 to 39 percent in 1929; that figure reached 55 percent by 1939. Tuition increased from $100 in 1919 to $300 in 1933, and dormitory rates soared.[19] When these increases could not make up for the loss in endowment income, the college was forced to postpone its building program, cut faculty salaries 5 to 15 percent, and place a freeze on hiring, although enrollment increased from 628 in 1933 to 799 in 1939.[20] Seeking to interest alumni in making annual contributions, the college created an alumni newsletter in 1926, produced a motion picture of the campus in 1930 to show to regional alumni groups, hired alumni and alumnae directors, placed alumni trustees on the board, and inaugurated annual homecoming and quinquennial reunions. The Depression seriously limited this effort, however, and alumni gifts were minimal until after World War II.[21]

As income from tuition became the principal support in the interwar period, the trustees apparently encouraged increased enrollment as a means of financing the college, particularly during the Depression. With a growing percentage of young Americans attending college after World War I, Middlebury was able to recruit a larger student body, and Moody's stated plans to emphasize quality and downplay growth were largely nullified by a phenomenal postwar increase in enrollment—from 387 in 1919 to 643 in 1927 and to 803 in 1941 (see Table 2). This naturally produced a constant need for more dormitory space and academic facilities.

The housing problem was particularly acute in the immediate postwar era. The college bought or leased several village houses close to campus—Halpin House (later named Hillcrest) in 1918, Cartmell House (later named Weybridge House) and the Logan House in 1920, the Atwood House and the Wilcox House in 1921, and others—to house the women. For the men, Painter and Hepburn were renovated to house greater numbers.[22] The fraternities provided housing for a good percentage of the men, particularly in the postwar years, when Delta Upsilon and Delta Kappa Epsilon moved into fine large houses on South Main Street near McCullough Gymnasium.[23]

TABLE 2
Student Enrollment, 1921–1941

Year	Men	Women	Total
1921–1922	241	246	487
1922–1923	268	260	528
1923–1924	278	254	532
1924–1925	299	253	552
1925–1926	310	276	586
1926–1927	329	281	610
1927–1928	350	293	643
1928–1929	336	284	620
1929–1930	342	274	616
1930–1931	352	273	625
1931–1932	364	291	655
1932–1933	346	292	638
1933–1934	316	294	610
1934–1935	331	303	634
1935–1936	332	294	626
1936–1937	375	333	708
1937–1938	423	354	777
1938–1939	413	357	770
1939–1940	426	357	783
1940–1941	429	356	785
1941–1942	422	381	803

Figures are for fall-term enrollment, based on numbers listed in the original typed manuscript, Middlebury Attendance Records, 1800–1951, Middlebury College Archives.

The college also constructed three new buildings to help meet the housing needs: the Chateau, Forest Hall, and Gifford dormitory.

Miss Frederika G. Holden (later Mrs. John Proctor) of Proctor, Vermont, informed President Moody in January 1923 that she would provide $62,500 toward the construction of a French house on campus if Middlebury contributed an equal amount.[24] Miss Holden, a wealthy student in the 1922 French Summer School session, had been enormously impressed by the work of the school's director, Henri P. Williamson de Visme '96. He had discussed with her his dream of building a real French chateau on campus similar to the one in Soisy, France, in which he had directed the Ecole du Chateau de Soisy.[25] The trustees agreed to Miss Holden's plan, and Moody commissioned a young architect and friend, J. Layng Mills, to design the building, which was constructed in 1924–1925. Stephen Freeman, director of the Language Schools for many years and author of a detailed history of the Schools, stated that the chateau "is still the finest French House in the country, the longest in continuous operation, the oldest but one, and the model of all others." The outside architecture is a "close copy" of the sixteenth-century Pavillon Henri IV of the Palace of Fontainebleau, and inside,

> the architecture and furnishings are generally of the XVIIIth century. On the ground floor, the Grand Salon is used as the "common room" of the house, as a lounge for meetings and all the social gatherings—teas, musicales, amateur dramatics. The Petit Salon, with the fine crystal chandeliers, was for a time the private salon of the Directress. Now it has become the working library of the house, since the former library became the authentic Salon Louis XVI from the Hotel Crillon in the Place de la Concorde. Offices, seminar rooms, and two forty-place classrooms occupy the rest of the ground floor. The offices of the Dean of the French School were for many years at the right of the center door. The two upper floors have single and double rooms for about 45 students. The dining room of 70 places is in the basement.[26]

The Chateau greatly eased the women's housing shortage and provided outstanding facilities for the study of French during both the regular school year and the summer session.

Although the Chateau, Hillcrest, and other small houses acquired in the 1920s temporarily solved the women's housing problems, by 1934, when more than 300 women were enrolled, the trustees agreed that a large new residence hall was needed.[27] Since a capital campaign was out of the question, the board decided to finance the dormitory by selling to the federal government most of the Battell forest lands the college had obtained in 1915. Terms were agreed upon after several years of bargaining. Some 21,858.9 acres were sold for $435,906.41, which provided more than enough cash to construct the new $355,000 Forest Hall dormitory. Since the trustees intended to make an annual profit of 4 to 6 percent from operating it, Forest Hall replaced the Battell Forest as a part of the income-producing endowment.[28]

The residence hall, designed by Dwight J. Baum of New York City, was to be the first major building of the proposed $3,500,000 women's campus.[29] The large white stone structure, which blended in well with the older buildings, was located on the north side of College Street, about 100 yards east of Pearsons Hall. It housed over 120 women, and its size, facilities, modernity, and location soon made Forest Hall the center of the women's college.[30]

Male enrollment more that doubled during these years, from 209 in 1920 to 429 in 1940. Although the new fraternity houses and the

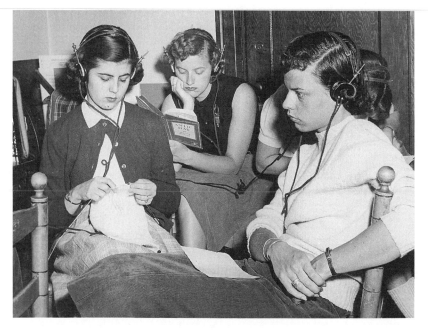

From 1925 until the construction of the Johnson Arts Center in 1968, the Music Studio was the locus of music enjoyment at the college.

renovation of Painter Hall had proved helpful, a new residence — the most recent being Hepburn, in 1916 — was clearly needed.[31] When Hepburn's friend and fellow trustee, James Gifford '77, passed away in 1939, his widow informed the college that she would contribute nearly $300,000 for a new men's dormitory, "the construction of which shall, according to his [Gifford's] wishes, follow the plan used by Mr. A. Barton Hepburn."[32] The new James M. Gifford Memorial Hall for Boys was built in 1940 on top of the college hill, to the north of Hepburn and Mead Chapel. Designed by John Muller of New York City, Gifford resembled Hepburn, except that it was constructed of limestone (from the same quarry that supplied Painter Hall in 1815), with "very fine neo-Georgian woodwork detailing inside and out."[33]

Increased enrollment also necessitated an expansion of academic facilities. Accordingly, during President Moody's tenure the college constructed (along with the Chateau) the Music Practice Studio, two recitation buildings, and two wings on Starr Library.

Mrs. Emily Proctor Eggleston, daughter of the late Vermont governor, Fletcher D. Proctor '81, gave $20,000 in January 1923 toward the construction of a music practice hall, "with the idea that this branch should be further developed."[34] Mrs. Eggleston was a devoted admirer of Miss Minnie Hayden, the college voice instructor who was also dean of the summer music school from 1913 to 1925. Aristocratic, strong-minded, and talented, Miss Hayden was feared and respected by all. One colleague remembered her as "a real dowager," and a student of that era recalls (without condescension) that she "was a bit of a campus character . . . but a very good soul."[35]

Mrs. Eggleston later wrote that she had originally desired to build a structure purely for Miss Hayden's work in voice instruction, "but in deference to her [Miss Hayden's] wishes, I joined in the plan of making the house for the use of the whole music department."[36] The music department had been housed in the crowded and inadequate facilities of the old Catholic church building on Weybridge Street that the college had bought in 1910 as a temporary gymnasium.[37] The new brick colonial Music Practice Studio, which contained a large room for glee club, band, and orchestra rehearsals; many small rooms for practice; and studios for the teachers, was an extremely helpful addition.[38] The final cost of the studio, located where the Johnson Arts Center now stands, was $30,000, and Mrs. Eggleston graciously contributed the remaining $10,000 as well.[39] The building was completed in 1925.

Although the Music Practice Studio was a fine addition, the major academic need after 1915 was more recitation facilities and classroom space. As early as 1917, President Thomas had urged the construction of a recitation hall for the humanities and social sciences.[40] Nothing was done, however, until 1922 when a wooden recitation building was erected at a cost of $8,500. The "temporary" structure (finally destroyed by fire in 1970) was built on the north side of College Street, just east of the present location of Carr Hall. Although it accommodated up to two hundred students and somewhat eased overcrowding in Old Chapel and the Chemistry building, faculty members still dreamed of the day they could have adequate classroom and office space.[41] Finally, in 1939, Charles A. Munroe '96, a wealthy utilities magnate and college trustee who had been born and educated in Middlebury, gave $150,000 for a new recitation building. Munroe Hall was constructed in 1940 on the south side of

Two new wings were added to Starr Library during President Moody's tenure to accommodate the growing needs of the college and the rapid increase of publications in every field.

College Street, between Chemistry and the site of Gifford Hall.[42] The four-story structure had native limestone facing and featured fifteen classrooms, an auditorium, and seventeen faculty offices (most of them doubles). For decades, the faculty had used "corners of classrooms, vacant tables at the Library, the stacks, dormitory rooms, and the family parlor as office accommodations."[43] The new building was obviously a welcome addition. Yet in some respects the situation remained far from perfect. Private offices were still the exception. The building's "ventilation [system] never worked, the basement floor was always damp and cold in winter, the acoustics were bad, and the planning of the rooms generally poor."[44] On the other hand, the new facilities in Munroe allowed the chemistry department to take over all four floors of the Chemistry building after twenty-seven years of sharing their "home" with other departments.[45]

Aside from recitation facilities, the most pressing academic need at Middlebury after World War I was more library space. Starr

Library, constructed in 1900 for the tiny turn-of-the-century college, was soon as overcrowded as the recitation rooms.[46] Fortunately, Dr. M. Allen Starr agreed in 1926 to provide most of the funds necessary for the construction of two new wings on the building his father, Egbert, had built for the college thirty years earlier.[47] Dr. Starr had served as a professor of diseases of the mind and nervous system (and later, of neurology) at Columbia University from 1889 to 1917. He was elected a Middlebury trustee in 1898, a year after the death of his father, continuing his family's long tradition of service to the college. In 1916, Dr. Starr demonstrated his interest in the library by paying for a third-floor addition and a set of stacks in the stack room, at a cost of some $5,000.[48] And ten years later he offered to defray most of the cost of the new west wing, providing reading rooms on both floors, and the cost of a new east wing, which would house the Julian W. Abernethy collection of American literature. Abernethy '76, a college trustee who had taught for many years at Adelphia Academy and Berkely Institute in Brooklyn, had willed his collection of seven thousand volumes, including many rare first editions, to Middlebury in 1923. His brother, Frank D. Abernethy, also provided funds to enhance the Abernethy wing and for additional equipment.[49] The new wings greatly expanded the library's capacity, allowing an increase in holdings from 40,000 volumes in 1921 to 140,000 in 1941 and a jump in annual circulation from 11,000 to 40,000.[50] They enabled the library staff to serve the college adequately until after World War II, when enrollment and use again rose dramatically.

The other major addition to the physical plant, Porter Hospital, served a different need: the college (and the town) were dependent on the hospitals more than thirty miles away in Burlington and Rutland, and a nearby facility had long been desired.[51] William H. Porter, a wealthy New York banker who had (like Munroe) grown up in Middlebury, gave $50,000 in May 1918 in memory of his mother, Martha Sansom, for the construction of a hospital and infirmary to be used and administered jointly by the college and the town.[52] Although Porter, who had contributed the funds for the Porter Athletic Field and grandstand several years earlier, had originally wished to acquire land on South Main Street (just south of McCullough Gymnasium and next to the old cemetery), there was some objection to locating the hospital so near a cemetery. "There is so close an affinity between these two objects," James Gifford wrote, "that I quite concur with that view."[53] Instead, the hospital was built in 1925 on land across South Street from the Porter Athletic Field. Porter eventually doubled his bequest to cover costs and contributed additional money as an endowment to help defray annual expenses.[54] After Porter's death in 1926, his widow, Esther Porter, paid for extensive additions and improvement in 1929, including a nurses' home, a tunnel connecting it with the main building, an annex for isolation cases in emergency, and elevator service. Capacity was increased from twenty-two beds to forty-seven.[55]

Porter's rather ambiguous desire to include the townspeople in the administration of the hospital, along with the college's reluctance to assume the inconvenience of operating it, led to the formation of a board of directors consisting of six members chosen by the college and six county members chosen through the Addison County Hospital Association.[56] In its early years, Porter Hospital had annual deficits, which the college covered, and nearly 90 percent of the patients were county residents. This eventually led to a change, whereby the college shed its responsibilities for managing and operating the facility, leasing it after 1941 to the Porter Medical Center Corporation, electing three of the new eighteen-member board of directors, and maintaining ownership only of the land.[57] In the end, the college had the advantages of a nearby hospital and improved town–gown relations by its early involvement in the project, which gave county residents their first convenient medical facilities.

The major additions of the interwar period—Gifford, Forest, Munroe, the Chateau, the Music Practice Studio, the new library wings, Porter Hospital—meant that Middlebury could for the most part adequately accommodate a student body of eight hundred. But the Depression made it impossible to obtain funds for other desired facilities, particularly a men's gymnasium, as well as the renovation of Old Chapel and Starr Hall and the planned women's campus, of which Forest Hall was just a beginning.[58] Only after World War II, when prosperity returned and enrollment again increased, was the college able to expand its facilities appropriately.

CHAPTER 3

COEDUCATION AT MIDDLEBURY, 1921–1941

If you will review the history of the College you will recall that for the first 83 years of its life, the period when it made its greatest contribution, no women were admitted, more than anything else because of the fact that feminine education was not popular. In comparing the progress of Middlebury since that time with the colleges with which it should normally be grouped (Williams, Dartmouth, Amherst, and Wesleyan), you will see how it has stood still in many respects while those other colleges have gone on.

> —Paul D. Moody to Miss Grace M. Ellis, April 12, 1923, Moody Papers, MCA

The hardihood and pluck which we see upon the athletic field is nicely balanced by the gentler manners, and perhaps finer ideals evidenced by the Women's College.

In this respect it is much like a large family. How unbalanced a home would be if given over entirely to the husband's smoking-rooms, horses, dogs, guns, fishing-rods, or any of the other implements which typify masculinity about a place. How equally distressing the pink and blue daintiness of the feminine boudoirs would seem if they crowded the atmosphere of the rest of the home.

> —*Middlebury Campus*, November 21, 1923

The average woman teacher is a greater problem than three average men teachers. They can be secured for less money, but that is not a distinct advantage. What I should deplore most of all would be a tendency to introduce by women teachers a development of a certain kind of feminism which we see at Mount Holyoke, which I think is the most unhappy of the larger women's colleges. Of the two evils, I would rather have men taught by a woman than women taught by a woman.

—President Paul D. Moody to James Gifford
'77, April 18, 1930, Moody Papers, MCA

In addition to affirming a preference for quality over quantity, President Moody's inaugural address emphasized his intention to change Middlebury from a coeducational to a segregated or coordinate institution.[1] Indeed, Moody had been elected with the instruction that he "carry out this policy of building an affiliated college for women," and for the next twenty years he faithfully (if unsuccessfully) worked to achieve that goal.[2]

There were numerous and powerful reasons that the college desired to separate the men and women. The slow pace of segregating the sexes during Thomas's administration had cost Middlebury an opportunity to obtain millions of dollars from Hepburn for a women's college.[3] Moody also argued that other potential donors, who would gladly contribute to men's colleges or women's colleges, were reluctant to give money to coeducational schools, which many educated Americans looked upon with increasing disfavor after 1900.[4] This included a belief that men and women had different intellectual strengths and weaknesses and should be taught with different methods and follow distinct curricula.[5] As Moody explained to Trevor Arnett of the General Education Board:

There is a tendency in many classes for the women to be slowed up to the men. This is particularly true in courses such as the languages, history and the sciences. But equally important is the fact that in some subjects like economics, political science and so forth, the women fall below the men. Where, in any field, one sex shows preeminence, the other seems to give up. The women are strong in work calling for detail and weak in work calling for a grasp of principles. The reverse is true of the men. . . . The education of the men calls, with us, for an emphasis in exactly the opposite direction. The women need a broader grasp, and the men a more detailed grasp.

To us the answer has always been segregation, with two totally different curricula.[6]

The difference in academic aptitudes at Middlebury was accentuated by the fact that the women were a highly select group, whereas the men, according to Moody, were "too largely unselected, averaging mediocre."[7] In 1929, for example, the college accepted 75 freshmen women from the 316 who applied, whereas 146 men were accepted from only 253 applicants. Not surprisingly, the women regularly swept Phi Beta Kappa and other college honors, much to the chagrin of certain trustees such as James Gifford, who used the small number of Phi Beta Kappa men to justify his arguments for segregation.[8] Ironically, the women's facilities—particularly housing—were decidedly inferior to the men's, and Moody claimed that Middlebury women would "never have a square deal" until they had a school of their own.

> It is not because we do not believe in the higher education for women that we would exclude them from the corridors of a man's college. We prefer to state it another way. We believe in it so much that we desire to give them equal opportunities, which they can never have under the existing system. We would build a college for them, in which men are the excluded aliens.[9]

Finally, many men regarded coeducational colleges as inherently inferior to men's colleges, and this may have further discouraged some good male students from applying to Middlebury.[10] Indeed, Moody went as far as to imply that the college had suffered a relative decline in status after 1883 because of coeducation:

> If you will review the history of the College you will recall that for the first 83 years of its life, the period when it made its greatest contribution, no women were admitted, more than anything else because of the fact that feminine education was not popular. In comparing the progress of Middlebury since that time with the colleges with which it should normally be grouped (Williams, Dartmouth, Amherst, and Wesleyan), you will see how it has stood still in many respects while those other colleges have gone on.[11]

Segregation would supposedly reverse the trend by attracting money and students as well as improving the educational environment for both sexes.

Moody therefore began in the early 1920s to segregate the sexes in freshmen classes.[12] By 1925, separate sections of the same course were arranged for men and women whenever possible, and professors who violated this rule were scolded. The president promised to push segregation further when he had the necessary funds.[13] These plans precipitated a debate among students, faculty, alumni, and friends of the college over the question of coeducation.

Apparently, Middlebury students in the 1920s were divided on the question. On one hand, Moody claimed in 1923 that 95 percent of the men probably favored segregation. Yet a campus straw poll (of dubious statistical significance) of twenty-four men and twenty-four women later that year revealed that over two-thirds of those sampled, both men and women favored the "education of the sexes together at Middlebury."[14] Certainly, there was some opposition. One male student argued in the *Campus* in November 1923 that segregation in the classroom was an excellent idea since it would relieve "a condition of unequal progress and . . . increase the efficiency of the professor's work." He noted that there would still be coeducation outside the classroom, and he questioned whether "the two groups have a good effect upon one another" in the social life of the college. "It is axiomatic," he wrote, "that a man can concentrate on but one thing at any given time. When his mind is occupied with thoughts of the other sex, it can hardly be grappling with bigger things. When social diversions grow to be paramount, they become a nuisance." Not only were women keeping men from engaging in important pursuits; according to this student, the college had neither the atmosphere of "wholesome femininity of an independent women's institution of learning" nor "the upstanding virility and spontaneity of a men's college." Middlebury instead reflected a "compromised atmosphere" that he viewed as unfortunate.[15]

His views were contested in the next issue by a female student who argued that Middlebury's supposedly "compromised atmosphere" was actually "a very well worked-out compromise, a combination of masculine strength and substantial femininity."

> The hardihood and pluck which we see upon the athletic field is nicely balanced by the gentler manners, and perhaps finer ideals evidenced by the Women's College.
>
> In this respect it is very much like a large family. How unbalanced a home would be if given over entirely to the husband's smoking-rooms, horses, dogs, guns, fishing-rods, or any of the other implements which typify masculinity about a place. How equally distressing the pink and blue daintiness of the feminine boudoirs would seem if they crowded the atmosphere of the rest of the home.[16]

These students were not arguing (as some would forty years later) the question of sexual attributes; indeed, they seemed to accept the idea that the sexes were quite different and had different interests, tastes, and abilities. Rather, they were disagreeing over whether men and women, with their varying attributes, should be educated together or separately.

Some women students and alumnae obviously interpreted Moody's drive for segregation as an attempt to downgrade the position of women at the college. Three alumnae—Harriet Cole '06, Anne Freeman Smith '06, and Harriet Hopkins Steele '95—sent out a questionnaire in 1923 to alumnae and friends of the college in an attempt to alert them to the possible ramifications of segregation at the college as well as to ascertain their opinions. Moody was furious when he saw the questionnaire, which he found "utterly misleading," and he wrote to one alumna urging her to use her influence on the other three to "get them to play fair." [17] The questionnaire reached Dorothy Canfield Fisher, an influential Vermont author who had recently written a favorable newspaper article about Middlebury College. She wrote Moody that she wished to record her opinion "as being wholly against the proposed segregation of women (if it is seriously contemplated) as a very great and lamentable step backward." She found arguments "in favor of a full and free sharing of academic life infinitely more cogent, American, and forward-looking than anything that can be said against it." [18]

Several male faculty members also opposed segregation. John Bowker, a mathematics professor and later dean of the faculty, commented years later that he found the "dual sectioning procedures were wasteful and unsound." [19] And Professor Frank E. Howard of the education department argued (according to his daughter) that coeducation was particularly good for the men because it forced them to compete with "the more conscientious female students," with the result that "the men produced much better work than they would have otherwise." [20]

Those most immediately affected by segregation were the female faculty members. Moody removed all but one of the female instructors in the early 1920s. "We have practically eliminated women from the faculty," he reported in 1925, "except in those departments like Home Economics and Physical Education for Women . . . the policy followed is that women shall teach only women." [21] Since women could not teach men, he wrote in 1927, "this worked out as a distinct handicap and made them a little too expensive a luxury for us."[22] As he informed James Gifford:

> The average woman teacher is a greater problem than three average men teachers. They can be secured for less money, but that is not a distinct advantage. What I should deplore most of all would be a tendency to introduce by women teachers a development of a certain kind of feminism which we see at Mount Holyoke, which I think is the most unhappy of the larger women's colleges. Of the two evils, I would rather have men taught by a woman than women taught by a woman.[23]

He might have added that women were not only paid less than men for entry-level positions but also that the maximum salary for women in 1930 (excluding Dean Ross) was only $2,500, one-half of the men's maximum. Moody also discouraged female applicants for faculty positions,[24] as this answer to a woman's inquiry in 1926 suggests:

> Middlebury is primarily a men's college and the faculty is made up of men except in the departments of peculiar interest to women. . . . Such women as have in the past been on the faculty have been replaced by men when they have withdrawn. So you see, there is not only no opening now, but there is not apt to be unless the Women's college should develop unexpectedly into a more complete entity than it is at present.[25]

Between 1929 and 1935, Moody and the trustees did seriously contemplate developing the women's college into "a more serious entity" and—over the objections of some faculty, students, alumnae, and friends of the college—pressed for the further segregation of the sexes.

The goal of creating a separate women's college had been stalled since the end of World War I by a lack of funds. Hopes that an individual donor might leave several million dollars to endow such a college came to naught; Hepburn, as we have seen, had apparently wearied of Middlebury's inaction on this issue, and his millions went elsewhere. After his death, the college attempted to obtain funds from his widow, who unfortunately was not a Middlebury supporter.[26] A few people argued that northern New England needed a women's college and that perhaps Middlebury could perform this role.[27] Moody, however, encouraged and supported the group who eventually founded Bennington in southern Vermont as a distinct women's college.[28] By 1929, Bennington was in operation and Middlebury had done little toward establishing a women's college except segregate some freshman classes.

James Gifford wrote Moody in November 1929 that he was tired of the college's slow pace in this direction. "Any steps which we have already taken," he added sadly, "do not in any way affect the fact that Middlebury is a Coeducational Institution. . . . It is certain that we will never accomplish anything definite unless this matter is taken up vigorously and pushed to some definite conclusion." Gifford also argued that Brown University had "solved the problem entirely" and called for a coordinate system akin to that of Brown and Pembroke.[29] Moody agreed that action should be taken. He had written to the General Education Board earlier that year for advice on this problem (and undoubtedly with the hope of more financial aid).[30] He informed Gifford that he had identified and was actively pursuing five wealthy prospects, any one of whom could have provided much of the money to endow a women's college. Middlebury, he added, should boldly announce its plan to end coeducation, begin a vigorous campaign to raise the $2 million necessary to endow and build the coordinate institution, and plan to open it by 1931.[31]

At the urging of Moody, Gifford, and others, the trustees discussed the question of coeducation and a separate women's college at length in 1930.[32] Allen Nelson urged the conversion of Middlebury into a women's college, while the University of Vermont would become an all-male institution.[33] Apparently, several trustees suggested the complete exclusion of women from Middlebury.[34] They voted on April 12 "to go on record as saying that a continuance of coeducation as practiced at Middlebury at present is undesirable." However, they rejected Nelson's proposal to eliminate men from the college, and Gifford moved to establish a coordinate system:

> . . . that women be admitted to the incoming class, but that no admissions after the class of 1934 to Middlebury College as such be allowed but that such be admitted into a College to be organized by a distinctive name either under the charter heretofore granted, or such charter as may be procured, which shall be devoted to the education of women and shall be separate and distinct from Middlebury College as such though it may be affiliated with or a part of same under the

Charter granted by the Legislature of Vermont and approved December 4, 1902.[35]

The trustees called a special meeting on June 5 to discuss Gifford's motion and the whole question of coeducation.

At that meeting, the board discussed a broad range of related issues, including the probable expense over the next few years of carrying segregation into effect, the legal problems involved in taking funds from Middlebury College to support a college for women, the experience of other institutions, and the necessity to obtain expert counsel before taking final action. The trustees then voted to turn the whole matter over to the president and the board's Committee on the Women's College, who, in turn, would report to the full board at its annual meeting on June 21.[36]

At this meeting, the committee urged the board to pass Gifford's motion, and the trustees, "with little discussion and slight opposition," voted to do so. They proposed to "raise money for additional dormitories and a recitation hall for women, and that, in the meantime, Middlebury College should loan to the new college for women the recitation halls and other facilities used at the present time."[37]

Although the trustees did not spell out details of the new coordinate arrangement, Moody revealed his own ideas to Gifford in April 1930.[38] The president was opposed to organizing the women's college as a distinctly separate institute. Instead, he envisioned an "imperium in imperio" with "Middlebury becoming in one respect a university with a Men's College, a Women's College, and a Summer Session." He would serve as president of all three, the faculty of the men's and women's colleges would overlap, and a united board would run both schools through two smaller bodies "which need not be interlocking, but under which would come some who were not trustees of the College." An entirely separate women's organization would "endanger the parent institution in less than a generation." The trustees apparently agreed with Moody in this regard. After 1930, the president and Fellows of Middlebury controlled both the men's college and The Women's College at Middlebury (as it was formally named in 1931),[39] the faculty for both units was nearly identical (except that most women taught only in the women's college), and Moody was president of both schools and chief officer of the summer sessions.

Administration of the women's college, which lacked its own separate trustees, faculty, or chief executive officer, was significantly affected by the activities of the Women's Advisory Committee and the power of the women's college dean, Eleanor Ross '95. President Moody had reestablished and restructured the Women's Advisory Committee in the mid-1920s to include three alumnae, three trustees, and three other prominent women who would serve as permanent members. This committee, with the encouragement of the board, successfully recommended several measures to improve the women's college in the 1930s and 1940s. They advocated strengthening the curriculum in the humanities and social sciences, including the addition of courses in oral English and the appreciation of art. They pressed for modernized entrance requirements, a placement bureau, more women professors, more scholarships, a separate admissions committee, and the conferring of only one final degree, the B.A. They also recommended that the college hire matrons for the women's dormitories, a full-time alumnae secretary, and a social director.[40]

Although the Women's Advisory Committee played an important role and effected many alterations and improvements, it was clear that they were an *advisory* body, not a separate board of trustees. On the other hand, Dean Eleanor Ross '95 functioned, in a very real sense, as president of the women's college. Moody himself admitted that Dean Ross "now runs the Women's College and is to all intents and purposes the president of that institution except that she does not confer degrees and does consult me in most matters, exactly as I in turn consult the trustees."[41] Indeed, from 1915, when President Thomas asked her to leave her successful twenty-year career as a secondary school educator and become dean of women at Middlebury, Eleanor Ross achieved dominance in her area and, according to Stephen Freeman, "was the real builder of the Women's College at Middlebury, the creator of its quality and strength."[42]

Her intellectual stature, high standards, and great concern for each woman under her charge were admired by students, faculty, and trustees alike. Physically, she was a large, handsome woman with an abundance of white hair and a beautiful melodious voice. She was dignified, straightforward, and formidable: nobody called Miss Ross "Eleanor"! Indeed, most students who admired her also held her in awe and were even a bit afraid of her.[43] Yet many alumni

Appointed dean of women in 1915 by President Thomas, Eleanor Ross, class of 1895, enlarged that position for twenty-nine years. President Moody admitted in 1930 that Dean Ross "now runs the Women's College and is to all intents and purposes the President of that institution." In 1949 she married John Thomas, who had appointed her, never imagining how she would shape the college.

also remembered critical occasions during their undergraduate days when Dean Ross successfully counseled them about important personal problems or gave them crucial advice concerning career plans. For twenty-nine years she gave much of her life and incredible energy to the women's college, and everyone was saddened by her death in 1953.

Dean Ross did not oppose segregation and the development of a separate women's college.[44] She undoubtedly hoped that such a change would mean better facilities for the women than they had experienced at coeducational Middlebury. For example, women's housing facilities were often very poor, and Ross recommended strongly in 1933 that women's admissions be restricted until adequate housing could be provided.[45] Indeed, while the trustees had made the verbal commitment to a coordinate system, it was clear that Middlebury would remain a coeducational institution—with inferior accommodations for women—until funds were found to construct appropriate educational facilities and residence halls.

Unfortunately, the trustees had chosen the early years of the Great Depression to embark on dismantling coeducation. In October 1930 the board authorized Moody to raise money for a women's residence hall, but a two-year search produced no funds. The General Education Board turned him down, and few people in those years had money available for college residence halls.[46] In 1933, as we have seen, the sale of twenty thousand acres of Battell's mountain estate provided enough money to construct Forest Hall.[47] The board also approved architectural plans in 1935 for a women's campus that would cost about $3 million.[48] But the only construction between 1936 and 1945 was on the men's campus (Munroe and Gifford). Except for Forest Hall in 1936 and an infirmary in 1937, the women's physical facilities were ignored, and the Women's College of Middlebury (the *at* was changed to *of* in 1937)[49] could not be considered a separate physical entity.

The Depression and World War II thwarted President Moody's high hopes for segregation and a coordinate system, and both ideas were scrapped in the postwar years. Indeed, one of the most exciting developments in the period after 1945 was the complete integration of the sexes at Middlebury and (with few exceptions) the creation of a truly coeducational college with equal facilities, equal treatment, virtually equal enrollment, and no double standard.

CHAPTER 4

CULTURE AND CURRICULUM: EDUCATIONAL CHANGE, 1915–1941

Students need to be protected from their immaturity. We believe that this is best accomplished by a reasonable prescription, especially in the first two years of the course. The weakness of the elective system is that students do not always choose wisely or with the best of motives. Even the most serious students sometimes show a narrow or scattered aim.

—Faculty statement, quoted in *Middlebury Campus*, June 1, 1927

Andre Morize was the chief architect of the Middlebury Foreign Language Schools as graduate schools of university quality and an international reputation. With vision, skill, and a tremendous energy, he developed the formula of Dr. Stroebe into a superb institution for the training of graduate students and teachers of foreign languages. . . . He had the enthusiasm and personal magnetism of de Visme, together with an acute sense of tact, sound judgment and good organization. He was a distinguished scholar, a literary historian of the first rank, a brilliant lecturer, an exacting teacher, a devoted counselor and loyal friend to his host of students. Under his direction, the French Summer School became the model for all the Middlebury Schools, and was imitated by all other summer language schools.

—Stephen Freeman, *The Middlebury College Foreign Language Schools: The Story of a Unique Idea* (Middlebury, Vt., 1975) 63

Slight in physique, Professor Davison was an intense and genuinely committed teacher, far above the average in talent, ambition, insight, and devotion. In the classroom, he represented a rare combination of intellectual energy and wholehearted dedication to his students. He had the Promethean spark which ignited young minds. His class hours were organized, he read well, had a distinction of the italicizing phrase, and communicated an electric excitement that gave the classroom a nimble and alerted air. The hours seemed over before they had actually started, and invariably students left the classroom anticipating the next meeting. . . . He was a brilliant teacher who kept the focus directly on the spiritual element in the human spirit. He was one of the best teachers I've ever known, both at Middlebury and at Oxford University.

—Reginald Cook to David Stameshkin, March 18, 1980, MCA

In addition to stressing quality over quantity and segregation over coeducation, Paul Moody also tried to emphasize culture over vocation as the major educational aim. He consistently attacked the notion that a college education was supposed to "fit men for specific vocations."[1] A Middlebury education, which would encourage independence of thought, scholarship, seriousness of purpose, a broad exposure to the liberal arts, and, in particular, a strong concentration in one area of study, should produce cultured individuals with a desire to serve society. In order to attain these goals, he supported a series of curricular reforms, hired a number of excellent faculty members, and greatly improved the quality and breadth of the college's academic offerings, especially the innovative summer programs. Yet, as in his struggles for quality and segregation, Moody faced difficult obstacles and had mixed success in trying to move the college away from the more utilitarian and "progressive" educational ideas introduced by President Thomas.

Many liberal arts colleges initiated curricular reforms after World War I, attempting among other things to attract students who were academically rather than vocationally oriented.[2] Here Middlebury followed the lead of Harvard, Swarthmore, and other outstanding colleges by adopting curricular changes designed to establish a stronger major with fewer electives and more prescribed courses and to create an atmosphere more conducive to independent study and serious scholarship. Thomas's system of majors, minors, and distribution requirements (which had divided college courses into three groups—languages and English, social sciences and humanities, and sciences and home economics) was modified. Students had been required to complete two majors in different groups (eighteen hours each) and a minor (twelve hours) in the third group and to satisfy distribution requirements (at least six courses in each group and not more than twenty in any one group).[3] Although the system had allowed students a good deal of freedom in choosing courses, the faculty decided in 1927 that so many electives were not helpful:

> Students need to be protected from their immaturity. We believe that this is best accomplished by a reasonable prescription, especially in the first two years of the course. The weakness of the elective system is that students do not always choose wisely or with the best of motives. Even the most serious students sometimes show a narrow or scattered aim.[4]

Moody agreed with this view and also knew that electives added expense and uncertainty to the college budget. At a time when as many freshman and sophomore classes as possible were being segregated, the college simply could not hire enough professors to handle a fully developed elective system and meet the added demands of segregated (duplicated) classes.[5] The solution was prescription.

In 1922, Middlebury had introduced a required one-year freshman course, contemporary civilization (modeled after a similar course first offered at Columbia in 1917), which examined a myriad of world problems and some of the proposed solutions.[6] The faculty was ready by 1927 to increase the number of freshman–sophomore course requirements:

> Our present curriculum is arranged in three groups. . . . We now attempt to secure adequate distribution of studies by requiring students to take not less than eight hours in each group. However, the subjects are very loosely grouped and students may meet this requirement without getting the broad background of basic subjects so necessary for subsequent specialization. We therefore propose to abolish our present system of distribution and substitute a program of required work during the first two years. An outline of this plan is given below:

PLAN OF WORK REQUIRED IN FIRST TWO YEARS

A.B.	B.S.
2 yrs. Latin or Greek	2 yrs. math., or math. and science
2 yrs. English	2 yrs. English
1 yr. contemp. civ.	1 yr. contemporary civilization

1 yr. history, pol. sci., econ., ped., or phil.	1 yr. history, pol. sci., econ., ped., or phil.
1 yr. math, physics, chem., or biology	1 yr. foreign language.[7]

This plan went into effect with the class of 1931. While some of the prescription was dropped in 1936, all students were still required to complete a "Field of Planned Study" (twenty-four to thirty-six hours in a major and twenty-four to thirty-six hours in a cognate subject), pass a comprehensive exam in the major during the senior year, and satisfy a distribution requirement of at least twelve hours in each of three divisions (languages, social sciences, and natural sciences).[8]

Prescription appeared to narrow student choices but only at the lower end of the curriculum. A primary aim of the new requirements was to strengthen the major; this in turn led to innovations variously designed to stress serious scholarship and implement one of Moody's major goals: that of giving students greater responsibility for their own education.[9] In the process they also acquired greater latitude and independence.

One important corollary of the strengthened major was the comprehensive examination, one of the group of curricular reforms instituted during the interwar years. Supporters of the comprehensive system argued that it encouraged students, through independent study, to take a broader perspective on a more concentrated body of material.[10] Stephen Freeman, a young French professor, proposed comprehensives as a requirement for all departments. The faculty was apparently not ready for such a major departure, but Freeman was allowed to employ them in his department as an experiment in 1927.[11] Professor Douglas Beers, another early advocate, was "chiefly responsible for the innovation of the comprehensive examination, Independent study, and Honors program in the English Department."[12] The system proved successful, and comprehensives were adopted for most seniors in 1931.[13]

A related innovation was independent study. The faculty approved a plan in 1928 that allowed a few seniors to do work "wholly outside of the classroom or in combinations of class work and independent study as they and their advisors may decide."[14] In addition, more students began to engage in honors work. This might previously have stigmatized them as "bookworms" or "grinds," but the increasingly serious intellectual atmosphere on campus conferred acceptance.[15]

The idea of involving students more significantly in their own education went a step or two further. The Student Curriculum Committee was formed in 1926, "privileged to confer with the similar committee of the faculty and to offer suggestions."[16] Although some faculty members objected to student involvement in an area that had been their special province, the student committee took its charge seriously and made several recommendations that the faculty adopted.[17] The principle was extended in 1927 to class attendance. Students previously had been allowed only three cuts per class per semester, but after an experiment in unlimited cuts with a few of the best upperclassmen, the new "voluntary absence" proposal (already in operation at Harvard, Yale, and elsewhere) was extended to all seniors and juniors and the best sophomores and freshmen, and it proved fairly successful.[18]

Students and faculty generally applauded all these changes. Educational quality seemed clearly on the rise even though the caliber of many incoming male students continued to disappoint reform-minded professors.[19] The *Campus* trumpeted Middlebury in 1928 as "one of the most progressive of Eastern colleges," and Professor Burrage hailed "a new and more bracing intellectual atmosphere."[20]

President Moody improved the quality and breadth of the academic program in three additional ways: by hiring a number of outstanding young faculty, some of whom had great influence well into the 1960s; by expanding the offerings of several departments; and by encouraging the development of the summer programs.

Some of Moody's most effective appointments were in the languages. In 1925 he called Stephen Freeman, a brilliant young Harvard Ph.D. from Brown University, to teach French at Middlebury. Freeman contributed mightily to the college's language programs for nearly half a century. Between 1926 and 1936 he was instrumental in establishing the "first continuous 'Language Laboratory' in the country, organized by a college for the individual study of foreign language pronunciation and intonation."[21] He helped organize Middlebury's Italian Summer Language School (1932) and the Russian School (1945), founded the Chinese (1966) and Japanese (1970) schools, and established the Middlebury Graduate Schools

French, and an abiding dedication to the teaching of foreign languages, united Edward C. Knox, director of the Language Schools from 1982 to 1993, and Stephen A. Freeman, director from 1947 to 1970, in the Salon Louis XVI of the Chateau.

Abroad Program (1949). He served as acting president of the college on several occasions and as vice president from 1946 to 1966. His intelligence, discretion, tact, and academic savoir-faire made him one of Middlebury's most powerful faculty members and administrators. Professor Cook has written that "Steve Freeman's service to the College is like a brilliant gold thread of loyalty, performance, and distinction running through three college administrations."[22]

Moody also hired Claude Bourcier (1937) in French, Juan Centeno (1931) and Samuel Guarnaccia '30 (1940) in Spanish, and Werner Neuse (1932) in German. These men taught in the college and frequently directed the summer language school in their respective disciplines during their long Middlebury careers. Guarnaccia, an outstanding scholar-athlete, taught Italian as well as Spanish.[23]

Moody also made several key appointments in the humanities. He helped create a good English department by hiring Douglas S. Beers (1925), Harry G. Owen '23 (1926), Richard L. Brown (1931), and Erie Volkert (1941).[24] In 1929 he persuaded Reginald "Doc" Cook '24 to return to his alma mater and join Professor Wilfred E. "Davy"

Reginald L. Cook '24 and Robert Frost walked in conversation when Cook was director of the School of English. "Doc" Cook was a bridge to Burgess Meredith's embodiment of Robert Frost in his 1983 film, The Afterglow.

Davison '13 in what was probably the first separate department of American literature established at an American college or university; Moody had founded it in 1923 to allow Professor Davison to chair a department in his specialty.[25] A marvelous teacher, Davison (as we shall see) left his mark on the Bread Loaf School of English as well as on the college, and "Doc" Cook had been one of his most outstanding and devoted students. The community was greatly shocked when Davison unexpectedly passed away in September 1929, just days before the fall term and Cook's appointment were to begin.[26]

Cook continued the tradition of great teaching in American literature at Middlebury. With a master's degree in 1926 from Bread Loaf and a B.A. in 1929 from Oxford, which he attended as a Rhodes scholar, Cook dazzled students for four decades with his brilliant lectures and exacting classes. Even in the late 1960s he "towered" over the institution, according to Peter Harris '69, and was undoubtedly its most popular and revered teacher during his long and active career. As director of the Bread Loaf School of English from 1946 to 1964, he also demonstrated administrative and leadership skills.[27] He persuaded one of his finest students, Howard Munford '34, to join the American literature faculty in 1941, thereby ensuring that the department would continue to be one of the stronger ones into the 1970s.

In other areas, Moody improved the faculty in the natural sciences by recruiting Raymond L. Barney to join Samuel Longwell in biology (1924) and Ben Wissler to assist the brilliant Ernest C. Bryant '91 in physics (1930). He also hired Bruno Schmidt in geology (1925) and Burt Hazeltine (1924) and John Bowker (1926) in mathematics. Hazeltine served as dean of men from 1926 to 1939; Bowker was dean of the faculty from 1953 to 1967.[28] While the number of faculty in the social sciences doubled (from eight in 1921 to sixteen by 1941), a greater increase than in any other division, the quality here may have been somewhat weaker on the whole than in the languages and humanities. A major exception was Harry Fife (1925), who helped establish the economics department as one of the best.[29]

Although Moody brought other successful professors to Middlebury, he usually hired people he considered "teachers" and, unlike his successors, placed less emphasis on a candidate's professional qualifications and research interests.[30] The result was a faculty devoted to teaching, to Middlebury, and to Moody but (with some notable exceptions) only secondarily interested in professional research.

Although Moody was moderately successful in implementing curricular reforms and improving the quality of the faculty, his stated goal of emphasizing culture over vocation was somewhat thwarted. The materialistic 1920s and the Depression forced the college (and many other schools) to emphasize the practical as well as the cultural virtues of collegiate training. Moody was careful to soften his verbal attacks on practical higher education and could write by 1931 that Middlebury was trying to harmonize the two ideals "by making the vocational courses as largely as possible cultural, and the cultural courses as far as possible vocational." [31]

Middlebury's willingness to countenance an emphasis on "vocational" or "practical" education was apparent in several areas. The men's and women's colleges developed vocational guidance and placement programs conducted by the deans in the early 1920s. [32] The B.S. degree was discarded in 1935–1936 (all graduates would receive an A.B.), and courses in Latin and Greek—the symbolic core of the old liberal arts curriculum—were no longer required. [33] Finally, the college's publicist, W. Storrs Lee '28, wrote a booklet, "To College with a Purpose," which explained how various four-year curricula at Middlebury could prepare students for specific careers. [34] This apparent concession to the rising tide of practical ideas was clothed in the rather defensive rhetoric of the liberal arts:

> It is the business of a liberal arts college to prepare men for careers—not jobs—and it can be accomplished only through a three-fold program: intensive work in the special field in which a student chooses to concentrate; a general survey of many subjects as they relate to the field of concentration; and the studying of certain cultural courses which alone can give definitive meaning and perspective to vocational purpose. In a liberal arts college, it cannot be overstressed that all truth is one, all problems are related. Probably the most acute need of the country is career-minded men, graduate leaders having a sympathetic understanding of problems not ordinarily recognized as being inter-related or even tangent. . . . Its [the booklet's] purpose is to stress the liberal education of students and at the same time to show how this liberal education may lead toward definite vocational ends. It answers at last that old accusation that the liberal arts college leads nowhere in particular. It defines our present aims at Middlebury. [35]

Thus did the college respond to the pragmatic demands of American society between the wars by developing a more tolerant attitude toward utilitarian ideals in higher education.

The most important and far-reaching curricular and educational phenomenon of this period was the growth and development of the college's innovative summer programs—the foreign language schools, the Bread Loaf School of English, and the Bread Loaf Writers' Conference.

Stephen A. Freeman has written a richly detailed history of the language schools; therefore, only a brief survey will be offered here.[36] According to Freeman, "the Middlebury Language Schools were the first summer schools in any college in the country which gave only advance courses concentrated upon a single language, and which required exclusive use of that language in the entire life of the school." [37]

It was mainly by chance that the schools were founded at Middlebury. Fraulein Lilian Stroebe, professor of German at Vassar, accidentally learned of the facilities at Middlebury College in 1914; here, she decided, were the ideal physical plant and summer climate to accommodate her innovative two-year-old German summer school.[38] With President Thomas's approval, Fraulein Stroebe began the first of three summers of German language training at Middlebury in 1915. The school, which was highly unusual in its emphasis on isolation, advanced training, and intensiveness, was successful until the United States entered World War I in 1917, when anti-German sentiment swept the country and many schools discontinued the teaching of German. As high school German teachers switched to other subjects, attendance at the Middlebury German School fell dramatically. The trustees reluctantly told Fraulein Stroebe that her school would not operate in 1918 and thanked her warmly for her services. It was reestablished in 1931 in nearby Bristol, Vermont, under the direction of Ernest Feise (1931–1948) and returned to the Middlebury campus in 1951.

Fraulein Stroebe's idea of an isolated, advanced, and intensive language training program struck a responsive chord at Middlebury. Soon after the conclusion of the initial German school session, President Thomas asked H. P. Williamson de Visme '96 and his associate, Paul Louis Jeanrenaud, to come to Middlebury in the summer of 1916 and operate a French school similar to Stroebe's German school.[39] Williamson de Visme, a dynamic Middlebury native, had been an assistant professor of French at the University of Chicago until moving to France in 1912 to operate a school at which Americans could learn French. He and Jeanrenaud, a Swiss, founded the Ecole du Chateau de Soisy for that purpose. (Few Americans went abroad after the outbreak of the World War I, and the school primarily attracted French students preparing for the baccalaureate examination.) De Visme and Jeanrenaud taught the French courses at the Middlebury summer session in 1914 and accepted Thomas's invitation to organize a French summer school in 1916. It was an immediate success, although the war prevented de Visme from leaving France to direct the 1917 session. Enrollment grew from twenty in 1916 to two hundred in 1920. De Visme accepted a Middlebury appointment in June 1919 as professor of French and head of the department of Romance languages, and a year later he opened the second college French house in the United States (the first was at the University of Wisconsin) and the first such house, according to Freeman, in which only French could be spoken anywhere on the premises.[40]

Williamson de Visme resigned in 1924 after several years of internal conflict and jealousy within the French program. His departure led to two new appointments. Professor Andre Morize of Harvard, a nationally known expert on French literature and civilization, was named director of the French summer school, and one of his prize students, Dr. Stephen A. Freeman, became chair of the French department and dean of the French School. (The division of responsibilities between a director who handled the academic program and a resident dean who dealt with publicity, admissions, housing, food, and all material arrangements began about this time.) According to Freeman, Morize's appointment was a landmark:

> Andre Morize was the chief architect of the Middlebury Foreign Language Schools as graduate schools of university quality and an international reputation. With vision, skill, and tremendous energy, he developed the formula of Dr. Stroebe into a superb institution for the training of graduate students and teachers of foreign languages. . . . He had the enthusiasm and personal magnetism of de Visme, together with an acute sense of tact, sound judgment and good organization. He was a distinguished scholar, a literary historian of the first rank, a brilliant lecturer, an exacting teacher, a devoted counselor and loyal friend to his host of students. Under his direction, the French Sum-

Andre Morize, the son of a Huguenot pastor in Dordogne, led the French School each Sunday of the summer program in a nonsectarian "Heure Spirituelle," with readings in French from philosophers and thinkers of many nations.

mer School became the model for all the Middlebury Schools, and was imitated by all other summer language schools.[41]

Morize attracted an outstanding, loyal, hardworking faculty and staff to the French School, upgraded the quality of the curriculum and the extracurricular program, and watched enrollment expand from 190 in 1926 to 306 in 1929 and 359 in 1940. This relatively large size was attained despite the Depression and a belief by most American academics (reversed during World War II) that, in foreign language study, concentration on reading proficiency was superior to oral training.[42] The French School, with an enrollment often double that of all the others combined, dominated the Middlebury campus each summer.

The early success of the German and French schools persuaded Middlebury to open a Spanish school in 1917 under the director-ship of an aristocratic Filipino, Julian Moreno-Lacalle, instructor in Spanish at the United States Naval Academy.[43] The wartime switch from German to Spanish instruction in many American schools was a major factor in this decision and an important reason for the

Created in 1927, the Experimental Laboratory of the French School was the first language laboratory in the nation. Besides wax cylinder Dictaphones, the laboratory had a kymograph (the machine with the large black cylinder presided over by Marcel Vigneron at far right) that cut a trace of the speaker's voice on smoked paper, which could then be compared with the track of a fluent speaker.

good attendance in the early years (an average of eighty-five students each summer between 1917 and 1929). President Thomas appointed Moreno-Lacalle the year-round head of the Spanish department and dean of the Spanish School in 1920, a post he retained until 1929, when he accepted a similar position at Rutgers.

Spanish School enrollment declined to an average of sixty-two students per session during the depressed 1930s. It was run by a succession of visiting directors until 1935, when the hardworking Juan Centeno agreed to take charge. Centeno, trained in medicine and Spanish literature at Madrid and the University of Wisconsin, had come to Middlebury in 1931. Under his leadership, enrollment increased and the atmosphere was greatly improved. The quality and status of the school were further enhanced in the late 1930s by the addition of several prominent Spanish intellectuals who emigrated to the United States with the defeat of the Republican forces in the Spanish Civil War: Don Fernando de los Rios, a Republican cabinet member; the poets Enrique Diez-Canedo, Pedro Salinas, and Jorge Guillen; and the famed phonetician, Tomas Navarro Tomas. During World War II the Spanish School enjoyed perhaps its greatest suc-

Even in the depths of World War II, the German School continued in Bristol, teaching Goethe's language and celebrating that nation's traditions.

cess, becoming "a rallying point and focus for the leading men and women of letters and intellectuals of Hispanic culture from all over the world."[44] Enrollment rose dramatically each year, from 60 in 1937 to a record 326 in 1942, as the hard-pressed Centeno strove to accommodate the avalanche of new students and faculty. In 1943–1945, because of the presence of the V-12 navy units on the Middlebury campus, the Spanish School was moved to Bread Loaf, where a room shortage limited enrollment to about 225.

Middlebury opened its fourth summer language program, the Italian School, in 1932, under the direction of Professor Gabriella Bosano (1932–1938), chair of the Italian department at Wellesley College.[45] At first it was a stepchild of the French School with a few courses, a Casa Italiana for conversation, and a small but growing enrollment (twenty-two in 1932, fifty-two in 1935). The college upgraded the program to a full-fledged Italian School in 1935, under the directorship of Camillo Merlino (1938–1947). The school expanded its faculty and its size (eighty-two students in 1939) and managed to survive the dwindling wartime enrollments intact.

All of the language schools developed social and extracurricular programs—plays, folk singing, literary contests (such as the Juegos Florales of the Spanish School), and picnics—that helped create strong bonds between students and faculty and greatly enhanced the range and depth of the learning experience.[46] These popular activities, when coupled with the standard formula—advanced courses, intensive training, and isolation—helped ensure an exciting and unusual atmosphere for many foreign-language students.

The unique nature of the language schools was underscored by the introduction of the degree of Doctor of Modern Languages in 1927. Morize, with some assistance from Moreno-Lacalle and Freeman, was responsible for proposing the new degree.[47] He argued that American graduate students in Romance languages were not prepared to teach or speak foreign languages adequately when they completed their Ph.D. programs, having spent most of their time in literary research and rather narrow philological and linguistic problems. Middlebury now hoped to develop a degree which would guarantee

> that the holder is able to impart to others a usable knowledge of a foreign language and its culture; that he is not only a scholar but a linguist with a mastery of the spoken and written language of his special field; that he is familiar by personal contact with the foreign country or area, its civilization and culture; that he possesses the pedagogical training and experience necessary to teach effectively.[48]

The requirements for the Doctor of Modern Languages degree were imposing: a master's degree, thirty credits while in residence, two semesters of study and residence abroad, and, in the major language, oral and written examinations, a semester's study of phonetics, a year of supervised teaching, and a thirty-five-thousand-word dissertation, plus an oral and a written examination in a minor language and a reading knowledge of German. Although most of academe accepted the new degree, only seven were awarded before 1945 (the first two in 1931). But it symbolized the way in which the mission of the Middlebury summer language schools differed from that of traditional Romance language graduate programs.

The early success of foreign-language training also helped inspire the formation of the Bread Loaf School of English in 1919–1920.[49] Actually, several concurrent developments spurred its birth. Middlebury had long offered a potpourri of summer courses, primarily for teachers, ministers, and other adults, in areas as diverse as Greek, food study, and wood carving—all under the rubric of an "English" school. By 1919, Provost Collins considered these summer courses as a "bargain basement type of education," unsatisfactory "for either revenue, reputation, or educational service," and he was looking for a superior alternative. By this time the success of the French School had led to crowded accommodations during the summer, and there was no longer room for the English school students. Furthermore, as we have seen, the trustees had just voted to sell or lease Joseph Battell's financially troubled Bread Loaf Inn. Collins was concerned about each of these problems. Then Stanley Williams, an English instructor at Yale and a summer instructor at Middlebury's English school, purportedly suggested that the college create a legitimate English summer school on the lines of the foreign language schools and house it at Bread Loaf. According to legend, Collins replied sarcastically, "What would you do, teach them all to speak English?" [50] But he soon became convinced that a school devoted entirely to English language and literature would be an excellent educational innovation and that utilizing Bread Loaf would preserve Battell's scenic legacy for the college while alleviating the summer school crowding on the main campus.

On a lazy summer afternoon in 1919, Collins, President Thomas, Dean de Visme, and (most likely) Professor Wilfred Davison, who was secretary of the summer school, met on a slope of the Widow's Clearing at Bread Loaf to discuss the establishment and location of an English school. Soon after this crucial meeting, the college decided to open an English school in the summer of 1920, Bread Loaf was chosen as the site, and Thomas persuaded the trustees not to sell the inn.[51] Professor Charles Baker Wright, who had taught in the English department since 1885, was named dean, and Davison was appointed assistant dean. Davison, who had attended the German School in 1915 and had taught German at Middlebury from 1913 to 1918 before joining the English department, became dean the following year and served in that post until his death in 1929.[52] Davison had a profound influence on the development of the school. "Doc" Cook has offered a vivid portrait of his former mentor:

> Slight in physique, Professor Davison was an intense and genuinely committed teacher, far above the average in talent, ambition, insight, and devotion. In the classroom, he represented a rare combination

Wilfred Davison '13 wanted the School of English "to do for teachers of English something similar to what was being done for teachers of modern languages in the schools at Middlebury . . . to be so organized that students and teachers should have the advantage of intimate association, the genuine contact of mind with mind—that was the plan."

of intellectual energy and wholehearted dedication to his students. He had the Promethean spark which ignited young minds. His class hours were organized, he read well, had the distinction of the italicizing phrase, and communicated an electric excitement that gave the classroom a nimble and alerted air. The hours seemed over before they had actually started, and invariably students left the classroom anticipating the next meeting.

I don't think Professor Davison could ever be measured by the conventional scale in a Bureau of Standards. If his lively, ranging, incisive, and independent mind drew closer to the conservative than to the liberal condition in culture, it is also no less true that he never enforced his viewpoint upon other intensities, other persuasions, other convictions. A moral idealist, he was far more concerned about practicing the art of pedagogy than he was in receiving the material rewards of teaching. He was a brilliant teacher who kept the focus directly on the spiritual element in the human spirit. He was one of the best teachers I've ever known, both at Middlebury and at Oxford University.[53]

To a great extent, Davison determined the purpose, curriculum, and staff of the school in its early years. He stated its objective in 1929, shortly before his untimely death:

The purpose of the Bread Loaf School was, in brief, to do for teachers of English something similar to what was being done for teachers of modern language in the schools at Middlebury. Those schools bring native instructors into intimate contact with American teachers, and in a friendly and informal atmosphere concentrate for six weeks on the language in question, at present French and Spanish. To have a school for teachers of English in which nothing but English should be taught, to have as instructors the best teachers who could be secured, and have a school limited in numbers and so organized that students and teachers should have the advantage of intimate association, the genuine contact of mind with mind—that was the plan.[54]

The majority of Bread Loaf students before World War II were women who taught English or hoped to do so, and Davison soon developed a curriculum for them that included courses in five areas: creative writing, dramatic production, English and American literature, public speaking and debate, and teaching methods. Enrollment grew quickly, from 51 in 1920 to 112 in 1923, then leveled out during the rest of the decade.

Davison attracted a strong faculty staff to Bread Loaf during the 1920s, including Edith Mirrieless of Stanford, Kenneth Murdock of Harvard, James Southall Wilson of the University of Virgina, Fred Lewis Pattee of Penn State (and later Rollins), Dallas Lore Sharp of Boston University, Katherine Lee Bates of Wellesley, Robert Gay of Simmons, Vernon Harrington of Middlebury, Leonora Branch of Mount Holyoke, and George Whicher of Amherst. By 1929, according to Bread Loaf's able historian, the faculty "could be called distinguished." [55] Davison also cajoled many famous writers to spend time at Bread Loaf in the 1920s and share ideas with students. The list of visiting authors included Willa Cather, Edwin Markham, Louis Untermeyer, and Dorothy Canfield Fisher. The name most closely associated with the school was that of Robert Frost, who maintained a Vermont summer residence and spent at least one day at Bread Loaf nearly every summer between 1921 and 1962. Frost stimulated students (particularly before World War II) with his brilliant and eclectic readings and discussions; Moody claimed in 1944 that Frost's "presence on the hill has been at all times an inspiration and generally its chief attraction." [56] Yet, as George Anderson has written, Frost in no way can be considered a founder of the school or a powerful influence on its operation, and after World War II, as the school became more consciously "academic," Frost's influence diminished.[57]

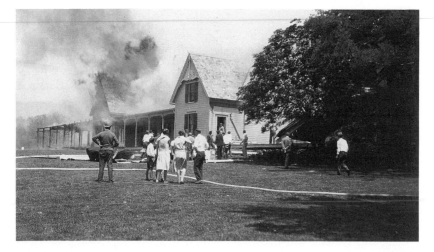

Although students and faculty deserted the baccalaureate service in 1931 to fight the fire that destroyed the recently built Davison Library, only a timely turn in the wind saved the Bread Loaf Inn.

Professor Robert M. Gay of the Simmons College English department was appointed director after Davison's death in 1929 and held that office until 1936. Gay, who had taught at Bread Loaf during the late 1920s, was more cosmopolitan than his predecessor and cultivated a somewhat more open atmosphere.[58] He faced two severe problems during his administration—the Depression, which cut enrollment nearly in half, and the disastrous Bread Loaf fire of June 7, 1931. The fire began in an electricity shed and spread quickly to the music hall, which was destroyed along with the bowling alley and the newly constructed Davison Memorial Library. Volunteer firemen came quickly to the scene from nearby communities, and when Moody, faculty, and students received word in Middlebury, they deserted the festivities of Baccalaureate Sunday and jumped into every available vehicle for a mad dash up the mountain to assist.

It was nature, however, that saved Bread Loaf. The wind was blowing in the right direction, and the rest of the inn was saved; the whole plant would otherwise have been destroyed. Nevertheless, three weeks before the opening of the summer session, a major portion of the facilities lay in ruin. The Bread Loaf School had not been a money-maker, and it would have been understandable if the trustees had allowed the school to expire rather than put funds into rebuilding it. But the board decided that the 1931 session would be held and arranged for the construction of new facilities.

When Gay resigned in 1936, after leading the school through the worst of the Depression and the postfire recovery, enrollments had risen to their previous levels and a new plant had been built. Furthermore, he had been instrumental in attracting several eminent faculty members: Walter Prichard Eaton of Stockbridge, Massachusetts; Donald Davidson of Vanderbilt; Theodore Morrison of Harvard; and George K. Anderson of Brown, as well as Hewette E. Joyce of Dartmouth, who would become director during World War II.

Gay was replaced by Harry Goddard Owen '23, the assistant director for seven years under Gay.[59] Owen had taught English and fine arts at Middlebury since 1932 and was one of three men appointed to run the college in 1940, when President Moody took a leave of absence. An able teacher and administrator, "both innovative and sophisticated in his approach," the new director of Bread Loaf was impressively described by "Doc" Cook:

> Professor Owen, as I remember him, was a tall, handsome, and extremely enlightened colleague of impeccable manners and courtesy. His passion for music, fine arts, and literature, in about that order, was most notable. The design of his life reflected a finely tuned sensibility in its intensity.
>
> As a teacher, he was able to stimulate vigorous discussions in his classes, and some of these discussions reverberated around campus. For example, when he presented the chapter on "The Grand Inquisitor" from *The Brothers Karamazov* in one of his literature courses, the intellectual excitement stirred up a large part of the college community.

Cook gives special credit to Owen for adding to the quality of Bread Loaf by "encouraging outstanding students to attend with scholarship aid, and by securing a brilliant faculty."[60] His interest in the arts and humanities led to "a widening of the horizon" as Owen secured faculty who would lecture or introduce courses in music, painting, and other areas outside English and American literature, strictly construed.[61] Enrollments soared as the Depression eased, averaging 181 students during Owen's directorship (1937–1942), with a high of 231 in 1941. Owen handled the enlarged school with a hitherto unseen care for detail. These years also saw the addition of Tamarack Cottage and the Barn of the Battell farm; the Barn, in particular, became an indispensable facility for a variety of functions.

Owen left in 1942 to join the armed forces, and Hewette Joyce, a Bread Loaf faculty member since 1932, was appointed acting director until Owen's expected return after the war.[62] Joyce capably brought the school through the war years. While enrollments slipped to about one hundred, and the size of the faculty was reduced by half to five or six members, the school continued to operate effectively, even though wartime shortages and anxiety may have disturbed people's concentration at times. Joyce's brief but successful stewardship set the stage for the successful postwar directorship of "Doc" Cook, who assumed the position after Owen decided to accept a deanship at Rutgers in 1945 when he returned from the war.

The Bread Loaf School of English, an innovative institution in its own right, spawned another unusual program only six years after it opened—the Bread Loaf Writers' Conference. The latter was developed, in part, as a response to Bread Loaf's financial exigencies.[63] The English School utilized the facilities for six weeks, from early July to mid-August, and the college was unable to turn a profit on this operation. John Farrar, editor of *The Bookman* (and later a major publisher), suggested in 1925 that Middlebury sponsor a special two-week program for writers in late August at Bread Loaf. Wilfred Davison seized upon the idea and sent a recommendation to President Moody in October:

> I recommend making the experiment next summer of a two week's course in creative writing, to follow the close of the regular session. I am doubtful whether we can secure for this special work a large number of students, but even a small number would materially assist the Inn in the later seasons. Mr. Farrar thought we might get 50 for such a short course. I should plan on 25, I think, in estimating the budget for such work. If you see fit to authorize me to go ahead with plans for such an experimental term, I shall be glad to work out details and submit the plans to you.[64]

Moody approved, and the first conference was held in August 1926. Farrar served as director for three summers. Robert Gay replaced him for a three-year stint and then gave way to Theodore Morrison, who began a twenty-four-year directorship in 1932. Enrollment reached sixty to seventy students in the late 1920s before shrinking to twenty (and nearly causing the cancellation of the program) in 1933, then rose as the economy improved in the late 1930s. The Writers' Conference continued during World War II (sharing facilities with the English School in 1943–1945), with attendance reaching a new peak of ninety students in 1945.[65]

Theodore Morrison points out that the Writers' Conference always had a dual philosophy, with the emphasis subtly shifting between the two purposes of encouraging the study of writing "as an art or an honorable craft" and the more practical goal of aiding participants in publishing their manuscripts.[66] Outstanding staff members and visiting lecturers included (to name only a few) Bernard DeVoto, Hervey Allen, William Hazlett Upson, Robert Hillyer, Archibald MacLeish, Robert Frost, James T. Farrell, John Crowe Ransom, Louis Untermeyer, Wallace Stegner, John Marquand, Fletcher Pratt, and Catherine Drinker Bowen. As these names suggest, fiction, poetry, and nonfiction were all subjects of discussion at the conference.

The development of the various summer programs in foreign languages, English, and creative writing greatly expanded the role of the college in American education and endowed Middlebury with a national and international reputation it would retain. Furthermore, the growth of the language schools after World War II continued to help distinguish—and differentiate—Middlebury from other liberal arts colleges.

CHAPTER 5

THE IMPACT OF WORLD
WAR II, 1940–1945

President Moody saw us through some dark days, and we felt very much grieved when we learned that not by his own volition he was leaving.

— John Bowker, former dean of faculty,
interview tape, October 15, 1974, MCA

Letters marked "Free Mail" arrive from odd corners of the world telling about places whose names are now linked with indescribable horrors . . . the Murmansk Run, Ardennes Bulge, Leyte Gulf, Guadalcanal. One girl receives three posthumous letters from the boy who took her to her prep-school prom. He talks about coming to Middlebury after the War and hopes she will still be there. Two weeks before the last letter arrives she receives a note from his mother telling her that an anti-tank gun blew his head off on one of the Philippines.

— June Brogger Noble '46, "Coming of Age in
World War II," *MCNL* 49 (winter 1975): 12–16

Although President Moody had been frustrated by economic imperatives and other obstacles from fully realizing his goals, he had experienced a number of successes by 1941 and was apparently quite happy with his job. He looked forward to retirement in 1944, when, at age sixty-five, he would have served nearly a quarter of a century as president.[1] But the Depression and World War II undermined Moody's position by sharply illuminating his weaknesses as president, and the trustees asked him to resign in 1942.

Moody had never been a good "money man," and Middlebury's

A triumvirate of W. Storrs Lee '28, Stephen A. Freeman, and Harry G. Owen '23, dean of the School of English, ran the college during President Moody's leave of absence in 1940.

economic fortunes, when compared with other New England colleges, declined markedly during his presidency.[2] He did not enjoy fund-raising and had not always been able to say no when he should have in fiscal matters. While his failure in the late 1930s to raise funds for a new field house (greatly desired by some influential alumni) was due in part to the Depression, a more dynamic fund-raiser might have succeeded. Moreover, the Depression necessitated cutting costs to the minimum. Yet when the trustees had ordered Moody to cut salaries, he had been opposed initially to anything that might hurt the faculty, and his reluctance to reduce spending and follow other trustee orders was apparently instrumental in his downfall.[3]

The war also may have played a role. Moody, an early and virulent opponent of fascism in Europe, was deeply committed to the Allied cause.[4] He received a four-month leave of absence in 1940 to help select Protestant chaplains for the armed forces under the auspices of the Wartime Commission of Churches and the Federal Council of Churches. (Except for a brief sabbatical in 1928, this was Moody's only leave of absence in his twenty years at the college.)[5] When he returned, he was angered by several *Campus* editorials that urged the United States to stay out of the European conflict.[6] At the 1940 commencement ceremonies, the president apparently remarked that he "had nothing good to say about this class" and shocked the audience by refusing to shake hands with Robert Pickard '40, the *Campus* editor who had written the editorials. Since it was customary for the president to shake the hand of each graduate, this incident was undoubtedly noticed by the trustees and may have added to their growing unhappiness with Moody's behavior.[7] Furthermore, they knew that if war did break out, the college would be in grave trouble unless military training units were brought there, as in World War I. They may have doubted whether Moody had the initiative or connections to ensure that similar arrangements would be made again.

Moody's relationship with the Middlebury board had always been quite different from that of President Thomas. Thomas was a strong-minded president who had, in a real sense, dominated the board. He organized majorities to support him on key issues and utilized his trustees to obtain critical advice and funds. Although less evidence is available for the Moody years, it is apparent that one trustee, Redfield Proctor, dominated the board as no one man had done in the Thomas years. Proctor, the wealthy executive of the Vermont Marble Company, had been elected chairman of the Middlebury board in 1933. Correspondence reveals that in the late 1930s Proctor had control over even day-to-day presidential decisions.[8] Moody's lack of power may have demeaned him further in the eyes of board members.

In any case, the board's prudential committee met secretly several times in the winter of 1941–1942 and recommended that Moody be replaced as soon as possible. The board officially received Moody's resignation on January 16, 1942, to take effect July 1, 1944, or earlier, if "so mutually arranged between him and the Board."[9] Two months later, the trustees secretly demanded a more immediate resignation, to take effect as soon as a replacement could be found.[10] A presidential selection committee was chosen, and it was announced publicly that Moody would resign July 1, 1944, or earlier.[11]

The community was, therefore, stunned and dismayed when a shaken Moody announced at a special faculty meeting directly following the May commencement ceremonies that he was resigning as of July 1, 1942. As John Bowker recalled years later, most of the faculty had a fond regard for Moody: "President Moody saw us through some dark days, and we felt very much grieved when we learned that not by his own volition he was leaving."[12] The town too had gained

Carolers from the German Club, led by Werner Neuse, celebrated the Christmas season of 1934 at the president's home.

respect and admiration for Moody, his wife, May, and his daughters Charlotte and Margaret, all of whom had participated actively in civic affairs. Moody had sharply reduced town–gown tensions, and a grateful chamber of commerce officially asked the trustees whether "something might be done to persuade Dr. Moody to withdraw his resignation." [13]

Although the town and the college community were upset by Moody's dismissal, it was Moody who was most deeply hurt; indeed, some feel that he never recovered from the blow.[14] He moved to New York City, where he served as assistant pastor of the First Presbyterian Church from 1942 to 1946, but he could never forget Middlebury.[15] "A considerable part of me is there . . . and always will be," he wrote in 1944. "They could take me out of Middlebury, but they could not take Middlebury out of me." [16] He died in Shrewsbury, Vermont, on August 18, 1947, at the lovely Tasheira house that the trustees had first helped him purchase and then given him in 1942 as a small consolation for the early resignation they had forced upon him.[17]

The trustees named Stephen Freeman, the forty-four-year-old chair of the French department and dean of the French School, as acting president. Freeman had been a member of the three-man Administration Committee selected to run the college in 1940 when Moody was on leave.[18] Freeman's administrative ability, his leadership in curricular affairs, his tactfulness, and his loyalty to the college made him a sound and obvious choice.[19]

Freeman faced difficult problems during his brief six-month administration. Because of the war, male applications for admission had dropped sharply: 352 male undergraduates were enrolled in September 1942, and that number would plummet to 74 by July 1943. To maintain a stable enrollment and tuition income, Freeman persuaded the board to accept more women and urged "a gradual strengthening of the curriculum for women."[20] He had heard, he told the faculty, that "army authorities are throwing the ordinary undergraduate college completely aside in their training plans." He warned that men would be increasingly hard to come by, and although an increase in women would ease the shock (and loss of tuition income), the college "must practice every possible economy. The lush, prosperous days are over, and we must now count our pennies."[21]

Freeman opened the 1942–1943 academic year by addressing a hushed and worried student body in Mead Chapel. He read the names of Middlebury students who had already died in conflict and warned that the "old leisurely comfortable patterns of college life" were gone. He urged the men to join one of the reserve corps units and reminded the women that they too would have a critical role in the war effort as they replaced men in traditionally male occupations.[22] He also promised alumni that while "it is the duty of the college to devote itself entirely to the service of our county," Middlebury would not sacrifice its ultimate goals:

> Every detail of our college life is being focused on the dual but inseparable purpose—of fitting young men and women to give their maximum service in winning this war, and in creating a stable peace thereafter. We insist on the duality of the purpose. We must win the

war, but we must not thereby sacrifice the civilization and the culture for which we are fighting. Far too many hysterical advisers and
false prophets are urging our youth to fill their entire college program
with war training courses. Some day this war will be over. We must
not allow this present generation of students to return to a peace-
time world, their life career sabotaged, their real talents untrained,
their best service to civilization spoiled by our shortsightedness. So
we are saying to them, proceed with your long-run plan for your life,
but make a place in your program for doing your duty in the present
emergency.[23]

Thus, even in the darkest days of the war, Freeman promised that
Middlebury would try to retain its character as a liberal arts college.

On December 12, 1942, the trustees elected Dr. Samuel S. Stratton, a professor of economics at the Harvard Business School, the
eleventh president of the college.[24] They undoubtedly believed that
Stratton, who resigned from an important wartime post with the War
Production Board in Washington to accept the Middlebury offer,
would have the necessary connections to bring a military training
unit to the college and thereby assure its continued operation during
the war. They also agreed with the presidential search committee's
recommendation that a new position of vice president be created for
Freeman, thereby demonstrating their approval of Freeman's recent
leadership and giving the new president an experienced associate to
help him break in. Stratton assumed his duties just three weeks after
his election. There was no formal inauguration ceremony. Freeman
merely introduced him to the students at daily chapel in early January 1943, and the new president spoke briefly before turning to the
difficult task of leading the wartime college.[25]

Samuel Somerville Stratton was born in Lynn, Massachusetts,
on February 23, 1898. He grew up in Newburyport and went to
high school there, serving as president of his senior class and editor of the school magazine. He entered Dartmouth in the middle
of World War I, left in 1918 to enlist and serve as an ensign in the
Naval Aviation Corps, and returned to college the following year
to become captain of the debating team and associate editor of the
daily newspaper. After graduating in 1920, he spent five years in
the steel business before entering Harvard as a graduate student in
economics. He utilized his knowledge of the steel industry in writing his doctoral dissertation — "The Economic Development of the

In 1943, at one of the bleakest moments of World War II, Stephen Freeman greeted the new president of the college, Samuel S. Stratton (left), in a brief ceremony in Mead Chapel.

Tool and Alloy Steel Industry in the United States" — and earned his Ph.D. in 1930. The Harvard Graduate School of Business Administration then appointed him an assistant professor of economics, and he remained affiliated with the school until 1943. During those thirteen years, Stratton collaborated on four economics books, and he also took several leaves of absence to conduct various surveys of the steel industry here and abroad. He was called to Washington in 1940 to assist Dartmouth president Ernest Martin Hopkins in setting up the agency that later became the War Production Board. Stratton held several positions with the board and was director of the Review Division in the Distribution Bureau when he resigned to accept the Middlebury presidency.[26]

While Stratton's academic credentials, business background, and administrative experience undoubtedly impressed the trustee search committee, his connections in Washington must have weighed in his favor; the college desperately wanted to attract a military training unit. Stratton did not disappoint the trustees. After some visits to Washington and a naval inspection of Middlebury's facilities, Stratton could announce on April 3, 1943, that a navy V-12 unit of approximately five hundred officer candidates would enter the college on July 1.[27] After two to six terms (the norm was four), navy men would go on to either medical schools, flight training, Naval Reserve Officer Training Corps, midshipman schools, or chaplain schools. Their time at Middlebury was thus a preliminary but important part of the officer training program. By the end of the war, over 1,200 navy men from twenty different states had studied there.[28]

The faculty and administration quickly made important changes to accommodate the new additions to the student body. Middlebury began to operate three terms a year without any significant break for vacations. Further, since the navy particularly desired that courses be offered for their men in mathematics, physics, drafting, and English, some faculty members in the humanities and social sciences were given refresher courses in physics and math by their colleagues so that they could instruct the navy men in those areas.[29] Philosophy professor John Andrews, for example, recalled that he enjoyed teaching courses in college algebra, trigonometry, and analytical geometry during the war.[30] Faculty members were forced to teach an unprecedented number of different courses.

The navy men were a varied group. Many had had previous college training and were often encouraged to take regular college courses with the Middlebury women and the dwindling number of civilian men. Others had no college background and required different courses. By 1944 some of them had matriculated for four terms, whereas others were just entering the program, which sometimes necessitated the teaching of courses at four levels in a discipline. Meanwhile, the presence of five hundred regular college students (about 85 percent of whom were women) required that the faculty offer a normal liberal arts curriculum as well. In short, the war meant heavy teaching loads, the loss of accustomed vacations, and no significant salary increases.[31] Patriotism and wartime morale saw them through this burdensome period, but dissatisfaction began to surface afterward; as we shall see, resentment over wartime pay and work loads was one of several faculty grievances raised against President Stratton.

The war also transformed student life.[32] Fraternities were forced to cease activities and finally, in 1943, to lease their houses to the women's college for the duration.[33] For the first time women assumed full responsibility for most college publications and for the Cultural Conference, which brought outstanding speakers to the campus each year to discuss world problems in open panels. With the temporary demise of the fraternities, the women initiated much of the campus social life, although the V-12 men did sponsor a "Navy Formal" each term. The athletic program was significantly curtailed.[34] Although the varsity basketball, baseball, and skiing teams continued to play a full schedule, other varsity, junior varsity, and freshman squads had to be eliminated because of the shortage of civilian males.[35] Many extracurricular activities were also dropped or curtailed; costs were one factor, and the accelerated academic pace was another. The popular Winter Carnival was still held, although the lack of fuel transferred the ski competition from the Snow Bowl to nearby Chipman Hill.[36]

   The quality of extracurricular and social activity was also diminished by the inability of the navy men to integrate completely into campus life. They usually had separate classes and faced a rigorous daily schedule that set them apart from the civilian students and gave them little time to engage in socializing or extracurricular pursuits.[37] Many were less academically oriented and socially adept than their civilian counterparts; indeed, some of them seemed more comfortable with the townspeople than with the student body. In short, most of the navy men considered themselves outsiders on campus throughout the war.[38] On the other hand, with five hundred women students and fewer than one hundred civilian male students, it is not surprising that some social interaction occurred.[39] Indeed, some Middlebury women may have dated young navy men in the V-12 unit who later became prominent, such as Daniel Patrick Moynihan, Harvard professor and later United States senator from New York; and Willard C. Butcher, chairman of the Chase Manhattan Bank.[40]

   The war was a constant presence, on- and offstage. Even on the

In 1943 the College News Bureau announced: "Ladies of the Press . . . Ruth R. Wheaton of Barrington, R.I., editor-in-chief, and Ingrid H. Monk of South Weymouth, Mass., business manager of the 113-year-old Middlebury Campus. The first coeds ever to head this undergraduate newspaper, they take office this week as their male predecessors join the Army Air Corps."

safe and secluded Middlebury campus, students faced constant and sometimes painful reminders. Women rolled bandages for the Red Cross, lecturers and professors related their topics and courses to the war, cigarettes and other items were scarce, and, as June Brogger Noble '46 has written, the mail brought the war to Middlebury every day:

> Letters marked "Free Mail" arrive from odd corners of the world telling about places whose names are now linked with indescribable horrors . . . the Murmansk Run, Ardennes Bulge, Leyte Gulf, Guadalcanal. One girl receives three posthumous letters from the boy who took her to her prep-school prom. He talks about coming to Middlebury after the War and hopes she will still be there. Two weeks before the last letter arrives she receives a note from his mother telling her that an anti-tank gun blew his head off on one of the Philippines.[41]

The Navy V-12 units, in formation in front of Munroe Hall, filled the college year-round and replaced the Middlebury men who had left to fight.

Even joy at the coming of peace in 1945 was tempered by the death of President Roosevelt, the specter of the atomic bomb, and the thought that fifty-seven Middlebury men had died in action during the war.

Whatever problems they encountered or created on campus, the V-12 men made a crucial difference; their presence during the twenty-eight-month period from July 1943 to November 1945 saved the college from taking a loss it could ill afford. Indeed, many of the 131 colleges and universities that were chosen to train V-12 units benefited enormously from the presence of the 120,000 navy men who occupied their otherwise empty classrooms.[42] At Middlebury, no faculty layoffs occurred (many faculty went into the service), facilities were utilized year-round to the utmost, and coeducation survived. Indeed, President Stratton has been credited with "saving the College" by bringing the naval training unit to the campus.[43]

Stratton faced difficult problems during the war. First, he had to find replacements quickly for staff who entered the armed forces or the war industry. He also had the unenviable task of convincing alumni and friends of the college that although the war had transformed Middlebury in many respects, it was maintaining its commitment to be a coeducational liberal arts college. As the navy slowly reduced the number of men training at Middlebury, from 495 in July 1944 to 215 in March 1945, Stratton was forced to increase the number of women to over five hundred to maintain total enrollments. "It is, I believe, regrettable to permit the number of women students to exceed the men," he apologized to the alumni, "but we hope that it is a temporary situation which can be quickly remedied at the end of the war. Any other decision at this time would have necessitated retrenchment that would have injured the quality of our educational standards."[44] He also attempted to reassure alumni that Middlebury had "preserved its academic standards" and that the presence of V-12 units had "not led to a dilution of our liberal arts program."[45] To bolster these contentions, Stratton appointed a faculty committee on educational policy to concern itself with "liberal arts objectives," approved the organization of a Spanish House (on the model of the French House in the Chateau), hired the first professor to teach Russian at the college (Mischa Fayer), supported the new interdisciplinary Great Books course, and, looking toward a fine arts program, brought Arthur Healy to Middlebury as Resident Artist.[46]

By early 1945, it was becoming clear that the war was nearing its end, and Stratton and the trustees were already planning for reconversion to a peacetime curriculum. It was during the forty-five years after the war that Middlebury College made its graceful leap from a regional New England school of reasonable respectability to an outstanding college with an excellent national and international reputation.

PART II

THE GROWTH OF THE MODERN COLLEGE, 1945–1990

I do not, however, believe that a liberal arts college like Middlebury will ever have a great stream of applications from returning veterans, since I believe many of them will wish more straight vocational work or will seek entrance into professional schools willing to waive the requirements of a bachelor's degree.

> —President Samuel Stratton, "The President's Page,"
> *MCNL* 19 (March–April 1945): 19

Personal acquaintance is a primary ingredient of community and collegiality. Given our purposes at Middlebury—liberal learning having primarily to do with values and their relation to the living of life—the College should remain a community small enough to gauge rightly character and ability, to bring out those authentic features which mark an individual. Thus, in the context of Middlebury College, its history and its educational purposes, size takes a central role; like the form of a poem it becomes a crucial part of the meaning of the college—its character and its quality.

> —James I. Armstrong, *Report of the President to the*
> *Board of Trustees, 1971–72* (Middlebury, Vt., 1972),
> 4–5

I have enormous pride in the College. This is my place. I have pride in our work together, what we have accomplished, what lies before us, and our capacity to face the future with great promise. I want to assure you of my continued and permanent commitment to Middlebury College. I cannot envision a time when my energies will not, in some measure, be devoted to its welfare.

> —Olin Robison, in a speech to the campus
> community, October 6, 1989, in *Middlebury College
> Magazine* 64 (autumn 1989): 9

In America the three decades after World War II were marked by national prosperity and a heightened interest in higher education. College enrollments expanded remarkably after 1945 as returning servicemen took advantage of the GI Bill to obtain an education they might never have otherwise enjoyed. The idea that a college degree was a ticket to economic and social success became more and more accepted, and applications for admission to institutions of higher learning rose steadily. Attendance soared further as the millions of children born in the postwar "baby boom" reached college age after 1963. Furthermore, the cold war between the United States and the Soviet Union sparked a national concern for improving American education, particularly after the successful Russian launching of Sputnik in 1957. During the 1950s and, particularly, the 1960s, colleges and universities had relatively little difficulty attracting funds. But the economy was hard hit by recessions, unprecedented long-term inflation, and declining productivity in the 1970s, and there was a simultaneous decline in the number of people of college age. These trends put a halt to the expansion of higher education, and colleges and universities entered a period of retrenchment and creative belt-tightening.

The history of Middlebury between 1945 and 1990 was in large part determined by these national forces. The desire of World War II veterans to attend schools such as Middlebury surprised officials and forced the administration to increase enrollment from 800 to 1,200 in a brief and difficult period after the war. For a few years Middlebury merely tried to provide adequate resources for this larger student body. But under the leadership of Presidents Samuel S. Stratton (1943–1963), James I. Armstrong (1963–1975), and Olin C. Robison (1975–1990), the college embarked in 1954 on a thirty-six-year period of planned capital growth and commitment to better educational quality that went far beyond anything previously attempted. Stratton and Armstrong took advantage of the national support for higher education, the larger pool of applicants for admission, and the increased number of qualified teachers to build a fine physical plant, to improve the quality of the student body, and to attract many outstanding faculty members.

The decision in the early 1960s to enlarge the student body to 1,800 and the decision in 1972 to remain at about that size were both immensely important, and they determined many subsequent actions. In 1975, although President Robison inherited a college that had rejected further enrollment increases, he continued to enlarge and improve the physical plant, endowment, curricular offerings, faculty, compensation, and national and international reputation. He also fought successfully against the national forces buffeting American colleges and universities, to bring Middlebury even more firmly into the ranks of the very best small colleges in the United States.

CHAPTER 6

THE STRATTON YEARS: FACULTY AND CURRICULAR CONCERNS, 1945–1963

[I]t was shown that a lack of understanding of human relationships, an autocratic and dictatorial manner, questionable integrity in actions, an attempt to make quantitative values take precedence over qualitative ones in liberal education, a failure to meet opposition and disagreements openly and squarely, a use of threat and intimidation, an apparent failure to recognize that academic and administrative problems cannot be dealt with separately, a failure to respect committees under assignment, a tendency to misrepresent issues, a coercive and restrictive attitude toward students and their affairs, and a personal attitude that is suspicious, critical, and negative constituted the major reasons for the feeling of disaffection on the part of the faculty toward the president.

> —Report of the Faculty Committee on
> Conference with the Trustees, in Middlebury
> College Faculty Minutes (1945–47): 123A,
> Old Chapel Archives

In order to avoid far more drastic action contemplated by some of the faculty I did take a part in proposing a compromise that the disagreements be properly investigated, but I was serving as conciliator not instigator. Since I had been taken into the confidence of members of the faculty in their discussions of grievances I was in no position to break that confidence by reporting on their discussions, nor did this appear necessary since the problems had already been discussed with you by faculty members concerned. It would be extremely difficult to remain at Middlebury if this misconception of leadership is not corrected and if the charge of disloyalty in voting for the activation of the Faculty Conference Committee is not removed.

> —W. Storrs Lee, Dean of Men, to President
> Samuel Stratton, April 9, 1947, Lee file, Old
> Chapel Archives

The immediate postwar years were difficult ones for Middlebury. Everyone was surprised by the deluge of returning servicemen asking for admission—including Stratton, who had not expected many veterans: "I do not, however, believe that a liberal arts college like Middlebury will ever have a great stream of applications from returning veterans, since I believe many of them will wish more straight vocational work or will seek entrance into professional schools willing to waive the requirements of a bachelor's degree."[1]

This prediction was dead wrong. They poured in, encouraged by a liberal GI Bill that paid tuition and a monthly stipend to each veteran attending college.[2] They comprised 45 percent of Middlebury male enrollment as early as November 1945, before the real influx began, and this percentage rose rapidly. Total student enrollment in 1946 was 1,158 (621 of them men), compared with a prewar (1937–1941) average of less than 800 (see Table 3).[3] Housing posed a constant challenge; students (some of whom were married veterans) occupied nearly every available room in town, and a few had to stay as far away as the Dog Team Tavern, five miles north of Middlebury. Housing for an increased teaching staff was also in short supply, and the college had to split up several houses into apartments.[4] Classroom and office space, too, was at a premium; this was hardly surprising, since a mere eight hundred students had crowded these facilities in 1941. Furthermore, the veterans had many unusual problems and needs, and each office adapted as best it could:

> The Registrar's Office took on new chores as an agency for the evaluation of service credits. The Business Manager went into the real estate business with the Dean as partner. The Superintendent of Buildings and Grounds found that his burden also included locating plumbers and carpenters to put in partitions and bathtubs in structures that never before came within his range of duty. The Treasurer's Office had one of the toughest jobs of trying to extract funds from a Veterans Administration that was overwhelmed with unexpected numbers of education-seeking veterans. The faculty were faced individually with

TABLE 3
Student Enrollment, 1945–1963

Year	Men	Women	Total
1945–1946	152	552	704
1946–1947	621	537	1158
1947–1948	682	499	1181
1948–1949	703	484	1187
1949–1950	699	492	1191
1950–1951	692	501	1193
1951–1952	674	524	1198
1952–1953	688	505	1193
1953–1954	693	502	1195
1954–1955	732	512	1244
1955–1956	739	519	1258
1956–1957	746	514	1260
1957–1958	748	516	1264
1958–1959	749	513	1262
1959–1960	748	525	1273
1960–1961	771	517	1288
1961–1962	757	512	1269
1962–1963	780	529	1309

Figures for 1945–1951 are from "Middlebury Attendance Records," typed manuscript, MCA. Figures for 1951–1963 are from the Middlebury annual catalogs. All figures are for the start of fall term.

academic challenges. New secretaries not infrequently, and not without embarrassment, confused younger professors with older veterans.

The Dean's Office became a Veterans Bureau where problems of housing, government benefits, immediate vocational objectives, divorce, marriage and babies were superimposed on what used to be the Dean's major job. Men in their late twenties and early thirties came for consultation more frequently than boys in their late teens. They brought with them perplexing adult questions in contrast with the worn, youthful inquiries.[5]

Those crowded and difficult postwar years had two important consequences: a faculty revolt against President Stratton and new construction between 1945 and 1963 that enabled the college to handle the increased enrollment. The focus in this chapter will be on the faculty revolt and other curricular issues; the building programs will be the subject of chapter 7.

Higher enrollments and crowded conditions bore most heavily on faculty and staff. They taught much larger classes than before the war, while their real income decreased as salaries could not keep pace with postwar inflation.[6] Many who had taught at Middlebury during the war were angry over the salaries they had been paid for their summer work with the V-12 units. And as "Doc" Cook remembered, they were tired from the continuous teaching they performed during those anxious years.

> It was a traumatic time, and, in part, the trauma can be attributed to the effects of trying to teach during the critical period of World War II. The war took its toll on all of us. We were fatigued from four years of round-the-clock teaching, and some of us had to cope with strange disciplines; for example, one French teacher taught physics, and an English teacher taught mathematics. I found it difficult enough to adjust to three kinds of students: the 4-Fs, and co-eds, and the Navy contingent. It was nightmarish trying to hold the line and succeeding only eventually. It was far worse than the Depression Era.[7]

Finally, many faculty members were unhappy with President Stratton. Most had served under President Moody, and they found Stratton terribly wanting in comparison with their beloved former "prexy." In 1946, when the talented political science professor, Robert Rafuse, was not offered a renewed contract, resentment bubbled over.[8] Faculty dissension shook the college for months.

On January 30, 1947, a petition of fifty-one faculty members requested that the Faculty Committee on Conference with the Trustees be activated and asked the board to inquire into faculty–administration relations.[9] The next day the Faculty Committee advised Stratton in person that the committee had been formed, and Stratton agreed to make arrangements for it to meet with the Trustee Committee on Conference. Although Stratton was very courteous, he told the Faculty Committee that he was deeply hurt, seeing the petition as an action behind his back. Particularly angry that Dean W. Storrs Lee '28 had signed the petition, Stratton charged him with disloyalty. Lee, who had been a powerful figure in the Moody administration and perhaps Moody's closest confidant, promptly wrote Stratton and denied any disloyalty. The college, he wrote, needed a "self-examination" that "would at least clear the air." "The proposal makes no charge," he went on; "it is directed at no one. It faces that fact that an unhappy state exists at Middlebury, and one is burying his head in the sand not to recognize that fact."[10]

The Faculty Committee (composed of Professors John Bowker, Waldo Heinrichs, and "Doc" Cook) and the Trustee Committee (Judge Walter Cleary, Redfield Proctor, George Allen, Dr. Elbert Cole, and Egbert Hadley) met on February 8, 1947. The trustees expected to hear faculty concerns about the salary situation and the Rafuse case, but most of the ninety-minute discussion concerned the disaffection with President Stratton. The situation, the professors said, had arisen early in Stratton's tenure and had "progressively worsened during the last two years." The gist of the complaint was that the administration was insufficiently cooperative and had allowed relations with the faculty to deteriorate, Stratton had acted autocratically and reprehensibly in his dealings with faculty, wartime salary arrangements were "definitely open to question," the best faculty were leaving, and the academic side of the college needed more emphasis and regeneration than the physical side. One committee member apparently convinced the trustees of the seriousness of the situation when he argued that after fighting a war for democratic procedures and against Nazism, he had been greatly saddened on his return to Middlebury to find conditions "undemocratic and actually Nazi-like."

The trustee committee then heard testimony from individual faculty members—twelve that evening until past midnight, fifteen more on the next afternoon, Sunday, February 9, and nine others about a month later.[11] The trustees listened attentively as the faculty members poured out their grievances. According to the Faculty Committee's report, many professors delivered blistering attacks on the president's general way of conducting business:

> [I]t was shown that a lack of understanding of human relationships, an autocratic and dictatorial manner, questionable integrity in actions, an attempt to make quantitative values take precedence over qualitative ones in liberal education, a failure to meet opposition and disagreements openly and squarely, a use of threat and intimidation, an apparent failure to recognize that academic and administrative problems cannot be dealt with separately, a failure to respect committees under assignment, a tendency to misrepresent issues, a coercive and restrictive attitude toward students and their affairs, and a personal attitude that is suspicious, critical, and negative constituted the major reasons for the feeling of disaffection on the part of the faculty toward the president.[12]

Faculty opposition emphasized particular Stratton policies. He was certainly opposed to dealing through a bargaining agent with the faculty as a whole. When a Middlebury chapter of the American Association of University Professors (AAUP) was formed after the war, Stratton reacted negatively—reportedly telling one faculty member that he was going to fire Professor Rafuse because Rafuse had supposedly set up the local AAUP chapter and "was boring from within, using C.I.O. tactics." [13] Stratton's fear of faculty opposition, according to one professor, was present all along:

> This leads me to suggest that Dr. Stratton from the first had it in mind that there would be opposition to him, and that a faculty purge, or to use his phrase—a house cleaning was inevitable and desirable. The opposition he imagined did not materialize at once. I can state that there never was any such opposition up to that time. . . . When Prexy Moody left there was deep regret among the faculty. But Dr. Moody had pledged the staff to carry on—to be loyal to Middlebury as the best loyalty to him. That he would fade out of the picture as completely as possible. I know that Prexy Moody kept his pledge, and I know that the faculty kept that pledge too. I did try to state this to Dr. Stratton, but he would not listen. . . . What I wish to say is that Dr. Stratton started out with an unfounded assumption. He has produced the thing he imagined. [14]

Indeed, according to the testimony, Stratton did not trust his faculty and staff. Some claimed he had "lied" to them, bypassed their committees on important issues, and tried to "buy" their support with salary increases and offers of job security.

Another professor maintained that the low salaries offered for teaching the wartime summer sessions was the critical issue. "My personal dissatisfaction, and I believe the point of crystallization of general faculty dissatisfaction, centers about the summer terms during the Naval Training period," he argued.

> In the beginning the President told us . . . that the situation of Middlebury College was critical in view of the war and reduced numbers of students, that the college hoped to obtain a service unit, but that he would assure us that he made no distinction between the college and the faculty; that the college was not interested in making a *profit* (note this word for later reference), and that the faculty would share in the fortunes of the college, whatever that turned out to be. [15]

The faculty had been promised remuneration ranging from $240 to $600 for summer teaching, the specific amount to be determined by four criteria. Yet most of the staff reportedly received the $240 minimum salary. [16]

Stratton apparently tried at first to deny that the college had benefited from the V-12 unit. He later implied that the surplus was plowed back into the reserve funds for necessary capital improvements after the war and stated that the faculty should be pleased at this strengthening of College finances.[17] One professor wrote that he would willingly have accepted this if he had been informed: "Had the President said to us frankly, in the beginning or at any subsequent time, that the college saw a chance to improve its endowment through the Naval Training period, and asked our cooperation in any sacrifice or personal effort or renumeration [*sic*], I believe it would have been unhesitatingly and freely given. I know mine would have been."[18]

Opposition to Stratton's policies seemed intertwined with a dislike of his methods and personality. One faculty member summed up the feelings of some senior staff when he wrote to former Dean Eleanor Ross:

> It is an hour to make strong men weep, and an hour that has brought almost the entire faculty together in a solidarity of despair, almost of desperation. It is not enough to suggest that if they don't like the situation, they can look for positions elsewhere. Many of us have given decades of service to Middlebury College. . . . One man, a comparative newcomer, who has evidenced no understanding of the values that make Middlebury what it is in the eyes of the academic world, would hardly seem endowed with wisdom or properly with authority to stand as the one person with right and logic on his side. In all fairness I think he has done the best he can, being the man he is, for I think he is by nature totally alien to the spirit of Middlebury as we know it.[19]

Faculty interviews with the trustees must have included considerable emotional outpouring.

After hearing the faculty's complaints, the Trustee Committee on Conference had to decide whether to recommend keeping President Stratton or not, and it met for that purpose on March 24. The trustees admitted that Stratton was a "martinet" at times and had to improve his personal relationship with the faculty. Still, they had been pleased with his operation of the college during "a very difficult time." They considered him "a good money man" who followed orders well and a decided improvement over Moody. Furthermore, key trustees believed that Dean Lee and a handful of faculty who had never completely accepted Moody's dismissal had fanned the flames of discontent "out of all proportion to their real importance" and had "kept this discontent alive, while under normal conditions it would have died a natural death."[20]

The trustee committee thus backed a chastened Stratton and informed the faculty committee of its actions. While the trustees conceded that "some of the criticisms of President Stratton appear to be justified," they claimed that "the President will do his best in the future to minimize" them. Various other criticisms were unjustified, they added, and "would not have arisen had there been more earnest good will on the part of various faculty members. The good of the College and the vital interest of the Faculty demand the utmost cooperation and understanding between the President and the Faculty."[21] In short, the trustees had bluntly told all parties to change and adapt: Stratton should be less dictatorial, the faculty more understanding.

A majority of the faculty had apparently hoped the trustees would ask for the president's resignation and were quite disappointed with their decision. On April 1, 1947, eight days after receiving the trustee committee's report, the faculty held a special unofficial meeting without Stratton present.[22] A vote of confidence or no confidence in Stratton was moved and seconded, and a long discussion ensued. Some of the older professors, near retirement, urged the faculty to drop its opposition and "iron out a difficult situation and make the best of it." They argued that the trustees had made the decision, and any further action would be divisive and not in the college's interest. A motion to table the vote of no confidence was defeated, 23–26, and the debate continued.

Then a compromise of sorts was apparently reached. The motion of no confidence was tabled by a vote of 31–14, but the faculty voted 43–11 to submit the following motion to the trustees: "The faculty has received a report of the Trustee Committee on Consultation with the Faculty and thanks them for the report but feels the report does not meet the issues which are at stake between the faculty and the administration."[23] There is little doubt, according to several who were present, that if the faculty had voted on the question of no confidence, a fairly large majority would have cast their ballots against Stratton. What the trustees would have done in that case is, of course, only open to speculation; several professors were certain that a publicized vote of no confidence in the president would have meant his dismissal.[24]

Once the faculty had declined to take the ultimate step, an uneasy truce was established. The faculty met again on April 3, this

In 1947, after faculty complaints to the Trustees about President Stratton's administrative conduct, the Faculty Advisory Council was established to give the faculty a voice in college governance. The first members were (left to right) Dr. Stratton; Donald H. Ballou, mathematics; Waldo H. Heinrichs, contemporary civilization; Richard L. Brown, English; John G. Bowker, mathematics; Reginald L. Cook, American literature; and Harold B. Hitchcock, biology.

time with Stratton present.[25] Stratton read a statement in which he admitted that some of the criticisms were justified. "I might plead the pressure of work during these particularly difficult years as an extenuating circumstance," he said. "I want to state to you with all frankness and sincerity that I shall endeavor at all times to minimize the basis of such criticisms in the future." He hoped the "unpleasant experience" of recent weeks would be judged later as "a constructive and successful transition to clearer and more satisfactory Faculty–Administration relations."

Although he appeared truly sorry and many of the faculty believed he had met them halfway, they were eager for institutional safeguards against what they saw as continued dictatorial behavior. Professor Holden, acting on a suggestion of Professor Andrews that Middlebury emulate a recent action of Amherst College, proposed the formation of a faculty advisory council, which would have "a voice to act with the President in making recommendations to the Trustees regarding faculty personnel." Stratton later accepted this idea.[26] The faculty and trustee committees on conference began to meet regularly. Finally, Stratton assured worried faculty members that he would propose no changes in the status of teaching faculty because of opposition to the president, and he stated that the AAUP chapter would be welcome to talk with him about any issue (though he reiterated his stand that he would not accept the group as a faculty bargaining unit).[27]

Although Stratton's magnanimous speech and assurances helped begin to heal the wounds, everyone knew there would not be peace until Stratton and Dean Lee reached some sort of understanding. Lee had been increasingly dismayed with Stratton's performance, and the president apparently considered him the "primary instigator of the disagreement."[28] Although Lee insisted he had been "conciliator not instigator,"[29] he apparently gave the trustees a good deal of damaging testimony concerning Stratton's administrative actions and also advised Cook and others on how to proceed in their attempt to obtain a hearing before the trustees.[30] If Lee were to remain as an important officer in the Stratton administration, an agreement between the two men would have to be negotiated.

On April 8, five days after Stratton's speech, Professor Arthur Healy called on him "to discuss some routine matters of appointment" in Healy's fine arts department.[31] Afterward, according to Healy, Stratton said he expected the trustees to censure Lee at their meeting of April 12 and perhaps even fire him. Healy "asked the President why he did not call on Mr. Lee to straighten out their differences." Pointing out Lee's enormous popularity with the faculty, Healy added "that nothing less than a pragmatic solution would bring any kind of peace to Middlebury." He further offered to prompt Lee to "state in writing, definitely, under what conditions he would continue to serve as Dean," and Stratton assured Healy of "his earnest reception of such a statement and its use in convincing the Trustees of a possibility of future concord." After a talk with Healy, Lee wrote to Stratton the following day.

Lee's letter vigorously defended his previous actions, set down certain demands that he expected to be met if he were to continue his affiliation with the college, and made professions of future loyalty to the administration. He denied having been leader in the drive to oust Stratton:

> In order to avoid far more drastic action contemplated by some of the faculty I did take a part in proposing a compromise that the disagreements be properly investigated, but I was serving as conciliator not instigator. Since I had been taken into the confidence of members of the faculty in their discussions of grievances I was in no position to break that confidence by reporting on their discussions, nor did this appear necessary since the problems had already been discussed with you by faculty members concerned. It would be extremely difficult to remain at Middlebury if this misconception of leadership is not corrected and if the charge of disloyalty in voting for the activation of the Faculty Conference Committee is not removed.[32]

Defending his actions as dean since the end of the war, Lee requested a competent guidance center for the men's college and more administrative support in dealing with married veterans. He demanded that he be included in discussions concerning the men's college and voiced resentment at not having been consulted at all on plans for the student union building. The dean did promise "to continue to represent the best interests of the College, the Administration, and the faculty" and "to defend any principles and policies set down by the Administration, Trustees, and Faculty." He also said he was eager for further discussion, which would "yield closer understanding than correspondence." The letter, though not overly compromising in tone, apparently had the desired effect. The trustees took no action against Lee, and he remained at Middlebury for eight more years as dean of men.

But the relationship between the two men never improved.[33] Lee and others continued to view Stratton as the wrong man for the job. As administrator since 1930 and student (1924–1928) before that, Lee had known only one other Middlebury president—Paul Moody. He had quickly gained Moody's friendship and became perhaps the president's closest colleague. Lee's institutional loyalty and devotion were unquestioned. He wrote a lively history of Middlebury, *Father Went to College*, in 1936; served as public relations officer in the 1930s; and immersed himself in all aspects of college life during the Moody administration. Faculty, alumni, and townspeople all held him in high regard.

*Dean W. Storrs Lee '28 spoke with veterans in Gifford Hall about their needs in return-
ing to civilian life and postwar education at Middlebury.*

Stratton's appointment as president ended Lee's special relationship to that office; and when he returned to Middlebury after the
war, he apparently could not accept the presence of so different a
leader. Moody was a warm and friendly man who showed great personal interest in his faculty, whereas Stratton was an intensely shy
man whom many saw as cold, distant, and defensive and who preferred to organize things on an impersonal basis. Lee was denied the
access he had enjoyed under Moody and resented the way he was
treated. Regarding his own actions between 1945 and 1955 as loyal to
the college he had known under Moody, Lee evidently never considered Stratton more than a pretender to the presidency, a temporary
aberration, a mistake to be corrected.

Many of the faculty who felt similarly could continue their professional activities and maintain only minimal contact with Stratton;
Lee, as a leading administrator, could not. The split became increasingly acrimonious and unproductive. Stratton, though he won over

other members of his staff after 1947 and effectively isolated Lee, was afraid to fire him because of Lee's great popularity. Finally, key trustees, weary of the struggle and perhaps fed up with Lee, ordered Stratton in June 1955 to ask for Lee's resignation. Stratton did so on June 29, and Lee tendered his resignation the next day.[34]

In response, the faculty printed a long "minute" in his honor, which included the following: "We express our sorrow at the removal of Storrs Lee from the Middlebury scene where he has lived usefully and creatively, and from the College he has served so capably, steadfastly, and loyally for over a quarter of a century."[35] Some angry alumni refused to give money because of Lee's dismissal.[36] The trustees had known this would occur, and one official stated that while "for the short range situation it would cause more trouble than good, nevertheless in the long range interest of the college it would be better to ask for Lee's resignation."[37]

Indeed, Stratton finally had a unified administrative team and was undoubtedly a happier man. As he wrote in 1956:

> Because of changes in the administration of men students, we had been prepared for a difficult year in certain respects. I am pleased to report that I have never experienced a year in which the general conduct and morale of men students has been better. . . .In no year of my incumbency have we had such a cooperative and effective administrative staff nor one which has worked so closely and harmoniously in arriving at its administrative decisions. I am informed by the staff that they share this opinion.[38]

Lee, meanwhile, reluctantly moved away and spent many fruitful years pursuing his favorite avocation—writing. Although he alternated winters and summers between Hawaii and Maine, he remained in close touch with his many Middlebury friends and retained a strong loyalty to the college.[39]

Stratton did change somewhat in response to his traumatic experience with the faculty in 1947. He became more sensitive to faculty opinion, less dictatorial, and more conciliatory.[40] The establishment of the Faculty Council in 1947 was an example of his willingness to share power. Whereas many of the faculty who had taught under Moody at best tolerated his successor,[41] professors whom Stratton brought to Middlebury had a different view. They and others who sympathized with his problems remember him as "painfully shy"

In 1958, Paul Cubeta, Robert Frost, and Ted Morrison found the unpastoral surroundings of the Bread Loaf parking lot the right place for a Writers' Conference discussion.

rather than cold and as a caring person who could give a young instructor the money for a topcoat just before a convention trip or who might drop by informally to see if a young faculty couple was doing all right. Averring that he was misunderstood by many, especially among the Moody loyalists, Stratton's supporters also point out that he raised salaries, allowed professors to build up departments, and increasingly demanded that instructors seeking to remain at the college earn their Ph.D.'s.[42]

Indeed, Stratton strengthened each of the four academic divisions, both by expanding and upgrading the teaching staff and facilities and by encouraging curricular reforms. In the social sciences division, which expanded during these years from eleven faculty members to twenty-three, new appointments improved each department; history, under the leadership of Thomas Hedley Reynolds (later dean of men at Middlebury and president of Bates after 1964), became one of the outstanding departments in the college.[43] The natural sciences division also benefited from staff additions. In the humanities division, Stratton established two new departments—fine arts and religion—under Professor Arthur Healy and Chaplain Charles Scott, both of whom he recruited. Other departments were expanded, which "allowed far greater opportunity for the exchange of ideas," and the English department was greatly strengthened by the addition of Paul Cubeta, a brilliant young teacher-scholar-administrator, who quickly became a leading figure at the college.[44] On the mountain campus, "Doc" Cook successfully guided the English School between 1946 and 1964 and encouraged Erie Volkert, chair of the drama department, to build an outstanding drama program at Bread Loaf.[45] Theodore Morrison, director of the Writers' Conference from 1932 to 1955, retired in favor of John Ciardi, who maintained the success of the program for the next seventeen years.[46]

In languages, Stratton accomplished much. He appointed Vice President Stephen Freeman the first director of the Middlebury College language schools in 1946 and assisted him in expanding and improving the various programs.[47] Mischa Fayer, hired in 1943, inaugurated a department of Russian and opened the Russian summer school in 1945. The new school quickly acquired a solid reputation, with enrollment averaging around eighty between 1947 and 1957. Aided by a Rockefeller Foundation grant, the college organized the summer Institute of Soviet Studies in 1958, integrating it into the Russian School ten years later. The purpose of the institute was to allow students of Soviet government, science, economics, and other areas to obtain instruction in those subjects in the Russian language. Between thirty and fifty students attended each summer.[48]

The other summer language schools maintained their good reputation through the Stratton years, although they suffered a temporary drop in enrollment in the early 1950s; the Italian School nearly disappeared as a separate entity when enrollment fell to twenty-two in 1951. The construction of new residence halls allowed the German School to return to the main campus from Bristol in 1951, and the French School and Spanish School were blessed with a continuation of fine leadership after the departure of Andre Morize and Juan Centeno.[49]

Perhaps the most significant innovation in the languages division was the establishment of the Graduate Schools Abroad Program. Freeman discovered that after 1945 American students who wished to undertake graduate study overseas had great difficulty in finding the necessary guidance and programs once they reached Europe. He proposed a plan in 1948 that would alleviate this problem (at least for students who wished to study in France) by utilizing Middlebury's experience in foreign-language education:

It was a unique plan, in keeping with the Middlebury character. No other institution had anything like it. Briefly stated, the proposal

Like many of Middlebury's most beloved teachers, Claude Bourcier seemed at times an actor manqué. In fact, each summer he flourished in French School productions of the classics of French theater. In 1972 he played Arnolph to Daniel Jourlait's Enrique in a production of L'École des Femmes *that put the director of the French School and its future director on stage together. M. Bourcier is at left.*

was to select a limited group of graduate students planning to teach French, to prepare them by a preliminary summer of study at the French School in Middlebury, and to send them to Paris in early October. They would spend the academic year from October to June in a coordinated and approved program of advanced instruction on French linguistics, phonetics, literature, history, institutions and culture. These courses would be followed in various institutes or schools of the University of Paris. The students would work under the close personal supervision and guidance of a resident Director of Studies representing Middlebury College. At the end of the year, final examinations would be administered under his direction by the French professors. The successful candidates would receive the Middlebury College Master of Arts degree, in addition to any French certificates or diplômes they might have been able to earn.[50]

The trustees agreed with Freeman's proposal in principle, and Stratton obtained a $6,000 grant to establish a Graduate School of French in France. Freeman went to Paris in 1949 to make the arrangements, and the first class of forty-five students met in Paris later that year. The success of the French School encouraged Freeman and Stratton to establish similar units in Spanish at Madrid in 1951, in German at Mainz in 1959, and in Italian at Florence in 1960. All the schools flourished, with average enrollments ranging from 15 in Florence to 45 in Paris, and by the early 1960s over 150 students were receiving M.A. degrees in these programs each year.[51]

Notwithstanding these achievements, one of the president's most important curricular goals—to reduce the number of courses that a student took each semester from five to four—was soundly rejected by the faculty. In 1959–1960, the Educational Policy Committee, under the direction of Paul Cubeta, investigated this question and placed before the faculty a recommendation that the college adopt a four-course curriculum. Cubeta and other young professors who hoped to improve the academic program strongly favored this change:

> By focusing upon four courses at a time, a student could be encouraged to experience the satisfaction of mastering a discipline more thoroughly than may now be possible. The emphasis of such a program would be upon training judgment and forming intelligent minds, on the formative as well as on the informative. For the Faculty these proposals would help establish a new pattern of faculty work with fewer class preparations and more time for study and for conferences with students.[52]

In essence, advocates maintained that the five-course curriculum led to superficiality and lack of intellectual commitment on the part of the students; opponents viewed the "superficiality" of a five-course curriculum rather as the key to a truly "broad" liberal arts education. They were worried that the reduction in the number of courses taken would mean exposing students to just that much less of the well-rounded Middlebury education they hoped to impart.[53]

Other reasons for opposition turned more on practical concerns than educational philosophy. Some professors feared that the reduction in the required number of courses might significantly reduce enrollments in their own areas, which in turn could lead to staff reductions. Indeed, Stratton's strong support of the four-course proposal was a major cause of its defeat; many faculty members, still suspicious of his motives, specifically foresaw a possibility that the college would use the curricular change as an excuse to cut the size of the teaching staff.[54] Even after the faculty rejected the proposal soundly, the trustees voted in 1962 to establish a four-course curriculum for freshmen. Objecting strenuously to what they perceived as an "abrogation" of their traditional rights, the faculty managed to convince the board that it would not be wise to force the change upon them.[55]

Yet even with this setback, Stratton had rebounded from his early troubles and markedly improved the college's educational quality, not only by enlarging the faculty and encouraging new programs but also, as we are about to see, by raising salaries and expanding and improving Middlebury's physical plant.

CHAPTER 7

THE STRATTON YEARS:
PHYSICAL GROWTH,
1945–1963

Even in relatively small towns and cities, the athletic facilities of high schools are today frequently far better than those we have to offer. Perhaps young men should select their colleges for very different reasons, but we do know that the lack of a modern athletic plant has too frequently discouraged promising boys from coming to Middlebury. If we are to achieve the post-war increase in enrollment of men which is our objective, it is absolutely essential that our facilities for physical education, intramural and intercollegiate athletics be brought up to the standards of other schools and colleges.

> —Samuel Stratton, "President's Page,"
> *Middlebury College News Letter* 19 (March–
> April 1945): 19

As a very human being, he was deeply aware of his own shortcomings. Such awareness disposed him gently and magnanimously toward others.

> —Chaplain Charles Scott, on the death of
> President Samuel Stratton, in *Middlebury
> College News Letter* 43 (spring 1969): 1

While President Stratton's efforts to improve the college's programs and staff and achieve harmony with his faculty were important aspects of the Middlebury story, they were generally of secondary importance to alumni, townspeople, and even students. What these constituencies did notice during the Stratton years were the more

The last building of the interwar period, Munroe Hall, was being completed when this aerial photograph was taken. New construction would resume in 1948 with the construction of the Memorial Field House.

tangible accomplishments, particularly the growth and improvement in both physical plant and endowment.

Due to the sudden rise in enrollment, the college's immediate post-war building needs were numerous, and the trustees decided in 1946 to open a Memorial Fund campaign to raise $2,700,000 for the construction of a gymnasium, field house, swimming pool, women's residence hall, fine arts center, and playhouse and for the remodeling of McCullough Gymnasium into a student union.[1]

The first project was an indoor gymnasium and field house. The Depression and World War II had long delayed the plans for such a structure, but the situation had worsened, as Joseph Kasper '20 reminded the trustees in 1944; there was now a "pressing need for new athletic facilities and a new gymnasium for men."[2] McCullough Gym may have been adequate for a college of 300 students, but it could no longer serve the 1940 population of 800 (much less the nearly 1,200 who would overrun the campus after the war). Addressing the question in 1945, the trustees advocated a three-unit structure, consisting of a field house, gymnasium, and swimming pool.

The complex—a memorial to the Middlebury men and women who fought and died in World War II[3]—was seen as the key to higher male enrollment; indeed, the field house campaign repeatedly emphasized that men might not apply unless adequate athletic facilities were available. President Stratton wrote to the alumni about this in 1945:

> Even in relatively small towns and cities, the athletic facilities of high schools are today frequently far better than those we have to offer. Perhaps young men should select their colleges for very different reasons, but we do know that the lack of a modern athletic plant has too frequently discouraged promising boys from coming to Middlebury. If were are to achieve the post-war increase in enrollment of men which is our objective, it is absolutely essential that our facilities for physical education, intramural and intercollegiate athletics be brought up to the standards of other schools and colleges.[4]

Of course, better facilities would also benefit women, but there was no shortage of women applicants; it was the men whom the trustees hoped to attract.

The initial goal was to raise $700,000 for the field house alone, which was to be completed by 1947. But building costs rose rapidly after the war, and contributions to the Memorial Fund lagged.[5] Therefore, when Middlebury officials learned that they could purchase a big navy surplus recreation building in Sampson, New York, for a reasonable price, they jumped at the chance. In March 1948, the board agreed to buy a 120-by-400-foot section of the building, demolish it, transport it, and re-erect it in Middlebury on South Main Street adjacent to Porter Field and south of the Chi Psi lodge.[6] The structure would provide 54,000 square feet of floor space, enough to contain a gymnasium, an indoor hockey rink with natural ice, basketball courts, a field cage, and other facilities, including offices, lockers, showers, and training rooms.

Since increased enrollments had made it impossible to hold a meeting of the entire student body in any of the college buildings, the new field house would also solve that problem and provide space for commencement exercises, dances, and other large functions. The college added a "fitting and appropriate memorial foyer and facade in keeping with the memorial purpose"[7] and completed the building in 1949. In addition, Mr. and Mrs. Fred P. Lang donated an intramural athletic field, 500 feet by 420 feet, at the rear of the new field

Under pressure to provide adequate athletic facilities for students after the war, the college purchased, moved, and reerected the field house, dedicating it to the alumni killed in the war.

house, in honor of their son, Fred D. Lang '47, who was killed in action in France.[8]

Middlebury also desperately needed a student union. The trustees had planned to convert McCullough Gymnasium for that purpose as soon as the new field house was completed, but this took longer than expected; and when the government offered an 11,000-square-foot war-surplus recreation center in February 1947, the college accepted the gift. Four months later, the building had been moved 246 miles from the Quonset Naval Air Station in Rhode Island and erected in Middlebury.[9] It was placed on the present site of the Proctor terrace and stood there until it was demolished to make way for the construction in 1960 of the modern student union, Redfield Proctor Hall.

More dormitory space for women was another pressing need. By the spring of 1950, 145 coeds were living in Hepburn Hall on the men's side, and many others were forced to find housing off campus.[10] Since the $2.7-million drive had not provided enough funds for a women's residence hall, the trustees decided to invest over $300,000 of permanent funds for this purpose—charging students a rate high enough to ensure a profit on the investment."[11]

The new residence unit actually consisted of two two-story buildings housing seventy-five students each. The structures, named Battell North and Battell South after the college's great benefactor, were built on the "women's campus" (which Battell had donated forty years earlier), east of Forest Hall, facing the town. Opened as part of the sesquicentennial celebration in the fall of 1950, the Battells featured "a modified Georgian style with slate roofs and faced with the native limestone from the same quarry which furnished the materials for Old Chapel, Forest, Gifford, Munroe, Painter, and Starr Halls."[12]

Other major additions and improvements included the renovation of Starr Hall in 1947 and the construction of a fine-arts building in 1951. The latter, located on the women's campus, east of Forest and south of the Battells, was named after Reid Carr '01, a trustee whose wife willed $152,000 to the college for the construction of the building. Carr Hall was another modified Georgian structure, faced with limestone that harmonized with nearby Forest and Munroe.[13] The chapel was enhanced by two gifts in 1952. Mrs. Philip Anson Wright gave money for the altar and cross in the chancel, and Edwin S. S. Sunderland '11 and his mother, Mrs. Anne Julia Stowell Sunderland Bingham, contributed funds for a small memorial chapel adjoining the main building.[14]

While this new construction filled many postwar needs, two natural disasters inflicted heavy damage on the physical plant. On November 25, 1950, a hurricane ravaged the northeastern United States and cut a wide swath through college property. Although every building except Starr Library suffered to some extent, the field house (estimated $50,000 damage) and Mead Chapel ($5,500 estimated damage) were hardest hit. The gale-force winds ripped off the flat sections of the field house roof, "exposing the hockey rink, basketball floor, and exercise room which were drenched by the rain."[15] Mead Chapel suffered extensive damage to its roof, spire, and windows. Two six-hundred-pound cement urns were dislodged from the steeple railing and crashed through the main roof of the chapel into the balcony below; one continued through the ceiling of the balcony and smashed a pew on the main floor. One hundred campus trees

Returning to the college in January 1954, F. Lynn Fisher '55 (left) and Leila Goodrich '56 found that the College Playhouse on Weybridge Street had burned and that the Carnival play, The Man Who Came to Dinner, *which they had been rehearsing, would have to find a new venue. Just as Lynn Fisher and Leila Goodrich were picking the sign from the ashes of the Playhouse, the college was planning a fund drive that would replace the Playhouse with Wright Theater in 1958.*

were felled by the storm, and many more had to be removed at the Snow Bowl to clear the skiing trails. All repairs had been made by the following spring, and insurance covered much of the $100,000 cost.[16]

On Christmas eve, 1953, three years after the hurricane, fire destroyed the old Playhouse on Weybridge Street. Although the college could collect $40,000 of insurance on the building, the trustees estimated that replacing it with a suitable speech and drama center would cost at least $200,000 to $400,000.[17]

Soon after the fire—and partly because of it—the trustees embarked on a major development campaign in 1954. They realized that the recent construction, valuable though it was, had accomplished only part of what Middlebury needed to keep pace with rival schools. In addition to building a new drama and speech center, the college planned to improve the science facilities, construct new dormitories, expand Starr Library, replace the student union with a modern structure, and expand the athletic facilities both on campus and at the Snow Bowl. The campaign also sought endowment funds to support higher faculty salaries and scholarship aid.[18]

On January 9, 1954, two weeks after the Playhouse fire, Stratton called for "bold action" and won the board's approval for a major fund drive. Trustee Edwin S. S. Sunderland '11 was elected chairman of the new development program and gave $15,000 to print a handsome brochure, "Middlebury—an Investment in Youth," to be sent to prospective donors. The goal was set at $3 million, and the campaign was given an official kickoff at a Homecoming Weekend dinner on October 2, 1954, with 175 persons in attendance.[19] At the dinner it was announced that Sunderland had given the development program an early boost with a $116,500 initial contribution.[20]

The first major project was the Drama and Speech Center, which the trustees decided in the spring of 1956 to locate on Chateau Road opposite the Battells.[21] The building, finally completed in 1958 at a cost of $525,000 and featuring a four-hundred-seat auditorium, was named for Professor Charles Baker Wright, a popular English teacher at Middlebury between 1885 and 1920.[22]

Facilities for physical education and extracurricular enjoyment were greatly enhanced during these years. Professor Wright's wife, who had contributed $50,000 in her husband's name for scholarships in 1949, gave the college another $50,000 just before her death in 1954 to finance an artificial ice rink for the field house. Since 1949, when the field house had been completed, the formation of ice had depended entirely on the weather, and mild winters had meant little or no skating. The new artificial rink guaranteed four months of ice time.[23] The winter sports program was further improved by the installation of a Poma ski lift at the Snow Bowl—a modern 3,185-foot overhead cable, the first such lift installed at an American college[24]—to replace the old rope tow. And C. V. Starr, a wealthy philanthropist who had financed the education of several foreign students at Middlebury and received an honorary LL.D. from the college in 1955, provided sufficient funds in 1962 to build the Neil Starr Shelter and complete the ski lodge at the Bowl.[25]

The college constructed one more addition to the physical education facilities in 1963—a large indoor swimming pool. The trustees

Completed in 1960, Redfield Proctor Hall contained a bookstore where incoming students could pick up the necessities for college life, including freshman beanies for the men.

had originally hoped to include a pool with the field house complex, but a shortage of funds blocked the project until contributions of $100,000 by Malcolm T. Anderson '25 and $200,000 by trustee Paul John Kruesi and his wife in the early 1960s made construction possible. The pool, built adjacent to McCullough, was named for Arthur M. Brown, Middlebury director of athletics from 1926 to 1955.[26]

The other major structure designed primarily for extracurricular activities was a modern student union building. In the late 1950s the college made several applications for a low-interest loan, the last being in the amount of $680,000, through the federal Housing and Home Finance Agency under Title IV of the Housing Act of 1950, "which enable[s] colleges and universities to build income producing buildings such as dormitories, dining halls, and student centers under very favorable long-term, low-interest, and self-amortizing loans."[27] The loan permitted construction of the new student center, completed in 1960 and located just behind the temporary union, between Hillcrest and the tennis courts. It contained two-and-a-half times the floor space of the old union, with a spacious lounge, a snack bar, an activities offices, and a dining hall large enough to accommodate the entire freshman class (thereby making possible Middlebury's first coed dining system). It was named for Redfield Proctor, former chairman of the board, who had died in 1957.[28]

The development program was unable to support the construction of a new science center, which would not be built until the mid-1960s. But several smaller science projects were funded, including a chemistry storage vault and the $12,300 Warner Greenhouse,

A student committee raised the seed money for the greenhouse attached to Warner Science. During a "Greenhouse Weekend," Robert DeLisser '55 and Lawrence Dietter '55 helped plant its foundation. The greenhouse provided facilities for the study of botany and plant physiology.

in which botany students could conduct experiments. The all-glass greenhouse, 14 feet by 31 feet, ran westerly from Warner Science and connected to the main building through a headhouse, which was faced with marble to conform with the lines of Warner.[29]

Enrollments continued to rise gradually during the 1950s, and the trustees responded by authorizing the renovation of two older residence halls and the construction of three new ones, two for women and one for men. Their first step—to provide safe, modern campus housing for all the women—was achieved by investing $300,000 in a dormitory unit that would link the two Battells. Battell Center, as it was called, was completed in early 1955 and allowed all women to live on campus.[30] The college also renovated Pearsons, the oldest women's dormitory, in 1961 and completed Allen Hall, a women's foreign language residence, two years later. Named for Cecile Child Allen '01, wife of the trustee and college treasurer, George Allen, the new dormitory was financed by a Housing and Home Finance Agency Loan of $445,000.[31] It was divided into several sections, each with its own study lounges and suites so that students wishing to speak a particular language could live together separated from the others. Allen Hall replaced three older frame buildings that had been used for this purpose.[32]

Not until 1957 were all Middlebury men able to live on campus or in fraternities. In that year the college completed construction of Stewart Hall, a men's residence with a capacity of 140 students, on a site just south of Hepburn. It was financed by a Housing and

By 1958 an expert at ground breaking, President Stratton sat at the controls of a track-mounted shovel for phase one of the expansion of Starr Library. Egbert C. Hadley '10 (chairman, at left) and Leon S. Gay represented the board of trustees.

Home Finance Agency loan of $525,000 and named for the Stewart family, one of the most influential in the college's history.[33] The administration arranged still another loan from the same source in 1958 to renovate Hepburn: the brick exterior was painted gray, an entrance terrace and portico were added, and the three-room suites were changed into doubles and singles, increasing occupancy from 97 to 139.[34]

The major building goal and most expensive project of the development program was the expansion of Starr Library. Starr had not been enlarged since 1928, when enrollment was about half of the 1958 figure. The number of volumes in the collection had grown steadily since World War II, from 105,954 to 126,838 in 1956, and the need for expanded facilities had become urgent.[35] The cost of the addition was estimated at $1,350,000. Since the trustees were concerned about the possibility of raising such a sum, they split the project into three phases and waited to begin each phase until after at least some of the funding had been assured.[36] The first two phases, completed in 1959–1960, added a new wing to the east side with one hundred study booths, four seminars, special collection rooms, more

A day before he retired in 1981 as vice president for development, Walter E. Brooker '37 smiled on a quarter century of successful fund-raising for his college.

stack areas, and modernized facilities. The third phase, which extended from the new wing toward the street, consisted of four floors of stacks and a two-level reading room connected to the stacks. It was completed between 1960 and 1962.[37]

Up to that time, the new library wing was the most expensive single structure the college had ever built, and credit for obtaining the money belongs in large part to Walter E. Brooker '37, who was hired in 1956 as Middlebury's first full-time development and public relations officer. Brooker had previously been an alumni fund chairman, and his volunteer efforts on behalf of the college were impressive.[38] He had been enjoying a successful career in advertising, and when Stratton offered him the Middlebury post, Brooker presented the idea to his wife as a good joke over which they could share a laugh. But Mrs. Brooker thought such a job would be an excellent change from the constant pressures and traveling of his present position. Much to Brooker's surprise, she soon convinced him, and he accepted Stratton's offer on February 11, 1956.[39] There are many knowledgeable observers who claim that this appointment may have been Stratton's most important single act, and the trustees showed their appreciation by promoting Brooker to vice president in 1962.[40]

He was an absolute marvel at the "development game." Under Presidents Stratton, Armstrong, and Robison, he was the indispensable man who knew just which alumni to tap for particular projects. Brooker could cajole money from the least likely individuals, and he gently guided the three presidents he served between 1956 and 1981 toward the right corporate and foundation doors.[41]

The development program, under Brooker's leadership, was not confined to physical facilities. From the beginning of the campaign (indeed, since the end of World War II), two other goals—increased faculty salaries and scholarship aid—had also been important, and Brooker and Stratton were successful here as well.[42]

Salaries were, as we have seen, one of the contributing causes of the discontent with Stratton in 1947. He fought consistently to increase faculty compensation during the rest of his tenure, and by the time of his retirement in 1963, salaries had risen 153 percent (some 50 percent in real terms).[43] Stratton wanted higher salaries so that Middlebury could compete with other schools for the best young instructors and retain the better professors, who might otherwise leave for higher compensation elsewhere. The college raised the cost of tuition from $425 in 1945-1946 to $1,300 in 1961-1962,[44] and much of this threefold increase was used to raise salaries.

Gifts to the endowment fund by individuals, foundations, corporations, and alumni were also important. The most lucrative of the individual gifts was received in the early 1950s, when the college learned that it would obtain four shares of the $75 million estate of Mrs. Hetty Sylvia Ann Howard Green Wilks, who died on February 5, 1951. On the advice of trustee Fred Lang '17, Stratton had visited Mrs. Wilks in July 1948 and persuaded her to remember Middlebury in her will, which she completed writing only ten days later.[45] Eventually, the college received $2,516,631.33 from the estate[46] and utilized the funds primarily to raise salaries. They were increased in 1952 by as much as 14 percent, and the following year Stratton could claim that salary increases since 1942-1943 had been 83 percent, while the cost of living during those years had risen only 58.3 percent.[47]

The development program of 1954-1963 made a further increase possible. Salaries were raised another 10 percent in 1956 after the college received an "endowment grant" of $336,200 for salaries as well as an "accomplishment grant" in excess of $100,000, both from the Ford Foundation.[48] The foundation had decided to spread its largesse among 615 institutions of higher learning for endowment grants, while another 126 "specially selected colleges and universities" received accomplishment grants as recognition of their leadership "in improving the status and compensation of American college teachers."[49] Still, rising enrollments around the country had increased competition for qualified instructors, and Stratton warned the board in 1956 that the 10 percent salary increase was only an interim solution. "We must find ways," he said, "to continue salary increases if we are to preserve the standards of instruction essential for our prestige and standing in the academic world."[50] He had made real progress in this area, and his successors would be able to build on his efforts and continue the process of raising salaries through tuition increases and earmarked gifts.

To compete successfully for outstanding students, Middlebury also sought funds for scholarship aid. The college had started an annual alumni fund in 1949, applying the proceeds to scholarships and unrestricted endowment.[51] This fund drew increasingly large sums from alumni ($16,000 in 1949-1950 to over $50,000 in 1958-1959). Although Brooker had some difficulty persuading donors during the development program campaign to continue to give to the alumni fund *and* still support the development effort, he eventually succeeded in this regard. The alumni fund goal was raised from $25,000 to $50,000 in 1954, with $25,000 of that amount earmarked for scholarship funds. Moreover, endowment for scholarships had increased by $90,000 between 1954 and 1958, and annual gifts and grants for scholarships (above the annual $25,000 from the alumni fund) totaled over $158,000.[52]

In January 1962, Stratton, who was nearing sixty-four years of age and had served nineteen years, informed the board that he would retire at the end of the 1962-1963 academic year.[53] He had worked diligently all those years with only two leaves of absence—to direct the government's Point Four Technical Cooperation Administration in Saudi Arabia and Yemen in 1952-1953 and to tour the Far East in the summer of 1960.[54] By the time of his retirement, Stratton could point proudly to several major advances in Middlebury's fortunes. The statistics bore him out: endowment up from $4,764,780 in 1943

In 1963, Middlebury's twelfth and thirteenth presidents joined under the portrait of its first to symbolically invoke his austere blessing on the transition to a new era.

to over $11,000,000 in 1963; faculty enlarged from 65 to over 100; salaries up 153 percent (about 50 percent in real terms); the operating budget expanded from $424,716 to $3,824,840; and plant assets (representing land, land improvements, buildings, and equipment) increased from $2,750,000 to $9,000,000. On the other hand, the college again lost ground (as it had in the Moody years) to similar colleges in comparative endowments. Middlebury's endowment was 38.7 percent of that of Williams in 1942 and only 25.1 percent by 1963; there were similar numbers for Amherst (from approximately 36 percent to 18.3 percent), Wesleyan (55.1 percent to 33.3 percent), and Colby (158 percent to 94.6 percent).[55]

Still, Stratton's accomplishments were real and proved to be essential in preparing the way for the truly significant gains made during the administration of his successor. And after facing intense faculty displeasure in his early years, Stratton had so moderated his policies and manner as to mitigate and ultimately to eradicate his unpopularity.[56]

After his retirement, Stratton was named vice president for education at Prentice-Hall, Inc. He died of a heart attack on a train near Petersburg, Virginia, on March 1, 1969, just a week after his seventy-first birthday.[57] Chaplain Charles Scott, whom Stratton had brought to Middlebury in 1951 and who became one of his closest colleagues and an influential figure in the administration, remembered Stratton in this way: "As a very human being, he was deeply aware of his own shortcomings. Such awareness disposed him gently and magnanimously toward others."[58]

Indeed, though Stratton's manner and habits caused him many difficulties during his years at Middlebury, he will be remembered more as a man who stabilized the college during World War II by bringing in the V-12 unit, as the man who enlarged the faculty and physical plant in response to the tremendous growth in postwar enrollment, and as the man who (with the assistance of departmental chairmen) significantly improved the quality of faculty and student body alike.

CHAPTER 8

THE ARMSTRONG YEARS, 1963–1975

The most important single effort over the next ten years will be to maintain and strengthen the faculty.

—President James I. Armstrong, "The President's Report, 1963–64," *Middlebury College Bulletin*, 59 (October 1969): 5

If the community is of a size so that a single voice whether of assent or dissent can gain a hearing, then there is a chance for firm footedness, a firm texture, a good morale—call it what you will—that is the mark of health and continuing life. I do not say that successful communities today cannot exist without conforming to this criterion of size; I do say that for what I think *we* are about, the criterion of encompassability or of hearing each individual seems right.

—President James I. Armstrong, *Middlebury College Report of the President, 1971–1972* (Middlebury, Vt., 1972), 4

In the past ten years we have all lived with the vision of expanding futures. . . . All of this is now drawing in.

—G. Dennis O'Brien, "1972–73 Dean of the College's Report to the President," typed manuscript, Old Chapel Archives

In early 1962, as soon as President Stratton had announced his plans to retire, the trustees chose a committee to select a presidential candidate. L. Douglas Meredith, then an executive officer of the National Life Insurance Company in Montpelier and later chairman of the college board of trustees, headed the presidential selection committee.

The faculty also chose a seven-person committee headed by "Doc" Cook '24 "to counsel" with the trustee committee on this matter.[1] The faculty suggested several names, including the committee's eventual first choice, James I. Armstrong, the forty-three-year-old classicist and associate dean of the graduate school at Princeton University.[2] Meredith approached Armstrong in November 1962 and discussed the presidency with him. Armstrong, in turn, consulted with Carlos Baker, a Princeton English professor who had taught at Bread Loaf for several summers, and with several other faculty members who had knowledge of Middlebury. Although larger schools were also seeking Armstrong, he was impressed with Middlebury's potential, and its size suited his personality better.[3] He accepted the offer in early March and was formally elected Middlebury College's twelfth president on April 13, 1963.[4]

James Isbell Armstrong was born in Princeton on April 20, 1919, the youngest of six children. His father was a professor of New Testament Greek and exegesis, and young James had an early introduction to the classics—receiving from his father, at age seven, a copy of Nestle's New Testament, which had Greek and Latin on opposite pages. James read the Latin; his father, the Greek; and the boy concluded soon after that he must learn Greek, too. His family was warm and religious. They regularly attended services at Princeton Theological Seminary, after which they returned home and often discussed theological points. With this upbringing, it is not surprising that all three of his sisters married ministers. But James did not want to be a minister, having no desire to be "an exhorter, to be hortatory." Rather, he "wished to lead people towards a perceptive and humanly responsive life by other paths." This desire eventually led him into education.[5]

He attended small private schools and graduated from the Taft School in 1937. He received his undergraduate degree from Princeton in 1941 and returned there after the war to earn his Ph.D. in classics in 1949. He was influenced by two "tiers" of Princeton professors: an older group, near retirement in the late 1930s, including David McGee and Charles Grovesnor Osgood (whom he used in his inaugural address as models of his concept of the master teacher); and a second group, headed by Whitney J. Oates ("Uncle Mike"), a student of Paul Elmer More. It was More who encouraged Armstrong to be a teacher when he returned to Princeton after the war.

After receiving his doctorate, Armstrong found himself drawn to administration, seeing it as "a way of enfranchising the learning process." Between 1950 and 1963 he was assistant and then associate dean of Princeton's graduate school. He returned to the classroom in 1962 and also received a fellowship to visit Rome and write a book on Homer's *Odyssey*. He later remarked that although he was happy teaching, he felt that "the world had narrowed a little when limited to the 'faculty point of view' and departmental perspectives." The Middlebury presidency would offer James Armstrong an opportunity to help a small college achieve new standards of excellence; the challenge attracted him, and in the summer of 1963 he and his wife, Carol, moved their young family from the familiar terrain of Princeton to an uncertain, yet promising new life in Middlebury.

Armstrong was not allowed the luxury of accustoming himself slowly to his new post. He was immediately presented with an opportunity to obtain funds that would help him meet his primary goals: to build an outstanding faculty by increasing salaries, providing research support, and initiating a generous leave program, and to enlarge and modernize the physical plant. The Ford Foundation had invited Middlebury to submit an application for a matching grant based on a projection of its needs for the next ten years. To prepare this projection (known as the Ford Profile), Armstrong and his staff had to engage in difficult and comprehensive long-term planning in the fall of 1963.[6] They utilized an earlier profile submitted to the Ford Foundation by President Stratton in 1961; Ford had rejected that request for a matching grant but remarked that they might reconsider at a later date.[7]

Armstrong, relying heavily on Business Manager (later Treasurer) Carroll Rikert, Vice President Walter Brooker '37, and the Faculty Educational Policy Committee for assistance, significantly altered some of the earlier profile's estimates. Stratton and the trustees had voted in 1961 to increase enrollment to 1,600 by 1971 and projected raising $7–8 million for new facilities during that period; Armstrong and his staff determined upon a goal of 1,800 students and $10 million. (See Table 4 for actual enrollment figures during the Armstrong administration.) The new profile also projected larger payments over the next ten years for tuition and room and board.[8]

The revised profile apparently impressed the Ford Foundation.

TABLE 4
Student Enrollment, 1963–1975

Year	Men	Women	Total
1963–1964	779	552	1331
1964–1965	786	566	1352
1965–1966	821	572	1393
1966–1967	816	561	1377
1967–1968	830	567	1397
1968–1969	895	662	1557
1969–1970	915	697	1612
1970–1971	967	693	1660
1971–1972	1057	802	1859
1972–1973	1019	798	1817
1973–1974	1078	854	1932
1974–1975	1028	850	1878

Figures are for the start of fall term, taken from the annual catalogs.

They informed Armstrong in June 1964 that they would provide up to $1.7 million if the college could match that amount on a 2:1 basis by raising another $3.4 million.[9] This $5.1-million total would still fall short of Armstrong's goal of $6.6 million, which he had presented to the board and the faculty that spring. He proposed increasing the endowment by $2,550,000 ($2 million of which would be for expending faculty resources) and raising $4,050,000 for new physical facilities, including $800,000 for a language center, $2 million for a science center, and $1,250,000 for an art–music center.[10]

The trustees, unsure whether they could raise so large a sum, retained Kersting, Brown, and Company as professional fund-raisers and asked them to study the college's fund-raising potential and recommend whether a capital gifts campaign of $6.6 million was realistic.[11] The consultants reported favorably. Though aware of the board's apprehensions due to lack of support in the past, they were optimistic that the campaign would be successful. "Other colleges comparable to Middlebury have found their alumni and friends responsive on an unprecedented scale when faced with the challenge of an urgent program," they wrote. The Ford challenge, they added, would make the difference. Armstrong also urged the trustees to make the attempt, and they agreed.[12]

The college officially accepted the Ford challenge in February 1965 and announced a $6.6-million capital campaign.[13] At the suggestion of Kersting, Brown, and Company, the trustees had earlier set up a Nucleus Fund Committee to collect pledges from the board

The Challenge Campaign was organized into regional committees. Here the New York City committee met with (left to right) Philip A. C. Clarke '51, chairman; Mary H. Cassidy '31; Carole Hoffman '65; Robert P. Youngman '64; William H. Kirby '55; Marilyn R. Bruhn '47. Robert Youngman, then co-captain with Carole Hoffman of the Regional Committee for Young Alumni, moved onto the board of trustees in 1980 and was elected chairman in 1993.

itself. Under the vigorous leadership of Ted Lang '17, this committee had already raised $725,000 when the campaign officially commenced.[14] Along with the Ford matching grant, the trustee contribution provided a powerful early momentum. Indeed, by September 1966, alumni, friends of the college, foundations, and corporations had combined with the Ford Foundation and the trustees to raise $8.3 million, and the campaign ended in an atmosphere of great happiness and optimism.[15]

The fruits of this success were quick to appear on campus during the next few years in the form of new buildings, larger academic departments, and, for the faculty, higher salaries, additional research support, and a new leave program. The money allowed the college to grow and improve its academic quality at the same time. Indeed, the period 1965–1969 was one of the most exciting in Middlebury's history. The capital campaign tapped a number of foundations, corporations, and individuals who were willing as never before to support a school that was attempting to join the ranks of the very finest liberal arts colleges in the nation.

The initial result appeared in 1965 with the construction of the first of three large instructional buildings, the Sunderland Language Center, named for Edwin S. S. Sunderland '11, who had earlier given much of the money for Wright Theater. Although the language center had been planned in Stratton's final years, the $800,000 for construction had not been forthcoming. Only about $80,000 had been raised by the summer of 1964, when the Charles A. Dana Foundation pledged $300,000 toward its construction on condition that Middlebury raise the rest.[16] This was the first of several generous gifts by Mr. Dana, who had made a fortune in automotive parts with the Dana Corporation.[17] Walter Brooker remembers his efforts to coax Dana, a well-known benefactor of many colleges and universities, to become interested in Middlebury:

> It was the summer of 1962, right after the Language Schools had closed, and I was the only one in Old Chapel. Dr. Henry Littlefield, president of the University of Bridgeport and vice-president of the Dana Foundation called me to tell me that he and Mr. Dana were near the campus and wondered if they could come and visit. Dana was quite old and had difficulty walking. It was a beautiful day, in the 70s, and we sat in Old Chapel and talked about building plans for the only thing we had going at the time—the Language Center. But Mr. Dana was interested in science, and I could feel that I was losing him. So, I said, "Let's go out and see the campus—it's such a beautiful day." I took them up to Mead Chapel, and as they looked out over the campus, Dana growled at me, "Brooker, this place looks the way I think a college ought to look!"[18]

Brooker kept in close touch with the philanthropist over the next few months, and when Dana returned to the campus in late 1963, Brooker and Stephen Freeman appealed again for help with the language center. Dana seemed particularly interested in the 270-seat auditorium. He finally agreed to provide the $300,000 matching grant; the college, in turn, later honored him by naming it the Charles A. Dana Auditorium.[19]

The Ford Foundation gave Middlebury $450,000 at the outset of the 1964–1967 challenge, $200,000 of which was earmarked for construction of the language center. With funding thus assured, the center was completed in 1965.[20] It was located on the corner of College Avenue and Chateau Road, facing south toward Painter Hall. Two old wooden structures—McGilton House and Voter House—were removed to make way for it. Stephen Freeman proudly asserted that the Sunderland Language Center was "without question the finest language center in this country and even in the world. No other institution has one like it."[21]

Sunderland had three separate, coordinated units. The first was the language laboratory: a master recording studio and control room plus sixty-three individual carrels or student practice rooms, five feet by seven feet each, all containing the most modern equipment. The master control room was connected electronically with the auditorium and the fifty-seat amphitheater, which together with other classrooms comprised the instructional unit. Dana Auditorium had excellent acoustics, a fine projection booth, and room for large audiences at public and campus lectures, movies, meetings, and other functions. The amphitheater and other classrooms were equipped with overhead projectors. The third unit included departmental and administrative offices, which provided adequate office space for faculty engaged in both the winter and summer programs. The college now had the physical facilities to match and enhance its language program, and Stephen Freeman, who had done so much to build that program into one of the nation's finest, was fittingly honored when the college named the language laboratory after him.[22]

The second new instructional building was the $1,600,000 Christian A. Johnson Memorial Building, a center for the fine arts and music departments. Completed in 1968 with funds provided by the Christian A. Johnson Endeavor Foundation, the structure was designed by the Boston firm of Shepley, Bulfinch, Richardson, and Abbott; and, as art professor Glenn Andres has written, "it proves that a building need not have a cupola to fit in with the Middlebury campus." Located on Chateau Road between Wright Theater and the new Sunderland Language Center, the Johnson building faced west across the mall toward the Battells. Although its contemporary architectural design was highlighted by raw concrete, exposed cement block, and natural wood, the building's scale and limestone exterior "permit it to co-exist quietly and naturally with other campus structures." The art department was located in the north half of the building, which included small galleries, classrooms, reference

The highlight of Homecoming in 1968 was the dedication of the Christian A. Johnson Memorial Building, which united music and art in a common building.

library, offices, and studios. The south half housed the music department, with practice rooms, offices, music library and listening center, and a large rehearsal hall on the third floor. A striking aspect of the building was the three-story central court, site of many concerts and showcase of many art exhibits.[23]

The third large instructional facility was the Science Center. President Armstrong stressed the urgent need for new science facilities in the spring of 1964:

> All of the physical and biological science departments are now housed in two buildings erected in 1901 and 1913. Past increases in enrollment, greater demands on the utilities . . . and the introduction of more independent laboratory projects and honors work, have strained these facilities beyond the limit of their capacities. That is, we have reached the point where admission to a number of courses must be refused to qualified students simply because of the physical limits of our science buildings. The projected increase in enrollment will make the space currently used by the sciences wholly inadequate. It is impera-

tive that a new Science Center—buildings and modern equipment—
be provided if Middlebury is to meet its obligations in the teaching
of science.[24]

That summer Grant Harnest, chairman of the chemistry department,
visited other schools that had recently built new science facilities.
Harnest, who was also charged with the task of evaluating the physical needs of Middlebury's natural sciences division, organized a Science Facilities Planning Committee with representation from each
department. This committee worked closely with Dean of College
Thomas Reynolds and other officers in developing a plan for a new
science center and later assisted the Architects Collaborative of Boston in the actual designs. The faculty envisioned two new buildings—
one for physics and chemistry, the other for biology and mathematics—constructed on the lower campus near Warner Science, which,
when completely renovated, would contain geography and geology.[25]

Armstrong vigorously searched for the necessary funds. He had
been spectacularly successful in his efforts to persuade the Christian A. Johnson Endeavor Foundation (particularly Mrs. Johnson)
to underwrite the new art and music center, but he had more difficulty with the $2.9-million science center. An application in 1965
for $2 million from the National Science Foundation was turned
down, and although Middlebury received several large gifts from
other groups, including $400,000 from the Alfred P. Sloan Founda-
tion and $300,0000 from the Dana Foundation, much of the money
eventually came from the government under Title III of the Higher
Education Facilities Act of 1963.[26]

Armstrong met some opposition to the idea of building the center
on the lower campus, because that would necessitate the realignment
of Storrs Avenue, the village street that bounded the college on the
east. One town resident, fearful that building the science center on
"the best street in our Village" would destroy some beautiful houses,
urged the college to consider other locations.[27] Armstrong had several reasons for the Storrs Avenue site. He wanted it close to Warner
so that the concept of a science center could be affirmed, he did not
want to infringe on the lower-campus green area between Old Stone
Row and Storrs Avenue, and he did not want to build on remote
college land because he wished to keep Middlebury a "six-minute
campus." In this case, as in others, the college planned carefully to
preserve green spaces and avoid the crowded and random appear-

ance of some schools.[28] The village trustees agreed to Armstrong's plan in the fall of 1965 and voted to close Storrs Avenue and later realign it.[29]

The science center, phase I, was completed in 1968. This was the first of two planned buildings; the second was never constructed due to financial considerations and enrollment patterns.[30] The center, Professor Andres writes, successfully combined modern design with materials used in other campus buildings: "Its exposed frame is of reinforced concrete in the vocabulary of the 'Brutalist' school of architecture and gives a sense of scale and order to the great mass. Its enclosing membrane of walls is of tinted glass and the local limestone, which will be met as a unifying constant of color and texture throughout most campus construction."[31] The four science departments that shared the facility enjoyed well-equipped laboratories, classroom space, a science library, offices, and storage areas.

The three new buildings were an impressive addition to the college, and their presence on campus supported President Armstrong's major goal: they had been built, in part, to attract superior faculty and enhance teaching effectiveness. This was particularly true of the sciences, where professors had long been hampered by limited space and outmoded facilities. As Dean Reynolds told the alumni in 1965, "it is obvious that we will not be able to recruit in the area of the natural sciences a faculty equal to any in the nation without the necessary equipment and facilities both to foster fine teaching at Middlebury and to enhance the future research of faculty members and students alike."[32]

Armstrong knew that facilities were a necessary but not a sufficient attraction for outstanding faculty, and he searched for funds to raise salaries and provide research money and paid leaves of absence. The Research Corporation and the Sloan, Charles A. Dana, Ford, and Old Dominion foundations all made contributions before 1969 that were earmarked for salaries and support for faculty research and professional development.[33] Armstrong also persuaded the trustees to raise tuition every year of his presidency in order to increase faculty compensation.[34]

The results were impressive. Salaries rose markedly at every rank, and differentials between ranks were increased: from 1963 to 1968 the average salary for full professors rose from $11,286 to $16,275;

Benjamin F. Wissler and James H. Baum '59 set up new physics apparatus, the result of a grant from the General Electric Company. This equipment, an e/m tube, allowed the measurement of the ratio of an electron's charge to its mass.

for associate professors, from $9,189 to $13,224.[35] Armstrong also initiated a popular new leave-of-absence program. Previously, the college only had the annual income from the $100,000 Walker Fund for this purpose, which could barely fund an annual leave for one professor. After 1965–1966, under the new plan, an average of nine or ten faculty members a year were granted one-semester or full-year leaves with full pay.[36] A Faculty Research Fund was established to support the continuance of scholarly work,[37] and the library's holdings were steadily increased under the leadership of John McKenna, whom Armstrong called from Colby College in 1964 to be the librarian.[38]

With improved facilities, higher salaries, new research funds, a generous leave program, a growing library, and high morale and institutional optimism, Armstrong was able to attract some bright new faculty. Increased enrollments enabled him to increase the faculty size from 104 in 1963 to 135 in 1968 and 154 in 1974. A larger faculty permitted individual departments to grow in size and range and allowed a greater variety of courses to be taught, thereby strengthening the offerings for majors and nonmajors alike.[39]

Not surprisingly, Armstrong looked to Princeton for people to help him improve the faculty. In 1964 he brought William B. Catton, a young American historian, to bolster the social sciences faculty, and a year later he cajoled G. Dennis O'Brien, a philosopher-administrator, to become dean of men and teach in the philosophy department. In 1966, Nicholas R. Clifford arrived to join Catton in the history department, and Kimberly Sparks, a well-known German-language scholar, was called to strengthen the foreign-language faculty. And in 1968, Armstrong recruited A. Richard Turner, a noted art historian, to enhance the college's fine-arts program.

While there were many other appointments, these five stand out because each of them quickly became an important member of the institution. Catton served as chairman of the social sciences division and, during a key period, as chairman of the Educational Policy Committee; O'Brien was chair of the philosophy department as well as dean of the faculty and dean of the college at various times during his eleven years at Middlebury; Clifford was chairman of the history department and later vice president for academic affairs, provost, and acting president in the Robison administration; Sparks served as chairman of the German department, the languages division, and a special Committee on Foreign Languages initiated in 1973; and Turner held several posts, including chairman of the art department and dean of the faculty.[40] For a time this group was known, not always affectionately, as the Princeton Mafia.[41]

The addition of these men and other vigorous teachers helped enable the college to initiate far-reaching curricular reforms in the period 1964–1970. Many of these changes had been pushed by some of Stratton's best appointees, such as Paul Cubeta and Thomas Reynolds. As we have seen, their effort to replace the five-course curriculum with a four-course schedule was defeated in 1960. But with Armstrong's support and a growing number of new faculty members sympathetic to reform, the balance tipped the other way.

The late 1950s and 1960s witnessed an increased seriousness about academic matters on the part of both students and faculty, and one of the clearest results was a growing emphasis on independent study.[42] In the opinion of its critics, the old five-course system allowed students little chance to investigate subjects deeply, whereas fewer courses would

> . . .lessen the fragmentation of intellectual effort and thereby provide additional time for more intensive study and deeper reflection in individual courses, and for more meaningful integration of the range of material encountered within and among the various courses. It will

also permit the student to pursue academic goals and interests that grow out of, but go beyond, what the curriculum requires of him.[43]

Many faculty also favored an end to the present semester system, with its many fall-term interruptions between November and January. Instead, they proposed a 4-1-4 calendar: students would take four courses instead of five in the fall and spring terms, with a reduction in semester length from fifteen to thirteen weeks, and a single course (to which they would "normally devote [their] entire academic energy") during a new one-month winter term between the regular semesters. The winter term represented, par excellence, the desire of some faculty to develop a curriculum that encouraged deeper intellectual commitment.

> In undertaking a single project during the Winter Session, he [the student] will encounter a change of pace from the rhythm of the conventional academic semester. He will experience the challenge of sustained absorption in a single endeavor, with no competing deadlines to divide his energy or concentration. He will be able to choose from a variety of new courses that offer material or approaches not normally encountered in regular departmental offerings. He will have increased opportunity for independent study, both within and outside of his departmental major.[44]

In February 1967 the Educational Policy Committee, which was dominated by the reform-minded element, presented a twelve-page document advocating a 4-1-4 calendar, pass–fail grading outside the major, and the possibility of dropping all distribution requirements. The faculty narrowly defeated this proposal on April 26, 50–46. Later, they voted 69–9 in favor of considering further the 4-1-4 calendar with the stipulations that language students might have to continue their first semester courses into the winter session and that the requirement for the A.B. degree would be successful completion of eight fall and spring semesters and four winter sessions. The faculty also made it clear to the Educational Policy Committee that they opposed the pass–fail system and the end to distribution requirements and that they wanted to take a final vote on the 4-1-4 proposal the following year. After months of discussion they voted 69–29 on February 8, 1968, to change the curriculum and calendar to a 4-1-4 program, beginning in the fall of 1968.[45]

President Armstrong was delighted and told the trustees that the 4-1-4 calendar "created a whole new dispensation for the College":

For the students it means a more reasonable rate of study, a change of pace in the winter program, and encouragement to greater independence. For the faculty, it offers an increased opportunity for experimentation in how teaching proceeds, [and] a revision of present offerings. For the College, it will bring about a better utilization of teaching resources, encouragement of interdepartmental and interdivisional curricular activity, and a more sensible calendar. In short, the program will create an atmosphere more hospitable and conducive to teaching. It is a major step forward that careful deliberations and the passage of time have brought into being.[46]

Armstrong had been a strong advocate of the proposal, and his influence had undoubtedly helped assure its passage. Unlike his predecessor, Armstrong had earned the faculty's confidence in the early years of his administration, and although some suspicious professors may have voted against the four-course curriculum in 1960 because Stratton favored it, Armstrong's relative popularity enabled him to play a more positive role.

In his early days at Middlebury, Armstrong had been surprised and hurt when the faculty (due in part to their lingering resentment of Stratton and in part to their desire for autonomy in curricular matters) refused him membership on the Faculty Educational Policy Committee. Armstrong argued that since the committee was the college's principal educational planning instrument, he should be a member if he was to meet his responsibilities as president.[47] He soon secured his objective. The faculty had told the trustees in April 1965 that they were "very pleased" with Armstrong and his impressive progress in meeting their needs, and they applauded his "procedure of consultation with the faculty in connection with the new building." The trustee committee on conference with the faculty could report by October 1966 "that an attitude of suspicion and apprehension on the part of the faculty members in previous years had changed to one of confidence in the President and the Board of Trustees."[48] Not surprisingly, Armstrong was elected to the Educational Policy Committee that fall while it was seriously discussing the 4-1-4 option.[49]

Two years after approving the 4-1-4 curriculum, the faculty voted in 1970 to end distribution requirements and lower the physical education requirement from two years to one. A subcommittee of the Educational Policy Committee had been set up in 1969 to examine all requirements (group, distribution, major, physical education).[50]

Students who favored ending the requirements formed a Student Investigating Committee (SIC) and tried to influence faculty voting on the issue by presenting them with a petition containing between nine hundred and one thousand signatures. Members of SIC even threatened to lead a student strike on May 5, 1970, if the faculty did not vote to implement the desired changes.[51] On May 4 the faculty voted 47–35 to end distribution requirements.[52]

Along with new buildings, an improved and more generously compensated faculty, and much curricular change came the decision to increase enrollment from 1,300 to 1,800 between 1963 and 1972. This had several major ramifications: the hiring of more faculty, as we have seen, an increase in residential and dining facilities, and significant structural change.

A growing college simply demanded a larger, more highly articulated, and more hierarchical administrative structure, and Armstrong created one. In 1964 he named Thomas Reynolds dean of the college, a new office to which the student deans, directors of admissions, chaplain, and several others reported. When Reynolds left in 1966 to become president of Bates College, Dennis O'Brien replaced him.[53] In the area of academic affairs, Armstrong revived the position of vice president (which Stephen Freeman had held from 1943 until his retirement from that office in 1963), and the position was assumed in 1970 by Paul Cubeta, who was given a great deal of power in the area of salaries and recruitment.[54] Cubeta had been named dean of the faculty in 1967 to replace John G. Bowker (who retired after serving in that capacity since 1953), and in 1970, A. Richard Turner replaced Cubeta in that office.[55] In another early move, Armstrong promoted Carroll Rikert, Jr., from business manager to treasurer. Formerly, the treasurer had been a trustee and the business manager had reported directly to the board; Armstrong wanted both business manager and treasurer to be full-time administrators responsible directly to the president, and the trustees agreed to this change in 1964.[56] As an "enormously talented" treasurer and a man who aggressively, often brilliantly, pursued what he saw as the best financial and educational interests of Middlebury College, Rikert was a dominant and sometimes controversial force on the campus during the Armstrong and Robison years.[57]

The administration grew in size, not only at the top but at the

College treasurer Carroll Rikert, Jr., assumed a hard hat in 1972 to explain to a Homecoming audience the bricks and mortar of the 175th Anniversary Campaign.

middle-management and staff levels, with the addition of a psychologist, a full-time physician, and numerous other employees necessary to serve the needs of the growing college.[58] The structure was also altered by Armstrong's decision to eliminate the vestiges of the coordinate system and thereby help establish a more truly coeducational college. He named Fred Neuberger '50 director of admissions for the entire College in 1964, thus ending the long practice of maintaining separate admissions offices for men and women, and he appointed Erica Wonnacott dean of students in 1969, eliminating the positions of dean of men and dean of women.[59]

Another necessary result of increased enrollments was the addition of residence halls and coeducational dining facilities. Four new residence halls were opened between 1969 and 1971. Located on the ridge just north of Pearsons Hall, they could house approximately 520 students. Although men and women initially lived in separate dormitories, two of the new buildings were connected by a lounge, which was designed to be coeducational. The four residence halls were named in honor of Elizabeth Baker Kelly, who had just retired as dean of women; Egbert C. Hadley '10, chairman of the board, 1944-1968; Fred P. Lang '17, treasurer, 1952-1964; and Gertrude Cornish Milliken '01, the college's first woman trustee. The lounge was named for the legendary Dean Eleanor Ross. These modern residence halls permitted the closing of a number of older houses that had been used as student residences during the 1960s.[60]

The college also constructed three social-dining units in the extreme northeast corner of campus. These units, named for Professor Reginald "Doc" Cook '24, Vice President Stephen Freeman, and President Cyrus Hamlin (1880–1885), provided alternative facilities for eating and socializing.[61] In the past, students had eaten either in large dining rooms on campus or (like most nonfreshmen males) in fraternities, and social life revolved around the fraternities. As we shall see in Part III, the decision to raise enrollment to 1,800 (which saw the male population far outstrip fraternity facilities), the drive to create equal facilities for women and a declining interest in traditional fraternity life led the college to seek other means of organizing social life and dining routine. The new social-dining complexes consisted of faculty offices, lounges, seminar rooms, and dining rooms in three units clustered around a central kitchen. The architects, Shepley, Bulfinch, Richardson, and Abbott of Boston, won a New England regional award from the American Institute of Architects for their design of the units. Professor Andres has remarked that the design of the social-dining units "combines contemporary forms and materials (such as the brutal, exposed concrete of the terrace) with a vocabulary that is at home in Middlebury and rural Vermont—limestone, wood pitched slate roofs, silos, and small-scale, picturesque massing."[62]

The college also renovated several buildings to accommodate the increased staff and student body. After completion of the Johnson building, Carr Hall was converted into a well-equipped infirmary in 1968. Chemistry (renamed Voter Hall for Perley Voter, longtime chairman of the chemistry department) was completely renovated in 1970, with administrative offices on the ground floor and dormitory suites on the upper floors. Warner, Munroe, and Old Chapel received comparable renovations.[63]

The first decade of the Armstrong presidency, taken all in all, was a remarkable era for Middlebury. Growth, change, and improvement in all areas—plant, endowment, faculty, enrollments, curriculum, calendar, administration—simply transformed the college. But external forces and internal decisions determined that the 1970s would be a period of less dramatic change and growth. Inflation demanded hefty tuition increases (the college switched to a comprehensive fee in 1970), and Middlebury still needed impressive alumni giving and enormous additions to endowment merely to maintain the recent gains in institutional and faculty quality.[64] On the other hand, the decision by President Armstrong and the trustees to keep enrollment at approximately 1,800 rather than permit further growth meant an end to the rapid expansion of the 1950s and 1960s. This was a reluctant decision. "It can be argued," Armstrong admitted, that "growth would insure financial stability, increase the 'range' of the educational program, in short bring all those 'benefits' which are usually ascribed to growth."[65] But the president was concerned that a college larger than 1,800 students might no longer be a community.

> If the community is of a size so that a single voice whether of assent or dissent can gain a hearing, then there is a chance for firm-footedness, a firm texture, good morale—call it what you will-that is the mark of health and continuing life. I do not say that successful communities today cannot exist without conforming to this criterion of size; I do say that for what I think *we* are about, the criterion of encompass-ability or of hearing each individual seems right.
>
> In colleges there is a working arrangement—a balancing of authority and responsibility by consent; it presumes a basis of trust among the various elements. This trust—so essential to the quality of life—derives, I believe, in some very large degree from acquaintance with one another.
>
> Personal acquaintance is a primary ingredient of community and collegiality. Given our purposes at Middlebury—liberal learning having primarily to do with values and their relation to the living of life—the College should remain a community small enough to gauge rightly character and ability, to bring out those authentic features which mark an individual. Thus, in the context of Middlebury College, its history and its educational purposes, size takes a central role; like the form of a poem it becomes a crucial part of the meaning of the college—its character and its quality.[66]

In short, Middlebury would not be able to maintain the special environment of a small liberal arts college if it expanded further.

Higher education underwent a period of retrenchment and difficulties in the early 1970s. Many schools were unable to balance their budgets, and calls for consolidation and retrenchment were uniformly heard. One scholar provocatively termed it "the new depression in higher education."[67] Middlebury was not immune. In-

Egbert C. Hadley '10 advised Middlebury's presidents and supported his college for most of this century. He had lunch with James I. Armstrong in the Johnson Arts Center during a Trustees' Weekend in 1973.

deed, due in large part to soaring costs and the decision to stabilize enrollment, the major efforts of the Armstrong administration after 1970 were directed toward the problems of a college more nearly at equilibrium than those of a growing institution: emphasizing endowment, faculty salaries, and current expenses rather than the more popular building campaigns; carefully analyzing the curriculum, identifying strengths and weaknesses to determine which programs should be bolstered and which possibly eliminated; and establishing a tenure policy that would ensure high quality and still maintain good morale among the younger faculty, many of whom now knew that they had no long-range future at Middlebury.

The financial picture in the late 1960s appeared increasingly troublesome. Operating costs were rising rapidly, and projections for the 1970s, with inflation showing no signs of abating, were not optimistic. Treasurer Carroll Rikert, Jr., reminded the board in 1969 that revenue had to rise an average of $600,000 annually to keep pace with expenses, and he warned that without substantial increases in endowment or other gifts, a tuition increase of $200 and a $25,000 rise in annual giving would not be sufficient to "permit even the same magnitude of expense increases made in 1969–70. This presents a prospect," he continued, "of sharply increasing fees and intense stress in making choices among strongly competing claims on the college's resources."[68]

This bleak picture had earlier persuaded the trustees to advance the opening date of the long-awaited 175th Anniversary Campaign to 1971, to obtain professional fund-raising assistance, to set a dollar goal, to seek precampaign trustee support, and to give the campaign a crucial early impetus by persuading some donor to supply a generous gift or matching grant. After setting the goal at $10.5 million, much of which was earmarked for endowment, the board again secured the services of Kersting, Brown, and Company as fund-raising consultants.[69] As in the 1964–1966 capital campaign, a trustee nucleus fund was organized, this time under the leadership of Arnold LaForce '35, which raised $942,869 at the outset and eventually over $2 million. Armstrong also secured a magnificent challenge grant from the Christian A. Johnson Endeavor Foundation, which promised one dollar for every four dollars Middlebury raised, with a maximum grant of $2 million if the college could obtain an additional $8 million from other sources. The Johnson grant and the board's generosity provided the necessary early push, and by October 31, 1975, when the campaign ended, Middlebury had raised $13,879,054, surpassing its goal by over $3 million.[70]

A large portion of this was designated specifically to endow professorships, including the Johnson Professorship of Art History and the Johnson Professorship of Studio Art, both in honor of the Johnson Foundation's $2-million matching grant. Other endowed chairs included the Starr Professorship of Linguistics, funded by a $750,000 gift from the Starr Foundation, and the William R. Kenan, Jr., professorship, established with a $650,000 grant from the William R. Kenan Charitable Trust. When those were added to the ones obtained earlier—the Dana Support Professorships, funded by a $250,000 gift from the Dana Foundation; and the Irene Heinz Given and John LaPorte Given Professorship in Premedical Sciences established in 1966 by a $500,000 grant—the result was a splendid achievement for Armstrong, Walter Brooker, and the fund-raising staff.[71]

Although most of the 175th Anniversary Campaign proceeds were earmarked for endowment or operating expenses, the drive also obtained funds for a major addition to the physical plant. By the early

1970s it had become evident that the Memorial Field House could not handle the demands of the growing student body, and athletic director Richard Colman noted that the old structure was "frightfully overcrowded and overused."[72] The trustees decided to include a new field house as a campaign goal and were heartened when the Dana Foundation agreed to provide a $250,000 challenge grant if the college could raise an additional $750,000 by December 15, 1973.[73] With substantial help from the Kresge Foundation ($150,000), the challenge was met, and ground breaking for the $1.2-million Paris Fletcher Field House, located just southwest of the old one, was begun in the spring of 1973. The building, named for an alumnus and active trustee who had been chairman of the Library Fund Development Campaign in 1958–1961, was designed by Daniel F. Tully Associates of Melrose, Massachusetts. Its most striking architectural characteristic was an unusual roof built up as a series of prefabricated and double-curved plywood planes.[74] The Fletcher Field House, fondly named by some local (Addison County) residents as "Addison Square Garden," greatly helped alleviate overcrowding in the athletic and recreational facilities.

The only other major addition during the final Armstrong years was the construction of two small residence halls north of the social-dining units. Completed in 1974 at a cost of $350,000 and named for the college's first two presidents, Jeremiah Atwater and Henry Davis, the two wood-frame buildings were designed to house thirty students. Atwater and Davis dormitories, like the Fletcher Field House, were designed by Tully Associates.[75]

Although Fletcher and Atwater-Davis were important additions, the building boom of the 1960s had clearly slowed. Faced by growing financial problems and an end to rising enrollments, the college turned away from further dramatic growth to concentrate instead on avoiding a deficit; plans for a large new library were reworked and later delayed due to lack of funds.[76]

Deciding it was time for taking stock, President Armstrong appointed a special committee in November 1971 to "undertake a searching examination of the College." Armstrong asked the committee "to look at the whole college (residential-social, curricular, extra-curricular, para-curricular) with an eye directed both internally and externally."[77] The committee, chaired by the dean of the faculty, Richard Turner, was composed of one professor from each academic division (Roger Peel from languages, Nicholas Clifford from the social sciences, Robert Hill from humanities, and Bruce Peterson from the natural sciences) and one student, Laura Reinertsen '73. Their wide-ranging report, after eighteen months of careful study, was issued on June 30, 1973. Although they offered recommendations in a number of areas, three in particular attracted attention.

First, the committee proposed a new curriculum, based on a belief that each student should take an integrated group of courses in both the sciences and humanities before pursuing more advanced or specialized study.

> In order to introduce the student to different ways of thinking, we propose that each student be exposed to the mode of thought of the sciences broadly conceived, a respect for objectivity, for precision and fact, cultivation of analytic process, and the formulation of hypothesis, theory, and law. Similarly, every student should be introduced to the mode of thinking of the humanities, which, in addition to a shared respect for objectivity, often relies heavily upon intuition and a process of synthesizing whose vehicle frequently is the language of analogy and metaphor.
>
> *We therefore recommend that the curriculum of the College be organized into two major groupings: 1) The Humanities (the present division of Humanities, plus Languages and History) and 2) the Natural and Social Sciences. We further recommend that each student be obligated to take one Concentration of five to seven courses in each of these two groupings and that this be regarded as the foundation of a Middlebury education.*
>
> A *Concentration* is a coherent sequence of five to seven courses in a traditional subject. It stresses the discipline and the method of the subject rather than striving for broad coverage. The fundamental questions posed by the Concentration are: *how* does a physicist (economist, art historian, etc.) think and why, and how do these processes of thought differ from other sorts of thinking that the student has experienced.[78]

In addition to the two concentrations, each student would complete an upperclass requirement of either (1) a third concentration, (2) an advanced major (similar to existing majors) built on one of the concentrations, or (3) a program such as teacher education, environmental studies, or creative writing.[79]

There was considerable opposition to this proposal. Many students argued that their freedom of choice would be greatly curtailed and that the concentrations were a thinly disguised attempt to restore the distribution requirements that a majority had opposed in the late 1960s. Many faculty members agreed. Indeed, much of the debate over the committee report centered on the curricular proposal, and on December 4, 1973, the faculty voted 71–34 to reject it.[80]

A second recommendation also stirred controversy: the committee proposed "a concerted effort to strengthen the languages at Middlebury, and recommend that with the library the languages have highest priority for the next capital campaign, which should be launched as soon after the conclusion of the 175th Anniversary Campaign as is practicable."[81] The committee argued that what primarily differentiated Middlebury from its competitors was its reputation in foreign languages, and this distinctive feature should not be weakened or compromised. The committee was concerned because of recent setbacks to the language programs. Many high schools had dropped their language requirements, causing a decline in the demand for foreign-language teachers and a decreasing enrollment at Middlebury's summer and overseas programs. The recommendation to strengthen the languages was prefaced by a plea: "We note the projected Summer School deficits in the years immediately ahead, and the increasingly less favorable financial status of the Overseas Schools in the face of inflation and dollar devaluation. We nonetheless believe that a failure of nerve at this point in Middlebury's history could lead to a serious mistake."[82]

Actually, the language programs under Armstrong had continued to expand and, up to that time, prosper. The five summer programs — French, German, Spanish, Italian, and Russian — all thrived in the 1960s, as did the overseas schools in France, Germany, Spain, and Italy. And two new summer language programs were founded. In 1966, after several years of trying, Armstrong and Stephen Freeman organized a Middlebury Summer School of Mandarin Chinese. Forty-nine students attended the first session, and under the leadership of the school's second director, Dr. Ta-Tuan Ch'en of Princeton University, enrollment rose to 114 by 1974. The early success of the Chinese School encouraged Freeman to investigate another possibility, and the Japanese Summer School was founded in the summer of 1970 with twenty-six students in attendance, directed by Professor Hiroshi Miyaji of the University of Pennsylvania. Under Miyaji's

In 1982, Dr. Ta-Tuan Ch'en visited the Chinese School. During the annual "China Night," when demonstrations of Chinese culture are mixed with comic sketches of the difficulties of Chinese School life, Dr. Ch'en gave a demonstration of t'ai chi, sword form. Through his demonstration of t'ai chi, Dr. Ch'en suggested the contrasting energies of thought and action moving together, the self-mastery needed for the study of Chinese.

guidance, enrollment jumped to sixty-six by 1974, placing the school on a firm footing. In the case of both Oriental schools, Middlebury offered intensive summer language training so that students could continue their studies at their home colleges the following fall at the next level of competency.[83]

Armstrong apparently accepted the view that languages were of prime importance and should be stressed: "The committee believes that Middlebury should lead from strength to greater strength for the whole College. Hence, the recommendations seek to develop the extraordinary potential for a total College language program involving the seven summer language schools . . . , the four schools aboard . . . , and the undergraduate departments."[84] In the fall of 1973, as a first step toward these goals, Armstrong appointed the eminent German professor, Kimberly Sparks, as chairman of a new Committee on Foreign Languages. This body, after examining the Special Committee's recommendations relating to languages, would try to assure the continued excellence of the summer and over-seas schools and strengthen the undergraduate language programs.[85] Armstrong named Roger Peel, dean of the Spanish Summer School, the new director of the language schools in 1973, replacing Andre Paquette, who had succeeded Stephen Freeman in that position three years earlier.[86] Under Paquette and Peel, the language schools added undergraduate courses both abroad and (beginning in 1973 with the intensive language programs) in the summer schools. These new offerings helped to increase enrollments and to bring in enough funds to assure financial solvency for the schools by the mid-1970s.[87]

Still, there was much opposition by faculty outside the languages to the idea that languages should have primacy, and although a good deal was said about this issue during the final Armstrong years, no significant changes took place.

The third important recommendation of the Special Committee was its proposal that the Faculty Council undertake a thorough review of tenure at Middlebury, "both in regard to its purposes and the rules now surrounding its practice."[88] The college had granted tenure in 1966 to all faculty members who had been there longer than the seven years prescribed by the AAUP as an upper limit on the length of appointments without tenure. Since that time, nearly two-thirds of those professors considered for tenure had been granted it. But as en-rollments — and necessarily, size of faculty — leveled off, the prospect of denying tenure to a larger percentage of junior people suddenly loomed. As Paul Cubeta argued in 1970, "with more than half of a faculty . . . on tenure, the College must be alert to the seriousness of the problem of granting tenure even to very fine young colleagues. The financial and educational dangers here are profound."[89] Cubeta feared that in a few years a mostly tenured faculty would become prohibitively expensive because salaries and benefits for the majority would be at the high end of the scale. And he also worried that with an overtenured faculty the college would have little flexibility to add new programs or strengthen existing ones and fewer opportunities to hire new instructors with fresh ideas. These fears led to a tougher policy in the early 1970s, which gave each department a tenure com-plement of about 50 percent (unless, of course, it had already passed that point, as several had).[90]

The tenure complement — in essence, a freeze — was not popular.

An exceptionally bright professor might not obtain tenure merely because he was in a department well over its complement, whereas a professor in another discipline could be tenured if his department had a slot available. Dean Dennis O'Brien expressed his anxiety for the College as a whole:

> No matter what abstract rationale may be given for the tenure freeze, no matter how impeccable the calculations and projections, I am hard pressed to see how it is to be lived through in human terms without a great depression of *enthusiasms*. Younger faculty are hired on and cannot see beyond the seventh year. Unlike Jacob, not even another period of servitude will earn them Rachel. For them, the future at Middlebury stops.[91]

O'Brien argued that a depression in the spirit of the faculty would "carry on through the student body." "Students," he wrote, "are birds of passage, and yet they come to believe that the roost should be permanently populated. If one creates a faculty and student class of transients, one swings the balance of the institution, I fear, in the direction of transience."[92]

The college wrestled hard with the tenure question. A new document, presented to the faculty in 1974 and passed in January 1975, stated that "strict mathematical quotas" (i.e., complements) were not "in the best interests of faculty development," but it went on to require an untenured professor to pass three separate reviews (during the second, fourth, and eighth years of service) before tenure could be granted. "Appointment with tenure," the document bluntly added, "is viewed as exceptional."[93] The process thus became lengthier and more rigorous, and the avowed intent of the new policy was to make tenure more difficult to obtain.[94] The faculty who supported this change may have been swayed by Vice President Cubeta, who presented disturbing statistics: if half of current untenured faculty received tenure by 1980, the college would be 67 percent tenured. Furthermore, of the twenty-four professors reviewed for tenure since 1970, fifteen had obtained it; if that trend continued, the percentage of tenured faculty would soon be even greater than 67 percent.[95]

While the decision to toughen tenure requirements may have been the proper course of action in the long run, it meant denying tenure during the next few years to a number of seemingly excellent teachers and scholars. This left a sour taste in the mouths of many professors, junior and senior alike, and seriously depressed the students, many of whom were naturally drawn to young and dynamic instructors. O'Brien's fears of the loss of "enthusiasms" was realized. Although it is impossible to assess exactly what the college paid for the financial gains and increased flexibility earned by its rigorous tenure policy, there is no doubt that faculty morale in 1975 (and after) was much lower than it had been ten years earlier.[96]

By 1974, Armstrong had served eleven years as president. The problems of the 1970s undoubtedly weighed heavily on him and went well beyond the normal challenges of fund-raising, recruitment, budget balancing, curricular reform, tenure policy, and general administration. Financial stringency and declining morale had replaced the expansive optimism of the 1960s. As we shall see in Part III, he also encountered critical and stormy social developments—a "revolution" in student life, a rancorous battle with fraternities as their influence declined, intense opposition to the war in Vietnam, and an emotional new commitment to increase black enrollment after Martin Luther King's death. All this had taken its toll.

Finally, on November 2, 1974, Armstrong informed the board of his intention to resign as of September 1, 1975, to become president of the Dana Foundation.[97] The trustees accepted this with reluctance: Armstrong's presidency had been one of the most productive periods in the college's history. Although his progress had been aided by a favorable educational environment, he had repeatedly demonstrated a keen ability to take advantage of available opportunities. Indeed, Armstrong has remarked that when he assumed the office of president, Middlebury's strengths and weaknesses were really one and the same: "[T]he college had great potential, but was too cautious and lacked the confidence to release its energies. It needed someone to uncoil the spring that had been readied during the previous administration."[98] Statistics can be cited to demonstrate the impressive gains made by Armstrong's Middlebury in endowment, value of plant, acreage owned, size of faculty, salaries, and other categories. During his presidency, for the first time in many years the college gained instead of losing ground to rival colleges in endowment: Middlebury's endowment was 18.3 percent of Amherst's in 1963 and 40.2 percent by 1975; and similar gains took place relative to Williams (25.1 percent to 49.7 percent), Colby (94.6 percent to 110.1 percent), and Bowdoin (50 percent to 88.3 percent).[99]

Scholar and alumnus Howard Munford '34 presented diplomas to his final class of American literature students in 1977.

In this regard and others, Armstrong's greatest achievements, perhaps, were in moving Middlebury solidly into the ranks of the country's first-rate liberal arts colleges and in improving its self-image.
Howard Munford '34, a faculty leader and spokesman during these
years, has said that it was only after Armstrong became president
and improved the college's academic reputation that Munford could
attend a professional conference or see colleagues from other schools
and not feel that he was teaching at an inferior institution.[100] It
was fitting that a professor should hold that view, since it had been
Armstrong's primary concern all along: "The most important single
effort over the next ten years," he announced in 1964, "will be to
maintain and strengthen the faculty.[101] In this and in much more,
Armstrong succeeded admirably.

CHAPTER 9

THE ROBISON YEARS, 1975–1990

[T]he Trustees continue to be aware of these concerns, and in large measure the College's vitality and strength now and in the future is dependent upon the College's having a faculty and staff who are fairly and competitively compensated. Increases in compensation have been discussed at length and are likely to continue to receive the sympathetic attention of both the administration and the Trustees in the years ahead.

> —Arnold LaForce, Chairman of the Middlebury College Board of Trustees, at the January 13, 1979, Trustee Meeting, in Minutes of the Corporation, Vol. 11, p. 1174, Old Chapel Vault

The 1983 Planning Document set as "the clear first priority" the enlargement of the faculty. We audaciously proposed that, by the academic year 1992–93, 23 new positions be created, thereby increasing the size of the faculty by 16%, reducing the student/faculty ratio to 12/1, and having 152 FTE's (full-time equivalents) in the classroom. In *five* years we have met or exceeded those goals. . . . Furthermore, the number of colleagues on leave has continued to grow, and the scholarly productivity of our faculty has increased dramatically. The 1983 Document looked to a day when one-twelfth of our faculty was on "research appointment" or leave. In 1987–88, 23 of our colleagues, far more than one-twelfth, are on leave, most of them for a full year at 75% of salary (another significant change in the last five years; full-year leaves were formerly available at $\frac{5}{9}$ of salary), and many of them unreplaced. This has not been done with mirrors but rather with a combination of boldness and planning that we can but applaud.

> —John McCardell et al., *Toward the Year 2000: A Basic Ten-Year Planning Document* (Middlebury, Vt., 1988), p. 1

Although Starr Library is so close to capacity that buying books at a normal pace promises to fill it before we could construct additional space, even if we started today, there is no evidence that the Board is concerned with library space. Although a valuable science collection deteriorates by the hour in a tiny and totally inadequate science library, there is no evidence that the Board has even addressed the problem. Although laboratory and teaching facilities for the sciences place us embarrassingly far behind all our competition, the Board has shown us no interest in better science space. . . .

What the Board does have to say is that we need a new football stadium. I disagree, and I believe their decision represents such a distortion of the proper priorities of this institution, such a complete misunderstanding of what we on campus want for this institution, that we must speak out. . . . What is the message? What is the symbolism when a Board of Trustees seems to have lost sight of the purpose of the institution, when the College seems but a plaything for wealthy trustees? What are we saying when the Board's direction is 180 degrees away from the faculty's? What does it mean when the Board concerns itself only with issues peripheral to the educational goals of the College?

> —Bruce Peterson, Professor of Mathematics, in
> an open letter to the faculty, November 6, 1989,
> copy in Faculty Minutes, November 6, 1989,
> Office of the Secretary of the Faculty

On November 2, 1974, on learning of Armstrong's decision to resign as of the following September, the board created a presidential search committee composed of seven trustees, four faculty members, two students, and one staff member. After careful consideration, the search committee asked the leading candidate, Dr. Olin C. Robison, the thirty-eight-year-old Bowdoin College provost, to visit Middlebury on April 12, 1975. Robison and his wife were pleased with the campus, and the committee was satisfied that Robison would be an excellent choice. On April 26, the trustees elected him the thirteenth president of the college.[1]

Olin Clyde Robison was born on May 12, 1936, in Anacoco, Louisiana.[2] He received his B.A. in history, religion, and philosophy from Baylor University in 1958, and while pursuing graduate study at Southwestern Theological Seminary from 1958 to 1960, he also served as pastor of a rural Baptist church in central Texas. He enrolled at Oxford University in 1960, receiving a D. Phil. in church history in 1963. He promptly returned to Texas, served a year as dean of students at San Marcos Academy, then accepted an administra-

Olin C. Robison welcomed James I. Armstrong back to Middlebury in 1977 to present him with an honorary doctorate of literature at Commencement.

tive appointment with the Peace Corps, where he became Director of University Affairs. From 1966 to 1968, he served successively as special assistant to Deputy Undersecretaries of State U. Alexis Johnson, Foy Kohler, and Charles Bohlen. While with the Department of State, Robison conducted regional conferences on classified policy issues, maintained liaison with counterparts in the military and intelligence communities, wrote speeches for Secretary Rusk and other notables, and handled various special assignments, including the American government's response to the revelations in 1967 that the CIA had been clandestinely involved in domestic educational and cultural organizations. He accepted the post of associate provost at Wesleyan University in 1968 and became provost at Bowdoin College in 1970, remaining in that office until moving to Middlebury in 1975.

Although he left full-time diplomatic work in 1968 for academe, Robison maintained his activities and interest in foreign affairs. He was a regular consultant to the Department of State, a foreign affairs advisor to presidential candidate Edmund Muskie, one of two public advisors in the preparation of *Diplomacy in the '70s* (an analysis of the government's organizational structure affecting our foreign policy in those years), and a lecturer and contributor to foreign affairs and educational journals. Even after assuming the presidency of Middlebury, Robison continued to serve his country in the diplomatic field. President Carter named him the first chairman of the United States Advisory Commission on Public Diplomacy in 1978, and he served in that capacity for three years, resigning the chair in 1981 and leaving the commission in 1984. Robison was also active in the affairs of the Council on Foreign Relations, the International Institute for Strategic Studies, the Institute for East-West Security Studies, and the Royal Institute for International Affairs. He was appointed a Rockefeller Foundation/Aspen Institute Fellow in 1978 and a Presidential Fellow at the Aspen, Colorado, Institute for Humanistic Studies a year later. President Reagan named Robison a charter director of the National Endowment for Democracy in 1983. He also continued to lecture and write on educational and diplomatic issues.

His special interest was the Soviet Union, and he traveled there frequently to speak to Soviet audiences, including the prestigious Academy of Sciences. Robinson served as advisor to the United States delegation to the Belgrade Conference on Security and Cooperation in Europe in 1977, and he was an important participant in the events that led to the widely publicized release from Russia in 1983 of the Pentecostal families, some of whom had been living for years in the American embassy in Moscow. Robison utilized his Soviet connections to help arrange an exchange of Russian and American undergraduates under the aegis of the American Collegiate Consortium of East-West Cultural Exchange in 1988 (see chapter 10). In short, Robison became Middlebury's most widely traveled and best-known president, and throughout his tenure he urged the college to continue to broaden its view and make Middlebury a more cosmopolitan and interesting place.

In his inaugural address on November 1, 1975, President Robison stated three major priorities: redefining the curriculum, expanding the library facilities, and increasing Middlebury's "capacity to extend scholarship and grant aid to students from middle-class families."[3] He told the trustees in January 1976 that he wanted increased salaries, to combat inflation and remain competitive; more money for faculty travel and research; and an accelerated renovation program of classroom and living spaces.[4] During his tenure, Robison succeeded remarkably in accomplishing all these tasks and achieved other advances as well: curricular and program development, a larger faculty, redesign of the administrative structure, improvement and modernization of the physical plant, and changes in the admissions and student services areas. Robison helped raise substantial funds in pursuit of these goals and spurred an unprecedented media coverage of Middlebury's progress.

Robison moved quickly, with wide faculty support, to encourage the development of a new curriculum. The defeat of the proposal presented by the Special Committee on the College in 1973 had not ended interest in curricular reform, and the Educational Council undertook a major study in 1975-1976 with an eye to redefining the curriculum and "developing proposals to insure that each student's education involved a certain breadth of knowledge." [5] The council, after interviewing many of the faculty and students and examining recent patterns of course distribution, explored "a variety of schemes for achieving breadth in each student's education." Rejecting the old distribution requirements and a limited pass/fail option, the council members arrived at a proposal that they argued "would reflect the will of the Faculty, would not be viewed as too restrictive for students, and would assure a significant amount of breadth." [6]

Each student, in addition to completing a major, would be required to take "foundation courses" in three of the four divisions and a "concentration" of four or more courses in a field substantially different from the major. The foundation courses would "offer introduction to major historical traditions, great ideas and great works, providing foundations for further learning." Since every student would take these courses in at least three divisions, they would "become an important factor in creating at Middlebury a community of discourse which would be one of its primary objectives as a small liberal arts college." [7] Concentrations, on the other hand, were "designed to generate coherence and substantial knowledge in a significant portion of the student's work outside the division of his major." [8]

Despite some opposition the faculty voted to implement the Educational Council's recommendations that each student complete a major, a concentration, and three foundation courses (in different divisions) in order to graduate. [9] The new curriculum received wide publicity as an example of the return to the ideal of "general educa-tion," including front-page coverage by the *New York Times*.[10]

Although the new curriculum was fairly well received for nearly a decade, Robison appointed a special committee in March 1985 to "address the perceived need for some kind of intellectual core to Middlebury's course of study."[11] Reporting in September, the com-mittee argued that the curriculum allowed "an imbalance between the twin goods of unrestricted choice and common educational ex-perience" and recommended dramatic changes: a 3-3-3 trimester sys-tem, freshman seminars, a sophomore core course, a revised founda-tions requirement, and required senior projects, while maintaining majors and concentrations.[12]

The faculty rejected this controversial package as a whole in the spring of 1986, but several of its components—freshman seminars, revision of the foundations requirement, and an end to winter term—met with much support.[13] In 1987, the faculty determined that, be-ginning with the class of 1992, each freshman would take two "fresh-man seminars"—one of them a writing seminar—before the middle of sophomore year.[14] And after a lengthy debate in the spring of 1988, the faculty abolished the foundations program by a vote of 43-40 and replaced it with a new distribution requirement: students would have to take at least two courses in each of the four divisions.[15]

Winter term, never universally popular among the faculty, came under increasing attack during the 1980s.[16] Many claimed that stu-dents did not take the academic component of winter term seriously enough. The faculty resolved in 1982 to replace pass/fail with A–F grades in most winter term courses in an attempt to raise "academic expectations," but this apparently did little good, and in 1985 the faculty recorded by a vote of 60–44–3 that it was "deeply dissatisfied with Winter Term as it currently operates."[17] While no action was taken for the next three years, the Educational Council was asked in February 1988 to review the winter term and determine whether it was worth saving.[18]

A fierce debate ensued in the pages of the *Campus* all spring, with students urging the retention of winter term and faculty arguing for its abolition. Professors Bruce Peterson and Robert Gleason claimed that students did too much "partying" during winter term and did not take their courses seriously and that the faculty also took it easy;

if winter term were abolished, the fall and spring semesters could be lengthened with good effect.[19] Students responded that winter term provided an opportunity to prepare for comprehensive exams and complete senior theses, offered a needed change of pace, and ensured that there would be important options for learning experiences.[20]

Not surprisingly, two alternatives emerged from the Educational Council's winter term review: keep winter term and revitalize it or change to a fall–spring semester system. The faculty decided in May 1988 to discuss the issue further the next fall and vote on it in the spring of 1989. Revitalization included several components: the faculty would teach every other year, and those not teaching would be required to prepare course proposals for the next winter term; team teaching, visiting professors, and student-led courses would be encouraged; students would evaluate courses; classes would meet for more hours; greater emphasis would be placed on seniors and juniors taking internships and off-campus courses, and winter term courses would be focused on underclassmen; February break would be lengthened to two weeks; and expectations of social responsibility would be heightened.[21] After much discussion, the faculty voted 98–90 in favor of the revitalized winter term in April 1989, thereby rejecting a two-semester curriculum.[22]

Although the 1976 curricular reforms and subsequent revisions were perhaps the most important academic changes during the Robison years, several important new programs also were implemented. Aided in several cases by large grants, the college created a variety of new majors and interdisciplinary programs: East Asian studies, with Chinese language study initiated in 1976 and Japanese in 1986; Northern studies, with a junior year in residence at the Center for Northern Studies in Wolcott, Vermont; classical studies; the international major, which enabled "a student majoring in a area other than a language or literature to do advanced work in that discipline in a foreign language"; literary studies (combining English literature and foreign languages); and Jewish studies.[23] The C. V. Starr Foundation established professorships in both linguistics and Russian and Soviet Area studies. Other new offerings included a computer science major, dance and film programs, and majors in women's studies and molecular biology.[24]

Many individual departments were strengthened. Economics was enriched by the establishment in 1977 of the Christian A. Johnson

*Michael P. Claudon (right), president of the Geonomics Institute, celebrates
with Raymond E. Benson (left), director of the American Collegiate
Consortium, and David A. Greene, of Office Environments,
the opening of the Geonomics Building.*

Distinguished Chair in Economics, which brought in outstanding scholars each year, and by the founding of the International Institute for Economic Advancement in 1988 (later renamed Geonomics). The institute, organized by Professor Michael Claudon and Robert A. Jones '59, held conferences on public policy issues.[25] The geography department, which had been weakened by a variety of forces (and at one point in 1981 momentarily voted out of existence), righted itself and stayed alive and independent.[26] The Department of American Literature became the Department of American Literature and Civilization, with two separate major tracks; and the theater department became the Department of Theater, Dance, and Film/Video.

The Christian A. Johnson professorships in art history and the performing arts brought scholars such as the renowned musicologist H. C. Robbins Landon to Middlebury for as long as a semester's stay. Indeed, the arts and humanities fared well under Robison. A visiting Committee on the Arts was convened in 1984–1985, and many of its recommendations for building new facilities, renovating older ones,

TABLE 5
Language Schools — Total Enrollment by Session, 1972-1986[a]

	Undergraduate-level enrollments[b]	Graduate-level enrollments[c]	Institute enrollments[d]	Workshop enrollments[e]	Total
1972	210	769	—		979
1973	295	823	—		1,118
1974	453	741	—		1,194
1975	505	652	—	28	1,185
1976	604	582	—	11	1,197
1977	521	535	—	13	1,069
1978	651	503	—	30	1,184
1979	690	448	—	49	1,187
1980	672	426	—	63	1,161
1981	788	409	—	82	1,279
1982	724	374	—	82	1,180
1983	835	367	—	70	1,272
1984	828	412	—	52	1,292
1985	734	384	—	43	1,161
1986	806	388	58	53	1,305

SOURCE: Report of the Director of the Language Schools, 1986-1987.
    [a] Excludes Bread Loaf School of English, Writers' Conference, Bread Loaf/Oxford, and Schools Abroad.
    [b] Nine-week and seven-week.
    [c] Six-week.
    [d] Five-week.
    [e] Two-week and three-week; for teachers and businessmen.

and providing greater faculty resources were accepted. The size of the permanent art collection grew so dramatically that Middlebury's first curator, Richard Saunders, was retained in the mid-1980s.[27]

Emphasis on study abroad and language education continued. Some 40 percent of the junior class elected to study abroad each year — one of the highest percentages in the country. Furthermore, because the college had stricter requirements in foreign language competence than most schools with similar programs had, students usually had better learning experiences abroad. The language schools continued to expand. Middlebury established a Russian School in Moscow in 1977 in cooperation with the Pushkin Institute, adding a master's degree program in the mid-1980s and granting the first four degrees in 1987.[28] A School of Arabic was organized in 1982 under the directorship of Peter Abboud — the first new language unit since the Japanese School in 1970.[29] Japanese was taught in the undergraduate college for the first time in 1986.

The major change in the language schools was the dramatic increase in undergraduate enrollments in the summer programs as the college compensated for the drop in attendance by graduate students (see Table 5). The eventual result was record summer enrollments. The language schools also moved to acquire video and computer resources, which had recently been made available for teaching foreign languages.[30]

The college expanded the Bread Loaf School of English in 1977 through a summer program at Lincoln College, Oxford, enabling students to obtain the same six graduate credits for a summer session at Lincoln that they could receive at Bread Loaf. The focus at Bread Loaf switched gradually as the college, supported by foundation money, initiated the Bread Loaf Program in Writing for Teachers of English from Rural Communities. This program brought teachers from culturally isolated and economically depressed regions to Bread Loaf each summer to learn how to teach more effective writing skills.[31] At the Writers' Conference, which continued to thrive, the addition of associate staff members in 1975 allowed more of the participants to have their manuscripts evaluated.[32]

In 1988–1990, as part of the decennial reaccreditation process, a campus task force, a long-range planning committee, several visiting committees, and the reaccreditation team evaluated all these curricular changes, as well as the status of divisions and departments.[33] The conclusions and recommendations were fairly consistent. First, they found that the general education curriculum was deficient in that it imposed "a broad set of requirements, but the purpose and the nature of those requirements seem little thought out."[34] Second, the immense power and independence of academic departments was noted as a negative aspect:

> At present, each of the literary departments operates so independently as to obscure, even prevent, any common intellectual aim. Departments are more than "strong" at Middlebury; their parochialism, and sense of "turf," exceed even that of some universities where the needs of professional graduate education prescribe a considerable degree of departmental autonomy. Middlebury's de facto constitution—"a loose confederation of inward-looking and defensive departments," as more than one of our members put it—seems both symptom and source of the lack of common identity and purpose among the several literary departments.[35]

On the other hand, the explosion of interdisciplinary programs was viewed as a positive way to break down these barriers, although it

J. Rowland Illick's breadth of expertise allowed him to teach cartography classes, such as this one in 1969, as well as regional and topical geography courses. His pioneering spirit launched the department, which now has interdisciplinary ties throughout the college.

was recognized that such programs demanded a great deal of administrative and pedagogical time and nurturing.[36] Finally, several reports noted that the one division that did not appear to share equally in the recent curricular flowering was the sciences:

> We gained from interviews that the larger College sees the sciences as "an expensive but necessary evil" and that the priority of the institution is really the languages and humanities. A large number of science faculty voiced to us the feeling that they are "second class citizens," existing to fulfill a service role. . . . The fact that the sciences are actually much stronger than perceived helps, but does not solve, the problem. . . . Having said this, the Committee has concluded, based on both internal and external evidence, that the laboratory sciences at Middlebury are significantly weaker than at comparable schools such as Williams, Amherst and Carleton College and that they do not share the same level of recognition or internal support as some other Middlebury programs.[37]

Several reports stressed that the curricular problems stemmed in part from the lack of a sense of shared institutional mission.[38]

These curricular developments, particularly the expansion of inter-disciplinary programs, necessitated a larger faculty, which grew from 144 in 1975–1976 to 161 in 1980–1981. Since enrollment remained at 1975 levels, the student–faculty ratio somewhat improved by 1980 (from 15:1 to 14.4:1).[39] Anxious to attract and keep talented people, Robison took several steps to improve conditions for the faculty. He sought significant salary increases and more money for leaves and professional activities. Funding for research, travel, and conference attendance, he told the trustees, was critical in order to get faculty "out into professional circles where the benefits are likely to be out of proportion to the relatively small amounts of money involved."[40] The Andrew Mellon Foundation gave $235,000 in 1976 to provide paid leaves for junior faculty; this grant would also be used to bring in faculty members on two-year "teaching residencies." An improved benefit package featured a new medical insurance plan, a new tuition remission–cash grant scholarship and credit program for faculty and staff children, and a salary supplement program for tenured faculty who wished to retire early without economic hardship.[41]

Although the college raised the comprehensive fee (see Table 9, chapter 10) in order to increase salaries and improve compensation and working conditions, the president admitted in 1980 that "salaries are not as competitive as they ought to be."[42] Several younger faculty claimed that they could barely make ends meet on starting salaries of $13,500, and senior professors complained that their increases had been insufficient. Professor Robert Ferm, AAUP chapter president, stated that the increases of the late 1970s "are below the inflation rate as it is, and with the inequality of salary increases, the situation for full and associate professors is steadily worsening."[43] Despite an expanded leave policy, some professors complained of insufficient leave time. The most divisive single issue continued to be the tenure and renewal decisions. Each year it seemed that several excellent junior faculty members were denied tenure or renewal, and the result was often a sorrowful, bitter time for the rejected teachers, their colleagues and supporters, and frequently their students.

One such decision was a major contributing factor to the organized student protests in 1979 (see chapter 14).[44]

For these reasons, faculty morale was quite low by the early 1980s. The 1980 reaccreditation report of the New England Association of Schools and Colleges urged Middlebury to improve salaries, increase sabbaticals, and further clarify the tenure process.[45] In response, Robison and the trustees agreed to work on solving these problems, as Arnold LaForce, chairman of the board, stated in January 1979:

> [T]he Trustees continue to be aware of these concerns, and in large measure the College's vitality and strength now and in the future is dependent upon the College's having a faculty and staff who are fairly and competitively compensated. Increases in compensation have been discussed at length and are likely to continue to receive the sympathetic attention of both the administration and the Trustees in the years ahead.[46]

Indeed, the trustees voted significant raises over the next few years in an attempt to catch up with other comparable institutions. Notwithstanding increases of 15 percent to 16.8 percent in salary and 31 percent in benefits in 1981–1982, Middlebury still "did not gain as much on other schools as we hoped because their percentage increases took off from a higher level."[47] The trustees therefore agreed in January 1982 to a $1,500 increase in the comprehensive fee (from $9,300 to $10,800) and commented that "the Administration should make every effort to increase compensation for faculty."[48] The administration followed through, and salaries went up 15 percent in 1982–1983. Robison noted that the decision to raise the fee by $1,500 when many schools held their increases to $500 was critical in making the college more competitive.[49]

Upon learning that the proposed increases for 1983–1984 were relatively modest, some of the faculty felt that "the progress in raising salaries over the past three years appeared to be halted short of its proper goal."[50] The faculty formed an ad hoc committee on compensation, which met with Provost Nicholas Clifford, Treasurer David Ginevan, and President Robison several times in the spring of 1983; and while the members attempted to execute their charge—improving salary and compensation for 1983–1984—they also maintained that "Middlebury College ought to compensate its Faculty at a level commensurate with its reputation among institutions of higher learning and according to its comparative resources."[51] The committee called for better communication between trustees and faculty and a regular review of salaries and benefits by a subcommittee of the Faculty Council—the Faculty Finance and Long Range Planning Committee (FLRP).

The Faculty Council had formed the FLRP in 1981–1982 to present a coherent set of views on long-range planning for compensation, salaries, and other general matters. The 1982–1983 FLRP, chaired by Professor Bruce Peterson, presented its report in April 1983.[52] It analyzed almost every aspect of college life and advocated average annual increases of 2 percent above the consumer price index (CPI) for the next decade plus "a special effort" to improve the benefit programs, which "lag far behind the competition."[53]

A new FLRP (composed of John Elder, John McCardell, and John Emerson) advocated in late 1983 that the college set its salary and compensation goals relative to a group of twenty-five selective liberal arts colleges rather than adopting an arbitrary formula such as the CPI plus 2 percent. The FLRP argued that the college should rank at the same level for salary and compensation among these twenty-five colleges that it did in endowment and financial aid, that is, about the middle of the second quintile (between 6th and 10th).[54] By the fall of 1983, thanks to three generous salary increases in a row, the college had moved up from twenty-fifth and last among these schools to a position near the middle of the pack, with salary levels about 9.1 percent below those schools in the second quintile. To reach the middle of the second quintile, the FLRP urged the board in January 1984 to exceed the salary increases of those schools by 3 percent a year for the next three years.[55] Robison and the board responded with continued increases, and by 1986 the salary and compensation goals had largely been reached. There was some slippage between 1986 and 1989, but Middlebury still ranked first among the twenty-five comparison colleges in the percentage increase in salaries between 1983 and 1989 for assistant professors, third for associate professors, and seventh for full professors.[56]

The 1983 FLRP report claimed that "the first priority for Middlebury in the next ten years is enlargement of the faculty."[57] Accepting this recommendation, Robison increased the faculty from 160 in 1981–1982 to 203 in 1986–1987. The expected benefits included the strengthening of departments (particularly the smaller ones), more upper-division courses, more leave opportunities and a need for fewer leave replacements, more equitable and bearable teaching loads, and reduction of the student–faculty ratio to 12:1.

In response to another complaint, the trustees increased the annual number of paid leaves from six to nine for the years 1984–1986. Most faculty members believed that heavy workloads made it virtually impossible to engage in research and publishing while teaching. By the end of the Robison years, the leave policy was more generous: the faculty had the option of a one-semester leave at full pay or a two-semester leave at 75 percent pay (as opposed to the previous five-ninths) and could reapply for leave after three full years of teaching. Many took advantage of the new policy; twenty-three people (one-twelfth of the teaching staff) were on leave in 1987–1988. It was, as John McCardell stated, a remarkable achievement, which had "not been done with mirrors but rather with a combination of boldness and planning that we can but applaud."[58]

The other matter of concern to many faculty members was the tenure process, which annually put the community through a wrenching psychological period. By 1983 the faculty was 56 percent tenured, and about 51 percent of the junior members who wished to stay were eventually granted tenure (73 percent of those who made it to the tenure review received a favorable recommendation).[59] Several decisions were particularly controversial. Economics assistant professor Paul Sommers was initially denied tenure in 1982, but his appeal for reversal was granted—apparently a first at Middlebury;[60] and Dale Cockrell, an assistant professor of music, charging that a colleague had "intentionally and improperly discounted and criticized his field of study, scholarship, and academic offerings without basis," sued to see his written evaluations. His case went to the Vermont Supreme Court in 1987, and the issue he raised—"academic privilege"—made it a landmark.[61]

By 1990, Middlebury's faculty was much larger and better compensated than it had been fifteen years earlier. Working conditions, including the sabbatical policy, were greatly improved. Indeed, Robison remarked that this expansion and improvement were two of the great achievements of his administration.[62]

Robison also expanded the administrative structure. The 1968–1969 reaccreditation report had commented that the college's administration was "dangerously lean," and Robison's early modifications

Like Ezra Brainerd a century before, John M. McCardell, Jr., was picked from the faculty to become Middlebury's president. He was elected Middlebury's fifteenth president in 1992, from his position as professor of American history and provost of the college.

pleased the New England team that visited the campus in 1980. He replaced the dean of the faculty with two deans—a dean of sciences and a dean of arts and humanities—both of whom reported to the vice president for academic affairs; and he created the position of the vice president of languages to oversee the language schools at Middlebury and abroad. He later added the title of vice president for administration to the office of treasurer; established the post of provost as the chief academic officer; combined the positions of dean of sciences and dean of arts and humanities back into one position— dean of faculty; and, in response to faculty requests and the visiting team recommendation, created the post of dean of academic planning and development to ensure communication between faculty and administration on issues of compensation, long-range planning, and fund-raising goals.[63]

Throughout Robison's presidency, most of the top administrators were recruited from the faculty. Three historians received key appointments: Nicholas Clifford, who served as vice president for academic affairs and later as provost; John Spencer, who became dean of the college; and John McCardell, who successively held the posts of dean of academic planning and development, dean of the faculty, and provost.[64] Steven Rockefeller (religion) and John Emerson (mathematics) also served as deans of the college; and several other prominent faculty members held significant administrative posts.[65] Paul Cubeta, in addition to his service as vice president, was director of the Bread Loaf School of English for twenty-five years before retiring under unfortunate circumstances in 1989.[66]

Several influential administrators retired during the Robison years. Walter Brooker, the vice president for development, who had served since 1956, retired in 1981, leading the board to remark: "For hundreds, indeed thousands of Middlebury alumni, Walter Brooker is Middlebury."[67] "Bud" Leeds was named to replace Brooker. Carroll Rikert retired in 1983, replaced by associate treasurer David Ginevan, who was promoted to the new position of treasurer and vice president for administration. Rikert, who had been treasurer for nearly twenty years and a key officer of the college since 1952, even won the respect and admiration of Dennis O'Brien, who as dean had often crossed swords with him:

> I consider myself very fortunate, indeed, to have had Carroll as a close colleague for twelve years. He is one of the most extraordinary academic servants I have ever met. As I say, I can't say that it was always pleasant, but it certainly was a bracing education. And finally, I really came to like the guy. No one worked harder, with more dedication and more loyalty for Middlebury than Carroll. My only apprehension as he retires is that he will now publish all those notes on our administrative conferences that he has been taking on yellow pads all these years. If he does, surely he will be shown to have been right more often than all us wayward deans.[68]

Charles Scott, college chaplain for thirty-five years, retired in 1986 but remained active on behalf of the alumni programs, visiting with some of the hundreds of former students whom he had counseled over the years.[69] And Erica Wonnacott, popular dean of students since 1970, retired in 1988, succeeded by Karl Lindholm '67, who had served as associate dean of students and associate dean of the college. Wonnacott, said Lindholm, was never a "theoretician or a systems person" like many of her counterparts at other schools. Rather, she was a friend to hundreds of students—"she likes to get into kids' lives."[70]

The size of the administrative staff increased markedly under Robison, from 351 employees in 1975 to 558 in 1990.[71] A major reason for this was the college's decision to improve the quality of its

Erica Wonnacott brought the urban pleasures of jumping rope to students who had slighted that part of their education before Middlebury.

services to students. The Career Counseling and Placement Office, which had primarily offered placement information and a dossier service, was transformed in 1979 into a more comprehensive career services center with a professional staff.[72] The Counseling Office, by adding a female psychologist in 1982 and a black counselor in 1988, was able to provide more outreach and educational service for such concerns as AIDS, sexually transmitted diseases, stress, sexual and racial harassment, date rape, eating disorders, and drug and alcohol problems; the name of the office was changed to Counseling and Human Relations.[73]

The death in 1977 of the college's first full-time medical officer, Dr. George Parton, led to a series of changes in health services. In 1982, after women students complained about the exclusively male staff of the health center, a woman was hired as director and nurse practitioner. By 1985 the college had determined that most inpatient needs could best be met at Porter Hospital through a cooperative arrangement, while the health center (which had been named for Dr. Parton) remained open during the day for outpatient visits.[74] The management of residential life was greatly improved after Frank

Kelley, a longtime Middlebury High School teacher and principal, was hired in 1983. Kelley, who quickly became one of the most popular administrators on campus, helped develop valuable new programs in the residence halls and fraternities.[75] The increase in security and safety concerns prompted the addition of a new position of director of campus safety.[76]

President Robison also oversaw a variety of additions and improvements to the physical plant. The first major addition was the $2-million Meredith Wing of Starr Library, dedicated in October 1979. Robison had stated in his inaugural that Middlebury was, for the most part, "well-housed." He had added, however, that the college needed "to proceed with dispatch" in expanding the library, which then had seating capacity for only 330 students and shelving space for only 300,000 volumes.[77] After months of debating whether to build a new library or enlarge the existing one, the board decided in 1977 that an addition would fill the bill more affordably.[78] The new wing, added to the east end of the library and named for L. Douglas Meredith, former chairman of the board, provided some 25,000 square feet of new space, shelving for another 200,000 volumes, 140 additional seats, and improved quarters for the microform collection.[79] Facilities were further enhanced when a new science library was constructed in 1978 on the top floor of the Science Center.[80]

Another important addition was the John and Barbara Kirk Alumni House Conference Center, also dedicated in October 1979. Built on the college golf course, the new center provided an alumni gathering place for a variety of events, as well as serving as a location for the annual Economics Conference and other activities.[81]

The college markedly improved its athletic facilities during the 1980s. A $2.6-million renovation of Memorial Field House in 1982–1983 provided top-quality athletic and recreational facilities, including an enlarged ice rink, expanded locker rooms, and more space for women's teams. The gymnasium portion of the field house, which was wholly remodeled, was named for Arthur D. Pepin '47 in recognition of a substantial gift to the project.[82] A five-thousand-square-foot addition to the field house, the $1-million two-story Fitness Center completed in 1989, provided a valuable array of training equipment.[83] Other additions included the 3.5-kilometer John "Red" Kelly '31 Trail for cross-country running or skiing through the ex-

Egbert C. Hadley '10 celebrated his ninetieth birthday in 1978 with a party at the president's home. The daughter of an earlier trustee, Jessica Stewart Swift (M.A. 1948, honorary) joined him in her 107th year.

panded eighteen-hole Ralph O. Myhre golf course into the nearby woods; a new four-field athletic complex just north of Fletcher Field House, between Lang Field and the golf course; three platform tennis courts; the Carroll and Jane Rikert Ski Touring Center at Bread Loaf; and snow-making equipment and new lifts at the Snow Bowl.[84]

Academic facilities also underwent improvement. The College Street School, located on the site in Storrs Park just below the Science Center where the original college academy building had been erected in 1798, was purchased from the town in 1984. The schoolhouse, constructed in 1867 after the old academy building had been razed, was renovated at a cost of $1.7 million to provide badly needed classrooms, seminar rooms, offices, a 109-seat lecture hall, and a new visitor information center. The building was named Twilight Hall in 1986 in honor of Alexander Twilight (class of 1823), generally considered America'a first black college graduate.[85] After retired board chairman Egbert Hadley's death in 1982, the college acquired the spacious Hadley House near the golf course and converted it to a guest house presided over by former dean Elizabeth Kelly.[86]

The construction of new arts facilities was another major priority.

The deficiencies and problems of the Johnson Building had become increasingly clear as the offerings, needs, and size of the arts departments continued to expand, and the growth of a thriving theater, dance, and film/video department required modern studios and performance facilities.[87] By 1987 the trustees had agreed to utilize a New York architectural firm, Hardy, Holzman, and Pfeiffer, to design a 91,000-square-foot fine-arts education and performance facility. The new center, completed in the fall of 1991, at a cost of $17 million, includes art galleries, rehearsal rooms, a concert hall, studio theater, dance performance space, and a new music library.[88] After Chipman Park residents protested the location of the arts center, (originally planned for the site of Porter House next to the Emma Willard House), Robison announced in 1988 that the site would be moved three hundred yards south to a location between Chi Psi house and the field house.[89]

The use of computers for administrative and academic purposes, which had begun in the 1960s,[90] increased greatly under Robison. Once it became clear that a combined computer/arts building was unworkable, the college proceeded to renovate the two lower floors of Voter and created a state-of-the-art computer complex. The Ballenger Computer Center, named for Middlebury parent and computer company executive John G. Ballenger, who provided a major gift, was dedicated on Parents' Weekend, 1988.[91]

The other major building project of the late 1980s was the conversion of McCullough Gymnasium into a student center. The declining importance of fraternities and the changes in Vermont's drinking laws (see chapter 11) had created an increasing need "for a large social space on campus that could comfortably hold between 300 and 600 students."[92] In 1983 the Residence Life Council sent President Robison a plan for an ideal residence life system, which included a "Wonnacott Barn" large enough to hold parties for six hundred to eight hundred students. But when the college announced its $60-million campaign for Middlebury in 1984, a new student center was not included in the plans.[93]

Much concerned, the Student Forum set up a student union committee in the fall of 1984, chaired by Tim Michaud '86 and Mike Neff '87. Utilizing the design of committee member Beatrix Esquerra '85, they made a successful presentation of their plan for a student center to the administration and later to the trustees.[94] The general outline of the Esquerra design so impressed the trustees that they approved the addition of twenty thousand square feet to the north side of Proctor for a student center in March 1985 and hired a consultant to explore the matter further.[95]

But actual construction was stymied. The board finally rejected Proctor and the social-dining units (SDUs) as potential locations and decided on McCullough Gymnasium instead. The firm of Hardy, Holzman, Pfeiffer was retained in 1987 to design additions and renovations for the old building at an estimated cost of $4 million.[96] The project continued to encounter roadblocks, including resistance in 1989 by the Governor's Commission on Historical Preservation. The commission was especially unhappy with the plan to add two octagonal towers onto McCullough, calling this "incompatible with the nice, quiet, classically referenced architecture around the green."[97] Finally, in the spring of 1990, the state's Board of Environmental Protection approved the plans, and construction commenced with a goal of completion by mid-1991. The new building includes a large space for dances and other activities, a snack area, a lounge, the chaplain's office, and offices for student organizations.[98]

Although enrollment remained fairly stable during the Robison years, at about 1,950 (see Table 7, chapter 10), the construction in 1986 of North Hall, a modern $4-million dormitory, allowed the college to embark on a twenty-five-year renovation of all of its residence halls, many of which were old and deteriorating. Designed by Edward Larrabee Barnes and Associates, the new hall, located east of the ridge between the SDUs and the chateau housed 130 students, almost entirely in singles. After its completion, the college was able to house everyone year-round and still take 125 beds out of use for renovation. The Chateau; Jewett, Homestead, and Weybridge houses; and Painter, Allen, Stewart, Gifford, Starr, Pearsons, Voter, and Hepburn halls had all been renovated by 1990.[99]

The college also modernized and improved other facilities. Warner Science, which had become shabby and in bad repair, was totally renovated in 1977 at a cost of $1 million. Dana Auditorium was overhauled in 1981 to provide a viewing facility for the growing program in film and video, and the Freeman language lab in Sunderland was modernized in 1983. The college purchased the fraternity houses in 1980 and upgraded them and also improved and expanded Proctor's dining areas. Seminar rooms were reintroduced into Old Chapel.

To the chapel he had just given, Governor John A. Mead, class of 1864, added a chime of eleven bells. Seventy years later, Allan R. Dragone, Sr., '50 offered to expand the chime to a full carillon of forty-eight bells. The original bells were taken down and shipped to France, where they were tuned and combined with new bells. In the spring of 1986 the completed carillon was returned to the steeple of Mead to enchant students with the more complex possibilities of the greatly increased range of tones.

Thanks to a gift from former board chairman Allan R. Dragone '50 and his wife, Jane, the Mead Chapel carillon was renovated and expanded to forty-eight bells at a cost of $150,000. At Bread Loaf the renovation of the Earthworm Manor Barn provided additional room for dramatic productions and teaching. Emma Willard House, containing the admissions and financial aid offices, was renovated, and a large pavilion wing was added on the north side along with a smaller connecting wing that became the main entrance.[100]

Important technological improvements took place. The library, which had developed a machine-readable record of its collections by 1985, went on-line in 1987–1988 with an automated operating system that allowed computer access to its holdings, borrower records, book orders, and other functions, Its half-million-volume collection was potentially quadrupled when Middlebury entered into a cooperative venture with other Vermont libraries in 1977. A new addition to the

Davison Library at Bread Loaf provided more room for computers and study space, and the music library in Johnson was expanded and modernized.[101]

The college successfully kept energy costs down by a series of innovative measures, many of which were instituted in the 1970s, when national energy concerns reached their height. Cogeneration of electricity on campus, "heat sinks" beneath the Meredith Wing of the library and the Kirk Alumni House Conference Center, and a new boiler capable of burning coal, fuel oil, or a mixture of coal and wood chips all provided greater flexibility in meeting energy needs. The college was therefore burning 22 percent fewer BTUs in 1980 than in 1975 even though more space was being heated. Indeed, Middlebury was selected by the Academy for Educational Development as one of ten institutions in the country to receive a $10,000 prize for its energy management program.[102]

Under Robison's leadership, Middlebury was notably successful in raising the money necessary—over $100 million—to complete all of this new construction and plant and program improvement. During Robison's first five years the college received major sums from the Dana Foundation ($300,000 challenge grant for library construction and other purposes and $100,000 for scholarships), the National Endowment for the Humanities ($550,000 as a challenge grant for library expansion), the Kresge Foundation challenge ($250,000 for the library), the National Science Foundation ($250,000 for the program in Northern studies), the Rockefeller Foundation ($100,000 for a rural teachers' program in writing), the Robert Sterling Clark Foundation ($40,000 for faculty leaves), and direct grants for library construction from the Alden Trust ($100,000), the George and Sybil Fuller Foundation ($100,000), the Stoddard Charitable Trust ($50,000), and the Gannett Newspaper Foundation ($29,335). The Mellon Foundation, in addition to its gift for faculty leaves and residencies, gave $150,000 for a program in Chinese; and the Christian A. Johnson Endeavor Foundation provided $250,000 for scholarships as well as the $1 million economics professorship. In 1976 the college also received $786,326 from Gertrude Cornish Milliken '01, the first woman to serve as a trustee.[103]

The greatest fund-raising accomplishment in Robison's early years may have been the big increases in alumni giving and endowment.

In 1975–1976 the annual giving program netted $427,708, and the average gift was under $40. By 1978–1979 the program raised $1,070,600 with 46 percent of all alumni participating, and the average gift exceeded $100. For the first time, Middlebury ranked among the top ten colleges in the country in the percentage of alumni giving annually.

To be sure, many postwar graduates had achieved financial success and could afford to be generous, but other developments mattered even more. An improved data processing system enabled the college to reach alumni and to identify prospects for major gifts more readily. Alumni activities were increased. In 1976, for example, the first annual Alumni College was held at Bread Loaf on Labor Day weekend. The program was expanded, and hundreds of graduates of all ages took advantage of the opportunity to explore intellectual topics with select faculty. The new Alumni Conference Center provided a special gathering place. Many more alumni became involved with annual reunions, volunteer fund-raising, and admissions interviewing.[104] Finally, and perhaps most important, Robison introduced a new style to alumni fund-raising. It had hitherto been considered inappropriate to ask directly for money at alumni dinners and gatherings, but Robison frankly emphasized the need for funds in his alumni talks and routinely recommended that every graduate should donate at least $100 annually. His approach apparently worked.[105]

The increase in alumni giving and the continuation of strong corporate and foundation support pushed the college's total gifts, grants, and other awards from $2,602,916 in 1974–1975 to $3,943,778 in 1980. After years of investing its permanent funds conservatively, the college, at Robison's prodding, undertook a complete review of the management of endowment and reserves in 1976 and adopted a goal of at least 10 percent total return per annum. That goal was reached each year, and along with additions from gifts, the result was a 100 percent increase (from $31 million to $62 million) in endowment between 1975 and 1980.[106]

Despite these impressive financial gains, it became obvious by the late 1970s that much more money was needed. Inflation had lowered real income, and the faculty was demanding increased compensation. The costs of a Middlebury education in a highly inflationary economy were soaring, and the comprehensive fee rose from $4,800 in 1974–1975 to $10,800 in 1982–1983. This was particularly worrisome to Robison because it impeded progress toward one of his primary goals, which we will examine in chapter 10: to diversify the predominantly upper-middle- and upper-class student body by admitting more lower-middle- and middle-class applicants; this required increases in financial aid awards, which the rising comprehensive fee made more difficult. Although the percentage of students receiving aid rose from 18 in 1974–1975 to 25 in 1979–1980 and the average grant nearly doubled, from $1,760 to $3,406, Robison reported in 1980 that "we are significantly more competitive today than we were in 1975; nevertheless, Middlebury continues to lag behind Amherst, Bowdoin, Wesleyan, and Williams in overall financial aid. This must continue to be a high priority." [107]

It was essential, therefore, to raise a substantial sum (over and above increases in the comprehensive fee) to meet the array of pressing needs—for faculty compensation, modernization of facilities, financial aid—that presented larger bills each year. In 1980 the college began to set long-term goals on which a large fund-raising drive could be based and retained a consultant to assess the responsiveness of Middlebury's constituencies to such an effort. A $50-million "Campaign for the '80's" was seriously discussed. [108]

Professor Bruce Peterson '56 presented the FLRP committee report in May 1983, and the trustees were impressed; indeed, they approved a $60-million campaign in January 1984 with goals and priorities based largely on the FLRP report. They planned on receiving $20 million from annual giving ($4 million per year from 1985 to 1989), with a major focus on reunion classes. Leadership and major gifts would provide another $25 million, and the advance goal was $15 million. [109]

The "Campaign for Middlebury College" was officially kicked off at Pepin Gymnasium at Homecoming, 1984, with over $13.8 million already pledged—a sum that exceeded the entire previous capital campaign of 1973–1975. By June 30, 1988, seventeen months ahead of schedule, the $60-million goal was reached. Pledges totaled $80.1 million by December 1989. [110] The largest single gift—indeed, the largest in the college's history—was a bequest of nearly $6 million from the estate of Alexander Hamilton Fulton, a former trustee (1964–1978) and longtime friend of the college, who died in 1986. Fulton's father, John Hamilton Fulton, was a successful New York

Alexander Hamilton Fulton was extraordinarily generous to Middlebury College. One of the pleasures he shared with the college community was listening to Beverly Sills, diva and director of the New York City Opera, deliver the John Hamilton Fulton Memorial Lecture in 1983.

banker. Alex used to visit the Champlain Valley from nearby Plattsburgh, New York, where he had settled in the 1940s, and when he came across Middlebury College, he was impressed. Numerous conversations with Walter Brooker slowly brought Fulton into the Middlebury fold. He donated $425,000 in 1963 to establish the Jean Thompson Fulton Professorship of Modern Languages (named for his mother) and made other significant gifts, named for his father. The $6-million Fulton bequest was named for his parents as well as himself.[111] (For other important contributions see Table 6.)

Alumni giving, which accounted for $29 million of the $80 million, increased sharply. In 1981, the class of 1956 became the first one to contribute more than $100,000 in a single year, and the class of 1958 set a twenty-fifth reunion record in 1983 of over $252,000; the college—with $4,922,340 in annual giving—was a winner in the CASE/US Steel Alumni giving Incentive Awards Program for the fifth consecutive year.[112] The banner year was 1987: the class of 1952

TABLE 6

Major Donations to Middlebury College $60-Million Campaign, 1984–1989

Donor	Amount	Purpose
Robert Jones '59	$1,850,000	Chair in monetary economics in the name of Federal Reserve official Alan R. Holmes
Mr. Bingham's Trust for Charity	$1,500,000	Bread Loaf Writing Program
Egbert C. Hadley '10 Estate	$1,500,000	Egbert C. Hadley Library Fund
Hiroshi Kawashima	$1,500,000	Kawashima Distinguished Visiting Professorship in Japanese Studies
C. V. Starr Foundation	$1,500,000	Starr Professorship in Russian and Soviet Area Studies
Paris and Marion Fletcher '24	$1,000,000	Fletcher Professorship in the Arts
Letitia Simons Pound Estate	$1,000,000	Ernest Simons Scholarship Fund
Frederick Dirks '30	$600,000	Faculty Residency in Economics and Political Science
Kresge Foundation	$500,000	New residence hall
Pew Memorial Trust	$500,000	Toward conversion of SDUs to international study center
Laurance S. Rockefeller	$500,000	New wing and renovation of Emma Willard House
Pew Memorial Trust	$487,337	Freshman seminars
Howard Hughes Medical Institute	$400,000	Improve undergraduate education in biological sciences
Pew Memorial Trust	$400,000	Renovation of College Street School
John and Marion Kruesi	$350,000	Trust for Elizabeth Baker Kelly Scholarship Fund
William and Flora Hewlett Foundation	$250,000	Toward $1 million addition to President's Discretionary Fund
Surdna Foundation	$150,000	Faculty leave program
Booth-Ferris Foundation	$100,000	Dance program
Stoddard Trust	Challenge grant for class of 1957	Toward $1 million to establish Pardon Tillinghast Professorship of History, Philosophy, and Religion
Donald Everett Axinn '51	Major gift	Donald Everett Axinn Chair in Creative Writing

Based on articles in *The Campaign Reporter*, vols. 1–5.

contributed over $500,000 (the first class to surpass that goal in a single year); the class of 1962 set a new twenty-fifth reunion record of $437,000, with 78.4 percent participating; the college raised its alumni participation rate 50 percent; the reunion classes contributed over $2.3 million; and annual giving was at the unprecedented level of $12 million.[113] The campaign thus succeeded remarkably in improving alumni support, but whether such increases would be maintained afterward was not clear. Furthermore, although the 50.2 percent alumni participation rate ranked Middlebury twenty-seventh in the country, rivals such as Williams (68.2 percent), Dartmouth (65.0 percent), and Amherst (62.4 percent) were still doing better.[114]

The endowment rose impressively during the campaign, from $100 million in 1984 to over $227 million in 1990, thanks in part to the overall performance of the stock market. Indeed, the college earned an annual return of 14 percent on the endowment in the late 1980s.[115] During Robison's tenure the endowment did quite well relative to other schools: Middlebury's was 40.2 percent of Amherst's in 1975 and 84.6 percent by 1990. Similar gains can be seen with Williams (up from 49.7 percent to 68.3 percent), Colby (110 percent to 293 percent), and Bowdoin (88.3 percent to 151 percent).

In the late 1980s the college was already beginning to contemplate the possible goals of the next big fund drive — perhaps a Bicentennial Campaign looking toward the year 2000. Could $200 million be raised? Could Middlebury maintain its quality otherwise?[116] As other colleges announced $100-million-plus campaigns, such a goal appeared more inevitable than unlikely. Few observers would have guessed in 1975 that Middlebury College, just fifteen years later, would raise $80 million in a capital campaign and increase the endowment sevenfold, to over $200 million.

On October 6, 1989, at an all-campus meeting in Mead Chapel, President Robison announced that he would be resigning at the end of the summer. After a leave of absence in 1990–1991, he planned on returning to the college as a professor. He remarked that he would have been president for fifteen years and an academic administrator for more than twenty-two consecutive years. "I look forward to teaching. I look forward to being a member of the community. And I look forward to having weekends off." After mentioning several of the tasks that remained to be completed, he concluded by describing his personal feelings for the college:

> There will be time later in the year to reflect on our time together. But I want to take this opportunity to say to you how grateful Sylvia and I are to all of you. . . . And I am deeply touched and deeply moved that this community saw fit to place confidence in us, to allow us the privilege of being stewards of this special place for a 15-year period.
>
> I have enormous pride in the College. This is my place. I have pride in our work together, what we have accomplished, what lies before

us, and our capacity to face the future with great promise. I want to assure you of my continued and permanent commitment to Middlebury College. I cannot envision a time when my energies will not, in some measure, be devoted to its welfare.[117]

President Robison could look back with pride at many accomplishments: the new curriculum and program offerings; the expanded faculty and the reduction in the student–faculty ratio; the many new endowed professorships; an improved benefit package and leave program; the new library wing, alumni conference center, and residence hall; the impressive modernization and renovation projects; the establishment of an aid-blind admissions program; the fund-raising efforts and management practices that swelled the endowment to unprecedented heights; and programs to increase the quality and quantity of the admissions pool. Robison had also succeeded in making Middlebury a more exciting place and in improving its self-confidence. He had hoped that increased research and travel, seminars, and academic visitors would stimulate the faculty to pursue their scholarly interests more vigorously and that a dramatic increase in the number and variety of speakers and cultural activities on campus would raise the vision of the entire community.[118]

Despite some success in these efforts, he made them at a time when American higher education was mired in a bitter pessimism that could not help but affect Middlebury. As we have seen, the period 1945–1972 was an era of great qualitative and quantitative gains for most colleges and universities. But thereafter growth and hope began giving way to contraction and anxiety. Younger scholars had difficulty finding a niche anywhere in the system; older faculty were beset by losses of real income and job security, guilt over the plight of junior colleagues, and a sense that the exciting postwar period of expansion and experiment had ended. In such an environment, Robison's initial efforts (particularly his attempt to improve the collective self-confidence) were probably not as successful as they might have been ten years earlier.[119] During much of the 1980s, however, the college was able to make important gains in faculty compensation and size and in improving the physical plant. The malaise of the 1970s was briefly transformed into an exciting era of construction, renovation, growth, and raised expectations.

For all these accomplishments, Robison frequently encountered criticism. Students, faculty, and administrators often commented

that he was away from campus too much and showed too little
interest in important aspects of college life and business. Robison
responded that he was usually in town on Mondays through Wed-
nesdays and that it was necessary for him to be away on other
days for fund-raising, other college-related events, or activities that
gave Middlebury positive publicity.[120] Indeed, Robison was a master
at generating national media coverage: early in his presidency the
New York Times, the *Washington Post*, the *National Observer*, *Time*,
Newsweek, the *Boston Globe*, the *Wall Street Journal*, and other publications carried stories about the college and Robison. When Russian pastor Georgi Vins arrived at Middlebury as Robison's guest in
1979, both television and newspapers gave the college wide national
coverage.

Robison's last year was in some ways one of the most difficult. In
the fall of 1989, the campus was in an uproar over the handling of the
Cubeta affair,[121] and some faculty and staff were upset that the board
had decided not to subsidize local day-care facilities (see chapter 15).
Furthermore, many professors were incensed when Robison and the
board announced their decision to build a new football and lacrosse
stadium and an all-weather track with money contributed solely for
the purpose. The old Porter Field stands were in continuous disrepair
and almost impossible to maintain, and the track surrounding the
field was in such poor condition that the college had not been able
to host a track meet in ten years.[122]

In response, Professor Bruce Peterson wrote a strongly worded
three-page statement, which he presented at the November 6 faculty
meeting. After berating the trustees for ignoring the faculty's wishes
on day care and fraternities, Peterson derided them for not attacking
what he considered more important problems:

> Although Starr Library is so close to capacity that buying books at a
> normal pace promises to fill it before we could construct additional
> space, even if we started today, there is no evidence that the Board
> is concerned with library space. Although a valuable science collec-
> tion deteriorates by the hour in a tiny and totally inadequate science
> library, there is no evidence that the Board has even addressed the
> problem. Although laboratory and teaching facilities for the sciences
> place us embarrassingly far behind all our competition, the Board has
> shown us no interest in better science space. Although faculty offices
> are too few and many totally inadequate (mine is tiny, too small for
> a computer and a typewriter, with a heating system which seldom

works—and it is the best in the building), I know from personal experience that the Board's reaction to the problem is to dismiss anyone who mentions it as a malcontent. Perhaps more important than any other problem on this campus is the salary structure for the hundreds of people who make our jobs possible; $5.00 an hour amounts to about $10,000 a year. Although Middlebury College continues to pay secretaries, custodians, kitchen workers and others at that rate, the Board is unconcerned.

What the Board does have to say is that we need a new football stadium. I disagree, and I believe their decision represents such a distortion of the proper priorities of this institution, such a complete misunderstanding of what we on campus want for this institution, that we must speak out. . . . What is the message? What is the symbolism when a Board of Trustees seems to have lost sight of the purpose to the institution, when the College seems but a plaything for wealthy trustees? What are we saying when the Board's direction is 180 degrees away from the faculty's? What does it mean when the Board concerns itself only with issues peripheral to the educational goals of the College? [123]

Peterson then offered a resolution urging the board to "initiate immediate and substantive discussions with a broad range of faculty, staff and student constituencies toward the end of reestablishing a basis of mutual trust and respect." The resolution also asked the board "to disavow publicly all plans for construction of a football stadium." It passed by a large majority.[124]

The faculty's unhappiness with Robison was reflected at their next meeting on December 11, when they voted to elect a faculty moderator (on a three-month trial basis) to run those parts of meetings having to do with faculty business. It had been a long-standing tradition at Middlebury to allow the president to chair faculty meetings in their entirety, and Robison argued strenuously against the new proposal. Three months later, the vote on permanent adoption of the moderator proposal received a simple majority but fell short of the two-thirds needed to change the rules.[125]

Finally, the college determined in 1989–1990 that the remarkable increases in expenditures during the Robison years had to be moderated. The budget had grown from $12.6 million in 1974–1975 to $68.4 million in 1989–1990, and even with large increases in the comprehensive fee and aggressive investment of the endowment, revenues could not keep up. The report of the 1989–1990 reaccreditation team described the problem clearly.

While operating revenues have grown at an average annual rate of 15.6% over the past three years, expenditures and mandatory transfers have grown even faster—at an average annual level of 19.3%. Between FY 1986 and FY 1989, the College's operating surplus has declined from over $3.3 million to less than $0.5 million. In addition, many of the expansions made possible by the recent revenue growth have longer-term operating implications that need to be addressed. A larger faculty population means more office and laboratory space, higher benefits costs, more support staff, more computers and scientific equipment, and more library resources. Larger physical facilities mean higher utilities costs, more maintenance and custodial care, and more pressure on the campus infrastructure. These costs and others have not been fully reflected in the past expenditure levels and will add further pressure for expenditure growth.[126]

Merely setting the comprehensive fee at whatever level was necessary to offset the massive increase in costs was no longer an acceptable option. Students protested vehemently in 1988 over a double-digit increase in the comprehensive fee; their response was a clear signal that the college had to try harder to reduce costs. It began that process in the spring of 1990 by asking each department to cut next year's nonsalary budget by 6 percent—the first such reduction in Robison's presidency—and a period of "consolidation" was unofficially declared.[127]

Although faculty resentments, financial stringency, and general uneasiness about the future all contributed to a difficult final year for Robison and the college, the trustees feted the outgoing president and his wife at a gala Texas-style barbecue and farewell party during the 1990 Commencement Weekend, at which staff, faculty, family, and friends (such as Bill and Judith Moyers) offered tributes.[128] Furthermore, the announcement that Dr. Timothy Light, the able linguist and highly regarded acting president at Kalamazoo College, had been elected Middlebury's fourteenth president gave everyone a new feeling of hope. Light, a 1960 Yale graduate, had taught in China for several years before earning his Ph.D. in linguistics from Cornell in 1974. After teaching Chinese for six years at the University of Arizona, he moved to Ohio State University as chairman of the Department of East Asian Languages and Literatures. In 1986 he accepted the position of provost at Kalamazoo College, returning to the city where he was born and raised and to the college where his father had been a trustee for twenty-four years.[129]

Students protested the rise in the tuition to $19,000 in 1989 with a march on Old Chapel.

As the reaccreditation team prophesied, President Light would face some serious problems in a period of consolidation: "As the College leaves a phase of rapid growth in the availability of resources and approaches more steady-state conditions, the tensions and competition between various academic units—departments or interdisciplinary programs—is likely to increase."[130] Furthermore, as Bruce Peterson pointed out in his shrill letter of November 6, 1989, the sciences needed attention, the library was nearing capacity, the faculty was clamoring for better classrooms and more seminar space, and offices were sometimes inadequate and in short supply.

Still, the college had made remarkable strides during Olin Robison's tenure, and Light inherited a first-rate institution. Indeed, Robison had successfully continued the mission of Stratton and Armstrong to make Middlebury competitive with the nation's very best liberal arts colleges. And unlike his two predecessors, Robison had to do much of his work against the prevailing winds.

PART III

A SOCIAL HISTORY OF CAMPUS LIFE, 1915–1990

The great majority of us had come from small towns or relatively small-city high schools—good, sound educational institutions but without the trappings and social "advantages" of exclusive, more expensive, more liberated prep schools—and we tended accordingly to overlook the fact that we had matriculated in a rather provincial college.

> —W. Storrs Lee '28, "In Retrospection," *Middlebury College News Letter*, 52 (summer 1978): 14

Our victory over UVM marks an EPOCH. It is significant because we have proved to our own satisfaction, as well as to the world at large, that Middlebury has entered again upon her own right. The place of honor which we once held but lost among the New England colleges is once more ready for us to go in and take possession.

For eight long years our beloved president Thomas has labored unflinchingly and with the deepest devotion to secure for Middlebury and her alumni this coveted and rightful glory. We as students will never know what has been the cost in the way of personal sacrifice, and his reward must ultimately consist largely in the knowledge of having served well his alma mater and humanity, for this has not been a slavish and prejudiced elevation to a one-sided cause. Our rejoicing and his does not consist in the mere fact of having won a long desired football victory, but in all which this victory symbolizes. Under his leadership, Middlebury has been preparing for the manifestation of her power.

> —*Middlebury Campus*, November 22, 1916

The strength of the small college is in the unity and solidarity of its community life. The whole argument of the personal relations between the faculty and student has by no means lost its force. There is no exercise which does so much to bring the college together and enable the institution to exert its deep and valuable personal influence as a daily assembly, and I feel very strongly that it must be maintained.

> —John Thomas to James P. McNaboe, June 1, 1917,
> Thomas Papers, Middlebury College Archives

Between 1915 and 1990, campus life at Middlebury was transformed. Until 1945, social activity revolved around the powerful fraternities, and class traditions were a significant part of college existence. The women's college, whose students were generally superior in academic ability and economic status to the men, was dominated by sororities, circumscribed by tight parietal hours, and characterized by a lack of social and political power in an unequal (and unrealized) coordinate educational system. Required daily chapel and intercollegiate athletics helped unify the predominantly unsophisticated white, Protestant, middle-class students, most of whom came from New England and New York, into a tight-knit, fairly homogeneous community.

The college was fundamentally altered after World War II. The changes were gradual at first, but in the 1960s the pace accelerated, and by 1990 college life bore little resemblance to that of forty years earlier. The reasons were varied but often related: the increased enrollment from 800 to 1,900 under Presidents Stratton and Armstrong, the growing emphasis on academic quality and a concomitant increase in costs, the commitment (particularly under Armstrong and Robison) to equal social facilities and opportunities for women, and the changing social mores and growing privatism of students. These factors contributed to the decline of the fraternities after 1965, the end of required chapel in the 1950s, the lessening of interest in class traditions, a growing student involvement in college governance, the increasing wealth and continued homogeneity of the student body, the disappearance of sororities and women's parietal hours, and the creation of a more truly coeducational college. Concerted efforts to diversify in the 1980s led to the matriculation of a growing number of African-American, Hispanic, rural, and foreign students.

This section is focused on the changing nature of the student body (chapter 10) and student life, particularly fraternities (chapter 11); athletics (chapter 13); student involvement in college government and "outside world" issues (chapter 14), and other extracurricular activities (chapter 12). The final chapter, ". . . And a Cast of Thousands," examines some of the changes in other Middlebury constituencies: the activities of faculty, staff, and administration; student–faculty relations; the contributions of Middlebury alumni; and, returning to a major theme of the first volume, town–gown relations.

CHAPTER 10

THE STUDENT BODY

We have been too cheap. Our low rates have given a wrong idea of the character of the college. Many people judge colleges by their prices, just as they do other things. Dartmouth increased its tuition to $200 and had a Freshman class of 700 the next year.

> —John Thomas to Carson H. Beane, April 19, 1920, Thomas Papers, Middlebury College Archives

With increased tuition and board and room charges, one of the urgent needs of the college is for increased sums available for loans or scholarships if we are to preserve opportunities for deserving and capable men and women students. During these post-war years, there has undoubtedly been a trend in the direction of accepting a larger proportion of students who can finance their education without college aid. I see no way of changing this trend unless our endowment is increased or annual gifts for scholarships and loan make more aid available for deserving students.

> —Samuel Stratton, President's Report, September 1, 1950, p. 8, MCA

This institution has committed itself to the diversity that is critical to a rich intellectual community. We have tried to build upon each new program and each success with an ever more heterogeneous student body and faculty. Whether this involves students from a Bronx high school, who along with their faculty regularly visit Middlebury and receive our students and faculty in return; whether it has to do with students from junior colleges throughout the country who demonstrate great promise and have places reserved for them at Middlebury; whether it is students from rural areas around the Northeast for whom a college like Middlebury was not even a dream a year ago; whether it is a Pakistani youth or a Soviet exchange student, or a 45-year-old artist from the People's Republic of China, Middlebury has

become a diverse institution where the mix of students is a pillar of
strength on which to build the future.

> —Olin Robison, "An Open Letter to the
> Middlebury College Community," *Middlebury
> College Magazine*, 64 (spring 1990): 30

The Middlebury student body changed markedly between 1915 and
1990. Before World War II the students came primarily from white
Protestant lower-middle- or middle-class homes in New England or
the upper Middle Atlantic region. Most of them needed financial
aid or jobs, or both, and a strong, self-conscious democratic feeling
existed on campus. The admissions pool of women at Middlebury,
since there were so few private coeducational colleges to which they
could apply, was far superior to that of the men; the college could
be more selective in its choice of female students, who tended to
be wealthier and abler than their male classmates. The college was
relatively unknown before World War II, and those students who
entered from outside Vermont often had heard about the place only
because an alumnus (or a teacher who had attended one of the summer schools) had recommended it. The influx of veterans after 1945,
many of whom might never have attended college without the GI
Bill of Rights, reinforced the democratic ethos of the prewar years;
and the presence of older, more worldly men (some of whom were
married) had a strong and salutary effect on campus life.

After midcentury an increasing number of students came from
well-to-do backgrounds. Presidents Thomas and Moody had initiated this process years before by raising tuition and asking more students to pay their way, but it accelerated sharply after 1945 as efforts
to improve academic quality and reputation drove tuition costs up-
ward. Indeed, in the postwar years, Middlebury consciously sought
upper-class students, particularly males, who could afford the rising
costs. At the same time, Middlebury's isolated and rural character, once considered a major handicap, became a positive attribute.
The beauty of the mountains and the pristine quality of the campus
and the Champlain Valley impressed a growing number of predominantly well-to-do Americans who sought to escape crowded urban
and suburban environments. The postwar skiing boom helped to attract the very students the college desired—those who could pay their
way. The enhanced tuition revenues eventually allowed Middlebury

to offer a higher-quality education, which, in turn, began attracting abler students, especially in the 1960s and after. The result was a more academically talented and wealthier student body; relatively few required financial aid. The poor man's college of the nineteenth century had been transformed; by the late twentieth century, Middlebury was drawing an increasing number of students from some of the wealthiest homes in America.

While the student body remained fairly homogeneous, Middlebury displayed increasing diversity after 1965. As more colleges became coeducational and the options for women multiplied, male and female students at Middlebury became increasingly equal in background and academic ability; indeed, by the 1980s they were admitted in almost equal numbers. The minuscule number of African-American and Hispanic students slowly increased, and more aggressive measures to diversify—such as "aid-blind admissions"—were inaugurated in the 1980s. And as the college consciously attempted, under Presidents Armstrong and Robison, to become a truly national and international institution, a greater proportion of students matriculated from regions outside the Northeast. By 1990, although it remained difficult to attract middle-class and lower-class applicants, the growing numbers of women, African-Americans, Hispanics, and students from abroad, from rural areas, and from every region of the United States made Middlebury a much more diverse and exciting school than it had been in the early twentieth century.

By the 1960s the great majority of Middlebury students—in sharp contrast to the profile in 1915—could be classified as upper-middle- or upper-class.[1] This striking change took place gradually, indeed almost imperceptibly until after World War II; and although implemented consciously, it was often done with regret, for it flew in the face of one of the college's primary missions in the nineteenth century: to train people of modest means for the clergy and other noble pursuits. Only the desire to improve quality and keep pace with rival schools finally shaped the decision to attract wealthier students and more income. Middlebury, of course, did not move on this track alone; many of the best liberal arts colleges in the Northeast and Midwest felt impelled to do likewise.

The story of Middlebury begins with President John Thomas, who discovered in the first year of his presidency (1908) that cash tuition payments from his 203 students (many of whom paid little or nothing) amounted to barely $1,000, and general income from students accounted for less than 20 percent of total college income. Thomas demanded that students begin to pay their own way. Between 1908 and 1915, while enrollment rose from 203 to 348, income from students increased more than fivefold.[2] In 1920, after raising tuition from $100 to $150, Thomas predicted that the new increase would probably not hurt enrollment either: "We have been too cheap. Our low rates have given a wrong idea of the character of the college. Many people judge colleges by their prices, just as they do other things. Dartmouth increased its tuition to $200 and had a Freshman class of 700 the next year."[3] The editor of the *Campus* agreed that "it has been recognized for some time that such a change was both inevitable and desirable."[4] (What Thomas and the editor did not say was that, whereas poor applicants might judge Middlebury more favorably if tuition rose, they might also be unable to afford to attend.) Thomas attempted to entice more affluent students with the construction of the modern Hepburn residence hall in 1915, which contained some relatively large and expensive rooms.[5]

President Moody continued these efforts by raising tuition several times and increasing the rates charged at Hepburn and other residence halls. He rationalized one increase (from $200 to $250 in 1929) by reminding the trustees that most comparable schools charged more than Middlebury did and that since an increasing number of male graduates were now entering business, the higher cost of education was a small investment for such students to pay in thus preparing themselves for a financially secure future.[6]

Indeed, according to an unusually candid and perceptive report by Dean of Men Burt Hazeltine in 1929,[7] the fact that a number of rival schools charged higher tuition was a major reason for Middlebury's relatively low position among New England private colleges. Hazeltine argued that low rates attracted students who were not only poorer in wealth but also in academic abilities and the social graces.

> In those colleges which had raised their tuition it was unanimously agreed that the type of student was much better than it has previously been. . . . In every case the colleges were very much gratified in the improvement in the student body following the increases. This brings up at once the relative position of Middlebury. . . . From the number of interviews which I have had this year it is apparent that

our own Freshman class is poorer financially than is ordinarily the case. Does this mean that we are getting those who are not able to go elsewhere? Are we getting the leftovers? Shall we continue to keep our own tuition in the low class and cater to that type of student? . . . We are at present in the very lowest line of New England Colleges as far as tuition charges are concerned. . . . Are we to try to maintain the standing of Williams, Amherst, Wesleyan and such institutions having tuitions of $400, or shall we content ourselves with the standing of Colby, Bates, and similar colleges? This is an important question for the future of Middlebury College and it is one that the Board of Trustees has got to meet.

Hazeltine understood that higher tuition would mean a smaller student body in the short run. But it would enable the college to attract better students and eventually eliminate those "from the lower rank of society" who "are outcasts among the fraternities and with the women of the other Colleges because of their insurmountable crudities and background." Second, more tuition income would allow the hiring of better faculty, which Hazeltine called "absolutely essential for the progress of the college."

At the present time the number of inspirational teachers on the faculty could be numbered on the fingers of the two hands. This is a serious state of affairs. But it is such a state of affairs that cannot be helped until we are able to pick and choose our faculty members in competition with other colleges of the type that we desire to become. This also is going to cost money. But it must be done if our scholastic prestige is to be maintained, if we are going to draw real students, and keep them contented after we have obtained them. Since the opening of college at least a dozen men have sought me out to complain that practically none of their instructors had the ability to interest them, or to keep them busy. Several members of the Freshman class have told me that they had dreamed of college as a place where one had to work to keep one's place in class but that here it was not necessary and they felt that they were wasting their time. Almost at the same time I had occasion to call in others who were failing. They said that their preparation had been such that it was almost impossible to adjust themselves. The first are the type we want, and the type we must keep if we are to be in the same class with the Little Three, but we must have a faculty that will appeal to them and make them happy, or they like many of last year's list will transfer elsewhere.

Hazeltine also recommended that Middlebury improve its admission process by hiring at least one officer who would travel widely to interview prospective students and "investigate the character of the candidate, his environment, and determine whether or not he has the qualifications to make him a desirable citizen in the college community," thereby ensuring that "the riffraff [are] discovered before enrolled, the standard of the college raised by just that amount and the mortality correspondingly lowered." The college duly hired an assistant admissions officer and raised tuition again, to $300 in 1931 and to $350 in 1939.[8] Between 1920 and 1941, while the average cost of living actually declined by nearly 20 percent, the basic price of a Middlebury education doubled—from less than $400 to $800.[9]

Notwithstanding these higher costs, the less affluent students still came in large numbers between the wars. W. Storrs Lee '28, who attended the college during Hazeltine's first years as dean, agreed that the student body lacked sophistication. "The great majority of us had come from small towns or relatively small-city high schools—good, sound educational institutions but without the trappings and social "advantages" of exclusive, more expensive, more liberated prep schools—and we tended accordingly to overlook the fact that we had matriculated in a rather provincial college."[10]

The relative homogeneity of Middlebury students was reinforced by an almost studied effort to create a "democratic" ethos at the college. Hazeltine wrote this florid paean to democracy on campus in 1932:

> Within a comparatively short time elections will be held to determine the new President of the Undergraduate Association and candidates are being discussed throughout the student body. Who will it be, and upon what will the election depend? Is Middlebury bound by its traditions to hold the chance of birth, position and inheritance sacred and hence to pick only those so chosen by Fate to fill its positions of trust and loyalty?
> The answer to this last query is one sonorous "NO" sounding simultaneously from the lips of every Middlebury man even from the oldest alumnus down to the youngest freshman. For everyone who has ever come in contact with the Spirit of Middlebury has been imbued with one never-to-be-forgotten lesson, that of Democracy.[11]

As W. Storrs Lee '28, Sam Guarnaccia '30, David K. Smith '42, and others have recalled, there were not many wealthy students on campus before World War II, and even those rarely put on airs. For example, only a handful displayed two of the most common symbols of upscale collegiate life in the 1920s and 1930s—the raccoon coat and the automobile.[12]

The majority of Middlebury students in this period required financial help, and many—perhaps three-quarters of the men and half of the women—sought employment at school and during vacations in order to pay their way.[13] During and right after World War I, jobs were fairly plentiful. Ray Mudge '18 apparently turned his college employment—four jobs at least—into a profitable venture, as he was able to deposit $12 each week into his bank account.

> I entered in September, 1914 with $40.00 plus some change, and graduated in 1920 with a substantial bank account. . . . As I recall Beany Parke and I were janitors at Chemistry Building (Oh! that Middlebury clay mud in the spring). I waited table at the A.S.P. House for my board, took care of the furnace for the Steam Laundry for spending money and term bill at one point. I was campus night watchman, turning out the lights at 1 a.m. . . . I milked Mr. Fletcher's cow and shoveled his paths (he was College Treasurer, I believe) for extra "ticket money" to Rutland to see my best girl.[14]

Students occasionally complained when ambitious men such as Mudge took on extra jobs just to earn spending money while "more worthy ones who are compelled to work their way" were seeking employment.[15]

Apparently, however, most students in the 1920s who needed work could find jobs, particularly as janitors, clerks, and waiters. Storrs Lee '28 recalled how students performed almost all of the menial work on campus.[16]

> Students were the janitors of the various buildings, and the choicest jobs they were—after table waiting, which was reserved for athletes, potential Phi Betes or the totally impoverished. . . . The toughest janitorial assignment was the Playhouse on Weybridge Street. The ancient furnace had to be stoked about midnight in winter and again before dawn, and it was a long trek down there.

For two years, Lee held the janitorship of Mead Chapel, a position he considered "the most coveted job on campus."

> It paid ten dollars a week, as I recall, and included snow shoveling of the portico, the steps and a wide area in front, sweeping the entire floor from choir loft to back balcony and vestibule (this was before the side balconies were added), dusting, scraping up the gobs of Addison County clay, safely stowing away the scarves, hats, textbooks, rubbers, class papers left behind by students, ventilation, turning on the portico lights at 5:30, though usually the chimes carillonneur could be counted on to do that, and double duty after every concert or eve-

ning week. . . . Assignment to jobs like this was considered something of an honor and fellow students were much more likely to be envious than disdainful of indulgence in such menial work.

Students sometimes stayed on campus during vacations to earn extra money:

An elderly town handyman, Billy Farrell, was in charge of buildings and grounds—a one-man post. With a part-time assistant or two, he supervised everything from a plumbing and janitorial service to snow plowing and campus mowing—with horse-drawn plow or mowing machine.

I assure you, the campus under Farrell was not very "kempt." The grass was mowed, like a farm field, for Commencement, and occasionally during the summer. The vast accumulation of maple leaves on lower campus was not raked in the fall. They remained matted on the ground until Easter vacation, when a dozen students or so were recruited to clean up the expanse. It was a major undertaking, for the compact drifts of leaves created perfect insulation, retaining the frost, and in places virtually had to be chopped off the frozen surface. Competition for this Easter vacation employment was keen, paying probably as much as 35 cents an hour.

Lee, Hazeltine, and others have claimed that students who worked were not looked down upon by their wealthier peers.[17] Indeed, letters and editorials in the *Campus* occasionally expressed the view that the experience of working one's way through school was an advantage in that it molded character.[18]

During the Great Depression, raising enough money to attend college became more difficult, and the demand for jobs on campus and in the community increased. Of the 132 men who applied for admission to the class of 1938, 107 asked for a scholarship or employment.[19] Student jobs were scarce until the government initiated several programs that directly benefited Middlebury; a number of students obtained part-time work in 1934 under the Federal Emergency Relief Administration. As part of that program, thirty men worked on the new ski jump, and others worked in the library or on special research projects. In 1935 the National Youth Administration (NYA) provided part-time jobs on campus for about 12 percent of the student body.[20]

Although these programs were helpful, there were never enough jobs or money to go around, and some students were unable to make ends meet. So many were in arrears on their bills by 1934 that Middlebury began requiring a $100 deposit from entering freshman, and demanded that upperclassmen pay all past balances and deposit $50 before they would be allowed to attend classes. Everett S. Allen '38 recalled that although he had done some NYA work, he ran out of money in his senior year and had to live in a "linen closet." He and his equally penurious roommate, Edward B. Haywood '38, lost out on social occasions. "In spring," he wrote, "through the open gymnasium door, we observed with envy those of our peers who could afford tickets to the formal ball, deriving penniless comfort from each other's situation."[21]

To make matters worse, the college began turning over some of the more dangerous or critical campus jobs to regular employees, a process that accelerated during the Stratton administration.[22] With campus jobs disappearing and enrollments rising, students found it harder and harder to obtain work, and dependence on direct financial aid increased markedly.

Middlebury had always offered scholarships (or waived tuition and fees) for poorer students in the nineteenth and early twentieth centuries.[23] Thomas and Moody modified that practice, but the continued influx of less affluent students in the interwar period put a continual strain on the small amount of scholarship aid available. Moody reported to the board in 1926 that the college had provided about $20,000 in scholarships—$7,000 more than was actually available from funds designated for that purpose.[24] The college announced in January 1930 that it would grant four-year scholarships of $1,000 to ten Vermont men to cover the cost of tuition. These Vermont scholarships were highly sought after and attracted excellent students, including Professor David K. Smith '42.[25] By 1932, 171 of the 372 male students were receiving annual scholarship aid ranging from $100 to $250, which, combined with employment income, was sufficient to pay for a Middlebury education during the Depression.[26] As one student who had managed to finance another year at the college wryly put it, "So for us the depression is over and we are assured of 3 meals a day."[27]

The fact that many individuals received financial aid and held campus jobs in the interwar period supports the observation that there were still numerous less affluent students at Middlebury. But, according to one student of that era, the increases in tuition and fees during these years had begun to change the character of the student body and the image of the college as well.

> Moody brought to Middlebury the first element of modern intellectual and social sophistication. Before him, it was a country — rustic — college; under him, it became a socially and intellectually accepted college in a country setting. There's a big difference. . . . Under his administration, it became a college that was difficult to get into, particularly for women, and a desirable, popular, growingly sophisticated college for the sons and daughters of parents of means and social prowess.[28]

When tuition was raised from $300 to $350 in 1939, the editor of the *Campus* feared that the college might no longer be able to accommodate less affluent students.[29]

Middlebury in the 1920s and 1930s enrolled large numbers of lower-middle-class men and a preponderance of middle-class or even upper-middle-class women.[30] The reason was quite simple: few private liberal arts colleges accepted women, and those who wanted to attend a good coeducational school had few options.[31] They therefore applied to Middlebury in fairly large numbers. Since the college always reserved fewer places for women than for men, the result was a much more selective group of women students — in terms of both academic ability and socioeconomic status.[32] In a normal year, anywhere from 50 percent to 75 percent of the female applicants would be rejected, whereas two-thirds of the male applicants would be accepted.[33] The admissions goal in the early 1920s was a class of one hundred men and sixty women. While these numbers were usually attained, the poorer quality of the male students resulted in a much higher attrition rate, and by junior and senior year, the gender breakdown was more nearly equal.[34] Although some men may have resented the superior status and academic abilities of their female classmates, others took advantage of this and married into a higher social class.[35]

As we have seen, President Stratton was well off the mark with his predictions that few veterans would attend schools like Middlebury after the war and that the college would therefore have to take extraordinary measures to attract men.[36] Instead, applications poured into the admissions office in 1945–1948 from veterans who were sup-

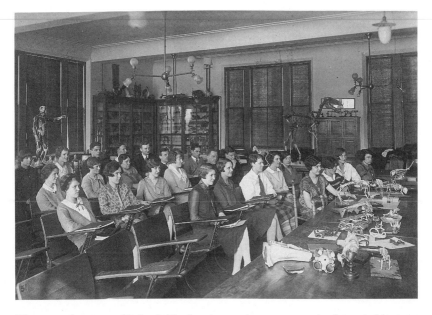

Women made up two-thirds of this class in vertebrate anatomy in the period between the two world wars.

ported by the GI Bill and anxious to make up for lost time. In the fall of 1946, 85.7 percent of the male students were veterans. College officials were overjoyed at this unexpected development and accepted as many as they could fit in; when they ran out of room, they found places to house students all over Addison County. Over 1,100 students were enrolled by 1948, about 300 more than before the war.[37]

Fred Neuberger '50, director of admissions from 1964 to 1990 and a veteran himself when he attended the college, recalled that the men who entered after World War II comprised some of the most diverse classes in the college's history.[38] Certainly, they brought with them experiences and circumstances that were without precedent. Many were older, married, and far more intellectually curious than the eighteen-year-olds to whom the faculty were accustomed.[39] Many had faced death and the privations of war, and they had emerged as more mature and focused than the ordinary college freshman. One veteran, when asked on his application to give a few highlights or colorful incidents in his service experience, answered:

What would you consider a "colorful incident" anyway? Going four days and four nights with about four hours sleep, marching through rain and climbing mountains through sleet and launching an attack afterward? Cowering in the goo in the bottom of your foxhole while the very earth quivers under the fury of an enemy artillery barrage? Dragging a steel assault boat through a mine field under mortar fire? Walking across an open field to draw enemy machine-gun fire and cause them to give away their positions? Watching four cold G.I.'s crowd into one hole to make a cup of coffee and staying there because a shell lands in the same hole? Returning to your own lines with a sense of relief because the night's work is nearly over only to see the red tongue of machine-gun fire lashing out of the shadows and feel hot bullets tearing through your body? To lie in an Italian ditch and gaze up at the stars and feel the warm blood trickling down your legs and think "It doesn't look like I'm going to make it back home after all"? The decorations I received don't mean anything. I can think of a dozen men more deserving of them.[40]

The great postwar influx of veterans allowed Middlebury to reduce women's admissions and ensure once again a substantial male majority in the student body.[41] The effect of this sudden drop in female acceptances was dramatic. To make up for the loss of men during the war, the college had accepted an unusually large number and percentage of female applications—an average of 158 freshman women from 1942 to 1945, compared with an average of 103 in 1937–1941. The war had therefore established a new level of expectations among those secondary schools that liked to send their female graduates to Middlebury. In 1946 and 1947, however, when only 88 and 98 freshman women students enrolled (respectively, out of 834 and 864 applicants), these schools were upset that many graduates who would have been admitted during the war years were being rejected.[42] Although female enrollment rose to 153 in 1948 (out of 875 applicants), President Stratton admitted that "in view of the very fine qualifications of our women applicants and the relatively few places available in next year's entering class, it is inevitable that many disappointments and some hard feelings will follow upon our decisions."[43]

Not surprisingly, the quality of the postwar women was extraordinary. The large number of veteran applicants allowed the college (for the first time in its history) to be somewhat selective in choosing men as well, and the quality of male students improved markedly after 1945.[44] But by 1949 the number of veteran applications had declined to a trickle, and Middlebury once again faced its perennial problem of finding good male applicants. Moreover, due to postwar cost increases (tuition rose from $350 in 1941 to $425 in 1946 and to $600 in 1951, and other costs escalated at a similar rate) and the lack of scholarship funds to serve a larger student body, Stratton informed the trustees in 1950 that most Middlebury students would have to pay their own way.

> With increased tuition and board and room charges, one of the urgent needs of the college is for increased sums available for loans or scholarships if we are to preserve opportunities for deserving and capable men and women students. During these post-war years, there has undoubtedly been a trend in the direction of accepting a larger proportion of students who can finance their education without college aid. I see no way of changing this trend unless our endowment is increased or annual gifts for scholarships and loans make more aid available for deserving students.[45]

Stratton determined, therefore, that it was necessary to go out and find people who could afford to attend Middlebury. The man he picked in 1947 to carry out this plan was Stanley Wright '19, who had directed the Memorial Field House fund drive of 1946–1947. Now director of admissions for men, Wright attempted to increase the pool of potential applicants by visiting schools Middlebury had rather neglected in the past; he called on a total of 164 schools in 1950–1951, compared with only 67 in 1949–1950.[46] He particularly courted preparatory schools that enrolled the type of wealthy students the college desired. Many of these prep school graduates did not have strong academic credentials, but the college accepted them anyway with the hope that they could attract better students from those schools in the future.[47]

As these academically inferior males appeared in increasing numbers in the early 1950s (some only briefly before they flunked out), the faculty was outraged, and Wright became a highly controversial figure.[48] Stratton, however, stood solidly behind him:

> Mr. Wright cannot be praised too highly for his achievements as Director of Admissions since 1947. Statistics give evidence of the sustained increase in applications and of the much larger number of schools from which men apply for admission. Statistics cannot, however, tell the story of the good will we have gained among parents, school principals, and headmasters as the result of Mr. Wright's

friendly but direct and honest handling of the affairs of the admissions office.[49]

Walter Brooker '37, Fred Neuberger '50, and Gordie Perine '49 have agreed that it was Wright who opened the doors of key preparatory schools to Middlebury's admissions efforts; and while the college did initially accept some students who were academically unprepared, better men enrolled from those schools in later years. "Wright, by sheer salesmanship and perseverance got Middlebury back on prep school lists," Brooker wrote. "It's ironic that for this he was hounded and pilloried by the faculty."[50]

The college indeed began to attract better male students during the 1950s and 1960s. Male applications increased consistently, from 628 in 1952 to 856 in 1958 to 1,127 in 1967, while enrollment of male freshman went up only from 227 to 306. SAT scores for men rose (as they did nationally at this time) from 1016 in 1952 to 1072 in 1956 and to 1279 in 1965.[51] Still, Middlebury women (who continued to apply in greater numbers than men) remained superior students, as *The Harvard Crimson* pointed out in 1954.

> The scholastic averages of two-thirds of all the girls at Middlebury fall within 93.8 and 80.4 points. Out of the 502 girls and 693 boys in the undergraduate body, there are 162 women on the Dean's List and 58 men. This is practically a three to one ratio, and in a small community it has powerful effects.
>
> Part of the problem can be traced to the atmosphere on both sides of the Middlebury campus. It begins with the fact that girls who apply to Middlebury apply to it as a first choice. Many are turned down who are accepted at Radcliffe, Wellesley, Vassar, Smith, and Bryn Mawr. But boys apply as their second or third choice, and if they end up there, it is generally because they were turned down elsewhere.[52]

On the other hand, due to Wright's efforts, the socioeconomic differences between men and women were less significant than they had been before the war. Indeed, as Stratton pointed out in 1956, Middlebury lacked the resources to attract academically talented but less affluent men, and this was a major reason for the gender disparity in academic ability:

> Our records again show a great difference in the academic standing of men and women students. . . . At Middlebury from approximately the same number of applications, we select 140 women but 220 men. Also we continue to lose many men students we have accepted be-

cause of higher scholarship awards offered to them by other colleges. I feel strongly we can narrow the academic gap between men and women students only by a substantial increase in scholarship awards for men students.[53]

By the late 1950s, Stratton and the board were ready to do whatever they could to attract better male students, even if it meant tuition increases. Tuition cost $650 in 1953–1954 and had more than doubled to $1,400 in 1962–1963, and Stratton urged these increases not only to "stay in line with colleges of its own kind on faculty and staff salaries" but also to increase financial aid.[54] In 1958, arguing for a tuition hike of several hundred dollars, he reasoned as follows:

> The increase to $1,200 envisions a dynamic and dramatic new program of financial aid for entering freshman men and women students. Under the proposed program, Middlebury will be able for the first time to compete effectively for academically superior students of great financial need by offering a limited number of scholarships for more than full tuition in the freshman and sophomore years, which in the junior and senior years will be converted in substantial part to loans.[55]

By 1963, Middlebury students were receiving $212,130 in various forms of aid, compared with $80,090 ten years earlier. Men got the lion's share of the aid, receiving $29,500 in college scholarships in 1957–1958, whereas women were granted only $10,725.[56]

The efforts to attract better men and thereby reduce the disparity in academic ability between the sexes were somewhat successful. The difference in SAT scores narrowed markedly in the 1960s, but observers still bemoaned the lack of good male applicants.[57] As Fred Neuberger remarked, coeducational Middlebury in the era of all-male Eastern colleges was not quite masculine enough for some applicants, and the college therefore continued at a disadvantage in recruiting men.[58]

The traditional gender characteristics of the student body—superior women but more men admitted and enrolled—were not completely altered until outside circumstances changed dramatically. It was only after a number of Middlebury's major competitors—Dartmouth, Williams, Yale, Amherst, Princeton, and other all-male schools—began admitting women in the late 1960s and after that Middlebury began to consider gender equality in admissions. Free at last from the old nagging fear that if 50 percent or more of the student body were women, the school would inevitably turn into

TABLE 7
Enrollment, by Gender, 1972–1990

Year	Men	Women	Total
1972–1973	1019	798	1817
1974–1975	1028	850	1878
1976–1977	1006	860	1866
1979–1980	995	919	1914
1981–1982	1013	911	1924
1983–1984	1012	935	1947
1985–1986	1022	916	1938
1986–1987	1039	1003	2042
1987–1988	1041	973	2014
1988–1989	991	986	1977
1989–1990	1045	986	2031

SOURCE: Reports of the Dean of the College, Middlebury College Archives.

a women's college, the administration slowly (and without much fanfare) moved toward a 50–50 male–female ratio between 1972 and 1990 (see Table 7). It was one of the most important changes in the nature of the Middlebury student body since the advent of coeducation a century earlier.[59]

The Stratton–Wright effort to enroll more men from affluent families was successful and changed the makeup of the student body. The number of students from preparatory schools jumped. The percentage from outside the Northeast also increased. Middlebury could not yet be called a national institution, but it was moving in that direction; Walter Brooker '37 recalled that when he returned in 1956 as an administrator, one of the major changes he noticed was a greater geographical diversity of the student body.[60]

In the nineteenth century, Middlebury had drawn a majority of its students from Vermont. Not until the early twentieth century did the number of Vermonters fall below 50 percent, and even then, 95 percent of the students came from New England and New York.[61] That figure gradually changed between the wars as the college became better known, but as Table 8 indicates, it was only after World War II that the percentage of students from areas outside of New England and the Mid-Atlantic states began to grow.

In the late 1970s, American colleges faced the dismal demographic truth that fewer eighteen-year-olds would be available to them in coming years. Middlebury was justifiably concerned, particularly since the decline was particularly steep in the Northeast. To counter

TABLE 8
Home Regions of Middlebury Students, 1915–1985

Region	1915–1916 (%)	1941–1942 (%)	1965 (%)	1985 (%)
New England	80.7	46.0	35.4	31.9
Middle Atlantic	16.9	49.1	39.6	33.2
Midwest	0.5	3.6	7.5	9.1
South	0.3	0.6	3.1	6.7
West	0.3	0.1	8.4	12.2
Abroad	1.1	0.6	6.0	6.9

SOURCES: *Middlebury Annual Catalogues*, 1915–1916 and 1941–1942; and *Report of the Admissions Long-Range Planning Committee, May 1, 1987.*

this potential shrinkage in its admissions pool, Middlebury began to tap the populous "Sun Belt." As Robison pointed out, "the demographic and financial center of the country has been moving away from the Northeast, toward the South and West."[62] The college therefore initiated a program (termed "Westward Ho!" by admissions director Fred Neuberger) that targeted several cities in the Midwest and Far West for special recruiting efforts.[63] The Admissions Office greatly expanded the Alumni Admissions Support Program, in which over one thousand alumni in thirty-eight cities across the country identified and interviewed prospective Middlebury students[64] These efforts were successful (see Table 8), and increasing numbers of western students enrolled after 1975.

Although the increase in geographic diversity after World War II was notable, many of the newcomers from California, Washington, Canada, and even England were quite similar in social and ethnic background to those from New York and Massachusetts. A major college goal in the late 1980s was not only to attract students from all over the country and the world but also to "increase diversity among its applicants, particularly economic and ethnic diversity," and "to attract the most able students from lower income and middle income families, and from black, Hispanic, Asian, and other minorities."[65]

The attempt to enroll and retain African-American students, in particular, had hitherto proved quite difficult. The story of the college's efforts in this regard began in 1963–1964, when students led by David Riley '64 formed a small civil rights group and held the first civil rights conference on campus.[66] Still, the *Campus* criticized Middlebury students in the fall of 1964 for lagging behind other

*Fred F. Neuberger '50 be-
nevolently guarded the gates
of admission to Middlebury
for thirty-two years.*

schools in responding "to the major social and political developments of the last decade," as "only a handful of Middlebury students
have been participants." [67] Later that fall, the pace of activity on
campus picked up. Students began to urge that more blacks be admitted, the Student Life Committee suggested an exchange with a
historically black college, nine hundred students joined in the fast
(sponsored by the National Student Association) to raise funds for
poor blacks in Mississippi, and, over Christmas, twenty-five students visited thirty largely black high schools to acquaint them with
Middlebury.[68] These efforts prompted twenty blacks to apply for
admission to the fall of 1965, and a small exchange program was
arranged with Talladega College for 1965–1966.[69]

In the spring of 1965 twenty-six students and faculty members
participated in the march from Montgomery to Selma, Alabama,
and another group of "deeply concerned" students and faculty held
a sympathy march in Middlebury from Mead Chapel, where a short
ceremony was held.[70] The students who had traveled to Alabama
were deeply affected by white hatred, black poverty, and the oppres-

sion of blacks by whites. As one dean commented, the participants "will never be quite the same again."[71] After the marches, some students formed a seminar during the last eight weeks of the term to study the civil rights movement; several others entered the Peace Corps after graduation to fight poverty and oppression in third world countries. It was also at this time that the sororities and Alpha Tau Omega fraternity took steps to end discriminatory clauses in their constitutions.[72]

The concern over civil rights was growing, but it encountered both opposition and restraint. Some criticized the "Self-Civil Righteous Group" for their "extreme" attitudes and "intolerance" of other viewpoints.[73] The administration was extremely wary of any militancy, trying, for instance, to persuade student leaders in 1963–1964 not to invite Malcolm X to campus.[74] President Armstrong and Dean Reynolds went to some pains to assure worried trustees in 1965 that the students had gone to Alabama as individuals, not as representatives of the college; that the students' interest was "orderly," "healthy," "affirmative," and constructive; and that the college had anticipated student actions and was thus fortunate to be in the position of leading rather than resisting.[75] Black enrollment grew very slowly, from three students in 1960 to twenty-three in 1967–1968 — still only 1.7 percent of total enrollment and somewhat lower than most comparable schools.[76]

The death of Martin Luther King, Jr., in April 1968 spurred a renewed interest in civil rights. At a memorial service for King on April 8 in Mead Chapel, President Armstrong announced that he would appoint a committee of students, faculty, and administrators to study and recommend the most appropriate role for Middlebury "in the national effort to seek remedies for the grievous problems of the urban ghetto, poverty, and racist discrimination."[77] The fourteen-member committee (quickly labeled the King Commission), chaired by Dean O'Brien, spent most of that spring discussing the possibility (and finally advocating) that the college help fund and administer a new summer program for underprivileged boys from Bedford-Stuyvesant, called Youths Opportunity for Understanding (Y.O.U.).[78]

The committee reported its recommendations to Armstrong in January 1969. They called, among other things, for "a much higher and more immediate priority" for admitting disadvantaged students (including "risk" students whose board scores were in the 300s) and finding funds to pay for their education; broadening the curriculum to include the study of race, poverty, and urban problems; offering precollege and freshman-year programs to aid in the transition to regular college work; and a larger financial commitment to the Y.O.U. program.[79] Black students met with Armstrong and O'Brien in March 1969 and with the trustees in April to urge speedy implementation of the King Commission recommendations. They also asked that the director of special programs be a minority group member and that black students be provided a room or an office as an organizational base.[80] After discussing at length the issues raised by the King Commission and the black students, the trustees approved "in principle" granting financial aid for disadvantaged students, funded Y.O.U. at a higher level, and approved the appointment of Arnold McKinney '70, a black junior, to be special assistant to the dean of the college for two years.[81]

Fifteen black freshmen entered Middlebury in 1969, raising the number of blacks on campus to a new high of thirty-six, and black enrollment continued to rise during the next few years.[82] Nevertheless, many of them had difficulty with their course work, and their attrition rate was generally two to three times higher than that of white students.[83] The college acceded to a request to set aside the main lounge in Adirondack House (the old Battell Cottage) for use by black students, who named their new social facility the Coltrane Lounge in 1973.[84] Many of the blacks felt more comfortable there, and white and black students, for the most part, kept a certain social and psychological distance from one another during these years.[85]

The goal of many liberal students and administrators in the 1960s had been to bring more blacks to campus because it was one way to lessen racial injustice in the United States and because it would be good for all Middlebury students to enjoy a greater cultural diversity on campus. Yet after the upsurge in black enrollment in the early 1970s, the number of blacks during the rest of the decade remained at about sixty, or 3 percent of the student body. Many of the other goals of the King Commission were still unrealized. In the fall of 1980, students, faculty, staff, and trustees began a two-year process of discussing and analyzing the problem of race relations at the college. The faculty concluded in September 1981 that Middlebury should attempt to "improve the quality of life for minority students and to increase racial awareness in the College community."[86]

President Robison appointed an ad hoc Committee on Minority Concerns (dubbed the Twilight Committee, after Alexander Twilight, class of 1823) to make recommendations. Their report, issued in October 1982, applauded the college for the progress it had made: it had hired a black staff member, increased black enrollment through intensive recruiting efforts and substantial financial aid packages, implemented a preenrollment program for minority freshmen, made efforts to hire more black faculty, increased curricular offerings in relevant areas, and elected a black alumnus to the board. But another series of recommendations stressed how far the college still had to go to meet the goals of the King Commission.[87]

Although the Twilight Report urged rapid and fundamental changes in some areas, relatively little change occurred until 1987, when the path-breaking *Report of the Admissions Long-Range Planning Committee* stated that race relations seemed to be on the back burner and that the college was failing in its mission to recruit and retain minority students. The report offered a wide range of recommendations, many of which were later approved and implemented.[88]

Several faculty, staff, and administrators who had been involved in the Long-Range Planning Committee's research formed a Minority Advisory Group and met almost weekly for two years in an effort to implement the goals that the report advocated. Perhaps its biggest accomplishment was organizing the successful Minority Advisory Workshops in the summers of 1987 and 1988. Eleven high school counselors attended the first workshop and made a series of suggestions about how to create programs to improve retention and recruitment of minorities.[89]

The college followed through on many of these recommendations in 1987–1989: the hiring of a black counselor, aggressive recruitment of minority faculty members, the implementation of a black studies concentration, the establishment of a Racial/Ethnic/Religious Harassment Policy, the creation of a summer science program for minority high school students (SCIENS), the opening of a Writing Center (later to be a Learning Center) and the hiring of a Coordinator for Academic Support Services to run it, and the development of an improved financial aid package for less affluent families that would include more grant and less loan funds.[90]

Another college group, the Human Relations Committee, also helped to improve the racial climate through a series of initiatives in 1987–1989, including organizing the popular Racial Awareness Lec-

Crispin O. Butler, laboratory supervisor, helps two students in the Sciens program demonstrate the Meissner effect, in which a small permanent magnet is levitated above a disk of high-temperature superconducting material that they made.

ture Series and a well-coordinated Martin Luther King, Jr., birthday celebration in January (jointly sponsored with the Winter Term Faculty Seminar, "Teaching the Black Experience"). The Black Student Union (which changed its name in 1990 to the African American Alliance) also organized programs promoting racial awareness.[91]

In January 1989, President Robison announced a goal of increasing the percentage of minority students to at least 10 percent of all graduates.[92] To reach that objective the college began to implement several other ideas that had emerged from the workshops, including recruiting more black and Hispanic students from urban high schools and community colleges. With the assistance of the New York Diversity Task Force, Middlebury established a partnership with DeWitt Clinton High School in the Bronx in 1988–1989. Middlebury faculty, students, and administrators regularly visited Clinton (which is 98 percent black and Hispanic), and Clinton students traveled to Middlebury for programs. The partnership sought to raise the interest of Clinton students in attending college and to assist those interested in enrolling. It also greatly increased the Middlebury community's understanding of minority high school students. The partnership was perhaps the first such liaison between an urban high school and a rural college.[93] Middlebury also developed articulation agreements with a number of community colleges from New York to Florida in an attempt to attract minority students.[94]

These innovative programs and aggressive recruiting techniques began to pay dividends. In the spring of 1989, 225 minority students (blacks and Hispanics) applied to the college; the largest previous number had been 138. When it entered in the fall of 1989, the class of '93 included 36 African-Americans and 26 Hispanic-Americans out of 500 members; in 1990, 258 minority students applied, and 47 blacks and Hispanics matriculated. These represented significant strides toward improved race relations and better minority recruitment and retention. The college had thus begun to meet one of its most important and difficult goals. As Dean of Students Karl Lindholm '67 put it: "If Middlebury is to survive in a competitive world, we can't be an all-white, upper-middle-class enclave."[95]

Middlebury also increased its efforts to attract international students. The number of individuals from foreign countries enrolled at Middlebury had been growing for two decades (see Table 8), and by the 1980s an average of 6 percent of the students were foreign nationals or international students holding American citizenship.[96] Their presence was highly desirable, according to the *Report of the Admissions Long Range Planning Committee*: "It is appropriate that Middlebury College, with its substantial international orientation, strive to be the home of significant numbers of international students."[97]

Until 1987–1988, the college required most foreign students to provide a minimum family contribution of $3,000 each year. In that year, however, Robison accepted the recommendation of the Admissions Long-Range Planning Committee and asked such students to pay the $3,000 only in their first year. Soon afterward, the number of applications from third world international students rose significantly.[98]

Middlebury took the lead in arranging for a path-breaking exchange of Russian and American undergraduates. Representatives of Middlebury and twenty-three other colleges, which had formed the American Collegiate Consortium for East-West Cultural and Academic Exchange, negotiated the exchange in March 1988 with the Soviet Ministry of Higher Education in a ceremony at Middlebury. In August, fifty-two Russian students arrived on campus for a month-long orientation program before leaving in groups of two or three to attend one of the member colleges. Three remained at Middlebury. More Russian students came to America in 1989, and sixty-four Americans went to Russia, including six from Middlebury.[99]

When these students returned from Russia, they brought back an international outlook that helped make the campus a more exciting place. They were not alone. By the 1980s nearly 40 percent of Middlebury students studied abroad at some point, one of the highest percentages in the country. This might have played havoc with the budget, except for the innovative and highly successful device (inaugurated in 1971–1972) of accepting approximately one hundred students as so-called February freshmen and delaying their matriculation until the spring semester each year.[100]

The increasing number of international students led to a greater cultural and religious diversity on campus. In 1988–1989, ten Islamic Middlebury students strictly observed Ramadan and attended an Islamic Symposium, and Chaplain Walsh helped them form a prayer group.[101] This was a remarkable change from the homogeneous religious community of earlier years. In 1920, out of 319 students, there were only 5 Catholics and 2 Jews. All of the rest of those who listed their religion (76 wrote "none") were Protestants.[102] Life for Jewish students in the interwar period was difficult at Middlebury but no different from that of Jewish students elsewhere. They were allowed social privileges in fraternities but could not be members, and they faced the normal antisemitism of that era. (At the annual halftime Homecoming "P-rade" in 1930, third prize for costume went to James Fish "who was made up as a Jew."[103])

By 1950 the percentage of Catholics (165 out of 1,193 students) had risen to almost 14 percent, and there were 18 Jewish students (1.4 percent). Still, the other 79 percent who identified their religious preference were Protestant (only 6 percent wrote "none").[104] Student religious preference by 1970, as Dean O'Brien wrote, tended to be determined by the proportion of those from affluent families; there were large numbers of Episcopalians, Congregationalists, and Unitarians; Baptists, Methodists, Lutherans, and Catholics (up to 18 percent) were underrepresented. Although the Jewish population

Daily chapel services were a fixture of Middlebury's life until the 1960s.

had risen to 5 percent, which was about the national average, it was well under the percentage at several other top colleges.[105] The percentage of Catholics and Jews had increased markedly by the 1980s; there were active Hillel and Newman Club organizations and a small but active Muslim group.[106] In short, the homogeneous white Anglo-Saxon Protestant campus of the prewar era had gradually changed over the years and was greatly altered by the college's recent concerted effort to attain a more diverse student body.

Many of the African-American, Hispanic, Asian-American, and international students who entered in the 1980s were not wealthy, and their enrollment allowed Middlebury to move closer to the goal of attracting more lower- and middle-income students. The Stratton and Armstrong administrations put more and more money into financial aid grants, but only 20 percent of the students received aid—this during a period (1962–1975) when tuition charges more than doubled, outstripping a 78 percent increase in the consumer price index. The college was increasingly perceived as a place for the wealthy, and academically able middle-class students were often drawn to other institutions.[107]

When Robison took office in 1975, only 18 percent of the student body was on financial aid, and he announced a determination to increase that percentage substantially and thereby diversify the socioeconomic mix. Two years later the situation had not improved, and Robison was frustrated: "We don't believe it's healthy for any college to attract only the affluent. But right now, we don't have the resources we need to help large numbers of middle class students to attend Middlebury."[108] As late as 1979, when the class of 1983 entered with only 18 percent receiving financial aid grants—compared with 43 percent at Bates, 31 percent at Colby, 37 percent at Bowdoin, 28 percent at Connecticut College, 33 percent at Trinity, 38 percent at Wesleyan, and 27 percent at Williams—the dean of the college expressed his concern: "We are behind our competition to the point where we hear that many high school guidance counselors are telling their less affluent students not to bother applying to Middlebury. I know you agree that this is exactly the reputation we do not want to get, but the comparison between us and colleges in our category is disquieting."[109]

Robison approached the trustees in December 1980 with a proposal to move toward an aid-blind admissions policy. Existing policy had been to admit some students but deny them financial aid even though they might qualify for it; Robison wanted to drop the admit/deny category completely and meet the full financial need of every admitted student. "Middlebury could thus take the final step," he argued, "to be recognized, without questions, as one of the half-dozen finest schools in the country."[110] The college implemented aid-blind admissions by the spring of 1982, and the number of entering students receiving aid quickly rose to more than 30 percent.[111] By 1989–1990, 37 percent of the student body was on financial aid, the average grant had increased to $9,000 (from $1,950 in 1976), and there were hopes of increasing the percentage on aid to 40 percent.[112]

In order to attract less affluent students, the college had to do more than promise sufficient financial aid. To overcome its reputation as an upper-class preppy college, Middlebury had to recruit students who might not otherwise attend. The innovative new programs to attract minority students helped in this regard. Another creative and successful effort to increase economic diversity was the Admissions Outreach Program, organized in 1987–1988 and brilliantly staffed by Caroline Donnan '75 of the Admissions Office. Just as Dean Walter Howard had scoured the hills and small towns of Vermont to find students in the early twentieth century, Donnan searched in the rural areas of northern New England (and other out-of-the way places across America) for gifted students who might otherwise not even think of attending a college like Middlebury. As she put it, she was looking for "diamonds in the rough" in rural Mississippi, Alaska, North Dakota, Vermont, and places such as Bullfrog Junction, Maine.

These students were often the first in their families to attend college, and there was sometimes little support (financial or psychological) at home for attendance at a selective, fancy, upper-crust school—a venture that, from the family's point of view, might result in unhappiness for a child who could not fit in or, worse, a radical change in the child that could lead to a permanent separation or estrangement from the family's values. Donnan talked to ninth- and tenth-graders as well as juniors and seniors ("talking to seniors is way too late in a rural school"); and once they were accepted and matriculated (approximately thirty-two students per year), she was there on campus, along with other members of the staff, to help orient, advise, and counsel them through the often difficult early period. This was essential; although Donnan's students were academically prepared (nearly half were valedictorians, and their SAT scores were usually higher than the Middlebury average), a number of them found the wealth and experience of some of their classmates intimidating at first and the general campus atmosphere a bit foreign.[113]

Another striking initiative, designed to induce more applications from minority, rural, Midwestern, and international students, was the decision in 1987 to allow admission applicants to submit achievement tests or the ACT in lieu of the SAT. As one of the first selective colleges to drop the SAT as a requirement (it was still recommended that most students submit their scores), Middlebury attracted much attention. Its seriousness regarding the issue of diversification could no longer be doubted.[114]

The remarkable changes in the student body in the late 1980s were the result of a genuine commitment. As Robison pointed out in 1990, it was a commitment driven both by the desire to do what was right for the betterment of American society and the world and by the need to improve the college by making the student body more diverse and interesting.

> This institution has committed itself to the diversity that is critical to a rich intellectual community. We have tried to build upon each new program and each success with an ever more heterogeneous student body and faculty. Whether this involves students from a Bronx high school, who along with their faculty regularly visit Middlebury and receive our students and faculty in return; whether it has to do with students from junior colleges throughout the country who demonstrate great promise and have places reserved for them at Middlebury; whether it is students from rural areas around the Northeast for whom a college like Middlebury was not even a dream a year ago; whether it is a Pakistani youth or a Soviet exchange student, or a 45-year-old artist from the People's Republic of China, Middlebury has become a diverse institution where the mix of students is a pillar of strength on which to build the future. The face of the College has changed in the past decade and it will continue to change. It is the best kind of growth and development.[115]

Dean of the College John Emerson reminded the trustees in 1987 that Middlebury "is now considered, in many ways, in the same league as Dartmouth, Brown, Princeton, Amherst, and Williams" but that "the major challenge for the next five years is to bring greater diversity, both ethnic and economic, to the College." [116] The marked increase of minority, international, middle-class, and rural students was a critical development, one that helped move Middlebury even more firmly into the ranks of the finest (and most interesting) small colleges as it entered the twentieth century's final decade.

This rosy picture of increased economic and ethnic diversity was clouded by growing parental and student concern over rising costs. Concomitant budgetary difficulties threatened to affect adversely some of the programs that had helped achieve the new diversity. As Table 9 indicates, Middlebury's comprehensive fee rose at an average annual rate of 10 percent during the 1980s. As we have seen, decisions such as the 16 percent increase in 1981–1982 were implemented primarily to raise faculty salaries.[117] But the college also needed funds to renovate the physical plant, mount new programs, and hire additional faculty and staff.[118] In short, Robison argued, as had his predecessors, that additional tuition income was needed for

TABLE 9
Comprehensive Fee Increases, 1979–1990

Year	Fee	% increase	% inflation rate
1979–1980	$6,900		
1980–1981	$7,800	13.0	13.5
1981–1982	$9,300	19.2	10.3
1982–1983	$10,800	16.1	6.1
1983–1984	$11,800	9.3	3.2
1984–1985	$12,600	6.8	4.3
1985–1986	$13,500	7.1	3.6
1986–1987	$14,500	7.4	1.9
1987–1988	$15,500	6.9	3.6
1988–1989	$17,000	9.7	4.1
1989–1990	$19,000	11.8	4.8

SOURCES: Middlebury College Trustee Minutes; and Office of Institutional Research, Franklin and Marshall College.

the improvements that would enable the college to compete successfully with its rivals. Although inflation was often cited as a major cause of fee increases, the consumer price index (CPI) rose only an average of 4.65 percent during much of the 1980s. On the other hand, most institutions were increasing their fees at a rate well above that of the CPI, and college officials often maintained that their costs were different from those considered in the CPI. Indeed, a study of twenty comparable liberal arts colleges reveals that the median increase for those schools, 9.9 percent, was only a bit below that of Middlebury.[119]

After 19.2 percent and 16.1 percent increases in 1981–1982 and 1982–1983, the annual rise in the Middlebury comprehensive fee averaged a relatively moderate 7.4 percent through 1987–1988. But in 1988–1989 the increase jumped to 9.7 percent and in the spring of 1989, when Robison announced an 11.8 percent rise (from $17,000 to $19,000) for 1989–1990, student and parental discontent boiled over.[120] Many parents were concerned that they could no longer afford the college and that Middlebury was pricing itself out of the middle-class market.[121] Students demanded an explanation, and Robison and Treasurer David Ginevan attempted one. They pointed out the marked advances in quality at the college—a lower faculty-student ratio, more competitive salaries and benefits, twice as many students on financial aid, renovated buildings, and much more—all of which cost money. They also noted that only 66 percent of the operating budget came from fees, so even students who were not on financial aid were, in a sense, receiving a large subsidy to attend the college.[122]

A number of students were not impressed, and they formed a group called STARTUP (Students Against the Rise in Tuition and Unjust Policies). STARTUP leaders David Milner '90 and Rob Gray '90 called for a boycott of classes on May 4, and approximately half the student body complied. There was a sit-in on Old Chapel steps, and Gray and Milner met with Robison to present the STARTUP demands: a reduction in the comprehensive fee increase to 7 percent, placement of an undergraduate as a voting member of the board and its budget committee, an itemized account for parents of how tuition dollars were spent, and a guarantee specifying tuition increases over a student's four-year residence.[123]

Robison and Ginevan promised to consider the proposals, and a committee was formed (composed of Ginevan, Gray, Milner, and Residential Life Director Frank Kelley) to look into ways to cut costs. The *Campus* gave the boycott and the general problem of rising costs a good deal of play in 1989, and officials were sensitive to the need to moderate costs and tuition increases in the future.[124] Indeed, the 1990–1991 fee was set at $20,300—up 6.8 percent, the lowest percentage increase since the 1970s.[125] Furthermore, as we have seen, the college asked each department to reduce spending by 6 percent in an attempt to cut costs.[126] There was some concern that budgetary difficulties might jeopardize the programs that had enabled the college to begin to diversify the student body.[127] If that were to occur, one of the greatest accomplishments of the Robison years would be negated.

CHAPTER 11

FRATERNITIES

Fraternities are the most powerful and partisan groups on the Middlebury campus. . . . They are the social center, the eating center, and, in varying degrees, the thinking center. The life of the average Middlebury man is focused upon his fraternity. There he eats and drinks and sleeps and lives. There he makes lasting friends and enemies.
— *Campus* editorial, October 21, 1954

With the increased emphasis on College level work in high school and ever widening attention to graduate school, the four years of college are becoming a compact and intensive time of study. Courses and study programs are demanding more and more of the student's time. The fraternity system, rather than being a thorn in the side of scholastic work must begin to make extensive contributions to the academic role of the college.
— *Campus* editorial, October 18, 1962

It is to be hoped that in the relatively near future fraternities may be removed from their present limbo. They should either be more encouraged as a vital part of the institution or done away with. If merely tolerated, they will, in the long run, be sources of constant disruption in student life.
— Dean Thomas Reynolds, Dean of College
1964–65 Annual Report, in President's Files,
1965 Folder, Old Chapel Attic

For many students who attended Middlebury during the twentieth century, fraternities were important, even critical campus organizations. The social life of the college often revolved around them. Even though the college attempted several times and in various ways after 1965 to abolish, reform, or deemphasize the Greek system, fraternities generally retained their prominence. Although by 1990 their future seemed in doubt, their historical significance remains.

In the period 1915–1941, fraternities continued to dominate the college's social and extracurricular scene, as they had since the 1870s. As enrollment rose from 343 to 803, the number of fraternities expanded from five to eight (with the addition of Sigma Phi Epsilon, Theta Chi, and Alpha Tau Omega), and the percentage of men who were fraternity members varied from 55 percent to 80 percent.[1] Their popularity is not difficult to understand. Fraternity activities were at the center of campus social life.[2] They offered men a congenial atmosphere for living, socializing, eating, intergroup competition, and even studying.[3] Furthermore, as one Chi Psi member wrote in 1939, the fraternity "enmeshes every member with a network of personal relations. They are friendships and more; they deserve the name of 'brotherhood.' "[4] They taught men how to coexist with others and within a group and provided certain practical experience:

> Fraternity life also gives valuable training in administrative affairs, since the offices of president, chairman, treasurer, steward, committee member and the like, all call for skill in dealing with men and things. Practical responsibility is a most efficient school, and the task of engineering a fraternity may help to prepare one for managing the business of a corporation.[5]

Fraternities could (and often did) utilize this energy and cohesiveness to serve their school and community by supporting college enterprises and participating in social welfare projects.[6] Nonfraternity men (also called neutrals or independents) were looked down on. W. Storrs Lee '28 recalled that he was not a member of a fraternity until his sophomore year, and during the unaffiliated period he "felt keenly the superiority of the fraternity class."[7] Indeed, neutrals frequently formed groups similar to fraternities in order to take part in athletic competition and organize social activities.[8]

Competition among fraternities for control of campus activities, indeed their absolute dominance in all extracurricular affairs, created problems. There were constant complaints that fraternities controlled the outcome of elections in organizations of any consequence and that, in some cases, "positions of responsibility are handed out to fraternity yes-men of distinct mediocre ability."[9] Although these fierce interfraternity battles for campus offices and influence may have sharpened the participants' political skills and understanding, the results were not always salutary.[10]

Rushing—the annual interfraternity competition for new members—could dominate the extracurricular life of the college for weeks at a time.[11] During most of the interwar period, the fraternities debated whether to rush freshmen immediately in the fall, halfway through the first semester in November, or during the second semester. Such a seemingly mundane matter caused Delta Upsilon to resign briefly from the Interfraternity Council (IFC) in 1925–1926, when their resolution for immediate rushing was vetoed.[12] Although rushing was often a painful and bruising experience, some argued that it could help train men for the world after college.

> Rushing is a competitive game. Think of it that way and you will find it to be an enjoyable experience. You are selling yourself and your fraternity in competition with other men and their fraternities. . . . Honestly concentrate on your rushing and you will find it an open sesame to a stronger and more effective personality. Today the art of selling yourself over as an individual at first notice, is a rare, and valuable possession. Through the practice of applied rushing it can be your possession.[13]

If rushing taught valuable lessons to members, some freshmen who were not chosen by their favorite fraternity were deeply hurt. For many, one member recalled, "rushing was traumatic, leaving deep emotional scars."[14]

Fraternities also were accused now and then of placing themselves first, before the welfare of the college. At such times, attempts were made to lessen their influence, restrain interfraternity competition, and encourage cooperation.[15] Two disgruntled fraternity men told Provost Collins in 1919 that it was "time we turned things around and ran the fraternities for the interest of Middlebury, and stop trying to run Middlebury for the interest of the fraternities."[16] Some complained that fraternities tended to limit student friendships because members failed to "realize that fraternity brotherhood does not necessarily make friendships and that friendship can exist just as well between men who do not wear the same badge."[17] Others claimed that men were classified by the type of fraternity they pledged so that by senior year, a man "was judged not on his own merits and qualifications but on the standards of those with whom he was affiliated."[18]

In November 1942 the men of Kappa Delta Rho fraternity scrapped their trophies and cups to support the war effort.

Although fraternities were occasional targets of criticism in the interwar period, expressed, sometimes by large numbers of students, the existence of the system was never "seriously questioned."[19] Indeed, as male enrollment rose from 187 in 1915 to 429 in 1940, it was correctly assumed that new fraternities would be formed to ensure that the majority of men could be members and that the system would continue its dominance.[20]

The fraternities closed during World War II, and the houses were used as women's dormitories. After the war, many of the returning veterans were not terribly interested in reorganizing the fraternities, and W. Storrs Lee '28, who was dean of men at the time, believed they, "could easily have been abolished in 1945–46."[21] There had been a spate of antifraternity articles in various periodicals during the war; at Middlebury, a "large proportion" of students were opposed to fraternities in principle, and several fought quietly for their removal. As Lee wrote: "Members of fraternities whose education had been interrupted for several years, in many cases, were ready to agree with the opponents of fraternities, unless their organizations were ready to take an immediate and strong stand to abolish the hokum, the campus politics, and some of the juvenile customs, remembered from pre-war days." Indeed, as one alumnus recalled, the returning veterans were in no mood to endure fraternity hazing. "How do you induce a man who is 27 years old and has just gotten out of a German prison camp to go through wearing a beanie or getting a paddling across his fanny?"[22] In the winter of 1945–1946, Dean Lee and the fraternity leaders set up a revitalized interfraternity council, which promised to end hazing, promote democratic membership practices, encourage scholastic achievement, and pursue other progressive policies. Under these arrangements, student opposition abated, and fraternities were officially back in operation by the fall of 1946. The administration was not unhappy with the continuance of the system: "The men's college has developed during the past quarter of a century with the assumption that the fraternities are to supply room and board for a majority of the upperclassmen. If they were to disappear as organizations and if the College did not take over the facilities as housing and dining units, a considerable economic readjustment would be necessary."[23] At the same time, Lee reminded the societies that they were on trial:

> Fraternities can be a significant adjunct to an educational institution, if the emphasis is educational as well as social. Fraternities cannot continue indefinitely if they return as social organizations intent on furthering their own interests on the campus rather than the interests of the college. The business of a college is education, and fraternities must fit themselves sensibly into the pattern.[24]

While the administration and faculty wanted emphasis on scholarship as well as social activities, some students were more concerned about racial or religious restrictions on membership. Near the end of the war, Phi Mu sorority members tried to pledge a Jewish woman but were told by their national leaders that they could not. June Brogger Noble '46 wrote searingly about the ugly contradiction involved:

> We find ourselves in an Alice-in-Wonderland situation, on the one hand fighting a madman who advances a theory to the superiority of a master Aryan race and on the other being party to schoolgirl bigotry. Schizophrenia does not prevail; Phi Mu chooses not to rush *anyone*, and it is only a matter of time before the oldest sorority in the nation leaves our campus.[25]

The same question faced the Alpha Delta chapter of Alpha Sigma Phi after the war.[26] J. David Hunt '49 and A. Gordon Miesse '20, representing, respectively, the group reactivating the Middlebury chapter and the fraternity's Middlebury alumni, met in December 1945 with Ralph Burns, executive secretary of the national Alpha Sigma Phi (ASP) fraternity. Hunt was interested in the attitude of the national "on the matter of initiating a Jewish boy into the chapter—something not permitted in the ritual."[27] Four years earlier, Robert E. Reuman '45 had asked the national for permission to initiate a Jewish student; that request had been denied on the grounds that only the convention of all the chapters could change the ritual. In 1945, Burns told Hunt again that only a vote of the national convention could change the ritual, which indeed was under review and would be reconsidered at the 1946 gathering.[28] Burns visited the chapter at Middlebury a few months later and was thought to give his "implied permission" to initiate a Jewish student.[29]

The chapter brothers were elated. They initiated the Jewish student and pledged twenty new members that winter, including two more Jewish students. But in January 1947 they received the revised ritual from the national with restrictions on Jewish and black membership still in effect, and they were "shocked and ashamed" when they read the pertinent section of the ritual: "Our requirements rigidly exclude members of the negroid and hebrew races. In this regard do you qualify for membership?" Chapter President George H. Booth '47 sent off a stinging letter to Burns, angrily reminding him that intolerance, prejudice, and bigotry were fascist and un-American and that if the section of the ritual pertaining to race and creed was not expurgated, "we will immediately take whatever steps are necessary" to drop from the rolls of the national fraternity.[30]

Burns restated his position that only a national convention could amend the ritual and urged Booth and other active members to consult with the more than two hundred alumni of the Middlebury chapter before doing anything hasty. He also defended the right of a social fraternity to select its members and reminded them that the rituals had been in effect for over a century.[31]

The Middlebury chapter was not satisfied by the response. They petitioned the national to poll other chapters across the nation and learned in May that the other chapters, by a vote of 41–26, did not favor the idea of a local option on racial or religious restrictions.

"That forced the issue," one alumnus wrote. "Either the chapter had to take a stand, or had to lose a valuable pledge class and its much more valuable integrity." [32] Several ambivalent alumni urged the local leaders to stay in the national and fight for reform from within. Booth, Reuman, and the others, however, decided that withdrawal was the right thing both morally and tactically.[33] A hurried vote of some of the chapter's alumni yielded a nearly two-thirds majority (29 out of 44) in favor of breaking with the national over the issue.

The chapter reorganized as a local fraternity on May 19, 1947, and, under some pressure from alumni, changed its name to Alpha Sigma Psi.[34] The Middlebury ASP chapter was apparently the first local in the nation to break with its national over racial and religious discrimination; members received some attention in the *New York Times* and were dubbed "Sluggers for Democracy" (later shortened to "Slug," which remained the fraternity's nickname into the 1980s).[35] In 1948, they invited Charles James, a black student who had earlier been granted house privileges, to be a member.[36]

The Middlebury fraternities maintained a somewhat better record in this area after the ASP controversy. When swollen postwar enrollments led to the formation of a new fraternity in 1949—a chapter of Phi Kappa Tau (PKT)—it was discovered that the national PKT allowed only white members, and the Middlebury IFC rejected a PKT chapter on campus by a 6–2 vote in May 1949. The PKT national soon voted to delete the discriminatory clause from its constitution, and PKT was approved that fall as a legitimate fraternity at Middlebury.[37] Ten years later, Sigma Phi Epsilon pledged a black student, Ron Brown '62 (later a college trustee, chairman of the Democratic National Committee and secretary of commerce). The local chapter was placed on probation by its national in the fall of 1959 for supposedly unrelated reasons. The local members, however, were sure that probation had resulted from their intent to recruit a black member. After Brown was initiated, the national eliminated its "white, Christian" restrictive clause but refused to reinstate Middlebury, and the chapter apparently operated as a local fraternity— Sigma Epsilon—until 1982, when it rejoined the national. It was not until 1964, when Alpha Tau Omega broke with its national (and became Delta Tau Omega) after failing in its attempt to end discrimination, that all of Middlebury's fraternities had discarded their discriminatory clauses.[38]

The World War II veterans in the Middlebury chapters were serious about democratic principles, their academic work, and minimizing fraternity traditions. But they did desire an active social life, and the fraternities once again became the heart of the campus social scene, a position they maintained for two decades. The 1950s and early 1960s were a heyday of fraternity dominance and popularity.[39] A tenth body, Phi Sigma (later to become Zeta Psi), was established in 1955 to accommodate the growing percentage of men who were joining. Only 11 freshmen out of 235 in 1960 did not wish to pledge.[40] The popularity of fraternities was not surprising, since the social life of a neutral at Middlebury was usually bleak to nonexistent.[41] As the *Campus* editorialized in 1954:

> Fraternities are the most powerful and partisan groups on the Middlebury campus.
> Middlebury may not be a fraternity school as such; there is not the bitter rivalry between houses such as on some campuses. Nevertheless, it is evident that frats at Middlebury are the center of college life.
> They are the social center, the eating center, and, in varying degrees, the thinking center. The life of the average Middlebury man is focused upon his fraternity. There he eats and drinks and sleeps and lives. There he makes lasting friends and enemies.[42]

Hazing also returned in this period. Paddling at initiations varied in intensity, and "brandings" were also used, as Karl Lindholm '67 recalled:

> In a pitch-black house, each pledge was blindfolded and led up from the cellar to the living room by a candlebearing brother. In the living room he was surrounded by members clad in white robes who chanted Greek words and DU [Delta Upsilon] songs. At this point, he was made to kneel in front of the fire place.
> When his blindfold was removed . . . he looked straight up at the largest, most muscular brother in the house, whose body was covered in shiny grease, reflecting the flames of the fire and accentuating every muscle. In his hands, he held the burning $\Delta\Upsilon$ brand and asked the pledge to pull down his pants so as to take the brand. As each pledge complied with his orders, he was touched by the hot object and sent back down to the cellar. Only later did he learn that he was touched by the candle, and not branded.[43]

Although fraternities were dominant in the postwar period, important developments were already working to undermine them. Indeed, between 1960 and 1990, a combination of fraternity mismanagement, administrative pressure, and the decline of student interest led to the near-demise of the system.

The fraternities helped immensely in their own downfall. Before the war, members took pride in their chapter houses and kept them in relatively good repair.[44] The houses began to deteriorate in the 1950s, even more so in the 1960s.[45] Here the fraternities were to some extent victims of the changing nature of the student body. Wealthier than their predecessors, students in the 1960s and 1970s were perhaps less likely to take pride in the condition of their quarters or care whether unsightly houses offended townspeople, college officials, or parents. These students were also less loyal (and thus less willing to sacrifice themselves) to institutions and large groups and more likely to form very small and intense circles of friends.[46] The results were obvious. The poor condition of most chapter houses embarrassed the college, damaged town–gown relations, and forced the administration to demand that the chapters install expensive safety equipment in their houses (some of which were deemed dangerously unsafe and unsanitary) and keep them in better repair.[47]

The faculty was becoming increasingly concerned about the negative educational influence of the Greek organizations. The younger professors who had arrived after the war, eager to improve the academic life of the college and involve students more closely with it, took an especially dim view. Yet the fraternities made only desultory efforts to modify their antiintellectual image. They only reluctantly stopped the practice of keeping files of old term papers to be used by members for last-minute plagiarizing.[48] They sponsored few, if any, educational, cultural, or intellectual programs, and thereby placed themselves outside the increasingly academic environment of the late 1950s and 1960s.[49] The *Campus* editor in 1962 urged them to improve in this area:

> With the increased emphasis on college level work in high school and ever widening attention to graduate school, the four years of college are becoming a compact and intensive time of study. Courses and study programs are demanding more and more of the student's time. The fraternity system, rather than being a thorn in the side of scholastic work must begin to make extensive contributions to the academic role of the college.[50]

In short, the not unrealistic image of fraternities as unkempt, antiintellectual anachronisms owed much to their unwillingness or inability to adapt meaningfully to the radical changes underway at Middlebury.

They did, however, effect some positive changes in the postwar years, in response to both administration demands and changing student desires. They gradually ended discriminatory practices in pledging, as we have seen. They occasionally replaced "hell week" with a "help week" during which pledges engaged in helpful projects around town.[51] After a thorough review in 1961–1962 by an evaluation committee composed of faculty, alumni, trustees, and administrators and chaired by Dean of Men Thomas Reynolds, the fraternities agreed to alter their rushing practices to alleviate two glaring problems: the rushing of freshmen, which arguably limited their early academic progress; and the exclusion of the 20 percent or more of men who wished to join.[52] Some of these neutrals (or "non-selected individuals") had formed the Jeremiah Atwater Club in 1955, with the assistance of Professor Paul Cubeta, so that they could enjoy social and athletic activities.[53] But the rejection by fraternities, according to Dean Reynolds and Professor Munford, continued to cause grave hurt to individuals and the transfer of good men.[54]

The evaluation committee recommended that most of the men who would not normally receive bids be offered membership or some sort of affiliation by at least one fraternity. They also recommended that students not be rushed until the beginning of their sophomore year.[55] The trustees approved both measures—sophomore rushing and "increased opportunity rushing"—and their adoption helped the fraternities appear less dominant and elitist than previously. Dean Reynolds even asserted that sophomore rushing in 1962 "has gone a long way in removing the stigma associated with fraternities."[56] The IFC, painfully aware of the need to improve the image, asked the faculty in 1963 to propose changes in the system and, at the faculty's suggestion, pressed individual chapters to destroy their old term paper files and improve the chaperoning system. The *Campus* applauded the IFC's action, and hoped that this was the beginning of a process that would elevate fraternities to "a position of social and academic usefulness complementary to other organizations within the college."[57]

Nevertheless, after Armstrong assumed the presidency in 1963, the fraternities had to fight for their place in the expanding college. The decision in 1964 to increase enrollment from 1,350 to 1,800 by

1975, in line with the Ford Profile, necessitated careful long-term planning on how those new students would be housed and fed and what arrangements would govern their social life. The Armstrong administration was not convinced that the fraternity system should remain the dominant social force. Indeed, Armstrong favored the action of President Sawyer at Williams, who had banned fraternities there in 1962.[58] Armstrong told a group of Middlebury chapter presidents in 1964 that he had "misgivings about the attitudes nurtured in fraternities toward the academic center." He called their tendency "centrifugal rather than centripetal" and worried that loyalty to fraternities was not consistent with loyalty to the college. Finally, he told them that he was concerned about the nonfraternity men's social life.[59]

By 1965, Dean Reynolds, too, had formed an increasingly negative view. "It seems to this observer," he wrote, "that the fraternities, as fraternities, are no longer providing their members with the emotional, or even physical outlets which once were their raison d'etre." He acknowledged that they still provided an important social service "which would have to be replaced were they to be eliminated or to disappear by their own default."[60] But fraternities, he told the trustees in 1966, were an inimical influence on the educational environment:

> Young men come to a college at a time when they are begging for information and orientation to the world around them. The fraternities have tended to teach them quick generalizations, sometimes in a superficial and detrimental way. They have given quick answers when they should be opening the student up to questioning at this time of his life. The fraternities have tried a number of cultural and academic programs with some success. Most fraternities have run study programs, sometimes for sophomores and at other times for the whole house; but this has not been a natural part of their existence and has tended to occur only when the fraternities were under attack.[61]

The new dean of men, Dennis O'Brien, who would replace Reynolds as dean of the college in 1966, also found the Middlebury chapters too antiintellectual for his tastes.[62]

Finally, there was growing concern about the negative effects of fraternities on the social experience of Middlebury's female students and on the development of a truly coeducational college. Fraternities controlled most social life and therefore denied women an active role in planning activities and consigned them to a secondary status. This obvious inequality bothered increasing numbers of students, faculty, and administrators during the 1960s and after.[63] Coeducational dining, which had been increasingly popular since its inception for freshmen around 1960, was an impossibility for upperclass students as long as most men ate at fraternities. A *Campus* editorial in 1965 raised the major issues that worried Armstrong and Reynolds:

> Yet Middlebury's students don't even receive exposure to the limited cross-section of national and international opinion already offered on the local campus. The present system of dining leaves the student body unfortunately fragmented by sex, by class and finally by fraternity.
> . . . Worse yet, the fraternity has become a refuge from the academic life of the college. Middlebury's ten houses play an important role in providing students with social facilities where they can "let off steam" without damage to college property. Yet when the fraternities define their function solely in terms of social life, each meal becomes an escape from the routine of thought associated with the classroom.
> The rigid antithesis drawn between Middlebury's academic and social life is a false one and prevents the growth of the atmosphere so necessary in a residential college. For learning in this small community, and in others like it throughout the country, is a continuous process. Mental development is not restricted merely to the classroom, and education can, and must, extend into both the extracurricular and social life of the college.[64]

In late 1964 the college considered the options available for housing and feeding the additional 450 students expected during the next decade and the role of fraternities in that process. Armstrong, Reynolds, and Dean of Women Elizabeth Kelly presented three possibilities to the board's prudential committee at its meeting in New York in January 1965: abolish fraternities, foster their expansion in proportion to the expansion of the college, or take over the feeding and housing of students completely and let fraternities continue in a social capacity. Armstrong and his staff favored the third option, and after much discussion, the committee agreed.[65] From that day until 1980, when the fraternities were finally forced to give up their dining function, the college's ultimate aim was to implement the third option. It would not be easy, and the fraternity controversy was heated and acrimonious for the next twenty-five years.

Armstrong knew that various constituencies, particularly many alumni and chapter members on campus, would strongly oppose his plans to ease fraternities out of the center of social life. Still, he wanted to include the entire community in the decision-making process and appointed the Ad Hoc Committee on Student Life in 1965 to make recommendations concerning ways of providing housing, dining facilities, and a proper social, cultural, and educational environment for the new expanded college. "Clearly," the president added, "the deliberations of this group will involve the future role fraternities will have at Middlebury." [66]

The committee, chaired by Reynolds, was composed of six alumni, four students, three deans, and one faculty member. They met frequently between November 1965 and the fall of 1966, when they sent their final report to Armstrong. They also issued two interim reports, which revealed the three major options they were considering: (1) expand the fraternities to house and feed upperclassmen; upperclasswomen would continue to eat and live in residence halls, and all freshmen would eat together in Proctor Hall; (2) house and feed all students in college facilities, with freshmen continuing to dine together in Proctor Hall and upperclassmen and women in coeducational "societies" designed around separate social and dining units, each with a capacity of about one hundred; and (3) a compromise plan in which 50 percent of the upperclassmen would live and eat in fraternities, while the rest would live in dormitories and eat with the women in coeducational societies; the freshmen class would continue to eat together in Proctor.[67] During the year in which the committee met, the college watched its progress carefully. As the *Campus* pointed out on March 31, 1966: "The quality of social life at Middlebury College from now to God-knows-when is being determined this semester. Everybody here knows this."[68] Not surprisingly, various constituencies made strong lobbying efforts to persuade the committee to see things their way. The IFC, whose president was a member of the committee, proposed alternative (3) above when it appeared that an expanded fraternity system was neither popular nor feasible.[69]

Indeed, the ad hoc committee's final recommendation, "that as soon as practicable the college undertake to house and feed all students in college facilities," was based in part on their belief that lack of funds prohibited an expanded fraternity system. Moreover, a system that allowed only half of the men to join fraternities would force the college "to relinquish the long established concept of equal opportunity for men; and not only relinquishing it but relinquishing it with the sure knowledge that a considerable number of men could not participate in an important and regular part of college life." The report also recommended "that fraternities be continued at Middlebury, and, if necessary, supported financially by the College through interim difficulties caused by loss of revenue from board and rent."[70]

After Dean Reynolds presented the report to the prudential committee on November 12, 1966, President Armstrong released it to the college community in December. The response from the fraternities and their supporters was one of anger and disgust. The chapter presidents argued that if the recommendation to end dining and living in fraternities were implemented, the fraternity system at Middlebury was dead. Another student wrote: "I believe that the Ad Hoc Committee's report should be exposed for what it is. It is an attempt by the college to secure control over fraternities by destroying them. This is no compromise report."[71] The IFC announced that it would urge the trustees to accept the 50 percent compromise plan rather than the ad hoc committee's recommendations. The Ad Hoc Alumni Interfraternity Committee also prepared a report, supporting the idea that fraternities and coeducational societies should coexist on campus with both offering eating and dining facilities.[72]

The board meetings in March and April 1967 were emotional affairs, with several members expressing deep positive convictions about fraternities and their place in the college. Armstrong replied that there was strong faculty support for the committee report.[73] But the board, perhaps because it did not want to alienate important segments of the community, rejected Armstrong's recommendations and voted: (1) to allow fraternities to continue to feed and house students as long as their facilities conformed to standards approved by the college and (2) to build social–dining units with which every student would be affiliated (although they could also join fraternities or sororities).[74]

Armstrong has said that the trustees' decision was "the great day of defeat for him" during an otherwise successful administration. He recalled that many trustees, while well-meaning, "were out of touch with the fraternities and the times in various ways."[75] In any case, the board had breathed new life into the system, and although the fraternities and the social dining units were to be coordinate, not competitive, students would choose between the two and their preferences would determine the fate of the fraternities. Neither Armstrong nor the trustees would have guessed that, in the next three years, students would not only completely reject the societies but also, increasingly, turn away from fraternities.

The social–dining units (or SDUs, as they were called) never caught on with the students. President Armstrong called it a "failure of concept not a failure of facilities";[76] and Dean O'Brien argued that student tastes were changing so rapidly in the late 1960s that, by the time the units were completed in 1970, the concept of eating and socializing in groups of approximately one hundred had become outmoded. "There is considerable question," O'Brien wrote, "about whether facilities with the concept of 'sociality' can sustain themselves in the current student mood of privatism. A much heavier direction from administration and faculty fellows is necessary if the units are to be more than 'facilities' or 'BOG North.'"[77] Since most students were forming small groups based on intense friendships, they had little need for membership in large organizations such as dining units.[78]

Lack of student interest also caused the decline of the fraternities. Ninety percent of the sophomore men were in fraternities in 1960, and 85 percent were members in 1965. But by the fall of 1969, only 50 percent of that class had pledged, and by 1973, only 20 percent of Middlebury men (including freshmen) were "brothers."[79] The change in student values was, of course, a major factor here. Students had become less interested in "frivolous" activities and tended to reject organizations that encouraged or even condoned selectivity, inequality, and antiintellectualism.[80] The *Campus* reported in 1973 that a common student image of a fraternity man at Middlebury was "a jock with a six-pack under one arm, a girl under the other, and with a football helmet on his head."[81] The change in Vermont's legal drinking age from twenty-one to eighteen and the liberalization of parietal hours (see chapter 14) ended the fraternity's near-monopoly on liquor and popular coeducational activities: students could now party and enjoy sexual intimacy in private rooms and engage in social drinking in town bars.[82]

The administration also played an important role. Its insistence that fraternities bring their facilities up to college standards placed heavy financial burdens on them. Expensive sprinkler systems were required after fires destroyed the Theta Chi annex in January 1968 and the Delta Kappa Epsilon house a year later.[83] Delta Tau Omega closed in early 1969 because it could not make the necessary financial investment, Theta Chi folded in 1970 due to heavy indebtedness, Phi Kappa Tau went bankrupt and disbanded after losing membership rapidly in the early 1970s, and Delta Kappa Epsilon did not reorganize after their fire because the cost of rebuilding was prohibitive.[84]

The administration continued to fight attempts by the more viable fraternities to enlarge their dining or housing capacity. As early as 1961, President Stratton and the trustees were on record as opposing any plans to build better facilities for the weaker chapters (ATO and PKT) if they included dining facilities.[85] In 1967–1968, Armstrong persuaded the trustees (over strong objections from some members) not to approve new or enlarged fraternity capacity that would "appear at the time to interfere with the College's own dormitory space and dining facilities, either existing or committed for."[86] Fraternities, whose ability to house and feed students was increasingly unrealistic, were seen as standing in the way of rational planning for college-wide dining and housing. To save money and encourage dining in its own facilities, the college returned only about one-half of the dining fee as a rebate to students who chose to eat off campus. Fraternity members vehemently protested this policy.[87]

The administration carefully kept the trustees informed of the slow collapse of fraternity housing, behavior, and morale. Armstrong told the board in 1969 that the fraternities were displaying "seriously vulgar and distasteful conduct recently, and the housekeeping conditions are still a grievous problem." He went on to state that "the whole question . . . may have to be reopened if the fraternities continue to act irresponsibly."[88] O'Brien also showed increasing impatience, noting in 1970 that most of the houses "continue to slide into ungenteel shabbiness," that there was a "[g]eneral demoralization and discouragement of fraternity life," and that fraternities were merely a "dive away from home."[89] Changing student values and administrative opposition hurt them, but the fraternities often damaged their own cause. Some of the houses were increasingly unsightly and maintained in a messy condition. Drug and parietal rules were constantly violated.[90] When the Delta Kappa Epsilon house burned down in the middle of the night, four Green Mountain College co-eds were forced to flee the building along with the brothers. "There was no doubt as to what the girls were doing in the building at that hour of the morning," Dean Bruce Peterson commented.[91]

Fraternity members tried to convince their fellow students that the houses had changed over the years, and that they were no longer selective, elitist, or interested in the traditional hazing and secret hocus-pocus involved with pledging and initiation. "The pledge system has died," one officer claimed in 1970. "We're just a bunch of guys living together and trying to get out from under college rule."[92] A fraternity announcement in the *Campus* in 1971 made a similar argument:

> The trend is away from hazing, beer blasts, and isolation to community involvement, closer ties with the hill, and a variety of social activities. . . . The structure of a fraternity offers one the alternative of living within the general structure of the college yet being able to decide for himself exactly how he wants to live and what he wants to eat. It is only in the fraternity that self-governance exists totally.[93]

While most of this was undoubtedly true (and indeed, the 1971 rush successfully netted eighty-nine new members), students still remembered that rumors ran rampant after a Delta Kappa Epsilon pledge was hospitalized in 1968 for getting "detergent in his eyes."[94] The fraternities were never able to shed their old image completely.

By 1972–1973, Armstrong and O'Brien were determined to bring the weakened and unwieldy chapters under college control. Armstrong told the trustees in December 1972 that "the president of the IFC submitted his resignation stating that in the past few years the fraternities have lacked the leadership and maturity to act as independent entities and that the college must supply direction."[95] Armstrong agreed, emphasizing that the chapters remained independent and were not really accountable to the college although they continued to feed and house students. O'Brien supported Armstrong's position.

> Moreover there is the problem of fraternities not living up to standards set. Five years of vigorous efforts have led to the conclusion that without college control it is an unrealistic approach. Insofar as fraternities serve a positive social function, it would seem wrong to force them out of existence. Dean O'Brien was also of the opinion that fraternities at Middlebury have never been the deeply negative influence as on other campuses, but are as good or bad as the current house leadership. He sees the issue as being one of independence

cited by the President, and stated that if fraternities are going to continue, their housing and feeding facilities need to become the college's responsibility.[96]

The administration had concluded, Armstrong told the board in April 1973, that the time had come "for the college to end the ambiguous relationship with the fraternities and acquire all their properties."[97] O'Brien informed the board in May that the fraternities had "sought to broaden their financial base and attractiveness by admitting women."[98] They had also asked for a "fair deal" in the distribution of room and board income collected by the college under the comprehensive fee. "In effect," O'Brien said, "the former men's selective fraternities seem about to be turned into coeducational, non-selective independent residences and dining halls. The notion of fraternities as they existed in the past is not a reality at Middlebury today. They are not used in the most efficient way and are financially in need of help." O'Brien recommended "that the college take over the legal and financial responsibility of the current houses, that the facilities continue to function as College residences and that they function as non-selective, coeducational houses, vacancies to be filled on a self-selecting basis rather than rush." After much discussion, the board agreed that "the college should proceed to bring the fraternities under college control and this meant in effect the end of fraternities at Middlebury College." Armstrong was authorized "to negotiate and conclude arrangements for control and/or ownership of all fraternity properties."

Armstrong sent letters to fraternity presidents and alumni boards that summer indicating the trustees' decision and his desire "to negotiate control and/or ownership of fraternity properties and to seek new ways of proceeding in small group living and eating for men and women."[99] The fraternities were shocked and angry, and many alumni were equally upset. During homecoming weekend that fall, the Alumni Council met at Bread Loaf with a large number of students and alumni. There was a long discussion of the fraternity question, and "considerable objection expressed . . . regarding the manner in which the administration had proceeded."[100] The fraternities were especially miffed that they had not even been consulted — merely presented with a fait accompli.[101]

Even many students not affiliated with fraternities came to their defense. Robin Cruise '73, an excellent student who had graduated several months earlier, expressed a widespread view in a letter to the *Campus*. "Somehow those occasional blowouts served a purpose," she wrote, "and proved to be a lesser of two evils when pitted against the prospect of spending another Friday night lost in the labyrinth of Egbert Starr [Library]. There was a lot of what you might call local color emanating mysteriously from Sig Ep, DU, and the other Greek houses. A little local color at Middlebury is not to be sneezed upon." [102] Many students who were not particularly fond of the fraternities resented the college's seeming desire to "control" student life and, as Cruise intimated, to homogenize it in the process.[103]

In response to this flurry of criticism, the Community Council suggested that a fact-finding committee look into the matter. This was done, and to the administration's surprise and disappointment, the committee reported that the six fraternities still operating on campus were in decent financial shape and (in its opinion) should neither be taken over nor abolished. Given the findings of the committee and the strong opposition to closing the fraternities, O'Brien told the trustees, it was "prudent and practical not to press for full ownership of the fraternity properties." [104] He did persuade them to authorize him to work on making contractual agreements with the fraternities that would allow their properties to revert to the college should a fraternity cease to function. Still, after months of wrangling, the fraternities refused to sign any agreement.[105]

Armstrong was upset that the issue of "control" had been misinterpreted. The college, he insisted, had only wanted "long-term control" of the properties so that planning for housing and dining facilities could be more rationally accomplished; it had not sought "proximate" control (i.e., curtailment of student independence).[106] Most students (particularly fraternity members), who were always a bit wary of the administration, could not see that distinction. Thus, the policies for which O'Brien and Armstrong had pressed for nearly a decade—ultimate college control of the fraternities—would have to wait another five years, when Olin Robison's administration finally accomplished their aim.

The change of presidents in 1975 did not alter the desire to bring fraternities under college control. Treasurer Carroll Rikert, Jr., in particular, desired a change in the relationship with the chapters, because their independent existence was costing Middlebury valuable money and planning capability.[107] Dean Wonnacott predicted in 1977 that fraternities would probably "die out" within a few years and be replaced, perhaps, by college-controlled "independent alternatives to living on the hill."[108] The administration had possibly helped this prediction along by raising the room and board rebates to fraternity members at a much slower rate than the increase in the comprehensive fee everyone paid after 1974. The IFC charged that the college was trying "to abolish fraternities gradually through a conscious policy of 'economic strangulation.'" Without an "equitable rebate," they argued, the cost of joining a fraternity would be so high that they would be forced to close."

Arnold McKinney '69, resigning as assistant dean of students in 1977 after five years on the job, agreed that the fraternities could not exist "with the present support they are getting from the college. The way it is now, there's no way they are going to survive." He called on the college to make up its mind—either treat the fraternities as integral members of the community by granting them a fair rebate or abolish them. "I think the fraternity situation at Middlebury is potentially so divisive that if it's not solved," he warned, "it's going to be very bad for the whole college."[109]

In September 1977, President Robison asked Judge Albert W. Coffrin '41, a prominent trustee, to head the Special Committee on Campus Social, Residential and Dining Arrangements with Special Attention to the Fraternities.[110] The committee met twenty-three times during the next year, gathered information from many sources, and, in the spring of 1978, revealed that they favored (by a 9–3–1 vote) the end of fraternity dining at the college.[111] Soon afterward five hundred to one thousand students demonstrated in front of Old Chapel in an attempt to change the administration's mind. During the fall of 1978 chapter members, alumni, and students generally continued to lobby (as they had in 1966 and 1974) for a decision more favorable to the fraternities.[112]

This time, however, they failed. Ironically, the profraternity forces appeared to be in a much stronger bargaining position than in 1974. The houses had shed much of their poor image and had even successfully invited women to eat and live there (although the national organization forbade full membership for women).[113] Delta Kappa Epsilon had been reorganized, and fraternity rushing had been successful.[114] The campus had taken on an increasingly more "conserva-tive" tone since 1969–1971, when the fraternities had reached their nadir in popularity, and general student support was strong.[115] On the other hand, the administration was convincing in its arguments that fraternity dining was costing Middlebury a lot of money. The Coffrin committee admitted that, on its merits, fraternity dining was a good thing; it was only *after* discussing financial matters that they recommended discontinuing it.[116]

The trustees agreed with much of the report and voted in Janu-ary 1979 to end fraternity dining as of June 30, 1980. In addition, they authorized the renovation of Proctor Hall to accommodate fra-ternity members who had formerly eaten off-campus and mandated that Robison negotiate with the houses to bring fraternity property and programs up to college standards.[117]

The Coffrin Committee report and trustee decision angered many fraternity members. Several chapters constructed manifestly hostile and particularly vulgar snow sculptures in 1979 as part of Win-ter Carnival activities. DU's contribution was entitled "shafted," and Chi Psi's entry was named "half moon." Townspeople report-edly complained about the sculptures as "disgusting and obscene," and when the fraternities refused to remove them, the college bull-dozed them.[118]

The faculty, most of whom had grown increasingly hostile toward the fraternities, were enraged at the behavior of the members who were protesting the trustees' action. On March 5, 1979, the faculty passed two resolutions. The first asked the dean of the college to in-vestigate and identify those responsible for "intimidation of guests of the college and also of members of the College staff while they at-tempted to carry out their duties; flagrant violation of College rules; and vandalism and thefts in the College library." The resolution passed almost unanimously. The second resolution, which passed by a 2–1 majority, asked the dean to initiate disciplinary action against those chapters that had "threatened the peace of the college" and, if such threats and disruption continued, to "begin procedures to close them down." (An attempt to strike this latter section was defeated.) Finally, the faculty voted to delete a passage supporting the Cof-frin Committee statement that "fraternities are an important part of Middlebury College life."[119]

After intensive negotiation, the dean of the college published

Document of Understanding: Fraternities in May 1980, which spelled out their new relationship with the college. The six major points were stated at the beginning:

> As of September 1, 1980, the following will be the new situation affecting fraternities and the new responsibilities assumed by the College with regard to fraternities:
>
> A. The College will have assumed the responsibility for providing dining services on campus for all students including those formerly dining at fraternities. Fraternity dining will have ceased by Trustee vote, and the financial rebate for those who formerly dined in fraternities will have been discontinued.
>
> B. Following the directive of the Trustees, the College will have achieved the renovation of the six fraternities so that the fraternity buildings meet standards of physical safety and repair comparable to those used by the College in maintaining College facilities.
>
> C. The College will have assumed the responsibility for the operation and maintenance of the physical plant of the six fraternities on a yeararound basis. The room rebates to fraternity members living in fraternities will have been discontinued.
>
> D. The College will have worked out with each fraternity corporation either an agreement whereby at the option of the fraternity corporation it will have purchased the fraternity property or some arrangement pursuant to the mandate of the Trustees whereby College funds used to renovate non-owned fraternity properties are protected.
>
> E. The College will have the responsibility for endeavoring to achieve full occupancy during the academic year of all fraternity buildings which it is operating and maintaining, and, by virtue of agreement with each fraternity, it will have the responsibility to determine who will live in and use the fraternity buildings during vacations including the summer months.
>
> F. The College will have reached an agreement with those fraternities whose buildings it has purchased, whereby each of those fraternities will be given assurance of use of their house as a fraternity headquarters for a minimum of one year.[120]

In short, the fraternities had retained the privilege to live and socialize together in their houses. They had lost the right of dining there, and the college, which spent over $1 million to purchase and renovate all the fraternity properties in 1979–1980, would henceforth maintain them.[121]

Although the fraternities were somewhat weakened by the new arrangement, they did not die out. They tried instead to adapt, aided among other things by a change in the legal drinking age back to twenty-one and a more conservative national ethos among college students that favored fraternity membership. Faculty and administrators continued to express displeasure with fraternity attitudes and behavior. Steven Rockefeller, dean of college, who like many of his colleagues disliked all-male social groups, attempted to turn the fraternities into coeducational organizations in the spring of 1980. The chapters balked, and Rockefeller finally agreed that the administration would not disband the all-male fraternities over this issue without a "call for action" from the Student Forum, the Community Council, and a significant number of women.[122] The administration, having just renovated and expanded Proctor Dining Hall to accommodate all fraternity men, was also irritated when Zeta Psi tried to set up a meal plan again in 1980–1981. Although Zeta Psi had a good deal of student support, the membership finally capitulated and stopped eating at the house in the spring of 1981.[123]

Fraternities grew in popularity in the early 1980s. Whereas only 17 percent of the men were members in 1979, affiliation jumped to 40 percent four years later. Large alcohol-centered parties were the rage in colleges across the country, and Middlebury chapters could offer them in an atmosphere that students obviously enjoyed.[124] The new success of the fraternities persuaded the Delta Kappa Epsilon alumni to forge an agreement with the college in 1985 by which they would build a new nonresidential house on the land where their former house had burned in 1969. A new undergraduate DKE chapter soon emerged.[125] When Vermont passed a law in 1986 that would raise the drinking age in gradual steps to twenty-one, fraternities (which pretty much ignored the new law at first) began to take the place of town bars as centers of the alcohol-based social life of underaged Middlebury students. In 1985–1986, there were some 20 registered fraternity parties; by 1988–1989, there were 240 such events. As one student wrote: "With the increasing role fraternities must play on this campus, it would seem healthy to have an administration more concerned with the preservation and not the destruction of fraternity life."[126]

As their popularity soared, their behavioral problems did likewise. Alpha Sigma Psi (Slug) was suspended indefinitely in 1983 for drug abuse at its annual dinner dance at Bread Loaf. That same spring, Delta Upsilon was placed on probation for the fall semester after members destroyed property, behaved obnoxiously in the dining hall, and overturned a student's car that was parked too close to the chapter parking lot.[127] Most of these incidents were drug- or alcohol-related, and late in the decade the college and the IFC sought to decrease legal liability by implementing new alcohol regulations and "dry rush" to encourage better behavior and less drunkenness.[128]

But incidents continued to occur. Sigma Phi Epsilon was placed on probation in 1987 for lighting a bonfire, and Delta Upsilon was suspended for a year in 1988 after they displayed a mutilated female mannequin with bloodied breasts during their annual toga party on the weekend of May 7 and 8.[129] Many members of the community were appalled. The Women's Union was incensed and asked the Community Council to disband the fraternity "on the grounds that its actions blatantly disregarded the rights, welfare, and safety of all members in the Middlebury community." [130] The brothers apologized to the community and claimed that the incident was not a "premeditated sexist action." [131] Although a number of people, including Dean of the College John Emerson, called for termination of the chapter, the Community Council conducted a hearing and recommended that the chapter be suspended for one year and placed on probation for the year after. Robison accepted the recommendation, acknowledging that the incident had been "traumatic" and that "there was an extraordinary intensity of emotion surrounding it." He also told the trustees that the "adult community at the College is basically fed up with the fraternities, although they still enjoy substantial support among the students." [132]

Indeed, the DU incident so upset the community that several professors and key administrators were moved in the fall of 1988 to question once again the existence of fraternities. For years the faculty had been dismayed by what they saw as the fraternities' institutionalized sexism, and the mutilated mannequin—which hung uncontested all weekend—demonstrated to many that misogyny and sexism had become the norm. Professor Victor Nuovo moved in September 1988 that the faculty recommend to the president and trustees that fraternities be abolished.[133] The faculty agreed to debate the issue at their November meeting; the Faculty Council, in the interim, determined that "the fraternity system as it is currently constituted does not serve a useful purpose in the life of the College and that it must be radically altered or abolished." The council informed the fraternities that the faculty would recommend abolition unless they agreed to cut all ties with their nationals, refrain from using the Greek letters and the gender-specific name "fraternities," and present a plan that would lead to equal representation of women in their organizations.[134]

Although many students and alumni reacted to these proposals with predictable anger, arguing that fraternities were a crucial center of campus life and that drunkenness would be even worse without them,[135] the chapters did appear to be taking the faculty's concerns seriously. Delta Upsilon organized a number of programs related to gender during their year of suspension and generally tried to mend their ways (and their image). Indeed, their penitential acts won them a probation for 1989–1990, a return to their house in the fall of 1989 (although kegs were banned indefinitely), and a spring rush in 1990.[136] The faculty's obvious concern with single-sex male organizations may have led Kappa Delta Rho to allow two women to pledge in the spring of 1989. They were "brotherized," although their status as "brothers" apparently was not recognized by the national organization.[137] But several incidents in 1989–1990 involving Delta Kappa Epsilon showed a lack of progress—illegal pledge activities and the hospitalization of four students for alcohol poisoning after a fraternity party.[138]

The argument over fraternities was being played out in similar fashion at a number of eastern liberal arts colleges. Amherst and Colby formally abolished their Greek systems early in 1984; Franklin and Marshall withdrew recognition from fraternities and sororities in 1988; and Wesleyan, Bowdoin, St. Lawrence, Gettysburg, and Dickinson, among others, carefully examined their relationship with fraternities. In each case, strong faculty opposition was a major reason for the intense scrutiny and occasional demise of the Greek organizations.[139]

The faculty certainly played a key role at Middlebury. By a vote of 113-13 in March 1989, they recommended that the college in effect "abolish" fraternities by ending their national affiliations and turning them into coeducational residential units.[140] In response, and in preparation for the decennial reaccreditation process, President Robison formed the Task Force on Student Social and Residential Life "to assess the degree to which student social life and behavior may have changed in the ten years since the issuance of the 'Coffrin Committee' report and in the course of this study, to take a particularly close look at the role played by fraternities."[141]

The task force, which issued its report in November 1989, offered twenty-four recommendations, all of which had unanimous support except the one to abolish fraternities by May 30, 1990, which passed by a vote of 11–5. The majority voted for abolition because they found that the structure of fraternities permitted "unacceptable behavior" and promoted "sexist attitudes" and that the fraternities were hindering the college's attempt to develop a truly "multicultural appreciation, understanding, and compassion." The five members who opposed abolition favored reforming the chapters by turning them into coeducational organizations. The majority, however, stated that reform had not worked in the past and that making the fraternities coeducational would not be successful.

> Furthermore, we believe that there is something inherently wrong with mandating a coeducational system through the current fraternity structure. It places women in the position of negotiating for concessions from the fraternities, a posture which places the fraternities in control and which ensures that women will continue to be second-class citizens. The reform approach also puts the College in the untenable position of having to encourage women to join organizations called fraternities.[142]

Reaction was immediate. Fraternity members and supporters angrily denounced the task force recommendations at an all-campus meeting in Mead Chapel. Others, such as the editor of the *Campus*, issued a verbal sigh and urged students to start looking beyond the fraternities for social life.[143]

On January 13, 1990, however, the board of trustees surprised both sides. After two lengthy discussions of the task force recommendations, the trustees voted to accept all of them except the one abolishing fraternities, stating that they could continue to exist if they became truly coeducational and called themselves "houses."

> 1) The Board believes that any social organization which discriminates on the basis of gender or whose practices have the consequence of exclusion on the basis of gender are antithetical to the mission of the College and not appropriate as a mode for our society at large. Ties with any national organization whose rules or practices are at odds with this belief should not be maintained. . . .
> 2) The Board will designate as "houses" the existing spaces now occupied by fraternities. . . . The Board expects that the house system, in fact as well as in name, will be coeducational, and that full and equal membership will be open to all students at Middlebury College.

The trustees gave each fraternity until the end of 1990 either to persuade its national organization to change its rules regarding women members or to sever all ties. Each fraternity had to declare by March 31, 1990, whether or not it would comply with this policy and become a coeducational house. Any chapter that announced that it could not comply would cease to exist on May 31, 1990.[144]

Many faculty members were angry that the board had overturned the task force recommendation, and a number of them drafted a letter to the trustees expressing their "deep dismay" at the decision. The letter once again noted the problems of fraternities—their exclusivity, sexism, intolerance, and "unacceptable anti-social behavior." Their continued existence, the letter added, sent all the wrong messages to the kind of prospective students the college hoped to attract.

> By maintaining any semblance of fraternities at a time when comparable institutions have moved to abolish them, Middlebury will perpetuate a "party school" image, and make it more difficult to move into the front rank of liberal arts colleges. If we are perceived by prospective applicants as a school where seriousness is compromised by indulgence, we will not be able to create a community united in the pursuit of knowledge and moral enlightenment. By continuing to attract students who seek a party atmosphere, we will hinder the growth of diversity and individuality within the student body, and will further alienate those students whose idea of a social occasion does not match the prevailing norms set largely by the fraternities.[145]

At a special meeting in January 1990 the faculty passed a formal resolution in which they attempted to implement further and make more specific the trustees' general policy statement. First, they called for the establishment of a deadline "by which time the fraternities must be fully integrated by gender in both their membership and leadership." Second, they asked that the "houses" be filled by regular room draw rather than "the mechanism of self-selection."[146]

The spring of 1990 was a difficult time for the fraternities. Their leaders were in a quandary as to how to proceed: most of them were not opposed to accepting women, but they knew that their nationals were unlikely to recognize their chapters if they became coeducational houses. For some, a split with the national would be particularly unfortunate—Kappa Delta Rho was founded at Middlebury and Chi Psi had one of its oldest chapters at the college. Moreover, the fraternities had been given a relatively short period in which to decide, and they resented the faculty's attempt to make compliance itself more rigorous and timely. While rumors circulated that several chapters would go underground rather than adopt the trustees' standards, by the summer of 1990 it appeared that most, if not all, might comply.[147]

The twenty-five years (1965–1990) during which Middlebury de-emphasized fraternities, brought them under college control, and moved to transform them into coeducational houses had been a long, painful, and divisive period. The fond memories that many alumni retained of their fraternity days, and the fears of undergraduates (members and nonmembers alike) that the college wished to "control" their lives more completely, convinced many that the administration was wrong in seeking to abolish fraternities or curtail their independence. Once the trustees refused to accept Armstrong's recommendations in 1966, they unknowingly ushered in a period of almost unrelieved hostility and bitterness between many students and the administration that soured campus life (at times considerably) for the next twenty-five years. Dean Reynolds had been prescient in 1965 when he argued: "It is to be hoped that in the relatively near future fraternities may be removed from their present limbo. They should either be more encouraged as a vital part of the institution or done away with. If merely tolerated, they will, in the long run, be sources of constant disruption in student life." [148]

CHAPTER 12

SOCIAL AND
EXTRACURRICULAR LIFE

Page after page of societies and clubs and records of organizations, each with its offices, committees, and statement of activities. In the sketches of students, note the number of officers and assignments after each name. Of course, I know that many of these things are merely nominal and demand little time or interest. But others are not nominal and require a great deal of both interest and time. I can imagine a thoughtful stranger turning over the page of that [yearbook] and saying—How in the name of twenty-four hours which make up a day [do] those young men and women find time to study? Probably a truthful answer would be that a good many of them don't.

—President John Thomas, *Middlebury Campus*,
September 24, 1919

In 1924 we, as freshman males, were a rather repressed submissive lot, kept in a state of subjection by sophomore paddles and volunteer upperclass gendarmes; never daring to appear in public uncrowned by our limp blue caps; . . . required to use the long-way-round paved walks, no matter how late to class we were, never daring to take the convenient, muddy shortcuts engraved across the campus greensward by upper classmen; restricted in wearing apparel to the least colorful garments—not knickers, no gay stockings, or sweaters; rounded up periodically like cattle for participation in P-rades, the Hat-scrap, and community prayers for rain under the windows of the women's dormitory. With more or less continuity all this hocus-pocus had survived for generations and we conveyed it to the next.

—W. Storrs Lee '28, *Middlebury College
Magazine* 3 (summer 1989): 60

What the College seems to ignore, or fail to admit, was that there has been a serious "drug problem" with Middlebury students since

the late 1960s. During my tenure at Middlebury [1970–1974], marijuana, acid, speed, and "downs" were as common as the Foley's truck
every Friday. Any student could partake of any of these things if he
or she had the bucks to spend—and most did. This was everyday
life. People dealt drugs, people bought drugs, and people did drugs—
some professors included.

> —David Y. Parker '74, letter to editor,
> *Middlebury College Magazine* 2 (summer
> 1988): 3

People come here and study hard, they play sports really hard, and
they go downtown really hard, but that's about it. That's our big three
and when it comes to extracurricular activities you have a small core
of people that really get out there, and then most other people really
don't give a damn.

> —Ari Fleischer '82, *Middlebury Campus*, April
> 23, 1982

Although fraternities dominated social and extracurricular life
from 1915 to the late 1960s, there were many other outlets for a student's time and energy: sororities, class and religious activities, a
myriad of clubs and organizations, and traditional all-college events.
(Athletics, political involvement in and beyond college affairs, and
social service endeavors will be considered in later chapters.) Of
course, changing student values and interests had a decisive influence
here. Sororities flourished in the relatively conservative and carefree
decades of the 1920s and 1950s but were nearly abolished by the
more sober and idealistic students of the 1930s and 1940s and were
finally terminated (along with many other traditional activities) in
the late 1960s by a particularly iconoclastic generation. Some activities and organizations—Winter Carnival, the Mountain Club, the
school paper, and others—proved their staying power by continuing
to flourish, while religion moved increasingly to the periphery.

Sororities were important at Middlebury until the late 1960s even
though they never approached the power or influence of the fraternities or, for that matter, of sororities at many other colleges and
universities.[1] The Middlebury sororities never had "houses" as such,
although they often rented rooms downtown for their use.[2] They
sponsored social activities, encouraged scholastic excellence through
intersorority competition, and engaged in a variety of social welfare

projects on and off campus.[3] Sororities were popular in the 1920s, with some two-thirds of the women belonging to one of the six chapters, each of which was affiliated with a national by the end of 1925: Kappa Kappa Gamma (formerly Alpha Chi), Pi Beta Phi, Sigma Kappa, Delta Delta Delta, Alpha Xi Delta, and Phi Mu.[4]

Although there was some student opposition to sororities in the 1920s, the majority apparently supported their continuation. This changed radically in the early 1930s; a student poll in 1932 revealed that students favored the abolition of sororities by a vote of 341–172. (The continuation of fraternities, on the other hand, was supported by a vote of 420–98.)[5] A resolution presented by the pledges of Kappa Kappa Gamma that spring revealed some of the reasons: first, "the vast majority of Middlebury women" were said to face financial problems that would prevent them from belonging were it not for a social stigma attached to nonmembership; second, in a small college like Middlebury there were other ways for a woman to gain experience in service and leadership through campus activities. The protestors were unhappy that sororities had the power to influence campus elections—and not always in the most helpful manner. They also disliked the antidemocratic character of the system, which mandated that women be chosen from an already select group and that "social privileges" be assigned to some but not to others. Shortly afterward a mass meeting of sorority women decided to defer rushing of freshmen for one year.[6]

The antisorority women demanded a vote in 1932–1933 on the question of the abolition of sororities. The vote was 72–61 for abolition, but it fell short of the required two-thirds majority.[7] Many sorority women were disappointed that their campaign to close the chapters had failed, and sixty-one freshmen women (about three-quarters of that class) successfully petitioned for indefinite postponement of sorority rushing.[8] Meanwhile, alumnae and national sorority leaders apparently brought pressure to retain the chapters.[9] President Moody told the trustees in June 1933 that "the present discussion regarding abolition of sororities at Middlebury College has reached a point where it is becoming detrimental to the best interests of the College," and the trustees authorized him to appoint a committee to investigate.

The committee, chaired by biology professor Raymond Barney, voted almost unanimously to abolish sororities.[10] Moody, apparently under pressure from some trustees, disregarded the report and announced in December that the sororities would once again resume their normal operation and conduct a rush for the first time in over two years. The sorority women, however, had other ideas. In January 1934 they presented Moody with a petition signed by 158 women (out of 294 enrolled) asking the college to abolish sororities.[11] The trustees were thereby forced to decide the issue. The prudential committee read the report of the investigating committee and reported back a motion on January 26 to abolish sororities; the full board, however, declined to "prohibit the existence of sororities at Middlebury College."[12] The sorority system therefore continued, but some felt that the chapters never entirely regained the strength they had attained before the 1932–1934 "revolt."[13]

Sororities came under attack again after World War II as elitist, discriminatory, and frivolous.[14] Once again, however, they survived and, like many other traditional activities, actually thrived in the 1950s.[15] But in the 1960s a new campus environment—greater student and college emphasis on academic excellence and growing student alienation from traditional group activities—proved fatal. Stratton informed the board as early as 1960 that a survey of upperclasswomen revealed that 25 percent of them thought sororities were not worthwhile. (Upperclassmen were nearly unanimous in their belief that fraternities were worthwhile.)[16]

The *Campus* argued in 1961 that the Middlebury sororities lacked any "vital function" that could not be performed at least as well by other groups. They encouraged "grade grubbing" and memorization rather than learning; they wasted valuable time holding "lengthy discussions on the relative merits of potential members and the planning of parties to impress and entertain them"; and they preserved "personality clans" instead of molding "individualistic young women." In short, the editorial concluded, many Middlebury women who had already "outgrown the Girl Scouts, feel they have passed the sophomoric stage of development represented by sororities." Those who still belonged should "take a serious look at the purpose of their organizations to determine whether they are clinging to a tradition antiquated by modern demands and actualities."[17] A member complained in 1962 that sororities were frivolous. "If we work according to the idea," she wrote, "that we spend our time and energy where our greatest interest lies, the value of being a sorority raised big doubts. We are not in college to make name tags or pour tea."[18]

Despite such criticism and declining student interest, the sororities might still have hung onto a precarious existence except for a
controversy over discrimination that hastened and ensured their dis-
solution.[19] In the early 1960s the Middlebury chapters tried to avoid
the issue of pledging blacks. One Sigma Kappa officer wrote in 1963:
"Although no Sigma Kappa chapter has ever pledged a Negro there
is no legal reason why we could not. We don't feel that the present
is the time to force the issue as feeling is still high among many of
our national members."[20] The five Middlebury sororities did vote in
1966 to send resolutions to their nationals affirming their commitment to nondiscriminatory membership policies, and one group—
Alpha Xi—left the national over the issue.[21]

Nevertheless, a black woman pledging Sigma Kappa charged in
the spring of 1968 that the sorority was discriminating against her.
The members told the administration that they were working on
changing the position of their national on this issue. Dean O'Brien
responded that that was fine but that if they did not succeed, the college would have to take steps to protect the rights of all students.[22]
After attempting without success that summer to modify the policies of their nationals, the Middlebury chapters were dealt a death
blow when the student senate voted in 1969 not to allow on campus sororities that discriminated against, blackballed, or had ritual
prayers that offended minorities.[23] The board's prudential committee approved the student senate resolution on February 8, 1969.[24]
Although they were given two years to comply with these regulations, the sororities decided they could not meet that deadline and
disbanded that spring.[25]

Students engaged in a wide variety of extracurricular activities in the
half-century after 1915. Indeed, President Thomas argued as early as
1919 that it was the "large number of subsidiary interests" that was
taking up "so large a proportion of the student's time." One only had
to look at the *Kaleidoscope* (the college yearbook) to see the trend,
he wrote:

> Page after page of societies and clubs and records of organizations,
> each with its officers, committees, and statement of activities. In the
> sketches of students note the number of offices and assignments after
> each name. Of course, I know that many of these things are merely
> nominal and demand little time or interest. But others are not nomi-
> nal and require a great deal of both interest and time. I can imagine

In 1931 the Mountain Club held a sugar-on-snow party at Bread Loaf. Students tapped the maples and boiled the sap for syrup, providing a sweet break after a long winter.

a thoughtful stranger turning over the page of that [yearbook] and saying—How in the name of twenty-four hours which make up a day [do] those young men and women find time to study? Probably a truthful answer would be that a good many of them don't.[26]

Student organizations abounded: musical groups such as Black Panthers, A Tempo, orchestra, band, college choir, and men's and women's glee clubs; academic-interest clubs like Le Cercle Francais, Der Deutsche Verein, English Club, El Club Espanol, Economics Club, and others; student publications, including the *Campus*, the *Kaleidoscope*, the *Saxonian* (literary magazine), and the handbook; honor societies such as Mortar Board, Waubanakee, Blue Key, and Phi Beta Kappa; and a myriad of others.[27] Perhaps the most popular and influential groups were the Mountain Club, founded in 1932, which arranged hikes and outings and organized the annual Winter Carnival; the Dramatics Club, which usually had the most members during the 1920s and 1930s; the Liberal Club and Women's Forum, both of which fostered debate and concern over such interwar issues as peace and the rise of fascism; the student-managed college radio station WRMC(S), which began operating out of a

Addresses by graduating seniors were a part of commencement celebrations from the time of Middlebury's first commencement in 1802. In 1955 Class Day provided the setting for seniors to address an audience of classmates and juniors on the lawn below Old Chapel.

converted chicken coop in 1949 and soon became an important part of campus life; and the men's and women's debating teams, which were particularly active between the wars.[28] There were thirty-seven student groups on campus in 1925 and sixty-seven by 1932 — an average of one for every nine students, one of the highest ratios of any New England college.[29]

Although there were occasional echoes of Thomas's fear that some students spent too much time in too many activities,[30] the Moody administration favored extracurricular involvement and even proposed in 1923 that participation in such activities be a graduation requirement.[31] The new rule was supposed to help students be more socially adept and better prepared for a life of service after graduation. It was generally agreed that a strong dose of extracurricular activities would help "make impossible the 'grind,' the nervous breakdown," and ensure each student a "well-rounded college life."[32]

Until the 1960s class activities and interclass rivalries also played an important role. Several of the principal annual occasions were at least in part class activities, including Senior Week (during commencement) and Junior Week (later Junior Weekend), which featured numerous social and athletic events each spring.[33] There was the memorable "tapping" of juniors, in chapel, for membership in the college's most prestigious honor societies: Mortar Board (formerly Banshees) for junior women, Waubanakee for junior men, and Blue Key, which tapped five graduating seniors, fifteen juniors, and five sophomores each year.[34]

To ensure that freshmen males understood their place at the bottom of the student hierarchy, they were immediately "admitted" into an intensive course in Middlebury traditions by the upperclassmen, highlighted by the "Midd-Nite" entertainments early in the fall and the "P-rade" at the Norwich or University of Vermont football game, during which the freshmen dressed up as co-eds, hula-hula maids, fairies, and the like.[35] They were forced to endure a variety of traditional undergraduate indignities, such as wearing beanies, walking only on sidewalks, dressing in strange costumes, being pelted with eggs and water balloons, being left at night miles from the college without transportation and directions, and withstanding physical abuse — ducking, hitting, tripping, and, in particular, paddling. Although the administration strongly disapproved of the more dangerous varieties of this "hazing,"[36] the *Campus* in 1929 supported paddling "unruly youngsters" who had not learned the college traditions:

> The results obtained were quite satisfactory. Paddling, when properly administered, it will be granted, does much more good than harm. It is the only way that things can be instilled in some people's minds. In such cases, physical impulses are necessary to bring about moral effects. We have come to school, not merely to get book learning, but also to learn how to get along with our fellowmen. Some people have this quality in their personalities and others must have it taught to them.[37]

College opposition made paddling and other forms of harsh physical hazing less prevalent after World War I, but more innocuous forms of hazing were allowed, as W. Storrs Lee has recently recalled.

> In 1924 we, as freshman males, were a rather repressed submissive lot, kept in a state of subjection by sophomore paddles and volunteer upperclass gendarmes; never daring to appear in public uncrowned by our limp blue caps; . . . required to use the long-way-around paved walks, no matter how late to class we were, never daring to take the

convenient, muddy shortcuts engraved across the campus greensward by upper classmen; restricted in wearing apparel to the least colorful garments—not knickers, no gay stockings, or sweaters; rounded up periodically like cattle for participation in P-rades, the Hat-scrap, and community prayers for rain under the windows of the women's dormitory. With more or less continuity all this hocus-pocus had survived for generations and we conveyed it to the next.[38]

In the 1920s only a freshman victory in the annual sophomore-freshman game would put an end once and for all to that year's hazing. Because of the stakes involved, everybody took the game seriously. Earl Hindes '28 has recalled that as freshmen in a French class in Old Chapel, he and Red Hill '28 saw through the open window a group of sophomores attempting to kidnap the star freshman lineman, Gordon Wiley '28. Hindes, Hill, Bill Donald '28, and others dashed out of the room, with class still in session, and thwarted the kidnapping. They also won the game.[39]

Some hazing was quite open, and even the faculty did not disapprove. Professor Myron Sanford was quite charmed in 1923 by the freshman who passed him on the way to chapel one day "turning handsprings up the slope, and saying with each handspring, "I'm a kangaroo, I'm a kangaroo." Indeed, Sanford felt that hazing "of an innocent nature" could be valuable in "helping a chesty high school graduate come down to his proper status."[40]

While freshmen and sophomore men continued their interclass rivalries such as cane-rushes and Hat-scraps in the 1920s and the rope-pull during Junior Week, the dominance of fraternities significantly weakened class ties and traditions among the men.[41] The Blue Key society was entrusted in 1931 with the "education" of the freshmen, and except in the immediate postwar years they attacked their duty with relish.[42] The veterans who returned to campus after 1945 would have none of the sophomoric paddles and other hazing.[43]

Students rebelled against the Blue Key hazing in the 1960s, and most of these traditions began falling by the wayside. As one student wrote: "The Freshmen are not taught humility that comes in the presence of great ideas and wise teachers; rather they learn the stubborn resistance characteristic of [the] oppressed."[44] The administration saw the need for a different kind of influence by upperclassmen, and Dean Reynolds initiated a Junior Fellows Program in 1958, which placed twenty-six outstanding upperclassmen in the freshman halls

to help orient the newcomers to college life. It was far more constructive than hazing. The results included a significant reduction in
academic failures among freshmen.[45]

Although both men and women engaged in hazing, the women
apparently developed a set of more elaborate and meaningful class
traditions. Unlike the men, the women's college was not dominated
by Greek organizations, and class distinctions and traditions, as
in women's colleges throughout the East, were important.[46] Freshmen women were hazed by the sophomores and forced to follow
a variety of rules, as Dorothy Tillapaugh Headley '25 wrote in her
freshman year:

> Then yesterday afternoon, the sophs at last gave us our rules. We
> had to march, the length of a corridor . . . between two rows of jeer-
> ing sophs, into a darkened room where we proceeded to fall all over
> ourselves, of course we did it gracefully. Then they called roll, gave us
> some supposedly good advice, handed us our rules, etc., made a few
> sarcastic remarks & sent us home. They wouldn't let you laugh on
> the outside (of you) but I never laughed so hard in my toes in all my
> life. Some of the girls, however, were properly impressed, & scared.
> Here are the rules—about the same as last year:—
>
> 1. Learn these rules & be able to recite them at any time.
> 2. Wear, at all times, the regulation green tam (Suns. excepted).
> 3. Always carry powder & a powder puff for the use of the wise
>   sophomores.
> 4. As a proof of your infancy, wear your napkin tied around your
>   neck at table. (I wish you could see us at table with our bibs &
>   tams!!!)
> 5. For your own welfare, innocent ones, obtain permissions from
>   some sophomore to attend movies.
> 6. Your inferior position demands that you assist the all-intelligent
>   Sophomores by carr[y]ing books, bundles, etc. with which they
>   may be laden.
> 7. Never use outside steps of Old Chapel, nor linger on steps of
>   New Chapel.
> 8. Never cut Campus. This privilege is reserved for your worthy
>   superiors.
> 9. Never form a group of more than two Freshman girls, on Cam-
>   pus. Keep moving!
> 10. Never use the benches on Campus.
> 11. Never pass thro a door in front of an upper classman.
> 12. Possessing a limited amount of intelligence, never ask a favor of
>   any Sophomore.[47]

The cane ceremony behind Forest Hall saw the passing of replicas of Gamaliel Painter's cane from the senior women to the women of the junior class, followed by a procession of the seniors under an arch of canes.

Junior and senior women performed certain class rituals during the final months of each year. The senior women would attempt to sneak away for a class breakfast at dawn, unmolested by the junior women, who would try to stop them or surprise them at their secret location.[48] During Junior Week, the juniors would gather on the steps of the senior women's dormitory and serenade them. At a separate ceremony (beginning in 1937) each senior woman would present her Gamaliel Painter cane to a junior, and on Class Day, the juniors would escort the seniors to a location on campus where a class tree would be planted.[49] The seniors also went to Bread Loaf to spend a last day and night alone as a class. "There, before a bonfire, each woman will confess to her sisters all the sins which she has committed during the past four years." Upon their return, the Old Chapel bell was tolled "to indicate their arrival and their reunion with the rest of the college."[50]

Although most class events, aside from dances and parties, were sex-segregated, there were a few class activities for men and women together. Although there was no formal orientation program in the 1920s to introduce freshmen to the college and to one another, there was occasionally a freshman weekend outing at Bread Loaf in the fall. Dorothy Tillapaugh Headley '25 enthusiastically wrote home about such an event in 1921. After walking up the mountain from East Middlebury on Saturday, the freshmen settled in their quarters, danced, ate some good meals, toasted marshmallows, hiked, posed (in the shape of an *M*) for an official class picture, and got to know one another. "There had been little previous opportunity for the 'men' and 'women' (as now we all, being so very grown-up, referred to each other) to get acquainted. Many freshman classes were segregated; I think I had only one class that first year that wasn't entirely female. Thus it was a big event to have all our classmates together." [51] Freshmen outings at Bread Loaf during Orientation were a big hit and served similar purposes in the 1970s and 1980s.

Arguably, the highlight of the social season was the Mountain Club's annual Winter Carnival, a popular college weekend event since it was first presented in its modern format in 1934. As early as February 1920 (and intermittently thereafter until 1934), Middlebury held a holiday or "carnival" of sports events and social activities modeled on the Dartmouth Winter Carnival. The site was either Chipman Hill and Noble's Grove in the village or Chapel Hill and Pearsons' Hill on campus. [52] In the early days there were obstacle races, snowshoe races along Storrs Avenue, cross-country and alpine ski races around campus, ski jumping, and other games. By the 1930s men's and women's teams began to compete against guests from other colleges in a variety of skiing events (moved to Bread Loaf in the 1940s). The occasion also featured hockey and basketball games, skating shows and snow sculpture competitions, a king and queen of the carnival coronation, and two big dances—a formal Carnival Ball and an informal Klondike Rush. [53]

Nearly all campus clubs and organizations had one thing in common—they held dances. In 1917 the faculty limited general college dances to one a month, and allowed each fraternity and sorority only one dance and two other entertainments during the entire year. [54] This changed dramatically in the interwar years, which featured both in-

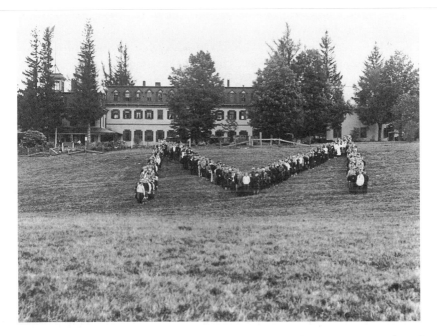

Forming an M *for a class picture faded from the program, but outings to Bread Loaf remained a feature of the first fall at Middlebury from the 1920s on.*

formal and formal dances by the score. Indeed, every weekly activity calendar was filled with opportunities for dancing. The most common affair was the small informal Saturday dance (twenty-five to thirty-five couples) at a fraternity, but there were also large dances held by the Saxonian Board, the French Club, the Hepburn Commons waiters, the "M" Club, each of the classes (the Frosh Frolic, the Sophomore Hop, the Junior Prom, the Senior Ball), and other groups. There were even informal "Depression" dances in the 1930s, with many participants wearing patched clothing "which lent the desired effect of poverty to the atmosphere." [55]

The dances and other annual events, such as the French Club's Halloween Party and the Spanish Carnival, all had to be chaperoned by faculty members or trustees, and there were stringent rules on curfews, conduct, and even lighting: "What a meeting the student life committee must have had when they passed that resolution about the minimum number of lamps and required candle power to be used at college informal dances. The idea—measuring human relations in watts and ohms!" [56] But lighting *was* critical. The great flood of 1927 temporarily cut off all electricity to the campus, and Dean Ross informed Fred Whittemore '28 that the dance that evening (which Fred had organized) would have to be canceled. Not easily deterred, Fred ventured down to Prexy Moody's house hoping for a different verdict. Moody was not home, but Mrs. Moody told him to go ahead with the dance and assured him that she and Prexy would be there to chaperone along with the Burrages and Dean Hazeltine. Fred remembered the evening as a grand success:

> A full moon guided our steps to the gym, the inside of which was ablaze with a multitude of candles. Mysteriously, by intermission time all the candles seem to have been extinguished, save for those in the chaperones' corner. Miss Ross arrived just in time to observe Prexy and Dean Hazeltine blowing out the last of the candles. The dance resumed and was one of the best and longest of our four years. [57]

The formal dances were usually highlighted by a live band, often the college's own Black Panthers, and the most important dances (Carnival Ball, Junior Prom, Senior Ball) often featured nationally known groups such as the Glenn Miller or Artie Shaw bands. [58] Yet one World War II veteran remembers the college dances as "sterile" affairs; after taking their dates home at a required (and usually early) hour, the men would return to their dorms or fraternities for long nights of "bull sessions" and carousing, while the women engaged in their own forms of sex-segregated conversation and entertainment. [59]

Student activities and interests changed markedly after 1965. Clubs and other organized activities became less popular as students looked for other outlets to "do their own thing." Class traditions and freshman hazing slowly disappeared and were dropped completely around 1970, as students simply ignored traditional activities. [60] Even interest in the Winter Carnival's nonathletic events dwindled. [61] The increased use of automobiles, the popularity of marijuana and other drugs, and the end of parietal hours (see chapter 14) all reinforced the students' rejection of big institutional activities in favor of intense relationships with small groups. [62] By 1976 the *Campus* noted that student interest in organized pursuits was at a low ebb and that hardly "any club or group on campus can boast a large or particularly loyal membership." [63]

Things improved somewhat in the 1980s. A popular and innovative May Days Festival, inaugurated in 1980, included the en-

Replacing a variety of more disorderly spring parties, Erica Wonnacott organized Middlebury's first "May Days" celebration in 1980.

tire community in its variety of events, and organizations such as WRMC, which was upgraded in 1981 from a ten-watt local station to a hundred-watt stereo station serving much of the Champlain Valley, continued to attract enthusiastic members. The college attempted to bolster student activities in 1987 by hiring six recent graduates as residence hall assistants, part of whose job would be to encourage more cocurricular programming. Middlebury, by circumstances and philosophy, was strongly committed to being a residential school, and only about fifty or sixty students lived off campus each year. "We're a residential college," Dean Erica Wonnacott stated in 1987, "and it's important that students live in and participate in the community here." The activities fee was increased from $80 to $160 in 1989 so that more student programming could be funded.[64] But the college in 1990 still looked less "organized" than it had in the 1950s. As Ari Fleischer '82 stated: "People come here and study hard, they play sports really hard, and they go downtown really hard, but that's about it. That's our big three and when it comes to extracurricular activities you have a small core of people that really get out there, and then most other people really don't give a damn."[65]

Middlebury students also enjoyed going to movies and an increasing number of college-sponsored concerts and lectures. Some students liked movies even before World War I, despite warnings that most movies, as the *Campus* argued in 1917, were "of no ultimate moral value, and by their very cheapness and misrepresentation of real life render callow the sensibilities and warp the moral perspective."[66] Yet a year later, as moral a group as the college YMCA was sponsoring motion pictures in McCullough Gym every Wednesday and Saturday evening, and they went so far as to invite "the girls to enjoy the pictures with them," thereby sacrificing their usual smoking and singing.[67] Students also went downtown regularly to see movies and savor an ice cream cone at Calvi's.

Given Middlebury's isolation, most cultural and intellectual programs had to be imported. Before World War I, little had been done in this regard except to secure occasional visiting ministers who would speak at Sunday vespers. But the trustees voted to spend $2,000 for lectures and entertainment in the 1919–1920 academic year. The students were understandably elated:

> ... the fact that Middlebury is three hundred miles "from Broadway" though fortunate in some respects, has certain disadvantages which are being removed with difficulty by the Board of Trustees. ... The committee [on student life] has secured expert aid in making selections, especially the musical, and it is highly probable that a number of concerts and lectures worthy to be heard and remembered will be arranged.[68]

The students were not disappointed. The entertainment series in 1921 included Williams Jennings Bryan, the Boston Symphony Orchestra, Pablo Casals, and the New York Chamber Music Society.[69] For Don Banks '24, who came from a small town in New York, Bryan's appearance was one of the highlights of his life. After Bryan mesmerized the overflow crowd in Mead Chapel with nearly an hour of his glorious vocal magic, he invited people to come forward and shake his hand. Banks, whose father idolized the famous orator, stood in line with hundreds of others and slowly made his way to greet him. When it was finally his turn to shake the great man's hand, he froze, and Bryan had to encourage him forward. Banks never forgot the incident, although he cannot remember at all what Bryan said that day![70] During the next seventy years, the college helped arrange an ever-increasing and varied program of speakers, concerts, artists, and other cultural and intellectual programs for the enjoyment of students, college staff, and townsfolk; and many young people, particularly those from rural or provincial backgrounds, such as Don Banks, received quite an education outside the classroom in the process.

During the Armstrong and Robison years, the quality and quantity of such occasions expanded at a high rate.[71] The list of events in "This Week at Middlebury" usually took up one page in 1975; ten years later it had expanded to both sides of two or even three pages. Indeed, staff and faculty in the 1980s were sometimes nearly overwhelmed at the prospect of supporting such an array of concerts, movies, lectures, and club and organization activities.[72] Several special events stood out, including two successful appearances by the humorist Garrison Keillor, who broadcast his popular *Prairie Home Companion* radio show on May 7, 1983, and May 28, 1988, from Mead Chapel.[73]

Even more memorable was the visit of the Dalai Lama in the fall of 1984 as part of the Symposium on the Christ and the Bodhisattva organized by Dean Steven Rockefeller and Professor Donald Lopez. By all accounts the symposium and the Dalai Lama's visit were an unprecedented occasion. Over thirteen thousand seats were filled during the various symposium events as visitors came from around the world to witness the Dalai Lama interact with students, faculty, children, his devoted followers, and (somewhat less auspiciously) Bill Buckley, who interviewed him in Mead Chapel as part of the conservative journalist's *Firing Line* television show. Students called the week "inspirational," "thrilling," and "eye-opening." "No visitor in recent years has left such a deep impression on Middlebury as the Dalai Lama," said the *Campus*, "and no one has ever captured the entire student body so completely."[74]

Six years later, in 1990, he returned to take part in another conference organized by Steven Rockefeller—"Spirit and Nature: Religion, Ethics, and Environmental Crisis." He was joined this time by five religious scholars, and the result was another remarkable experi-

During his second visit to Middlebury, the Dalai Lama ate lunch with students in Proctor Hall. William Arron Jenkins '94 shared lunch and conversation with him in 1990.

ence.[75] The two visits by the Dalai Lama symbolized the international flavor and outlook that Robison had helped bring to the college's programs year-round.

As in much of American society, "drinking" was almost always part of life beyond the classroom at Middlebury, particularly since 1865. Even during Prohibition, students found a way to consume alcohol. Zeke Bliss '28 recently recalled that during his undergraduate days, when he was in charge of closing Starr Library on weekend evenings, he often had to deal with some of the boys who "were able to secure a bottle or two" and had chosen the library for their "evening revelry."[76] Of course, styles change, and the large, open, alcohol-centered parties of the 1960s and after were not a common occurrence in earlier decades, when drinking was more of a private individual or group activity, often restricted to men. And although the legal drinking age in Vermont was twenty-one from the end of Prohibition until 1971, underage students found a way to drink, either in the fraternities or (particularly in the 1950s and 1960s) by crossing the border into New York, where the legal age was eighteen. The return rides, unfortunately, were occasionally fatal, and memorial services for students who died during those trips occurred much too often.[77]

After Vermont lowered the legal age to eighteen, students who wanted to drink could frequent bars downtown, attend the open fraternity parties, or just create their own private party in the dorms.

Indeed, campus drinking apparently increased substantially in the 1970s and after, due both to the lower drinking age and to changes in national drinking norms, including a greater consumption of beer and other alcoholic beverages by women. In addition, as the college became more demanding academically and many students felt under greater pressure to do well in courses, larger numbers of them may have begun to look forward to the weekend as a time to drink (heavily in some cases) to reduce anxieties.

While there were many cases of students in the 1950s and 1960s who abused alcohol, it was in the late 1970s that premeditated drunkenness among a significant percentage of the student body apparently took hold at Middlebury.[78] The college (along with most other schools that had dismantled their in-loco-parentis apparatus in the 1960s) did relatively little to regulate drinking until Vermont, under pressure from federal authorities, raised the legal drinking age back to twenty-one in 1986 (with a grandfather clause that delayed the full impact of the law until 1988–1989).[79]

In 1985, to prepare for this coming change, the college organized the "21" Committee, whose recommendations for innovative alternative programming, new social spaces, and increased alcohol education programs formed the basis for Middlebury's alcohol policy during the remainder of the decade.[80] Under the leadership of Jim Terhune '86, the college spent $75,000 in January 1988 to transform the old Zeppelin room in the Cook social–dining unit into The Undergraduate, a chic, nonalcoholic pub modeled on The Rosebud, a popular downtown bar that had recently closed. The Gamut Room, a nonalcoholic coffeehouse in Gifford South, was opened in the fall of 1989. It was hoped that the new student center, when completed, would provide space for nonalcoholic programming.[81]

The college also began tightening its drinking regulations. By 1987–1988, kegs were prohibited in dormitories, all students were "carded" before they could enter events (including fraternity parties) at which alcoholic beverages were available, and such events were more carefully monitored and structured.[82] Underage students were still able to obtain alcholic beverages for consumption in their rooms by using false identification or by enlisting the help of older students, but there apparently was a decrease in public drinking and drunkenness and a concomitant rise in private drinking and dorm damage in the residence halls. The administration informed the trustees that at least one hundred kegs of beer had been consumed during one spring weekend in 1988 and that "we have strong alcohol programs in operation on campus, but there is still a serious problem."[83]

Illegal drugs were also an important part of the social scene after about 1965.[84] Students experimented with marijuana, LSD, "speed," and a variety of other substances, as a 1974 graduate recently recalled:

> What the College seems to ignore, or fail to admit, was that there has been a serious "drug problem" with Middlebury students since the late 1960s. During my tenure at Middlebury, marijuana, acid, speed, and "downs" were as common as the Foley's Truck every Friday. Any student could partake of any of these things if he or she had the bucks to spend—and most did. This was everyday life. People dealt drugs, people bought drugs, and people did drugs—some professors included.[85]

Cocaine did not come into much use at Middlebury until the late 1970s. By 1980, however, a *Campus* poll revealed that 55 percent of the students smoked marijuana (most of them only rarely) and that 18 percent had tried cocaine and other drugs.[86] Cocaine became more popular on campuses all over the country during the 1980s, and on February 20, 1986, it became clear to the rest of the world that Middlebury College was no different. On that day, police arrested John Zaccaro '86, son of 1984 Democratic vice-presidential candidate Geraldine Ferraro, on charges of selling one-quarter of a gram of cocaine to undercover police. Authorities later searched his apartment and car and discovered eight grams of cocaine, drug paraphernalia, and notes allegedly documenting his drug dealing.[87]

The case received extensive national attention for the next two years, and the college was portrayed as a school that had not done much to halt drug dealings and abuse.[88] Indeed, after Zaccaro's trial and conviction in April 1988, an angry Mrs. Ferraro blamed Middlebury for her son's actions, denouncing it as "a place where drugs were available to so many students and continue to be so."[89] Some students were upset that the college was being portrayed in so bad a light. "This is no different than any other campus," Dwight Garner '88 told the *Rutland Herald*. "We don't deserve this. We hate to think people are thinking of us as a campus of drug addicts. People are being implicated who didn't even know John Zaccaro."[90]

As the community was reeling from the Zaccaro case, another

former student, Nick Lieder, who had left the college in 1985 with a severe cocaine addiction and $6,000 in drug-related debts, returned during the 1987 winter term to testify before the trustees' Drug Task Force, which had been set up after Zaccaro's arrest. He made a videotape to let the community know his story, and it made a strong impression on students and faculty alike. Reporting in May 1987, the task force made several recommendations that were accepted, including the hiring of a person who would be specifically responsible for coordinating drug counseling and education.[91]

Religious activities, a central aspect of college life—curricular and extracurricular—during the nineteenth century, became less important and more peripheral after 1915. The students—particularly the men—had difficulty maintaining active religious organizations; only a few exhibited a visible religious presence on campus, and compulsory daily chapel and sabbath services were finally abolished during the 1950s. There was a renewed interest in religion after midcentury, but it never came close to regaining its old importance.

Between 1915 and 1930 the only religious group that maintained a useful existence on campus was the YWCA. The women organized social activities, presented plays and musical programs, sponsored Bible discussions, and were active in community welfare projects.[92] The men's intermittent efforts to organize a YMCA chapter and an ongoing Bible discussion group were unsuccessful.[93] Indeed, as President Moody wrote resignedly in 1927, the Middlebury men were not strongly inclined toward organized religious activities:

> I am persuaded that we have the finest group of undergraduate men in New England but they are not the kind that give expression to whatever religious feeling they have. We have men who have been active in Sunday School, Christian Endeavor, and Y.M.C.A. work before coming here. They maintain a high standard of conduct and throw themselves heartily into work, but they do not identify themselves [openly?] with anything religious while they are here. I am unable to account for it.[94]

In 1927 the *Campus* tried to explain the lack of religious feeling and attributed it to peer influence: "There is little doubt that if one brings any religious intelligence or background with him to college, it will be entirely reconstructed and modified before he graduates."[95]

Still, a few religious men would preach at churches in nearby rural towns. W. Storrs Lee '28 has recalled a humorous incident concerning Jim McLeod '26, who sometimes substituted at a church in Whiting, Vermont, when the preacher was ill or absent. "To reach Whiting," Lee wrote, "[McLeod] took the early morning train to Leicester Junction and there transferred to a line that then ran to Whiting. On arrival at Leicester Junction one Sunday and finding the train engine out of operation, he borrowed one of those two-man hand cars and pumped the eight or ten miles by himself to Whiting. That was genuine religiosity." [96] There were other instances of religious interest. After the Senior Ball in 1923, for example, the students (with Moody's hearty approval) assembled at 4:00 A.M. for a worship service.[97]

Yet these were exceptions, and the college hardly had a Sunday-school atmosphere in the 1920s.[98] Although President Moody, an ordained minister, came from a distinguished religious family and encouraged religious activity on campus, he was not a fundamentalist, and he and the college had no trouble accepting evolutionary doctrines. In 1923, two years before the famous Scopes "monkey trial," Moody confidently saw no conflict between religious belief and the doctrines of modern science.

> Our own feeling is that the religious life here is strong and fine but it is modern, and it must be if it is going to be operative in a modern world. By modern I do not mean that it is opposed or contrary to that which is vital to the faith of the past, but boys cannot wear the faith of their fathers in exactly the same fashion and drapery any more than the mill can grind with water which is past. God is revealing Himself ever greater and greater at every new discovery of science.[99]

Moody had a daily opportunity to present his view of religion and scriptures to all the students in the required chapel service. "Chapel" was a midmorning (changed in 1916 to 10:00 A.M. from 8:15 A.M.) break in the academic day. And as Professor John Bowker pointed out in a fine reminiscence, daily chapel was the major opportunity for the entire student body to meet together.

> During my early years at Middlebury the life of the College centered in the Chapel. Attendance at daily chapel was compulsory, six days a week. . . . When the daily class bells rang at 10 a.m. it was the signal for everyone to start up the Hill. Students and faculty who were seeking to discuss some matter with the President lay in wait for his

company up the center walk and the opportunity for a question or two. I do not recall any protest to compulsory chapel prior to the war. Even though the side balconies had not been added the entire College could be seated. . . . Even though the center aisle separated the sexes, the event was referred to as "co-educational" chapel. . . . Following the organ prelude the daily uncensored news notices were read by a senior member of Blue Key. There was no printing of daily announcements. At times, the list of activities of the day was so long and amusing that Dr. Moody would almost despair of the reading of the Scriptures. On occasion a notice would deliberately be so in-volved that it would require several readings. Meanwhile, the student proctors lent more confusion to the scene by almost running up and down the aisles to take attendance. Before 10:30 a.m., however, Presi-dent Moody, the son of an evangelist, always managed to read and interpret a short section of the Scriptures and to lead the students in prayers. The brief periods of meditation were dutifully respected by the student body though there must have been many dissidents. The transition from the first to the second part of the daily chapel ser-vice was intuitive and traditional. This was Middlebury and no one wanted it otherwise.[100]

There was resentment of the rowdy behavior of some students during chapel, the mixing of secular and religious in service, and the fact that it was required.[101] Students also complained about the quality of the sermons delivered by visiting preachers, who led many of the required Sunday vespers services. There was the Yale minister, for example, who had been called to preach at Middlebury twice in one year. The second time, he barely had time to catch his train, and the sermon he grabbed happened to be the same one he had delivered previously. The minister did not realize this until he had returned home. He sent the Middlebury students an apology, "congratulating them on their deportment," and promised to deliver a brand-new sermon if he was invited back.[102] And then there were a few students, such as Fred Dirks '31, who tried all kinds of ploys to avoid chapel. Dirks has recalled how he told a dean that he had converted to Zoro-astrianism and wished to be excused from daily chapel on religious grounds. The dean replied enthusiastically that since Zoroastrians worshipped the sun, Dirks would be expected to be up before sun-rise every morning to pray. Dirks suddenly withdrew from the faith and rejoined the rest of the students in the chapel.[103]

Yet, as Professor Stephen Freeman has recalled, most students looked forward to the secular, if not the religious, ceremonies and rituals that made chapel such an important part of Middlebury life between the wars.

> Chapel in those days was the focal point of the campus life; the entire College met together, daily, for talks by special guests, and for "moving-up" at the year-end. Student Committees met "in the senior seats." Boys and girls made dates "on Chapel steps." These things created a cohesion, a unity of spirit which were not out of keeping with the devotional spirit, and which were a precious part of the College atmosphere. I know of nothing that has taken the place of daily Chapel.[104]

Chapel was also a time for individuals to find a moment of peace or a moment with someone close. "I never thought of daily chapel as a religious experience," a member of the class of 1933 recalled. "It was a chance to hear Red Yeomans '33 tell of daily events and a great opportunity to see my girl of the moment and arrange our next get-together. It was also a quiet respite from the day's busy activities." [105] By the mid-1940s several colleges were abolishing required chapel, and there was some opposition to it at Middlebury as well. Yet many probably agreed with the *Campus* writer who argued in 1942 that there "is time to have the college brought together once a day and to have it given something we as alumni will remember best about Middlebury." [106]

Due to the huge increase in enrollment after 1945, the entire student body could no longer sit together in chapel at the same time. Instead, they were divided into two groups—seniors and juniors in one, underclassmen in the other—and attended services on alternate Sundays and chapel every other weekday. Some wag labeled the new arrangement "varsity and j.v. chapel." [107] D. K. Smith '42, who returned to teach at the college in 1950, commented that the loss of the common daily chapel significantly reduced the sense of community he had felt as an undergraduate.[108] By 1950 most students opposed compulsory chapel. Indeed, 89 percent of those questioned said that required weekday chapel services were not "of any religious or spiritual value" to them, and 70 percent favored abolishing religious weekday services entirely.[109]

The pressures of increased enrollment and student opposition led to the gradual abolition of required chapel (and mandatory attendance at Sunday services) during the 1950s. In 1951 the trustees ap-

Chaplain Charles P. Scott knit many Middlebury families together and then, often, their children. Darren Zecher, whom Chaplain Charlie married in 1987 to Buchanan Lilley, was the daughter of Peter H. Zecker '55 and Jane Hollenbeck '56, whom he had married in 1956.

proved a report of the Advisory Committee on Chapel Attendance that each student be required only to attend one chapel service and assembly each week and a Sunday service every other week. There was also a twice-weekly voluntary devotional.[110] The new college chaplain, Rev. Charles P. Scott, also allowed students (beginning in the fall of 1950) to sit where they wanted to, and for the first time in Middlebury history, men and women sat next to each other in daily chapel.[111] Even more changes were in the offing. In 1953–1954, seniors were no longer required to attend, and a special freshman chapel was inaugurated. The trustees agreed by 1957 to make daily chapel entirely voluntary and to require attendance only at every other Sunday service.[112] Finally, in 1961, all chapel and Sunday service requirements were abolished.[113]

The trustees and college officials only grudgingly agreed to these changes. Indeed, President Stratton and Chaplain Scott apparently considered compulsory chapel essential to a Middlebury education as late as 1957.[114] It was Stratton, the first president who was not a clergyman, who created the post of college chaplain in 1943. He appointed the Rev. Marshall Jenkins that year and Rev. Robert Johnson '38 in 1947, before Scott came in 1951 to begin more than thirty-five years of service to the college.[115] Gratified by signs of a heightened student interest in voluntary religious activities, Chaplain Scott actively worked to build a strong religious program. With his assistance and encouragement, students organized a voluntary Tuesday

Rabbi Victor Reichert, long associated with Bread Loaf and Ripton, gave Middlebury a Torah in 1990. Robert S. Schine, associate professor of religion, organized a service to welcome it and invited students to read. Surrounded by her family, Juliet M. Sampson '90 read a blessing before reading from the Torah.

night vespers service, a strong Christian Association, and a Hillel organization for Jewish students.

As evidence that the community was taking religion more seriously as an intellectual and academic area of inquiry, Middlebury held its first annual Religion Conference in 1953, featuring lectures and seminars presented by outstanding religious scholars and ministers. The conference continued to be a successful college activity for many years.[116] A department of religion was organized, and Scott became its first faculty member. Religion added a second member in 1954 and became a full-fledged departmental major ten years later.[117] All these positive developments allowed the college to drop required chapel and Sunday services more gracefully than otherwise, since officials could now claim (as students had long maintained) that religion would still flourish on campus but in new, voluntary forms.

Nevertheless, religion at the college after 1960 held a central place in the lives of relatively few students, and in the absence of compulsory services, many had little or no contact with religious observance during their four years in residence. In 1986 the *Campus* noted the relative "invisibility" of any sort of religion on campus, although there were small but active Hillel, Newman Club, Christian Fellowship, and Muslim groups in 1988.[118] For most students, religion had become just one more potential activity that might or might not attract their interest.

This was a monumental change from the evangelistic days of the antebellum college. Moreover, the demise of required chapel was a critical modification, since the daily service had engendered strong community feeling from the very beginning. As President Thomas remarked in 1917:

> The strength of the small college is in the unity and solidarity of its community life. The whole argument of the personal relations between the faculty and student has by no means lost its force. There is no exercise which does so much to bring the college together and enable the institution to exert its deep and valuable personal influence as a daily assembly, and I feel very strongly that it must be maintained.[119]

Thomas would have been unhappy at the disappearance of daily chapel. Yet by midcentury the college had simply become too large — not only to fit in the chapel at one time but also too large to foster the kind of community life that had existed before 1940.

CHAPTER 13

ATHLETICS

One of the most dramatic scenes in the annals of the gridiron was enacted when a little group of boys came down from a small hamlet in
the Vermont mountains, overcame seemingly unsurmountable odds
and held the much vaunted gridiron legions of mighty Harvard to a
6–6 tie before 25,000 amazed and wild-eyed human beings in the big
Harvard Stadium.

> —"84 Years of Football Traditions," 1977,
> Middlebury College Public Relations Files

I sometimes have thought that we weren't as devastatingly bad as our
awful record signified, just especially unlucky. I've since resolved that
issue. We were bad. And unlucky. . . . We really tried so very hard. We
cried after losses, banged lockers, and rededicated ourselves to greater
effort—and continued to lose. And lose and lose. . . . We ran until our
tongues hung out. No team was better conditioned. Unfortunately,
we were a basketball and not a track team.

> —Karl Lindholm, "Also Plays," *Middlebury
> College Magazine* 60 (spring 1986): 20–21

Next year with a little more work and more enthusiasm we might
turn the snow and cold of winter months into advantage for the whole
college. . . . here in Middlebury, where there is so much territory to
tramp over, and where Breadloaf Inn and the cabins of the Green
Mountain Club are not far distant.

> —*Middlebury Campus*, March 3, 1920

Intercollegiate and intramural athletics were among the most popular activities at Middlebury between 1915 and 1990. Except during
World War II, when squads were not fielded, the intercollegiate
teams provided memorable competitive experiences for the partici-

pants and inspired strong feelings of loyalty from students, faculty, alumni, and townspeople. The teams were recognized as a major source of good public relations. Between the wars, men's football was the major sport. After 1945 a growing interest in winter sports (which had developed in the 1920s and 1930s) placed Middlebury in the forefront in men's and women's skiing and, briefly, ice hockey. Gradually, a spate of other men's sports were organized or upgraded in status, and women's intercollegiate sports grew rapidly after 1968 in number and importance. By the end of the 1980s more than one-third of Middlebury students were participating in intercollegiate athletics each year, and half of all students joined a team at some point in their undergraduate careers. Intramural sports, physical education programs, improved athletic facilities, and the development of the Snow Bowl after World War II helped ensure that all students would have opportunities for recreation.

Football has dominated most American college athletic programs since 1900, and this was also true of Middlebury, particularly between 1916 and 1945.[1] The struggles on the field were critical for the fans as well as the participants, as the games became symbolic struggles for institutional—not just team—superiority. In 1916, when Middlebury, captained by Ted Lang '17, won its first Vermont state football championship by defeating the University of Vermont (UVM) 6-2 on a sixteen-yard pass from James Bower '20 to Earle Good '20, the *Campus*, described the victory in monumental terms:

> Our victory over UVM marks an EPOCH. It is significant because we have proved to our own satisfaction, as well as to the world at large, that Middlebury has entered again upon her own right. The place of honor which we once held but lost among the New England colleges is once more ready for us to go in and take possession.
>
> For eight long years our beloved president Thomas has labored unflinchingly and with the deepest devotion to secure for Middlebury and her alumni this coveted and rightful glory. We as students will never know what has been the cost in the way of personal sacrifice, and his reward must ultimately consist largely in the knowledge of having served well his alma mater and humanity, for this has not been a slavish and prejudiced elevation to a one-sided cause. Our rejoicing and his does not consist in the mere fact of having won a long desired football victory, but in all which this victory symbolizes. Under his leadership, Middlebury has been preparing for the manifestation of her power. The spirit of Gamaliel Painter is once more abroad and

Dressed in the thin uniforms of 1919, Middlebury's state champions gathered on the bleachers for a commemorative photograph.

his cane is now an inspiration to the student body as well as to its honored possessor.[2]

Athletic victories not only provided hope for the future and solace for years of inferiority but also engendered intense feelings of loyalty. Rallies, bonfires, and parades brought students, faculty, and townspeople together in celebration of the college's successes.[3] The basketball team won one of the most important victories in the school's history by defeating UVM in 1928 for the first time in twelve years. The reaction was ecstatic: "Townspeople joined with students to riot over the campus in an impromptu celebration of the occasion. Everything available in the way of inflammable material was piled high near the gym and transformed into a mammoth bonfire.[4]

Successful athletic teams also generated greater publicity for many American colleges, thereby increasing alumni support and more applications for admission. With this in mind, A. Barton Hepburn 1871 gave the college $65,000 in 1920 for the support of football and baseball, then the major intercollegiate sports at Middlebury.[5] Hepburn told the grateful trustees that he donated the money in large part because "I particularly believe in successful athletics, as the best means of college advertising, and that is the particular feature which I wish to serve at this time."[6]

The Hepburn gift helped usher in a decade of football boom and bust. The college — to increase its visibility and prestige in the eyes of the public (and particularly high school students) — began in the early 1920s to schedule games with some of the most powerful schools in the East: Columbia, Penn State, Yale, and Harvard. Indeed, after the 1921 season, the school received a "wealth of flattering offers" from big football powers to play them in 1922, and the *Campus* urged Middlebury to accept.

> In preparing the 1922 schedule it will be well to remember that the varsity contests this year against teams of widely recognized standing were infinitely more valuable as advertising than were any of the games for the State Championship . . . the plain truth is that a strong fight against Harvard though a losing one, means more to a greater number of prospective freshmen than a victory over Norwich, Clarkson or St. Lawrence.[7]

Even a doubtful President Moody was temporarily convinced. "I am rapidly becoming reconciled to the idea of our football team playing a schedule of big teams throughout the East," he told a cheering student rally before the 1922 Penn State game.[8]

Fortunately, Middlebury also attracted some outstanding football players, and the team performed admirably between 1921 and 1924. Sparked by Stone Hallquist '25, Alfred Brosowsky '25, Herbert Riegelman '25, Aloys Papke '25, Joseph Novotny '26, and William McLaughlin '26, the 1923 team barely lost to Columbia (led by guard Lou Gehrig) 9–6 and played powerful Harvard to a 6–6 tie in Cambridge as Marshall Klevenow '25 kicked two late field goals. According to the *Boston Globe* report, David had undone Goliath again: "One of the most dramatic scenes in the annals of the gridiron was enacted when a little group of boys came down from a small hamlet in the Vermont mountains, overcame seemingly unsurmountable odds and held the much vaunted gridiron legions of mighty Harvard to a 6–6 tie before 25,000 amazed and wild-eyed human beings in the big Harvard Stadium."[9] Legend has it that President Moody called the team in Cambridge to hear the final score. "Six to six," he was told. "Sixty-six to what?" Moody replied, expecting the worst. Although Harvard won the next year, 16–6 before thirty-five thousand fans, that 1924 Middlebury team trounced all the rest of its opponents, won the Vermont state championship, piled up the most points in the East, and placed several of its members on the all-star teams picked by eastern sportswriters.[10]

Football was the major intercollegiate sport between the two world wars. President Moody strove to keep it no more than one part of a balanced education, but he enjoyed attending games such as this one, which he watched with Coach Benjamin H. Beck.

The euphoria was short-lived. Many of the best players graduated the following spring, Coach David Morey resigned to coach in the South, and a weakened squad could no longer compete with the best teams in the East. They were routed 53–0 by Yale to open the 1925 campaign and crushed 68–0 by Harvard the following week. For the next several years the stronger Ivy League and eastern university teams considered Middlebury a setup and gradually dropped the school from their schedules. Columbia, the last football power to play Middlebury, stopped in 1933 after severely drubbing the Panthers several years in a row.[11]

President Moody was apparently pleased when the college descended from the ranks of "big-time" football. He told entering freshmen in the late 1930s that he was greatly relieved that the 6–6 tie with Harvard had not led to greater emphasis on sports.[12] Indeed, Moody fought during the 1920s to keep athletics in perspective. In cooperation with the presidents of other New England colleges, he ended the practices of hiring high-paid seasonal coaches, of allowing athletically talented transfer students and freshmen to play immediately on varsity teams, and of making scholastic and financial concessions to athletes. Middlebury coaches worked year-round after 1923 and were paid on the same scale as faculty members. Transfer students and freshmen had to wait one year before playing, and varsity players were treated no differently from other students in receiving financial aid or other benefits.[13]

Between 1926 and 1929, the Carnegie Foundation for the Advancement of Teaching investigated intercollegiate athletics at 112 colleges and universities. Although Middlebury was cleared of any charges of recruiting athletes, it was not on the list of twenty-eight schools at which "no evidence was found that athletes were subsidized by any group or individual." [14] Moody was surprised at the intimation that the college was subsidizing athletics in some ways.

> This is rather amusing for one of the most frequently voiced criticisms has been that not enough was done here for athletes. Impartial investigators felt that we erred in the opposite direction.
> However the jacket fits, we have no alternative to wearing it. And while we would like to have been 100% impeccable, we are grateful that we are exonerated from any suspicion of recruiting. There was a time when this could not have been said of us, in those dear bye gone days when our standards of sportsmanship were not as high as our scores. It is more important to be 100% sportsmen than to be 100% victorious. Some prices are too high for the ephemeral value of athletic victories.[15]

Middlebury settled down to a small-college football schedule in the 1930s and, under Coach Ben Beck (1928–1941), fielded several fine teams. Sam Guarnaccia '30, Walter "Duke" Nelson '32, and Walt Boehm '35 (the college's first All-American) spearheaded Beck's early teams. In 1936, led by Captain Bill Craig '37, John Kirk '39, George Anderson '38, John Cridland '38, John Chalmers '38, Vic Seixas '37, Bobby Boehm '38, Swede Liljenstein '38, Paul Guarnaccia '38, John Golembeskie '39, and Randall Hoffman '37, the Panthers recorded the school's first perfect undefeated season.[16] The small squads of those days played "both ways"—offense and defense—and the fans seemed not to miss the "big-time" atmosphere of the 1920s. "In spite of occasional wailings from fanatically loyal alumni who weep at the death of the orgiastic era when 'football was football,' " a *Campus* editor commented in 1933, "we of Middlebury have come to realize that the greatest good to be gained from athletic competition comes from a season of comparable opposition, and not from futile expense of health and morale against a juggernaut of overwhelming weight and reserve." [17] Following the brief flirtation with big-time football, the most important games each year were with Williams, Norwich, and (until the series ended in 1968) the University of Vermont. [18]

After the war, Walter "Duke" Nelson '32 assumed the coaching duties (1946–1968) and led the club to 6–1 and 7–1 seasons in 1947 and 1948. "Duke" compiled a fine 83–75–10 record during his twenty-two years and coached many outstanding players, including Wendy Forbes '51, John Zabriskie '55, Dick Atkinson '60, Charles Brush, '69, and Lee Cartmill '71. Nelson introduced two-platoon football, which resulted in larger squads, more coaches, and greater emphasis on specialization. [19] Middlebury football had its greatest success in the 1970s, when, under the leadership of coaches John W. Anderson (1969–1972) and Michael G. Heinecken (1973–), the Panthers had the best record of any college-division team in New England and ranked eighth nationally. Men from the class of 1974, one of the most athletically talented in the school's history, helped anchor both the undefeated 1972 team (the first since 1936) and the 1973 squad, which lost only one (disputed) game to Norwich. Quarterbacks Peter Mackey '74 and Doug Cramphin '74, halfbacks Phil Pope '73 and Tom O'Connor '75, tackle Dave Uyrus '73, and linebacker Jim Barrington '75 were among the stars. Roy Heffernan '78, a fine halfback, set new rushing marks and, along with linebacker Duane Ford '78, led the Panthers to three excellent seasons.

The team continued to do well in the early 1980s, with a 7–1 record in 1981, after which Heinecken was named Coach of the Year in New England. Ted Virtue '82, Bill Genovese '82, Jim Loveys '82, Jon Good '84, Jon Peterson '86, Tom Mahon '84, and tight end Beau Coash '82 (who played for the Boston Breakers and later had a tryout with the New England Patriots) were among the outstanding players in those years. After 1985, however, the team did not fare as well (a record of 15–32–1 from 1985 to 1989), perhaps because of subtle changes in the admissions/recruiting strategy. [20]

Aside from skiing and hockey, no other sport approached football in popularity until the 1970s. Basketball never caught on at Middlebury as it did elsewhere; this was undoubtedly because of the popularity of outdoor winter sports and the generally poor performance of Middlebury teams over the years. Since 1918, when basketball was declared a major varsity sport, good seasons were rare. Coach Tony Lupien managed a winning record during his tenure (1951–1956), relying on the scoring of Alfred "Sonny" Dennis '55 and the rebounding of Tom Hart '56, who still holds college and NCAA rebounding records. But from 1956 to 1970 the team compiled an abysmal record, 49–232, including several winless seasons. Karl Lindholm '67, who played on several of these hapless teams (including the 1966–1967 squad, which had the worst record, 1–23, of any college team that year) has recalled the frustrations:

> I sometimes have thought that we weren't as devastatingly bad as our awful record signified, just especially unlucky. I've since resolved that issue. We were bad. And unlucky. . . . We really tried so very hard. We cried after losses, banged lockers, and rededicated ourselves to greater effort—and continued to lose. And lose and lose. . . . We ran until our tongues hung out. No team was better conditioned. Unfortunately, we were a basketball and not a track team.[21]

Later, under Coach G. Thomas Lawson (1970–1978), the fortunes were reversed, as outstanding players like Kevin Kelleher '80, David Pentkowski '75, Kevin Cummings '76, David Nelson '76, and David "Ben" Davidson '75, led the basketball team through its most successful decade.[22] The team returned to historical form in the 1980s (with a dismal 61–120 record between 1978 and 1987), although individual stars such as Paul Righi '82, Fain Hackney '83, John Thompson '87, and John Humphrey '88 (the school's all-time leading scorer) provided plenty of points and excitement.[23] Righi, a biopsychology major who graduated Phi Beta Kappa, with a grade point average of 3.84, and Pentkowski (a superb student and soccer player as well as a basketball star) were recipients of the prestigious NCAA Postgraduate Scholarship, awarded annually to only ten scholar-athletes.[24]

Spring comes late to Vermont, and spring varsity sports—baseball, tennis, golf, and track—usually attracted limited support from the college community. Baseball, a popular sport before World War I, declined in importance over the years. Schedules were limited and victories infrequent; the 1977 team (11–5) recorded the most wins since 1915.[25] Middlebury had its first intercollegiate tennis match in 1920 and was playing a nine-game schedule by 1926. The extraordinary growth in the popularity of tennis in America after 1960 was reflected in the large number of Middlebury students who played tennis on campus. The addition of indoor courts after the war enabled them to play in the colder months as well, and students such as Fain Hackney '83 (Middlebury's first tennis All-American) and Pete Bostwick '58 had outstanding careers on the men's team.[26] But tennis as a varsity sport remained relatively minor in importance. Varsity golf and track were first organized in the 1920s. Undergraduates were allowed to use the nine-hole Middlebury Country Club course in 1925, and a team had achieved minor sport status by 1928. The course itself was expanded to eighteen holes between 1974 and 1977 under the direction of Ralph O. Myhre (after whom the course was named following his death in 1979).[27] Although Middlebury had competed with Norwich and UVM in track and field for many years, the first modern schedule was completed in 1924, when Reginald "Doc" Cook '24 led the team to its eighth consecutive state championship.[28]

After 1970 the most important developments in athletics (aside from winter sports) were the introduction and growing popularity of new sports like soccer and lacrosse; a greater emphasis on intramurals, "life-time" sports, and physical fitness; and the extraordinary growth of women's intercollegiate athletics.

Football's postwar supremacy was finally challenged by the successful men's soccer program. In 1954, Frank Punderson '55, who was both captain and coach, led Middlebury's first soccer team to a 4-0-2 record. During the next fourteen years the team compiled a 75-24-16 mark and developed a spate of outstanding players, including Rich Miner '58, Tor Hultgren '60, W. Davis Van Winkle '63, A. Keith Van Winkle '64, David Nicholson '67, Peter Askin '62, George Rubottom '62, John Marks '68, Peter Kovner '67, John Garrison '66, and three-time All-American J. Davis Webb '66. Perhaps the most outstanding teams were fielded in 1972 and 1973 (again, the remarkable class of 1974 was instrumental here), when the college recorded 9-0-1 and 10-0 seasons. The team allowed only one goal during the entire regular season of 1973, as halfbacks David Pentkowski '75, Andy Jackson '74, and Kevin Candon '74 demonstrated outstanding skills.

Between 1975 and 1985, the team continued its winning ways by compiling a record of 71-31-22 and capturing several New England championships. These squads were sparked by Steve Sass '78, Grayle Howlett '81, Chip Doubleday '81, Jamie Hutchins '83, Mike Noonan '83, F. W. Nugent '84, Van Dorsey '86, Marty Wenthe '85, and Chris Parsons '87, who led the 1986 outfit to a 14-2-1 record and the ECAC Division III eastern championship. The success of the team over the years and the growing interest of Americans in soccer spurred a lively following for the three squads that came to compete for the college—men's varsity, women's varsity, and men's "B" teams.[29]

Lacrosse also gained a substantial following after the war, when, with the prodding of Curtis Cushman '50, it was first accorded minor sport status. Many football players became attracted to the lacrosse team in the spring, and this helped Middlebury win nine ECAC New England titles after 1973. Indeed, thirty-four Middlebury men won All-American honors or mention in lacrosse in the period 1960–1990. Powerful midfielder John Burchard '81 starred in both football and lacrosse and was considered by his coaches to be "one of the best college athletes in Division III."[30] Other lacrosse stars who helped the Panthers to a 105-30 record between 1975 and 1985 included Will Graham '76, Peter Boucher '76, Bill Kuharich '76, Tom Callanan '77, Roy Heffernan '78, Roger Nicholas '80, Eric Kemp '80, Chip Clark '80, Jeff Thomsen '83, Mark Chafee '85, David Hennessy '85, Kevin Mahaney '85, and Steve Kirkpatrick '87. In 1988, the team had a 13-1 mark, won the ECAC championship, and ranked seventh in the country in Division III.

Other sports caught on later in the century. Men's cross-country, first introduced in 1921, was reorganized in 1968 by skiing and cross-country coach John Bower and grew in popularity, undoubtedly helped by the national running and jogging craze of the 1970s and 1980s.[31] After several years as a club sport, men's swimming was elevated to varsity status in 1985. By 1990, a variety of men's club sports teams, including volleyball, squash, and rugby (as well as a coeducational rowing club) had been organized to compete on an ad hoc basis with other schools.[32]

Although only a minority could participate in varsity sports, most Middlebury students were involved in physical education and intramurals. Indeed, men and women were required to attend physical education classes—segregated by sex—for most of the years between 1921 and 1970.[33] There was a physical education major until it was eliminated in 1957–1958, after which every male still had to complete a four-semester phys ed requirement. In 1970 the board accepted a plan presented by the new director of athletics, Richard Colman, to integrate the men's and women's staffs and programs into one Department of Physical Education and Athletics.[34] Colman, with the assistance of Coach Mary Lick and the rest of his staff, also revised the unpopular four-semester men's physical education requirement by instituting a flexible (though still required) one-year coeducational curriculum, which emphasized (as the women's physical education program had previously done) lifetime sports and the recognition of previous athletic achievements.[35]

The physical fitness boom of the period 1960 to 1990 was particularly apparent among the type of upper-middle-class youth who attended Middlebury, and the demand for additional athletic and recreational facilities by varsity teams, individuals, and the intramural program led to the construction of Fletcher Field House in 1974 and its annex in 1989. Furthermore, Dean Steven Rockefeller arranged for the reopening of the outdoor skating rink at the base of Hepburn Hall, where it had been located until the construction of the Memorial Field House in 1949.[36]

An even more significant phenomenon after 1965 was the growing opportunity for women to compete in varsity athletics. From the founding of the Women's Athletic Association in 1912 until the late 1960s, women's athletics were a relatively unimportant and almost hidden part of college life. Instead of playing sports, the women were (according to the men) apparently expected to spend their time cheering for the men's teams. Indeed, as late as World War I, women were not supposed to appear in public in athletic garb, and only gradually were men allowed to attend women's games. A faculty member complained to the dean of women in 1919 that the "Department of Physical Education permitted women in gym costume, without skirts, to cross the public road" en route to Porter Field. After that, the women tried to use Porter at times they might "manage to escape the gaze of the men." The trustees finally allocated $2,500 in 1921 for a new athletic field next to Pearsons in the relative privacy of the women's campus.[37]

Customs changed somewhat between the wars, and women had more freedom to dress appropriately for athletic activities. They began to take up ice skating, horseback riding, archery, golf, volleyball, field hockey, basketball, badminton, tennis, skiing, tobogganing, and fencing.[38] However, except for skiing, they primarily participated in physical education classes, intramural sports, and in occasional "sports days" at which Middlebury women competed against teams and individuals from other schools in sports such as tennis, basketball, or field hockey.[39] The annual sum allocated to women's sports was relatively tiny: $300 in 1931–1932, for example, compared with nearly $21,000 for men's sports.[40]

Beginning in the late 1960s, however, the women's movement and, more specifically, the phenomenal rise of women's intercollegiate athletics, had a major impact. Middlebury women organized varsity teams in field hockey (1968), swimming (1969), lacrosse (1969), tennis (1971), cross-country (1975), track (1975), squash (1976), basketball (1977), soccer (1979), and ice hockey (1981). In several of these sports, enough women turned out to form "B" teams, which also competed with other schools. Women's rugby and riding were also organized on a club level in the 1980s.[41]

The field hockey team had particular success, posting several undefeated seasons and excelling in postseason play. Edie MacAusland '75, Deb Daniels '75, Lisa Hill '81, Sue Butler '81, Michelle Plante '83, Helen Ladds '81, Julie Ewing '80, Ann McCollum '86, and many other fine players contributed to this outstanding record.[42] Other outstanding athletes include Karin VonBerg '81, an All-American distance runner and one of the best collegiate cross-country performers in the nation; Tina Ilgner '86, an All-American middle-distance runner in each of her four years at the college; Dorcas Den-Hartog '87, a gifted long-distance runner and cross-country skier who won the NCAA Division III women's cross-country championship in 1986; Megan Kemp '88, an All-American lacrosse player who led her team to an 11–3 record and a regional championship in her senior year; Victoria Hoyt '89, the first Middlebury woman to earn All-American honors in squash; Caroline Leary '92 and Kathy Dubzinski '90, who helped the basketball team win eighteen games in 1989–1990; and Debbie Gow '90, a high-scoring tri-captain of the ice hockey team.[43]

Athletic facilities also improved after 1970, as coaches such as

Mary Lick spoke out in favor of equality for women. In 1973, a small addition to the Memorial Field House, which was used for women's office and locker space allowed women for the first time to have realistic access to facilities other than McCullough Gymnasium.[44] The trustees remained concerned that the college was not in compliance with Title IX, and the extensive renovations of the old field house in 1981–1982 and the four new practice fields were designed to give women and men more equal facilities.[45] Some students expressed concern in the 1980s that the college should have more women coaches, and a number of women athletes again complained in 1988 about inferior facilities and coaching. "Middlebury College guarantees us equal educational opportunities," lacrosse captain Megan Kemp '88 stated. "We just want equal athletic opportunities as well. We just want them to respect us as athletes." In the fall of 1988, the college promised to remedy the situation, particularly to ensure that coaches for the women's teams were qualified.[46]

Middlebury's location in the hills of northern New England permitted an emphasis on winter sports, particularly skiing and hockey, as key elements in the athletic and recreational programs. In particular, the development of the Snow Bowl as a ski area set Middlebury apart from other schools, even as the growing popularity of skiing among middle- and upper-class families enhanced Middlebury's desirability among the very class of people the college sought to attract (see chapter 10).

Before World War I, Middlebury students apparently did not, at least in any organized way, take advantage of the snow that blanketed the Champlain Valley and the Green Mountains for months each winter. But several men formed an Outing Club in 1917, on the model of Dartmouth's successful group, and hoped to send a team to participate in the Dartmouth Winter Carnival. One member urged every Middlebury man to "take an active part in some winter sport" and to try out for the team, not only for the benefit of the club but also because "this will do much to bring Middlebury to the front in New England as several of the larger colleges would be represented there at that time."[47] The major events in those early days of intercollegiate skiing competition involved various kinds of ski and snowshoe races, including dashes, cross-country, and obstacle races.[48] Throughout the 1920s, although its teams often suffered from "a lack of student interest" and poor organization and preparation, Middlebury men ventured to skiing meets and winter carnivals at Dartmouth, McGill, Norwich, and elsewhere.[49] Occasionally they even were victorious, as in 1922, when they swept the snowshoe race at McGill to become, as the *Campus* trumpeted, "the foremost collegiate snowshoers in this country." [50] Arthur Ferry '24, Roger Hall '22, Ray Noonan '21, and Cy Shelvey '23 (the first captain of a Middlebury ski team) were some of the stars of the early 1920s.[51]

The Outing Club also organized winter sports events just for Middlebury students, and the first Winter Holiday (forerunner of Winter Carnival) was held on February 23, 1920, on Chipman Hill (for the women) and at Noble's Grove (where the men competed). Although the affair was only a qualified success, the *Campus* urged (with some prescience) that it become an annual event. "Next year with a little more work and more enthusiasm we might turn the snow and cold of the winter months into advantage for the whole college. . . . here in Middlebury, where there is so much territory to tramp over, and where Breadloaf Inn and the cabins of the Green Mountain Club are not far distant." [52] After another Winter Holiday in 1921, the name was changed to Winter Carnival in 1922. Coach Morey expanded the activities the following year to include inter-class and interfraternity contests designed to "entertain" more of the college community.[53] The early carnivals, which included ski and snowshoe races for men and women, ski jumping, and toboggan sliding, really had two purposes, as the *Campus* explained: "If the Winter Carnival is established as an annual fixture in Middlebury's program of college activities, it will aid in developing spirit, and, we hope, will speedily place the Outing Club's teams on a par with those of our New England and Canadian neighbors." [54] By 1924, however, the interest in organized winter sports (other than ice hockey) was waning, and the carnival was held only occasionally until 1934.[55] On the other hand, Coach Arthur Brown, who came to Middlebury in 1926, agreed to coach the ski team (although he apparently knew almost nothing about skiing), and Middlebury continued to compete with other schools in an increasing number of meets.[56]

Interest in skiing grew rapidly in the 1930s, particularly after the 1932 Winter Olympics at Lake Placid. W. Wyman Smith '35, Coach Brown, and Professor Perley Voter brought back a blueprint of the Municipal Jump at Lake Placid, and a twenty-seven-meter ski jump

Interfraternity rivalry created confections of snow and ice during Winter Carnival.

was constructed on Chipman Hill in time for the college's first inter-collegiate Winter Carnival on February 10–12, 1934.[57] That carnival, organized by the Mountain Club, featured the first women's inter-collegiate meet at Middlebury, with women from UVM, McGill, and Skidmore competing.[58] In 1935–36, they improved the Chipman Hill trails and constructed a new ski jump. Although the new jump was a welcome addition, there was not much room to run out after the jump, and as Marion Holmes '33 has recalled, one jumper at the end of his run took a faculty wife with him over a fence.[59]

The first trails were cut (by people from both town and college) on Worth Mountain under the leadership of J. J. Fritz, the college's business manager, and R. L. Rowland, assistant district ranger. One of the men involved, Richard Hubbard '36, recalled that a Middle-bury Ski Club was organized in 1935 and that Robert Holmes, Beach Bly, Ellsworth Cornwell, Perley Voter, and others would go up to Bread Loaf with their families on Sundays in the late 1930s to en-joy picnic lunches and cut down trees to form the Worth Mountain Downhill Trail and a log cabin warming hut. According to Hubbard,

Middlebury's ski jump on Chipman Hill was patterned on the jump at the Lake Placid Olympic site of 1932. It was improved and resited to Bread Loaf after World War II. Ski jumping was a spectacular feature of Winter Carnival until the 1970s.

two "Rube Goldberg-types" — John Phillips and his brother Harry — rigged up the first rope tow on an old automobile.[60]

By the winter of 1935–1936, ski fever gripped the northernmost parts of the United States, and skiing became one of the most popular activities at the college, as W. C. Heinz '37 (later a well-known sportswriter) remarked in one of his *Campus* columns:

> Yes sir. Middlebury, it seems, has truly taken the time off to keep abreast of the times and go ski-crazy. An hour after the snow stops falling, Chapel Hill and all surrounding slopes are a maze of crisscross tracks and odd patterns. Daily and nightly, wherever you look, the eye falls on dozens of little "Ski-Boys" and "Ski-Girls" earnestly endeavoring to display the technique that will qualify them for membership in that great fraternity of Ski Heilers. . . . So it goes — Middlebury eats, breathes, walks, talks, and lives skiing.[61]

Dick Hubbard '36 was hired in 1937 as the first paid coach of the men's ski team, and by 1939, following the lead of several other colleges and ski schools, Middlebury imported a coach—Arthur Schlatter—from Europe. Schlatter was a big success. In 1939 he not only directed the men's team to its first Middlebury Carnival victory (over six opponents) but also organized (with Hubbard) the college's first women's ski team. Women students—eighty-seven of them—were taking lessons on Chapel Hill from the popular coach only a few weeks after he arrived at Middlebury.[62] The men's team continued its winning ways in 1940, led by tiny Eddy Gignac '43, captain Elbert "Mole" Cole '40, Ray Unsworth '41, Ike Townsend '42, and Bob '41 and John Gale '43.[63]

During the war there was little skiing activity at the college, but the legendary U.S. Army 10th Mountain Division was skiing up a storm in Europe, and one of its veterans, Joe Jones, was hired by President Stratton in 1945 to coach the ski team and manage the Snow Bowl. Jones recruited a number of his war buddies to join him, and for the next several years Middlebury was a power in American college skiing. Although Jones left in 1947, Robert "Bobo" Sheehan '44, an outstanding skier in his own right, took over the coaching reins, and under his leadership, the men's team of Joseph "Tink" Bailey '48, Phil Deane '49, Don Henderson '49, Paul Kailey '50, Tom Jacobs '51, Fred Neuberger '50, and Jack Valentine '49 won the North American Championships in Sun Valley in 1948.[64] The college did not have the funds to send that team on the three-day train trip to Sun Valley, but the student body raised most of the necessary expenses so that the team could compete.[65] The men's team repeated as North American champions at Aspen in 1949. The team was aided by improvements to the Snow Bowl after the war, as Dr. Stewart Ross '20 influenced his fellow trustees to underwrite the construction of new ski trails and a fifty-meter jump.[66]

The women's team was even more famous in the 1940s, due, first, to a raft of publicity in the *New York Times* and other papers about the star skier, Becky Fraser '46, who in 1948 became the first Middlebury athlete to compete in the Winter Olympics; and second, to a popular movie about Middlebury skiing—*Sno' Time for Learning*—which was produced in 1948 and featured Middlebury women skiers. President Stratton proudly told the trustees in 1949 that the movie had been shown in seven thousand theaters across the United States and in foreign countries and that the college was receiving unprecedented recognition.[67]

In the 1950s, although unable to win the Dartmouth Carnival or dominate eastern skiing until 1959, the men's team remained successful (third in the nation in 1955 and 1956, fourth in 1958), and individual students and coaches made their mark in international competition. Tom Jacobs '51 and Verne Goodwin '53, who competed in the 1952 Winter Olympics in Oslo, were the college's first (male) winter Olympians, while Doug Burden competed for the United States in the 1954 world championships, Les Streeter '55 skied on the 1956 Olympic team, and Bobo Sheehan was chosen to coach that team; Bob Beattie '55, who would coach the U.S. team in the 1960s, took over at Middlebury. At the end of the decade, Peter Lahdenpera '59, Gordie Eaton '65, and Herb Thomas '60 led the men's team to three undefeated seasons (1958–1960), as well as a victory at the Dartmouth Winter Carnival for the first time since 1948.[68]

Fred Neuberger '50 developed an outstanding women's program in the 1950s, and, at Squaw Valley in 1960, one of the most famous women to ski at Middlebury, Penny Pitou, became the first American to win an Olympic medal in downhill. In 1956, during the one year she was enrolled, Pitou tried to put in some extra training hours but was stymied, she later recalled, by contemporary attitudes toward women and sports: "In those days women didn't 'sweat' so it was a little difficult to train and still look 'preppy.' I lived in the Chateau and trained in my sweat suit in the brambles behind the dorm. Lots of fun?! More than once Mrs. Kelly (then Dean of Women) asked me to 'please try to fit in and not be so much of a jock.' I didn't heed her however."[69]

Women skiers continued to put the college on the map after 1960. Renie Cox Gorsuch '60 (a 1960 Olympian), Nancy Sise Auseklis '63, and Pamela Reed '72 were standouts, but the peak years were 1976–1981, when Middlebury women captured four national championships and one second-place finish while remaining undefeated in the East.[70] Among the many fine athletes of that era, alpine skier Sara McNealus '79 was particular successful. After winning the giant slalom and finishing second in the slalom at Nationals in 1979, she was named an All-American and National College Competitor of the Year by *Ski Racing Magazine* and was the first woman at a New England school to win the prestigious Broderick Award for excellence in skiing. Coach Terry Aldrich called McNealus "one of the finest athletes to ever attend Middlebury."[71] Foreign skiers began to domi-

The Women's cross-country relay team locked in Middlebury's Winter Carnival victory during the nearly snowless winter of 1980. Their victory was only sweeter for taking place at the site of the just completed Lake Placid Winter Olympics.

nate women's and men's skiing in the 1980s, but several Middlebury women, including Alice Tower '81, Sue Long '82, Tara McMenamy '82, Leslie Baker '84, Ingred Punderson '88, Claudia Stern '89, and Leslie Smith '83 (a 1976 Olympian and four-time All-American — the only Middlebury skier, male or female, to manage that) performed splendidly.[72]

Although the men's teams after 1960 did not fare quite as well as the women's, there were a number of outstanding individual performers. In 1961, Gordie Eaton '65 won the NCAA downhill championships at the Snow Bowl. At that same meet, John Bower '63, the finest Nordic skier ever to compete for Middlebury, won the NCAA championship in the Nordic combined. John Clough '64 also won national titles, in both the slalom and downhill and at the 1964 national meet at Dartmouth took the alpine combined title as well. After competing in the 1964 and 1968 Olympics, Bower won the Nordic combined trophy at Holmenkollen — a feat never before accomplished by a non-Scandinavian. Bower later was Middlebury's coach (1969–1975) and a member of the coaching staff for the U.S. Olympic teams in 1976 and 1980. Other graduates who competed or coached in the Olympics included John Morton '68, Joe McNulty

'72, Dennis Donahue '66, Don Henderson '49, Fred Neuberger '50, Terry Morse '65, Hank Tauber '64, Finn Gunderson '69, and Craig Ward '76. Other fine male skiers were Peter Swallow '65, Roger Buchika '66, Steve Lathrop '73, Paul "Rat" Reed '70, Hugh Barber '73, John Jacobs '78, and Jim Goodwin '79. In the 1980s, Mike Graham '84 (an excellent cross-country skier) and NCAA slalom champion Rob McLeod '88 were standouts.[73]

One of the reasons these skiers enrolled at Middlebury was the rapid improvement of the Snow Bowl. As President Stratton commented in 1954: "Winter sports activities undeniably are a feature which attracts students, both men and women, to Middlebury and certainly part of our educational objectives is to provide healthy recreational sports facilities during our Vermont winters."[74] The college proceeded to do so—by completing a 300-foot-wide, 1,500-foot slalom slope and a 1,300-foot rope tow and by widening the beginner's slope to 400 feet and servicing it with a double rope tow, all in 1946; by constructing a 50-meter ski jump—for many years the nation's largest collegiate jump—in 1947; by opening the Proctor, Ross, and Voter trails and installing a 3,185-foot Poma-lift in 1954; and by adding an 1,800-foot Pomalift ten years later.[75] Indeed, by 1971 the Snow Bowl could boast a 15-kilometer cross-country ski trail, three Poma ski lifts, a 4,200-foot double chair lift, 14 slalom and downhill trails and slopes, and 3 jumps.[76] These facilities, together with the Neil Starr Ski Lodge (see chapter 7), a base building with food service, library, and rest areas; and the Carroll and Jane Rikert Ski Touring Center, added in 1983, arguably made the Snow Bowl the finest college ski area in the country.[77]

The major driving force behind the development of the Snow Bowl was Ralph O. Myhre, its manager from 1951 to 1978. It was Myhre's insistence that rope tows were obsolete that led to the installation of the Poma lift in 1954 and the modernization of the Bowl thereafter. Myhre was also responsible for the development of the Ski Patrol and Ski School. In the mid-1970s he designed and built the 3.5-kilometer John "Red" Kelly '31 Ski Trail for cross country skiing and running. The trail, which circles the golf course, was named for a popular coach (1932–1970), who was also, at various times, director of intramural athletics and chairman of the physical education department.[78]

For nearly three decades the Bowl was the favorite skiing area for thousands of Middlebury students. In the 1960s and 1970s an estimated 30 percent of the student body purchased season passes, and some 90 percent of students who skied went frequently to the Bowl.[79] The lack of snow between 1980 and 1984, however, led to a dramatic decline in student use; in 1983–1984, only twenty-eight students purchased passes, as Middlebury facilities were being "outclassed by the newer ski resorts."[80] The ski team had to drive long distances just to practice, there had been only one Winter Carnival with a full complement of skiing events in five years, and the 1984 Eastern Collegiate Skiing Championship alpine events had to be moved from the Bowl to Pico Peak—with much embarrassment to the college—all because of lack of snow.[81] The trustees responded by appropriating nearly $850,000 in 1984 to purchase snowmaking equipment and to install more chair lifts and other necessary equipment. The improvements helped. In 1984–1985, 560 students bought passes, and the college was able to maintain its position as a top skiing institution.[82]

Ice hockey had its origins at the college in the early 1920s. At first, some pick-up games were played on Porter Pond off South Street, but a better rink was needed.[83] In 1922–1923, Paris Fletcher '24, Don Ross '25, and Malcolm Ross '23 took matters into their own hands and created the first successful boarded on-campus rink (a previous attempt near Voter had unfortunately been set up on the steam lines), as Fletcher later recalled.

> On the site of what is now Munroe Hall, there were three tennis courts cut into the side of the hill and they had square wooden posts to hold the nets. We secured an old two-handled cross-cut saw and cut them off nearly at ground level. I don't recall consulting the College authorities in advance, but once we had removed those obstacles, we had a nice flat area large enough for a hockey rink, and it was *fait accompli*. . . . I have some pretty vivid memories of sub-zero, moonlit nights holding the nozzle of a borrowed Middlebury Fire Department hose in the air watching the water freeze almost before it hit the ground.[84]

Fletcher helped organize an intercollegiate team in 1922–1923, and they ventured to Rensselaer Polytechnic Institute for their first game, which, as Max Petersen has written, was memorable: "There wasn't any coach, substitutes were unheard of, and the big Irish

Hockey was still a club sport when Middlebury defeated Clarkson in 1928. Enthusiastic audiences and a 9-1 season contributed to hockey's becoming a major sport in 1930. Games moved indoors with the completion of Memorial Field House in 1949, but the ice rink in front of McCullough was revived during the snowless winter of 1979-1980 by Dean Steven C. Rockefeller.

goaltender, who couldn't skate, relied on his first basemen's glove to stop the puck." [85] That goalie, "Rip" Gallagher '25, had practiced without a stick (the team did not have one for him), but Fletcher purchased one at R.P.I. just before the game. Gallagher, later a New York State Supreme Court judge, soon discarded it for the glove, however, and did a creditable job, giving up only five goals in the three games (all losses) that season. The first victory did not come until the team's third season, in 1924-1925 (after nine losses and one tie), with a 1-0 win over R.P.I.[86] In 1926-1927, after player-coach Carleton Simmons '28 and fellow linesmen Hal Whittemore '28 and Stillman Kelley '29 led the team to a 6-0 season and the Vermont championship (for the second consecutive year), hockey was granted minor sport status, and eight men were awarded "M" sweaters.[87] After a 7-1 season in 1927-1928, the Panthers settled into nearly two decades of solid but unspectacular records.

From 1946-1964, however, under Coach Walter "Duke" Nelson '33, a superb defenseman and 1930 honorable mention All-American, Middlebury became a dominant force in eastern hockey, winning the

"Duke" Nelson '33 advised the women's ice hockey team in 1980, long after he had officially retired from coaching.

Vermont championships for five consecutive years in the late 1940s and compiling a 47-23-2 record. The college competed in the old Tri-State League, with St. Lawrence, R.P.I., Clarkson, and Williams until 1959, and played strong Division One schools such as Clarkson, Army, Yale, Dartmouth, Northeastern, Boston College, and Boston University in the 1950s and early 1960s, an era that has been called the "Golden Age" of Middlebury hockey.

The peak years were 1959-1961, when the team recorded 16-7 and 19-2 seasons. Those squads were led by three-time All-American Phil Latreille, the greatest college hockey scorer of all time; Mike Karin '59, who still holds the NCAA assist record for one season (sixty-two in 1958-1959); and the Fryberger brothers—Bob '61, Jerry '61, and Dates '63—who in 1960-1961 formed the only all-brother line in college hockey. That 1960-1961 squad, which lost only to Clarkson and R.P.I., outscored its opponents by an astounding 192-59, as Latreille set the NCAA single season mark of 108 points (80 goals and 28 assists). That record still stands, as does Latreille's career scoring record of 346 points and career goals record of 250. Dates Fryberger, whose 236 points ranks him among the fifty top college scorers, went on to be an All-American in 1962 and 1963 and started on the 1964 U.S. Olympic hockey team.[88]

Coach Nelson, a cum laude graduate, compiled a record of 210-163-7 before giving up the reins in 1964 to one of his best players, Wendy Forbes '51. Nelson, who also coached football (1946-1968), golf (1947-1962, 1964-1972), and lacrosse (1954-1958), even came out of retirement briefly in 1982-1983 to coach the women's hockey team (which later developed into a regional power with an 11-3 record in 1988 and 12-4-1 in 1990). The college honored Nelson in 1981 by naming a lounge in the Alumni Center after him and, in an even more fitting dedication, named its artificial ice rink in the field house the Duke Nelson Arena in 1986. Participating in college and community athletic activities almost until his death in 1989, "Duke" will long be warmly remembered as a fine human being and a great asset to Middlebury, town and college alike.[89]

Forbes, who compiled a 254-232-18 record before he retired in 1985, was named national coach of the year in 1975 and took his team to the ECAC playoffs seven times, winning the ECAC Division II West title in 1978-1979. His successor, Bill Beaney, directed the 1989-1990 team to a 21-5-1 record—the most wins ever for a Middlebury hockey team—and was named Division III National Coach of the Year by his fellow coaches.[90]

The winning tradition of Middlebury teams in winter sports, particularly skiing, helped put the college on the map after 1945. Its northern and mountainous location, so great a detriment in earlier years, now became an enormous magnet that attracted skiers and skaters, and Middlebury built proper winter sports facilities to take advantage of this. The mountains became not only a backdrop to the beauty of the valley but also the center of most extracurricular life in the winter months. Many students—notably, wealthy eastern youngsters who enjoyed skiing—came because of the hills, and the college was transformed.

CHAPTER 14

STUDENT INVOLVEMENT: COLLEGE GOVERNANCE AND THE WORLD OUTSIDE

Greatly liberalized parietal hours would create social pressures in the area of sexual conduct which would encroach on individual freedom and might cause serious psychological impairment to some students.
—Dean Dennis O'Brien, *Middlebury Campus*, March 2, 1967

The deeper issue is that of the student role in the decision-making process at Middlebury. Students sense a growing movement to revoke privilege and restrict freedom, and the natural reaction is to resist the tendency. . . . The intent of the Administration is not to deceive or subvert, and Old Chapel is not insensitive to student concern, but perhaps merely unaware or inattentive. . . . At any rate, students should be shown what is happening, not told; the rationale should be presented and explained when action is taken; and student input should be solicited.
—Lucy Newell '78, *Middlebury Campus*, April 20, 1977

It would be dishonest to say that this judgment to turn aside from ROTC in favor of national needs closer to home is unrelated to the war in Vietnam. When ROTC came to this campus, United States military forces operating under a United Nations mandate were attempting to check a war of aggression. Today, the bulk of our armed forces are engaged in a war regarded by many as unjustified and which lacks even the clear sanction of the United States Congress. One cannot talk about the need for military forces entirely in the abstract; today that need is related to a war which is increasingly destructive of two societies, Vietnam and our own.

>—Minority Report of Ad Hoc Committee on
>R.O.T.C., quoted in Faculty Minutes, 1969–70,
>p. 33

What began to emerge here, over the past few days, was visible, palpable, compelling, and in its small way magnificent—or so many of us thought. I refer to the spirit which, despite continuing differences of opinion (of all shades) as to the size and nature of the problems at hand and the best ways of dealing with them, provided a common denominator, a unifying bond, and a sense of direction for nearly all out efforts. . . . If what we saw happening has the meaning and the potential—I am tempted to say the beauty—that so many of us glimpsed, it will not dissipate or disappear because of a blackened building.

>—Professor William Catton, in a speech to the
>Middlebury Community during the student
>strike of 1970, printed in the *Weekly News
>Calendar*, vol. 1 (May 13, 1970)

There were two other extracurricular activities of intermittent importance at twentieth-century Middlebury: student interest and participation in college governance and periodic student involvement in national and international political and social issues. In both areas the times of greatest concern occurred after 1960; the earlier decades, with a few exceptions, featured a prevailing contentment with (or willingness to accept) the status quo.

Between 1915 and 1960, separate student governments in the men's and women's colleges exercised some control over internal matters but commanded only mild student interest or support. The men's government, in particular, was often viewed as a mere arena for fraternity politics.[1] Under the rules of the Undergraduate Association, which replaced the Student Union as the men's governing body in 1919, the men had some power in devising freshman rules and, briefly, athletic policy.[2] In 1927 the presidents of the men's and women's student governments were allowed to sit on the Student Life Committee, which had wide-ranging control over campus activities. This decision to include students in the governing process was hailed as the removal of the "last vestige of administrative conservatism."[3] Students were also involved in judging and punishing those who violated some of the myriad college rules and regulations.[4]

Indeed, the list of rules was almost endless, particularly for the women, yet for the most part students went along with the college's in loco parentis role. June Brogger Noble '46 recalled her reaction to the rules set down by the college regarding the mixing of Navy V-12 men and Middlebury women at "the Lodge," the temporary wartime student union in Chi Psi:

> Opening Day at the Lodge goes a long way to aid fraternization between the saddle shoes crowd and the apprentice seamen, but a trembling Administration with visions of petting and fornication issues an edict to the Women's College: "Until such time as we can secure suitable permanent chaperones, you will be able to use the Lodge only when faculty chaperones are present."
>
> The Administration *in loco parentis* had spoken, and, brain-washed as we are into believing that each new privilege must be tediously earned, we go along with it.[5]

Before 1960 women were expected in at 12:30 A.M. on Saturday evenings and at 10:00 P.M. on all other nights, and they needed a chaperone if they went to dine with a man at a hotel unless it was one of the eleven inns on the approved list. Coeds could not walk alone in the evening off campus and were not allowed to smoke "while walking, attending athletic events, in the living room or entrances of halls of dormitories, or outside of buildings." There were dress codes (no slacks for women in Old Chapel, the library, or downtown), behavior codes (no card playing or dancing in public places on Sundays), and nearly undecipherable codes ("Driving between dormitories is permitted to one couple when going to and from a dance.") Of course, men and women were not allowed to visit each other's rooms, and after 10:00 P.M., woe to the individual who was spotted on the wrong side of College Avenue (the dividing line between the two campuses).[6]

For the most part, as late as the 1950s, students took for granted that the administration should impose rules on them, and they rarely questioned the regulations or gave them a second thought.[7] Furthermore, the rules were enforced. Under the firm hand of Deans Eleanor Ross (1915–1944) and Elizabeth Baker ("Ma") Kelly (1951–1970), the women generally conformed, as Dean Kelly once recalled: "If a

Dean Elizabeth Kelly reinforced the college's regulations governing women with the milder influence of tea at her home.

girl wasn't in her room at night and you didn't know where she was, she wouldn't really need to bother to tell you because she wouldn't be here long enough to do it." [8]

But the sexual urge was strong, and students found spots to neck in out-of-the-way places in nearby fields, on Chipman Hill, in fraternity houses, and in automobiles. Nevertheless, as one coed put it, virginity was still "as native to Middlebury as maple syrup," and premartial sexual intercourse appears to have been relatively rare before the mid-1960s. Most students who matriculated before World War II recall a rather innocent student body, in which fraternity men would serenade the women in their residence halls. By 1967, 61 percent of the men and 34 percent of the women reported that they had experienced sexual intercourse. Ironically, many women found the old rules convenient at times: being forced to return to one's dormitory by 10:00 P.M. could provide a wonderful excuse to end an otherwise dreary date or to fend off an overeager suitor. [9]

The whole system of regulations was gradually discarded during the 1960s; in its stead came coed residence halls, unlimited visitation hours, and few if any restrictions on the conduct or activities of women students. The 1960s were a truly revolutionary decade in this regard, and it was the students, at every juncture, who, demanding that they be treated as adults, won their "freedom." The fact that the struggle against paternalistic administrations was a nationwide phenomenon helped greatly in spurring students on and, ironically, gave hard-pressed officials one good answer to the angry questions from parents, trustees, and alumni who disapproved of the changes: everybody else was doing it, and the colleges that refused to accede to student demands were facing insurrection or a precipitous drop in applications for admission, or both.[10]

The agitation to end parietal rules and other regulations began innocently enough in 1960–1961 when women petitioned success-fully to extend their nightly curfew from 10:00 to 11:00 P.M. Re-quired chapel was also abolished that year, as we have seen. The *Campus* claimed that the later curfew, the abolition of required chapel, and the addition of independent study and honors projects to the curriculum were all part of a national trend toward giving students more freedom and responsibility.[11] In 1963, although the Student Life Committee again extended the curfew for women to midnight each evening and to 1:00 A.M. on Saturdays, there was growing discontent with the lack of any place on campus to engage in discreet private contact. "Where does one go to improvise, listen to music with friends, make love?" wrote one student.[12] The *Campus* agreed. "Student complaints basically concern a lack of privacy on the campus. There are no places where students can find privacy ex-cept outside in the grass or in cars. Sophomores and freshmen only have the grass, and the winters in Vermont are long and cold."[13]

For the next five years, students continually nagged the adminis-tration to liberalize the rules, and a few changes were made, allowing unchaperoned females in men's fraternity and dormitory lounges for a few hours each week; by 1966–1967, women could be in men's rooms with doors open, no alcohol present, and proctoring.[14] The administration was reluctant to go any further. As Dean Reynolds stated in 1966, "the college feels very strongly that at the present time the privacy for students to retire into a room and close the door is not something the college wants to condone."[15] He and Dean O'Brien both argued that "greatly liberalized parietal hours would create social pressures in the area of sexual conduct which would encroach on individual freedom and might cause serious psychological impairment to some students." [16]

The gradual change was not nearly fast enough for many, and the frustration showed itself in several ways. The Student Association, the coeducational student government formed in 1961, complained that it was powerless to change anything on campus and agreed to allow students to vote on whether to dissolve the organization. As one member put it just after resigning, "There really isn't any sort of student government at Middlebury." Things are changed, he continued, only when the administration wants them changed. The student body agreed and dissolved the Student Association in March 1967 by a vote of 407-70.[17]

It was clear that students wanted both a real voice in college governance and more freedom from college restrictions. In response, President Armstrong appointed the Commission on Student Life in the fall of 1967, to reexamine the conventions, customs, and rules of the community "to see whether these make sense as guidelines for student life today." [18] The commission, composed of four students, three deans, and three professors, reported to the trustees on April 13, 1968, and advocated sweeping changes: no more curfews for upperclasswomen, expanded hours for sophomores and freshmen women, residence halls to determine their own parietal hours, and students allowed to be with each other in their rooms with the doors closed. Although some trustees were upset over the "closed doors" policy, two student on the commission—Gilbert Kujovich '69 and Susan Shattuck '69—apparently convinced the board that the new system would permit greater responsibility through self-governance and that the social rules were not keeping up with the educational changes. Dean Kelly, who had opposed liberalization of the rules in the past, admitted that the students had changed her mind over time.[19]

The trustees finally agreed to these proposals with certain reservations, including the assurance that a new student government would be formed to replace the dissolved Student Association. The commission had also developed a plan for student government with dormitory councils as the basic unit, a student senate as the representative body (primarily elected through the dormitories), and a College

Council (later renamed Community Council) comprising four student officers of the senate, three faculty members, and three deans,
which would have the final say on all proposals passed by the Senate.
The College Council was viewed "as the fundamental meeting place
of the various competencies and concerns of the college—student,
faculty, and administration." [20]

While this new system was acceptable to the trustees, there were
some initial difficulties in defining spheres of power. When each dormitory submitted its proposal for social rules to the Student Senate,
Gifford Hall asked for complete autonomy in all matters concerning social life in the dormitory. The College Council denied the
request, arguing that autonomous dorms would weaken the community. Eight of the eleven members of the Gifford Dormitory Council
resigned in protest, but finally the dormitory gave in and submitted
rules for senate and council approval. [21]

The students continued to press for further liberalization. Over
the next few years, they sought twenty-four-hour parietals, coeducational dormitories, the end of all curfews, and unrestricted driving
privileges. [22] Gradually, they succeeded; by the mid-1970s most students lived in coeducational dormitories, many of them unaware of
the tremendous changes that had been wrought during the previous
decade. [23] The immediate results of the new freedom were not all
positive. The incidence of abortions and venereal disease rose dramatically, until Dr. George Parton, the school physician, began to
dispense birth control information and contraceptives. The Student
Sex Information Service, formed in the early 1970s, was also helpful
in this regard. [24] Dean Kelly worried about several other unfortunate
effects of the removal of most student rules—the shy person's rights
were no longer protected, the women's dorms might no longer be
quiet because the men (who had never known a quiet dormitory)
would bring their noise to the coeducational residences, and students were displaying a growing lack of consideration toward each
other and toward college property. [25]

On the other hand, the well-intentioned demands based on principles of freedom and responsibility were difficult to deny. President
Armstrong, looking back on the revolutionary changes, concluded:
"We did move beyond the woodenness of rules. Once we saw 18 as
the age of majority, we came gradually (rapidly in history's eye) to

understand that these young people—these young adults—must live as young adults." [26]

Students also pressed for a greater voice in college affairs after the formation of the new government apparatus in 1968. They prodded the faculty in 1969 into allowing student representation on all faculty committees;[27] and they persuaded the trustees in 1971 to elect two "young" trustees for two-year terms, to be nominated by the ballots of the current graduating class and the two most recent classes.[28] And when the institution, at President Armstrong's request, completed a full-scale reexamination of college governance in 1969–1970 and recommended that four councils—faculty, community, resources, and education—should replace or oversee the work of twenty-one existing committees, students were awarded representation on each of the councils except resources.[29] Students also flexed their collective muscle by pressing the faculty to eliminate distributional requirements (see chapter 8), and as we shall see, by persuading the faculty to abolish the R.O.T.C. requirement.[30]

Thereafter, except for some halfhearted demonstrations in favor of fraternities, divestment (see below), and more moderate tuition increases (see Chapter 10) the only major displays of organized protest against college policies and requests for greater control over decision making occurred in the late 1970s and early 1980s. Some students were upset in 1976–1977 when President Robison would not elaborate on the sudden and mysterious resignation of Gordon B. Bridges, director of dining halls.[31] When the administration decided to end rebates to nonfraternity students living on campus, who did not eat on campus, and to reduce the number of room blocks and suites available in the dorms, one thousand students signed a petition calling for more consultation and conversation before decisions were made. Lucy Newell '77, co-chairman of the Community Council, ably invoked the issue of college governance:

> The deeper issue is that of the student role in the decision-making process at Middlebury. Students sense a growing movement to revoke privilege and restrict freedom, and the natural reaction is to resist the tendency. . . . The intent of the Administration is not to deceive or subvert, and Old Chapel is not insensitive to student concern, but perhaps merely unaware or inattentive. . . . At any rate, students should

be shown what is happening, not told; the rationale should be presented and explained when action is taken; and student input should be solicited.[32]

A compromise was arranged, but some students were unhappy with Robison's leadership and the "atmosphere of distrust" on campus, and they called for a student trustee to sit on the board so that they could learn the truth about and have a greater say in college policies.[33]

Another group of unpopular decisions in 1978–1979 caused the usually apathetic student body to protest in earnest.[34] When students learned that the popular French professor, Susan Hayward, had been denied tenure, they staged a sit-in at Old Chapel. They also were angry over the Coffrin Committee report eliminating fraternity dining. They were unhappy about the crowded conditions in Proctor Dining Hall; the discontinuance of the program in Bath, England; the administration's unwillingness to break down the comprehensive fee; and the necessity to register all parties. Generally, the students did not feel they were being heard or having any impact in college decisions.[35]

On March 22, 1979, over six hundred of them attended a "student-wide meeting" sponsored by the ad hoc group Middlebury Awareness Development (MAD). The meeting considered six areas of concern: student activity space, tenure and reappointment, women's union and *Artemis Magazine*, programs abroad, treatment of fraternities, and student representation on the board. They also approved "solutions." They sought more activity space, greater and more timely input in tenure decisions by each department's student advisory committee, more active recruitment of women and minorities, standardized requirements for the study-abroad program, more contact with President Robison "in order to better inform the Trustees of Middlebury College of prevailing student opinion," a statement by the college supporting fraternities as an integral part of the community, and the annual election of a student to serve as a nonvoting member of the board's Undergraduate Life Committee.[36]

President Robison responded directly to the MAD proposals on March 26 in an address to seven hundred students in Mead Chapel. Robison, who had described the MAD agenda to the trustees two days earlier, agreed that nonvoting student representation on trustee committees was a good idea, and he promised that he would urge the board to place two students on the Undergraduate Life Committee and two on the Athletic Committee. Otherwise, Robison primarily defended current policy. He pointed out that they had tried diligently to hire more minorities and women, that the college would most likely renovate Proctor to provide more activity space, that student input into the tenure-decision process was welcome but that in the end such decisions called for peer-group review, and that while the programs-abroad committee and MAD representatives could discuss problems, Middlebury would remain rigorous in its academic standards for study abroad.[37] Although Robison had acceded to few of the MAD demands, his straightforwardness and the promise of possible student representation on trustee committees (later approved) apparently defused much of the unhappiness.[38]

Two years later, however, another set of issues led to the organization of Students Concerned about Middlebury (SCAM), and on March 24, 1981, students again filled Mead Chapel to express their displeasure. This time the issues included the administration's unwillingness to allow Zeta Psi fraternity members to have a meal plan in the house, divestment of college funds in South Africa, low faculty and staff salaries, minority concerns, and the lack of student input into the redesign of Proctor. The Student Forum discussed these matters somewhat vehemently with members of the administration, and by the next fall, some progress had been made in addressing the students' concerns.[39]

Aside from MAD and SCAM (and the "strike" in 1989 in response to the increased comprehensive fee, described in chapter 10), there were no major bursts of student interest in campus governance per se. The great majority remained "completely indifferent to or uninvolved in" student government.[40] Moreover, representation on three trustee committees and several faculty committees, departmental student advisory bodies (with input on tenure and hiring decisions), and the perception that the college was responding to student demands in a variety of areas helped to keep protests regarding governance to a minimum in the 1980s.

After 1960, Middlebury students also devoted more attention than their predecessors had to national and international issues, particularly civil rights and the Vietnam War in the 1960s and early 1970s and a variety of other topics in the 1980s, especially apartheid in South Africa.

Students in earlier years were not, for the most part, particularly interested in national and world affairs. The men organized a Discussion Club in 1919, and a Student Forum met in 1924 to discuss issues, but both groups were short-lived.[41] By the 1930s many students were more seriously concerned about national and international developments and were becoming somewhat more liberal in outlook. In the spring of 1928, over two-thirds of the students polled favored the Republican Herbert Hoover over Democrat Al Smith and all other candidates. But in 1932 the Socialist Norman Thomas finished second to Hoover in the student poll by a vote of 318 to 144, with Democrat Franklin Roosevelt trailing badly with 45 votes. In 1934, when students were asked, "To the beliefs of which party do you most closely subscribe?" 179 answered Socialist, 162 Republican, and 40 Democratic. This represented but a momentary loss in Republican hegemony; in 1936 students favored the Republican Landon over FDR by 398 to 175, with Socialist Norman Thomas polling only 33 votes.[42]

International peace became a concern in the 1930s. The Liberal Club, formed in 1932, discussed political issues and attempted to educate the rest of the community about certain matters, particularly peace and war, through questionnaires, speakers, and even participation in a national collegiate peace strike in 1936.[43] The strong antiwar sentiments of many students were occasionally expressed in the *Campus* until shortly before Pearl Harbor.[44]

During the war, students were naturally more concerned with international and national issues than before, forming the liberal Student Action Assembly and organizing the first Middlebury Conference in 1943.[45] June Brogger Noble '46 recalled that Granville Hicks, "who would later be termed a parlor pink by the reactionary right," came to campus as part of the conference, and "[led] us beside the still waters of unchecked capitalism and [showed us] the starving people on the other side."[46]

The veterans returned with firsthand knowledge of foreign lands and the horrors of combat and a strong antipathy toward undemocratic and elitist views.[47] President Stratton, a political conservative, had watched warily the activities of student liberals during and after the war and shared his observations with the trustees in 1947:

> On my arrival in Middlebury there existed a strong and fairly numerous group of students of various degrees of Left of Center opinions. They gave voice to their ideas in the Student Action Assembly and the Cultural Conference which had been organized by joint faculty and student groups. They were equally critical of the "undemocratic" organizations of the college and the lack of "economic democracy" in our capitalistic system. It is my impression that this group is now fewer in number and less bitter in their attacks than four years ago. There are, of course, a group of students under the influence of a few professors who are antagonistic toward the administrative policy of the college.[48]

After the veterans departed, this liberalism waned. The increased number of men from preparatory school backgrounds restored the moderate-to-conservative Republican mood that had existed during the 1920s. Although there continued to be discussions of politics, particularly around election times, and occasional conference speakers like Ralph Flanders, who discussed McCarthyism, the general tone of political life in the 1950s was self-satisfied, conservative, and apolitical. There were no crusades and few crusaders.[49]

In the 1960s the mood of the nation changed, and reform impulses began to appear on college campuses. Young people were especially active in the civil rights movement, and Middlebury students (as we saw in chapter 10) were no exception. They also worked to effect changes on campus that were consistent with the goals of the broader movement. This same pattern occurred later in the decade, when many students participated in the national protests against the Vietnam War and simultaneously urged the faculty to deemphasize the Reserve Officers' Training Corps (ROTC) program.

In the spring of 1965, eight Middlebury students joined in the March on Washington to protest the war, along with twenty-five thousand other students from across the nation. It was followed a week later by a confrontation between the administration and some forty students who wanted to demonstrate their dissatisfaction with the compulsory ROTC program. The administration persuaded the demonstrators not to march and assured them that the college was seriously considering changes in the requirement that each male student participate in the ROTC program during freshman and sophomore years.[50]

The army had established an ROTC unit at Middlebury in 1952 at the urging of President Stratton, who believed that such a program would help stabilize male enrollment during the Korean War.[51] It apparently worked. The program allowed students to fulfill part of their military obligation as undergraduates, and between 1952 and 1969 the Middlebury unit produced 623 commissioned officers, all of whom completed an optional two-year advanced course during junior and senior year and a stint at summer camp after the required work as underclassmen.[52] By the early 1960s, however, many students were opposed to the compulsory nature of the program's first two years. "Compulsory ROTC at Middlebury is an anachronism," argued Howard B. Tolley, Jr., the *Campus* editor, in January 1965.

> No longer can Middlebury afford to dilute its academic curriculum with compulsory courses in Military Science and Tactics. . . . A Reserve Officers Training Corps unit is undoubtedly a convenience for the 113 junior and senior men currently enrolled in the advanced program. But consider the 448 freshmen and sophomores required to drill each week so that upperclassmen can gain practical experience. Since a mere one-third of those in the lower classes will opt to continue army training, the majority are little more than guinea pigs for their more military minded classmates. Too many valuable hours each week are devoted to course materials of no intrinsic merit or relevance for the liberal arts student.[53]

The faculty and trustees, in apparent agreement, voted in April 1966 to retain ROTC but on a totally voluntary basis.[54] But opponents of the war in Vietnam favored the more drastic option of discontinuing ROTC altogether, and for the next two years, as they demonstrated against the war, these students and faculty also lobbied for the end of ROTC.[55] Between 1967 and 1970, Middlebury students and professors organized antiwar teach-ins, demonstrated against Dow Chemical interviews, staged a large sit-in at the local draft board, and participated in activities associated with the October 15, 1969, moratorium against the war. Some traveled to Washington to march against the war in 1967 and 1969; others worked in 1968 for antiwar presidential candidate Eugene McCarthy, who was a heavy favorite among Middlebury students. Although only a minority were actively involved in these activities, 65 percent of those polled in

March 1968 felt that the war was not in the country's best interests, and 32 percent called it unjust.[56]

The faculty began to consider further action against the ROTC in the fall of 1968. They were badly divided over the issue. Some wanted to eliminate it entirely; others hoped to relegate it to a noncredit, paracurricular program; a minority favored keeping it as it was. A large majority of students—71.4 percent—also favored a downgrading of the ROTC role, although only about 25 percent favored its total elimination.[57] In 1968–1969 the debate revolved around the question of whether to continue granting credit for ROTC. On February 3, 1969, the faculty voted tentatively (46–42) to deny ROTC representatives faculty voting privileges and (46–43) to stop granting credit for ROTC courses.[58] An ad hoc committee, composed of six professors, one student, and an ROTC representative, was formed to consider the issues further and report. A petition presented by 250 students at the May 5 faculty meeting urged that ROTC become merely an extracurricular activity. The army let it be known that they would not accept that status but were willing to negotiate. On May 14, the ad hoc committee met with an officer, who assured them that the army's main concern was to keep the unit on campus, even if it meant changing its status.[59]

The committee gave its final report at the May 26 faculty meeting.[60] Four members favored a "modified" system, which would allow the ROTC to remain on campus but would downgrade it in several ways: the Department of Military Science would cease to exist as a college department and would remain only as a "program," no ROTC courses would carry credit, none of the ROTC staff would have full faculty status or voting rights, and the program would be conducted by a faculty-student committee. Three members—two professors and the student—asked for elimination of the program entirely, and the ROTC representative, not unexpectedly, voted for no change in the program's status.

Since the May 26 meeting was so close to final exams, it was decided to vote on the question in the fall. President Armstrong was worried that the delay would hurt the chances of the "modified" plan because Vietnam was becoming an increasingly volatile issue.[61] Indeed, the rationale presented by the three committee members who favored total elimination of ROTC was essentially based on opposition to the war:

> It would be dishonest to say that this judgment to turn aside from ROTC in favor of national needs closer to home is unrelated to the war in Vietnam. When ROTC came to this campus, United States military forces operating under the United Nations mandate were attempting to check a war of aggression. Today, the bulk of our armed forces are engaged in a war regarded by many as unjustified and which lacks even the clear sanction of the United States Congress. One cannot talk about the need for military forces entirely in the abstract; today that need is related to a war which is increasingly destructive of two societies, Vietnam and our own. In rejecting the necessity of the Vietnam war, we must, in part, diminish the argument for the necessity of ROTC at Middlebury.[62]

This threesome also argued that the army, not the faculty, would be controlling the content of courses, and pointed out that the "inherent logic of a program in Military *training* can never be made to fit the criteria applicable to a liberal arts *education*."

The four supporters of the "modified plan" countered with several arguments, the most telling of which was simply that it was rash and possibly injurious to the college to eliminate the program completely.

> In recommending the retention of ROTC at Middlebury College on a modified basis, we are primarily concerned about the welfare and interests of the College *in the long run*. We make no claim to powers of clairvoyance, but we hope that events of the past can throw some light on the future. We fear that an urge to terminate ROTC at this time is a response to current pressures which are highly subject to change. Within the last thirty years Middlebury College has been twice sustained by the presence of military organizations: first by the V-12 unit of the Naval Reserve Program during World War II, and then by the establishment of the Army ROTC unit in 1952, during the Korean War; both events insured that the College could retain its chosen coeducational status at times when this status was very much in doubt.[63]

After lengthy discussions during the fall of 1969, the faculty voted on October 7 to accept the "modified plan" by a vote of 53–51. The *Campus* claimed that students had heavily influenced the voting and may have signaled a new emphasis on student input into the decision-making process.[64] ROTC continued as a voluntary program until 1976, when it was phased out due to lack of participation.[65]

Student participation in the antiwar movement reached its height in 1969–1971. The peak occurred in May 1970, after United States

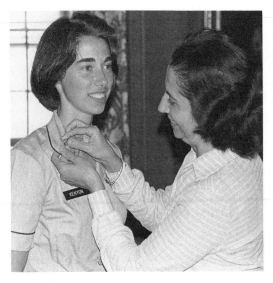

At the penultimate ceremony commissioning ROTC officers, Susan Kenyon '77 became Middlebury's first woman to receive her second-lieutenant's bars. Her mother pinned them on.

forces entered Cambodia and students and onlookers were killed at Kent State University on Monday, May 4, during demonstrations against the Cambodian invasion. On the morning of May 5, hundreds of Middlebury students signed a petition protesting the deaths at Kent State and the invasion of Cambodia.[66] The College Council responded immediately by holding a special noon meeting at which they resolved that the college should "suspend normal activities" for the next six days:

> WHEREAS our nation is in a state of crisis precipitated by the expansion of the war in Southeast Asia and by the deaths of four Kent State University students, and WHEREAS we are in a state of personal and community distress.
>
> Be it resolved,
> that the Middlebury College Community shall suspend normal activities until Monday, May 11, 1970.
> *First*, for the purpose of striking against the expansion of the war in Southeast Asia;
> *Second*, for the purpose of mourning the deaths of the four Kent State University students; and
> *Third*, for the re-examination of our collective and individual directions and purposes.
> We recognize the right of individuals to teach and learn according to the dictates of their consciences without being subject to communal criticism or penalty.[67]

Students and faculty protested the draft in March 1970 with a march into town.

That evening the faculty approved the council proposal by a vote of 79-11 with 4 abstentions. Immediately after the faculty meeting, an overflow crowd assembled in Mead Chapel for a service in memory of the people who died at Kent State. President Armstrong (who had rushed back from New York to chair the faculty meeting) gravely told the hushed crowd that he had joined a large number of other college and university presidents in an appeal to President Nixon to end the war. The presidents told Nixon that they shared the "severe and widespread apprehensions on our campuses" raised by the invasion of Cambodia and the resumption of the bombing of North Vietnam: "We implore you to consider the incalculable dangers of an unprecedented alienation of America's youth and to take immediate action to demonstrate your determination to end the war quickly." [68] After the memorial service, a rally in the chapel was addressed by Dean O'Brien, history professor Nicholas Clifford, and a number of students. On Wednesday, another rally was held, with Lieutenant Governor Hayes as the keynote speaker.

Plans were made to canvass the Middlebury area against the war and continue the activities of the strike (as it was styled by some of the more radical members of the student–faculty ad hoc committee) or "extraordinary session" (as it was termed by the administration).

A candlelight procession following the burning of Recitation Hall in 1970.

One observer described it as "a confusing array of meetings, informational workshops, planning sessions, and projects." The more radical students and faculty formed a "strike committee," which was busy, as one student wrote, "discussing various ways of extending the strike at Middlebury, aligning the College with the goals of the national movement and organizing more efficiently the efforts of the hundreds of students who daily crowded into the strike headquarters in Proctor Hall."[69]

At dawn on Thursday, May 7, the community received a frightening jolt when Recitation Hall, the old wooden structure just east of Carr Hall, was virtually destroyed in a fire set by an arsonist. The culprit was a former student with apparent psychological problems. Although Recitation Hall had been scheduled for demolition, the loss of the building and the threat of similar acts cast a pall over the institution. After the fire was put out, President Armstrong, fearful that "things might fall apart," held a staff meeting at his house at 5:30 A.M. Over breakfast, it was decided that the president should address the entire college community and assure them that Middlebury "could sustain itself under these trials."

Armstrong was greatly encouraged by the reception he was given at the speech before a jam-packed chapel ("I have never seen the Chapel so full," he remarked later).[70] He told the audience that the loss of a college building reminded the community of its vulnerability to force and violence and that perhaps there was "real danger" in continuing in extraordinary session. However, he argued that "we have witnessed a great outpouring of good will, even when in strong disagreement, an openness all deeply felt, and this may be a basis for our carrying on in extraordinary session until Monday."[71] History professor William Catton supported the president's remarks, and urged the college not to be deterred from its purposes by the work of an arsonist:

> What began to emerge here, over the past few days, was visible, palpable, compelling, and in its small way magnificent—or so many of us thought. I refer to the spirit which, despite continuing differences of opinion (of all shades) as to the size and nature of the problems at hand and the best ways of dealing with them, provided a common denominator, a unifying bond, and a sense of direction for nearly all our efforts. . . . If what we saw happening has the meaning and the potential—I am tempted to say the beauty—that so many of us glimpsed, it will not dissipate or disappear because of a blackened building.[72]

Several students also spoke, urging that the extraordinary session continue despite the fire. The student–faculty ad hoc committee issued a statement that characterized the arson as a "wanton, irrational, manifestly apolitical" act. Later that day the College Council, in open meeting, voted to continue the suspension of classes until Monday as planned. During the meeting, the audience was shocked and dismayed at the report that someone had defaced the set for the play *Alice in Wonderland*, which was to be produced during the week. That evening, Dean Bruce Peterson organized a number of students and faculty to help the campus security team guard all the college buildings against further damage. They continued this surveillance throughout the week and were applauded for their efforts by the grateful chief of campus security, Fred Spencer, Jr.: "We would have been lost without the students; there are only four of us in Security. We depended upon them and they did not fail us."[73]

The rest of the extraordinary session was busy and, for many, exhilarating. Later that month, Armstrong told the trustees that "education was going on" during that week although most classes were not held: "The achievement of the week was not that students did not disrupt, rather it is that they took positive and concerned steps to improve their understanding of themselves and the world around them. . . . There was a free flow of ideas, a spirit of profound concern both political and moral." [74] Efforts to extend the strike past May 11 were not successful, but the faculty voted to be flexible and lenient in handing out incompletes to students who wished to pursue political activities during the rest of the semester. [75]

While the strike of 1970 was undoubtedly the high-water mark of the Middlebury protests against the war, some students continued to be active in various causes. A few weeks after the strike, an ROTC classroom was vandalized (apparently by a small group of students), and in 1971 fifty Middlebury students participated in May Day demonstrations in Washington; twenty-six of them were arrested. [76] The following spring, after the United States resumed the bombing of North Vietnam and mined Haiphong Harbor, a strike was called on April 27 by the Radical Education Action Projection (REAP), a left-wing student group that had been formed in early 1971. REAP took over the ROTC building and turned it into a "peace center." A strike was not called, but on May 9, 1972, the faculty declared (by a vote of 46–12, with 28 abstentions) that it deplored the resumption of bombing and the mining of the harbor. [77]

Other groups now began to compete with antiwar activists for support. Many students became interested in the struggle for environmental quality during the 1970s and 1980s, and the student group EQ was often active, sponsoring a week-long series of lectures and discussions in 1989, for example, that culminated in a Saturday afternoon festival. [78] After 1972, however, Middlebury (along with other American campuses) settled down into a more conservative and apolitical—some might say apathetic—mood. It was not until the mid-1980s that the college awakened again over apartheid in South Africa, the activities of the CIA, and the rights of women and gays.

The faculty expressed its support in 1978 for the struggle for human rights and civil liberties in South Africa and asked the trustees to determine whether the companies in which the college had investments were adhering to the Sullivan Principles. By 1981 the faculty was calling for complete divestment, but the trustees agreed only to end investments in firms not adhering to the Sullivan Principles. [79] The students came around more slowly; it was not until 1985 that representatives of the Black Student Union met with the Undergraduate Life Committee to ask the college to divest.[80] Although other students and faculty also urged divestment, the trustees held firm in their stance.

During the winter of 1986, students formed several antiapartheid groups, including the Armadillos, who built a small rock wall on campus to symbolize the South African cause, and the Students against Apartheid, who organized a sit-in in President Robison's office in February.[81] The board, while influenced by campus pressure, was even more concerned with the deteriorating situation in South Africa during 1986. As President Robison put it: "The tragic unfolding of events in South Africa has sharply focused our energies, and our consciences. With each new outrage, each life surrendered, each freedom denied, we find ourselves, as citizens and human beings, baffled by the complexity of the situation yet still hoping for a path to peace in that troubled land."[82] For this reason, the board moved away from its previous policy of selective divestment and finally voted, on July 28, 1986, for full divestment over a two-year period.[83]

The question of whether the Central Intelligence Agency should be allowed to recruit at Middlebury also activated the campus in the mid-1980s. CIA recruitment became an issue because the organization supposedly would not hire gays and was allegedly involved in controversial covert activities in Latin America. A number of faculty, staff, and students demonstrated in February 1987 against CIA recruitment on campus. Several months later, the Student Forum and the Community Council passed a proposal that the CIA no longer be allowed to recruit at Middlebury. President Robison rejected this proposal in October on the grounds that the campus should remain open to "those organizations whose recruiting policies conform to federal laws."[84] But CIA recruiters would be asked to hold an open educational session and answer questions about their hiring procedures and activities.

Disappointed, the anti-CIA forces quickly organized a teach-in to discuss the issues, and the faculty voted 63–23 in December that "the College should permit recruitment on campus only by employers who will sign statements affirming a policy of hiring and promoting personnel without discrimination on the basis of race, religion, gender, or sexual orientation."[85] Although concerned students made their case before the Trustee Committee on Undergraduate Life in the spring of 1988, the college's position did not change, and CIA recruitment continued in 1988–1989 even though the *Campus* and the Community Council continued to oppose it. Not surprisingly, protests and counterprotests accompanied the appearance of CIA recruiters in the fall of 1988, despite the claim that the organization no longer discriminated against homosexuals.[86]

CIA representatives signed the Middlebury employment policy statement in the fall of 1989, thereby formally affirming that they would not discriminate against homosexuals. The protests continued, now focusing directly on the agency's activities. On October 17, fifty faculty members, students, and townspeople, some of them members of the activist group ACT NOW, entered the Career Counseling and Placement offices and attempted to stop the CIA representatives from holding their scheduled interviews. The protest group sang and chanted so loudly that the recruiters were unable to go on. Finally, a deal was struck. The chief recruiter agreed that the organization would not return to Middlebury as long as he was in charge of the Northeast region if the protesters would quiet down so that he could finish the interviews that day. The students concurred and wrote up the verbal agreement in the form of a document for the recruiter to sign. He was at first reluctant but eventually signed it.[87]

These protests, in part touched off by the alleged CIA policy of discrimination against homosexuals, marked one of the few times in the college's history when the issue of homosexuality had been a focus for campus discussion. Until the mid-1970s, gay men and lesbian women kept their sexual orientation pretty much to themselves. Some "came out of the closet" on September 16, 1975, when gay and lesbian students held their first open meeting.[88] The Gay People at Middlebury, as they called their group, was relatively successful for a few years but went downhill in the early 1980s and disappeared in 1983–1984 as homophobia grew and gay students claimed they were too uncomfortable to meet as a group.

The gay community reorganized itself in 1988–1989 as the Middlebury Lesbian and Gay Alliance (MLGA).[89] A major difference then, according to Professor Richard Cornwall, was the presence of some support from heterosexual members of the community, who believed that homophobia could have deleterious effects on the college and the educational process. In 1985, Cornwall and Professor

David Prouty helped persuade the faculty to pass (by a vote of 58–21–5) a recommendation that the trustees include sexual orientation in the college's official nondiscrimination statement.[90] The trustees argued that "since the nondiscrimination statement is simply a statement of compliance with the law, it would not be advisable to go beyond such compliance."[91] The CIA protests also allowed gay and lesbian students and faculty to ally themselves with people who opposed the CIA for reasons other than that of discrimination. The result was at least a momentary end to the political isolation of the gay movement, and in 1989–1990 the MLGA became the MGLSA — the Middlebury Gay Lesbian Straight Alliance.[92]

Another important area of student involvement—women's rights—deserves a little background. One of the most remarkable changes at Middlebury between 1915 and 1990 was the development of a more truly coeducational college. Since much of this transformation is chronicled in other chapters, only a brief analysis and summary will be attempted here.

Until the 1960s, the situation of Middlebury women was similar to that of most women in American society—they were second-class citizens, discriminated against and segregated on the periphery of a college that concentrated primarily on the activities of its men.[93] Middlebury women were not allowed to direct (or sometimes even participate in) the major political, social, and athletic aspects of college life. In those few cases outside the classroom where they worked with men, they served in traditionally subordinate roles; otherwise, they engaged in sex-segregated social and athletic activities that were of much less importance than those of the men.

Only after 1960 did women begin to gain an equal place at Middlebury College. This had several causes: the decline of the fraternities, the end of curfew hours and discriminatory social regulations, the integration of dining and living facilities and of many extracurricular activities, the crumbling of the last vestiges of the coordinate college system, the increased support for women's intercollegiate athletics, and the hiring of more female faculty members and administrators.

Fraternities were the center of campus social life before 1965, which excluded women from most of the social decisionmaking.[94] Until 1955, when coeducational freshman dining began on an experimental basis, men and women had eaten separately—most of the men in fraternities and the women in campus dining halls.[95] When Armstrong determined in 1964–1966 that fraternities should be abolished or deemphasized, he made clear that his decision was based in part on the desire to provide an equal social life and dining opportunities for women.[96] Progress toward this goal accelerated in the 1980s as fraternity dining facilities were closed and women began to be integrated into the formerly all-male chapters.

Women gained equality slowly after World War II. Not until the 1970s did they begin to have similar opportunities to compete in intercollegiate athletics. The sexes maintained separate student governments from 1915 to 1961, with the men's organization receiving much greater *Campus* coverage, especially before the war. The Men's and Women's Undergraduate Associations merged in 1961 to form the Student Association (SA), but the president was required to be a male.[97] Indeed, the *Campus*, *Kaleidoscope*, and other coeducational clubs and activities traditionally elected men as president (or editor-in-chief) and treasurer (or business manager), while women held the subordinate offices of secretary, vice president, assistant business manager, and assistant editor. Women ran all the activities and publications during the war but were once again consigned to their subordinate stations after the men returned to campus. As late as 1966 a study sponsored by the National Institute of Mental Health called Middlebury a masculine college run primarily by men with women in the background. The authors pointed out that a man headed the SA and most other important organizations. Still, there were exceptions. Women were co-chairs (or co-editors) of the Middlebury Conference (founded by women as the Cultural Conference during the war), the Religion Conference, and *Kaleidoscope*. Explanations for male dominance included the claims that men could not work for women and that women tended to be submissive in their relations with men.[98]

Male domination began to decrease after 1965, due in part to the influence of the national women's movement, which sensitized college women (and some men) to the many-sided issue of sexist assumptions and practices. The end of parietal and curfew hours for women and the opening of coed dorms helped eliminate some of the artificialities of the segregated system and allowed men and women to form friendships and closer attachments more naturally and in a more egalitarian atmosphere.

All of this is not to say that Middlebury women were unhappy prisoners of a discriminatory system. For the most part, they were happy to be at Middlebury, proud of their college, and fairly active in campus activities. One observer claimed in 1941 that women at Middlebury were better treated than their counterparts elsewhere. "In most institutions with an arrangement of this sort, the women still remain secondary to the men, but that is far from the case here. Probably in no other college in the country where women and men tread the same campus walks is there the same spirit of equality in social and educational prerogatives."[99] What equality there was should be attributed to the dignified efforts of Dean Ross (1916–1944), who apparently believed that women were discriminated against at Middlebury and may have encouraged the separation of the two colleges in the hope that women would do better on their own.[100]

It was during Armstrong's presidency that the dual structure of the coordinate college was dismantled. Armstrong created a single dean of students office, a unified admissions office, and a single department of physical education. Discrimination against women in admissions diminished after 1970, as nearly equal numbers of men and women began to be admitted for the first time, and the men and women admitted were of equal academic potential.

The struggle for equality and an end to discrimination against women engulfed American society and academe in the 1970s and 1980s; not surprisingly, it had an impact on the college as well. Women at Middlebury made important gains. The number of female faculty members increased dramatically (from twenty-two in 1976 to sixty-six by 1987), and several women were appointed or elected to important positions—such as chemistry professor Jane Margaret O'Brien, who became associate provost in 1988; Ann Hanson, appointed acting dean of the college in 1989; and Professor of Spanish Chela Andreu, who, in 1989, was the first woman elected to the powerful Committee on Reappointment.[101] By 1989 the college was considering a proposal for a woman's studies major; the Women's Culture Series, featuring a schedule of lectures and presentations by female artists and writers, was in its fourth year; faculty members were being trained (in a winter term seminar) on how to teach women's studies in their classes; a feminist magazine, *Womyn*, was about to appear; Fletcher House had been set aside as an all-female

In 1976, Marjorie Lamberti became the second woman at Middlebury to be appointed full professor; Clara Blanche Knapp had been appointed professor of home economics in 1925. Marjorie Lamberti's scholarship, in nineteenth- and twentieth-century German educational systems, as well as her animated classes in modern European history, made her an exemplar of the teaching scholar to her colleagues and a model to the women who entered the faculty in significant numbers in the years after her appointment.

residence; and some of the inequities in the athletic program were being addressed. Robison announced at the start of the 1988–1989 academic year the formation of a committee of students, faculty, and staff to look at "attitudes toward gender."[102]

Still, equality had not been reached. Sociology professor Margaret Nelson stated in 1989 that women—faculty and students— "are made to feel like they are not full-fledged members of the community."[103] The bloodied mannequin at Delta Upsilon in the spring of 1988 reminded everyone that mindless, even unconscious misogyny existed at Middlebury; as one female student put it at the hearings following that incident: "I have been afraid of you [fraternity men] since my freshman year . . . why does the social space on this campus almost all belong to men?"[104] As we have seen in chapter 13, women athletes complained of unequal treatment—less money for their teams, inexperienced coaches, inferior facilities and equipment.

The report of the Special Committee on Attitudes toward Gender, appearing in the spring of 1990, painted a rather dismal picture. Surveys revealed that younger women faculty did not appear to be advancing as quickly as their male counterparts, that female staff members saw serious gender inequities in the workplace, and that many students described "social life" at Middlebury as approaching a meat market. The committee offered fourteen recommendations, including the formation of a standing committee on gender issues to address the problems raised in the report. President Robison hailed it "as the basis for discussion and action" and hoped that it would provide "the proper setting for correction and change." [105]

Historians, like journalists, sometimes tend to overemphasize the importance of political activities, and I plead guilty: in this chapter I have certainly written at length about those rather rare periods when Middlebury students, happily ensconced in rural Vermont, overcome their normal lack of interest in the political world. Countless *Campus* editorials and letters during the past century have blamed Middlebury's isolation for this lack of student concern; a political forum was organized in 1977 to "combat isolation and apathy, caused by living in a location such as Middlebury." [106]

Although location may have been a factor, there are perhaps other explanations for the customary student apathy. Some studies suggest that student activists—those who are "protest-prone"—are from homes in which parents have liberal or radical political leanings.[107] But most Middlebury students have traditionally come from conservative or apolitical families. One could also argue that the type of student who would choose to attend a small school in a beautiful and isolated setting is not as likely to be an activist in the first place. Only when large numbers of students at other schools have already initiated an organized political cause—the peace movement of the 1930s, the civil rights and antiwar movements of the 1960s, the South African divestment issue in the 1980s—do Middlebury students tend to become involved. That seems unlikely to change in the near future.

CHAPTER 15

"... AND A CAST OF THOUSANDS"

Improvement and recruitment of fine faculty continues to be the College's principal area of concern. The first is recruitment, the second is improvement, and third, very close to it but slightly different, the creation of an atmosphere and working circumstances which make maximum use of a faculty's many talents. . . . In the area of faculty improvement, the new programs for research grants to faculty members and for leaves of absence for self-improvement are making a magnificent contribution. The morale of the faculty, in this respect, is higher this year than I have ever known it.

> —Thomas Reynolds, Report of the Dean of the College, 1965, pp. 11-12

Counsel from townsmen was free, and in those days [1924-1928] they offered a generous supply of enlightenment that wasn't to be found in textbooks. The College was still an enclave of the town—or vice-versa. Together they composed the community, one dependent on the other. Then, symbolically, we were graduated from Middlebury, Town and College, when we were handed our diplomas on the platform of the Congregational Church, whence they had been dispensed for a century and a quarter.

> —W. Storrs Lee '28, "In Retrospection," *Middlebury College News Letter*, 52 (summer 1978): 15

The previous five chapters have been dominated by students, because I believe that campus life is essentially determined and played out by students. But the social history of Middlebury College has had other key players—faculty, administrators, staff, trustees, alumni, and townspeople. In this final chapter, they will all receive some well deserved (if relatively brief) attention.

When President John Thomas and Paul Moody went looking for new faculty, they often searched for men (and a few women) with good character, experience in the real world, and strong teaching skills. If the candidates had a doctorate or research interests, that was fine but not necessary. This changed significantly after World War II, as Presidents Stratton, Armstrong, and Robison increasingly looked for scholarly potential and productivity in candidates. In the Stratton years, the Ph.D. and a solid attempt to stay current in one's field was usually considered sufficient for a faculty member to remain at Middlebury.[1] But by the 1960s faculty members were expected to continue publishing beyond the dissertation, and tenure decisions came to be based as much (or more) on scholarly output as on teaching ability or community service. Untenured faculty began feeling tremendous pressure to publish, which led them to seek sabbaticals and leaves of absence during their early years at the college.[2] The period 1960–1990 witnessed a subtle shift away from emphasizing excellence in teaching and assisting students; junior faculty, faced with a difficult job market after 1970, tried instead to maximize their chances for tenure (at Middlebury or elsewhere) by conducting research and publishing. In 1989 the *Report of the Visiting Committee on Literature* remarked upon this sea change:

> The criteria for appointment and for promotion at Middlebury appear to have undergone a marked, but largely unacknowledged and unarticulated, change in the past decade or so. This has not been a conscious decision so much as a response to the fact that, in a buyer's market, it has been possible to insist on a Ph.D. from a major research institution and, subsequently, to look for a scholarly output consistent with promotion within such an institution. Whether such possibilities will remain in what promises, at least until the end of this century, to be a "sellers market," is less the question than whether Middlebury can or should continue on this path without a careful reassessment of its policies. Already, it would seem, tendencies have evolved that seriously compromise Middlebury's identity as a first-class liberal arts college. . . .
>
> Obviously teaching and research are complementary, not contradictory; each informs and enriches the other. . . . Just as obviously, scholarly productivity is essential to junior faculty should they need to place themselves on the market again. But meanwhile an emphasis (however unintended and, because uncertainly expressed, ambigu-

ous) encourages identification with the profession rather than with the institution. . . .

Whatever one's notion of the nature and purposes of undergraduate education, however, what should be of concern to Middlebury is that this tilting of the earlier balance of teaching and research has occurred seemingly without institutional self-awareness and, quite clearly, unevenly as among the several departments.[3]

These changes undoubtedly accelerated in the 1980s, but they date back much farther than the report suggests. Before World War II, the faculty felt a strong identification with Middlebury College and with institutional goals. The shift toward professional and away from institutional identity and orientation began around midcentury, continued gradually for some two decades, and was present in full force by 1970. Although their goals and institutional expectations changed markedly, Middlebury faculty demonstrated an enduring interest in institutional governance. They sought a strong voice not only in internal faculty matters but also in setting general college policies. This produced recurrent tensions, since some members of the board of trustees (and even an occasional administrator or two) did not always view the faculty as partners but rather as employees.

The faculty naturally showed a continuing and at times intense interest over the years in matters relating to compensation and in the general questions of promotion, appointment, reappointment, and tenure. Both subjects have been discussed in earlier chapters, but a short review (with some additional examples) of policies and reactions concerning appointment and tenure might still be in order. For example, President Thomas's decision in 1917 not to retain three teachers greatly disturbed the faculty, and Professor Vernon Harrington wrote Thomas about his concerns.

> I most earnestly hope that a method of concluding a teacher's work in the College may be devised which is not so abrupt & painful & which will not so unsettle the whole teaching staff as the one now in operation. . . . The stigma of having been dismissed follows the man for years & maybe for life. . . . anyone who understands human nature knows that the fact of an abrupt dismissal follows a man like an avenging spirit & over & over shuts him out of being considered for positions for which he may be perfectly fitted.[4]

Harrington argued that the men dismissed should have been warned at least a year in advance, for job-hunting purposes, and proposed giving the faculty member a chance "to make statements as to his plans, methods, & theories of teaching. To pass a sentence on a man without his having had opportunity to present his side of the case, to be heard in his own behalf, is un-American—contrary to all American law." He also suggested that "in every case a conference with at least his colleagues of his own & closely related departments is indispensable." He concluded by describing the general reaction:

> As to the spirit & morale of the Faculty as a whole, I need only touch upon the unfortunate effect of the method which has been pursued. Nothing could be more unsettling. The feeling which has been present since a year ago must be immensely intensified by the recent events. It cannot help having a sort of paralyzing effect on the Faculty's endeavors. The faculty cannot tell where this is going to stop—whose turn comes next.

Thomas and the trustees wrestled with these issues during 1917–1918, met with a group of faculty members, and developed the college's first official policy of appointment and tenure. It included the creation of a three-member faculty Committee on Conference with whom the trustees would meet "before recommending the dismissal of any member of the permanent teaching staff of the College." In addition, the trustees or president might confer with this committee "as to changes in the teaching staff of the College, or as to any matter affecting its work or influence." [5]

The trustees further refined the rules in 1933 and 1941, and after the revolt against Stratton in 1947, he gave faculty members an advisory voice in personnel matters.[6] But Stratton's tenure policies were apparently idiosyncratic, and it was never completely clear what the actual rules were. An instructor with twenty years of service might still not have been granted tenure. Furthermore, although promotion to full professor was supposed to confer "appointment without limit of tenure," as the phrase went, Professor Howard Munford recalled that when he was promoted to full professor, Stratton told him he did not yet have tenure because he had been disloyal.[7]

The faculty never completely trusted Stratton and asked the board in 1955 to give the Faculty Committee on Tenure more than just advisory powers. The trustees declined, but after Armstrong took over in 1963, the college moved quickly to set more precise rules on tenure and reappointment and to give more power to the faculty in these matters. The faculty wrote a new set of rules, approved by the board in April 1966, which allowed a number of faculty who met the new criteria to be granted tenure almost automatically.[8]

Fears of overtenuring the faculty mounted, and new rules were passed in 1975 that, among other things, extended the length of time that junior faculty remained in a probationary status. It was clearly becoming more difficult to attain permanent status at Middlebury, as evidenced by several controversial decisions denying tenure or reappointment to Professors Bruce Carroll, Joan Peters, Peter Stitt, and John Conron.[9] In the meantime, the de facto power of the faculty Committee on Reappointment grew steadily after 1963, and only rarely were its personnel recommendations overturned.[10]

Faculty interest in obtaining more power and influence extended to other areas of institutional governance. They asked the board in 1955 to allow them to elect the entire membership of the Faculty Council and the majority of the Educational Council and requested that the membership of the Administration Committee be determined by faculty vote. The trustees agreed only to allow faculty to elect all members of the Educational Council. The board also turned down a request that the trustees direct the president to consult with faculty on administrative appointments.[11]

Faculty members continued to meet with the trustee Committee on Conference and express their concerns, frequently urging greater expenditures for improving the library and other academic facilities, for attracting the best possible students, and for bettering the college's intellectual environment.[12] Frustrated at times by trustee predilections and policies, the faculty periodically called for membership on the board. When they asked for six seats on the board in 1968, Armstrong offered the compromise of placing faculty (and some students) on certain board committees without granting actual board membership. They requested it again in 1990 over dissatisfaction with board and presidential actions. The faculty also sought a voice in the hiring of the president and were instrumental in finding James Armstrong.[13]

Sabbatical leaves and teaching conditions were another concern. As we have seen, leave policy was simple and extremely limited until the 1960s and after, when Presidents Armstrong and Robison greatly enlarged and improved the leave program.[14] Teaching conditions before World War II were not onerous. Many faculty did have to share offices until (and even after) Munroe Hall was competed in 1940. Still, since there was no publishing requirement under Thomas or Moody, life was less pressure-packed than in later years.[15] Moreover, teaching loads (nine to fifteen hours) and class size (10:1 student-faculty ratio in 1938–1939 and 13.5:1 in 1939–1940) were not particularly heavy.[16] Prewar professors therefore had a bit more time for coffee and relaxation than their successors did, but they faced the usual time-consuming responsibilities: teaching, student conferences, committee work, advising and assisting student groups, attending extracurricular events, and chaperoning student parties.

One of the most onerous tasks—grading—was, of course, a constant, and registrars often had to take unusual measures to collect grades from those teachers who tended to be slow in turning in their grade sheets. Registrar Frank Cady once became so frustrated that he rowed out into the Middlebury River to remind a professor, who was fishing there, that his grades were inexcusably late. And Marion Holmes '33 recalled traveling out to Weybridge seeking late grade reports from Professor John P. "Sleepy" Davison. After some stalling, Davison sheepishly confessed that the grade sheets had been eaten by his dog, Baby.[17]

In later years the faculty often complained of the pressure placed on them to complete their research and publish articles and books while still teaching a full load and doing committee work. Changes in the American family produced additional pressures. Before 1970 most of the faculty were men, and most of them had wives who stayed at home and took care of family responsibilities. By the 1980s a growing number of faculty members—most of them younger and untenured—were men and women with working spouses; they therefore had more family responsibilities while simultaneously being expected to do more to gain tenure.[18]

These various changes also affected social life. Before midcentury, the faculty was small in size and tightly knit, with little turnover. Good camaraderie existed between younger and older faculty, and there was less jealousy and "striving to get ahead" than in later times. Not only did groups of professors and their spouses socialize often, but there were many occasions when the mostly male faculty sought

*President Moody wasn't above a hand of bridge with faculty members
and their spouses.*

opportunities for companionship.[19] Stephen Freeman recalled that
in the Moody years there was a group among whom

> there was an even closer bond of common interest, and cooperative
> activity—in college business, in social diversions, and family friend-
> ships. A dozen of us—Ray White, Sam Longwell, Ray Barney, Allen
> Cline, Julius Kingsley, Harry Fife, Reginald Cook—formed a discus-
> sion group, meeting monthly in our homes. One of us would read
> a paper, and discussion, relevant or not, would follow. Before the
> evening was over, we were swapping stories, President Moody in
> the lead.[20]

The wives formed a group (the Sewing Bee) that organized various
social activities. Indeed, aside from strong church associations enjoyed by some professors, most of a faculty member's closest friendships were with other faculty.[21]

Faculty members continued to find their best friends among colleagues and college employees, but job and family pressures after
1970 apparently reduced socializing somewhat. The great difficulty
in achieving tenure strained relationships between junior and senior
faculty.[22] As the faculty grew in number, the tight-knit relationships
of prewar years became harder to form, but the community's con-

tinued isolation and small size provided faculty with relatively few alternatives in the search for friends and social outlets.

Changing faculty goals and interests affected student–faculty relations as well. Interaction between students and their teachers has always been a complex subject. For the great majority, the most natural and frequent interaction with faculty took place in the classroom, and the best learning experiences were memorable. "Doc" Cook '24 recalled that his physics professor, Ernest Bryant, was "an artist-showman (in the best sense of the word) at the lectern, conducting his experiments with considerable flair and eclat," and that "he probably taught more undergraduates how to think clearly than any other teacher during the years of his professorship."[23] And Dorothy Wunner Woodward '34 remembered what drama professor V. Spencer Goodreds "could accomplish on our tiny stage. . . . He taught us the fundamentals of good play production with humor and a driving force for perfection. . . . And how many of us left Middlebury to emulate his teaching?"[24] Numerous other examples could be offered.

Some students, because they attended a small college, apparently expected not only more attention inside the classroom but also closer relationships with professors outside the classroom. This expectation led generations of students and faculty to explore ways of strengthening this aspect of their relationship. At open forums in 1917 and 1919 on key issues of the day, the student–faculty relationship was always one of the subjects discussed.[25] One problem, as the *Campus* noted in 1924, was that important differences in background and interests often created a social barrier.

> Why, then, should there be a gap between student and instructor? Is the instructor, or professor, so much further advanced intellectually, so much more learned, that his sense of superiority forbids him to associate with his students except in the classroom? Or does his greater learning impose a natural barrier between him and the student? These answers fit only in particular cases. Students and faculty are separated because there is nothing to bring them together. They naturally draw apart, and adhering to those of their respective ages, form two distinct social groups. To become a college professor, it appears that much study is necessary, and much study not only is "a weariness of the flesh" but tends to become a barrier to companionships.[26]

Students sometimes viewed their professors as just another group of adults who were out of touch with modern times and incapable of understanding young people's needs and interests. In 1928 the *Campus* editor attempted to improve such perceptions:

> Droop-mouthed professors with single track minds, perpetually absent-minded professors with hungry looks, lanky professors always pictured with nets chasing butterflies, naive professors that shun women and barber shops, most of them have been relieved by time, trustees, or the undertaker. They are old fashioned, a product of 1900, and have, with a few exceptions, disappeared.
>
> To take their place has come a quite different type of teacher, one with social experience, wide contacts, and varied interests. Versatility characterizes the teacher of this new regime. He is the cheering section at varsity games, has seen the latest plays, knows art, has read the latest fiction, can repeat the wisest cracks appearing in Judge last week. He is acquainted with life. . . .
>
> The monk-professor has already become vestigial; colleges are introducing the Gentleman-and-the-scholar, a jolly good fellow.[27]

Still, most Middlebury students and faculty found it difficult to maintain good social relationships with each other, and there was a bit of distrust on both sides. The level of distrust changed often, depending on circumstance; in the years right after World War II, the faculty was impressed with the maturity and experience of veterans attending under the GI Bill, and relations were excellent.[28] During the Vietnam War, the fact of shared antiwar views and a similar perspective on social change again brought many students and faculty closer together. But in the 1980s the faculty tended to hold more liberal views than did the students, many of whom were keenly interested in seeking lucrative careers. The situation worsened after a series of acrimonious discussions between students and college officials concerning fraternities, comprehensive fees, and social life; and the dean of college reported that

> we must restore constructive and trusting relationship between students and faculty and administration. Student perspectives on such issues as social life, the student center, budgeting priorities, and the comprehensive fee must be heard and taken seriously in our deliberations. Conversely, students must have an opportunity to consider, understand, and weigh perspectives and positions that differ from their own.[29]

One infrequently attempted solution was to have faculty living with students or having their offices in the residence halls. There were good instances. When President Thomas's house was hit by fire in the winter of 1917, he stated, "I'll go with my boys in Hepburn Hall" and temporarily moved into the new dormitory with his family. The *Campus* hailed this as "another striking example of the kind of democracy that should prevail" at Middlebury.[30] Professor Blanche Knapp, who headed the home economics department during much of her tenure at Middlebury 1922–1947), lived with the women students who resided in the Homestead, the practice house where women had an opportunity to learn sewing, cooking, and home decorating. Juanita Pritchard Cook '26 remembered Professor Knapp as a gently authoritative and motherly woman who had nearly as much positive influence as Dean Ross.[31] A few staff members such as Mrs. Maud O. Mason—"Mother Mason" to the hundreds of boys she befriended as the live-in supervisor of Hepburn Hall from 1915 to 1938—formed close relationships with students.[32]

Nevertheless, although most administrators over the years agreed that an adult presence would be helpful in the residence halls, few of the faculty were willing to serve in that capacity. The problems of having a married faculty member living in the dorms are fairly obvious; football coach David Morey and his wife lived for a time during the 1920s in the all-male Hepburn Hall. An alumnus recalled that one of the men who lived on the same floor as the Moreys

> decided to proceed to the shower room in the "buff" as usual. When finished with his shower, he burst out and started for his room, only to spot Mrs. Morey rounding the corner at a good clip. Non-plussed (as were all Middlebury men in those days), he hurriedly placed the towel over his head and roared past a startled Mrs. Morey who was never able to identify the culprit.[33]

The administration attempted in the 1980s to move several faculty offices into the residence halls in an attempt to integrate academic and residential life more effectively. The experiment failed; students showed little interest in a regular faculty presence, and the professors (who also served as advisors to those students) felt isolated from their colleagues.[34]

The dramatic change in faculty interests and life-styles also affected their relations with students. Between the wars faculty generally demonstrated more of an interest in student affairs, and there apparently were more formal and informal social occasions at which the two groups interacted. Faculty and faculty wives sometimes entertained students in their homes or at the college. There were afternoon teas for women students, faculty receptions for freshmen, and Christmas parties for seniors.[35] Students often took the initiative and challenged faculty to sporting events, made up holiday food baskets for favorite professors, and entertained them at meals or receptions, particularly around holiday time.[36] With students in control, the results were sometimes unpredictable. Zella Cole Hibbert '28 recalled that she and Jane French Douglass '28 were in charge of cooking the turkey when President and Mrs. Moody had been invited to a dinner with all the trimmings at the Homestead: "All went well until, trying to get the bird out of the oven without burning ourselves, we tipped the roasting pan too much to one side. The bird fell out and skidded across the floor. Fortunately, it did not fall apart. As we squelched our laughter, we quickly picked it up, put it on the platter and served it to our illustrious guests, from whom we heard no complaint."[37]

Before 1960, the faculty was more involved with extracurricular activities, particularly the Winter Carnival, in which they helped by acting as judges, timers, and chaperones.[38] They showed more interest in varsity athletics. At a rally before the Norwich football game in 1922, Professor de Visme was a major speaker, and Professor LaCalle led the snake dance that climaxed the rally. The faculty wrote reviews of students' dramatic productions and performed in vaudeville shows to raise money for a stage curtain.[39]

Faculty chaperones, although they were bored and mostly ignored, were de rigeur at fraternity parties and many other functions until the late 1960s. Marion Holmes '33, a longtime staff member and mountain enthusiast, recalled that she and a young professor were the chaperones for a Mountain Club overnight outing at a cabin on the Long Trail. When she woke up in the morning, she and the professor were the only ones remaining in the cabin.[40] Although most faculty and students treated chaperoning as an unfortunate necessity, it still provided an opportunity to get a feel for student social life.[41] After 1970 few professors had close contact with fraternity parties or other social affairs; and as we have seen, when they entered into the fraternity issue in the 1980s, students not only resented it

When he received tenure, the Campus *called him "the talking typewriter," but Pardon Tillinghast also led intense, though more Socratic, seminars at his home.*

but doubted that faculty had more than a superficial understanding of the situation.[42]

We have also seen that some faculty members were more concerned with research and leaves of absence than with their students.

> The status of a faculty member seems in some measure to be determined by the number and frequency of outside grants or fellowships. Such a policy (whether or not unstated) would, again, seem to place a premium on scholarly credentials (for peer review) and meanwhile create disruptive discontinuities in both staffing and curriculum. Not a few students, by the way, even while they rejoiced in the additional "voices" they could hear by reason of visiting or substitute faculty, lamented the lack of familiar voices from year to year. Especially for students abroad for all or part of the junior year, returning to Middlebury seeking a "thesis" advisor, the faculty often seems less given to a local habitation than they.[43]

In other ways, though, relations improved somewhat over the years. Middlebury faculty occasionally wanted the students to adopt, implement, and regulate an honor code; such proposals did not receive sufficient student support when discussed in 1922, 1927, 1933, or 1962, but an honor code was finally adopted in 1965.[44] Faculty also

Before the passage of the honor code, final exams were held in the field house at tables carefully spaced to forestall cheating.

allowed students a measure of participation in shared governance, curricular discussions, and eventually—through surveys, interviews, and departmental advisory committees—in providing feedback for assessing teaching effectiveness and tenure decisions.[45] Increased interest in research led to more faculty–student interaction on research projects; between 1985 and 1989, with college encouragement, the number of students in the Summer Work Program rose from 30 to 120, and many of them worked as faculty research assistants.[46] Finally, the establishment of events like May Day allowed students, faculty, staff, and administrators to interact in various ways.[47]

Despite some positive episodes and developments, however, the comment of the *Campus* in 1979 came close to describing the prevailing situation: "Interaction between professors and students beyond the classroom and short conference of formality is a rare occurrence here."[48]

Until the twentieth century the president and the rest of the faculty performed all of the administrative and many of the staff tasks on campus (every Middlebury president prior to Thomas taught). As the college grew, however, help in running it effectively was clearly needed. Between the wars a few full-time administrators appeared on campus—registrars, librarians, deans, directors, controllers, and editors.[49] The administration and staff grew from fourteen in 1915 to fifty-eight in 1941. In response to the large postwar increase in enrollment, the college raised the number of staff members and administrators to 104, outnumbering the faculty (for the first time) and nearly double the prewar figure. The increase in later years was even more remarkable—from 129 staff employees and 85 hourly employees in 1968 to 323 and 235, respectively, in 1989; the faculty increase (107 to 171) was less than 60 percent.[50]

Whole new sections were created. Before 1956 the president and a few members of his staff would occasionally give over some time to fund-raising; by 1990 the two lower floors of Forest Hall were filled with people who did little else. In the Moody years a dean of men and dean of women handled most of the problems created by students; by the 1980s the student services area included counselors, directors, coordinators, advisors, and a gaggle of deans able to help with career counseling, psychological problems, residence hall concerns, medical ailments, party planning, advice on studying abroad, working off-campus or volunteering, and much more. Every area of the college had witnessed astounding growth in the size and specialization of the staff—truly one of the more significant changes in Middlebury (and other liberal arts colleges) in the twentieth century.

Many staff members and administrators, although they might identify strongly with their professions—librarians, counselors, computer specialists—also had a strong identity with the college and the community. Some of them gave their time to advise student groups and often became closer to some students than the faculty did. Many professors before 1950 were leaders in Middlebury churches, volunteers in the community, and members of service organizations. While some faculty members remained active in those areas, such roles were increasingly assumed by staff members.

Staff and administration concerns were similar to those of the faculty, particularly their interest in better wages and benefits. During times of economic trouble, the Middlebury staff felt the effects and reacted accordingly. In 1947, sixty-eight buildings, grounds, and maintenance employees, unhappy with low wages in a time

During the strike of buildings, grounds, and maintenance employees in 1947, students were forced to change the sheets on their own beds. In all likelihood this pleased their parents and may have surprised some.

of postwar inflation, walked off their jobs.[51] The simultaneous impact of recession and inflation ("stagflation") in the period 1978–1982 wrought hardship and dissatisfaction among Middlebury staff. About one-third of them responded to a questionnaire in 1981 with expressions of concern over low salaries, distribution of raises, job classification, vacation policy, and benefits for part-time employees.[52] Many were still concerned, five years later, about salaries and job conditions, and the Staff Council was formed in 1986 "to provide a forum that will regularly address staff-related concerns and ideas and thus contribute to the well-being of the Middlebury College community."[53] The Staff Council, some felt, did not win sufficient responses from the college, and in the winter of 1987–1988, several staff members advocated bringing in a union to represent them. The college discouraged this idea, and many of the staff believed that a strengthened council would be preferable to a union.[54]

One of the leaders of the union movement, April Jin, resigned her position at the college in 1988 and asked President Robison in an open letter for a variety of improvements in working conditions, benefits, and salaries. The college responded by increasing the minimum hourly wage and declaring part-time employees eligible for health care coverage, with the college paying part of the premium. The staff, apparently influenced by these favorable initiatives and their own intrinsic antiunion views, voted overwhelmingly to reject union representation and constitute the Staff Council as an advisory group to the administration.[55]

Problems of finding a place to park (with space at a premium) and a place to smoke (with nonsmokers ascendant) produced much discussion,[56] but an even more important concern in the 1980s—shared by faculty, staff, and administration—was that of assisting those parents who needed day care for their dependent children. For a time the college subsidized the Otter Creek Child Center and the Mary Johnson Day Care Center, but the trustees were concerned about the cost of the program and the problem of equity in providing employee benefits. Although there was strong sentiment for some form of subsidized day care, the college ultimately balked. Instead, after a year of study, the trustees announced in 1990 that the institution would offer employees $500 each to use for whatever benefits they desired.[57]

The growth of the college in the twentieth century changed the job of the president markedly. The nineteenth-century president spent much of his time teaching; dealing directly with students, faculty, and parents; and occasionally raising money. His duties thereafter became more specialized. After John Thomas asked not to teach and thus became the first full-time president, the expectation of teaching disappeared. Still, Thomas and Moody presided over the college as father-figures—counseling students, leading daily chapel, hiring new teachers. Both could even be stern and paternalistic with the faculty; Moody warned them during the Depression not "to rock the boat," that is, to make radical statements and bring down the wrath of the conservative board of trustees.[58]

Swollen enrollments after 1945 ended the possibility of much presidential interaction with parents and students—there were, after all, other administrators and staff hired to do just that. Even in the critical area of faculty hiring—a responsibility that Thomas, Moody, and Stratton took on themselves—Armstrong and Robison allowed individual departments and faculty deans to manage. Indeed, the last two presidents had to administer things through their vice presidents and senior officers because the institution had become much too large to micromanage. Armstrong and, particularly, Robison found that, in order to succeed they had to spend a good deal of time off campus raising money; cultivating trustees, alumni, and foundations; and generally spreading the word about Middlebury College. Assured that their staffs could take charge of day-to-day operations, these presidents were able to spend an increasing amount of time away from Middlebury.

One thing that did not change in the president's job description was the importance of working with the board of trustees. The relationship of each president with his board was quite different: Thomas and Armstrong were strong presidents who led their boards through successful administrations; Moody and Stratton were relatively weak presidents, controlled to a great extent by powerful trustees. Armstrong, it will be recalled, successfully curtailed the power that several local trustees had exerted during the Stratton era by placing the treasurer (formerly a board officer) under his control and by politely but firmly informing those trustees that he hoped they would let him run his administration. By focusing the board's attention on fund-raising and long-range planning and away from day-to-day administration, Armstrong helped to define the trustee's role more clearly. Robison also worked to strengthen the office of the president, as well as to broaden the base of support for the college, by persuading the trustees to limit their terms to fifteen years and by forming the Council of Overseers to allow former trustees to remain a part of the governance system.[59]

With the expanded opportunities for women to work in American society after 1970, the role of the president's wife became less clear-cut. Formerly, she was expected to be a spouse, mother, hostess, and community leader. Her place was usually in the home supporting her husband in any way she could, often as an important confidant and adviser. Margaret "Tib" Moody Rice '28 recently wrote a remembrance of her mother, Charlotte Hull Moody, the wife of President Moody.

> Mother's first concern was always for [President Moody], and in these days of latchkey children and working mothers, it's interesting to look back and realize that she was always home. Groceries were

ordered by phone, and though she would go calling on new faculty wives or to faculty teas, she always walked. Home was where she wanted to be, and she loved the usual domesticities—cooking and silver polishing, but above all gardening and having flowers all over the house. She was quiet and self-effacing, but of great perception, and father sought her opinion before all others.[60]

Mrs. Thomas, Mrs. Stratton, and Mrs. Armstrong more or less followed Mrs. Moody's pattern. However, when Olin Robison came in 1975, his wife, Sylvia, had different ideas about her role. First, she took a job in the development office, where her responsibilities included registering nonmonetary gifts, writing, and cultivating prospects and donors. While she supervised the nearly endless entertaining at the president's house, she gradually professionalized the running of it so that she would not be spending hours lettering placecards, planning the table settings, and arguing "about whether there should be separate salad plates."[61] She used her extra time to become the "College's chief interior designer, supervising the refurbishing of most of the College's major public spaces." During her fifteen years "in office" she worked on the president's house, the deanery, the Chateau, Pearsons, Adirondack House, Mead Chapel, the field house, Emma Willard House, Painter House, and the Hadley House. In a sense she created guest housing at the college with her work on the deanery in 1976 and the Hadley House. While doing all of this, she still managed to help raise three boys and served on numerous community boards, including a term as president of the Vermont State Orchestra.[62] She was, in short, continuing to fulfill some of the former responsibilities of the president's wife while breaking much new ground, and in so doing she became one of the more visible and productive members of the college staff.

Another key Middlebury constituency is the alumni, who over the years found or were given many opportunities to become more involved in college affairs. Alumni volunteers were repeatedly helpful in recruiting students. A "100 Freshman Men Club" was organized in 1921; one hundred alumni would each attempt to recruit one young man to enter Middlebury.[63] Such activities were later expanded and more carefully articulated.[64] Similarly, alumni historically helped graduating students and one another in fulfilling career objectives; a formal program, Middnet, was initiated in 1985 to ex-

In January 1941, alumni of Middlebury gathered for a banquet at the Longchamps restaurant in Manhattan.

pand and improve that effort.[65] Alumni also became more active in raising money. There was talk of initiating an alumni annual fund in the late 1920s, but it was not until 1949 that Cap Wiley, William Edmunds '17, and Dorothy Nash Brailey '19 organized the first one.[66] Early alumni fund totals were fairly modest, but in later years, aided by a fine reunion class organizational effort, the annual fund became a great success, with over half of the alumni contributing a total of several million dollars each year.[67] As noted in chapters 7 and 8, the fund-raising achievements of Walter Brooker '37, long-time vice president for development, were truly outstanding. Finally, many alumni served with distinction on the board of trustees, most of them elected by the Alumni Association.[68]

To maintain alumni loyalty and interest, Middlebury created numerous opportunities for them to see each other and return to the campus. Homecoming, first organized in 1928, became a successful event under the leadership of Edgar "Cap" Wiley '13 and his wife, Pruda Harwood Wiley '12. The Wileys organized the Homecoming, and a highlight of the weekend was the Wileys (Pruda at the piano) leading everyone in the singing of college songs.[69] For later generations, Gordie Perine '49 was the mainstay and symbol of Homecoming. After 1976 alumni were also enticed back to campus

While Robert Stafford '35 was governor of Vermont, his daughter Madelyn entered the class of 1963. She carried on a tradition that included her mother, Helen Kelley '38, and her grandfather, Bert L. Stafford '01. Governor Stafford moved to Congress and then to represent Vermont in the U.S. Senate. For this picture, Governor Stafford wore his football sweater.

by the successful Alumni College program, at which Middlebury professors offered four-day courses at Bread Loaf during Labor Day weekend. A Spring Alumni College and an Alumni Winter Weekend were launched a few years later.[70] Regional alumni associations, some dating back to the 1920s, held social and educational events each year.[71] The college started an alumni newsletter in 1926 and hired W. Storrs Lee '28 to edit it and other publications in 1929. The *Middlebury College Newsletter*, published ever since, changed its name to *The Middlebury College Magazine* in 1981.[72]

Middlebury alumni made great contributions, not only to the college but to society was well. Their career choices changed considerably during the twentieth century.[73] Although nearly half of the graduates entered the field of education until about 1920, that number declined steadily thereafter, with some one-third going into education between the wars and only 15 percent to 20 percent in the postwar years. Many Middlebury women, however, continued to enter the field. It was more the exception than the rule for nineteenth-century graduates to become business leaders, but more and more of them did so in the twentieth century: in 1920 some 20 percent of the class chose business careers, and the number rose steadily, reaching nearly 40 percent in the 1950s and 1960s before tailing off slightly after 1970. The college always attracted students who wished to enter the professions, and they entered a host of them after 1915, including architecture, law, social work, and economics. Some 5 percent became doctors or scientists; several made their mark in government and politics. The number entering the ministry, which attracted nearly half of some classes in the pre–Civil War years, declined steadily to around 12 percent in the late nineteenth century and to one or two a year after 1900. Many graduates pursued successful careers as writers or journalists; others, as artists, musicians, entertainers, and athletes. Middlebury also produced fourteen Rhodes Scholars over the years.

In the nineteenth century it was the town's college; in the twentieth, as the institution grew in size, wealth, and prominence, it seemed in certain ways to become more self-sufficient and isolated from the town. But a closer examination reveals that the college's physical expansion and needs continued to tie its fortunes inextricably with those of the town. Construction of new facilities (and a strong desire to protect the beauty of the campus) occasionally resulted in conflict with members of the community. Moreover, the college remained a major employer and consumer of services; indeed, its growth and financial success eventually helped transform parts of the village and some surrounding areas into a relatively wealthy and upscale community. The college also provided a growing number of cultural and athletic programs, students organized a variety of social welfare projects in and about the area, and faculty and staff were frequently active in local religious, social, and political activities.

Relations had been very close in the nineteenth century. Students and townspeople socialized often, and the young men (and later women) of the tiny college were well known in town. Residents took pride in the accomplishments of students after graduation, which were often recounted in the local press. As the college grew in size and wealth after 1900, the student body became increasingly self-sufficient, and contacts slowly diminished in both quantity and intensity. Fraternities, which had been a good source of income for some "local tradesmen," started buying cooperatively in the late 1930s and bypassing the town merchants.[74] Whereas before midcentury a number of students had attended local churches, lived in town, held part-time jobs there, and knew some townspeople—particularly true of many of the married veterans who enrolled after 1945—this changed radically after 1950. The college was able to house almost all students on campus and offer them dining facilities, increased social opportunities, and a good bookstore, all of which reduced the ties between students and town.[75]

In 1938 the college ended the tradition of holding commencement in the village's Congregational church, turning instead to the greater capacity of recently renovated Mead Chapel. The colorful march of the graduates and college officials through the village to the church on Commencement Day had been an impressive annual event between 1809 and 1937, and many townspeople had watched the parade and attended graduation exercises. The use of its own facilities rather than the church for Commencement was an important symbol of the college's growing self-sufficiency.[76]

Still, students continued to patronize town merchants after mid-century, and, according to the local editor, "the summer Language Schools students literally take over the village each summer, some returning for so many years that lasting friendships have been formed with year-round residents."[77] There was still plenty of interaction—both positive and negative—in the twentieth century.

Student behavior, as in the nineteenth century, occasionally constituted a problem. In 1916, after an important athletic victory during Junior Week, a group of students led a noisy "shirt-tail" parade through the village only to be met by a stream of water from the fire hoses of some local police. After an important basketball victory in 1928, students built a huge bonfire on campus and some pranksters called out the local fire department. The volunteer firemen were not amused to find only a controlled bonfire and sent the college a bill. Townspeople also complained when students made disturbances in movie theaters or stole street signs.[78] In the 1960s and 1970s some of the fraternity houses located in the village began to deteriorate, and several in particular became eyesores and an embarrassment. The sight of half-naked, long-haired fraternity men revving up their motorcycles and cavorting on the village green was upsetting to many residents in the late 1960s, as Dean Bruce Peterson noted:

> . . . It is certainly the case that College-Town relations have been severely damaged by the presence of a group like Theta Chi in the

center of town. In a time when students are increasingly concerned with their role and image in the community, this is an increasingly important consideration. By their actions, appearance, poor maintenance, and financial irresponsibility, Theta Chi has severely damaged the fraternity system and certainly contributed to poor Town-Gown relations.[79]

The obscene snow sculptures constructed at times by some fraternities for Winter Carnival did not sit well either.[80]

The enormous change in the type of student who attended Middlebury also affected relations. Particularly after 1950, students were increasingly wealthy, sophisticated, and mobile. Some had flashy cars, expensive ski equipment, and an attitude of superiority that rankled area residents. Many townspeople were put off by the drinking, rowdiness, and use of drugs.[81] The *Campus* complained in 1979 that some students acted obnoxiously in local restaurants and intruded without thought on the lawns of village residents.[82] Some students, in turn, had always felt that Middlebury was too rural and isolated, as one wrote just before leaving for Christmas holiday in 1920: "Tomorrow we go back to the land of the trolley cars, musical comedies, evening papers, telephones that do not require cranking, and movies that we have not seen before."[83] As late as 1938, the editor of the *Campus* was complaining (as had his nineteenth-century predecessors) that nobody knew where Middlebury was.[84] This attitude gradually diminished, however, as more and more students and parents searched for a rural college and as Middlebury became a more sophisticated and interesting town.

Of course, there is another side to this: Middlebury students were consistently active in community social welfare projects. As early as 1916 the college YWCA chapter ran a story hour every week for town children, and during the 1920s students organized or were involved in a variety of activities that benefited local organizations.[85] In one instance, the efforts of the YWCA's Rural Discussion Group, which "adopted the public school at Ripton as a practical experiment," helped the school meet "standarization requirements."[86] The contribution was often less noticeable, like the concert given by two female students in the winter of 1925 for an elderly shut-in. "There is a good deal of beneficent service rendered in this community by college students—and others connected with the college—which often

Students renovated three rooms of the Home for the Destitute in Middlebury in May 1952 as part of a national cleanup period.

passes unacknowledged," wrote one student.[87] In the Depression, students collected warm clothing for local families.[88]

The Women's Forum, organized in 1936 as primarily a discussion group, included a small social welfare committee that ran Christmas parties for the children of nearby Ripton. The forum became increasingly involved in community work during the 1940s. It opened a thrift shop in 1941 at the Middlebury Community House, where clothing donated by students was sold cheaply. By the 1950s about 70 percent of the women's college students belonged to the forum, and twenty-six committees of the group organized a wide variety of programs, primarily for children, at the Community House.[89]

Each sorority also sponsored community projects after World War II. Even fraternities occasionally stopped socializing long enough to clean out barns or spruce up Chipman Hill park, the Sheldon Museum, the Porter Hospital Annex, and local churches. Delta Upsilon sponsored a road race in 1979 to raise money to send a

A Delta Upsilon Christmas party in 1950 with a brother dressed as Santa Claus exemplifies the ways the fraternities reached out to the children of the town.

local handicapped young adult to camp.[90] Although there may have been a slight decrease in student involvement in the period 1960 to 1980, some students still actively worked with town children in Big Brothers/Big Sisters, Girl Scouts, and recreational programs.[91] After the "strike" of 1970 and the burning of the Recitation Building, many students who had wanted to canvass the townspeople and bring them into the antiwar movement realized, as one of them wrote: "For too long we had remained isolated in the college community. It would be insincere to suddenly take an interest in the townspeople merely because we wanted to build a broader base of opposition to the war. It had been this kind of insensitive self-serving approach which had created much of the friction that already existed between the town and the college."[92] These students accordingly began Head Start programs in nearby Bristol and Cornwall.

The level of volunteer activity rose in the 1980s, particularly after the college hired a volunteer services coordinator, Tiffany Nourse Sargent '79, in 1985.[93] By 1990 over six hundred students were

In the spring of 1985, Dorothy S. Paynter '87 found herself at Bread Loaf with a delighted burden of Community Friends.

helping out in community activities such as a local soup kitchen, a cleanup and a volleyball tournament (with donations for both events targeted at feeding the hungry), tutoring programs for local youngsters, an Adopt-A-Grandparent program organized through the Addison County Community Friends group, and a community breakfast for ninety elderly residents.[94] Several hundred students were among the one thousand volunteers who assisted in 1987 in the construction of KIDSPACE, a local children's play area, and the Interfraternity Council sponsored field days in 1988 and 1989 for local youths. The Middlebury Alliance, formed in 1989 to help coordinate the work of the various student groups involved in community action programs, sponsored a charity dance to raise money for needy local families.[95] By 1990, wrote Tim Etchells '74:

> Just about anywhere you look in Addison County, when you see organizations that require volunteers, you'll usually see Middlebury students.
>
> Of course, coaching little kids in soccer doesn't have quite the same cachet as working against the war in Vietnam, or rallying for

women's reproductive rights. But Middlebury, the town and the College, wouldn't be the kind of place it is without the involvement of college students, in both political and social spheres. It's something we don't often celebrate, but something we can't imagine doing without.[96]

There were occasions when the town was particularly proud of the students. When the great flood of 1927 devastated numerous Vermont river communities, the town of Waterbury called for help. As President Moody recalled: "Two hundred fifty students volunteered and 150 (all that could be accommodated) were allowed to go, to clean cellars, and generally to help the people of Waterbury to get back to normal living conditions. The expression of gratitude we have received from Waterbury people are such as to fill us with pride in our student body." [97] The cleanup work was not easy. Fred Whittemore '28 and Bill Donald '28 remembered helping dig out cellars in Waterbury after the water receded. On those cold early-November nights, Fred slept with just a blanket on the floor of the local schoolhouse, and Bill attempted, without much success, "to heave galvanized wash tubs half full of mud out of a cellar window and to keep up with Steve Hendricks and other football strongmen," until his "trackman back" gave out and he asked for different work.[98]

While relations between the town and the students were mixed and somewhat complicated, the larger picture of the economic ties between town and school is even more complex. In the twentieth century the college increasingly bought its supplies from businesses outside Middlebury.[99] But as the number of people employed by the college kept increasing, the indirect effects of their salaries on local business and tax revenues became significant. The development of the Snow Bowl and the summer language schools drew more business and tourists to the area.[100] Moreover, while many townspeople employed at the college were often unhappy with their wages, improvements in fringe benefits and treatment of staff in the 1980s helped improve relations.[101]

The college's growth and success in the twentieth century spurred growth, prosperity, and change in the town. After midcentury, more than a few suburban housing developments, condominiums, and fine country homes began to dot the outskirts of the village and the surrounding towns and countryside. A small "suburban-type" shopping center, dozens of new stores in the downtown area (many of them in several new developments on both sides of the falls, such as Frog Hollow and the Marble Works Shopping District developed by Towny Anderson '75), traffic lights, upscale restaurants, and other trappings of "urban" growth changed the town.[102] When Paul Vaughn '57 came back in 1985, he was amazed: "The town of Middlebury is no longer the tiny borough we knew. Although still 'country,' it now has specialized shops and is far more sophisticated than we could have imagined."[103] This change owed much to the college's success.

The college was also one of the town's biggest landowners. Its size and influence were not always viewed kindly by the townspeople, and occasionally, when interests clashed, relations were strained. In 1927, for instance, the college invested heavily in the renovation of the Addison House (now the Middlebury Inn). The trustees argued that the school needed a good hotel in the village for guests, alumni, prospective students, and parents, and they were willing to fund the restoration. Many residents also thought it a good investment and subscribed to the capital stock of the "Middlebury Hotel Corporation." Unfortunately, the Depression arrived soon after, the value of the stock dropped from $100 in 1927 to $1 in 1938, and some local people lost a good deal of money. Many blamed the college for their losses, and some residents remained bitter for decades.[104]

Although college expansion had rarely bothered the town before the 1960s, a series of later projects brought opposition. The first such controversy occurred in 1965, when the college wanted to close off Storrs Avenue on the eastern edge of the campus to build a science center. As we saw in chapter 8, some residents objected strongly, and the village trustees approved the action only on condition that the college build a new road and deed it to the town.[105]

The major conflict in the 1970s concerned the location of a proposed bypass of U.S. Route 7 around Middlebury. Many townspeople favored a route that would pass just to the west of the college over college land. The westerly bypass had two major advantages: it would include construction of a new bridge over Otter Creek, and it would inconvenience only a few landholders. The college feared that if a bypass were determined upon, the westerly route would be chosen by default unless another option were available. The college therefore began to buy up land along a potential eastern bypass corridor, and President Robison publicly announced this policy. By 1990 the college had purchased approximately two thousand acres for that purpose.[106] Many residents were angered by this apparent attempt to determine town policy; the Middlebury *Valley Voice* claimed in 1979 that the institution was using its wealth and influence to prevent consideration of a westerly route.[107] The college again responded that it merely wanted to present an alternative to the westerly bypass. Certainly, Middlebury College would prefer not to have a high-speed highway running just below the western ridge of the campus, disturbing its pristine rural character. There were intermittent bypass discussions during the 1980s, but no decision was made. In general, President Robison was proud of the success of the policy of purchasing tracts of land that would protect and enhance the college's (and the town's) beauty and ambience, for he was well aware of the importance of Middlebury's beautiful location and environment.[108]

In the late 1970s the new Kirk Alumni House and Conference Center was another source of conflict. The college claimed that the center was an educational structure and therefore entitled to tax exemption. The town disputed this claim in 1979, and the college paid over $11,000 in taxes that year under protest. Later, it was determined that only certain areas of the facility, such as the snack bar, were taxable.[109]

Two potential building projects in the late 1980s upset local residents. The college, seeking a new location for a student center, briefly considered renovating the social–dining units (SDUs) for the purpose in 1987. When residents on Gorham Lane, behind the SDUs, learned of the proposal, they protested loudly. Since students and faculty also were opposed to this location, the idea quietly died.[110] The second controversial project was the construction of a new performing arts center between Emma Willard and the Sig Ep fraternity house, directly adjacent to the houses in Chipman Park. Homeowners there became particularly upset about prospects of ground water drainage, noise and dust from blasting, and the loss of the view to the southwest. After meeting with residents, the college changed its plans and moved the location several hundred feet south to a site between Chi Psi and Memorial Field House.[111]

Although these disagreements may have weakened town–gown relations on occasions, ties remained strong. The college renovated the old Painter mansion in 1988 and arranged for it to be used by a group of nonprofit organizations. This decision earned high praise

Townsend Anderson '75 explains his plans for the renovation of the monitor of Painter House to (left to right) James D. Ross '51, business manager of the college; David W. Ginevan, vice president for administration and treasurer; and Stephen Freeman.

in the community, and the renovation, directed by Townsend Anderson '75, won a recognition award from the Vermont Preservation Trust.[112] A segment of the town population continued to enjoy the college's cultural offerings and recreational opportunities.[113] After the completion of the Johnson Arts Building, Friends of Art was organized in 1968 to fund new acquisitions for the college, and a similar organization was formed for the library; both groups were successful.[114] Most of their members were local residents who carried on the tradition of town financial support for the college that had been so important before 1915. The historic involvement of faculty families in church work, local politics, public and organizational meetings, benefit performances, and other activities diminished after midcentury, but a number of college employees (particularly administrators and staff) continued to be active members of such groups.[115]

Middlebury College was founded, nurtured, and sustained during the nineteenth century by the residents who first cut the town out of the forests and hills of the Vermont frontier. Certainly the Middlebury College of 1990 was no longer "the town's college" it had been a century earlier. Yet perhaps as much as any other major American college, the school remained highly dependent on its geographical context—the charming village, the beauty and recreational advantages of the surrounding mountains, and the rural ambience—for its popularity and its unique character and mission. Indeed, the strength of the hills continued to support Middlebury College.

NOTES

ABBREVIATIONS

CM   Minutes of the Corporation of Middlebury College, 1915–1990, Old Chapel vault, Middlebury College

CR   *The Campaign Reporter*

DEKE   Delta Kappa Epsilon fraternity

DU   Delta Upsilon fraternity

FM   Faculty Minutes of Middlebury College, 1915–1990, Old Chapel vault, Middlebury College

GC   *Middlebury College in the State of Vermont, General Catalogue, Sesquicentennial Edition*, ed. Duane L. Robinson (Middlebury, Vt., 1951)

GEB   General Education Board

HEQ   *History of Education Quarterly*

JIA   James I. Armstrong, president of Middlebury College, 1963–1975

JT   John M. Thomas, president of Middlebury College, 1908–1921

KDR   Kappa Delta Rho fraternity

MAR   Middlebury Attendance Records, 1800–1951, typescript, Middlebury College Library

MC   *Middlebury Campus*

MCA   Middlebury College Archives

MCB   *Middlebury College Bulletin*

MCL   Middlebury College Library

MCM   *Middlebury College Magazine*

MCNL   *Middlebury College News Letter*

MP   The Paul D. Moody Papers, Middlebury College Library

MR   *Middlebury Register*

PM   Prudential Committee Minutes, Old Chapel vault, Middlebury College

SK   *The Sesquicentennial Kaleidoscope, Being an Account of the One Hundred and Fifty Years of a New England College* (Middlebury, Vt., 1951)

TP   The John Thomas Papers, Middlebury College Library

UVM   The University of Vermont

INTRODUCTION (PAGE xvii)

1. *MCM* 59 (summer 1985): 25.

CHAPTER 1. JOHN THOMAS AND THE GREAT WAR, 1915-1921
(PAGES 5-21)

1. On the desire for additions to the physical plant, see JT, "Report of the President of Middlebury College," *MCB*, 9 (November 1916): 9-14. In addition, see *MC*, September 27, 1916; and Rossiter and Muller Architects to JT, October 31, 1916, TP. The new recitation building was to be called Vermont Hall. See CM, 3:79. For early discussion of an infirmary or hospital, see *MC*, March 12, 1913; JT, Statement to the Board of Trustees . . . January 22, 1915, p. 4, typescript, MCA; JT to Charles G. Barnum, March 13, 1914, TP; JT to Rev. Arthur H. Bradford, July 15, 1915, TP; William H. Porter to JT, June 18, 1915, TP; and JT to Porter, June 21, 1915. The eventual funding and construction of the hospital is described on pp. 34-35.

2. See JT, "Report of the President," *MCB*, 9 (November 1916): 14-16.

3. Ibid.; JT to Hepburn, January 23, 1917, TP; and JT, "A Confidential Letter to Middlebury Alumni," December 3, 1917, printed copy, TP.

4. See, for example, *MC*, May 31, 1916, October 25, 1916, and June 13, 1917.

5. J. Glenn Anderson '15 to Board of Trustees [spring 1917?], TP.

6. See JT to W. H. Porter, December 1, 1913, TP; E. C. Sage to JT, January 23, 1914, TP; JT to General Education Board, June 15, 1914; TP; Hepburn to JT, September 18, 1915; JT to Hepburn, December 22, 1915, TP; E. C. Sage to JT, January 31, 1916, TP; CM, 3:58, Henry S. Pritchett to Hepburn, February 6, 1917, copy in TP; and JT to Hepburn, February 2, 1917, and February 9, 1917, TP.

7. JT to Hepburn, June 12, 1917, TP. For Hepburn's offer, see Hepburn to JT, June 4, 1917, and June 7, 1917, TP.

8. Wiley to JT, November 19, 1917, and November 28, 1917, TP; *MC*, February 27, 1918, and April 3, 1918; JT to Percival Wilds, March 2, 1918, TP; and "The Argument for Middlebury," *MCB*, 12 (January 1918), supplement. Two of the campaign circulars, "A Fight for a College" and "A Confidential Letter to Alumni" are in the College Archives.

9. "A Confidential Letter to Alumni," MCA.

10. JT to Hepburn, November 5, 1917, TP; and *MC*, October 31, 1917.

11. JT to E. C. Sage, January 22, 1918, TP; E. C. Sage to JT, March 2, 1918, TP; and *MC*, March 20, 1918.

12. For example, Colonel Silas Ilsley willed $10,000 to the college, and Mrs. Ilsley promised she would give the last $5,000. See *MC*, February 13, 1918; JT to E. C. Sage, January 22, 1918, TP; JT to James Gifford, January 17, 1918, TP; and JT to Hepburn, June 10, 1918, TP. On local giving, see also JT to F. D. Abernethy, June 7, 1918, TP. Thomas was sometimes disappointed in alumni support, but he gave them credit at the end of the drive. See JT to Harold D. Leach, May 21, 1918, TP; and JT to Barton, June 29, 1918, and July 2, 1918, TP.

13. JT to Barton, June 29, 1918, TP. Thomas, urged on by Hepburn, consciously went for an oversubscription of $15,000 to $20,000. See Hepburn to JT, May 2, 1918, and JT to Barton, July 2, 1918, TP.

14. CM, 3:104, 108.

15. *MC*, February 21, 1917, and February 6, 1918; CM, 3:81; JT to Hepburn, April 5, 1917, and April 25, 1917, TP.

16. JT to Hepburn, April 25, 1917, TP. See also JT to President Ira Reeves, Norwich University, April 13, 1917, TP; and *MC*, February 6, 1918.

17. E. J. Wiley '13, "College Army Post, 1918 Model," *MCNL*, 18 (September 1942): 8-10.

18. The wording of the recruiting agreement enabled Thomas to block the students from leaving until the end of the school year. JT to Reeves, April 13, 1917, TP; and JT to J. W. Abernethy, April 12, 1917, TP.

19. *MC*, May 30, 1917; and JT to Hepburn, May 4, 1917, TP.

20. *MC*, October 24 and October 31, 1917, December 5 and December 12, 1917, January 23, 1918, and February 27, 1918.

21. *MC*, October 3, 1917, January 2, 1918, and January 23, 1918; and "Why Go to Middlebury in War Time," *MCB*, 12 (October 1917), supplement. For the effect of the war on American colleges, particularly the depopulation of schools, see Parke Rexford Kolbe, *The Colleges in War Time and After: A Contemporary Account of the Effect of the War upon Higher Education in America* (New York, 1919), 127–30.

22. *MC*, May 30, 1917, October 10, 1917, October 17, 1917, October 31, 1917, November 21, 1917, December 12, 1917, January 30, 1918, and April 24, 1918.

23. *MC*, November 14, 1917, and April 10, 1918.

24. Wiley, "College Army Post," 8–10; "The Coming of the S.A.T.C.," *MCB*, 13 (December 1918):7; "To Young Men," *MCB*, 12 (July 1918), supplement; and CM, 3:104. A fairly thorough study of the SATC can be found in Kolbe, *The Colleges in War Time and After*, chap. 6; and Carol S. Gruber, *Mars and Minerva: World War I and the Uses of Higher Learning in America* (Baton Rouge, 1975), chap. 6.

25. JT to Fish, September 2, 1918, TP.

26. Wiley, "College Army Post," 8–10; *MC*, October 16, 1918, October 23, 1918, November 20, 1918, February 26, 1919, and June 24, 1919. A few curricular changes had been made during 1917–1918 but nothing on the order of the alterations under SATC. See *MC*, January 2, 1918, and February 27, 1918.

27. "The Coming of the S.A.T.C.," 8.

28. *MC*, November 13 and November 27, 1918, and December 4, 1918.

29. Wiley, "College Army Post," 10; and *MC*, January 8, 1919.

30. See pp. 75–80.

31. On the conservative postwar reaction, the standard study is Robert K. Murray, *Red Scare: A Study in National Hysteria, 1919-1920* (Minneapolis, 1955). Aside from a brief discussion on pp. 169–70, Murray barely touches on the impact of the Red Scare on colleges. Also see John Higham, *Strangers in the Land: Patterns of American Nativism, 1860-1920* (New York, 1973).

32. The documents on which my account is based are in three large folders, marked "Lawrence Controversy" in MCA.

33. See Exhibit 6, Lawrence Files, MCA; and JT to Rufus Flagg, December 8, 1919, Lawrence File, MCA.

34. Swift to JT, November 10, 1919, Lawrence Files, MCA. The letter by Lawrence on labor can be found in *MR*, November 7, 1919.

35. Lawrence's dossier is in the Lawrence Files, MCA.

36. *MC*, February 25, 1920; Lawrence to JT, December 26, 1919, Lawrence Files, MCA.

37. See Lawrence to JT; and exhibit 6, Lawrence Files, MCA. These are the notes Lawrence took of the meetings he had with Thomas.

38. Thomas's view of the conversations can be found in *MC*, March 3, 1920, and JT to Professor Tenney Frank, November 12, 1920, Lawrence Files, MCA.

39. See JT to Frank; Charles B. Wright, "Memorandum," Lawrence Files, MCA; and interview with Joseph Kasper '20, August 6, 1974, MCA.

40. Judge F. L. Fish to JT, January 9, 1920, TP. Also see JT to Ralph M. Easley, March 17, 1920, TP. Stevens was granted an interview with the faculty-trustee conference committee. See JT to Fish, January 9, 1920.

41. Lawrence to JT, February 7, 1920, February 22, 1920, and March 9, 1920; and JT to Lawrence, February 13, 1920, and March 1, 1920, Lawrence Files, MCA.

42. "Putting Metternich to Shame," *The New Republic*, 21 (February 18, 1920): 357.

43. MC, February 25, 1920, and March 3, 1920, containing the speech. There is also a copy in the Lawrence Files, MCA.

44. See MC, March 3, 1920, and April 21, 1920; and Lawrence Files, MCA. For more on Kasper's role, see interview with Joseph Kasper, August 6, 1974, taped recording, MCA.

45. *Springfield (Mass.) Union*, May 10, 1920.

46. MC, April 28, 1920, and April 21, 1920.

47. JT to Willard D. Carpenter, May 3, 1920, TP.

48. The AAUP apparently approved of the way Middlebury had handled the Stevens episode since he had been granted an appearance before the faculty–trustee committee. Except for the final AAUP report, most of the documents concerning the investigation are in the Lawrence Files, MCA. The final report was published as "Report of the Sub-Committee on Inquiry for Middlebury College," *AAUP Bulletin*. 7 (May 1921): 28–37.

49. See, for example, Thomas's speech in MC, February 11, 1920. On postwar inflation, see Neil A. Wynn, *From Progressivism to Prosperity: World War I and American Society* (New York, 1986), chap. 8.

50. MC, February 11, 1920, and April 28, 1920.

51. John Mead '64, a prominent college trustee, may have influenced Walker to make the bequest. See Mead to JT, January 2, 1917, TP. Thomas was pleased but a little unhappy at the uses to which it had been restricted. See JT to Dr. James L. Barton, August 30, 1917, TP.

52. Brainerd's pamphlet was printed as *Emma Willard's Life and Work in Middlebury* (Middlebury, Vt., 1918). On the Sage bequest, see George W. Ellis to Ezra Brainerd, December 12, 1893, and December 18, 1893, Brainerd Papers, MCA; MC, November 20 and November 27, 1918; and CM, 3:120. On earlier attempts to obtain money from Mrs. Sage, see James Gifford to JT, May 11, 1908, TP; Junius Mead to JT, July 2, 1908, TP; JT to Mrs. Sage, February 2, 1911, TP; and JT to President John H. Finley, January 10, 1918, TP.

53. A copy of the will is in the Battell File, MCA. See also Hepburn to JT, January 9 and January 12, 1917, TP; and JT to James Gifford, June 21, 1917, TP.

54. See, in particular, Frank C. Partridge to JT, March 4, March 6, and March 21, 1916, TP. Thomas based his interpretation of the will on Partridge's letters. See JT, "Report of the President of Middlebury College," *MCB*, 11 (November, 1916): 20–30; and JT to Partridge, March 9, 1916, TP. Also see CM, 3:79, 91; JT to Gifford, June 21, 1917, TP; and JT to Frank L. Greene, May 11, 1916, TP. It was initially hoped that the use of scientific forestry and conservation on the commercial areas might permit the development of a forestry school in connection with the college, another of Battell's aims. See JT to James Gifford, September 9, 1910, TP; and F. Hubbard to Battell, March 15, 1910, copy in TP.

55. Thomas E. Boyce '76, Battell's indispensable private secretary and co-executor of the estate, was retained by Thomas to help manage the lands. See JT to F. C. Partridge, December 10, 1915, TP; and *Burlington (Vt.) Free Press*, March 22, 1943, obituary notice of Boyce. In 1920, Middlebury Professor E. I. Terry and six assistants surveyed the property and estimated that the forest lands would yield a net income of $100,000.

56. See, for example, JT to C. S. Page, February 24, 1917, TP; JT to Frank L.

Greene, October 30, 1916, TP; JT to Hepburn, January 16, 1917, TP; and JT to Thomas E. Boyce, June 17, 1920, TP.

57. CM, 3:106; see also F. D. Abernethy to President Paul D. Moody, June 22, 1931, copy, Moody Papers, MCA.

58. Collins, a pedagogy professor and effective administrator, was serving as acting president during this period while Thomas was on temporary leave of absence (from October 1918 until early April 1919) as an army chaplain in New Jersey. Ill health had forced Professor Charles Baker Wright, the initial acting president, to relinquish his duties to Collins in December 1918. Collins was given the permanent position of provost in January 1919. See CM, 3:74–75, 103, 111–12; MC, April 9, 1918, October 16, 1918, November 13, 1918, December 4, 1918, and February 12, 1919; and JT to Hepburn, April 7, 1919, TP.

59. Boyce had begged Collins to keep the inn as a hotel in deference to Battell's memory. JT to T. E. Boyce, November 13, 1919, TP. On Collins's role, also see MC, June 17, 1925.

60. CM, 3:118. On the founding of the Bread Loaf School, see the excellent study by George K. Anderson, *Bread Loaf School of English: The First Fifty Years* (Middlebury, Vt., 1969).

61. MC, June 2, 1920. Apparently, Thomas had asked for $350,000. See JT to James L. Barton, June 3, 1920, TP.

62. CM, 3:132.

63. MC, December 8, 1920, and June 22, 1921.

64. MC, February 11, 1920; and CM, 3:126.

65. See, for example, JT to Carson H. Beane, April 19, 1920, TP.

66. On Thomas's early fears about coeducation, see David Stameshkin, *The Town's College: Middlebury College, 1800–1915* (Middlebury, Vt., 1985), 239. On the general tendency of schools to shy away from coeducation and move toward segregation in this period, see Thomas Woody, *A History of Women's Education in the United States* (New York, 1929), 2:280–95; Lynn D. Gordon, "Coeducation on Two Campuses: Berkeley and Chicago, 1890–1912," in *Woman's Being, Woman's Place: Female Identity and Vocation in American History*, ed. Mary Kelley (Boston, 1979), 171–93; and Rosalind Rosenberg, "The Limits of Access: The History of Coeducation in America," in *Women and Higher Education in American History*, ed. John Mack Faragher and Florence Howe (New York, 1988), 107–29.

67. CM, 3:100; and Gifford to JT, September 24, 1917, TP.

68. Dr. James L. Barton to JT, May 18, 1918, and May 21, 1918, TP; JT to Barton, May 20, 1918, TP; and JT to Wallace Buttrick, May 20, 1918, TP. E. C. Sage of the General Education Board visited the college on June 4, 1919, and issued a report later that month that urged the "centralization and improvement of the facilities for the education of women," including a new women's residence hall and dining hall. However, the report stopped short of advocating an affiliated college as such. See E. C. Sage, "Notes on a Visit to Middlebury College, Middlebury, Vermont," June 1919, typescript, MCA. Appended to the Sage report are two analyses by trustee J. W. Abernethy of questionnaires that faculty and administrators had been asked to complete regarding coeducation. The first analysis is a summary of all the responses; the second carefully reviews only Thomas's responses. Abernethy, a strong advocate of coordinate education who hoped the college would develop an affiliated women's college, was bitterly unhappy with Thomas's opinions on this subject; indeed, Abernethy provided angry and sometimes sarcastic comments on some of Thomas's questionnaire responses in the appendix to the Sage report.

69. Hepburn to JT, November 6, 1919, TP.

70. JT to Herbert K. Twitchell, October 23, 1919, TP. See also JT to Judge F. L. Fish, January 9, 1920, TP; and JT to Herbert K. Twitchell, January 12, 1920, TP. Thomas articulated many of his views on coeducation in his responses to a questionnaire circulated in 1919. See note 68 above.

71. See CM, 3:123–26.

72. Gifford to JT, February 21, 1920, TP. The Carnegie Foundation, an organization Hepburn wholeheartedly supported, had already developed "with great care" a plan for a teachers college in Vermont, which probably included substantial financial assistance from the state. See Gifford to JT, February 21, 1920, TP. For more on this issue, see JT to James Barton, June 3, 1920, TP; and JT to Gifford, June 23, 1920, TP.

73. See Paul D. Moody to Miss Grace Ellis, May 31, 1923, MP.

74. JT to Gifford, June 23, 1920, TP. Also see CM, 3:131–32; and JT to Gertrude Cornish, June 26, 1920.

75. Paul D. Moody to Miss Grace Ellis, May 31, 1923, MP; and Moody to Mrs. Dorothy Canfield Fisher, June 2, 1923, MP.

76. CM, 3:138–39.

77. MC, September 27, 1916; JT to Judge Charles H. Darling, May 17, 1919, TP; JT to Olin Merrill, December 5, 1919, TP; Wayland Fuller Dunaway, *History of the Pennsylvania State College* (Lancaster, Pa., 1946), 219–33; MC, February 9, 1921. There is no evidence that the loss of the Hepburn money or any other issue over which some trustees may have been displeased had anything to do with Thomas's resignation.

78. JT to George Harding, August 6, 1918, TP; and JT to Henry Seely White, May 6, 1919, TP.

79. MC, April 13, 1921.

80. MC, March 2, 1921; and CM, 3:148–49.

81. CM, 3:148–49.

82. Dunaway, *History*, 219–33.

83. GC, 234; MCNL 26 (April 1952): 11, 19; and 27 (July 1953): 16, 18.

CHAPTER 2. PAUL MOODY AND COLLEGE GROWTH, 1921–1942 (PAGES 22–35)

1. MC, February 23, 1921, and April 13, 1921; and CM, 3:149.

2. Reginald Cook to David Stameshkin, January 28, 1982, MCA. See also GC, xliii. Collins also founded the Ecole Champlain in nearby Charlotte, Vermont, which was later directed by his daughter, Mrs. E. Sheridan Chase '25.

3. CM, 3:151, 153.

4. See GC, xxxviii; MC, September 28, 1921, March 5, 1924, and March 25, 1942; and W. Storrs Lee to David Stameshkin, July 30, 1976, in my possession.

5. The following description of Moody has been drawn from a variety of sources, particularly interviews, all of which are preserved as taped recordings and/or notes housed at MCA. See the following interviews: with Howard Munford '34 and Marian Munford '32, March 3, 1975; with Joseph Kasper '20, August 6, 1974; with David K. Smith '42, March 10, 1975; with Eleanor M. Benjamin Clemens '32, February 25, 1975; with Juanita Pritchard Cook, February 24, 1975; and with Egbert Hadley '10, July 31, 1975. Also helpful were W. Storrs Lee '28 to David Stameshkin, July 30, 1976, MCA; reminiscences of Margaret Moody Rice '28 in MCM, 63 (sum-

mer 1989): 59–60; and "In Memory of Paul Dwight Moody, 1979-1947: A Service Held in the First Presbyterian Church . . . November 16, 1947," a printed program in possession of W. Storrs Lee.

6. "Dr. Freeman Recalls 45 Years of College History and Language Growth at Middlebury," *MCNL* 44 (summer 1970): 39.

7. "The Inaugural Address of President Paul Dwight Moody of Middlebury College," *MCB* 16 (June 1922): 19–36. The quotation is on pp. 33–34. For restatements of this thesis, see *MC*, September 28, 1921, October 19, 1921, November 16, 1921, May 10, 1922, September 28, 1922, and September 23, 1925.

8. "The Inaugural Address," 30.

9. Ibid., 33.

10. CM, 3:132, 143–44; E. C. Sage (GEB) to JT, June 4, 1910, TP.

11. CM, 3:157; Paul D. Moody to E. C. Sage, March 14, 1922, MP. On May 25, 1922, the GEB finally extended the college's time by one year, to July 1, 1923. See W. W. Brierley to Moody, May 27, 1922, copy, MP.

12. Hepburn gave two separate gifts, one of $100,000 and one of $150,000. He intended that the latter sum be used to construct a men's dormitory; however, since the GEB would count only money earmarked for endowment toward their conditional grant, Hepburn agreed to allow the $150,000 to be so used. The college (hoping they would raise enough to free Hepburn's $150,000 for its intended use) kept the gift a secret until the end of the drive. Unfortunately, they did not obtain the extra funds and had to use the $150,000 to qualify. The dormitory had to wait until 1940, when James Gifford's estate provided the necessary funds for the structure Hepburn had hoped to build. See Hepburn to Moody, November 15, 1921, MP; Moody to Wallace Buttrick, February 8, 1922, MP; Buttrick to Moody, February 11, 1922, MP; Moody to Trevor Arnett, June 20, 1923, MP; Arnett to Moody, June 27, 1923; MP; and *MC*, October 10, 1923. A general breakdown of who gave what to the campaign is appended to Moody to Arnett, June 20, 1923, MP. It was also called the 2-6-1 campaign because the goal was to raise $261.00 from each living alumnus. Five-year pledges of $52.20 were eagerly sought. See 2-6-1 fund-raising file, MCA. On the campaign, also see W. Storrs Lee, *Father Went to College* (New York, 1936), 230–31; *MC*, all issues April 25–June 18, 1923; and *Burlington (Vt.) Daily Free Press*, May 2, 1923. At some point Hepburn contributed additional stock, which had enhanced in value by 1929 to over $800,000. See "The President's Report, 1928-1930," *MCB*, 24 (January 1930): 87.

13. "Middlebury's Million," *MCNL* 2 (January 1928): 12; and Lee, "Twenty Years A-Growing," *MCNL* 15 (June 1941), 5–8, 17.

14. The maximum salary for full professors was raised immediately from $2,400 to $3,000 and climbed to $4,500 by 1930. See Moody to General Education Board, October 23, 1922, MP; and "The President's Report, 1928-1930," 12. The endowment figure for 1921-1922 is in *MAC* (1921–22): 15.

15. On Hepburn's gifts, see "President's Report, 1928-1930," 87; and *Treasurer's Report, Middlebury College, June 30, 1930* (n.d., n.p.), 21. The endowment is listed each year in *MAC* (1920–31), usually on p. 15 or 16.

16. Two useful studies of the effects of the Depression on American higher education are David O. Levine, *The American College and the Culture of Aspiration, 1915-1940* (Ithaca, N.Y., 1986), chap. 9; and Malcolm M. Willey, *Depression, Recovery, and Higher Education* (New York, 1937).

17. *Treasurer's Report, June 30, 1930*, 18–35; and J. J. Fritz, "Depression and the College," *MCNL* 6 (December 1931): 2. There were some large additions to

endowment in the 1920s and 1930s. Hepburn's will provided $200,000 for a professorship in 1923; and Frank Abernethy gave $200,000 in 1932, as well as his store in 1937, which the college later sold for $130,000. See *MAC* (1923-24): 18; CM, 4:184; and *MC*, April 20, 1932. For other gifts, see CM, 3:25-51, 112, 327; and *MC*, February 11, 1931.

18. Fritz, "Depression and the College," 2; and "The President's Report, 1926-27," *MCB* 21 (January 1926), 25-26.

19. *MCNL* 14 (March 1940): 4, 10-11; "The President's Report, 1928-1930," 84; CM, 3:110, 126, 187-88, 234, 259, 265, 286; Fritz, "Depression and the College," 20; and *MC*, April 12, 1939.

20. Paul D. Moody, "Seven Lean Years," *MCNL* 14 (December 1939): 10; CM, 4:39, 49, 50, 83, 99, 101, 152, 165, 186, 217-18, 221; and John G. Bowker, "Middlebury College in Retrospect," *MCNL* 41 (spring 1967): 12. The faculty–student ratio was up to 13:1 by 1939-1940.

21. CM, 3:182, 247, 257-58, 273, 285, 286; *MC*, January 22, 1930; Lee, "Twenty Years A-Growing," 7; William H. Carter, "Challenge from the Alumni President," *MCNL* 14 (December 1939): 11; Edgar J. Wiley '13, "Making a Start," *MCNL* 9 (March 1935): 2-3, 22.

22. *MC*, October 16, 1918, April 30, 1919, September 24, 1919, May 5, 1920, September 29, 1920, September 28, 1921, November 23, 1921, September 28, 1922, January 17, 1923, and May 20, 1925; and CM, 3:133.

23. "It would be hard to see where and how the present student body could be provided for were it not for the aid rendered by the fraternities in this way," President Moody wrote in early 1927. "The President's Report, 1926-27," 19.

24. The following account of the building of the chateau depends heavily on Stephen Freeman, *The Middlebury College Foreign Language Schools: The Story of a Unique Idea* (Middlebury, Vt., 1975), 42-43, 64-67. The cost of the building was about $183,000, and another $31,000 was apparently expended on furnishing and equipping it. Miss Holden gave an additional $10,000 for that purpose. The college used money from the Hepburn bequest to pay the balance of the costs ($140,500). See CM, 3:175, 216, 226, 233; *MC*, June 17, 1925; and "The President's Report, 1926-27," 18.

25. On Williamson de Visme, see *GC*, 254; and Freeman, *Foreign Language Schools*, 30-48.

26. Freeman, *Foreign Language Schools*, 65-66. Also see Glenn Andres, *A Walking History of Middlebury* (Middlebury, Vt., 1975), 63-64; and *MCM* 60 (spring 1986): 8. In recent years, the Petit Salon has also been used as a seminar room.

27. "Second Middlebury College," *MCNL* 10 (September 1935): 9; and Paul D. Moody, "Mountains for Dormitories," *MCNL* 9 (May 1935): 6-7.

28. Moody, "Mountains," 6-7; CM, 4:50, 51, 58, 69, 70, 71, 87, 149, 162, 168; and PM, 1:1, 56.

29. "Second Middlebury College," 8, 9, 20; and Mary Ruth Yoe, "The Campus That Might Have Been," *MCM* 62 (winter 1988): 16-19.

30. Interview with members of the class of 1939 at their 35th reunion, June 1974, MCA.

31. On the renovation of Painter Hall, see *MC*, September 30, 1936; and CM, 4:229. In 1938, Moody had recommended the construction of a new men's dormitory. See CM, 4:185, 204.

32. *MCNL* 14 (September 1939): 2; CM, 4:216, 228, 233, 278; and PM, 1:50-52.

33. Andres, *A Walking History of Middlebury*, 61. Also see *MC*, October 2, 1940, and November 13, 1940.

34. CM, 3:176.

35. I rely heavily here on interviews with Stephen Freeman and notes from Reginald "Doc" Cook '24, typed notes, MCA. Miss Hayden was instructor of voice from 1921 to 1933. On Miss Hayden, see *GC*, xlviii.

36. Emily Proctor Eggleston to John A. Fletcher, July 1, 1925, MP.

37. The church was converted into the college playhouse after the music department moved into the new Music Practice Studio.

38. "The President's Report, 1926–27," 18–19; and *MAC* (1926–27): 99.

39. CM, 3:184. She remarried in the mid-1920s and became Emily Proctor Telfer.

40. See, for example, CM, 3:79. Also see E. C. Sage, "Notes on a Visit to Middlebury College, Middlebury, Vermont," June 1919, typescript, MCA.

41. CM, 3:160–61; 4:185, 208; and *MC*, March 1, 1922, and September 28, 1922.

42. CM, 4:230. On Munroe, see *GC*, 252; *MCNL* 14 (June 1940): 2; *MR*, January 25, 1907; CM, 4:278. The cost was $151,000.

43. See notes from Stephen Freeman and Reginald "Doc" Cook, MCA.

44. Ibid.

45. *MC*, September 27, 1939, and April 24, 1940; and *MCNL* 14 (June 1940): 2.

46. "The President's Report, 1926–27," 36–37; and *MC*, March 14, 1923.

47. Dr. Starr first agreed to give $20,000 if the college contributed an additional $50,000, then generously raised his bequest to one-half of the total cost. Finally, he announced he would pay for everything except for the equipment furnished by Frank D. Abernethy for the Abernethy wing. See CM, 3:233, 243, 252, 274, 284; and *MCNL* 2 (January 1928): 14.

48. *MCNL* 2 (January 1928): 14; and JT, "Report of the President of Middlebury College," *MCB* 11 (November 1916): 19–20.

49. On the Abernethy Collection, see CM, 3:186–87; "The President's Report, 1928–30," 55–57; *MAC* (1927–28): 92–93; and *MCB* 23 (August 1928). On Julian Abernethy, see *GC*, 201. On the west wing, see *MAC* (1927–28): 92–93. On Frank Abernethy's contribution, see CM, 3:274.

50. Lee, "Twenty Years A-Growing," 8, 17.

51. See *MC*, March 12, 1913, and April 3, 1918; JT to Charles G. Barnum, March 13, 1914, TP; and JT to Rev. Arthur H. Bradford, July 15, 1915, TP.

52. See "The President's Report, 1926–27," 16–17; W. H. Porter to JT, June 18, 1915, TP; JT to Porter, June 21, 1915, and May 1, 1916, TP; and JT to Rev. J. W. Atwood, May 7, 1918, TP. Earlier in 1915, Emily Proctor had agreed to pay the architect's commission and one-fourth of the cost of a hospital, which would cost $20,000 to $30,000 to build. See JT, "Statement of the President to the Board of Trustees . . . January 22, 1915," p. 4, MCA; and JT to Porter, June 21, 1915, TP.

53. Gifford to JT, May 28, 1918, TP.

54. "The President's Report, 1926–27," 17.

55. "The President's Report, 1928–30," 79; and CM, 3:283–84.

56. CM, 3:239, 246; Charles I. Button to Moody, January 24, 1926, MP; and Moody to Wright Caswell, August 14, 1926, MP.

57. CM, 3:263–64, 276–77; CM, 4:158; and interview with David Ginevan, July 3, 1986, notes in MCA. The buildings revert to the college only if they cease to be used as hospital or medical facilities.

58. See *MC*, September 28, 1938; "Building Plan," *MCNL* 13 (September 1938): 6–7; Wiley, "Making a Start," *MCNL* 9 (March 1935): 2–3, 22; CM, 4:1, 185, 204, 234, 265; and CM, 3:268, 274, 290, 348.

CHAPTER 3. COEDUCATION AT MIDDLEBURY, 1921–1941
(PAGES 36–46)

1. "The Inaugural Address of President Paul D. Moody," *MCB* 16 (June 1922): 33.

2. Paul Moody to Dorothy Canfield Fisher, June 2, 1923, MP. Even before Moody arrived, there was great pressure to begin segregation after Thomas's departure. See J. W. Abernethy to Dr. Collins, June 29, 1921, TP; and Collins to Abernethy, July 1, 1921, TP.

3. See pp. 17–20; Moody to Grace Ellis, May 31, 1923, MP; and Moody to Douglas Beers, memorandum, September 30, 1926, MP.

4. Moody to Dorothy Canfield Fisher, June 2, 1923, MP; and Moody to Ellis, April 12, 1923, MP. On the antagonism toward coeducation in this period, see, in particular, Thomas Woody, *A History of Women's Education in the United States* (New York, 1929), 2:280–95; Lynn D. Gordon, "Co-education on Two Campuses: Berkeley and Chicago, 1890–1912," in *Woman's Being, Woman's Place: Female Identity and Vocation in American History*, ed. Mary Kelley (Boston, 1979), 171–93; and Rosalind Rosenberg, "The Limits of Access: The History of Coeducation in America," in *Women and Higher Education in American History*, ed. John Mack Faragher and Florence Howe (New York, 1988), 107–29. Also useful are works (cited in full in the Bibliography) by the following authors: Barbara Solomon, Helen Lefkowitz Horowitz, Mabel Newcomer, Carol Lasser, and Patricia Albjerg Graham. While the following discussion is informed to some extent by each of these works, Woody, in particular, is useful in understanding the arguments against coeducation.

5. W. Abernethy '76 to Moody, October 21, 1922, MP; J. W. Abernethy '76, "Courses in Women's College," *New York Evening Post*, November 29, 1919, copy in TP.

6. Moody to Trevor Arnett, GEB, May 22, 1929, MP.

7. Ibid. On the superiority of the women, also see interview with John Bowker, October 15, 1974; *MC*, January 17, 1923; and interview with Jane Howard Fiske '39, March 10, 1975, MCA.

8. Gifford to Moody, November 18, 1929, MP.

9. "Inaugural Address of Paul Moody," 33. See also Moody to Grace Ellis, April 12, 1923, MP; Moody to J. W. Abernethy '76, October 22, 1921, MP; CM, 3:139, 4:42.

10. See, for example, *To the General Education Board* (n.p., n.d.), copy in MP.

11. Moody to Ellis, April 12, 1923, MP.

12. *MC*, December 14, 1921, June 14, 1922, and February 7, 1923.

13. Moody to Professor Douglas Beers, memorandum, September 30, 1926, MP; and Moody to Robert Kelly, September 24, 1925, MP.

14. Moody to Ellis, April 12, 1923, MP; and *MC*, December 5, 1923. Joseph Kasper '20 claimed that male students after World War I were not opposed to coeducation. See interview with Kasper, August 6, 1974, MCA.

15. *MC*, November 14, 1923.

16. *MC*, November 21, 1923. Also see *MC*, June 18, 1923, November 28, 1923, and May 7, 1924, for student opinion on coeducation.

17. Moody to Ellis, May 31, 1923, MP. Unfortunately, I have been unable to find a copy of this questionnaire.

18. Dorothy Canfield Fisher to Moody, May 31, 1923, MP. For Moody's response, see Moody to Fisher, June 2, 1923, MP.

19. John G. Bowker, "Middlebury College in Retrospect," *MCNL* 41 (spring 1967): 11.

20. Interview with Jane Howard Fiske '39, March 10, 1975, MCA. On faculty opposition to segregation, also see Moody to Gifford, December 19, 1929, MP. For faculty comments on coeducation, see Stephen Freeman, "Thirty-eight Years at Middlebury," *MCNL* 38 (autumn 1963): 15; and interview with Samuel Guarnaccia '30, October 8, 1974, MCA. Guarnaccia stated that many people belived during the interwar period that women knew how to mimic and memorize better than men, and that is why they were better students.

21. Moody to Robert Kelly, September 24, 1925, MP.

22. Moody to Miss Emily Dutton, February 5, 1927, MP.

23. Moody to Gifford, April 18, 1930, MP.

24. Moody to Miss Ellen Wiley, July 18, 1930, MP.

25. Moody to Mary Linehan, January 5, 1926, MP.

26. Moody to J. W. Abernethy, October 23, 1922, and Gifford to Moody, November 18, 1929, MP.

27. Abernethy to Moody, October 21, 1922; Abernethy to Collins, June 29, 1921, TP; and Moody to Abernethy, October 11, 1922, MP.

28. Moody to Miss Julia H. Farwell, October 30, 1923, MP; and *MC*, October 2, 1923.

29. Gifford to Moody, November 18, 1929, MP.

30. Moody to Trevor Arnett, May 22, 1929, MP.

31. Moody to Gifford, December 19, 1929, MP.

32. The board discussed the issue at three meetings (January 31, April 12, and June 5). Each time they referred the matter to their Committee on the Women's College, all in preparation for the annual meeting on June 21, 1930, at which they voted to establish a coordinate system. See CM, 3:303, 308–11, 314–15; and Moody to Gertrude E. Cornish, July 22, 1930, MP.

33. Moody claimed that Nelson was a strong "friend of segregation" who supported eliminating the men from the campus only because it was expedient and the college "could make more headway toward segregation by doing so. However, since Nelson was a "loyal graduate" he "does not favor this any more than the rest of us." Moody to Gifford, March 12, 1930, MP. On Nelson's idea, also see CM, 3:298; and Moody to Cornish, July 22, 1930, MP.

34. *To the General Education Board* [November 8, 1930?], copy in MCA.

35. CM, 3:308–9.

36. CM, 3:310–11.

37. CM, 3:314–15. See also Moody to Cornish, July 22, 1930, MP.

38. Moody to Gifford, April 16, 1930, MP.

39. CM, 3:336.

40. This paragraph is based primarily on Gertrude C. Milliken, et al., "Brief History of the Advisory Board of the Women's College of Middlebury (1913 to 1949)," typescript, MCA; and Evelyn Plumley Adams '25, "Mother Went to College Too (1914–1943)," *MCNL* 36 (winter 1962): 19, 60.

The advisory board was originally set up by President Thomas in 1913, primarily to convince the American Association of University Women that although Middlebury College had no women trustees and few female faculty members, the college still valued the opinions of women and should be granted a chapter. Among the most prominent members of the committee were Mrs. Charles Burrage, Ruth Bryant '18, Mrs. Cecile Child Allen '01, Mrs. Hazel McLeod Willis '09, Mrs. Marjory Wright Upson '15, and Mrs. Gertrude Cornish Milliken '01. See also CM, 3:210, 254, 258, 4:78, 169–70.

41. Moody to Gifford, April 16, 1930, MP.

42. Freeman, "Thirty-eight Years," 16.

43. See interviews with Jane Howard Fiske '39, March 10, 1975; David K. Smith '42, March 10, 1975; John Andrews, October 15, 1975; and Howard Munford '34 and Marian Munford '32, March 3, 1975, MCA.

44. "Eleanor Ross Thomas '95, 1874–1953," *MCNL* 27 (July 1953): 16, 18.

45. CM, 4:42, 49. See also Moody to J. W. Abernethy '76, October 22, 1921, MP; and CM, 3:139.

46. CM, 4:321–22; GEB to Moody, January 29, 1931; "To the General Education Board" [November 9, 1930?], MCA.

47. CM, 4:43–44, 104–6, 115–16.

48. CM, 4:104–5; Mary Ruth Yoe, "The Campus That Might Have Been," *MCM* 62 (winter 1988): 16–19; and W. Storrs Lee '28, "Second Middlebury College, *MCNL* 10 (September 1935): 8–9, 20.

49. CM, 4:169–70.

CHAPTER 4. CULTURE AND CURRICULUM (PAGES 47–68)

1. "The President's Report, 1927–1928," *MCB* 22 (January 1928): 13.

2. On curricular reform in the interwar period, see, for example, R. Freeman Butts, *The College Charts Its Course* (New York, 1939), chaps. 14–22; Frederick Rudolph, *Curriculum: A History of the American Undergraduate Course of Study Since 1636* (San Francisco, 1981), chap. 7; Robert M. Hutchins, *The Higher Learning in America* (New Haven, Conn., 1936); and David O. Levine, *The American College and the Culture of Aspiration, 1915–1940* (Ithaca, N.Y., 1986), chap. 5.

3. See *MAC* (1919–1929) for course requirements. In 1923–1924, the faculty modified the curriculum from two minors and one major to two majors and one minor. See *MC*, May 23, 1923.

4. *MC*, June 1, 1927.

5. *MC*, April 26, 1922; and Moody, "Problems on a College President's Desk," *MCNL* 3 (April 1929): 2–4.

6. *MAC* (1922–23): 45. On the Columbia course and its impact, see Daniel Bell, *The Reforming of General Education: The Columbia College Experience in Its National Setting* (New York, 1966), 14–15; and Levine, *The American College*, 96–97.

7. Report of Curriculum, p. 4, n.d., typed copy, MP.

8. *MAC* (1935–36).

9. See, for example, *MC*, September 28, 1927; and John G. Bowker, "Middlebury College in Retrospect," *MCNL* 41 (spring 1967): 14.

10. President's Report, Middlebury College, January 26, 1933, p. 2, printed copy, MCA; and Hazeltine to Moody, January 23, 1929, p. 4, MP.

11. Stephen Freeman, "Thirty-eight Years at Middlebury," *MCNL* 38 (autumn 1963): 18, and interview with Stephen Freeman, August 27, 1981, MCA.

12. Cook to Stameshkin, January 28, 1982, MCA.

13. CM, 3:349. Also see *MC*, October 19, 1927, November 16, 1927, December 7, 1932, December 14, 1932, February 15, 1933, March 1, 1933, June 14, 1933, March 7, 1934, and May 27, 1936.

14. *MAC* (1926–27): 40–41.

15. *MC*, November 25, 1925, December 7, 1932, and March 11, 1936.

16. Statement by Professor William Burrage in 1927, quoted in Bowker, "Middlebury College in Retrospect," 14.

17. Burt Hazeltine to Moody, January 23, 1929, p. 4, MP; *MC*, November 29, 1921, April 21, 1926, November 16, 1927, February 22, 1928, and March 1, 1933.

18. *MC*, February 3, 1926, February 10, 1926, April 14, 1926, and March 6, 1929. There were problems, too. Some students complained that their classmates tried to take courses with easy graders so that they could qualify for the Dean's List in their first two years and thereby obtain unlimited cuts. Some of the faculty also apparently reacted negatively. See *MC*, February 8, 1933; and Hazeltine to Moody, January 23, 1929, MP.

19. Although admission requirements were changed slightly in these years and the quality of entering students thereby enhanced somewhat, there was still room for improvement in the men's college. See *MC*, October 5, 1932; Edgar J. Wiley '13, "How's the Enrollment?" *MCNL* 9 (September 1934): 9–10; Burt A. Hazeltine, "Proposed Report to the Board of Trustees, "undated typed manuscript, MP; *MC*, January 15, 1936; and W. Storrs Lee '28, "College with a Purpose," *MCNL* 10 (June 1936):14–15, 20.

20. *MC*, June 18, 1928; and Bowker, "Middlebury College in Retrospect," 14.

21. Stephen A. Freeman, *The Middlebury College Foreign Language Schools: The Story of a Unique Idea* (Middlebury, Vt., 1975), 198; see also *GC*, xlix-1.

22. Cook to Stameshkin, January, 28, 1982, MCA.

23. *GC*, lii-liii; and *Freeman, Foreign Language Schools*, 91-105, 265-85, 287-305, 337-57.

24. See *GC*, 722, 506, 1, lii, liv.

25. See Reginald Cook to David Stameshkin, March 18, 1980, MCA; and John Smith Lewis, Jr., "The History of Instruction in American Literature in Colleges and Universities of the United States, 1827-1939" (unpublished Ph.D. diss., New York University, 1941).

26. George K. Anderson, *Bread Loaf School of English: The First Fifty Years* (Middlebury, Vt., 1969), chap. 2.

27. The claim of his popularity is based on countless informal conversations I have had over the past fifteen years with alumni, faculty, and townspeople. Also see *GC*, 516; Anderson, *Bread Loaf*, chap. 6; and *MC*, September 4, 1984.

28. *GC*, xlix. On Bowker, see interview with John Bowker, October 15, 1974, MCA.

29. The quality of the division was assessed as inferior to the others by the great majority of faculty I interviewed, most of whom asked not to be quoted or cited. On Fife, see *GC*, 1.

30. See interview with Howard Munford '34, March 5, 1975, MCA.

31. Paul D. Moody, "Liberal Arts Limitations," *MCNL* 6 (December 1931): 8. See also "The President's Report, 1926-1927," 33-34; JT to Harold Leach, May 12, 1920, TP; *MC*, October 15, 1919, March 10, 1920, January 11, 1922, and January 25, 1922. The student teacher program also continued to operate. See CM, 3:306, 4:186. On the national debate over the practical versus the cultural, see Butts, *The College Charts Its Course*, chap. 19; and Levine, *The American College*, chap. 5.

32. See, for example, *MC*, October 15, 1919, December 17, 1919, March 10, 1920, January 11, 1922, and January 25, 1922.

33. CM, 4:118-19; *MC*, October 30, 1935; and Lee, "College with a Purpose," 14-15, 20. In the 1920s, about 80 percent of the A.B. candidates were women, and 80 percent of the B.S. candidates were men. See *MAC* (1925-26): 131, 133.

34. W. Storrs Lee, "To College with a Purpose," *MCB*, 30 (June 1936). For a similar version for the women's college, see *MCB*, 31 (April 1937).

35. Lee, "To College with a Purpose," 14-15. In 1935, the college went so far as to offer a course in aviation, which, the editor of the *Campus* argued, somewhat defensively, did not make Middlebury into a "technical college." See *MC*, December 11, 1935, and December 18, 1935. The college agreed in 1939 to cooperate with the government in offering a ground school course for civil aeronautics.

36. Freeman, *Foreign Language Schools*.

37. Ibid., 9.

38. On the origins of the German School, see ibid., 21-29.

39. On the origins of the French School, see ibid., 30-48.

40. Ibid., 40.

41. Ibid., 63, 67.

42. Ibid., 78-79.

43. On the origins of the Spanish School, see ibid., 49-62.

44. Ibid., 101, 91-105.

45. Ibid., 121-32.

46. For example, see ibid., 53-54, 58, 66, 73-74.

47. Ibid., chap. 6; and interview with Stephen Freeman, August 27, 1981, MCA.

48. Freeman, *Foreign Language Schools*, 210.

49. I relied heavily on Anderson, *Bread Loaf*, for the following account. On the origins of the school, see pp. 1-14.

50. Ibid., 11-12.

51. Ibid., 12. De Visme had successfully opposed suggestions that the French School be moved to Bread Loaf.

52. Ibid., 13-14.

53. Cook to Stameshkin, March 18, 1980, MCA.

54. Quoted in Freeman, *Foreign Language Schools*, 38.

55. Anderson, *Bread Loaf*, 29.

56. Quoted in Anderson, *Bread Loaf*, 32; see also Reginald L. Cook, "In the Councils of the Bold," in *Robert Frost and Bread Loaf* (Middlebury, Vt., 1964).

57. Anderson, *Bread Loaf*, 32. Reginald "Doc" Cook commented: "Yes, Frost certainly stimulated the Bread Loaf students, . . . Pretty definitely, though, Frost was not, as Storrs Lee has stated, the godfather of Bread Loaf." Cook to Stameshkin, January 28, 1982, MCA.

58. Anderson, *Bread Loaf*, 66, and chap. 3. The name of the position had been changed in the 1920s from dean to director.

59. Ibid., chap. 4.

60. Cook to Stameshkin, January 28, 1982, MCA.

61. Anderson, *Bread Loaf*, 67.

62. Ibid., chap. 5.

63. For this account I relied heavily on the fine work by Theodore Morrison, *Middlebury College Bread Loaf Writers' Conference: The First Thirty Years* (Middlebury, Vt., 1976). Since I was fortunate enough to work as a research assistant on this project, I was able to become acquainted with the primary sources more intimately than in the case of the language schools or the English school.

64. Davison to Moody, October [?] 1925, MP. I found this remarkable letter two years after Morrison and I had searched diligently for such a document while researching his history of the Writers' Conference.

65. Morrison, *Writers' Conference*, 6-24, 83-86.

66. Ibid., 9.

CHAPTER 5. THE IMPACT OF WORLD WAR II, 1940-1945
(PAGES 69-80)

1. Paul Moody to W. Storrs Lee '28, November 21, 1944, in Lee's possession; interview with Howard Munford '34 and Marian Munford '32, March 3, 1975, MCA; and CM, 4:290.

2. A comparison of the endowment funds at Middlebury and other New England colleges during the interwar years reveals that Middlebury lost ground to those schools President Thomas had hoped to "catch." Middlebury's endowment was 51.4% of Williams's in 1920-1921, only 38.7% by 1942. Middlebury's relative standing (based on the single criterion of permanent funds) dropped when compared with Amherst (42.4% to 36.0%), Bowdoin (60.6% to 50.0%), Dartmouth (32.0% to 21.9%), and Wesleyan (62.9% to 55.1%) between 1921 and 1942. Information was obtained from the colleges' 1921 and 1942 annual catalogs.

3. The assertions and theories presented here were arrived at after interviews with many people. Some of them would undoubtedly disagree with my conclusions. The most informative interviews were with Stephen Freeman, August 27, 1981; Eleanor Mitchell Benjamin (Clemens), February 25, 1975; Howard Munford, March 5, 1975; John Andrews, October 15, 1974; W. Storrs Lee, July 2, 1976; John Bowker, October 15, 1974; Joseph Kasper, August 6, 1974; and, particularly, Egbert Hadley, July 31, 1975. Tapes or notes of these interviews are in MCA.

4. Interviews with Howard and Marian Munford, March 3, 1975, John Andrews, October 15, 1974, and D. K. Smith, March 10, 1975; tapes or notes in MCA.

5. PM, 1:75, 77; MC, October 9, 1940, and April 9, 1941; and "Three Thirds of a President," *MCNL* 15 (February 1941): 9, 18.

6. In particular, see *MC*, May 22, 1940. Also see *MC*, September 27, 1939, October 4, 1939, and November 8, 1939. On the popularity of pacifism on campus, see "War and Peace," *MCNL* 14 (December 1939): 3-4.

7. Interviews with John Andrews, October 15, 1974, and D. K. Smith, March 10, 1975, tapes or notes in MCA. Moody's comment about the class is mentioned in *MCM* 64 (summer 1990): 65.

8. See Redfield Proctor file, MP. On Proctor, see *GC*, xxxi; *CM*, 4:39, 113; and Stephen Freeman, "Thirty-eight Years at Middlebury," *MCNL* 38 (autumn 1963): 17.

9. CM, 4:290, see also interview with Egbert Hadley, July 31, 1975, MCA.

10. Paul Moody to Redfield Proctor, March 5, 1942, Proctor file, MP.

11. CM, 4:291; and MC, March 25, 1942.

12. Interview with John Bowker, October 15, 1974, MCA. See also *MC*, May 26, 1942; *MCNL* 16 (June 1942): 2-3; and Moody to Proctor, May 7, 1942, MP.

13. The chamber of commerce also stated that the "residents of this community are deeply disturbed and grieved by the announcement of the resignation of Paul D. Moody." John O. Williams and James W. Shea to the Board of Trustees of Middlebury College [April 3, 1942?], in possession of W. Storrs Lee.

14. Interviews with Howard and Marian Munford, March 3, 1975, and W. Storrs Lee, July 2, 1976, MCA.

15. On Moody's work in New York City, see "Address by the Rev. J. V. Moldenhawer, D. D.," in *In Memory of Paul Dwight Moody, 1879-1947: A Service Held in the First Presbyterian Church, Fifth Avenue at Twelfth Street, New York, November 16, 1947* (New York[?], 1947[?]), 5-7. Storrs Lee graciously loaned me a copy of this pamphlet.

16. Moody to W. Storrs Lee, November 21, 1944, in Lee's possession.

17. Interview with Lee, July 2, 1976, notes in MCA. Lee stated that he had been instrumental in obtaining the Tasheira property for the college. See PM, 1:87, for earlier decision to sell it to Moody in 1940; and PM, 1:129, for the decision to pay off the $6,150 Moody still owed on the property.

18. CM, 4:315; "Three Thirds of a President," 9, 18. The other two members were College Editor W. Storrs Lee '28 and Harry G. Owen '23, director of the Bread Loaf School of English.

19. GC, xlix-1; and interviews with John Bowker, October 15, 1974, and W. Storrs Lee, July 2, 1976, MCA.

20. Stephen Freeman, "As the Year Begins," MCNL 17 (September 1942): 7, 19; CM, 4:315, 325; MAR(1800–1951).

21. FM, October 8, 1942, pp. 66–68.

22. Ibid., 7; and June Brogger Noble '46, "Coming of Age in World War II," MCNL 49 (Winter 1975): 12–16.

23. Freeman, "As the Year Begins," 7.

24. CM, 4:326.

25. "The Eleventh President of Middlebury College," MCNL 17 (March 1943): 5–6, 19; MC, January 13, 1943. Also see interviews with Egbert Hadley, July 31, 1975; Joseph Kasper, August 6, 1974; John Bowker, October 15, 1974; and Stephen Freeman, August 27, 1981, MCA; CM 4:326; FM (1943–45): 88.

26. This account is drawn from "The Eleventh President," 5–6, 19; and GC, xxxviii.

27. Boylston Green, "Middlebury's Task," MCNL 18 (September 1943): 7; "The President's Message Page," MCNL 17 (March 1943): 2; FM (1943–45): 111; and MC, April 7, 1943, and May 3, 1943. On the V-12 program and its dealings with colleges, see James C. Schneider, The Navy V-12 Program: Leadership for a Lifetime (Boston, 1987), 1–35.

28. For a full account of the navy experience at Middlebury, see Boylston Green, "A Framework for Reconversion," MCNL 19 (January 1945): 5; and Russell G. Sholes, "Navy at Middlebury," MCNL 20 (February 1946): 8–9, 19.

29. Middlebury had initiated a twelve-week third semester summer session in science in 1942, and, according to Latin professor Raymond White, "[t]he establishment at that time of what was a conservative form of a three-term system was to prove of great help when the College was chosen in 1943 for a V-12 Navy Unit. The Navy required a three-term system for all V-12 units, and when the Navy men arrived on July 1, 1943, our problem was the relatively simple one of adjusting these dates for the beginnings of the three terms." See White, "The War and the Curriculum," MCNL 20 (February 1946): 12–13; and MCNL 18 (December 1943): 4.

30. Interviews with John Andrews, October 15, 1974, and John Bowker, October 15, 1974, MCA.

31. Sholes, "Navy at Middlebury," 8–9; interview with John Bowker, October 15, 1974, MCA; FM (1943–45): 14; and PM, 1:145, 152, 160.

32. On life at Middlebury during the war, see Noble, "Coming of Age," 12–16. On life at V-12 schools, see Schneider, The Navy V-12 Program, 244–86. On civilian life, see John Morton Blum, V Was for Victory: Politics and American Culture during World War II (New York, 1976).

33. In July 1943 the college leased the fraternity houses for a seven-week period for civilian men and language school students, then decided to lease the houses for

use by the women's college. Theta Chi, Delta Kappa Epsilon, Delta Upsilon, and Sigma Phi were respectively given the temporary names of Seely, Eaton, Howard, and Sanford. See PM, 1:150, 156; *MC*, September 22, 1943; and Correspondence, September 23, 1940–May 31, 1946, Chi Psi Archives, Middlebury College. See also Margaret L. Fayer, "Seely, Eaton, Howard, Sanford," *MCNL* 18 (December 1943): 14-15.

34. Juanita Cook, "The Women's College," *MCNL* 20 (February 1946): 10-11.

35. "Physical Education Program," *MCNL* 20 (February 1946): 16-17.

36. Noble, "Coming of Age," 14; and *MC*, January 14, 1942, March 18, 1942, and March 9, 1943. On the origins and development of Winter Carnival, see chap. 13 below.

37. Sholes, "Navy at Middlebury," 9; "A Year of V-12," *MCNL* 18 (June–July 1944): 8-9; and *MC*, February 8, 1945.

38. Interviews with Jane Howard Fiske '39, March 10, 1975, and John Bowker, October 15, 1974, MCA; *MC*, February 8, 1945.

39. *MC*, December 16, 1943; and Noble, "Coming of Age," 14-15.

40. Schneider, *The Navy V-12 Program*, p. 379.

41. Noble, "Coming of Age," 12-16.

42. Schneider, *The Navy V-12 Program*, 327-31.

43. Samuel Stratton, "The President's Page," *MCNL* 18 (September 1943): 2; interview with Stephen Freeman, August 27, 1981, MCA.

44. Samuel Stratton, "The President's Page," *MCNL* 19 (September–October 1944): 2; see also MAR(1800-1951).

45. Stratton, "The President's Page," *MCNL* 18 (September 1943): 2.

46. Samuel Stratton, "The President's Page," *MCNL* 18 (December 1943): 2, 16. Freeman gives Stratton credit for hiring Professor Mischa Fayer and also for founding the Russian School. Interview with Stephen Freeman, August 27, 1981, MCA.

CHAPTER 6. THE STRATTON YEARS: FACULTY AND CURRICULAR CONCERNS (PAGES 85-102)

1. "The President's Page," *MCNL* 19 (March–April 1945): 19.

2. For the national picture, see Keith W. Olson, *The G.I. Bill, the Veterans, and the Colleges* (Lexington, Ky., 1974), chap. 3 and *passim*.

3. See Tables 2 and 3, above; MAR (1800-1951). Other college officials had also underestimated the number of veterans seeking admission. See Olson, *The G.I. Bill*, chap. 2; FM (1945-47): 15.

4. Interviews with Fred Neuberger, February 3, 1975, and Gordon Perine, February 28, 1975, taped copies, MCA; W. Storrs Lee, "Buildings and Grounds," *MCNL* 21 (January 1947): 8-9; *MC*, November 22, 1945; and Interim Report of the President to the Trustees of Middlebury College, January 12, 1946, pp. 3-4, 6, President's Reports File, MCA.

5. W. Storrs Lee '28, "The Men," *MCNL* 20 (February 1946): 6. Also see Lee to Stratton, April 9, 1947, Lee file, Old Chapel archives; and Olson, *The G.I. Bill*, chap. 4.

6. See, for example, *MCNL* 21 (July 1947): 13; and FM (1945-47): 60-62, 80-81; and FM (1948-50): 118.

7. Reginald "Doc" Cook to David Stameshkin, January 28, 1982, MCA. Also

see FM (1945–47): 61; and Confidential Files, President's Office Safe, Old Chapel (hereafter cited as Conf.). These files contain materials relevant to the 1947 trustee investigation into faculty–administration relations. Much of the file consists of summary notes by members of the faculty committee involved in the investigation. I am grateful to former president James I. Armstrong for allowing me to view these files. Unless otherwise stated, all of the following is based on materials in Conf.

8. "Doc" Cook has stated: "The motivations in Professor Rafuse's conflict with President Stratton were not solely economic (salary), or psychological (i.e., temperamental difference), or ideological (autonomy, etc.), but also familial. Mrs. Dorothy Rafuse, Professor Rafuse's wife, had been a long-standing friend and favorite of the Moodys." See Conf.

9. The petition and the names of the signers are in Conf. Some faculty members wanted the petition to ask directly for Stratton's ouster. Of the fifty-one professors who signed the petition, thirty-five "expressed a positive opinion that the best interests of Middlebury College would be served by the resignation of the President." Also see Lee to Stratton, April 9, 1947, Lee file, Old Chapel Archives.

10. Lee to Stratton, January 31, 1947, Lee file, Old Chapel Archives.

11. Memorandum, "To The Trustees of Middlebury College, The President, the Faculty Conference Committee, from the Trustee Committee on Conference, March 24, 1947," copy in Conf., claims the date of the last interviews was March 8; the faculty notes in Conf. give the date as March 15, 1947.

12. See Report of the Faculty Committee on Conference with the Trustees, in FM (1945–47): 123A.

13. Conf. For more on the Rafuse case, see MC, January 23, 1947, and February 20, 1947. Stratton was particularly sensitive to labor organizing. In September 1947, the staff of the college went on strike and won. See MC, October 3, 1947.

14. Conf.

15. Ibid.

16. See ibid. for one professor's lengthy statement on this issue.

17. Ibid.; and FM (1945–47): 61. On the development of the reserve program, see interview with Carroll Rikert, August 3, 1979, MCA.

18. Conf.

19. A copy of the letter is in Conf.

20. Memorandum, "To the Faculty Committee on Conference, from the Trustee Committee on Conference, March 24, 1947," copy in Conf. See also interview with Egbert Hadley, July 31, 1975, transcribed notes in MCA.

21. Memorandum, "To the Trustees of Middlebury College, The President, the Faculty Conference Commitee, from the Trustee Committee on Conference, March 24, 1947," copy in Conf.

22. The following account is based on the minutes of the meeting in FM (1945–47): 116–19. As many as fifteen faculty members might not have attended. There were apparently seventy-five faculty members and assistants who had a right to vote at meetings, and at least fifty-four of these attended this unofficial meeting (note vote of 43–11). Several of the missing faculty were on leave, and according to Doc Cook, some of the absentees may have been assistants who "were not at all concerned and some perhaps never attended a faculty meeting while in the service of Middlebury College." The argument of the trustees (echoed by Stephen Freeman in recent years) that a small minority were opposed to Stratton appears to be incorrect. A solid majority apparently desired his removal. Cook has written that those senior faculty who declined to join the majority in criticizing Stratton included Professors

Perley Voter, Phelps Swett, Bruno Schmidt, Arthur Brown, and A. M. Cline. See Cook to Stameshkin, January 28, 1982; and interview with Freeman, August 27, 1981, MCA.

23. FM (1945–47): 118.

24. Based on interviews with Professors John Andrews, October 15, 1974, Howard Munford, March 5, 1975, Sam Guarnaccia, October 8, 1974, and John Bowker, October 15, 1974, tapes and notes, MCA.

25. The following is based on the minutes of the meeting in FM (1945–47): 124–26.

26. Ibid.; and interview with John Andrews, October 15, 1974, MCA. See also FM (1945–47): 140, 141, 144, 145.

27. Based on materials in Conf. and interview with Howard Munford, March 5, 1975, MCA.

28. Lee to Stratton, April 9, 1947; interview with W. Storrs Lee, July 2, 1976, MCA.

29. Lee to Stratton, April 9, 1947.

30. See Conf.

31. Healy's notes of this meeting are in Conf.

32. Lee to Stratton, April 9, 1947.

33. The following analysis, informed by sixteen years of interviewing many people and examining all the relevant documents I could unearth, is my own. I am sure most (if not all) of the people I have interviewed will not agree totally (or even in part) with it.

34. Interview with Egbert Hadley, July 31, 1975, MCA; and PM, 1: 419–20. Also see *MC*, September 25, 1955.

35. FM (1955):131–32.

36. See Gordon Perine to Miss Mary-Elizabeth Oetjen, February 13, 1956, original in possession of W. Storrs Lee. Mr. Lee graciously allowed me to see this letter and other related materials.

37. Minutes of the Joint Meeting of the Alumni and Alumnae Councils, October 9, 1955, copy in possession of W. Storrs Lee.

38. Report of the President to the Trustees, July 1, 1955, to June 30, 1956, typed copy in Old Chapel Archives.

39. Interview with W. Storrs Lee, July 2, 1976, MCA.

40. Based on interviews with Egbert Hadley, July 31, 1975, John Bowker, October 15, 1974, and Stephen Freeman, August 27, 1981, MCA.

41. Interview with Howard Munford, March 3, 1975, MCA.

42. Based on interviews with Fred Neuberger, February 3, 1975; Chaplain Charles Scott, July 31, 1975; Gordon Perine, February 28, 1975; Joseph Kasper, August 6, 1974; Thomas Reynolds, October 3, 1975; and, particularly, David K. Smith, March 10, 1975, MCA.

43. Interviews with John Andrews, October 15, 1974, and Thomas Reynolds, October 3, 1975, MCA; and "The Stratton Era," *MCNL* 37 (spring 1963): 12–14.

44. "The Stratton Era," 11.

45. George K. Anderson, *Bread Loaf School of English: The First Fifty Years* (Middlebury, Vt., 1969), 85–112.

46. Theodore Morrison, *Bread Loaf Writers' Conference: The First Thirty Years* (Middlebury, Vt., 1976), 91–94.

47. On Freeman's appointment, see Stephen Freeman, *The Middlebury College Foreign Language Schools: The Story of a Unique Idea* (Middlebury, Vt., 1975), 157–58.

48. On the Russian School, see ibid., 133–54. On the institute, see ibid., 145–54, 331–32.

49. See ibid. for a full account of these years, in particular, pp. 180–81, 287–304, 312–29.

50. Freeman, *Language Schools*, 223–25.

51. Ibid., 223–63.

52. Report of the Educational Policy Committee, April 1960, in FM (1959–61): 27.

53. FM (1959–61): 48.

54. Based on interviews with Paul Cubeta, March 14, 1975; John Andrews, October 15, 1974; Howard Munford, March 3, 1975; and John Bowker, October 15, 1974; MCA. For Stratton's view, see *MCNL* 34 (summer 1960): 7.

55. FM (1961–63): 150–51; and *MC*, September 20, 1962.

CHAPTER 7. THE STRATTON YEARS: PHYSICAL GROWTH
(PAGES 103–17)

1. *MC*, May 2, 1946; and CM, 6:393.

2. PM, 1:166. On earlier efforts to raise money for a gymnasium, see CM, 3:268, 274, 290, 348, 4:1; *MC*, March 13, 1935, and September 28, 1938; and Edgar J. Wiley '13, "Making a Start," *MCNL* 9 (March 1935): 2–3, 22.

3. Joseph P. Kasper '20, "A Lasting Memorial," *MCNL* 20 (June 1946): 12–13, 27.

4. "President's Page," *MCNL* 19 (March–April 1945): 19. See also PM, 1:166, and "President's Page," *MCNL* 20 (February 1946):18.

5. "Work Starts on World War II Memorial," *MCNL* 22 (April 1948):12; and *MC*, February 19, 1948. Only $400,000 had been raised by January 1948. See CM, 6:429. The campaign was run by Edgar "Cap" Wiley and, particularly, Stan Wright. See CM, 8:1001–2; *MC*, February 2, 1956; *MCNL* 21 (January 1947): 7.

6. "Work Starts," 12. Even with the reduced cost, the trustees could not raise enough money to offset the costs and had to dip into reserves to pay the $159,974.33 remaining due on the field house. See CM, 6:484.

7. "Work Starts," 12.

8. See CM, 6:442; *MC*, September 23, 1948; and *MCNL* 23 (October 1948): 3. The elder Lang '17 was a trustee and later treasurer of the college. See GC, 420, and CM, 9:1303.

9. *MC*, February 27, 1947, and September 25, 1947.

10. CM, 6:471, 474–75; and "Women's Dormitory Unit Will House 150 Students," *MCNL* 24 (April 1950): 5.

11. Ibid.

12. "Women's Dormitory," 5. On the celebration, see *MC*, September 21, 1950, and September 28, 1950.

13. *MC*, September 21, 1950; and CM, 6:492, 500. On the renovation of Starr Hall, see W. Storrs Lee, "Buildings and Grounds," *MCNL* 21 (January 1947): 8–9.

14. CM, 6:545. On Sunderland, see CM, 8:954.

15. *MC*, November 30, 1950.

16. *MCNL* 25 (January 1951): 1–3; CM, 6:500, 507.

17. *MC*, January 7, 1954; and CM, 6:579. Also see "The President's Page," *MCNL* 28 (April 1954): 2.

18. "The President's Page," *MCNL* 28 (April 1954): 2, and 29 (February 1955): 2.

19. CM, 6:578, 587, 595.

20. *MCNL* 29 (November 1954): 3-4.

21. PM, 1:401-2; CM, 6:624, 643. The board had first considered and then rejected the idea of buying and converting the old high school gymnasium.

22. The cost, originally (1955) estimated at $325,000, had risen to $392,500 by the following spring and to $478,908 by October 1956. The trustees voted not to go higher than $450,000, and it took a vote by mail for approval to raise the appropriation to $525,000 in January 1957. See CM, 6:624, 643, 661, 670, and PM, 1:428, 476. According to Walter Brooker, Edwin Sunderland gave much of the money for Wright Theater. See interview with Brooker, June 11, 1975, tape in MCA. On Wright, see David Stameshkin, *The Town's College: Middlebury College, 1800-1915* (Middlebury, Vt., 1985), 214, 276, 277.

23. *MC*, November 11, 1954; *MCNL* 29 (February 1955): 4. On the artificial ice, see *MCNL* 29:4; CM, 6:579; PM, 1:367; *MC*, January 14, 1954; and *MCNL* 28 (July 1954): 6.

24. Dr. Stewart Ross '20, an avid skier and generous benefactor of skiing facilities at Middlebury, contributed $2,000; the rest of the cost was defrayed by funds restricted (under terms of Battell's will) for the improvement of the area. See *MCNL* 28 (July 1954): 6; PM, 1:384; " 'Where the College Champions Ski,' " *MCNL* 35 (winter 1962): 8-9; and *MAC* (1958-59): 22.

25. MAC (1958-59): 22. He apparently gave $85,371. See CM, 7:873. On Starr, see " 'Where the College Champions Ski,' " 8-9; and President's Report to the Board of Trustees, 1959-60, p. 1, MCA. "Neil" was Cornelius V. Starr's nickname.

26. CM, 7:857, 873, 884, 889, 9:1302; PM, 2:696, 705, 712, 719; *MC*, September 21, 1961; *MCNL* 37 (winter 1963): 7; and *MCNL* 36 (spring 1962): 62.

27. See *MCNL* 33 (spring 1959): 6; CM, 7:696, 714, 723, 739; and PM, 2:560.

28. *MCNL* 33 (spring 1959): 6; *MC*, December 11, 1958, and October 15, 1959; and CM, 7:677, 685, 773.

29. For years, botany students had been unable to complete or even undertake many experiments due to the lack of adequate plants. Many thought that a greenhouse would rectify this problem, and a student committee raised $300 toward its construction in 1955. Later that spring, a "Greenhouse Weekend" was held, and a group of students, faculty, and staff gathered at the west end of Warner Science to begin the excavation. The college's development program soon provided a professional contractor and the balance of $12,000 necessary for construction. See *MCNL* 30 (November 1955): 4; and PM, 1:418.

30. CM, 6:585; and PM, 1:415. Also see Walter E. Brooker '37, "A Progress Report on Your Development Program," *MCNL* 30 (August 1956): 18.

31. CM, 7:841, 864, 883, 890. On Allen's role with the college, see CM, 7:922, and interview with Carroll Rikert, Jr., June 11, 1975, MCA.

32. Glenn Andres, *A Walking History of Middlebury* (Middlebury, Vt., 1975), 64; and *MCNL* 38 (winter 1964): 55.

33. On the Stewarts, see Stameshkin, *The Town's College*, 66, 187; and "New Chair Recalls Oldest Family Ties to the College," *MCNL* 45 (winter, 1971): 11-13. See also *MC*, May 3, 1956, October 3, 1957; CM, 6:631, 653, 696-97; and PM, 1:431, 458, 484-87.

34. *MC*, March 13, 1958; CM, 7:707, 714, 732-32a, 758; and PM, 2:558-59. One other major building constructed in the Stratton years was the 70-by-146-foot addition to the Service Building, "designed to give adequate space for functions

now taking place in crowded and scattered quarters." The cost was $73,928. See CM, 7:902, and *MC*, May 9, 1963.

35. See FM (1947–49): 82; President's Report to the Board of Trustees, 1948–49, p. 9, MCA; President's Report to the Board of Trustees, September 15, 1953, p. 11, MCA; and President's Report to the Board of Trustees, August 24, 1956, p. 15, MCA.

36. CM, 6:670, 682, 683, 714, 740–41; PM, 2:559; and *MCNL* 35 (fall 1960): 14. The college hired a library consultant, Dr. Joseph Wheeler, in 1953 to study the situation and offer proposals. See PM, 1:344.

37. See *MC*, September 22, 1960; and "President's Page," *MCNL* 36 (fall 1961): 8. Necessary funds for the third phase were obtained during the summer of 1961.

38. As early as July 1955, Sunderland had urged Stratton to create a permanent public relations and fund-raising post. See PM, 1:421, 426, 431, 436, 442. On Brooker's earlier work for the college, see *MCNL* 28 (July 1954): 7.

39. Interview with Walter Brooker '37, June 11, 1975, tape in MCA.

40. Based on numerous interviews with college officials.

41. See, for example, typed notes of my interviews with JIA; and taped interview with Walter Brooker '37, June 11, 1975, MCA.

42. *MCNL* 32 (winter 1958): 4.

43. "The Stratton Era," *MCNL* 37 (spring 1963): 6.

44. The annual figures for tuition are in *MAC* (1819–1987). The consumer price index rose from 19.5 in 1946 to 30.2 in 1962, an increase of 54.8 percent. The increase in tuition at Middlebury in those years was 205.8 percent. See the data on consumer price indexes in *Economic Report of the President . . . January, 1989* (Washington, D.C., 1989), Table B-58, p. 373.

45. *MCNL* 25 (April 1951): 3. On Mrs. Wilks, see *New York Times*, February 6, 1951, and November 16, 1951; and *Facts on File, 1951* (New York, 1951), 56 E-F, 392-G.

46. CM, 6:503, 519, 527–28, 537, 573, 582; and *MC*, October 30, 1952.

47. PM, 1:340; *MC*, October 30, 1952. For utilization of the Wilks money, see PM, 1:294; and FM (1951–53): 14.

48. *MCNL* 30 (August 1956): 2, 19. Only 40 percent of the 10 percent raise was attributed directly to the Ford money. The other 60 percent came from other gifts and a tuition increase.

49. *MCNL* 30 (February 1956): 15.

50. Report of the President to the Trustees, July 1, 1955 to June 30, 1956, p. 2, MS, Old Chapel Archives.

51. "The Alumni Fund and Its Purpose," *MCNL* 24 (October 1949): 12, 24.

52. *MCNL* 28 (July 1954): 7; and *MCNL* 32 (winter 1958): 4, 6.

53. CM, 7:858. He asked that no publicity whatsoever about the decision be made until after June 1962. Also see *MCNL* 36 (summer 1962): 11.

54. CM, 6:524; *MC*, February 5, 1953; and "The Stratton Era," 5.

55. "The Stratton Era," 6. Endowment figures for other colleges were obtained either directly from catalogs or from an appropriate administrative officer.

56. Interview with Howard Munford, March 5, 1975, MCA.

57. *MCNL* 43 (spring 1969): 1; CM, 7:896.

58. *MCNL* 43 (spring 1969): 1.

CHAPTER 8. THE ARMSTRONG YEARS, 1963–1975
(PAGES 118–45)

1. L. Douglas Meredith, "How Will Middlebury College Select a New President?" *MCNL* 37 (autumn 1962): 14–15.

2. Interview with Howard Munford, March 5, 1975, MCA. Also see FM (1962–63): March 6, 1963, p. 16.

3. Interview with James I. Armstrong (hereafter cited as JIA), April 30, 1975, p. 2, corrected notes, MCA.

4. PM, 7:796; and CM, 7:892.

5. This and the following are based on interview with JIA, April 30, 1975, pp. 1–2, corrected notes, MCA.

6. Interview with Walter Brooker, June 11, 1975, MCA.

7. CM, 7:848, 851, 856, 872.

8. JIA to James W. Armsey, January 11, 1964, Ford Report file, File Drawer 2, Old Chapel attic; interview with JIA, April 30, 1975, MCA.

9. Joseph M. McDaniel, Jr. (Ford Foundation) to JIA, June 25, 1964, in CM, 7:952, appended letter.

10. CM, 7:938; and "Brief Statement of Middlebury Future Plans," in FM (1963–64):108.

11. On Middlebury's initial tentativeness regarding the campaign, see interview with JIA, April 30, 1975, p. 3.

12. Kersting, Brown, and Company, Inc., "Middlebury College: Report of Study and Recommendations Relating to a Capital Gifts Campaign," August 3, 1964, unpublished mimeographed copy, President's Report files, Old Chapel Archives; CM, 8:954.

13. *MC*, February 11, 1965.

14. See "The Middlebury College Challenge Fund," *MCNL* 39 (winter 1965): 4.

15. On the campaign, see *MC*, September 16, 1965, and October 14, 1965; "$4.5 Million in Construction Gets Underway," *MCNL* 41 (spring 1967): 18. When the challenge period (1964–1967) was finished, the college had actually raised $10,151,431. See JIA, "Middlebury College, 1963–1968, Report of the President," p. 16.

16. The name of the building was determined in 1962. See CM, 7:883. On Sunderland, see CM, 8:954. For early plans, see "The Language Program and the Future," *MCNL* 37 (autumn 1962): 9. Also see "Plans Completed for Language Center," *MCNL* 38 (winter 1964): 54.

17. On Dana, see *MCNL* 38 (spring 1964): 3; and *MC*, December 7, 1977.

18. Interview with Walter Brooker, June 11, 1975, MCA.

19. Ibid., and *MCNL* 38 (spring 1964): 3.

20. See CM, 7:921, 926, 941, 952, 959, 967, 968, 978, 991.

21. Freeman, *The Middlebury College Foreign Language Schools, 1915–1970; The Story of a Unique Idea* (Middlebury, Vt., 1975), 206.

22. Ibid., 206–9; and Andres, *A Walking History of Middlebury* (Middlebury, Vt., 1975), 65–66.

23. Andres, *A Walking History*, 64–65; and CM, 8:1048, 1120. There were problems with the building, which will be discussed in chap. 9.

24. FM (1963–64):109.

25. Thomas H. Reynolds, "Our Need for Faculty and Facilities in the Natural

Sciences," *MCNL* 40 (autumn 1965): 8, 10; and Grant Harnest, "Program Calls for Expansion of Physical Facilities for Sciences," *MCNL* 40 (autumn 1965): 9, 11.

26. See CM, 8:958, 981–83, 1030, 1048, 1117, 1119; and *MC*, January 12, 1967.

27. *Addison County Independent*, September 24, 1965.

28. *MC*, September 30, 1965, and October 7, 1965.

29. Ibid., November 4, 1965.

30. Interview with Walter Brooker, June 11, 1975, MCA.

31. Andres, *A Walking History*, 55.

32. Reynolds, "Our Need for Faculty," 8.

33. Middlebury applied to the Sloan Foundation for funding in the natural sciences in 1966. See PM, 3:938. Sloan gave $400,000 for, among other things, a program to allow an eminent visiting professor to be in residence for one year at a time. The Dana Foundation gave a $250,000 matching endowment grant (to be matched equally), the income of which was to supplement the salaries of four professors. The Research Corporation gave $70,000 in 1966 and $175,000 in 1968, all earmarked for the sciences. The Ford Foundation donated $46,500 for support of faculty development in the humanities. The Old Dominion Foundation gave $50,000 to provide supplements to salaries of senior professors during 1967–1972. See JIA, "President's Report, 1963–1968," 5–7.

34. See interview with JIA, April 30, 1975, p. 3.

35. JIA, "Report of the President, 1969–1970," *MCB*, 65 (November 1970):18; and JIA, "President's Report, 1963–1968," Appendix A.

36. JIA, "President's Report, 1963–1968," 4–5 and Appendix B; JIA, "Report of the President, 1972–1973," *MCB*, 69 (January 1974): 4; and CM, 8:961.

37. JIA, "President's Report, 1963–1968," 5 and Appendix B.

38. In 1963–1964, the college library held 149,874 volumes aside from government documents; by 1967–1968, that figure had increased to 180,557; ibid., 8. On McKenna, see CM, 10:1545.

39. JIA, "President's Report, 1963–1968," 4, and "1963–1975: A Record of Achievement," summary card, MCA.

40. For faculty appointments, see *MAC* (1963–70). Also see interview with JIA, April 30, 1975, p. 2. On O'Brien, also see CM, 10:1857. On Turner, also see CM, 10:1494–95. O'Brien left in 1976 to become president of Bucknell University (and later of the University of Rochester); Turner was named president of Grinnell College in 1974. Conversation with William Catton, March 29, 1991.

41. Conversation with William Catton, March 29, 1991.

42. Based on interviews with Paul Cubeta, March 14, 1975, Howard Munford, March 5, 1975, and Thomas Reynolds, October 3, 1975, MCA.

43. Report of the Educational Policy Committee, January 8, 1968, in FM (1967–68): 31.

44. Ibid., 31.

45. The final proposal is in FM (1967–68): 29–43. See also *MC*, February 16, 1967, April 27, 1967, and May 4, 1967.

46. CM, 8:1094–95.

47. PM, 2:836; CM, 7:939; and interview with JIA, April 30, 1975, p. 3.

48. CM, 8:970, 1026.

49. PM, 3:948; and FM (1965–67): 112. Doc Cook has written that the "opposition to President A[rmstrong] serving on the Educational Policy Committee was based solely on principle, and that principle was one of faculty autonomy (i.e., that at least *one* faculty committee ought to be free of direct administrative influence)." See Doc Cook to David Stameshkin, January 28, 1982, MCA.

50. Previously, students had to take "two term courses of a literary and humanistic rather than a technical character," "two term courses chosen from the social and behavioral sciences," "two term laboratory courses chosen from among the natural sciences," and a fourth term course or more advanced course in ancient or modern languages. See *MCB* (1967–68): 22; and *MC*, October 23, 1969.

51. *MC*, April 16, 1970, and April 30, 1975; and interviews with Marshall Forstein '71, April 20, 1974, and SIC member Laureen Miner Cox '71, July 17, 1986, MCA.

52. There was a sense of the meeting that this was a temporary measure and that the faculty would address the question of curricular requirements at a later time. See FM (1970): 168.

53. Interview with Thomas Reynolds, October 3, 1975, MCA; PM, 2:832; and *MC*, March 5, 1964. On O'Brien, see CM, 10:1587.

54. Interviews with G. Dennis O'Brien, April 30, 1975, and Paul Cubeta, March 14, 1975, MCA; and PM, 3:1089.

55. PM, 3:1089; and interview with John Bowker, October 15, 1974, MCA. On Turner, see CM, 10:1494–95.

56. Interview with JIA, April 30, 1975, pp. 3–4.

57. This assessment is based on numerous interviews, conversations, and personal observation during the period 1972–1987.

58. See, for example, Report of the Dean of the College to the President, 1972–73, manuscript, Old Chapel Archives.

59. New England Association of Colleges and Secondary Schools, *Re-Evaluation: Middlebury College, 1968-1969* (n.p., n.d.), pp. 3–4; CM, 9:1214; and interview with G. Dennis O'Brien, April 30, 1975, MCA.

60. See CM, 8:969, 1034, 1058, 1086, 1119, 1123–26, 9:1141, 1162, 1196, 1212–13, 1227; PM, 3:1106; and *MC*, January 16, 1969.

61. CM, 9:1212.

62. Andres, *A Walking History*, 63.

63. On Carr Hall, see CM, 8:1114, and PM, 3:1035. On Voter Hall, see PM, 3:1078, 1091, and CM, 9:1212. Also see JIA, "Report of the President, 1972–1973," 8.

64. JIA, "Report of the President, 1972–1973," 10.

65. JIA, "Report of the President. 1971–1972," 4.

66. Ibid., 4–5.

67. See Earl Cheit, *The New Depression in Higher Education* (New York, 1971); and Earl Cheit, *The New Depression in Higher Education—Two Years Later* (Berkeley, Calif., 1973).

68. CM, 9:1206.

69. CM, 9:1156, 1252, 1257–59.

70. CM, 9:1353, 10:1553; and "Report of the President, 1971–1972," 9.

71. CM, 8:1010, 1036, 9:1400, 10:1258–59. On the contribution of Dana and the Given Family to Middlebury, see interview with Walter Brooker, June 11, 1975, MCA.

72. *MC*, May 14, 1970.

73. PM, 3:1183.

74. CM, 9:1282, 1391–92, 1400, 1401, 1426–28, 1434, 1511; Andres, *A Walking History*, 66. On Fletcher's role in the campaign, see *MCNL* 31 (autumn 1956): 4.

75. CM, 10:1448–49, 1452; and PM, 3:1252.

76. CM, 10:1449, 1515.

77. *Report of the Special Committee on the College* (Middlebury, Vt., 1973), vii.

78. Ibid., 3–4.

79. Ibid., 4–5.

80. MC, September 20, 1973, October 11, 1973, and December 6, 1973; and FM, December 3, 1973.

81. *Report of the Special Committee*, 6.

82. Ibid.

83. Freeman, *The Middlebury College Foreign Language Schools*, 264–383.

84. JIA, "Report of the President, 1972–1973." 12.

85. PM, 4 (September 8, 1973).

86. CM, 9:1213.

87. *Report of the Special Committee*, 7; CM, 9:1382, 11:1687.

88. *Report of the Special Committee*, 19.

89. Report of the Dean of the Faculty, 1969–1970, to President Armstrong, manuscript, Old Chapel Archives.

90. Based on interviews with many administrators and faculty. Also see Paul Cubeta to faculty, memorandum, in FM (1974–75): 42.

91. Report of the Dean of College, 1972–73, MCA.

92. Ibid.

93. *1978 Middlebury College Handbook* (Middlebury, Vt., 1978), 5.

94. FM (1974–75): 75–76. This statement is based on my own notes on attending faculty meetings during 1974–75 when tenure was discussed.

95. FM (December 2, 1974): 42–45.

96. This statement is based on my own interviews with numerous faculty members and administrators.

97. CM, 10:1484–86.

98. Interview with JIA, April 30, 1975, p.3; and CM, 10:1484–86.

99. The one exception here was Wesleyan, whose endowment rose unusually quickly during this period. Information concerning endowment income for these colleges was obtained either directly from their catalogs or from an appropriate official.

100. Interview with Howard Munford, March 5, 1975, MCA.

101. JIA, "The President's Report, 1963–64," *MCB*, 59 (October 1964): 5.

CHAPTER 9. THE ROBISON YEARS, 1975–1990 (PAGES 146–79)

1. CM, 10:1484–86; PM, 3:1259; and Olin Robison, *A Report to the Board of Trustees: Middlebury College, 1975–1980* (Middlebury, Vt., 1980), 1.

2. Biographical material was kindly provided by the president's office and the Middlebury Office of Public Affairs. I checked this with the public records whenever possible. Also see *MCNL* 52 (spring 1978): 2; *MCNL* 53 (fall 1978): 2; *MCNL* 53 (summer 1979): 11; and *MCNL* 56 (spring 1982): 3. I also conducted interviews with President Robison, including those of August 7, 1979, July 9, 1986, and July 3, 1990. On the Russian-American student exchange, see *MC*, September 11, 1987, November 20, 1987, February 19, 1988, September 16, 1988, and April 14, 1989; and *MCM* 62 (summer 1988): 32–34.

3. "President Olin C. Robison's Inaugural Address," *MCNL* 50 (winter 1975–76): 8.

4. CM, 10:1558–59.

5. FM (1975–76): 71.

6. Ibid., 72.

7. Ibid., 73; and CM, 10:1593.

8. CM, 10:1593; and FM (1975–76): 74. Concentrations had been a major part

of the 1973 curricular package. See *Report of the Special Committee on the College* (Middlebury, Vt., 1973), 4.

9. For student opinion, see *MC*, March 25, 1976, April 1, 1976, and May 6, 1976. The faculty voted 83–21 in favor of the foundations requirement and 77–27 in favor of the concentration requirement. See *MC*, May 6, 1976; and FM (1975–76): 103. On Robison's support for the proposal, see CM, 10:1592–93. In general, also see "A Return to Breadth: The New Middlebury Curriculum," *MCNL* 51 (fall 1976): 14–17.

10. Edward B. Fiske, "Concept of a 'General Education' Is Revived on College Campuses," *New York Times*, October 26, 1976, p. 1.

11. Donald S. Lopez, et al., *Toward Greater Educational Community: Recommendations to the President and Faculty, Middlebury College, The Report of the Special Committee on the Curriculum* (Middlebury, Vt., 1985), p. 1.

12. Ibid., *passim*.

13. For faculty action on the committee's report, see FM, October 14, 1985, pp. 25–32; December 2, 1985, p. 45; February 17, 1986, pp. 72–75; March 3, 1986; and April 7, 1986.

14. A grant from the Pew Memorial Trust enabled the college to develop and implement this program. See *MC*, February 20, 1987, March 6, 1987, March 13, 1987, and November 20, 1987; and *MCM* 62 (autumn 1988): 36.

15. FM, February 8, 1988, March 8, 1988, and April 4, 1988; and *MC*, February 12, 1988, and April 8, 1988.

16. In 1971 the Educational Policy Committee voted 7–6 against dropping winter term. See *MC*, December 9, 1971. For proposed changes in winter terms, also see FM, April 30, 1974, pp. 94–113.

17. FM, February, 1985, p. 81. See also FM, November 3, 1980, p. 25; March 25, 1982, p. 116; and May 9, 1983; and *MC*, March 26, 1982, April 16, 1982, May 7, 1982, November 5, 1982, and February 18, 1983.

18. FM, February 8, 1988.

19. For Peterson's view, see *MC*, February 12, 1988. Gleason's arguments can be found in *MCM* 62 (spring 1988): 41–42.

20. *MC*, February 19, 1988, and April 22, 1988.

21. FM, May 4, 1988. The Educational Council printed two documents as a basis for discussion: "A Revitalized Winter Term" and "A Preliminary Draft of a Proposal for a Semester System," dated May 2, 1988.

22. For discussion of winter term during 1988–1989, see *MC*, December 2, 1988, January 20, 1989, January 27, 1989, and April 28, 1989; FM, March 20, 1989; and *MCM* 63 (summer 1989): 43. Also see *MC*, September 29, 1989, for further changes in winter term procedures.

23. On East Asian studies, see CM, 9:1407; Robison, *A Report to the Board*, 4–5; *MCM* 56 (spring 1982): 11–13; FM (January 7, 1985): 65; and *MC*, April 18, 1986. The origins of the Northern studies program can be found in "Beyond the Trees . . . One Last Opportunity," *MCNL* 51 (winter 1977): 19–23. The international major quote is from *MAC* (1987–88): 46. On Jewish studies, see *MC*, January 22, 1981, November 22, 1985, and October 17, 1986. On the literary studies program, see *Report of the Visiting Committee on Literature* (Middlebury, Vt., 1989), 25–28.

24. A Russian Soviet studies major was developed in 1985 and the professorship obtained for $1.5 million in 1987. See *MC*, March 8, 1985, November 13, 1987, and January 22, 1988. The C. V. Starr Professorship in Linguistics was announced in 1973 and actually funded in 1979 at $750,000 after the Starr estate was distrib-

uted. See CM, 9:1400; *MC*, December 6, 1979; and *MCNL* 54 (winter 1980): 2. The computer science major was approved in February, 1988. See FM (February 8, 1988), addendum; *MCM* 62 (spring 1988): 33; and *MC*, February 19, 1988. After a tenuous existence as a nonprofit organization called the Dance Company of Middlebury, dance moved from the music to the theater department in 1980, offered a concentration in 1981–1982, and was approved as a major in 1983–1984 (with a tenurable faculty position) in the theater, dance, and film department. Three faculty members were teaching dance in 1989. See FM (September 8, 1980): 7; *MCNL* 55 (spring 1981): 3–4; *MCM* 58 (winter 1984): 10; "Dance Comes of Age," *MCM* 59 (winter 1985): 14–19; and *MC*, September 29, 1989. A women's studies major was proposed in 1988–1989 and approved for the 1989–1990 academic year. See *MC*, October 7, 1988, March 3, 1989, and September 22, 1989. The molecular biology major was proposed in the spring of 1989. See *MC*, March 3, 1989. A variety of grants, particularly one from the Dana Foundation, allowed the college to increase its interdisciplinary professorships and offerings. See *MC*, March 9, 1984; *MCNL* 55 (fall 1980): 9; and *MCM* 59 (winter 1985): 22–26.

25. On the Johnson chair, see *MC*, March 16, 1977; CM, 10:1613, and 1618 appended; *MCNL* 51 (spring 1977): 4; and *MCNL* 52 (winter 1978): 2. On the institute, see *MCM* 62 (spring 1988): 32, 34; *MC*, September 16, 1988, and December 2, 1988; and CM, March 10, 1989.

26. The geography saga is long and complicated. After Professor Vincent Malstrom left the college in 1975, Robison did not immediately make an appointment at the professorial level to replace him. However, Robison did appoint an ad hoc committee chaired by history professor William Catton to recommend the fate of the geography department. Although the committee recommended that geography should continue with an appointment at the professorial level and a four-person department, the college appeared to be moving toward incorporating it into a larger unit (as, for example, in the 39–37 faculty vote in 1981 to end the independent existence of the department). In 1979–1980 the announcement that Perry Hanson, who had been hired to create a new curriculum for the department, had been denied tenure led some to believe that geography would not survive as an independent unit. See PM, 3:1286; *MCNL* 51 (spring 1977): 3; FM (1976–77): 74–76; FM, November 3, 1980, February 2, 1981, September 7, 1981, and October 5, 1981; and *MC*, November 11, 1975, January 22, 1976, March 9, 1977, January 24, 1980, January 31, 1980, March 27, 1980, May 1, 1980, May 15, 1980, November 13, 1980, February 5, 1981, April 24, 1981, May 1, 1981, and October 9, 1981.

27. See CM, 13:2027–28. On the Johnson professorships, see Robison, *A Report to the Board*, 5. On Landon, see *MCM* 57 (winter 1983): 3.

28. "The Robison Years," pp. 28–29; *MC*, March 9, 1977, September 21, 1977, and September 11, 1987; *MCNL* 51 (spring 1977): 8; CM, 10:1613; and Report of the Director of the Language Schools, 1986–87, MCA.

29. A faculty committee determined in 1981 that a summer Arabic language program was preferable to other options (i.e., a school abroad or undergraduate programs in Arabic and Middle Eastern studies). See Committee on the Feasibility of Arabic Studies to Olin Robison, March 20, 1981, MCA; CM, 12:1835; *MCM* 56 (autumn 1981): 2; *MCM* 57 (autumn 1982); and *MC*, September 18, 1980, October 23, 1980, and October 2, 1981. Also see *MC*, November 1, 1979.

30. As early as 1973, Roger Peel, director of the language schools, reported that budget deficits were growing and the applicant pool was declining. Steps were taken to turn this situation around by adding undergraduate courses. See CM, 11:1697;

John McCardell et al., *Toward the Year 2000: A Basic Ten-Year Planning Document, May, 1988* (Middlebury, Vt., 1988), p. 25; and Reports of the Director of the Language Schools, 1982–87, MCA. Also see *Reports of the Director* for the increased interest in video technology.

31. CM, 10:1600; *MC*, April 20, 1977; *MCNL* 52 (summer 1977): 2; *MCM* 59 (autumn 1984): 4–5.

32. See David Haward Bain, "Bread Loaf at Sixty," *MCM*, 59 (spring 1985): 22–27.

33. *Report of the Visiting Committee on the Sciences* (Middlebury, Vt., 1989); *Report of the Visiting Committee on Literature* (Middlebury, Vt., 1989); *Middlebury College: Self-Study Report, January, 1990* (Middlebury, Vt., 1990); *Full Report of the Task Force on the Curriculum . . .* (Middlebury, Vt., 1990); *Report to the Faculty, Administration, Trustees, Students of Middlebury College . . . by . . . the New England Association of Schools and Colleges* ([Swarthmore, Pa.?] 1990); *Toward the Year 2000: A Basic Ten-Year Planning Document, May 1988* (Middlebury, Vt., 1988).

34. *Self-Study Report,* 54.

35. *Report of the Visiting Committee on Literature,* 3.

36. For positive remarks on the strengthening of interdisciplinary programs, ibid., 19–20, 27; and *Report to the Faculty,* 7–8.

37. *Report of the Visiting Committee on the Sciences,* 3, 5. The college was aware of this problem. The 1988 planning document made it clear that the needs of the sciences had to be given first priority. See *Toward the Year 2000,* 12–13.

38. *Toward the Year 2000,* 2; *Report to the Faculty,* 2–3; *Report of the Visiting Committee on Literature,* 3. Interestingly, the college had formed a Task Force on Institutional Mission, whose recommended statement was not approved by the board. See *Self-Study Report,* 8–12 and Appendices I and II.

39. The information is based on data in the files of the Provost's Office, Middlebury College.

40. CM, 10:1558.

41. Robison, *A Report to the Board,* 14, 15, 17, 18; *MC*, January 22, 1976; and CM, 10:1557–59.

42. Olin Robison, "A Five Year Report on the State of the College," *MCNL* 54 (summer 1980): 16. On the direct tie between increases in the comprehensive fee and faculty salaries, see CM, 10:1558–59.

43. *MC*, May 1, 1980. My conclusions are based on interviews conducted in the summer of 1979 with sixteen Middlebury faculty members—eight tenured and eight nontenured. Also see *MC*, February 28, 1980, May 1, 1980, and May 15, 1980. Faculty also complained about high rents charged by the college and asked for a subsidy for housing. See *MC*, October 2, 1980.

44. Faculty interviews, 1979; and *MC*, January 22, 1976, January 12, 1977, January 26, 1977, and January 13, 1979, February 28, 1979, March 7, 1979, and February 28, 1980.

45. Richard F. Gross to Robison, October 1, 1980, President's Office files; and *Report . . . New England Association,* 2–3.

46. CM, 11:1714. Also see CM, 11:1687, 1691, 1741, 12:1781; PM, 12:1328, 1336, 1339; FM (February 12, 1979): 59; and FM (September 4, 1979).

47. PM, 12 (December 4, 1981).

48. CM, 12:1855.

49. Interview with Olin Robison, July 3, 1990, MCA; *MCM* 64 (spring 1990): 33; *MC*, October 28, 1983.

50. *Report of the Faculty Ad Hoc Committee on Compensation,* May 18, 1983, p. 2, MCA. See CM, 12:1929 for report of Committee on Conference. On faculty discontent in the spring of 1983, see FM, April 20, 1983.

51. FM, April 20, 1983, p. 1.

52. *Middlebury College, 1983-1993, Inventory and Prospect: A Basic Ten Year Planning Document* (n.p., n.d.). It has the subtitle *A Report to the President of the College by the Faculty Committee on Long Range Planning, 1982-83.* A copy is in the Provost's office.

On formation of a FLRP, see FM, September 1, 1981, and December 7, 1981; and MC, November 6, 1981. The New England Association's 1980 reaccreditation report had urged the college to "consider ways in which to involve the faculty in longer-range financial planning." See Gross to Robison, October 1, 1980; and *Report . . . the New England Association,* 2-3.

53. *Middlebury College, 1983-1993 . . . Ten Year Planning Document,* 10.

54. On the evolution of this view see, in particular, FLRP to Robison, October 19, 1983; FLRP to Nicholas Clifford, October 31, 1983; FLRP to the Faculty, November 7, 1983; and FLRP to Robison, January 9, 1984, November 27, 1984, and February 28, 1985. These documents are in the possession of John McCardell.

55. See John McCardell's handwritten notes for his presentation to the board at their January 1984 meeting, in his possession; and FLRP to Robison, January 9, 1984.

56. FLRP to Faculty, October 1, 1984; PM, 12:1377, 1381; CM, 13:1965, 2004, 2121; PM, 13:1386, 1388, 1391; MC, April 18, 1986, and April 15, 1988; and FM (1985-86): 54. The Provost's Office supplied the data on comparison colleges and Middlebury's progress during the years 1983-1989.

57. *Middlebury College, 1983-1993,* 6.

58. McCardell et al., *Toward the Year 2000,* 1. The New England Association's reaccreditation report in 1980 specifically called for a sabbatical leave program. Indeed, this is the one area in which the college did not improve as requested by the Association visitation in 1968-1969. See *Report the New England Association,* 5. On the more generous leave policy of recent years, see *Self-Study Report,* 38; and McCardell et al., *Toward the Year 2000,* 1. For a fairly critical review of the leave policy, see the *Report of the Visiting Committee on Literature,* 6-8.

59. PM, 13:1387. The tenure policy had been mildly criticized by the 1980 New England Association accreditation team. They asked the college to clarify the tenure process "by informing successful candidates in the pre-tenure [four-year] review of the reasons and by replacing the term 'exceptional' in the list of qualification." See Gross to Robison, October 1, 1980; and *Report the New England Association,* 4-5.

60. MC, March 19, 1982.

61. MC, November 20, 1987.

62. Interview with Robison, July 9, 1986.

63. Robison, *A Report to the Board,* 15-16; MC, May 6, 1976; *Report . . . the New England Association,* 1, 4. "Notes for a Ten-year Report," unpublished manuscript, p. 42, Office of Public Affairs files. The first vice president for foreign languages was Hiroshi Miyaji, who served from 1980 to 1982 after which Ed Knox took over. See *MCNL* 54 (summer 1980): 2; *MC* October 22, 1982; *MCM* 57 (autumn 1982): 28; and *MCM* 58 (autumn 1983): 28-29.

64. The position of provost and vice president for academic affairs was established so that Robison could spend more time away from the college raising funds.

Clifford's appointment would "ensure that day to day administration . . . is not adversely affected by his travel." See FM (November 1981): 26; *MCM* 56 (winter 1982): 2. On Spencer, see *MC*, May 8, 1981. On Rockefeller, see *MCNL* 55 (summer 1981): 3.

65. Among these were Bruce Peterson (mathematics), George Saul (biology), Margaret O'Brien (chemistry), Robert Gleason (chemistry), Roger Peel (Spanish), Ed Knox (French), Stanley Bates (philosophy), Victor Nuovo (religion), Stephen Donadio (American literature), Russ Leng (political science), and Ted Perry (theater). Officers of the college are listed annually in the *MAC*. On Peel, who resigned as director of the language schools in 1979, see *MC*, November 1, 1979. On Perry, see FM (September 10, 1979): 6.

66. Professor James Maddox of George Washington University took Cubeta's place as director at Bread Loaf. See *MCM* 63 (spring 1989): 44; and *MC*, March 3, 1989. Cubeta had been accused of sexually harassing several male students and assistants at Bread Loaf. On the controversy over Cubeta and the college's handling of the incident, see *MC*, September 29, 1989, October 6, 1989, October 13, 1989, November 3, 1989, November 10, 1989, and December 1, 1989; and FM, December 11, 1989.

67. CM, 12:1877. On Brooker's retirement and Leeds's appointment, see *MC*, January 15, 1981, and February 19, 1982; *MCM* 56 (winter 1982): 6–7; and *MCNL* 55 (spring 1981): 2.

68. *MCM* 57 (spring 1983): 11. See also CM, 7:936; and *MCM* 57 (winter 1983): 2.

69. *MCNL* 60 (spring 1986): 4.

70. *MCM* 62 (spring 1988): 9–12, 14–15. On Wonnacott and Lindholm, also see *MC*, March 6, 1981, and April 22, 1988; and CM (May 21, 1988): 2132–34.

71. Based on information in the Office of the Treasurer. See Jane Bingham to David Stameshkin, August 10, 1990, MCA.

72. See CM, 12:1786. The first professional career counselor, Joan O'Connell, was hired in 1980–1981. See PM, 12:1320.

73. See *MC*, September 17, 1982, and September 25, 1987. On AIDS education, see *MC*, September 19, 1986, October 3, 1986, January 16, 1987, and September 25, 1987; and *MCM* 61 (winter 1986): 9.

74. On Parton, see *MCNL* 51 (spring 1977): 6; CM, 10:1612; and *MC*, January 26, 1977. On the changes in the health center, see *MCM* 57 (autumn 1982): 2; *MC*, September 17, 1982; and Steven Rockefeller and David Ginevan to Olin Robison, May 24, 1985, memo, appended to CM, 13:2029.

75. PM, 12:1365.

76. On security and safety issues, see *MC*, September 25, 1987, October 2, 1987, February 12, 1988, and April 8, 1988.

77. "Inaugural Address," 8. Also see Ronald Rucker, "Conquering Time and Space: Defining a College Library," *MCNL* 52 (spring 1978): 12–13; "The Middlebury Library: Planning for the 21st Century," *MCNL* 52 (spring 1978): 14–16; *MC*, October 23, 1975, March 11, 1976, and September 27, 1979; and *MCNL* 54 (winter 1980): 7.

78. In January 1975, a twenty-year projection of facilities and space for acquisitions convinced JIA to seek money from foundations for a new free-standing library. See CM, 10:1500. Robison told the trustees in October 1975 that the library was "the one place where the College does not have the facilities sufficient for the mis-

sion the College has designed for itself." No decision was made at that time about whether to construct a new building. See CM, 10:1553, 1561. For indications that decisions had been made, see *MC*, April 27, 1977; PM, 3:1297; and CM, 11:1665.

79. Robison, *A Report to the Board*, 6; PM, 3:1297.

80. The science library was completed in late 1978 at a cost of $358,150. See PM, 3:1297, 1707 appended; CM 11:1665, 1717 appended; and *MC*, September 21, 1978, and November 8, 1979.

81. See CM, 11:1665, 1717 appended; PM, 3:1297, 1307 appended; "A Place for All Seasons: A New Alumni House and Conference Center," *MCNL* 52 (spring 1978): 17–18; and *MCNL* 54 (winter 1980): 8.

82. The concern over college compliance with Title IX provided an initial impetus for examining the need for the field house renovations. See CM, 11:1726, 12:1769. On the renovations, see CM, 12:1784, 1838, 1954; *MC*, September 18, 1981; and *MCM* 56 (autumn 1981): 7–8.

83. *MC*, October 14, 1988, and January 27, 1989; and *CR* 5 (April 1989): 3.

84. *MCNL* 55 (fall 1980): 29; and see chap. 13 below. The trail, named for the college's longtime intramural director, John Kelly '31 (the husband of Dean Elizabeth Kelly), was dedicated in September 1977. See *MC*, September 21, 1977; and CM, 10:1602.

85. PM, 12:1369; *MCM* 60 (summer 1986): 6–7; and *CR* 2 (December 1985): 2. On Twilight, see Stameshkin, *The Town's College: Middlebury College, 1800–1915* (Middlebury, Vt., 1985), 108–9.

86. On Hadley House, formerly known as Starrfield, see *CR* 1 (May 1985): 1, 3; and PM, 12:1353–54.

87. On the problems with Johnson Arts, see, for example, notes from an interview with Glenn Andres, September 20, 1986, MCA. On the new building, see *CR* 5 (November 1988): 2.

88. *CR* 5 (November 1988): 2; *MC*, January 23, 1987, October 23, 1987, November 6, 1987, and March 3, 1989; CM (October 17, 1987), appended, 2110–11; and CM, May 27, 1989.

89. CM (January 16, 1988): 2118; PM (May 19, 1988); and *MC*, May 6, 1988, September 30, 1988, and October 7, 1988. Also see chap. 15, p. 349.

90. In 1968 it was determined that academic and administrative computer systems should be kept separate, and the college used a succession of increasingly sophisticated and powerful IBM systems for administrative purposes. The first computer course, offered by Professor Donald Ballou in 1963, relied on punch cards sent to UVM for batch processing. On November 2, 1966, the first time-sharing teletyping equipment (connected to a computer at Dartmouth) was installed in Munroe Hall. During the mid-1980s, the college utilized a DEC VAX 11/780 system and compatible terminals throughout the college for academic computing. On the early use of computers, see Donald Ballou, "The Beginning of Computing at Middlebury—Personal Recollections," MCA.

91. CM, 14:2045; *MCM* 60 (summer 1986): 9; *MC*, April 15, 1988; PM (May 19, 1988): 1445; and *CR* 5 (January 1989): 1. The trustees had briefly considered a combined arts/computer building in 1985. See PM, 13:1395–96; and CM, 13:2013.

92. *CR* 5 (November 1988): 2.

93. *MC*, December 9, 1983, and February 3, 1984. On the campaign, see below.

94. *MC*, November 2, 1984, November 9, 1984, and January 25, 1985.

95. *MC*, March 15, 1985; PM, 13:1395–96; Robison to Board of Trustees, February 27, 1985, in CM, 13:2006; and CM, 13:2013.

96. MC, March 20, 1987, April 24, 1987, May 1, 1987, October 23, 1987, November 6, 1987, January 15, 1988, and February 12, 1988; and PM (May 22, 1987): 1432.

97. MC, September 15, 1989.

98. On the construction of the center, see CM, May 27, 1989; MC, March 16, 1990, and May 4, 1990; and MCM 64 (spring 1990): 15-16.

99. PM, 12:1374-75; CM, 13:1964, 1988, 1997; MC, September 23, 1983, February 22, 1985, September 19, 1986, December 4, 1987, October 7, 1988, September 22, 1989, and April 20, 1990; and MCM 59 (winter 1985): 5-6. Also see *Self-Study Report*, 97.

100. On Warner Science, see MC, October 5, 1977; CM, 10:1500; and PM, 3:1290. On Dana and the language lab, see MC, September 25, 1981; and MCM 56 (autumn 1981): 4. On the fraternities and Proctor, see chap. 11; and MC, September 18, 1980. On the bells, see MC, March 8, 1985; MCM, 60 (autumn 1986): 20-25; and CR 1 (May 1985): 4. For the Willard House addition, see CR 3 (May 1987): 1. Other projects completed in the early Robison years are described in Robison, *A Report to the Board*, 26; and MC, September 18, 1975, September 22, 1976, and October 13, 1976.

101. MCM 61 (winter 1986): 10; and MC, September 25, 1987.

102. Robison, "A Five Year Report," 18; Richard Wolfson, "Energy Recycling: Heat from the Ground," MCNL 52 (spring 1978): 19; MCNL 53 (spring 1979): 2; "Thinking Energy: The Middlebury Story," MCNL 54 (winter 1980): 13; MCNL 55 (fall 1980): 4.

103. Robison, *A Report to the Board*, 21-22; MCNL 52 (summer 1977): 2; and MCNL 54 (winter 1980): 7. On Milliken's gift, see MCNL 51 (summer 1976): 46.

104. Robison, *A Report to the Board*, 19-21. On the Alumni College, see also CM, 10:1575.

105. "The Robison Years," MCM 64 (spring 1990): 32; and interview with Olin Robison, July 3, 1990.

106. MCNL 54 (winter 1980): 4; CM, 12:1810; Robison, *A Report to the Board*, 22, 24; "The Robison Years," 32; and interview with Olin Robison, July 3, 1990. Surveys of return on investment conducted by the National Organization of College and University Business officers showed that, prior to 1976, Middlebury usually did not do well compared to other schools.

107. Robison, *A Report to the Board*, 13. Also see MC, March 25, 1976, and April 1, 1976; and CM, 10:1576, 12:1811, 1839, 1857-58.

108. CM, 12:1811, 1839, 1857-58; and MC, March 5, 1982. The FLRP report was titled *Middlebury College, 1983-1993, Inventory and Prospect: A Basic Ten-Year Planning Document*.

109. CM, 12:1940; CM, 13:1966-67; and MCM 59 (autumn 1984): 18-19.

110. MCM 59 (winter 1985): 4-5; and MCM 64 (spring 1990): 14. On the progress of the campaign, see CM, 13:1016, 14:2041; MC, September 16, 1988; and CR, vols. 1-5.

111. On Fulton's bequest, see MCM 60 (autumn 1986): 8; MC, September 11, 1987; and CR 3 (January 1987): 1. On his earlier gift, see "President's Report to the Trustees, 1961-62," 19.

112. MCM 58 (autumn 1983): 4; MCM 64 (spring 1990): 14; and CR 4 (August 1987): 5. The class of 1956's $100,000 gift was particularly significant in that the money was all paid in one year. Later class gifts were larger, but they often consisted of numerous multiyear pledges.

113. ~~*CR* 4 (August, 1987): 5; and *MC*, November 13, 1987.~~

114. *MC*, November 13, 1987; and CM, October 21, 1988.

115. Files in Development Office; *CR* 4 (November 1987): 2; *MCM* 62 (spring 1988): 32, and minutes of the Trustee Development Committee in CM, January 15, 1988, March 12, 1988, and October 28, 1988. The college was fortunate that only 60 percent of the endowment was in equities at the time of the market's plunge, rather than the usual 80 percent. See CM, October 28, 1988. On the 14 percent figure, see "The Robison Years," 32.

116. PM (March 10, 1988): 1437.

117. *MCM* 64 (autumn 1989): 9.

118. Interview with Olin Robison, August 7, 1979, MCA; and Robison, "A Five Year Report," 14.

119. Based on interviews with faculty.

120. This is based on my interviews with faculty and administrators during the 1980s. Also see *MC*, October 9, 1987, March 3, 1989, and especially October 13, 1989. For several criticisms of Robison near the end of his presidency, see *MC*, January 19, 1990, and February 23, 1990.

121. See note 66 above.

122. The new stadium was to be named for Trustee Emeritus William Young-man '31 and built between Fletcher Field House and the golf course on Route 30. The track was to be named after outgoing board chairman Allan Dragone '50. On the plans for the new facilities, see CM, May 27, 1989; *MC*, November 10, 1989; McCardell et al., *Toward the Year 2000*, 16-17; and *MCM* 64 (winter 1990): 14.

123. A copy of the letter is in FM, November 6, 1989.

124. FM, November 6, 1989.

125. FM, December 11, 1989, and April 2, 1990; and Minutes of the Faculty Council, December 13, 1989.

126. *Report to the Faculty*, p. 5. Also see Report of the Task Force on Curriculum, p. 6; interview with Robison, July 3, 1990; and interview with David Ginevan, July 3, 1990, MCA. Also see Jane Bingham to David Stameshkin, August 10, 1990, MCA.

127. See, for example, Bingham to Stameshkin, August 10, 1990; and *Report of the Task Force on Curriculum*, p. 6.

128. *MCM* 64 (summer 1990): 13.

129. CM, March 10, 1990. On Light, see *MCM* 64 (spring 1990): 9-11; *MC*, March 16, 1990.

130. *Report to the Faculty*, 7.

CHAPTER 10. THE STUDENT BODY (PAGES 185-214)

1. This assertion is based primarily on anecdotal evidence, articles in the campus paper, reports by college officials, and analysis of tuition and fee increases. There has been no attempt to ascertain the wealth of individual students, except indirectly through the reports of college officials. This obviously weakens any conclusions I may draw. Still, the evidence from other sources is overwhelming, and I am confident that the changes I describe took place.

2. On the early Thomas years, see David M. Stameshkin, *The Town's College: Middlebury College, 1800-1915* (Middlebury, Vt., 1985), chap. 9.

3. JT to Carson J. Beane, April 19, 1920, TP.

4. *MC*, February 11, 1920.

5. Hepburn rates, which varied from $50 to $100 in 1916, were increased during the Moody years. See *MC*, March 16, 1916, May 10, 1916, and April 14, 1926; and *MAC* (1919-41).

6. "The President's Report, 1927-1928," *MCB* 22 (January 1928).

7. "Proposed Report to Board of Trustees," typed manuscript, Moody Papers, Box 2, MCA.

8. CM, 3:303; and *MC*, April 12, 1939. On the work of the assistant director, see *MC*, April 15, 1936.

9. Basic costs include tuition, room and board, heat, lights, other fees, and books. See *MAC* (1920-41) for annual costs. Also see *MC*, December 17, 1930, and February 15, 1939; and Interchurch World Movement of North America Survey, TP, MCA. On changes in the cost of living, see *Historical Statistics of the United States, Colonial Times to 1970* (Washington, D.C., 1976), 1:210-11.

10. W. Storrs Lee '28, "In Retrospection," *MCNL* 53 (summer 1978): 14.

11. Dean Burt A. Hazeltine, "Democratic Middlebury," *MCNL* 6 (April 1932): 2.

12. Lee, "In Retrospection," 15; W. Storrs Lee to David Stameshkin, September 6, 1976, MCA; interview with Howard Munford '34, March 5, 1975; interview with Sam Guarnaccia '30, October 8, 1974; and interview with David K. Smith '42, March 10, 1975, MCA. Erwin Warren '37 recalled that he was very popular with his Chi Psi brothers because he had permission to have a car on campus. He was the only guy with a car. See *MCM* 59 (spring 1985): 38.

13. See, for example, *MC*, May 28, 1919, and February 15, 1922; and Interchurch World Movement of North America survey, TP, MCA.

14. *MCNL* 52 (summer 1977): 31.

15. *MC*, March 26, 1924.

16. All of the following Lee quotations are taken from Lee to Stameshkin, September 6, 1976, in the author's possession.

17. Ibid.; and Hazeltine, "Democratic Middlebury," 2-3.

18. See, for example, *MC*, February 22, 1922, and October 28, 1925.

19. CM, 4:66.

20. *MC*, April 25, 1934, October 16, 1935, and November 6, 1935.

21. *MCM* 60 (autumn 1985): cover; *MC*, May 23, 1934.

22. Hazeltine, "Democratic Middlebury," 2-3; and Lee to Stameshkin, September 6, 1976.

23. Stameshkin, *The Town's College*, 180, 181, 218, 220-21, 222, 234-35, 239, 250, 272, 281.

24. CM, 3:234. The total annual income available for scholarships from vested funds was approximately $6,500 in 1928-1929. In addition, the state provided $7,200 in aid for Vermont students. If the college paid out an additional $7,000, then the total financial aid was about $20,000. See *MAC* (1928-1929): 107. For a listing of the scholarships, see *MAC* (1928-1929): 102-6.

25. CM, 3:302; *MC*, February 22, 1933, and May 13, 1936; see also interview with David K. Smith, '42, March 10, 1975.

26. Hazeltine, "Democratic Middlebury," 3.

27. *MC*, September 28, 1932.

28. Lee to Stameshkin, September 6, 1976.

29. *MC*, April 19, 1939.

30. This statement is based on many interviews with students and faculty from

the interwar period, who are in complete unanimity on this point. Other indirect evidence includes the relatively smaller number of Middlebury women who obtained scholarships and held jobs. See *MAC* (1920–1941) for scholarship offerings; and Hazeltine, "Democratic Middlebury," 3, for statistics on student employment by gender.

31. On coeducation in the early twentieth century, see Thomas Woody, *A History of Women's Education in the United States* (New York, 1929), Vol. 2, chap. 5.

32. See *MC*, February 26, 1936; and chap. 3.

33. See, for example, chap. 3, pp. 37–38; FM, September 18, 1922, p. 52; and interview with D. K. Smith '42, March 10, 1975.

34. *MC*, March 22, 1922. The class of 1928 entered with 108 men and 80 women. By their junior year, the class had 59 men and 67 women. See *MC*, October 8, 1924, October 7, 1925, October 6, 1926.

35. Interview with Sam Guarnaccia '30, October 8, 1974.

36. On Stratton's views, see above, chap. 6, pp. 86–87.

37. Interim Report of the President, January 10, 1948, exhibit 2, MCA; Stanley Wright '18, "Admissions Problems: The Men," *MCNL* 22 (July 1948): 5, 18; Report of the President to the Trustees of Middlebury College, 1948–49, 6–7, MCA; and MAR (1800–1951).

38. Interviews with Fred Neuberger '50, February 3, 1975, and July 16, 1986, MCA.

39. President's Report, September 1, 1950, p. 5, MCA; W. Storrs Lee '28, "The Men," *MCNL* 20 (February 1946): 6–7, 18; and Lee to Stameshkin, September 6, 1976, p. 5.

40. *MCNL* 20 (February 1946): 7.

41. Interviews with Fred Neuberger, February 3, 1975, and July 16, 1986; Ruth E. Cann '19, "Admissions Problems: The Women," *MCNL* 22 (July 1948): 5, 18; and interview with Barbara Wells '41, February 10, 1975.

42. Interview with Wells; President's Report, September 15, 1953, p. 5, MCA; and MAR (1800–1951).

43. Interim Report of the President to the Trustees of Middlebury College, January 10, 1948, p. 2, MCA.

44. See ibid., on the women's credentials. On the men's situation, see Wright, "Admissions Problems," 5; and interview with D. K. Smith '42, March 10, 1975, MCA.

45. President's Report, September 1, 1950, p. 8, MCA. In June 1950, only $18,567 was available for scholarships, whereas $640,555 in tuition income had been collected that year. See exhibit 11. On college costs, see *MAC* (1941–42, 1946–47, and 1951–52). Also see President's Report, September 1, 1951, pp. 3–4, MCA.

46. President's Report, September 1, 1951, p. 3, MCA. On Wright, see *GC*, 448; interview with Fred Neuberger, July 16, 1986; interview with Howard Munford, March 5, 1975; and Lee to Stameshkin, September 6, 1976, p. 6.

47. Walter Brooker to George Huban, June 22, 1981, MCA; interview with Fred Neuberger, July 16, 1986; interview with Howard Munford, March 5, 1975; *MC*, May 18, 1950; and Lee to Stameshkin, September 6, 1976, p. 6.

48. On the increase in academic problems in the men's college in the early 1950s, see President's Report, September 1, 1950, exhibit 6, MCA; *MC*, September 21, 1950, February 15, 1951, and May 24, 1951; President's Report, September 15, 1953, p. 2, MCA; and CM, 6:553. On the faculty's response, see President's Report,

September 1, 1951, pp. 1-2; Report of the President to the Board of Trustees, September 15, 1953, p. 2, MCA; FM, March 25, 1953; and Lee to Stameshkin, September 6, 1976, p. 6.

49. Report of the President to the Trustees of Middlebury College, September 15, 1954, p. 3, MCA. Also see President's Report, September 1, 1951, pp. 1, 2.

50. Brooker to George Huban, June 22, 1981, MCA; interview with Fred Neuberger, July 16, 1986, MCA; and interview with Gordie Perine '49, February 28, 1975, MCA.

51. President's Report, August 24, 1956, p. 4a, MCA; and admissions office files. Enrollment figures are from *MAC* (1952-63). SAT scores are from Admissions Office files and Dean of the College files.

52. "Middlebury College, Myths of Coeducation," *The Harvard Crimson*, May 21, 1954. Fred Neuberger has said that the good male students of the 1950s were equal in quality to the good female students, but that the worst men students were inferior to the worst of the women. See interview with Neuberger, July 16, 1986.

53. Report of the President to the Trustees, July 1, 1955 to June 30, 1956, manuscript, MCA.

54. Quotation is from CM, 7:687. On tuition increases in the period, see CM, 6:583, 7:705, 712, 809; PM, 1:409, 431, 481; 2:540, 667.

55. PM, 2:590.

56. *Report of the President, 1972-1973* (Middlebury, Vt., 1973), 10; *MCNL* 32 (spring 1958): 12.

57. When the class of 1966 entered in 1962, the men's SAT score mean was 1199; the women's was 1226. When the class of 1973 entered in 1969, the men's mean was 1300 and the women's was 1301. Scores varied in the 1970s, but there were no significant gender differences in total mean scores; women averaged 10-40 points higher in verbal scores, whereas men scored higher in math by a similar amount. See Admissions Office files.

58. Interview with Fred Neuberger '50, February 3, 1975.

59. In the 1950s and 1960s, approximately 58 percent of Middlebury students were males. Although several entering classes in the 1970s and 1980s had more women than men, total enrollment was still about 55 percent male in the 1970s and just under 52 percent in the 1980s. By 1988-1989 there were 991 men and 986 women enrolled. Based on enrollment statistics in annual reports of the Dean of the College, MCA; and *MAC* (1950-1973).

60. Brooker to George Huban, June 22, 1981.

61. Stameshkin, *The Town's College*, 271.

62. Olin Robison, *A Report to the Board of Trustees: Middlebury College, 1975-1980* (Middlebury, Vt., 1980), 10.

63. The three cities initially targeted were Denver, San Francisco, and St. Louis. Ibid., 11; and CM, 11:1697.

64. Olin Robison, "A Five-Year Report on the State of the College," *MCNL*, 54 (summer 1980), 15-16.

65. *Report of the Admissions Long-Range Planning Committee* (Middlebury, Vt., 1987), 14.

66. MC, May 21, 1964, September 9, 1964, and October 15, 1964; interview with Roth Tall '65, June 3, 1975, MCA. Riley went to Vicksburg, Mississippi, after graduation to volunteer in organizing and running a newspaper. Also see MC, May 23, 1963, for earlier action. On college students and the civil rights movement

in the 1960s, see Doug McAdam, *Freedom Summer* (New York, 1988), and the review essay by Jack Weinberg, "Students and Civil Rights in the 1960's," *HEQ* 30 (summer 1990): 213-24.

67. *MC*, September 24, 1964.

68. *MC*, October 29, 1964, November 5, 1964, November 19, 1964, and January 14, 1965.

69. *MC*, February 18, 1965, and May 6, 1965; and Annual Report of the Dean of Men, June, 1965, p. 8, typed copy, MCA.

70. Annual Report, 8; and *MC*, March 25, 1965.

71. Annual Report, 8; *MC*, April 1, 1965.

72. Interview with Roth Tall '65, June 3, 1975.

73. *MC*, November 5, 1964, and April 15, 1965.

74. Interview with Roth Tall '65, June 3, 1975.

75. CM, 8:966; and Annual Report, Dean of the College, July, 1965, copy in Old Chapel attic.

76. "The Negro Revolution and Middlebury," *MCNL* 43 (autumn 1968): 5.

77. Ibid., 4; CM, 8:1096; and *MC*, April 18, 1968.

78. *MC*, January 30, 1969. The college gave a $2,500 matching grant to Y.O.U. in 1968.

79. *MC*, October 17, 1968, and January 30, 1969.

80. *MC*, March 13, 1969, and April 17, 1969.

81. CM, 11:1162, 1134. The college also agreed to participate in the ABC (A Better Chance) program sponsored by the Rockefeller Foundation, which helped minority students attend prep schools in the Northeast.

82. PM, 3:1087-88; and Dean's Office records.

83. For attrition data, see *Report of the Admissions Long-Range Planning Committee, May 1, 1987* (Middlebury, Vt., 1987), II.F.15, Appendix A; *MC*, October 16, 1980, and January 29, 1981; and *Report of the Task Force on the Composition of the Student Body* (Middlebury, Vt., 1989), pp. 25-26. The faculty offered courses during winter term to help and approved special interdivisional compensatory programs for disadvantaged students. See *Report of the Task Force on the Composition of the Student Body*; CM, 9:1208, 1213; and *MC*, March 5, 1970.

84. *MC*, February 22, 1973. Adirondack House had been named, over the years, Battell Cottage, Willard Hall, Alumni Center, and Economics House. See CM, 9:1057.

85. Based on my own observations during 1972-1975. At that time (1972-1974), I taught Afro-American history classes and had contact with many of the black students. Also see *MC*, February 26, 1976; "Erica," *MCM* 62 (spring 1988): 12; and *Report of the Ad Hoc Committee on Minority Concerns*, October 1982, pp. 12-14.

86. FM, September 1, 1981, pp. 1-2. See also *Report of the Ad Hoc Committee*, 1-2; CM, 12:1817-18; and *MCM* 57 (summer 1983): 2-4. Enrollment statistics on minority students are in the Office of Admissions files and in *Report of the Task Force on the Student Body*, 13.

87. *Report of the Ad Hoc Committee*, 1-24.

88. *Report of the Admissions Long-Range Planning Committee*. One of the reasons for the lack of progress before 1987 was faculty concern over minority hiring initiatives. See FM, April 6, 1983 (executive session minutes, in 1983-84 folder), and May 7, 1984, p. 117. Also see *MC*, May 6, 1983, April 27, 1984, and April 19, 1985.

89. Elizabeth Karnes, "The Minority Advisory Group—the Minority Advisory Workshops," in John Emerson to President Olin Robison, January 4, 1989, Presi-

dent's Office files, p. D. Also see *MC*, October 14, 1988, and November 4, 1988; and John Emerson, *An Update on Minority Concerns: Postscript to the Twilight Report* (Middlebury, Vt., 1988), pp. 11–12. A summary of Emerson's work can be found in *MCM* 62 (summer 1988): 34, 36.

90. On the hiring of a black counselor and psychologist, see Emerson, *An Update*, p. 7; and *MC*, February 26, 1988, and September 23, 1988. New rules on faculty hiring in 1988–1989 helped in the recruitment of additional minority faculty. For example, after screening applications, departments were required to rank their top four candidates, one of whom had to be a woman or a member of a minority group. If a department identified, "a qualified minority candidate" and a position did not exist, a regular tenure-track position—an increment—could be created for that person. (But if a member of that department subsequently left the college, the increment would not automatically be retained.) See John McCardell, "Recruiting Minority Faculty," in Emerson to Robison, January 4, 1989, p. I. Also see Emerson, *An Update*, 7–8. On the Racial/Ethnic/Religious Harassment Policy, see copy in Emerson to Robison, p. B; *MC*, October 2, 1987, October 9, 1987, and November 6, 1987; Emerson, *An Update*, 8–9 and Appendix IV. On SCIENS, see Emerson to Robison, January 4, 1989, pp. F and M2–3. On academic support services, see Emerson to Robison, January 4, 1989, pp. K and M2; *MC*, November 4, 1988, April 28, 1989, and March 16, 1990; and *MCM* 64 (spring 1990): 16. On recruitment and retention of minority students, see Emerson to Robison, January 4, 1989, pp. G, H, J, and M1; Emerson, *An Update*, 3–6; and *MC*, January 15, 1988, March 11, 1988, and May 6, 1988. On the aid package, see CM, October 17, 1987, p. 2107. The trustees supported all of these initiatives in January 1989. See CM (January 14, 1989): 2155.

91. On the Human Relations Committee, see Emerson to Robison, January 4, 1989, p. C; and *MC*, January 20, 1989. On the change of the name of the Black Student Union, see *MC*, February 23, 1990. Also see *MC*, April 29, 1988, and January 27, 1989.

92. "Middlebury's Agenda for Minorities: Priorities and Goals," attached to Emerson to Robison, January 4, 1989.

93. On the DeWitt Clinton partnership, see *MCM* 64 (winter 1990): 10, 12; *Report of the Task Force on the Composition of the Student Body*, 14–15; *MC*, February 24, 1989, April 14, 1989, February 23, 1990, and March 16, 1990; and Herbert F. Dalton, Jr., *To Share a Dream: The Clinton-Middlebury Partnership* (Middlebury, Vt., 1990).

94. On articulation agreements, see *Report of the Task Force on the Composition of the Student Body*, 18.

95. Quoted in Dalton, *To Share a Dream*, 25. On minority enrollment in the late 1980s, see *MC*, April 15, 1988, September 22, 1989, and December 1, 1989; *MCM* 63 (summer 1989): 24–29; and Recruitment Plan and Report: Students of Color, June 12, 1990, draft copy, Admissions Office.

96. *MAC* (1915–72); and Admissions Office files.

97. Appendix III-Q.

98. Ibid.; and *Report of the Task Force on the Composition of the Student Body*, 16.

99. On the consortium, see *MC*, September 9, 1989; *MCM* 62 (winter 1988): 28; 62 (summer 1988): 32–34; 62 (autumn 1988): 37; and 63 (autumn 1989); 18–25.

100. On February freshmen, see *MCM* 58 (autumn 1983): 42; and 59 (spring 1985): 2–4.

101. Dean of the College Report, 1988–89.

102. Interchurch World Movement of North America survey, March 29, 1920, TP.

103. Interview with Walter Brooker, June 11, 1975; and MC, November 19, 1930. On the experience of Jews at other colleges, see Dan A. Oren, *Joining the Club: A History of Jews and Yale* (New Haven, Conn., 1985); and Marcia G. Synnott, *The Half-Opened Door: Discrimination and Admissions at Harvard, Yale, and Princeton, 1900-1970* (Westport, Conn., 1979).

104. Report of the President, September 1, 1951, p. 10c.

105. Report of the President, 1969-70, pp. 34-35.

106. Because the college does not ask students to reveal religious affiliation, only estimates can be made. Chaplain John Walsh estimated that in 1990 perhaps 12 percent of the student body was Jewish and at least twice that number were Catholic. Telephone interview with Chaplain John Walsh, November 19, 1990.

107. The amount of financial aid increased during the Armstrong years, from $212,130 to $724,875, but the number of people assisted was not sufficient to change the prevailing perception of the college. See President's Report, 1962-63, p. 10; and the relevant appendices from the draft of an unpublished ten-year report on the Robison administration, copy in the author's possession.

108. *MCNL* 52 (summer 1977): 2. See also "President Olin C. Robison's Inaugural Address," *MCNL* 50 (winter 1975-6): 8.

109. Report of the Dean of the College, 1978-79, p. 4, MCA.

110. PM, 12:1336. Also see PM, 12:1339.

111. *MCNL* 56 (summer 1982): 2; and 58 (autumn 1983): 2.

112. Report of the Dean of the College, 1988-89; and John McCardell et al., *Toward the Year 2000: A Basic Ten-Year Planning Document, May, 1988* (Middlebury, Vt., 1988), 21.

113. For information on the Admissions Outreach Program, see *Report of the Task Force on the Composition of the Student Body*, pp. 9-12, Appendices IIIA-D; "Middlebury Admissions Outreach Representative Profiles: Matriculating Rural Students 1988" (copy in MCA); MC, January 22, 1988, and November 11, 1988; CM, October 22, 1988, p. 2147; Fred M. Hechinger, "About Education," *New York Times*, October 26, 1988; and interview with Caroline Donnan, July 13, 1990, MCA.

114. See *MCM* 61 (summer 1987): 5; and *MC*, April 17, 1987.

115. Olin Robison, "An Open Letter to the Middlebury College Community," *MCM* 64 (spring 1990): 30.

116. CM, May 23, 1987, p. 2099.

117. See chap. 9, pp. 157-59.

118. For information on early comprehensive fee increases under Robison, see, for example, *MCNL* 51 (spring 1977): 3; and 52 (spring 1978): 3; *MCM* 61 (summer 1987): 5-6; and 62 (spring 1988): 31-32; CM, 12:1558-60, 1772, 1797, 1815, 1911; and PM, 3:1314, 1359-60.

119. Files of the Office of Institutional Research, Franklin and Marshall College. The comparative colleges were Amherst, Bowdoin, Carleton, Colby, Colgate, Davidson, Franklin and Marshall, Grinnell, Hamilton, Haverford, Kenyon, Knox, Lafayette, Oberlin, Pomona, Reed, Swarthmore, Trinity, and Williams.

120. The following summary of the reaction to the fee increase is based on the report in *MCM* 63 (summer 1989): 42. Also see *MC*, May 5, 1989, and September 15, 1989; and Report of the Dean of the College, 1988-89, p. 3, MCA. On the decision to set the fee at $19,000, see CM, March 11, 1989, p. 2163.

121. See, for example, *MC*, March 17, 1989.

122. *MC*, April 14, 1989.

123. *MC*, September 15, 1989; and Report of the Dean of College, 1988–89, p. 3.

124. See, for example, *MC*, March 17, 1989, April 14, 1989, April 28, 1989, May 5, 1989, September 15, 1989, September 22, 1989, September 29, 1989, October 13, 1989.

125. For information on how the fee was set for 1990–1991, see *MCM* 64 (spring 1990): 11–13; CM, March 10, 1990, p. 2187; and *MC*, February 23, 1990, March 9, 1990, and March 16, 1990.

126. See chap. 9, p. 177.

127. Interview with David Ginevan, July 3, 1990; and telephone conversation with John Emerson, August 29, 1990.

CHAPTER 11. FRATERNITIES (PAGES 215–42)

1. Enrollment figures are in MAR (1800–1951). The original five fraternities, Chi Psi, Delta Upsilon, Delta Kappa Epsilon, Kappa Delta Rho, and Alpha Sigma Phi (which affiliated with its national in 1925), were still going strong. Sigma Phi Epsilon was organized in 1921 as Sigma Phi Iota. In 1925 it became a Sigma Phi Epsilon affiliate. See *MC*, May 24, 1922; and *SK*, 73–74. Theta Chi was originally present on campus in 1923 as Chi Kappa Mu and, in 1925, Epsilon of Beta Kappa. Beta Kappa and Theta Chi national merged in 1942. See *SK*, 74–75; and *MC*, March 14, 1923, February 18, 1925, and June 17, 1925. From 1938 to 1947, Alpha Tau Omega was a local fraternity—Sigma Alpha. See *SK*, 75; and *MC*, April 12, 1939. Other fraternities existed for short periods in the interwar years, including Delta Sigma (1911–1929?). See *SK*, 75; *MC*, March 10, 1926; and the *Kaleidoscope* (1925). The percentage of men in fraternities was obtained from interviews and occasional statistical sources. See *MC*, September 26, 1923; and *Kaleidoscope* (1927, 1933, 1934). The number of fraternity men was counted from the names and pictures in *Kaleidoscope*, and that number compared with the total number of men enrolled as listed in MAR (1800–1951). See also *MC*, January 19, 1921.

2. See interviews with Joseph Kasper '20, August 6, 1974; Howard Munford '34, March 5, 1975; Egbert Hadley '10, July 31, 1975; D. K. Smith '42, March 10, 1975; and Sam Guarnaccia '30, October 8, 1974, among others, MCA. For examples of fraternity parties, dances, sleigh rides, etc., see *MC*, April 17, 1918, February 27, 1924, December 3, 1924, January 21, 1925, and April 8, 1936.

3. Intergroup competition was very important. The fraternities competed in intramural athletics, in homecoming activities, in scholastics, and, most important, in rushing potential members. For examples of nonrush competition, see *MC*, March 21, 1917, February 23, 1921, May 14, 1924, December 3, 1924, October 16, 1935, and June 15, 1936.

4. "The Value of the Fraternity," "The Chaos" (1939), typed manuscript in Chi Psi Archives, Middlebury College chapter house.

5. Ibid.

6. For example, see *MC*, October 2, 1935.

7. W. Storrs Lee to David Stameshkin, September 6, 1976, MCA. Also see, *MC*, October 11, 1916.

8. See *MC*, February 19, 1919, May 18, 1938, and October 19, 1938. The Philians of the 1920s were perhaps the longest-lasting organization of this type. See *SK*, 75; and *MC*, January 11, 1922.

9. *MC*, September 21, 1938. Also see *MC*, May 18, 1921, April 1, 1925, January 20, 1926, February 10, 1926, May 19, 1926, March 27, 1929, February 26, 1936, and May 6, 1936.

10. Joseph Kasper '20 and Doc Cook '24, among others, emphasized that fraternities helped develop the political abilities and sensibilities of their members. See interview with Kasper, August 6, 1974; and interview with members of the class of 1924, May 25, 1974, MCA. For examples of fraternity influence on elections, see *MC*, November 23, 1922, February 10, 1926, April 17, 1929, October 23, 1929, and September 21, 1938.

11. For concern over rushing procedures, see *MC*, May 12, 1926, November 16, 1927, and October 30, 1935.

12. *The Middlebury Campus* ran frequent articles about rushing almost every year. For the IFC-DU flap, see *MC*, June 17, 1925, and May 12, 1926.

13. Carroll J. Atwood, *A Manual to Guide Each Future Chi Psi in the More Effective Performance of his Fraternity's Most Vital Function: Rushing* (n.p., 1939), i, 5.

14. Interview with Howard Munford '34, March 5, 1975.

15. See *MC*, January 22, 1919, February 26, 1919, June 4, 1919, March 9, 1921, December 3, 1924, April 14, 1926, April 26, 1926, May 5, 1926, October 27, 1926, February 26, 1936, and March 18, 1936.

16. Provost Collins to J. W. Abernethy '76, March 8, 1919, TP.

17. Editorial in *MC*, April 14, 1926.

18. Letter to editor from "Wall Flower" in *MC*, January 20, 1926. Also see *MC*, April 14, 1926.

19. *MC*, October 9, 1935, and June 4, 1930.

20. *MC*, May 27, 1936, and April 12, 1939.

21. W. Storrs Lee '28, "Fraternities on Trial," *MCNL* 20 (June 1946): 9. This paragraph is mainly derived from Lee's article. Also see Lee to Stameshkin, September 6, 1976, MCA; and *MC*, November 29, 1945, and February 7, 1946.

22. Interview with W. Spencer Wright, February 26, 1975, MCA.

23. Lee, "Fraternities on Trial," 9–10; FM (1945–47): 28–31. Also see Lee to Stameshkin, September 6, 1976.

24. Lee, "Fraternities on Trial," 10.

25. June Brogger Noble '46, "Coming of Age in World War II," *MCNL* 49 (winter 1975): 15.

26. This account of the Alpha Sigma Phi struggle to end racial and religious requirements for membership is based primarily on materials (hereafter cited as RER) loaned to me by Robert E. Reuman '44, Waterville, Maine, an ASP brother. The main item is a 14-page mimeographed mailing to all Middlebury ASP alumni by A. Gordon Miesse '20, the chapter's alumni secretary, dated April 30, 1947 (hereafter cited as RER/AGM). These materials are in the MCA. For the broader picture of fraternity prejudice in the United States during this period, see Alfred McClung Lee, *Fraternities without Brotherhood* (Boston, 1956).

27. For the meeting of Hunt, Miesse, and Burns, see RER/AGM, p. 1.

28. RER/AGM, pp. 1, 6.

29. RER/AGM, pp. 1, 7, 12; and Donald S. Putnam '42 to Alumni [Alpha Sigma Phi, Alpha Delta chapter], [spring 1948?], RER.

30. George H. Booth to Ralph Burns, January 16, 1947, in RER/AGM, pp. 6–7. Also see Booth to Reuman, January 30, 1947 in RER.

31. Burns to Booth, January 22, 1947, copy in RER/AGM, pp. 8–10.

32. Putnam to Alumni, RER. Earlier that winter the Middlebury chapter had taken its own informal poll of the ASP chapters, and by a "bare majority" local option had lost. See Putnam to Alumni, RER.

33. See notes on the meeting of Robert Reuman and George Booth with the Grand Council of ASP on March 29, 1947 in RER. For the alumni's reaction, see RER/AGM, p. 2; Miesse to Reuman, February 10, 1947, RER/AGM; and Miesse to Reuman, May 16, 1954, RER. Also see *MC*, May 22, 1947.

34. See Miesse to Alumni, September 15, 1947, copy, RER.

35. *New York Times*, May 23, 1947. I have tried in vain to find the original source of the term "Sluggers for Democracy."

36. Putnam to Alumni, RER.

37. See *MC*, January 27, 1949, April 21, 1949, May 26, 1949, and September 22, 1949. On the efforts of the IFC to end discrimination, see *MC*, November 23, 1949, February 12, 1953, February 28, 1957, and February 13, 1958. On the college's success in integrating Jews into the fraternities after World War II (and thereby eliminating the possibility of a "Jewish" fraternity at Middlebury), see Lee to Stameshkin, September 6, 1976, MCA.

38. FM (1963–65), 128. For further developments in this area, see *MC*, September 29, 1960, and November 2, 1961. On the Ron Brown '62 story, see Ed Ernst, "Democracy Is Not a Spectator Sport," *MCM* 63 (winter 1989): 24–25; *MC*, February 24, 1989; and *MCM*, 64 (summer 1990): 6.

39. Interviews with Fred Neuberger '50, February 3, 1975; Ken Nourse '52, February 13, 1975; Gordie Perine '49, February 28, 1975; and Russell Leng '60, February 26, 1975, MCA.

40. Thomas H. Reynolds, "Fraternities at Middlebury Today," *MCNL* 35 (winter 1961): 7; *MC*, February 24, 1955.

41. Paul Cubeta, "With Our Faculty," *MCNL* 29 (August 1955): 11; President's Report to the Trustees, September 15, 1955, p. 2, MCA; interview with T. Richardson Miner '58, October 22, 1974; and interview with Eugene Sapadin X'61, July 10, 1975, MCA.

42. *MC*, October 21, 1954.

43. *MC*, February 28, 1980.

44. Interview with David K. Smith '42, March 10, 1975.

45. Interview with Fred Neuberger '50, February 3, 1975; and interview with Gordie Perine '49, February 28, 1975. One of the contributing factors was the disappearance of housemothers who had encouraged cleanliness and orderliness in earlier generations of men.

46. See the excellent synthesis of published materials on this topic presented by Helen Lefkowitz Horowitz in *Campus Life* (New York, 1987), chap. 10. Russ Leng '60 has remarked that when he returned to the campus to teach in the later 1960s, the biggest change he noticed in the fraternities was the near collapse of "brotherhood"—the idea that "brothers" would always help each other. Instead, he saw the growth of small-group friendship and loyalty to that group rather than to the fraternity. See notes on interview with Russ Leng '60, February 3, 1975, MCA.

47. *MC*, September 19, 1963, and October 16, 1970.

48. Delta Upsilon, for example, argued that it would not alter its "scholastic files" because it was up to the individual not to plagiarize. The files themselves, they contended, were not evil; how the material was used was another question.

Such logic did not endear the fraternities to the faculty. The IFC did try to convince DU that they were wrong, and other fraternities complied. See *MC*, April 25, 1963, May 2, 1963, May 9, 1963, and May 23, 1963; and FM (1949–51): 25.

49. See *MC*, January 14, 1960; interview with Thomas Reynolds, October 3, 1975; and interview with Howard Munford, March 5, 1975, MCA.

50. *MC*, October 18, 1962.

51. *MC*, March 13, 1952, November 26, 1952, May 4, 1961, and April 12, 1962.

52. *MC*, September 19, 1963, October 21, 1964, January 14, 1960, January 21, 1960, February 11, 1960, February 18, 1960, April 21, 1960, May 5, 1960, and May 12, 1960; and Reynolds, "Fraternities at Middlebury Today," 6–7, 59.

53. On the Atwater Club, see Cubeta, "With Our Faculty," 11, 26; and *MC*, April 21, 1955, April 28, 1955, December 13, 1956, and October 10, 1957. The Atwater Club used Weybridge House for its activities. See CM, 6:610. It dissolved in 1963. See *MC*, March 28, 1963.

54. *MC*, April 21, 1960.

55. Students who had been polled supported this measure, 244–59. See *MC*, May 26, 1960. See also Reynolds, "Fraternities at Middlebury Today," 6–7, 59.

56. *MC*, October 25, 1962.

57. *MC*, February 11, 1963. See also Robert A. Gay, "The Middlebury Fraternity System," *MCNL* 35 (winter 1961): 8, 59.

58. Interview with JIA, May 20, 1975, transcribed notes, MCA. On Middlebury's reaction to the Williams decision, see *MC*, September 9, 1962, and October 11, 1962.

59. *MC*, December 3, 1964. For the independents' view on fraternities, see *MC*, October 7, 1965.

60. Dean of the College 1964–65 Annual Report, in President's Files, 1965 Folder, Old Chapel Attic.

61. PM, 2:951.

62. *MC*, October 21, 1965.

63. See Dean Elizabeth Kelly's remarks on this topic in PM, 2:961; and interview with JIA, May 20, 1975.

64. *MC*, March 4, 1965.

65. PM, 2:871–73.

66. *MC*, September 30, 1965; PM, 2:950; and "Interim Report of the Ad Hoc Committee on Student Life," *MCNL* 40 (spring 1966): 15.

67. *MCNL* 40 (summer 1966): 4, 5, 45; and PM, 2:949–50.

68. *MC*, March 31, 1966.

69. "2nd Interim Report of the Ad Hoc Committee on Student Life," *MCNL* 40 (summer 1966): 5.

70. *A Recommendation and Report to the President of Middlebury College by the Ad Hoc Committee on Student Life* (Middlebury, Vt., [1966?]), 1, 5.

71. *MC*, December 15, 1966. See also PM, 2:949–52; and *MC*, December 8, 1966.

72. *MC*, January 12, 1967, January 19, 1967, and March 23, 1967. The fraternity alumni apparently alerted all their brothers to the plight of the fraternities. See *New Horizons* [1967?], of Alpha Sigma Psi, p. 2, copy in possession of Robert Reuman '44.

73. Interview with JIA, May 20, 1975; and CM, 8:1039–40, 1042–45.

74. CM, 8:1050 appended; and "Statement of Policy," April 8, 1967, copy, Presi-

dent's Files, MCL. Also see interview with Dean Dennis O'Brien, April 30, 1975, MCA.

75. Interview with JIA, May 20, 1975.

76. Ibid.

77. Dean of the College's Report, 1969-70 Academic Year, manuscript MCA.

78. Ibid.; interview with Russell Leng '60, February 26, 1975; and interviews with several students from that era, MCA.

79. MC, October 16, 1970, and February 22, 1973.

80. Interview with Russell Leng '60, February 26, 1975; and MC, October 16, 1970.

81. MC, February 22, 1973.

82. MC, October 16, 1970, and March 6, 1980; and interview with Karl Lindholm '67, July 9, 1986, MCA.

83. MC, October 16, 1970; and CM, 9:1162.

84. MC, January 11, 1968, January 10, 1969, and January 28, 1971; and interview with Karl Lindholm '67, July 9, 1986. On Theta Chi, see Theta Chi file, MCA, particularly Bruce Peterson, Dean of Men, to Albert F. Gollnick, Jr., May 29, 1970.

85. CM, 7:801, 844, 851; and MC, September 22, 1961, and September 25, 1961.

86. CM, 9:1144 (quoted), 1115-16. Several trustees argued that they understood that the April 8, 1967, decision meant that the college should help the fraternities remain in existence by allowing them to increase their numbers to make construction of new facilities feasible and at the same time to correct the bad housekeeping practices.

87. Interview with O'Brien, April 30, 1975; MC, October 16, 1970, and February 22, 1973; and Dean of the College's Report, Academic Year 1969-70, Old Chapel Attic.

88. CM, 9:1151-52. Also see CM, 8:1060, 1083-84.

89. Dean of College's Report, Academic Year, 1969-70.

90. Ibid.; and informal interviews with students of that period.

91. MC, December 3, 1970.

92. MC, October 16, 1970.

93. MC, March 25, 1971.

94. MC, November 21, 1968, October 16, 1970, and April 29, 1971.

95. PM, 3:1192-93.

96. PM, 3:1193.

97. CM, 9:1401-2.

98. The material in this paragraph is derived from CM, 9:1416-17. On attempts to bring women into the fraternities, see MC, January 18, 1973.

99. CM, 9:1434.

100. Ibid., 1434. Also see MC, October 4, 1973, and October 11, 1973.

101. MC, October 4, 1973.

102. MC, October 18, 1973.

103. Based on my own observations and numerous conversations with students during the 1973-74 academic year at Middlebury.

104. CM, 10:1434, 1453. The Student Forum Working Committee also came out against college ownership of fraternities. See MC, December 6, 1973.

105. CM, 10:1453, 1469. Also see PM, 3:1246; and CM, 10:1500. Aside from reversionary rights, O'Brien asked each fraternity (in return for college support): (1) to make clear and continued progress toward an open rush, (2) to allow the col-

lege to place students in chapter houses when there was need and available space, and (3) to allow a college representative to sit on each fraternity corporation board. See *Middlebury College Self-Study Report . . . February 1980* (Middlebury, Vt., 1980), H-15, copy in MCA.

106. CM, 10:1435.

107. MC, May 11, 1977; and interview with Dennis O'Brien, April 30, 1975.

108. Quoted in *MC*, May 11, 1977.

109. MC, May 11, 1977.

110. The Coffrin Report can be found in *Middlebury College Self-Study . . . February, 1980*, Section H. Also see *MCNL* 52 (winter 1978): 2. On Coffrin, see CM, May 21, 1988, pp. 2127–28.

111. CM, 11:1691, 1715; *MC*, May 3, 1978; and *MCNL* 53 (winter 1979): 2–3.

112. MC, September 21, 1978, October 4, 1978, and January 11, 1979.

113. MC, October 23, 1975, and February 2, 1977. The college declared that if women were denied equal rights (full membership) at the fraternities, they could not eat there and receive rebates for off-campus eating. See *MC*, November 30, 1977, and January 25, 1978.

114. MC, May 6, 1976, and March 13, 1977.

115. MC, September 21, 1978.

116. CM, 11:1715–17.

117. Ibid. The board also ordered the college not to commit any funds to properties it did not own or control in any manner that did not afford protection for such funds.

118. MC, February 28, 1979.

119. MC, March 7, 1979.

120. *Document of Understanding: Fraternities* (Middlebury, Vt., May 30, 1980), pp. 1–2. Also see "Fraternities: A New Understanding," *MCNL* 55 (fall 1980): 5; and *MC*, May 2, 1979, May 9, 1979, March 6, 1980, March 13, 1980, and March 20, 1980.

121. MC, September 18, 1980.

122. MC, May 15, 1980.

123. On the Proctor renovations, which increased dining capacity by about 150, see *MCNL* 53 (spring 1979): 2; *MCNL* 54 (winter 1980): 3, and CM, 12:1784. Members of Zeta Psi wanted to cook meals at the house three nights a week and pay for the meals themselves. The Students Concerned about Middlebury (SCAM) movement in the spring of 1981 focused on the Zeta Psi dining issue. See *MC*, March 27, 1981, and April 3, 1981; and chapter 14, below. The Community Council even supported the idea. The administration, however, was concerned that the rebate issue would inevitably be raised again if they allowed this option; therefore, they favored an end to this last gasp of fraternity dining. See *MC*, January 29, 1981, March 27, 1981, and May 1, 1981; and PM, 12:1343. Faculty and administrators also found fault with the KDR "little sister" program (a designation that many considered degrading to women). See *MC*, October 28, 1983; and FM (January 4, 1982): 55.

124. See *MCNL* 52 (winter 1978): 2; *MC*, December 6, 1979, October 2, 1980, November 20, 1981, March 19, 1982, March 11, 1983, and November 16, 1984.

125. See *MC*, February 3, 1989, January 25, 1985, February 22, 1985, September 27, 1985, and October 11, 1985. The agreement stated that the college would own the land and the alumni would own the house but that no undergraduate members could live there. See *MCM* 60 (autumn 1985): 4–5; and CM, 14:2033.

126. MC, March 18, 1988. Also see MC, April 24, 1987. On the change in the drinking law, see MCM 61 (winter 1986): 10. On the fraternity parties, see *Report of the Task Force on Student Social Life* (Middlebury, Vt., 1989), 6.

127. See MC, September 23, 1983. On a hazing incident that apparently was drug- and alcohol-related, see MC, March 11, 1988.

128. MC, October 30, 1987, January 15, 1988, February 26, 1988, September 23, 1988, and September 30, 1988.

129. On Sigma Phi Epsilon, see MC, September 11, 1987. On the DU incident, I relied heavily on a DU file in the possession of Frank Kelley in the Dean of Students' Office in Old Chapel at Middlebury (hereafter cited as DU File). Also very useful is MCM 62 (winter 1989): 42–46. For a view more sympathetic to the fraternity, see the letter by Barry McPherson '88 in MCM 65 (winter 1991): 4–5.

130. Memo from Women's Union, May 13, 1988, DU File. See also Emerson to Robison and Peterson, May 11, 1988, DU File; and letters from Gary Margolis (May 11, 1988), Yonna McShane (May 10, 1988), and Ed Ernst (May 13, 1988) in DU File.

131. Delta Upsilon Brothers to Middlebury College Community, May [13?], 1988, DU File.

132. PM (May 19, 1988): 1445; CM (May 21, 1988): 214; and Robison to Middlebury College Community, May 17, 1988, copy in DU File. On the hearing, see documents in DU File.

133. MC, September 23, 1988; and MCM 63 (winter 1989): 42–46.

134. MCM 63 (Winter 1989): 42–46, and MC, November 11, 1988.

135. See, for example, MC, September 23, 1988, September 30, 1988, October 7, 1988, October 14, 1988, October 21, 1988, November 18, 1988, and January 20, 1989; and MCM 63 (spring 1989): 4–9.

136. On Delta Upsilon during their year of probation, see MC, January 27, 1989, March 10, 1989, and March 17, 1989. On the decisions to allow them back into the house and to end the probationary status, see MC, October 13, 1989; and MCM 63 (summer 1989): 43.

137. MC, May 4, 1989.

138. MC, January 19, 1990, and March 16, 1990.

139. See David Stameshkin, "Recent Actions of Other Schools Regarding Fraternities," unpublished manuscript, spring 1988, and David M. Stameshkin, "A History of Fraternities and Sororities at Franklin & Marshall College, 1854–1987," unpublished manuscript, spring 1988, both in Franklin and Marshall College Archives.

140. MC, March 10, 1989; and FM, March 6, 1989.

141. MCM, 63 (spring 1989): 41–42; and *Report of the Task Force on Student Social Life* (Middlebury, Vt., 1989), 1–2.

142. MCM, 63 (Spring 1989): 41–43.

143. MC, December 1, 1990.

144. Board of Trustees to Middlebury Community, January 13, 1990, MCA; MC, January 19, 1990; and Dwight Garner '88, "Frats under Fire," MCM 64 (spring 1990): 21–23.

145. Ellen Basu et al. to Board of Trustees and President Robison, January 23, 1990, in FM (1989–90), attached to January 23 minutes.

146. FM, January 23, 1990.

147. On the spring 1990 deliberations, see MC, February 23, 1990, March 2, 1990, April 6, 1990, April 13, 1990, and April 27, 1990; Garner, "Frats under Fire,"

21–23; and *MCM* 64 (summer 1990): 13. Although total compliance appeared probable, the head of the Delta Kappa Epsilon alumni group, John L. Buttolph III '64, stated in the summer of 1990 that the DKE chapter had not yet determined what they were going to do. See *MCM* 64 (Summer 1990), pp. 5–6.

148. Annual Report of the Dean of the College, 1964–65, p. 7, President's Files, 1965 folder, Old Chapel Attic.

CHAPTER 12. SOCIAL AND EXTRACURRICULAR LIFE
(PAGES 243-69)

1. There has been very little written about the history of sororities that is useful. Even the outstanding study of college youth in the 1920s by Paula Fass, *The Damned and the Beautiful* (New York, 1977), contains a good deal about fraternities but almost nothing regarding sororities. For some information, see Helen Lefkowitz Horowitz, *Campus Life: Undergraduate Cultures from the End of the Eighteenth Century to the Present* (New York, 1987), chap. 9.

2. See *MC*, January 2, 1918, March 6, 1918, and May 10, 1922. Pi Beta Phi sorority had rooms in the Battell Block for fifty-three years. See *SK*, pp. 81, 82.

3. For examples of sorority social events, see *MC*, January 2, 1918, March 29, 1922, April 9, 1924, and May 14, 1924. For a defense of sororities, see the section of a Panhellenic Council booklet for freshmen quoted in *MC*, October 5, 1961. On social welfare activities, see Report of the President to the Trustees, July 1, 1955, to June 30, 1956, manuscript, p. 3, Old Chapel Attic.

4. The number of women in sororities is based on membership figures listed in the annual *Kaleidoscope*, occasional mention of the number of women pledged in *MC*, and information in individual biographical accounts in the *GC*. Also see *MC*, October 26, 1921, November 29, 1922, October 29, 1924, October 27, 1926, November 23, 1927, and February 26, 1936. The Gamma Lambda chapter of Kappa Kappa Gamma was organized in 1923 from the Alpha Zeta chapter of Alpha Chi. Pi Beta Phi had been at Middlebury since 1893. Sigma Kappa was founded in 1911 after Pi Mu Epsilon decided to disband and become a national affiliate of Sigma Kappa. Delta Delta Delta emerged in 1917, about the time Phi Mu Gamma died a natural death. Alpha Xi Delta was organized from Theta Chi Epsilon in 1925, and Phi Mu was formed from a local chapter, Delta Omega Delta, also in 1925. See *SK*, pp. 80–84; and *MC*, May 10, 1922, June 18, 1923, June 17, 1925, and September 23, 1925.

5. Results printed in *MCNL* 6 (June 1932): 3. Also see interview with Juanita Pritchard Cook '26, February 24, 1975; and interview with Marian Munford '32, March 3, 1975, MCA.

6. *MC*, May 4, 1932, May 18, 1932, and May 25, 1932.

7. *MC*, February 22, 1933. The students had petitioned the administration to have a numerical vote (rather than a vote by sorority) with a two-thirds majority required. Also see *MC*, January 18, 1933, January 24, 1933, and February 8, 1933.

8. *MC*, March 1, 1933, March 8, 1933, and March 15, 1933.

9. Interview with Marian Munford, March 3, 1975; *MC*, December 6, 1933; and interview with Eleanor Benjamin Clemens, February 25, 1975, MCA.

10. See relevant documents in Sororities—Abolition file, S5/104, MCA. Also see CM, 4:46.

11. *MC*, December 13, 1933, and January 10, 1934.

12. CM, 4:59, 63, 65.

13. Interviews with Marian Munford, March 3, 1975, and with Eleanor Benjamin Clemens, February 25, 1975; and *MC*, November 6, 1935.

14. *MC*, November 8, 1945, November 15, 1945, April 4, 1946, February 20, 1947; and June Brogger Noble '46, "Coming of Age in World War II," *MCNL* 49 (winter 1975): 15.

15. See President's Report, 1954, manuscript, p. 10, MCA.

16. President's Report, 1959-60, pp. 25-26, MCA.

17. *MC*, October 5, 1961.

18. *MC*, March 8, 1962.

19. On this issue, see Elizabeth Kelly interview tape, A13/59, MCA.

20. *MC*, May 9, 1963.

21. *MC*, January 13, 1966.

22. *MC*, May 9, 1968, and May 16, 1968.

23. *MC*, October 3, 1968, January 16, 1969, and January 23, 1969.

24. PM, 3:1055.

25. *MC*, February 20, 1969.

26. *MC*, September 24, 1919.

27. For student groups in the interwar period, I have consulted the *MC*, and the annual *Kaleidoscope*. A particularly good roster of clubs and activities appears in *MCNL* 6 (April 1932): 11.

28. On the Mountain Club, which was organized following a climb up Lincoln Mountain by students and faculty to take publicity shots for the college, see *MC*, January 21, 1931, and January 28, 1931. By 1938 the Mountain Club was the largest club on campus. See *MC*, November 16, 1938. The Outing Club had been formed in 1920, modeled after one at Dartmouth. See *MC*, May 28, 1919, March 3, 1920, and February 9, 1921. On the drama club, see *MC*, October 10, 1923, June 1, 1927, March 27, 1929, and *MC*, April 28, 1949. On the Liberal Club and Women's Forum, see *MC*, November 20, 1935, April 15, 1936, and April 29, 1936. The origins of the radio station are described in "WMCRS Is on the Air," *MCNL* 24 (January 1950); 18, 21; *MC*, March 31, 1949; and interview with Ken Nourse '52, February 13, 1975, MCA. Debate can be followed through the 1920s and 1930s by using the card file prepared for that period by Deborah Clifford, in MCA.

29. See *MC*, December 16, 1925; and "Extra Curricular," *MCNL* 6 (April 1932): 10.

30. See, for example, *MC*, December 3, 1919, March 12, 1930, May 15, 1935, and September 28, 1938.

31. FM (1923): 89-93; and *MC*, April 18, 1923.

32. *MC*, May 9, 1923, October 3, 1923, and September 24, 1924.

33. On Senior Week, see *MC*, May 29, 1929. Junior Week originally was intended to show off the college to prospective students. Later, it became a week-long period of interclass and intercollegiate sporting events and numerous social events, particularly the junior prom. By the 1940s, it had been concentrated into a "weekend." See *MC*, May 10, 1922, May 13, 1936, and May 15, 1940; and *SK*, 170-71.

34. On tapping, see *MC*, May 14, 1932; and interview with Gordie Perine '49, February 28, 1975, MCA. On Mortar Board (which had been Banshees until 1928), see *MC*, May 16, 1928. Blue Key was formed from two class societies—Delta Tau and Sages—in 1930. See *SK*, 113.

35. On the desire to retain class distinctions, see *MC*, February 26, 1919, and November 1, 1962. On Midd-Nite, see *MC*, October 2, 1935, and September 23,

1948. On early P-rades, see *MC*, May 7, 1919, and October 19, 1921. On the history of the P-rades in the 1930s, see *SK*, 164.

36. *MC*, November 3, 1926, October 2, 1929, October 29, 1953, and September 26, 1968. The *Campus* frequently reported on college opposition to hazing. See also FM (1924): 40; FM (1927): 9; FM (1929): 9.

37. *MC*, October 29, 1929.   38. *MCM* 63 (summer 1989): 60.

39. *MCM* 63 (autumn 1989): 62.   40. *MC*, May 2, 1923.

41. *MC*, October 31, 1917, April 23, 1919, April 30, 1919, November 4, 1921, and May 18, 1938.

42. *MC*, March 14, 1923, and October 10, 1923. On Blue Key, see *MC*, April 4, 1931, December 2, 1931, September 28, 1938, October 12, 1938, November 7, 1946, October 27, 1960, November 3, 1960, May 21, 1964, and September 26, 1968.

43. On veterans' attitudes in the late 1940s, see chap. 11, pp. 218–20.

44. *MC*, October 27, 1960.

45. See President's Report to the Board, 1958–59, p. 3, MCA; "President's Report to the Board, 1959–60," p. 5; and interview with Thomas Reynolds, October 3, 1975, MCA.

46. Women lived in dormitories by class, which reinforced class feelings. See *MC*, March 5, 1953. On life at other schools, see Helen Lefkowitz Horowitz, *Alma Mater: Design and Experience in the Women's Colleges from Their Nineteenth-Century Beginnings to the 1930s* (New York, 1984).

47. Dorothy Tillapaugh Headley, "Dorothy Goes to College: The Letters of a Coed from Middlebury to Her Family, 1921–1924," pp. 16–17, typed copy in MCA.

48. *MC*, May 21, 1924.

49. *SK*, 190–91; *MC*, June 14, 1922, May 25, 1938, and May 5, 1955.

50. *MC*, May 25, 1938.

51. *MCM*, 60 (autumn 1986): 30–31.

52. See *MC*, January 24, 1917, February 18, 1920, March 3, 1920, February 16, 1921, and February 22, 1951; and *SK*, 166–68.

53. *SK*, 166–68; and *MC*, February 7, 1934, February 5, 1936, February 12, 1936, and February 19, 1936. For faculty reminiscences of early carnivals, see *MC*, February 25, 1965.

54. FM (1917): 17–18.

55. *MC*, December 14, 1932, and November 15, 1933. On other dances, see *MC*, November 8, 1916, February 11, 1920, December 7, 1932, January 15, 1936, and November 4, 1936.

56. *MC*, October 12, 1932. One faculty or trustee couple had to be on the list of chaperones for any affair after 1933. For the Halloween party at the chateau, see *MC*, October 28, 1925. For Spanish Carnival, see *MC*, December 7, 1927.

57. *MCM* 63 (spring 1989): 59.

58. See, for example, *MC*, December 14, 1938, and May 18, 1938 for big band appearances.

59. See interview with Fred Neuberger '50, February 3, 1975, MCA. On bull sessions, see *MC*, February 11, 1925, October 26, 1927, and May 30, 1928.

60. Interview with T. Richardson Miner '58, June 3, 1975; "Interview with Elizabeth Kelly," *MCNL* 44 (spring 1970): 9, MCA; *MC*, May 14, 1964, September 26, 1968, and November 2, 1972; and interview with Gordie Perine, MCA; The introduction by Dean Reynolds of the Junior Fellow system in the residence halls gave freshmen a better way to learn about Middlebury. See interview with Reynolds, October 3, 1975, MCA; and "President's Page," *MCNL* 34 (fall 1959): 11.

61. *MC*, January 28, 1971.

62. Restrictions on the use of automobiles were steadily lifted after 1945. See *MC*, June 1, 1927, May 7, 1930, and October 2, 1954; Harris Thurber, "Automobiles at Middlebury," *MCNL* 32 (autumn 1957): 11, 30; FM (1949–51): 21–22, 125–26, 133; *SK*, 162; CM, 6:604–5, 8:1014; *MAC* (1967–68): 129; and *MAC* (1969–70): 36.

63. *MC*, November 10, 1976.

64. On the origins of May Days, an idea attributed to Dean Steven Rockefeller and Professor Victor Nuovo, see CM, 12:1794; and interview with Erica Wonnacott, July 16, 1986, MCA. On WRMC, see *MC*, March 27, 1981; interview with Ken Nourse '52, February 13, 1975, MCA; and Donald M. Kreis '80, "And Now for the News . . . ," *MCNL* 52 (spring 1978): 8–9. On off-campus living, see *MC*, November 20, 1987, and April 22, 1988. On college actions, see *MC*, September 25, 1987, January 20, 1989, and March 17, 1989.

65. *MC*, April 23, 1982.

66. *MC*, February 21, 1917.

67. *MC*, November 6, 1918.

68. *MC*, May 28, 1919. For trustee action, see CM, 3:112, 122. The sum was raised to $2,500 for 1920–21.

69. *MC*, September 28, 1921. On the success of the early entertainment series, see *MC*, March 2, 1921, and June 22, 1921.

70. *MCM* 60 (summer 1986): 28.

71. Each administration seemed to increase the number of concerts and other programs. See President's Report to the Trustees, October 20, 1969, manuscript, MCA, in which Armstrong remarked that ninety-one lectures and discussions, eighty-five films, and fifty-five concerts and recitals were held in 1968–1969, compared to only fifty-eight lecturers, thirty-one films, and ten concerts in 1964–1965. On further increases in the Robison years, see Olin Robison, *A Report to the Board of Trustees, 1975–1980* (Middlebury, Vt., 1980), 8.

72. Robison's Ten-Year Report, unpublished draft, in author's possession; and interviews with administrators and faculty over a fifteen-year period.

73. Paul Desruisseaux, "A Lake Wobegon Weekend," *MCM* 57 (summer 1983): 12–16; and *MC*, March 18, 1988, and April 8, 1988.

74. *MC*, October 5, 1984; and "A Man with a Heart," *MCM* 59 (autumn 1984): 10–17.

75. "Spirit and Nature," *MCM* 65 (winter 1991): 22–34.

76. *MCM* 63 (autumn 1989): 62.

77. *Report of the "21" Committee: Middlebury College and the Legal Drinking Age* (Middlebury, Vt., April 19, 1985), pp. 1–2.

78. I have no statistical data to back up my claim of increased drinking at the college; it is based on personal observation and interviews over the past twenty years. Certainly, there was a good deal of drinking and abuse. See, for example, ibid.; *MC*, October 25, 1978, and November 6, 1980; and *Report of the Drug Task Force* (Middlebury, Vt., May 1987), pp. 3–4, MCA.

79. On the change in Vermont law and its impact, see *MCM* 61 (Winter 1986): 10; and *MC*, September 19, 1986. On college attitudes toward alcohol and alcohol policy in the early 1980s, see *Report and Recommendations of the Middlebury College Alcohol Committee* (Middlebury, Vt., October 9, 1981), MCA.

80. *Report of the "21" Committee*, p. 10.

81. On The Undergraduate, see *MCM* 62 (spring 1988): 44; and *MC*, November 6, 1987, January 15, 1988, and January 22, 1988. On The Gamut, see *MC*,

October 20, 1989. For one early statement that the new center might help with the alcohol problem, see Robison to Board of Trustees, memorandum, February 27, 1985, appended to Board minutes, March 9, 1985.

82. *MC*, May 8, 1987, September 11, 1987, October 2, 1987, February 26, 1988, April 29, 1988, and September 30, 1988.

83. See *MC*, October 31, 1986, October 2, 1987, and February 19, 1988; and *MCM* 61 (spring 1987): 8. The quotation is from PM, May 19, 1988, p. 1443.

84. Marijuana was smoked covertly in small (but increasing) quantities by a growing number of students in the period 1964–1968. In 1968–1969 and after, it was much more widespread and smoked less guardedly. This statement is based on a number of interviews with students of that period (most of whom wished to remain anonymous). Administrative reports agree with these observations. See *MC*, March 2, 1967, October 24, 1968, and April 17, 1969. In 1967 only 33 percent had tried marijuana. By 1970, 75 percent of the students had probably used it. See Annual Report of the Dean of the College, August 16, 1968, MCA; PM, 3:1116; and CM, 9:1260.

85. David Y. Parker '74, letter to editor in *MCM* 62 (summer 1988): 3.

86. *MC*, November 6, 1980.

87. *MC*, February 28, 1986, September 19, 1986, and March 6, 1987; and *MCM* 60 (summer 1986): 6.

88. *Report of the Drug Task Force*, p. 1. On national coverage, see, for example, *New York Times*, February 23 and 24, 1986; and the *Providence Journal* article reprinted in the *San Diego Tribune*, February 27, 1986. I also found useful the two thick folders of press clippings regarding the Zaccaro affair that are in the Middlebury College Public Affairs office.

89. *MC*, April 15, 1988.

90. *Rutland (Vt.) Herald*, February 25, 1986.

91. *MC*, February 27, 1987, October 17, 1987, and March 18, 1988; CM, 14: 2048–51; and *Report of the Drug Task Force*.

92. On the YWCA in the years 1910–1930, see, for example, *MC*, January 10, 1917, September 28, 1921, October 26, 1921, November 2, 1921, November 16, 1921, November 30, 1921, December 14, 1921, February 22, 1922, April 5, 1922, November 1, 1922, November 21, 1923, December 5, 1923, April 9, 1924, September 24, 1924, October 1, 1924, November 25, 1925, March 9, 1927, June 20, 1927, and February 6, 1929.

93. On YMCA affairs, see *MC*, June 14, 1916, December 6, 1916, June 11, 1919, September 28, 1921, October 31, 1923, April 9, 1924, December 17, 1924, January 14, 1925, and November 3, 1926. From 1919 to 1923, there was a Sunday men's club, but that folded, too. See *MC*, December 10, 1919, February 7, 1923, and September 26, 1923.

94. Moody to Phillips P. Elliott, November 9, 1927, MP, MCA.

95. *MC*, October 19, 1927.

96. W. Storrs Lee '28 to David Stameshkin, September 6, 1976, MCA. On student preachers, also see GC, 447, for the work of Robert Taylor '19.

97. Moody to Charles E. Crane, June 20, 1923, MP, MCA.

98. Lee to Stameshkin, September 6, 1976.

99. Moody to George W. Parker, February 12, 1923, MP, MCA. Moody did strongly believe in studying Scriptures, and, for a brief time in the early 1930s, students apparently were required to pass an examination in Bible in order to graduate. See CM, 3:302; and *MC*, October 1, 1930.

100. John G. Bowker, "Middlebury College in Retrospect," *MCNL* 41 (spring 1967): 13. On the time change in 1916, see *MC*, June 21, 1916.

101. See *MC*, December 12, 1923, March 4, 1925, March 10, 1926, March 17, 1926, and January 29, 1936.

102. *MCM* 60 (spring 1986): 29; *MC*, November 3, 1926, and November 17, 1926. For examples of vespers preaching, see *MC*, November 9, 1921, September 24, 1924, and October 30, 1935.

103. *MC*, February 20, 1987.

104. Stephen Freeman, "Thirty-eight Years of Middlebury," *MCNL* 38 (autumn 1963): 20.

105. *MCM* 59 (summer 1985): 38.

106. *MC*, September 30, 1942. On opposition to required chapel during World War II, see Noble, "Coming of Age in World War II," 15.

107. See *MCNL* 32 (autumn 1957): 19; Charles P. Scott, "Religion at Middlebury College," *MCNL* 29 (April 1954): 15–17, 21; and interview with Charles Scott, June 24, 1975, MCA.

108. Interview with D. K. Smith '42, March 10, 1975, MCA.

109. *MC*, April 20, 1950, April 27, 1950, May 11, 1950, and May 18, 1950.

110. CM, 6:511; and *MC*, October 9, 1952.

111. Interview with Charles Scott, June 24, 1975.

112. CM, 7:686–87, 700; *MC*, September 24, 1953, April 25, 1957, May 2, 1957, May 9, 1957, and September 19, 1957.

113. *MC*, November 10, 1960, November 17, 1960, December 8, 1960, January 12, 1961, January 19, 1961, and September 21, 1961; and PM, 2:719.

114. *MC*, May 9, 1957.

115. Scott, "Religion at Middlebury College," 15.

116. Ibid., 15–17; *MC*, December 9, 1954; interview with Charles Scott, June 24, 1975; President's Report, 1955–56, p. 3, MCA; and *MC*, January 22, 1982. In 1957 the conference was endowed by Don Mitchell, chairman of Sylvania Corporation. See *MAC* (1959–60). The student who worked with Scott to start Hillel at Middlebury, Gerald B. Zelermyer '61, later became the first Middlebury graduate to become a rabbi. See *MCM* 58 (summer 1984): 47. On Hillel and Jewish students in the 1980s, see *MC*, October 16, 1987, and January 27, 1989.

117. Interview with Charles Scott, June 24, 1975; and Scott, "Religion at Middlebury College," 16–17.

118. *MC*, October 17, 1986, and March 11, 1988.

119. JT to James P. McNaboe, June 1, 1917, TP, MCA.

CHAPTER 13. ATHLETICS (PAGES 270–93)

1. On the dominance of football at most American colleges, see Benjamin G. Rader, *American Sports: From the Age of Folk Games to the Age of Spectators* (Englewood Cliffs, N.J., 1983), 209–15, 266–75; and Douglas A. Noverr and Lawrence E. Ziewacz, *The Games They Played: Sports in American History, 1865–1980* (Chicago, 1983), 44–47, 80–83, 113–17, 142–44, 161–64, 179–80, 202–10, 246–55, 309–16.

2. *MC*, November 22, 1916.

3. On college spirit in the interwar period, see *MC*, May 14, 1919, October 15, 1919, October 20, 1926, October 3, 1928, and November 20, 1935.

4. *MC*, February 29, 1928.

5. Athletics were supported primarily by an athletic tax and college subsidies in the early decades of the twentieth century. See *MC*, February 23, 1916, and January 9, 1918; and CM, 3:131, 136, 148, 195, 198.

6. *MC*, February 11, 1920. On the connection between athletics, publicity, and attracting men to the college, also see JT to E. Kendall Hewlett, July 14, 1909, TP; and Hewlett to JT, July 10, 1909, TP.

7. *MC*, November 23, 1921.

8. *MC*, October 25, 1922.

9. "84 Years of Football Traditions," 1977 Public Relations Files. Also see *SK*, 126–29; *MC*, October 17, 1923; *MCNL* 55 (fall 1980): 28–29.

10. *MC*, October 15, 1924, November 26, 1924, and December 3, 1924.

11. *MC*, February 25, 1925, October 7, 1925, October 14, 1925, and October 4, 1933; and interview with Sam Guarnaccia '30, April 24, 1975, MCA.

12. Interview with D. K. Smith '42, April 25, 1975, MCA.

13. *MC*, March 15, 1922, April 19, 1922, October 4, 1922, November 29, 1922, and January 24, 1923; FM (December 14, 1922): 67; and CM, 3:176. The one-year rule was later amended to one semester. See *MC*, December 5, 1923; and CM, 3:190. President Thomas had condoned athletic scholarships. See JT to Philip Condit, August 19, 1915, TP. Also see the letter of Dean Wiley in *MC*, December 15, 1926.

14. Howard J. Savage et al., *American College Athletics* (New York, 1929), 229, 242.

15. [Paul Moody?], "The Carnegie Report," typescript, Moody Papers, MCL.

16. *MC*, February 15, 1928, November 29, 1933, and December 6, 1933; *SK*, 126–29; "84 Years of Football," 5; and W. C. Heinz, "Pittsburgh Won the Rose Bowl—but Who Cared," *MCM* 61 (winter 1986): 43.

17. *MC*, November 22, 1933.

18. On the end of the UVM series, see CM, 8:1035.

19. On Nelson, see *MCM* 57 (winter 1983): 42; and 60 (spring 1986): 2.

20. See "Middlebury Posts Best Record in 1970s N.E. College Football," in *Middlebury-Norwich official program*, Saturday, November 8, 1980, p. 17; *MCNL* 55 (fall 1980): 26; *MCM* 56 (autumn 1981): 24, 56 (winter 1982): 28–29, 56 (spring 1982): 32, 56 (summer 1982): 29, 57 (summer 1982): 29, 57 (autumn 1982): 34, 58 (winter 1984): 26, and 60 (spring 1986): 23–24. On the problems of the late 1980s, see *MC*, December 2, 1988.

21. Karl Lindholm "Also Plays," *MCM* 60 (spring 1986): 20–21. Also see *MCM* 60 (summer 1986): 12–13. The 1951–1970 figures are based on information contained in the files of Middlebury College's Sports Information Director, (hereafter, SID files); and interview with G. Thomas Lawson, August 26, 1981, MCA.

22. Interview with G. Thomas Lawson, August 26, 1981; and *MCNL* 54 (spring 1980): 27.

23. See Athletic Report, 1976–85, Dean of the College's files; *MCM* 56 (spring 1982): 33, 57 (summer 1983): 30, and 61 (summer 1987): 13. On Humphrey, see *MC*, March 4, 1988; and *MCM* 62 (summer 1988): 6–10. Humphrey set a career record of 1,844 points, a single-season record of 456 points, and a single-game record of 46 points.

24. *MCM* 56 (summer 1982): 28; and interview with G. Thomas Lawson, August 26, 1981.

25. *MCNL* 52 (summer 1977): 28.

26. *MCM* 57 (summer 1983): 29. Also see *SK*, 146.

27. *SK*, 147. The course was purchased outright in 1963. See CM, 3:217. On Myhre and the course, see *MCNL* 51 (summer 1976), and 53 (winter 1979): 5.

28. *MC*, May 21, 1924; and *SK*, 142.

29. SID files; interview with G. Thomas Lawson, August 26, 1981; Athletic Report, 1976–85; *MCM* 56 (spring 1982): 34, 57 (spring 1983): 30, 58 (winter 1984): 20–23, 59 (summer 1985): 3, 60 (spring 1986): 22, and 61 (spring 1987): 18. At the 1989 Homecoming, Punderson was recognized for his contribution to the founding of varsity soccer at Middlebury. The Frank Punderson Cup is to be awarded each year to the winner of the alumni–varsity soccer game. See *MCM* 64 (spring 1990): 67.

30. *MCNL* 55 (summer 1981): 24–25. For Cushman and early lacrosse, see *SK*, 150–51.

31. See *SK*, 148; and *MC*, October 24, 1968.

32. On men's swimming, see *MCM* 59 (spring 1985): 29. On the origins of rugby, see *MC*, October 5, 1967, and October 19, 1967. On recent problems with rugby, see *MC*, October 9, 1987, and October 14, 1988. On rowing, see *MCM* 64 (winter 1990): 9, and 64 (summer 1990): 15–16. Other men's club sports organized in recent years included ultimate frisbee, martial arts, wrestling, winter track, synchronized swim, water polo, cycling, and fencing. See Athletic Report, 1976–85; *MC*, March 21, 1979.

33. See *MCB* (1921-70); *MC*, April 13, 1921, and February 22, 1928. Men's intramurals were very popular; in 1923-1924, 162 of the 260 male students were regularly involved in athletics. See *MC*, April 9, 1924. For other evidence of men's intramurals, see *MC*, April 17, 1918, February 9, 1927, February 1, 1934, and March 4, 1936.

34. PM, 3:1087; and CM, 9:1231.

35. Mary E. Lick, "Report on Leave of Absence," typed manuscript, mimeo copy in MCA; interview with Mary Lick, August 24, 1981, MCA; and *MC*, September 22, 1976. There had been a men's physical education major until 1957–58, when the trustees decided to require all men to complete a four-semester physical education program. See CM, 6:640. On Colman, see *MC*, September 22, 1976, and March 16, 1977; *MCNL* 51 (fall 1976): 73, and 56 (spring 1982): 35.

36. *MC*, September 22, 1976, October 14, 1988, and January 27, 1989; and *MCNL* 54 (spring 1980): 4.

37. Marion L. Young '24, "Development of Women's Sports," *MCNL* 6 (April 1932): 6–7, 18; and CM, 3:148. On the expectation (and reality) of women as cheering spectators, see *MC*, December 1, 1915, November 22, 1916, October 3, 1917, November 21, 1917, November 12, 1919, and November 1, 1922.

38. See Young, "Development of Women's Sports," 6; *Kaleidoscope* (1926, 1938–39, 1939–40); and *MC*, February 7, 1917, September 24, 1924, and June 18, 1928.

39. *MC*, March 21, 1934, April 29, 1936, and May 6, 1936; and interview with Mary Lick, August 24, 1981. On physical education classes, see Women's Athletic files, MCA.

40. *MC*, January 11, 1933. Also see *MC*, October 24, 1922, and March 27, 1929.

41. See, for example, interview with Mary Lick, August 24, 1981; *MCNL* 55 (winter 1981): 27; *MCM* 56 (fall 1981): 23; *MC*, April 24, 1981; and Athletic Report, 1976–85. On riding, see *MC*, October 30, 1987. On rugby, see *MC*, May 4, 1989.

42. Interview with Mary Lick, August 24, 1981; and "Middlebury College 1980 Field Hockey Squad," typed manuscript, copy, mimeo, Women's Athletic Files, MCA. The latter contains a historical record of the field hockey team.

43. On Von Berg, see *MCNL* 55 (summer 1981): 24. On Ilgner, see *MCM* 59 (summer 1985): 32, and 60 (autumn 1986): 12. On DenHartog, see *MCM* 60 (spring 1986): 12–15, 60 (summer 1986): 24, 26, and 61 (spring 1987): 19. On Kemp, see *MCM* 62 (summer 1988): 1. On Hoyt, see *MCM*, 62 (summer 1988): 39. On Leary and Dubzinski, see *MC*, March 10, 1989, and March 2, 1990; and *MCM* 64 (spring 1990): 18. On Gow, see *MCM* 64 (spring 1990): 19.

44. See Lick, "Report of Leave of Absence," 6–9; CM, 9:1405; and *MC*, March 18, 1973, and March 15, 1973.

45. CM, 11:1674, 1726, 1769; and interview with G. Thomas Lawson, August 24, 1981, MCA.

46. When students were invited to attend a joint meeting of the Undergraduate Life and Athletic committees of the board in October 1982, they asked that the college hire more female coaches. See CM, 23:1906. On the 1988 criticisms, see *MC*, April 29, 1988 (the Kemp quote is from that issue), May 6, 1988, and November 4, 1988 (the college's response is in that issue).

47. *MC*, January 24, 1917. A similar trip to Dartmouth was planned the next year. See *MC*, February 20, 1918.

48. *MC*, January 24, 1917.

49. *MC*, February 23, 1921, February 8, 1922, February 15, 1922, March 1, 1922, February 21, 1923, January 16, 1924, January 21, 1925, November 18, 1925, February 3, 1926, February 10, 1926, and February 22, 1928. Several colleges formed ski associations to govern these competitions. See *MC*, February 23, 1921, and February 21, 1923.

50. *MC*, March 1, 1922.

51. Mike Schoenfeld, *The 50th Anniversary Celebration of Skiing at Middlebury, November 10, 1984* (Middlebury, Vt., 1984), p. 1.

52. *MC*, March 3, 1920. Also see, *MC*, February 18, 1920.

53. *MC*, February 8, 1922, February 22, 1922, March 1, 1922, January 10, 1923, January 24, 1923, February 14, 1923, January 16, 1924, February 20, 1924, and February 27, 1924.

54. *MC*, February 28, 1923.

55. *MC*, February 27, 1924, February 11, 1925, February 10, 1926, February 24, 1926, and February 16, 1927.

56. Max Petersen, "History of Skiing at Middlebury" (1968), Public Relations files, p. 1. According to Petersen, Brown started coaching the ski team in 1926. The number of meets increased as follows: 1927, one; 1928, five; 1933, seven; 1934, nine; and 1936, eleven. See *MC*, January 11, 1939. For the claim that Brown "knew nothing about skiing and [to him] slalom was just an odd-sounding foreign word, but neither did the players and that evened everything up," see *MC*, January 11, 1939.

57. Schoenfield, *50th Anniversary*, p. 1; and *MC*, October 4, 1933, and November 29, 1933. There is some disagreement about the year of the first carnival, and some have (mistakenly, I believe) placed it in 1931. See, for example, *MC*, February 25, 1965; and Petersen, "History of Skiing at Middlebury," 1.

58. *MC*, December 6, 1933, January 31, 1934, and February 14, 1934.

59. *MC*, January 9, 1935, and December 4, 1935; Schoenfeld, *50th Anniversary*, p. 2; and interview with Marion Holmes, May 4, 1986, A13/59, MCA.

60. Interview with Richard Hubbard '36, August 21, 1981, MCA. Also see inter-

view with Marion Holmes, May 4, 1986; Schoenfeld, *50th Anniversary*, 1–2; and *MC*, December 11, 1935. On the early development of the Bowl, also see CM, 4:158; PM, 1:13, 19; and *MCNL* 36 (winter 1962): 9.

61. *MC*, January 15, 1936.

62. *MC*, January 11, 1939; interview with Hubbard, August 21, 1981; and Schoenfeld, *50th Anniversary*, 2. Men's skiing became a minor sport in 1936 and a major sport in 1939. See Schoenfeld, *50th Anniversary*, 2; and *MC*, February 12, 1936. On women's intercollegiate skiing before an actual team was formed, see *MC*, December 18, 1935, January 15, 1936, and February 5, 1936.

63. Schoenfeld, *50th Anniversary*, 2.

64. Ibid., 3.

65. Interim Report of the President, January 10, 1948, pp. 4–5, manuscript, Old Chapel Attic.

66. Schoenfeld, *50th Anniversary*, p. 3.

67. Report of the President to the Trustees, July 1, 1948, to June 30, 1949, manuscript, Old Chapel Attic. Also see Schoenfeld, *50th Anniversary*, p. 3.

68. Schoenfeld, *50th Anniversary*, 3–4; and Max Petersen, "History of Skiing at Middlebury," pp. 1–3.

69. Quoted in Schoenfeld, *50th Anniversary*, 4.

70. Ibid., 5.

71. On McNealus, see *MCNL* 53 (summer 1979): 26–27, and 54 (winter 1980): 23.

72. *MCNL* 53 (spring 1979): 25, and 54 (spring 1980): 27; *MCM* 56 (winter 1982): 29, 61 (summer 1987), and 62 (summer 1988): 39; *MC*, March 18, 1988; and Schoenfeld, *50th Anniversary*, 5.

73. Schoenfeld, *50th Anniversary*, 4–7; Petersen, "History of Skiing," pp. 1–3; *MCM* 58 (spring 1984): 24, and 61 (summer 1987); and *MC*, March 18, 1988, March 10, 1989, and March 17, 1989.

74. Report of the President to the Trustees of Middlebury College, September 15, 1954, p. 1, File Drawer 1, Old Chapel Attic.

75. The ski jump was destroyed in the 1950 hurricane but was rebuilt and named as a memorial for Eddy Gignac '43, the former Middlebury skier who died in World War II. The trails were named for Redfield Proctor, Stewart Ross, and Perley Voter. The Pomalift, dedicated on February 19, 1955, served thousands of skiers until 1988, when it finally went to the scrap heap. See "Where the College Champions Ski," *MCNL* 36 (winter 1962): 9; *MCNL* 28 (July 1954); *MAC* (1958–59): 22; and *MC*, January 15, 1988.

76. *MAC* (1958–59), 22; *MAC* (1971–72); and *MCNL* 38 (winter 1964): 71. On trustee action regarding expansion and improvement of the Bowl in the 1950s and 1960s, see CM, 7:941; PM, 1:384, 391, 398, 2:904, and 3 (September 14, 1968); and CM, 9:1196.

77. "Where the College Champions Ski," 8; CM, 7:873; and *MAC* (1963–65).

78. On Myhre, see *MCNL* 53 (winter 1979): 5; CM, 11:1708; and *Addison County Independent*, January 4, 1979. On the Kelly trail, see "Skiing on the Level," *MCNL* 51 (winter 1977): 8.

79. Interview with John Myhre, Jr., August 13, 1981, MCA.

80. *MC*, March 16, 1984, and January 27, 1984.

81. Schoenfeld, *50th Anniversary*, 7; and *MCM* 58 (spring 1984): 4.

82. *MCM* 58 (spring 1984): 4, and 59 (spring 1985): 7, and CM, 13:1972–73.

83. *MC*, December 7, 1921, and January 11, 1922.

84. Quoted in Max Petersen, "History on Ice," *MCM* 59 (winter 1985): 29–30.

85. Ibid.

86. Derived from files of the Sports Information Director, Public Relations Office, Middlebury College.

87. *MCM* 59 (summer 1985): 15; and *MC*, March 23, 1927.

88. Petersen, "History on Ice," 30; Petersen to Stameshkin, July 12, 1990, MCA; and President's Report, 1959–60, p. 35, Old Chapel Archives.

89. On Nelson, see Petersen, "History on Ice," 30; *MCNL* 55 (spring 1981): 4; *MCM* 57 (winter 1983): 42 CM, 14:2035; *MCM* 60 (spring 1986): 2; *MC*, November 3, 1989; and tribute by Fred Neuberger '50 in *MCM* 64 (winter 1990): 7. On the rink's construction, see *MCNL* 28 (July 1954): 6. On the women's hockey team, see *MCM* 62 (summer 1988): 38.

90. On Forbes, see Petersen, "History on Ice," 30; and *MCNL* 53 (spring 1979): 25; and *MC*, September 11, 1975. On Beaney, see *MCM* 64 (summer 1990): 23; and *MC*, March 9, 1990.

CHAPTER 14. STUDENT INVOLVEMENT (PAGES 294–320)

1. See *MC*, November 1, 1933. On the lack of interest, see *MC*, January 18, 1933; and interview with Russ Leng '60, MCA.

2. On the men's Student Union, see *MC*, January 26, 1916, and June 7, 1916. On the origin and early years of the men's Undergraduate Association and Student Council, see *MC*, April 9, 1919, April 30, 1919, May 21, 1919, January 12, 1921, May 9, 1923, and May 19, 1926.

3. *MC*, September 28, 1927. On the good relations between faculty and students on the committee, see *Kaleidoscope* (1939), p. 116.

4. See the Middlebury *Handbooks*, copies in MCA; and Report of the President to the Trustees, September 15, 1953, typed copy, MCA.

5. June Brogger Noble, "Coming of Age in World War II," *MCNL* 49 (winter 1975): 15. For an example of one of the few early protests, see the letter to the editor in *MC*, June 16, 1926. The student argued: "No one is asking for the privilege of running wild. We merely want the right to develop our own consciences by being allowed in so far as is in any way possible to decide for ourselves, as self-respecting women, what will bring honor and what disgrace to the name of our Alma Mater." Also see the editorial in *MC*, April 12, 1939.

6. See Middlebury *Handbooks*, MCA, for the period in question.

7. Interview with Stephen Freeman, August 11, 1981, and interview with Judith Allen Peterson '55 and Bruce Peterson '56, June 19, 1975, MCA.

8. Interview with Elizabeth Baker Kelly in *MCNL* 44 (spring 1970): 8.

9. Based on interviews with members of the class of 1924, Sam Guarnaccia '30, Fred Neuberger '50, and Bruce Peterson '56 and Judith Allen Peterson '55, June 19, 1975, MCA; and *MCM*, 63 (autumn 1989): 62.

10. Interview with JIA, May 20, 1975, MCA.

11. *MC*, November 3, 1960, November 10, 1960, and September 21, 1961.

12. *MC*, October 17, 1963, and November 21, 1963.

13. *MC*, October 31, 1963. Also see *MC*, November 21, 1963, and February 20, 1964.

14. *MC*, March 5, 1964, March 26, 1964, May 21, 1964, November 18, 1965, January 13, 1966, and February 16, 1967.

15. *MC*, March 10, 1966.

16. *MC*, March 2, 1967.

17. *MC*, November 10, 1966, February 9, 1967, February 16, 1967, February 23, 1967, March 2, 1967, March 9, 1967, March 16, 1967, and October 5, 1967.

18. *MC*, September 28, 1967.

19. *MC*, February 29, 1968; and CM, 8:1102–04. Dennis O'Brien had also changed his mind. He admitted that parietal hours would offer an "easier opportunity for pre-marital sexual activity." But he was convinced that "the restrictive policies of the past" were "unwise and unenforceable." See Annual Report, Dean of the College, August 16, 1968, p. 5, MCA.

20. *MC*, February 29, 1968.

21. *MC*, October 10, 1968, and each succeeding issue through November 23, 1968.

22. See, for example, *MC*, January 16, 1969, February 27, 1969, March 20, 1969, April 27, 1972, and September 14, 1972; PM, 3:1052–53, 1076; and CM, 9:1199–1200.

23. The first coed dorms apparently were Allen and Le Chateau in 1970. See CM, 9:1223. But see *MC*, September 25, 1975, for conflicting data and other information. By 1975 only two residence halls were single-sex dormitories. See also *MC*, March 2, 1977.

24. *MC*, November 6, 1970, November 12, 1970, September 14, 1972, and March 8, 1973; PM, 3:1177; and CM, 9:1348.

25. Interview with Dean Kelly in *MCNL* 44 (spring 1970): 8.

26. Interview with JIA, May 20, 1975.

27. FM (1967–69): 233–35; and *MC*, April 17, 1969.

28. PM, 3:1070; CM, 9:1207, 1217–18, 1284; and *MC*, January 14, 1971, and February 25, 1971.

29. CM, 9:1306–7, 1321 appended; and *MC*, February 26, 1970 and October 2, 1970.

30. See pp. 130–32; and pp. 305–8.

31. *MC*, November 17, 1976, December 8, 1976, January 26, 1977, and May 11, 1977.

32. *MC*, April 20, 1977.

33. *MC*, April 27, 1977.

34. The *Campus* editor admitted in April 20, 1977, "that students are not readily aware of who their representatives are, make no effort to find out, and do not actively attempt to express their opinions to them."

35. *MC*, January 11, 1979, and March 7, 1979.

36. The increase in activity space could be realized, they argued, by building a new student union or expanding Proctor Hall. *MC*, April 18, 1979.

37. *MC*, April 18, 1979; and CM, 11:1723.

38. *MC*, September 27, 1979.

39. *MC*, March 27, 1981, April 3, 1981, September 18, 1981, and October 30, 1981.

40. The quotation is from an article in *MC*, March 13, 1981, regarding a student poll in which 90 percent expressed their lack of interest. For other moments of student interest in governance matters, see *MC*, February 25, 1983, and May 6, 1988.

41. *MC*, October 29, 1919, and November 19, 1924. On the students' lack of knowledge of domestic and foreign affairs, see *MC*, January 19, 1927, and February 22, 1928.

42. *MC*, March 7, 1928, October 19, 1932, May 23, 1934, and October 21, 1936.

43. *MC*, April 18, 1928, October 26, 1932, November 16, 1932, April 26, 1933, April 18, 1934, and April 15, 1936. On campus political activity in the 1930s, see Eileen Eagan, *Class, Culture, and the Classroom: The Student Peace Movement of the 1930's*, (Philadelphia, 1981); Philip G. Altbach, *Student Politics in America: An Historical Analysis* (New York, 1974); and James Wechsler, *Revolt on the Campus* (New York, 1935).

44. See chapter 5 above for Moody's unwillingness to shake hands with the *Campus* editor because of the latter's antiinterventionist and antiwar views.

45. The idea for the Middlebury Conference apparently came from a similar conference at Williams in 1941. See *Kaleidoscope* (1946), p. 74; and *MC*, March 11, 1954.

46. Noble, "Coming of Age in World War II," 16.

47. For veteran attitudes and the Alpha Sigma Psi controversy, see above, chapter 11.

48. Report of the President to the Trustees of Middlebury College, April 12, 1947, MCA.

49. See interview with Bruce Peterson '56 and Judith Allen Peterson '55, June 19, 1975; and interview with T. Richardson Miner, Jr., '58, October 22, 1974, MCA.

50. *MC*, April 22, 1965, and April 29, 1965.

51. PM, 1:317; Lt. Col. Stuart G. Williams, "The Army Comes to Middlebury," *MCNL* 27 (November 1952): 25; *MC*, May 15, 1952, and May 22, 1952. Initially, students had hoped to have an ROTC unit from the air corps. See PM, 1:288-90 and also for the strong student and faculty support for establishing an ROTC unit in 1951. Also see interview with Stephen A. Freeman, August 11, 1981; FM (1969-70): 27; and "The President's Page," *MCNL* 25 (April 1951): 2.

52. FM (1969-70): 27.

53. *MC*, January 14, 1965. Also see *MC*, February 12, 1959, October 19, 1961, October 26, 1961, and November 14, 1963 for student opinion on ROTC.

54. *MC*, April 21, 1966; and CM, 8 (June 4, 1966).

55. *MC*, October 13, 1966, February 22, 1968, March 7, 1968, October 10, 1968, and October 17, 1968; and FM (1967-68): 49, 54.

56. *MC*, October 26, 1967, November 9, 1967, March 14, 1968, March 28, 1968, April 18, 1968, September 26, 1968, April 24, 1969, October 9, 1969, November 20, 1969, March 22, 1970, and May 6, 1971; and FM (1969-71): 41. Student sit-ins and demonstrations were becoming common. In 1967 students staged a sit-in to draw attention to their demand that visiting hours be extended. The action was successful. See *MC*, March 9, 1967, March 16, 1967, and March 23, 1967. The administration responded by setting up a student–faculty committee, which issued a carefully drawn statement on campus order. See CM, 9:184. On the college view of early demonstrations, see Annual Report of the Dean of Men, August 26, 1968.

57. *MC*, January 16, 1969; and FM (1969-70): 28. By the fall of 1969, 61 percent wanted it downgraded and another 25 percent asked for its elimination. See *MC*, September 26, 1969.

58. FM (1967-69): 167-68. Also see *MC*, November 7, 1968, November 14, 1968, December 12, 1968, January 16, 1969, January 30, 1969, February 20, 1969, and February 27, 1969; PM, 3:1059; and PM (1969-70): 28.

59. FM (1967-69): 246-48; *MC*, May 9, 1969; and CM, 9:1185.

60. The report is in FM (1967-69): 270-82.

61. PM, 3:1076. Also see "Report of the President, 1969-70," *MCB* 65 (November 1970): 7.

62. FM (1969-70): 33.

63. Ibid., 27.

64. *MC*, October 9, 1969. Also see *MC*, September 18, 1969, and September 25, 1969. The trustees agreed to accept the faculty position. See CM, 9:1199.

65. *MCNL* 51 (summer 1976): 2–3, and 52 (summer 1978): 7.

66. Except when noted, the following account is based primarily on the accounts of the strike in *MC*, May 14, 1970; the *Weekly News Calendar*, Vol. 1 (May 13, 1970); interview with JIA, May 20, 1975; "Report of the President," *MCB*, 65 (November 1970): 7–12; CM, 9:1243–45; Steve Early '70, "The Strike," *MCM* 64 (spring 1990): 34–41; and FM (1969–71): 205–8.

67. The resolution is printed in *MC*, May 14, 1970.

68. Ibid.

69. Ibid.

70. Interview with JIA, May 20, 1975.

71. The full address is printed in the *Weekly News Calendar*, Vol. 1 (May 13, 1970). The next day, the prudential committee met and commended JIA for "his strong leadership." See PM, May 8, 1970.

72. See the *Weekly News Calendar*, Vol. 1 (May 13, 1970) for the text of Catton's speech.

73. Quoted in ibid.

74. CM, 9:1244.

75. FM (1969–71): 207–8.

76. *MC*, May 6, 1971. On the ROTC classroom incident, see Early, "The Strike," p. 40. Although the vandals were not caught, Early asserts that they were Middlebury students; given his activist role in the antiwar movement, he may have been in a position to know that for a fact.

77. CM, 9:1363.

78. From my reading of the *MC*, Environmental Quality (EQ) seems to have taken off in 1971–72. On the festival, see *MCM*, 63 (summer 1989): 43. On early activity in the women's movement, see *MC*, March 5, 1970, April 25, 1970, October 2, 1970, February 25, 1971, and November 2, 1972.

79. *MCNL* 52 (summer 1978): 2; FM, April 13, 1981, pp. 84–85; September, 1981, p. 6; and March 14, 1983. The faculty voted to divest in January 1986. See FM, January 6, 1986, pp. 55–56. On the trustees, see PM, 13:1392; and CM, 13:2009. The Sullivan Principles, a series of seven principles designed in 1977 and augmented in 1984 by Rev. Leon Sullivan, committed signatory companies to implementing a variety of fair employment and black advancement practices in their South African operations. For a full text of the prinples, see Jennifer D. Kibbe, Investor Responsibility Research Center, *Divestment on Campus: Issues and Implementation* (Washington, D.C., 1989), 83–86.

80. CM, 13:2006; and *MC*, January 25, 1985.

81. *MC*, October 16, 1981, December 7, 1984, April 26, 1985, September 20, 1985, October 11, 1985, November 8, 1985, and September 26, 1986. The board's decision to stand firm is included in "Statement by the Board of Trustees of Middlebury College, January 25, 1986," memorandum, MCA. For a picture of the Armadillos' wall, see the article on divestment in *MCM* 60 (summer 1986): 2–5. On the SAA sit-in, see *MC*, February 28, 1986. On March 7, 1986, the Undergraduate Life Committee of the board met with members of SAA and the Community Council to discuss divestment. See *MC*, March 14, 1986.

82. Olin Robison to the Middlebury College Community, September 2, 1986, memorandum, MCA.

83. The trustees slowly changed their minds, moving from partial divestment

to full divestment during 1986. See *MCM* 60 (spring 1986): 3, 60 (summer 1986): 2-5, 60 (autumn 1986): 7-8; and Olin Robison to the Middlebury College Community, September 2, 1986, memorandum, MCA. Also see *MC*, September 19, 1986, October 30, 1987, and January 15, 1988.

84. *MC*, October 30, 1987.

85. FM, December 7, 1987. For the teach-in, see *MC*, November 6, 1987.

86. *MC*, March 4, 1988, March 11, 1988, March 18, 1988, October 14, 1988, and October 21, 1988.

87. *MC*, September 29, 1989, and October 20, 1989; and *MCM* 64 (winter 1990): 14-15.

88. On early gay and lesbian group activities, see *MC*, September 25, 1975, November 20, 1975, November 10, 1976, and November 30, 1977. On antigay letters and responses, see *MC*, December 7, 1977, and January 11, 1978.

89. *MC*, November 14, 1986, November 13, 1987, and March 3, 1989; and telephone interview with Professor Richard Cornwall, April 17, 1989, MCA. In 1984, Cornwall requested in the alumni magazine that gay and lesbian students send him historical information on what it was like to be gay at Middlebury. He only received one response. See *MCM* 58 (winter 1984): 41; and interview with Cornwall, April 17, 1989, MCA.

90. FM, January 7, 1985, p. 61. At the same meeting, the faculty also unanimously recommended the addition of the words "sexual preference" to the sexual harassment statement.

91. PM, 13:1391 (January 17, 1985). Members of the board met with several faculty members to discuss the issue. See *MC*, March 1, 1985, March 15, 1985, and March 22, 1985.

92. Telephone interview with Cornwall, April 17, 1989; and *MC*, February 23, 1990.

93. There are numerous works on the recent history of women in American life. See, for example, William Chafe, *The American Woman: Her Changing Social, Economic, and Political Roles, 1920-1970* (New York, 1972); Sheila M. Rothman, *Woman's Proper Place: A History of Changing Ideals and Practices, 1870 to the Present* (New York, 1978); and Lois W. Banner, *Women in Modern America: A Brief History* (New York, 1974).

94. Based on interviews with Sam Guarnaccia '30, October 8, 1974; Fred Neuberger '50, February 3, 1975; Walter Brooker '37, June 11, 1975; and Gordon Perine '49, February 28, 1975, among others, MCA.

95. *MCNL* 30 (November 1955): 9. After Proctor was completed in the fall of 1960, freshmen ate together there.

96. Interview with JIA, May 20, 1975.

97. *MC*, November 4, 1954, October 27, 1955, September 27, 1956, January 17, 1957, April 27, 1961, May 11, 1961, and March 15, 1962.

98. The study is reported in *MC*, November 10, 1966. On women in World War II activities, see, for example, *MC*, December 9, 1942.

99. W. Storrs Lee '28, "Twenty Years A-Growing," *MCNL* 15 (June 1941): 7.

100. Interview with Juanita Pritchard Cook '26, February 24, 1975, MCA.

101. See *MC*, February 26, 1988 on O'Brien; *MCM* 64 (summer 1990): 2 on Hansen; and *MC*, March 10, 1989 on Andreu. On the number of female faculty members, see John McCardell et al., *Toward the Year 2000: A Basic Ten-Year Planning Document, May, 1988,* (Middlebury, Vt., 1988), 4.

102. Leslie Virostek, "Taking Measure of Women's Work," *MCM* 63 (spring

1989): 30–34; *MC*, November 4, 1988, November 18, 1988, January 20, 1989; *MC*, October 30, 1987, and October 20, 1989; and *MCM* 63 (winter 1989): 2. The college dietitian formed a support group in 1989 for women who were preoccupied with food or weight. See *MCM* 63 (winter 1989): 2.

103. Quoted in Virostek, "Taking Measure of Women's Work," 33; also see *MCM* 63 (winter 1989): 2.

104. Quoted in Brett Millier, "Some Lessons," *MCM* 63 (spring 1989): 36.

105. The report was printed as *Special Committee on Attitudes toward Gender: Final Report* (Middlebury, Vt., 1990). For comments, see *MC*, March 2, 1990, March 9, 1990, and March 16, 1990; and *MCM* 64 (summer 1990): 12–13. Also see Robison to Middlebury College Community, memorandum, March 12, 1990, MCA. It should be noted that, except for the statement that the number of women faculty had increased over the past ten years, the report said nothing about the major changes during the past thirty years; indeed, a major weakness of the report was the lack of any historical perspective on the issues or any feeling that things were in the process of changing, as indeed they were.

106. *MC*, March 9, 1977.

107. See Kenneth Keniston and Michael Lerner, "Campus Characteristics and Campus Unrest," *Annals*, 395 (May 1971): 39–53; Richard E. Flacks, " 'The Liberated Generation': An Explanation of the Roots of Student Protests," *Journal of Social Issues*, 23 (1967): 52–75; and A. W. Astin, "Personal and Environmental Determinants of Student Activism," *Measurement and Evaluation in Guidance* (fall 1968): 149–162.

CHAPTER 15. ". . . AND A CAST OF THOUSANDS" (PAGES 321-51)

1. In 1949–1950, fourteen of the forty-eight Middlebury faculty members above the rank of instructor held the doctorate; in 1960–1961, thirty-five of fifty-one. See *MCNL* 36 (fall 1961): 9.

2. *Report of the Visiting Committee on Literature* (Middlebury, Vt., 1989), 7.

3. Ibid., 7.

4. Vernon C. Harrington to JT, March 7, 1917, TP.

5. CM, 3:93–94; and CM, 4:301–2. Also see JT to Percival Wilds, March 9, 1917, TP; JT to F. L. Fish, March 15, 1917, October 18, 1917, and April 26, 1918, TP; and CM, 3:91.

6. CM, 4:38–39, 299–302. On the revolt against Stratton, see chapter 6, above.

7. Interview with Howard Munford, March 5, 1975, MCA.

8. CM, 6:625, and 8:1002.

9. See *MC*, November 21, 1968; CM, 9:1201, 1275; and 10:1506, 1546; PM, 3:1130–31; FM (1969–70): 102–6; FM (1971–72): 40; and FM (1973–74): 127–64. The new rules passed in 1975 set up two-year, four-year, and eight-year reviews of probationary faculty, the last being the tenure review. Up to that time, tenure decisions were made after a six-year review. See CM, 8:1085, 1105, and 1117; *MC*, January 18, 1968, March 28, 1968, April 4, 1918, May 16, 1968, April 19, 1973, January 22, 1976, and January 26, 1977; PM, 3:1200; and FM (1972–73): 65–66, 88–94.

10. One of the few examples I found was in 1985, when President Robison apparently overturned a recommendation of the Committee on Reappointment.

The president's action was viewed by the faculty as "an erosion of the Committee's power," and the members temporarily resigned from the committee. See FM (1985–86): 62.

11. CM, 6:624–25.

12. For the issues over which the faculty expressed discontent to the board, see CM, 13:1968, 1976; 10:1565–67, 1611; 11:1708; and CM (October 17, 1987): 2108. On the library, see FM (1946–47): 90; Dean of Women's Report in President's Report to the Board of Trustees, 1954, p. 10; and MC, March 10, 1955, MCA. With the increased interest in research and publication in the 1970s and 1980s, demands on the library grew steadily; the 1988 ten-year plan claimed that "the most common complaint heard from faculty has been their dismay over the inability to acquire what in some cases is regarded as basic journal literature in a field." See John McCardell et al., *Toward the Year 2000: A Basic Ten-Year Planning Document, May, 1988*, (Middlebury, Vt., 1988), 29.

13. Interview with Howard Munford, March 5, 1975. Also see CM, 9:1150, 1303–94; PM, 3:1033; and FM (May 14, 1990).

14. See chapter 8, p. 127–28, and chapter 9, pp. 157–60. On the Walker Fund, whose $4,000 annual interest was the only available leave money for the entire faculty until the 1950s, see CM, 3:96, 163, 173.

15. Based on interviews with many faculty members who worked before and after 1950. See, for example, taped interview with Pardon Tillinghast, MCA. On conditions in the late 1980s, see McCardell et al., *Toward the Year 2000*, 10–15.

16. On faculty loads and class size, see the various presidents' reports to the board of trustees, particularly January 12, 1946, August 12, 1947, and January 10, 1948, MCA; MC, March 8, 1951; and "For Your Information," *MCNL* 30 (November 1955): 12.

17. Interview with Marion Holmes, May 4, 1987, A13/59, MCA.

18. There were twenty-two women faculty by 1976 and sixty-six in 1987–1988. See McCardell et al., *Toward the Year 2000*, 4.

19. Interview with John Bowker, October 15, 1974; interview with John Andrews, October 15, 1974; and interview with Jane Howard Fiske '39, March 10, 1975. Also see Pardon Tillinghast's comments in MC, April 16, 1982. All in MCA.

20. Stephen Freeman, "Thirty-eight Years of Middlebury," *MCNL* 38 (autumn 1963): 16. There was also a faculty club in the interwar period. See MC, November 23, 1921, and March 25, 1925.

21. On the Sewing Bee, see, for example, MC, December 14, 1921. On faculty friendships, also see Marion P. Harris to David Stameshkin, February 4, 1982, MCA.

22. See "Full Report of the Task Force on Junior/Senior Faculty Relations for the Middlebury College Self-Study Report," January 1990, pp. 2–3; and interview with Provost John McCardell, July 2, 1990, MCA.

23. Doc Cook to David Stameshkin, January 28, 1982, MCA.

24. MCM 60 (autumn 1985): 32.

25. MC, February 7, 1917, January 29, 1919, and February 5, 1919.

26. MC, January 23, 1924. D. K. Smith '42 stated that student–faculty relations were limited in his era because the students tended to be relatively uncultured and unsophisticated and held faculty in some awe. See MC, March 25, 1983.

27. MC, February 1, 1928.

28. Interview with John Andrews, October 15, 1974. Also see MC, May 25, 1927, for questionnaire on student–faculty relations.

29. Report the Dean of the College, 1988–89, p. 8, MCA.

30. *MC*, January 23, 1918.

31. Interview with Juanita Pritchard Cook, February 24, 1975, notes and tape, MCA.

32. *MCNL* 12 (June 1938): 2. Also see W. Storrs Lee to Committee on Freshman Counseling, in President's Report, September 15, 1954, MCA.

33. *MCM* 61 (summer 1987): 38.

34. PM, 12:1381; Dean Steven Rockefeller to Olin Robison, in CM, May 24, 1985; and *MC*, May 4, 1984, and May 10, 1985.

35. *MC*, October 6, 1920, December 18, 1920, April 27, 1921, October 16, 1935, and December 11, 1935; and CM, 4 (October 10, 1931).

36. See, for instance, *MC*, January 30, 1918, February 6, 1918, June 24, 1919, January 28, 1920, and December 1, 1920; and *MCM* 64 (winter 1990): 60. Also see interview with Joseph Kasper, August 6, 1974, tape, MCA.

37. *MCM* 63 (summer 1989): 60.

38. See, for example, *MC*, February 20, 1958.

39. *MC*, May 11, 1921, November 1, 1922, and May 20, 1936.

40. Interview with Marion Holmes '33, May 4, 1986, A13/59, MCA.

41. *MC*, May 12, 1926, April 29, 1936, and January 11, 1962.

42. See chapter 11.

43. *Report of the Visiting Committee of Literature*, 8.

44. On the honor code, see *MC*, December 10, 1919, February 16, 1921, November 30, 1921, January 18, 1922, March 15, 1922, May 17, 1922, April 20, 1927, May 4, 1927, November 15, 1933, November 16, 1961, February 22, 1962, April 12, 1962, and May 24, 1962; Annual Report of the Dean of Men, June 23, 1965, MCA; and CM, 8:975. In 1975–1976 there was talk of eliminating the honor code because of massive violations, but no change was made. See *MC*, October 9, 1975, and January 22, 1976.

45. See *MCNL* 23 (October 1948): 9; and *MC*, March 15, 1962, April 12, 1962, April 19, 1962, and January 17, 1963. Also see chapter 14, p. 303.

46. Report of the Dean of College, 1988–89, 7.

47. *MC*, May 4, 1989.

48. *MC*, October 11, 1979.

49. The office of controller was added in 1923, the associate dean of men in 1925, the director of admissions and personnel in 1927, and the director of public relations in 1928. See *MC*, April 18, 1923, March 25, 1925, October 26, 1927, and January 11, 1928.

50. I derived these figures by counting the names in the Middlebury College directories (in MCA) for those years. Complete personnel records apparently do not exist before 1968. See Jane Bingham, Treasurer's Office, to David Stameshkin, August 10, 1990, MCA.

51. *MC*, September 25, 1947.

52. A copy of the staff questionnaire is in File A15/1, MCA. On staff concerns in 1978–1982, see *Valley Voice*, June 21, 1978; petitions in the possession of Robert Buckeye; Carroll Rikert to Members of the Staff, June 6, 1978, in Buckeye's possession; and *MC*, November 8, 1979, September 25, 1980, February 27, 1981, March 27, 1981, February 26, 1982, November 5, 1982, and November 12, 1982.

53. A copy of the Staff Council Statement of Purpose is in A15/5/1, MCA.

54. *MC*, September 25, 1987, November 13, 1987, December 4, 1987, January 15, 1988, February 12, 1988, and March 18, 1988.

55. *MC*, April 15, 1988, April 22, 1988, September 16, 1988, January 27, 1989, March 17, 1989, October 6, 1989, and March 2, 1990. Also see PM, May 19, 1988.

56. On the parking problems of the late 1980s, see *MC*, October 2, 1987, October 30, 1987, December 4, 1987, February 12, 1988, and February 19, 1988. On the controversy over smoking on campus, see *MC*, October 17, 1986, January 16, 1987, April 24, 1987, and January 15, 1988; and *MCM* 62 (spring 1988): 32.

57. On the day-care controversy, see *MC*, March 4, 1988, September 15, 1989, and March 2, 1990; CM, March 11, 1989, May 27, 1989, and March 10, 1990; PM, May 25, 1989; FM, May 24, 1989; Olin Robison to Middlebury College Community, May 12, 1989, and June 2, 1989, MCA. Also see the "need for affordable child care for staff, especially for staff at the lower end of the pay scale" expressed by staff in the *Special Committee on Attitudes toward Gender: Final Report* (Middlebury, Vt., 1990), 16.

58. FM (April 11, 1935): 75–78.

59. On the changes in the rules regarding membership of the board under Robison, see PM, 12:1322, 1328; CM, 12:1881; PM, 13:1383–88; CM, 13:1995–96, 2003, 2021. On the role of the trustees, see Arnold B. LaForce '35, "Middlebury and the Trustee's Role in Its Governance," *MCNL* 44 (winter 1970): 3–9.

60. *MCM* 63 (summer 1989): 60.

61. Sylvia Robison to David Stameshkin, September 13, 1990, MCA; and interview with Olin Robison, July 3, 1990, MCA.

62. *MCM* 64 (spring 1990): 26; Sylvia Robison to Stameshkin, September 13, 1990.

63. *MC*, April 21, 1920. Also see *MC*, April 22, 1936, for an announcement that the Boston area alumni association would host a reception for local high school preparatory students.

64. See chapter 10, pp. 200–1.

65. *MCM* 60 (autumn 1985): 8.

66. CM, 3:285, 286; Mrs. Earle W. Brailey to David Stameshkin, November 30, 1981, MCA; and W. Ransom Rice to David Stameshkin, April 17, 1982, MCA.

67. In 1953, only $22,000 was raised. See *MC*, February 4, 1954. On the beginnings of the reunion class effort, see Susan Christopher Leist '76 to David Stameshkin, April 14, 1982, MCA. Susan credits her mother, Jane Hyde Christopher '51, who was national chairman for annual giving from 1976–1978, with several of the innovative ideas that were crucial to the program's success. On more recent success, see chapter 9, pp. 169–74.

68. Alumni were first elected to the board by the Alumni Association in 1925. See CM, 3:182, 211–13. Under the rules instituted by Robison in the 1980s, the number of alumni trustees was dropped from eight to six but with five-year terms. Two recently graduated alumni were also to be elected for two-year terms, to give current students some representation without actually placing undergraduates on the board. See CM, 12:1881; and 13:2021.

69. CM, 8:1001–2; *MC*, November 6, 1929; *SK*, 164; and *MC*, January 18, 1933.

70. See *MCNL* 51 (fall 1976): 18; and brochures describing the Alumni College in the MCA. For the later alumni occasions, see *MCM* 60 (summer 1986): 49.

71. Boston and New York City were two of the first regional groups, and many others followed. A Philadelphia group was formed in 1930, a New Hampshire group in 1938, and many other clubs, including the Middlebury Alumni Association of Japan, were started over the years. See *MC*, January 26, 1921, January 26, 1930, and October 26, 1938; and *MCM* 64 (spring 1990): 51. A Student Alumni Asso-

ciation was formed on campus in 1979 to encourage interest in such activities by undergraduates. See *MC*, October 18, 1979; and *MCNL* 53 (winter 1979): 3.

72. CM, 3:247, 257-58, 273; *MCNL* 51 (summer 1976): 13-15; and *MC*, December 18, 1929.

73. The college does not have a complete and accurate listing of graduates and their occupations, but I have been able to piece together what I hope is a fairly accurate picture of career patterns from a variety of sources. Statistics on graduates before 1915 are in Stameshkin, *The Town's College: Middlebury College, 1800-1915* (Middlebury, Vt., 1985), 259-60. The 1950 *GC* has a listing of all Middlebury graduates (and some nongraduates) with the jobs they held during their careers. Although not perfectly accurate, the *GC* is a fairly good source for graduates before the class of 1940; after that it is less helpful. The Alumni Office attempted to ascertain the occupations of living alumni in 1922 and 1955. See *MC*, March 22, 1922; and *MCNL* 30 (November 1955): 12-14. Both of those studies, particularly the latter, are useful. In 1986 I requested a class-by-class breakdown of occupations by gender. The information was flawed because it was self-reported and incomplete, but it was consistent with other sources. See, for example, *MC*, June 13, 1938, and November 21, 1939; *MCM* 64 (summer 1990): 65; and *MCNL* 52 (summer 1977): 34.

74. *MC*, November 2, 1938.

75. Interviews with Spencer Wright, March 6, 1975; Juanita Pritchard Cook '26, February 24, 1975; Eleanor Mitchell Benjamin Clemens, February 25, 1975; and Richard Hubbard, August 21, 1981, MCA. See also *MC*, February 5, 1919, and October 16, 1935.

Fewer college men were dating or marrying town women; apparently, they were marrying college women instead. As late as World War I, it was common for college men to marry local residents. See *MC*, October 10, 1917, October 1, 1919, and October 22, 1919. On the question of students living off campus, in the late 1960s a group of students successfully petitioned to reside off campus. In 1970, however, the Student Senate voted overwhelmingly to limit the number living off campus because "Middlebury students, by moving off campus in increasing number, are depriving low-income families of needed housing and driving up housing costs." The administration, which believed in the residential college principle, supported the senate. See *MC*, May 4, 1967, May 11, 1967, May 18, 1967, and January 22, 1970.

76. PM, 1:18; and Thomas H. Noonan '91, "New Commencement Tradition," *MCNL* 12 (June 1938): 14. The other major change in commencement exercises occurred in 1918, when the college began importing an outside speaker to deliver the address in place of all-student addresses. Only the valedictorian and salutatorian spoke thereafter. See *MC*, May 31, 1916, for list of addresses at that Commencement.

77. William J. Slator, "Town and Gown," *MCNL* 37 (spring 1963): 21.

78. *MC*, May 10, 1916, March 7, 1928, May 8, 1929, and April 22, 1936.

79. Bruce B. Peterson to Albert F. Gollnick, May 29, 1970, Theta Chi File, MCA.

80. Based on my conversations with townspeople, 1972-1975. Also see *MC*, September 27, 1979, October 4, 1979, January 24, 1980, and November 13, 1981.

81. Based on my conversations with townspeople, 1972-1975.

82. *MC*, September 27, 1979, and October 4, 1979.

83. *MC*, December 15, 1920. Also see *MC*, September 24, 1919, and March 2, 1921.

84. *MC*, November 9, 1938.

85. MC, May 24, 1916, January 14, 1925, February 11, 1925, May 4, 1927, May 25, 1927, and November 23, 1927.

86. *Kaleidoscope* (1929), 252.

87. MC, February 11, 1925.

88. MC, November 12, 1930, and December 11, 1935.

89. Nancy Warner '56, "Women's Forum: The College—the Community," *MCNL* 30 (May 1956): 13–14, 22; MC, July 14, 1943, and May 2, 1957.

90. *MCNL* 53 (summer 1979): 27. Also see interviews (all in MCA) with Bruce and Judy Peterson, June 19, 1975; Roth Tall, June 3, 1975; and Gordie Perine, February 25, 1975; and MC, March 13, 1952, November 26, 1952, February 18, 1960, May 4, 1961, and April 12, 1962.

91. For example, college students, under the direction of Laurie Miner Cox '71, taught art to elementary students. See MC, October 17, 1969. Also see interview with Erica Wonnacott, July 9, 1986; and MC, October 5, 1977, May 10, 1978, and November 13, 1981.

92. MC, October 2, 1970.

93. Interview with Tiffany Nourse Sargent '79, July 11, 1990.

94. *MCM* 60 (autumn 1985): 12–15; MC, October 3, 1986, January 15, 1988, October 21, 1988, January 20, 1989, April 28, 1989, February 23, 1990, March 2, 1990, March 9, 1990, March 16, 1990, and April 13, 1990.

95. MC, September 25, 1987, November 10, 1989, and January 19, 1990.

96. "Editor's Note," *MCM* 64 (spring 1990): 2.

97. MC, March 21, 1928.

98. *MC* 64 (winter 1990): 60. On the students and the flood, see MC, November 23, 1927; and George W. Mead, "Flood Days," April, 1929, typescript, MCA.

99. Interview with Richard Hubbard, August 21, 1981; and interview with Jim Ross, August 25, 1981, MCA.

100. Slator, "Town and Gown," 20.

101. MC, September 25, 1980, and October 16, 1981; interview with President Olin Robison, August 11, 1981, MCA; and my conversations with college employees in 1974–1975, 1979, and 1981.

102. On Anderson's work, see MC, November 3, 1989, January 19, 1990, and January 26, 1990; and Debby Hodge '60, "Something Old, Something New," *MCM* 64 (winter 1990): 38–49.

103. Paul Vaughn '57, "First Words," *MCNL* 58 (spring 1984): inside cover.

104. CM, 3:223, 237–38; 4:122, 153, 189; and conversations with townspeople conducted in 1974–1975.

105. See MC, September 16, 1965, September 30, 1965, October 7, 1965, November 4, 1965, and March 2, 1977; *Addison County Independent*, September 24, 1965; and CM, 8:990.

106. On the Route 7 bypass conflict, see, for example, CM, 8:1076; PM, 3:1273, 1298; interview with Olin Robison, August 11, 1981; and MC, November 12, 1970, November 3, 1976, January 11, 1978, March 8, 1978, and January 26, 1979. On the land that the college bought, also see interview with David Ginevan, July 3, 1986; and Jane Bingham to David Stameshkin, August 10, 1990, MCA.

107. *Valley Voice*, April 25, 1979. Also see *Addison County Independent*, January 26, 1979; and interview with John Michael White, July 16, 1986, MCA.

108. See, for example, PM, October 21, 1988, p. 1448; interview with President Robison, July 3, 1990, MCA; and MC, October 2, 1981, and March 17, 1989.

109. *MC*, October 11, 1979; and interview with James Ross, August 25, 1981, MCA.

110. *MC*, May 1, 1989; and PM, May 22, 1987, p. 1432.

111. CM, October 17, 1987, pp. 2110–11, and appended; CM, January 16, 1988, p. 2118; PM, May 19, 1988; and *MC*, May 6, 1988, September 30, 1988, and October 7, 1988.

112. CM, 12:1844, 1854; 13:2014, 2026; PM, 12:1345, 1353; and *MCM* 56 (autumn 1981): 2–3.

113. See, for example, *MC*, March 2, 1921.

114. *MCNL* 54 (fall 1979): pp. 9–10; and interview with Robert Buckeye, July 3, 1990, notes in author's possession.

115. On early examples of faculty involvement in the community, see *MC*, January 23, 1918, February 26, 1919, June 2, 1920, January 13, 1926, January 11, 1928, December 18, 1935, March 18, 1936, and May 18, 1938; and interview with John Bowker, October 15, 1974. In recent years administrators such as Gordie Perine '49 (longtime treasurer of St. Stephen's Church) and Bob Peskin (president of the board of trustees of the United Way of Addison County) have been particularly active members of the community. See *MCM* 63 (summer 1989): 31, and 60 (summer 1986): 10.

SELECTED BIBLIOGRAPHY

A. UNPUBLISHED MANUSCRIPTS

Lancaster, Pennsylvania. Franklin & Marshall College. Office of the President. David M. Stameshkin, "A History of Fraternities and Sororities at Franklin & Marshall College, 1854–1987."

Lancaster, Pennsylvania. Franklin & Marshall College. Office of the President. David M. Stameshkin, "Recent Actions of Other Schools Regarding Fraternities."

Lancaster, Pennsylvania. Franklin & Marshall College. Office of Institutional Research. Comparison College Files.

Middlebury, Vermont. Middlebury College. Chi Psi Archives. Rush Files.

Middlebury, Vermont. Middlebury College Admissions Office files.

Middlebury, Vermont. Middlebury College. Dean of Students Office. Delta Upsilon file.

Middlebury, Vermont. Middlebury College Library. Battell File.

Middlebury, Vermont. Middlebury College Library. "Brief History of the Advisory Board of the Women's College of Middlebury (1914–1943)."

Middlebury, Vermont. Middlebury College Library. Donald Ballou, "The Beginning of Computing at Middlebury—Personal Recollections."

Middlebury, Vermont. Middlebury College Library. Dorothy Tillpaugh Headley, "Dorothy Went to College: The Letters of a Coed from Middlebury to her Family, 1921–1924."

Middlebury, Vermont. Middlebury College Library. E. C. Sage, "Notes on a Visit to Middlebury College."

Middlebury, Vermont. Middlebury College Library. George W. Mead, "Flood Days," April 1929.

Middlebury, Vermont. Middlebury College Library. John Thomas Papers.

Middlebury, Vermont. Middlebury College Library. Lawrence Files.

Middlebury, Vermont. Middlebury College Library. Middlebury Attendance Records, 1800–1951.

Middlebury, Vermont. Middlebury College Library. Paul Moody Papers.

Middlebury, Vermont. Middlebury College Library. Report of the Faculty Ad Hoc Committee on Compensation.

Middlebury, Vermont. Middlebury College. Office of Public Affairs. "Eighty-Four Years of Football Traditions."

Middlebury, Vermont. Middlebury College. Office of Public Affairs. Max Petersen, "History of Skiing at Middlebury."

Middlebury, Vermont. Middlebury College. Office of Public Affairs. "Notes for a Ten-Year Report (1975–1985)."

Middlebury, Vermont. Middlebury College. Office of Public Affairs. Sports Information Director's Historical Files.

Middlebury, Vermont. Middlebury College. Office of Public Affairs. Zaccaro File.

Middlebury, Vermont. Middlebury College. Old Chapel. Dean of the College, Annual Reports, various years.

Middlebury, Vermont. Middlebury College. Old Chapel. Minutes of the Corporation of Middlebury College, 1915–1990.

Middlebury, Vermont. Middlebury College. Old Chapel. Minutes of the Prudential Committee of the Corporation of Middlebury College, 1915–1990.

Middlebury, Vermont. Middlebury College. Old Chapel. Reports of the President, various years.

Middlebury, Vermont. Middlebury College. Old Chapel, President's Office Safe. Confidential files.

Waterville, Maine. Personal Papers of Robert Reuman. Alpha Sigma Phi files.

B. MAGAZINES AND NEWSPAPERS

The Campaign Reporter, 1987–1988.
The Middlebury Campus, 1915–1990.
Middlebury College Magazine, 1981–1990.
Middlebury College News Letter, 1926–1981.

C. INTERVIEWS

Andrews, John. Middlebury, Vermont. October 15, 1974.
Armstrong, James I. Middlebury, Vermont. April 30, 1975.
———. Middlebury, Vermont. May 20, 1975.
Bowker, John. Middlebury, Vermont. October 15, 1974.
Brooker, Walter. Middlebury, Vermont. June 11, 1975.
Buckeye, Robert. Middlebury, Vermont. July 3, 1990.
Class of 1924 members. Middlebury, Vermont. May 25, 1974.
Class of 1939 members. Middlebury, Vermont. May 25 1974.
Clemens, Eleanor B. Middlebury, Vermont. February 25, 1975.
Cook, Juanita Pritchard. Middlebury, Vermont. February 24, 1975.
Cox, Laurie Miner. Ripton, Vermont. July 17, 1986.
Cubeta, Paul. Middlebury, Vermont. March 14, 1975.
Fiske, Jane Howard. Middlebury, Vermont. March 10, 1975.
Forstein, Marshall. Middlebury, Vermont. April 20, 1974.
Freeman, Stephen. Middlebury, Vermont. August 11, 1981.
———. Middlebury, Vermont. August 27, 1981.
Ginevan, David. Middlebury, Vermont. July 3, 1986.
Guarnaccia, Samuel. Middlebury, Vermont. October 8, 1974.
Hadley, Egbert. Middlebury, Vermont. July 31, 1975.
Holmes, Marion. Middlebury, Vermont. May 4, 1987.
Hubbard, Richard. Middlebury, Vermont. August 21, 1981.
Kasper, Joseph. Middlebury, Vermont. August 6, 1974.
Lawson, G. Thomas. Middlebury, Vermont. August 26, 1981.
Lee, W. Storrs. Pemaquid Point, Maine. July 2, 1976.

Leng, Russell. Middlebury, Vermont. February 26, 1975.
Lick, Mary. Middlebury, Vermont. August 24, 1981.
Lindholm, Karl. Middlebury, Vermont. July 9, 1986.
McCardell, John. Middlebury, Vermont. July 2, 1990.
Miner, T. Richardson. Middlebury, Vermont. October 22, 1974.
Munford, Howard. Middlebury, Vermont. March 5, 1975.
Munford, Howard, and Marian Munford. Middlebury, Vermont. March 3, 1975.
Myhre, John, Jr. Middlebury, Vermont. August 13, 1981.
Neuberger, Fred. Middlebury, Vermont. February 3, 1975.
———. Middlebury, Vermont. July 16, 1986.
Nourse, Kenneth. Middlebury, Vermont. February 13, 1975.
O'Brien, G. Dennis. Middlebury, Vermont. April 30, 1975.
Perine, Gordon. Middlebury, Vermont. February 28, 1975.
Peterson, Bruce, and Judith Allen Peterson. Middlebury, Vermont. June 19, 1975.
Reynolds, Thomas H. Lewiston, Maine. October 3, 1975.
Rikert, Carroll. Middlebury, Vermont. August 3, 1979.
Robison, Olin. Middlebury, Vermont. August 7, 1979.
———. Middlebury, Vermont. August 11, 1981.
———. Middlebury, Vermont. July 9, 1986.
———. Middlebury, Vermont. July 3, 1990.
Ross, James. Middlebury, Vermont. August 25, 1981.
Sapadin, Eugene. Middlebury, Vermont. July 10, 1975.
Sargent, Tiffany Nourse. Middlebury, Vermont. July 11, 1990.
Scott, Charles. Middlebury, Vermont. July 31, 1975.
Smith, David K. Middlebury, Vermont. March 10, 1975.
Tall, Roth. Middlebury, Vermont. June 3, 1975.
Wells, Barbara. Middlebury, Vermont. February 10, 1975.
White, John Michael. Middlebury, Vermont. July 16, 1986.
Wonnacott, Erica. Middlebury, Vermont. July 16, 1986.
Wright, W. Spencer. Middlebury, Vermont. February 26, 1975.

D. COLLEGE PUBLICATIONS AND REPORTS

Catalogue of the Corporation, Faculty, and Students of Amherst College. Amherst, 1916, 1921, 1943, and 1963.
Catalogue of the Officers and Students of Bowdoin College. Brunswick, 1916, 1921, 1943, and 1963.
Catalogue of the Officers and Students of Dartmouth College. Hanover, 1916, 1921, 1943, and 1963.
Catalogue of the Officers and Students of Middlebury College. Middlebury, 1915– . Under various titles.
Catalogue of the Officers and Students of Wesleyan University. Middletown, 1916, 1921, 1943, and 1963.
Dalton, Herbert F., Jr. *To Share A Dream: The Clinton-Middlebury Partnership.* Middlebury, 1990.
Document of Understanding: Fraternities, May 30, 1980. Middlebury, 1980.
Emerson, John. *An Update on Minority Concerns: Postscript to the Twilight Report.* Middlebury, June 1988.
Full Report of the Task Force on the Curriculum . . . Middlebury, 1990.

Full Report of the Task Force on Junior/Senior Faculty Relations for the Middlebury College Self-Study Report. Middlebury, January 1990.

Kaleidoscope, 1915–90.

Lopez, Donald S., et al. *Toward Greater Educational Community: Recommendations to the President and Faculty, Middlebury College, The Report of the Special Committee on the Curriculum.* Middlebury, 1985.

McCardell, John, et al. *Toward the Year 2000: A Basic Ten-Year Planning Document.* Middlebury, 1988.

Middlebury College, 1983–1993, Inventory and Prospect: A Basic Ten-Year Planning Document. Middlebury, 1983.

Middlebury College Bulletin, 1915–90.

Middlebury College Handbook. Various years.

Middlebury College in the State of Vermont, General Catalogue, Sesquicentennial Edition. Edited by Duane L. Robinson. Middlebury, 1951.

Middlebury College: Self-Study Report . . . February, 1980. Middlebury, 1980.

Middlebury College: Self-Study Report, January, 1990. Middlebury, 1990.

New England Association of Colleges and Secondary Schools. *Re-Evaluation: Middlebury College,* 1968–69.

A Recommendation and Report to the President of Middlebury College by the Ad Hoc Committee on Student Life. Middlebury, [1966?].

Recruitment Plan and Report: Students of Color. June 12, 1990 (draft copy). Admissions Office.

Report and Recommendations of the Middlebury College Alcohol Committee, October 9, 1981. Middlebury, 1981.

Report of the Ad Hoc Committee on Minority Concerns. Middlebury, 1982.

Report of the Admissions Long-Range Planning Committee, May 1, 1987. Middlebury, 1987.

Report of the Director of the Language Schools. 1970–1990.

Report of the Drug Task Force, Middlebury, May 1987.

Report of the President, Middlebury College. Various years, 1915– .

Report of the Special Committee on the College. Middlebury, 1973.

Report of the Task Force on Student Social Life. Middlebury, 1989.

Report of the Task Force on the Composition of the Student Body. Middlebury, 1989.

Report of the "21" Committee: Middlebury College and the Legal Drinking Age. Middlebury, April 19, 1985.

Report of the Visiting Committee on Literature. Middlebury, 1989.

Report of the Visiting Committee on the Sciences. Middlebury, 1989.

Report to the Faculty, Administration, Trustees, Students of Middlebury College . . . by . . . the New England Association of Schools and Colleges. Swarthmore, 1990.

Report to . . . Middlebury College by . . . The New England Association of Schools and Colleges, March–April, 1980.

Robison, Olin. *A Report to the Board of Trustees: Middlebury College, 1975–80.* Middlebury, 1980.

Schoenfeld, Mike. *The 50th Anniversary Celebration of Skiing at Middlebury, November 10, 1984.*

Special Committee on Attitudes Toward Gender: Final Report. Middlebury, 1990.

Treasurer's Report, Middlebury College. Various years, 1915–90.

The Weekly News Calendar. Various years and titles.

E. BOOKS

Altbach, Philip G. *Student Politics in America: An Historical Analysis.* New York, 1974.

Anderson, George K. *Bread Loaf School of English: The First Fifty Years.* Middlebury, 1969.

Andres, Glenn. *A Walking History of Middlebury.* Middlebury, 1975.

Atwood, Carroll J. *A Manual to Guide Each Future Chi Psi in the More Effective Performance of His Fraternity's Most Vital Function: Rushing.* N.p., n.d.

Banner, Lois W. *Women in Modern America: A Brief History.* New York, 1974.

Bell, Daniel. *The Reforming of General Education: The Columbia College Experience in Its National Setting.* New York, 1966.

Blum, John Morton. *V Was For Victory: Politics and American Culture During World War II.* New York, 1976.

Brubacher, John S., and Willis Rudy. *Higher Education in Transition: A History of American Colleges and Universities, 1636-1976.* New York, 1976.

Butts, R. Freeman. *The College Charts Its Course.* New York, 1939.

Brainerd, Ezra. *Emma Willard's Life and Work in Middlebury.* Middlebury, 1918.

Chafe, William. *The American Woman: Her Changing Social, Economic, and Political Roles, 1920-1970.* New York, 1972.

Cheit, Earl. *The New Depression in Higher Education.* New York, 1971.

———. *The New Depression in Higher Education—Two Years Later.* Berkeley, 1973.

Clark, Burton R., ed. *The Academic Profession: National, Disciplinary, and Institutional Settings.* Berkeley, 1987.

DeVane, William Clyde. *Higher Education in Twentieth-Century America.* Cambridge, Mass., 1965.

Dunaway, Fuller. *History of the Pennsylvania State College.* Lancaster, Pa., 1946.

Eagan, Eileen. *Class, Culture, and the Classroom: The Student Peace Movement of the 1930's.* Philadelphia, 1981.

Fass, Paula. *The Damned and the Beautiful: American Youth in the 1920's.* New York, 1977.

Freeman, Stephen A. *The Middlebury College Foreign Language Schools: The Story of a Unique Idea.* Middlebury, 1975.

Gordon, Lynn D. "Coeducation on Two Campuses: Berkeley and Chicago, 1890–1912." In *Woman's Being, Woman's Place: Female Identity and Vocation in American History,* edited by Mary Kelley, pp. 171–93. Boston, 1979.

Higham, John. *Strangers in the Land: Patterns of American Nativism, 1860-1920.* New York, 1973.

Horowitz, Helen Lefkowitz. *Alma Mater: Design and Experience in the Women's Colleges from Their Nineteenth Century Beginnings to the 1930s.* New York 1984.

———. *Campus Life: Undergraduate Cultures from the End of the Eighteenth Century to the Present.* New York, 1987.

Hutchins, Robert M. *The Higher Learning in America.* New Haven, 1936.

In Memory of Paul Dwight Moody, 1879-1947: A Service Held . . . November 16, 1947. [New York?], [1947?].

Kolbe, Rexford Parke. *The Colleges in War Time and After: A Contemporary Account of the Effect of the War upon Higher Education in America.* New York, 1919.

Lasser, Carol. *Educating Men and Women Together: Coeducation in a Changing World.* Urbana, 1987.

Lee, Alfred McClung. *Fraternities Without Brotherhood.* Boston, 1956.

Lee, W. Storrs. *Father Went to College*. New York, 1936.

Levine, David O. *The American College and the Culture of Aspiration, 1915–40*. Ithaca, N.Y., 1986.

McAdams, Doug. *Freedom Summer*. New York, 1988.

Miller, J. Hillis, and Dorothy V. N. Brooks. *The Role of Higher Education in War and After*. New York, 1944.

Morrison, Theodore. *Middlebury College Bread Loaf Writers' Conference: The First Thirty Years*. Middlebury, 1976.

Murray, Robert K. *Red Scare: A Study in National Hysteria, 1919–1920*. Minneapolis, 1955.

Newcomer, Mabel. *A Century of Higher Education for American Women*. New York, 1959.

Noverr, Douglas A., and Lawrence E. Ziewacz. *The Games They Played: Sports in American History, 1865–1980*. Chicago, 1983.

Olson, Keith W. *The G.I. Bill, the Veterans, and the Colleges*. Lexington, Ky., 1974.

Oren, Dan A. *Joining the Club: A History of Jews and Yale*. New Haven, 1985.

Rader, Benjamin G. *American Sports: From the Age of Folk Games to the Age of Spectators*. Englewood Cliffs, N.J., 1983.

Rosenberg, Rosalind. "The Limits of Access: The History of Coeducation in America." In *Women and Higher Education in American History*, edited by John Mack Faragher and Florence Howe, pp. 107–29. New York, 1988.

Rothman, Sheila M. *Woman's Proper Place: A History of Changing Ideals and Practices, 1870 to the Present*. New York, 1978.

Rudolph, Frederick. *The American College and University: A History*. New York, 1962.

———. *Curriculum: A History of the American Undergraduate Course of Study Since 1636*. San Francisco, 1981.

Savage, Howard J., et al. *American College Athletics*. New York, 1929.

Schneider, James C. *The Navy V-12 Program: Leadership for a Lifetime*. Boston, 1987.

Solomon, Barbara. *In the Company of Educated Women: A History of Higher Education in America*. New Haven, 1985.

Stameshkin, David. *The Town's College: Middlebury College, 1800–1915*. Middlebury, 1985.

Synnott, Marcia G. *The Half-Opened Door: Discrimination and Admissions at Harvard, Yale, and Princeton, 1900–1970*. Westport, 1979.

Wechsler, James. *Revolt on Campus*. New York, 1935.

Willey, Malcolm M. *Depression, Recovery, and Higher Education*. New York, 1937.

Woody, Thomas. *A History of Women's Education in the United States*. 2 volumes. New York, 1929.

Wynn, Neil A. *From Progressivism to Prosperity: World War I and American Society*. New York, 1986.

F. ARTICLES

Adams, Evelyn Plumley. "Mother Went to College Too (1914–43)." *Middlebury College News Letter* 36 (Winter 1962):19, 60.

Astin, A. W. "Personal and Environmental Determinants of Student Activism." *Measurement and Evaluation in Guidance* (Fall 1968):149–62.

Bain, David Harward. "Bread Loaf at Sixty." *Middlebury College Magazine* 59 (Spring 1985):22–27.

Bowker, John G. "Middlebury College in Retrospect." *Middlebury College News Letter* 41 (Spring 1967):11–15.

Cann, Ruth. "Admissions Problems: The Women." *Middlebury College News Letter* 22 (July 1948):5, 18.

Cook, Juanita. "The Women's College." *Middlebury College News Letter* 20 (February 1946):10–11.

Desruisseaux, Paul. "A Lake Wobegon Weekend." *Middlebury College Magazine* 57 (Summer 1983):12–16.

"The Eleventh President of Middlebury College." *Middlebury College News Letter* 17 (March 1943):5–6, 19.

Ernst, Ed. "Democracy Is Not a Spectator Sport." *Middlebury College Magazine* 63 (Winter 1989):24–25.

Fayer, Margaret L. "Seely, Eaton, Howard, Sanford." *Middlebury College News Letter* 18 (December 1943):14–15.

Flacks, Richard E. " 'The Liberated Generation': An Explanation of the Roots of Student Protests." *Journal of Social Issues* 23 (1967):52–75.

"Dr. Freeman Recalls 45 Years of College History and Language Growth at Middlebury." *Middlebury College News Letter* 44 (Summer 1970):38–47.

Freeman, Stephen A. "As the Year Begins." *Middlebury College News Letter* 17 (September 1942):7, 19.

———. "Thirty-eight Years at Middlebury." *Middlebury College News Letter* 38 (Autumn 1963):15–21.

Fritz, J. J. "Depression and The College." *Middlebury College News Letter* 6 (December 1931):2, 20.

Garner, Dwight. "Frats Under Fire." *Middlebury College Magazine* 64 (Spring 1990): 21–23.

Graham, Patricia Albjerg. "Expansion and Exclusion: A History of Women in American Higher Education." *Signs* 3 (Summer 1978):759–73.

Green, Boylston. "A Framework for Reconversion." *Middlebury College News Letter* 19 (January 1945):5–6, 31.

Harnest, Grant. "Program Calls for Expansion of Physical Facilities for Sciences." *Middlebury College News Letter* 40 (Autumn 1965): 9, 11.

Hazeltine, Burt. "Democratic Middlebury." *Middlebury College News Letter* 6 (April 1932):2–3, 21.

Hodge, Debby. "Something Old, Something New." *Middlebury College Magazine* 64 (Winter 1990):38–49.

"The Inaugural Address of President Paul Dwight Moody of Middlebury College." *Middlebury College Bulletin* 16 (June 1922):19–36.

"Interim Report of the Ad Hoc Committee on Student Life." *Middlebury College News Letter* 40 (Spring 1966):15.

"Interview with Elizabeth Kelly." *Middlebury College News Letter* 44 (Spring 1970): 3–10.

Kasper, Joseph. "A Lasting Memorial." *Middlebury College News Letter* 20 (June 1946):12–13, 27.

Keniston, Kenneth, and Michael Lerner. "Campus Characteristics and Campus Unrest." *Annals* 395 (May 1971):39–53.

Kreis, Donald M. "And Now for the News . . ." *Middlebury College News Letter* 52 (Spring 1978):8–9.

[Lawrence, Henry?]. "Putting Metternich to Shame." *The New Republic* 21 (February 18, 1920):357.

Lee, W. Storrs. "Buildings and Grounds." *Middlebury College News Letter* 21 (January 1947):8–9.

———. "Fraternities on Trial." *Middlebury College News Letter* 20 (June 1946):9.

———. "In Retrospection." *Middlebury College News Letter* 52 (Summer 1978):14.

———. "The Men." *Middlebury College News Letter* 20 (February 1946):6–7, 18.

———. "Second Middlebury College." *Middlebury College News Letter* 10 (September 1935):8–9, 20.

———. "To College with a Purpose." *Middlebury College Bulletin* 30 (June 1936).

———. "Twenty Years A-Growing." *Middlebury College News Letter* 15 (June 1941):5–8, 17.

Lindholm, Karl. "Also Plays." *Middlebury College Magazine* 60 (Spring 1986):20–21.

Meredith, L. Douglas. "How Will Middlebury College Select a New President?" *Middlebury College News Letter* 37 (Autumn 1962):14–15.

"Middlebury College, Myths of Coeducation." *The Harvard Crimson,* May 21, 1954.

Moody, Paul D. "The Inaugural Address of President Paul D. Moody." *Middlebury College Bulletin* 16 (June 1922):

Moody, Paul D. "Mountains for Dormitories." *Middlebury College News Letter* 9 (May 1935):6–7.

Moody, Paul D. "Seven Lean Years." *Middlebury College News Letter* 14 (December 1939):10.

Noble, June Brogger. "Coming of Age in World War II." *Middlebury College News Letter* 49 (Winter 1975):12–16.

Petersen, Max. "History on Ice." *Middlebury College Magazine* 59 (Winter 1985):29–30.

"The President's Report, 1928–1930." *Middlebury College Bulletin* 24 (January 1930).

"Report of the Sub-Committee on Inquiry for Middlebury College." *AAUP Bulletin* 7 (May 1921):28–37.

"A Return to Breadth: The New Middlebury Curriculum." *Middlebury College News Letter* 51 (Fall 1976):14–17.

Reynolds, Thomas H. "Fraternities at Middlebury Today." *Middlebury College News Letter* 35 (Winter 1961):7.

Reynolds, Thomas H. "Our Need for Faculty and Facilities in the Natural Sciences." *Middlebury College News Letter* 40 (Autumn 1965):8, 10.

Robison, Olin C. "A Five-Year Report on the State of the College." *Middlebury College News Letter* 54 (Summer 1980):13–18.

———. "An Open Letter to the Middlebury College Community." *Middlebury College Magazine* 64 (Spring 1990):30–31.

[Robison, Olin]. "President Olin C. Robison's Inaugural Address." *Middlebury College News Letter* 50 (Winter 1975–76):5–8.

"The Robison Years." *Middlebury College Magazine* 64 (Spring 1990):24–33.

Rucker, Ronald. "Conquering Time and Space: Defining a College Library." *Middlebury College News Letter* 52 (Spring 1978):12–13.

Scott, Charles P. "Religion at Middlebury College." *Middlebury College News Letter* 29 (April 1954):15–17, 21.

Sholes, Russell G. "Navy at Middlebury." *Middlebury College News Letter* 20 (February 1946):8–9, 19.

Slator, William J. "Town and Gown." *Middlebury College News Letter* 37 (Spring 1963):21.

"Spirit and Nature." *Middlebury College Magazine* 65 (Winter 1991):22–34.

"The Stratton Era." *Middlebury College News Letter* 37 (Spring 1963):12–14.

Thomas, John. "Report of the President of Middlebury College." *Middlebury College Bulletin* 9 (November 1916):9–14.

[Thomas John?]. "The Argument for Middlebury." *Middlebury College Bulletin* 12 (January 1918), supplement.

"Three Thirds of a President." *Middlebury College News Letter* 15 (February 1941):9, 18.

Virostek, Leslie. "Taking Measure of Women's Work." *Middlebury College Magazine* 63 (Spring 1989):30–34.

"War and Peace." *Middlebury College News Letter* 14 (December 1939):3–4.

Warner, Nancy. "Women's Forum: The College—The Community." *Middlebury College News Letter* 30 (May 1956):13–14, 22.

Weinberg, Jack. "Students and Civil Rights in the 1960s." *History of Education Quarterly* 30 (Summer 1990):213–24.

" 'Where the College Champions Ski.' " *Middlebury College News Letter* 35 (Winter 1962):8–9.

White, Raymond. "The War and the Curriculum." *Middlebury College News Letter* 20 (February 1946):12–13.

Wiley, E. J. "College Army Post, 1918 Model." *Middlebury College News Letter* 18 (September 1942):8–10.

———. "Making a Start." *Middlebury College News Letter* 9 (March 1935):2–3, 22.

[Wiley, E. J. ?]. "The Coming of the S.A.T.C." *Middlebury College Bulletin* 13 (December 1918).

[Wiley, E. J. ?]. "To Young Men." *Middlebury College Bulletin* 12 (July 1918), supplement.

[Wiley, E. J. ?]. "Why Go to Middlebury in War Time?" *Middlebury College Bulletin* 12 (October 1917), supplement.

Wolfson, Richard. "Energy Recycling: Heat from the Ground." *Middlebury College News Letter* 52 (Spring 1978):19.

Wright, Stanley. "Admissions Problems: The Men." *Middlebury College News Letter* 22 (July 1948):5, 18.

Yoe, Mary Ruth. "The Campus That Might Have Been." *Middlebury College Magazine* 62 (Winter 1988):16–19.

Young, Marion L. "Development of Women's Sports." *Middlebury College News Letter* 6 (April 1932):6–7, 18.

INDEX

AAUP. *See* American Association of
  University Professors
Abboud, Peter, 154
Abernethy, Frank D., 34
Abernethy, Fred, 359–60(n17)
Abernethy, Julian W., 34, 357(n68)
ACT NOW, 315
Addison County Hospital Association, 35
Ad Hoc Alumni Interfraternity Committee, 228
Ad Hoc Committee on Student Life,
  227–28
Administration and staff, 334–36,
  417(n49); and Armstrong presidency,
  132–33; presidency position, 336–38;
  during Robison presidency, 160–64,
  382–83(n64), 383(n65); staff strike
  in 1947, 335(photo), 370(n13); and
  Stratton presidency, 94–97, 113–14,
  374(n38); town relations with, 350,
  421(n115); women members, 318, 319–
  20. *See also* Faculty-administration
  relations; *individual presidents*; Student-
  administration relations
Administration Committee, 325
Admissions: aid-blind policy, 210; gender issues in, 194–200, 200(table);
  geographical diversity in, 200–201,
  201(table); and student quality/
  diversity, 189–90, 210–12. *See also*
  Enrollment; Recruitment
Admissions Outreach Program, 210–11
African Americans, 187, 201, 203–7,
  390(n83); and sororities, 247; and
  South African apartheid, 314
Alcohol abuse, 260–62, 403(n78); and
  fraternities, 237–38
Alden Trust, 169
Aldrich, Terry, 287
Allen, Cecile Child, 111, 363–64(n40)
Allen, Everett S., 193

Allen, George, 88
Allen, Hervey, 68
Allen Hall, 111
Alpha Sigma Phi, 220–21, 393(n1),
  395(n32)
Alpha Sigma Psi, 221, 237
Alpha Tau Omega, 221, 393(n1). *See also*
  Delta Tau Omega
Alpha Xi Delta, 245, 247, 400(n4)
Alumni: and coeducational issue, 40;
  facilities for, 164, 170; and fraternities, 228, 232, 396(n72); gifts and
  Armstrong presidency, 122, 135;
  gifts and Robison presidency, 169–
  70, 172–74, 385(n112); gifts and
  Thomas/Moody/Stratton presiden-
  cies, 28, 115, 354(n12); involvement
  and annual events for, 170, 338–41,
  339(photo), 418(nn 67, 68), 418–
  19(n71); and Lee dismissal, 97; and
  sororities, 245; student recruitment by,
  201, 338, 418(n63)
Alumni Admissions Support Program,
  201
Alumni College, 170, 340
American Association of University Pro-
  fessors (AAUP): and Lawrence-Stevens
  controversy, 14, 356(n48); and Stratton,
  89–90, 94
American Collegiate Consortium for
  East-West Cultural and Academic
  Exchange, 207–8
Anderson, George K., 64, 66, 275
Anderson, J. Glenn, 7–8
Anderson, John W., 276
Anderson, Malcolm T., 110
Anderson, Townsend, 348, 350,
  350(photo)
Andres, Glenn, 124, 127, 134
Andreu, Chela, 318
Andrews, John, 76, 93

Arabic program, 154, 380(n29)

Armadillos, 314

Armstrong, James I., xvi–xvii, 81, 116(photo), 148(photo); administration, 132–33; and civil rights/minority issues, 203, 204; faculty and curriculum, 127–32, 138–44, 322, 324–26; and fraternities, 225–33, 242, 317; fundraising and physical facilities, 120–27, 133–38; and gender segregation issues, 318; and parietal rules, 299, 300–301; as president, 82, 119–20, 144–45, 337; and Vietnam antiwar protests, 307, 310, 311–13, 413(n71)

Arnett, Trevor, 37

Art history, 153

Arts. *See* Dance program; Fine arts/ music; Theater

Askin, Peter, 278

Athletic Committee, 303

Athletics: baseball, 277–78; basketball, 276–77, 406(n23); facilities for, 104–6, 106(photo), 107, 109–10, 138, 164–65, 176, 280, 281–82, 293, 386(n122); football, 271–76; funding, 406(n5); golf, 278, 407(n27); ice hockey, 290–93; participation in, 270–71, 406(n13); physical education and intramurals, 279–80, 407(nn33, 35); skiing, 282–90, 293, 408(n56), 409(nn 62, 75); soccer, 278–79, 407(n29); sports clubs, 279, 281, 407(n32); and women, 280–82, 284, 286, 287–88, 288(photo), 293, 317, 319, 408(n46); during World War II, 77

Atkinson, Dick, 276

Atwater Hall, 138

Auseklis, Nancy Sise, 287

Bailey, Joseph "Tink," 286

Baker, Carlos, 119

Baker, Leslie, 288

Ballenger, John G., 166

Ballenger Computer Center, 166

Ballou, Donald H., 93(photo), 384(n90)

Banks, Don, 258–59

Barber, Hugh, 289

Barney, Raymond L., 54, 245

Barrington, Jim, 276

Bates, Katherine Lee, 64

Bates, Stanley, 383(n65)

Battell, Joseph, xvi, 15–17, 356(n54)

Battell complex, 107, 111

Baum, James H., 128(photo)

Beaney, Bill, 293

Beattie, Bob, 287

Beck, Benjamin, 274(photo), 275

Beers, Douglas S., 50, 52

Bennington College, 42

Benson, Raymond E., 153(photo)

Bequests: and Armstrong presidency, 123; for athletics, 272; Battell land, xvi, 15–17, 30, 46, 356(nn 54, 55); during Moody presidency, 29, 31, 32, 34, 35, 359(n12), 359–60(n17), 361(n47); and Robison presidency, 169, 171–72, 173(table); during Stratton presidency, 105–6, 107, 109–10, 114, 373(nn 22, 24); and Thomas presidency, 15, 354(n12), 356(n51). *See also* Endowment fund; Grants

Bingham, Anne Julia Stowell Sunderland, 107

Black Student Union, 314

Bliss, Zeke, 260

Blue Key society, 248, 250, 251

Bly, Beach, 284

Board of trustees: and Armstrong, 118–19, 337; and Battell bequest, 16–17; and Bread Loaf, 65–66; coeducation issue, 18–20, 42–43, 45, 363(n32); curricular additions and reforms, 100, 102; drug abuse issue, 263; extracurricular activities and, 258; faculty issues, 12–13, 88–92, 158–60, 323, 324–25; and fraternities, 224, 228–29, 235, 240–41, 242, 397(n86), 398(n117); fund-raising, 121–22, 137, 171; and Lee, 95, 97; membership, 34, 339, 418(n68); and Moody, 25, 70, 71, 337; and physical facilities, 104–5, 108–9; political controversies and, 204, 314, 316, 413(n64), 413–14(n83), 414(n91); and required chapel, 266–67; and Robison, 147, 337; and sororities, 246; and Stratton, 75–76, 337; and Thomas, 5, 337

Boehm, Bobby, 275

Boehm, Walt, 275

Bookman, The, 67

Booth, George H., 220, 221

Bosano, Gabriella, 60

Boston Globe, 273

Bostwick, Pete, 278

Boucher, Peter, 279

Bourcier, Claude, 52, 100(photo)

Bowen, Catherine Drinker, 68
Bower, James, 271
Bower, John, 279, 288
Bowker, John G., 40, 54, 69, 71, 88, 93(photo), 132, 264–65
Boyce, Thomas E., 356(n55), 357(n59)
Brailey, Dorothy Nash, 339
Brainerd, Ezra, 15
Branch, Leonora, 64
Bread Loaf Inn, 16, 357(n59); fire, 65, 65(photo)
Bread Loaf Program in Writing for Teachers of English from Rural Communities, 155
Bread Loaf School of English, 366(n58); Alumni College, 170, 340; and Battell bequest, xvi, 16–17; and Davison, 54; establishment/development of, 61–67, 99, 168, 169; freshmen outing at, 254, 255(photo); during Robison presidency, 155
Bread Loaf Writers' Conference, xvi, 67–68, 99, 155
Bridges, Gordon B., 301
Brooker, Walter E., 113(photo), 113–14, 115, 120, 123, 137, 162, 172, 198, 339
Brosowsky, Alfred, 273
Brown, Arthur M., 110, 283, 370–71(n22), 408(n56)
Brown, Richard L., 52, 93(photo)
Brown, Ron, 221
Bruhn, Marilyn R., 122(photo)
Brush, Charles, 276
Bryan, Williams Jennings, 258–59
Bryant, Ernest C., 54, 328
Bryant, Ruth, 363–64(n40)
Buchika, Roger, 289
Buckley, Bill, 259
Burchard, John, 279
Burden, Doug, 287
Burns, Ralph, 220
Burrage, Mrs. Charles, 363–64(n40)
Butcher, Willard C., 77
Butler, Crispin O., 206(photo)
Butler, Sue, 281

Cady, Frank, 10, 326
Callanan, Tom, 279
Campaign for Middlebury College, 171–74
Candon, Kevin, 278
Career Counseling and Placement Office, 163

Carnegie Foundation: Advancement of Teaching, 275; General Education Board (GEB), 8–9, 17, 18, 27, 37, 42, 45, 357(n68); and a Vermont teachers college, 358(n72)
Carr, Reid, 107
Carr Hall, 107, 134
Carroll, Bruce, 325
Cartmill, Lee, 276
Cassidy, Mary H., 122(photo)
Cather, Willa, 64
Catholic students, 208–9
Catton, William B., 128, 129, 295, 312, 380(n26)
Centeno, Juan, 52, 59, 60, 99
Center for Northern Studies, 152
Central Intelligence Agency (CIA), 314–15
Chafee, Mark, 279
Challenge Campaign, 120–23, 122(photo), 375(n15)
Chalmers, John, 275
Chapel, required attendance, xx, 182, 264–67, 269
Ch'en, Ta-Tuan, 140, 141(photo)
Chinese School, 51, 140, 141(photo)
Chi Psi, 241, 393(n1)
Christopher, Jane Hyde, 418(n67)
Ciardi, John, 99
Civil rights movement, 201–3, 305
Clark, Chip, 279
Clark (Robert Sterling) Foundation, 169
Clarke, Philip A. C., 122(photo)
Class attendance, 51, 365(n18)
Classical studies, 152
Class traditions, xix, xx, 182, 249(photo), 249–54, 253(photo), 255(photo), 256
Claudon, Michael P., 153, 153(photo)
Cleary, Walter, 88
Clifford, Nicholas R., 129, 139, 158, 161, 310, 382–83(n64)
Cline, A. M., 370–71(n22)
Clough, John, 288
Coash, Beau, 276
Cockrell, Dale, 160
Coeducational issues, 17–20, 26, 27, 37–46, 133, 357(n68), 362(nn 2, 14), 363(nn 20, 32, 33); and fraternities, 225–26, 239, 240–42. *See also* Women
Coffrin, Albert W., 234
Coffrin Committee, 234–35, 302
Cole, Elbert "Mole," 88, 286
Cole, Harriet, 40

College Council, 299–300, 309–10, 312. *See also* Community Council

Collins, Edward Day, 16–17, 22–23, 62, 357(n58), 358(n2)

Colman, Richard, 138, 280

Coltrane Lounge, 204

Commencement, 342, 419(n76)

Commission on Student Life, 299–300

Committee on Foreign Languages, 141–42

Committee on Minority Concerns (Twilight Committee), 205

Committee on Reappointment, 415–16(n10)

Committee on the Arts, 153

Community Council, 238, 314, 315, 398(n123)

Comprehensive examinations, 50

Computer facilities, 166, 384(n90)

Computer science major, 379–80(n24)

Conron, John, 325

Cook, Juanita Pritchard, 330

Cook, Reginald "Doc," 53(photo), 93(photo), 134; and Armstrong, 119; career positions, 52–54, 67, 99; on Collins, 23; on Davison, 47–48, 62–63; on effects of World War II, 88; and faculty-Stratton dispute, 88, 370(n8), 370–71(n22); on Owen, 66; on Robert Frost's influence, 366(n57); on Stephen Freeman, 52; on student-faculty relations, 328; and track, 278

Cornwall, Richard, 315–16, 414(n89)

Cornwell, Ellsworth, 284

Council of Overseers, 337

Counseling and Human Relations Office, 163

Craig, Bill, 275

Cramphin, Doug, 276

Cridland, John, 275

Cross-country, 279, 281

Cruise, Robin, 233

Cubeta, Paul, 98, 98(photo), 101, 129, 132, 142, 143, 162, 224, 383(n66)

Cultural Conference, 77, 304, 305. *See also* Middlebury Conference

Cummings, Kevin, 277

Curriculum: and Armstrong presidency, 128, 129–32, 139–42, 377(nn 50, 52); and minorities, 390(n83); Moody presidency and, 48–51, 55–56, 364(n3), 365(n33), 366(n35); and Robison years, 150–57, 379(nn 9, 16); Stratton presidency and, 101–2; and World War I, 355(n26); during World War II, 76, 80. *See also* Departments/programs

Cushman, Curtis, 279

Dalai Lama, 259–60, 260(photo)

Dana, Charles A., 123

Dana Auditorium, 167

Dana (Charles A.) Foundation, 123, 126, 127, 137, 138, 169, 376(n33), 379–80(n24)

Dance program, 152, 153, 379–80(n24)

Daniels, Deb, 281

Davidson, David "Ben," 277

Davidson, Donald, 66

Davis Hall, 138

Davison, John P. "Sleepy," 326

Davison, Wilfred E. "Davy," 47–48, 52–54, 62–64, 63(photo)

Deane, Phil, 286

DeLisser, Robert, 111(photo)

de los Rios, Fernando, 59

Delta Delta Delta, 245, 400(n4)

Delta Kappa Epsilon, 230, 234–35, 237, 239, 393(n1), 398(n125), 399–400(n147)

Delta Tau Omega, 230

Delta Upsilon, 217, 238, 239, 344–45, 345(photo), 393(n1), 395–96(n48)

Den-Hartog, Dorcas, 281

Dennis, Alfred "Sonny," 277

Department of American Literature and Civilization, 153

Departments and programs: and Armstrong presidency, 128–29, 140–42; founding of summer programs, 2, 61–67, 67–68; graduate, 61, 99–101; and Moody presidency, 51–55, 56–61; physical education, 280; religion, 268 (*see also* Religion); and Robison years, 152–56, 379–80(n24), 380(n26), 381(n37); science program for minority high school students (SCIENS), 205, 206(photo); and Stratton presidency, 98–101. *See also* Bread Loaf School of English; Bread Loaf Writers' Conference; Curriculum; Foreign language schools; *individual departments*

de Visme, Henri P. Williamson, 29, 56–57, 62, 331, 366(n51)

DeVoto, Bernard, 68

DeWitt Clinton High School, 206–7
Dietter, Lawrence, 111(photo)
Diez-Canedo, Enrique, 59
Diplomacy in the '70s, 148–49
Dirks, Fred, 265
Distribution and foundations require-
    ment, 49–50, 131–32, 151, 377(n52),
    379(n9)
Document of Understanding: Fraternities,
    236
Donadio, Stephen, 383(n65)
Donahue, Dennis, 289
Donald, Bill, 251, 347
Donnan, Caroline, 211
Dorsey, Van, 279
Doubleday, Chip, 279
Douglass, Jane French, 331
Dragone, Allan R., 168, 168(photo),
    386(n122)
Drama. *See* Theater
Drama and Speech Center, 108, 109
Drug abuse, 237, 256, 262–63, 404(n84)
Dubzinski, Kathy, 281

East Asian studies, 152
Eaton, Gordie, 287, 288
Eaton, Walter Prichard, 66
Economics, 152–53
Eddy, Stanton S., 11
Edmunds, William, 339
Eggleston, Emily Proctor, 32, 361(nn 39,
    52)
Elder, John, 159
Emerson, John, 159, 161–62, 212, 238
Employment, student, 191–93
Endowment fund: and Armstrong presi-
    dency, 121, 135, 144, 378(n99); and
    faculty chairs, 137, 152–53, 172; and
    Moody presidency, 27, 30, 359–
    60(n17), 367(n2); and Robison presi-
    dency, 170, 174, 385(n106), 386(n115);
    and Stratton presidency, 114–15, 115–
    16; and Thomas presidency, 7–9, 15–17,
    20; in war/Depression years, 2, 91. *See
    also* Bequests; Fund-raising; Grants
Energy management, 169
English department, 52–54, 98, 152. *See
    also* Bread Loaf School of English
Enrollment: during Armstrong presi-
    dency, 121(table), 132, 135; and Bread
    Loaf School of English, 66, 67; and
    Bread Loaf Writers' Conference, 67–

68; by gender, 200(table) (*see also*
    Admissions, gender issues in); in lan-
    guage schools, 57, 58–59, 60, 99, 101,
    140, 141, 154(table), 154–55; minority,
    203, 204; during Moody presidency,
    28, 29(table); postwar growth in, 82,
    86, 87(table), 369(n3); and Thomas
    presidency, 7(table), 10–11, 15, 20;
    and tuition increases, 188; world
    wars/Depression years and, 2, 10–11,
    15, 73, 80. *See also* Recruitment
Environmental Quality (EQ), 313,
    413(n78)
Esquerra, Beatrix, 166
Etchells, Tim, 346–47
Ewing, Julie, 281
Expenditures, 177–78. *See also* Income,
    operating
Extracurricular activities, 247–49; faculty
    participation in, 331; movies/concerts/
    lectures, 258–60, 268, 318, 403(nn 68,
    71); student government, 295–96, 299–
    300, 301–3, 317, 411(nn 34, 40). *See
    also* Athletics; Political activism; Social
    life; Student clubs/organizations

Facilities. *See* Physical facilities
Faculty: appointment and tenure issues,
    142–44, 157–58, 160, 323–25, 382(n59),
    415(n9), 415–16(n10); Armstrong
    presidency, 119, 128–29, 145; Bread
    Loaf School of English, 64–67; and
    coeducational issue, 40–41; and col-
    lege governance, 323–25, 382(n52)
    (*see also specific committees*); and cur-
    riculum issues, 49–51, 130, 131–32,
    139–40, 142, 150, 151–52, 377(n52);
    endowed chairs for, 137, 152–53, 172;
    in foreign language schools, 56–
    60; and fraternities, 223, 235, 237,
    238–39, 241, 395–96(n48); minority,
    391(n90); Moody presidency, 24–
    25, 51–55, 71; political activism by,
    306–8, 309–13, 310(photo), 314, 316,
    413(n79), 414(n90); quality of, 322,
    415(n11); research and sabbaticals, 127,
    128, 157, 160, 322–23, 325–26, 332,
    382(n58), 416(nn 12, 14); Robison
    presidency, 157–60; social life, 326–28,
    416(n20); Stratton presidency, 87–94,
    97–99, 101–2, 116; Thomas presidency,
    20; women, 318, 319, 319(photo),

415(n105), 416(n18); work loads, 76–77, 322–23, 326, 360(n20); and World War II, 76–77, 79. *See also* Faculty-administration relations; Faculty salaries; Student-faculty relations

Faculty-administration relations, 323–25; and Armstrong presidency, 131, 376(n49); Lawrence-Stevens controversy, 12–14; and Robison presidency, 176–77; and Stratton presidency, 88–92, 97–98, 116, 270–71(n22), 370(nn 8, 9), 370–71(n22)

Faculty Advisory Council, 93(photo), 93–94, 97

Faculty Committee on Conference with the Trustees, 85, 88–92, 94, 324

Faculty Committee on Reappointment, 325

Faculty Committee on Tenure, 324

Faculty Council, 325

Faculty Educational Policy Committee, 101, 120, 130, 131–32, 150, 151, 325, 376(n49), 379(n16)

Faculty Finance and Long Range Planning Committee (FLRP), 159, 171

Faculty Research Fund, 128

Faculty salaries: Armstrong presidency, 127–28, 376(n33); Moody presidency, 27, 28, 359(n14); postwar/Stratton presidency, 87–88, 98, 109, 114–15, 116, 374(n48); Robison presidency, 157, 158–59, 381(n43); Thomas presidency, 7–8, 9; for women, 41; and World War II, 76, 90–91

Farrar, John, 67

Farrell, Billy, 192

Farrell, James T., 68

Father Went to College (Lee), xv, 95

Fayer, Mischa, 80, 99, 369(n46)

Federal Emergency Relief Administration, 192

Feise, Ernest, 56

Ferm, Robert, 157

Ferry, Arthur, 283

Field hockey, 281

Fife, Harry, 54

Film and video program, 152, 153

Financial aid: and Armstrong years, 392(n107); during interwar period, 193, 387(n24); and minority students, 204, 205; and Robison years, 171, 209–10; in Stratton years, 109, 115, 197–99, 388(n45). *See also* Employment, student

Fine arts and music: facilities for, 31(photo), 32, 107, 124–25, 125(photo), 165–66; and Robison presidency, 153–54; and Stratton presidency, 98

Fisher, Dorothy Canfield, 40, 64

Fisher, F. Lynn, 108(photo)

Fleischer, Ari, 244, 257–58

Fletcher, Paris, 290, 291

Fletcher Field House, 138, 280

FLRP. *See* Faculty Finance and Long Range Planning Committee

Football, 271–76, 272(photo), 274(photo)

Forbes, Wendy, 276, 293

Ford, Duane, 276

Ford Foundation, 115, 120–22, 123, 127, 376(n33)

Foreign language schools, xvi, 56–61, 68, 380–81(n30); under Armstrong, 140–42; facilities, 123–24; and Freeman, 51–52, 99; and Robison presidency, 154(table), 154–55. *See also specific language programs*

Foreign students, 207–8

Forest Hall, 30, 46

Fraser, Becky, 286

Fraternities, xix, xx, 182, 393(n1); community welfare projects, 344–45, 345(photo); and discriminatory clauses, 203, 208, 218–22; exclusion of women and, 225–26, 316–17, 398(n113); and housing/dining facilities, 28, 167, 219, 227–29, 230, 236, 360(n23), 395(n45), 397(n86), 398(n123); intergroup rivalry, 393(n3); 1915–1941 period, 216–18, 251; 1960–1990 decline of, 222–42, 395(n46), 395–96(n48), 397–98(n105); and student governance, 295, 394(n10); and town relations, 342–43; during World War II, 77

Freeman, Stephen A., 52(photo), 70(photo), 75(photo), 134, 350(photo); and Chinese School, 140; and comprehensive examinations, 50; on faculty social life, 327; fund-raising and Language Center, 123, 124; and Graduate Schools Abroad Program, 99–101; on language schools, 29–30, 56; on Moody, 22, 24; on Morize, 47, 57–58; positions and contributions, 51–52, 61, 73–74, 99, 132; and required chapel, 265–66; on Eleanor Ross, 44; and World War II, 2

French House, 29–30, 360(n24)
French School, 56–58, 58(photo), 59(photo), 99, 100(photo), 366(n51); and Graduate Schools Abroad Program, 100–1
Fritz, J. J., 284
Frost, Robert, 53(photo), 64, 68, 98(photo), 366(n57)
Fryberger, Bob, 292
Fryberger, Dates, 292–93
Fryberger, Jerry, 292
Fuller (George and Sybil) Foundation, 169
Fulton, Alexander Hamilton, 171–72, 172(photo)
Fulton, John Hamilton, 171–72
Fund-raising: by alumni, 339, 418(n67) (*see also* Alumni); and Armstrong presidency, 121–23, 126, 137–38, 375(n15); and Brooker, 113–14; and coeducational issues, 37; and Moody presidency, 26–27, 70, 359(n12); and Robison presidency, 169–74, 173(table); staff participation in, 334; during Stratton presidency, 104, 105, 108–9, 372(n5), 374(n38); during Thomas presidency, 8–9, 17, 354(nn 12, 13). *See also* Alumni; Endowment fund; Grants; Income, operating; Tuition and fees

Gale, Bob, 286
Gale, John, 286
Gallagher, "Rip," 291
Gannett Newspaper Foundation, 169
Garner, Dwight, 262
Garrison, John, 278
Gay, Leon S., 112(photo)
Gay, Robert M., 64, 65, 66, 67
Gay People at Middlebury, 315
Gay rights movement, 314–16, 414(nn 89, 90)
GEB. *See* Carnegie Foundation, General Education Board
Gender. *See* Admissions, gender issues in; Women
General Education Board (GEB). *See* Carnegie Foundation, General Education Board
Genovese, Bill, 276
Geographical diversity, 200–201, 201(table)
Geography department, 153, 156(photo), 380(n26)
Geonomics Institute, 153, 153(photo)

German Club (Deutscher Verein), 11
German School, 56, 60(photo), 72(photo), 99; and Graduate Schools Abroad Program, 101
Gifford, James, 18, 19, 31, 35, 38, 42–43
Gifford (James M.) Memorial Hall for Boys, 31
Gignac, Eddy, 286, 409(n75)
Ginevan, David W., 158, 162, 213, 214, 350(photo)
Given, Irene Heinz and John LaPorte, 137
Gleason, Robert, 151, 383(n65)
Golembeskie, John, 275
Golf, 278, 407(n27)
Good, Earle, 271
Good, Jon, 276
Goodreds, V. Spencer, 328
Goodrich, Leila, 108(photo)
Goodwin, Jim, 289
Goodwin, Verne, 287
Gorsuch, Renie Cox, 287
Governance, college: and faculty, 323–25, 382(n52); and staff issues, 334–36; and students, 245, 295–96, 299–300, 301–3, 317, 411(nn 34, 40). *See also* Administration and staff
Governor's Commission on Historical Preservation, 167
Gow, Debbie, 281
Graduate programs, 51–52, 61, 99–101, 154
Graduate Schools Abroad Program, 51–52, 99–101, 154
Graham, Mike, 289
Graham, Will, 279
Grants: and Armstrong presidency, 120–22, 123, 124, 126, 127, 137, 138, 376(n33); during Robison presidency, 157, 169, 173(table), 379(n14), 379–80(n24)
Gray, Rob, 214
Great Depression, 27–28, 45, 55, 65, 70, 192–94
Greene, David A., 153(photo)
Guarnaccia, Paul, 275
Guarnaccia, Samuel, 52, 190, 275, 363(n20)
Guillen, Jorge, 59
Gunderson, Finn, 289

Hackney, Fain, 277, 278
Hadley, Egbert C., 88, 112(photo), 133, 136(photo), 165, 165(photo)

Hadley House, 165, 338

Hall, Roger, 283

Hallquist, Stone, 273

Hamlin, Cyrus, 134

Hanson, Ann, 318

Hanson, Perry, 380(n26)

Hardy, Holzman, and Pfeiffer, 166, 167

Harnest, Grant, 126

Harrington, Vernon, 64, 323-24

Harris, Peter, 54

Hart, Tom, 277

Harvard Crimson, The, 198

Hayden, Minnie, 32, 361(n35)

Hayes, Lieutenant Governor, 310

Hayward, Susan, 302

Haywood, Edward B., 193

Hazeltine, Burt, 54, 188-90

Headley, Dorothy Tillapaugh, 252, 254

Health services: 1918 influenza epidemic, 11; Porter Hospital, 34-35; and Robison presidency, 163

Healy, Arthur, 80, 94, 98

Heffernan, Roy, 276, 279

Heinecken, Michael G., 276

Heinrichs, Waldo H., 88, 93(photo)

Heinz, W. C., 285

Henderson, Don, 286, 289

Hennessy, David, 279

Hepburn, A. Barton, 272; and Battell Trust, 16; bequests from, 8, 15, 17, 27, 359(n12), 359-60(n17); and women's college, 5, 18, 19-20, 37, 41

Hepburn Hall, 112, 188

Hibbert, Zella Cole, 331

Hicks, Granville, 304

Higher Education Facilities Act, 126

Hill, Lisa, 281

Hill, Red, 251

Hill, Robert, 139

Hillyer, Robert, 68

Hindes, Earl, 251

Hispanics, 187, 207

History department, 98

Hitchcock, Harold B., 93(photo)

Hoffman, Carole, 122(photo)

Hoffman, Randall, 275

Holden, Arthur John, Jr., 93-94

Holden, Frederika G. (Mrs. John Proctor), 29, 360(n24)

Holmes, Marion, 326, 331

Holmes, Robert, 284

Honor societies, 248, 250

Housing and Home Finance Agency, 110, 111-12

Housing and dining: and Armstrong presidency, 133-34, 138; coed, 300, 316-17, 411(n23), 414(n95); and fraternities, 28, 167, 219, 227-29, 230, 236, 360(n23), 368-69(n33), 395(n45), 397(n86), 398(n123); and Moody presidency, 28-31, 360(n23); off-campus, 419(n75); and Robison presidency, 163-64, 167; and Stratton presidency, 86, 106-7, 111-12; for women, 45-46, 316-17, 318-19

Howard, Frank E., 40

Howard, Walter E., 6(photo), 211

Howlett, Grayle, 279

Hoyt, Victoria, 281

Hubbard, Richard, 284-85

Hultgren, Tor, 278

Humanities: grants for, 376(n33); and Moody presidency, 52-54; and Robison presidency, 152-53, 154-56; and Stratton presidency, 98. *See also specific departments*

Human Relations Committee, 205-6

Humphrey, John, 277, 406(n23)

Hunt, J. David, 220

Hutchins, Jamie, 279

Ice hockey, 281, 290-93, 291(photo), 292(photo)

IFC. *See* Interfraternity Council

Ilgner, Tina, 281

Illick, J. Rowland, 156(photo)

Ilsley, Colonel and Mrs. Silas, 354(n12)

Income, operating, 20, 27-28, 135-37, 187-90. *See also* Tuition and fees

Independent study, 50-51, 129

Institute of Soviet Studies, 99

Interdisciplinary programs, 155-56

Interfraternity Council (IFC), 217, 224, 227, 228, 234, 346

International Institute for Economic Advancement, 153, 153(photo)

Italian School, 51, 60, 99; and Graduate Schools Abroad Program, 101

Jackson, Andy, 278

Jacobs, John, 289

Jacobs, Tom, 286, 287

James, Charles, 221

Japanese School, 51, 140-41, 154

Jeanrenaud, Paul Louis, 56–57
Jenkins, Rev. Marshall, 267
Jenkins, William Arron, 260(photo)
Jeremiah Atwater Club, 224, 396(n53)
Jewish students, 208–9, 268, 268(photo),
    405(n116)
Jewish studies, 152
Jin, April, 336
Johnson, Rev. Robert, 267
Johnson (Christian A.) Endeavor Founda-
    tion, 124, 137, 169
Johnson (Christian A.) Memorial Build-
    ing, 124–25, 125(photo), 166, 169
Jones, Joe, 286
Jones, Robert A., 153
Joyce, Hewette E., 66, 67
Junior Fellows Program, 251–52,
    402(n60)

Kailey, Paul, 286
Kaleidoscope, 317
Kappa Delta Rho, 218(photo), 239, 241,
    393(n1)
Kappa Kappa Gamma, 245, 400(n4)
Karin, Mike, 292
Kasper, Joseph, 14, 104, 362(n14)
Keillor, Garrison, 259
Kelleher, Kevin, 277
Kelley, Frank, 163–64, 214
Kelley, Stillman, 291
Kelly, Elizabeth Baker ("Ma"), 133, 165,
    226, 287, 296–97, 297(photo), 299,
    300
Kelly, John "Red," 384(n84)
Kelley ("Red") Ski Trail, 164–65, 289,
    384(n84)
Kemp, Eric, 279
Kemp, Megan, 281, 282
Kenan (William R.) Charitable Trust, 137
Kenyon, Susan, 309(photo)
Kersting, Brown, and Company, 121, 137
King Commission, 203–4
Kirby, William H., 122(photo)
Kirk, John, 275
Kirk Alumni House and Conference
    Center, 164, 170, 349
Kirkpatrick, Steve, 279
Klevenow, Marshall, 273
Knapp, Clara Blanche, 319(photo), 330
Knox, Edward C., 52(photo), 382(n63),
    383(n65)
Kovner, Peter, 278

Kresge Foundation, 138, 169
Kruesi, Paul John, 110
Kuharich, Bill, 279
Kujovich, Gilbert, 299

Lacrosse, 279, 281
Ladds, Helen, 281
LaForce, Arnold, 137, 146, 158
Lahdenpera, Peter, 287
Lamberti, Marjorie, 319(photo)
Landon, H. C. Robbins, 153
Lang, Fred P., 105–6, 114, 133, 372(n8)
Lang, Ted, 122, 271
Lathrop, Steve, 289
Latreille, Phil, 292
Lawrence, Henry W., 12–14
Lawson, G. Thomas, 277
Leary, Caroline, 281
Leave policy. *See* Research and sabbati-
    cals
Lee, W. Storrs, xv, 70(photo), 96(photo);
    and alumni newsletter, 340; on class
    traditions, 243, 250–51; on frater-
    nities, 216, 218, 219; on interwar
    years, 190, 191–92, 264, 321; and
    Moody presidency, 368(nn 17, 18); and
    Stratton-faculty dispute, 85–86, 88, 91,
    94–97; on vocational education, 55
Leeds, "Bud," 162
Leng, Russ, 383(n65), 395(n46)
Levine, David O., 1
Liberal arts emphasis, 26, 48, 55–56, 74,
    80
Liberal Club, 304
Liberty Endowment Drive, 8–9, 354(nn
    12, 13)
Lick, Mary, 280, 282
Lieder, Nick, 263
Light, Timothy, 178–79
Liljenstein, Swede, 275
Lincoln College, Oxford, 155
Lindholm, Karl, 162, 207, 222, 270, 277
Linguistics, 379–80(n24)
Literary studies, 152
Loans, federal, 110, 111–12
Long, Sue, 288
Longwell, Samuel, 54
Lopez, Donald, 259
Loveys, Jim, 276
Lupien, Tony, 277

MacAusland, Edie, 281

Mackey, Peter, 276
MacLeish, Archibald, 68
Maddox, James, 383(n66)
Mahaney, Kevin, 279
Mahon, Tom, 276
Malstrom, Vincent, 380(n26)
Markham, Edwin, 64
Marks, John, 278
Marquand, John, 68
Mason, Mrs. Maud O., 330
Mathematics, 54
May Days Festival, 256–57, 257(photo), 333
McCardell, John M., Jr., 146, 159, 160, 161, 161(photo)
McCollum, Ann, 281
McCullough Gymnasium, 167
McFarland, Raymond, 9, 10
McGee, David, 119
McKenna, John, 128
McKinney, Arnold, 204, 234
McLaughlin, William, 273
McLeod, Jim, 264
McLeod, Rob, 289
McMenamy, Tara, 288
McNealus, Sara, 287
McNulty, Joe, 288
Mead, John, 356(n51)
Mead Chapel, 107, 168, 168(photo)
Mellon (Andrew) Foundation, 157, 169
Memorial Field House, 104–5, 106(photo), 107, 109, 138, 164, 282, 372(n6), 384(n82)
Memorial Fund campaign, 104, 105, 372(n5)
Meredith, L. Douglas, 118, 119, 164
Merlino, Camillo, 60
Michaud, Tim, 166
Middlebury (town). *See* Town-gown relations
Middlebury Alliance, 346
Middlebury Awareness Development (MAD), 302, 411(n36)
Middlebury Campus: and coeducational issues, 36, 39; on curriculum and quality, 47, 51, 151; on faculty-student relations, 328, 329, 330; and football, 271–72, 273, 275–76; and fraternities, 215, 222, 223, 224, 226, 227, 229, 231, 240; and Lawrence-Stevens controversy, 13, 14; on parietal rules, 298; and political issues, 70–71, 78(photo), 201–2, 304, 306, 308, 315, 320, 412(n44); on religion and required chapel, 263, 266, 269; and social life/extracurricular activities, 250, 256, 258, 259, 262; and sororities, 246; on student employment, 192; on student government, 411(n34); and town-gown relations, 343; and tuition increases, 188, 194, 214; and winter sports, 270, 283, 285; women on staff of, 317
Middlebury College Magazine, 340
Middlebury Conference, 317, 412(n45). *See also* Cultural Conference
Middlebury Gay Lesbian Straight Alliance, 316
Middlebury Inn, 348
Middlebury Lesbian and Gay Alliance (MLGA), 315
Middlebury Register, 12
Middnet, 338–39
Miesse, A. Gordon, 220
Milliken, Gertrude Cornish, 133, 169, 363–64(n40)
Mills, J. Layng, 29
Milner, David, 214
Miner, Rich, 278
Minorities, 187, 201–7, 390(nn 81, 83); and fraternities, 219, 220–21; and sororities, 247. *See also* African Americans; Religious minorities
Minority Advisory Group, 205
Mirrieless, Edith, 64
Mitchell, Don, 405(n116)
Miyaji, Hiroshi, 140–41, 382(n63)
Monk, Ingrid H., 78(photo)
Moody, Charlotte Hull, 337–38
Moody, Dwight L., 14, 23, 245–46
Moody, Paul D., 2, 3, 23–26; and athletics, 273, 274(photo), 274–75; and campus religion, 263, 264–65, 404(n99); and coeducational issue, 19–20, 36–46; curriculum under, 48–51, 55–56; and extracurricular activities, 249; and faculty, 24–25, 51–55, 322, 327(photo); fund-raising under, 26–28; and great flood of 1927, 347; and increasing tuition, 186, 188, 193; physical facilities under, 28–35; and presidency position, 336; resignation, 69–73, 367(n13), 368(n17); student relations, 412(n44); summer programs/Bread Loaf, 56–68
More, Paul Elmer, 119
Moreno-Lacalle, Julian, 58–59, 61

Morey, David, 274, 283, 330
Morize, Andre, 47, 57-58, 58(photo), 61, 99
Morrison, Theodore, 66, 67, 68, 98(photo), 99
Morse, Terry, 289
Morton, John, 288
Mountain Club, 248, 248(photo), 254, 284, 401(n28)
Moynihan, Daniel Patrick, 77
Mudge, Ray, 191
Muller, John, 31
Munford, Howard, 24, 25(photo), 54, 145, 145(photo), 224, 324
Munford, Marian, 24
Munroe, Charles A., 32
Munroe Hall, 32-33, 134
Murdock, Kenneth, 64
Music. *See* Fine arts and music
Music Practice Studio, 31(photo), 32
Muslim students, 208, 209
Myhre, Ralph O., 278, 289

National Endowment for the Humanities, 169
National Science Foundation, 169
National Youth Administration (NYA), 192
Natural disasters and fires, 65, 65(photo), 107-8, 311; great flood of 1927, 347
Natural sciences: facilities for, 110-11, 125-27, 128(photo), 373(n29); grants for, 376(n33); library for, 164, 384(n80); molecular biology major, 379-80(n24); and Moody presidency, 54; and Robison presidency, 156, 381(n37); and Stratton presidency, 98
Neff, Mike, 166
Nelson, Allen, 42, 363(n33)
Nelson, David, 277
Nelson, Margaret, 319
Nelson, Walter "Duke," 275, 276, 291, 292(photo), 293
Neuberger, Fred F., 133, 195, 198, 199, 201, 202(photo), 286, 287, 289
Neuse, Werner, 52
Newell, Lucy, 294, 301
New England Association, 382(nn 52, 58, 59)
New Republic, 13
New York Times, 151, 221, 286
Nicholas, Roger, 279
Nicholson, David, 278

Noble, June Brogger, 69, 78, 219, 296, 304
Noonan, Mike, 279
Noonan, Ray, 283
Northern studies, 152
North Hall, 167
Novotny, Joseph, 273
Nucleus Fund, 121-22, 137
Nugent, F. W., 279
Nuovo, Victor, 238, 383(n65)

Oates, Whitney J., 119
O'Brien, G. Dennis, 118; and antiwar protests, 310; career positions, 128-29, 132, 376(n40); and fraternities, 225, 229, 230, 231-33, 397-98(n105); and parietal rules, 294, 298-99, 411(n19); on Rikert, 162; and sororities, 247; and student diversity, 203, 204, 208; on tenure issues, 143
O'Brien, Jane Margaret, 318, 383(n65)
O'Connell, Joan, 383(n72)
O'Connor, Tom, 276
Old Chapel, 134, 167
Old Dominion Foundation, 127, 376(n33)
175th Anniversary Campaign, 137-38
Osgood, Charles Grovesnor, 119
Outing Club, 282-83, 401(n28)
Owen, Harry G., 52, 66-67, 70(photo), 368(n18)

Pack, Robert, 25(photo)
Painter House, 349-50
Papke, Aloys, 273
Paquette, Andre, 142
Parietal rules, 296-301, 317, 410(n5), 411(n19); and dances, 255-56, 402(n56)
Parker, David, 243-44
Parsons, Chris, 279
Parton, George, 163, 300
Partridge, Frank C., 16
Pattee, Fred Lewis, 64
Paynter, Dorothy S., 346(photo)
Pearsons Hall, 111
Peel, Roger, 139, 142, 380-81(n30), 383(n65)
Pennsylvania State College, 20, 21
Pentkowski, David, 277, 278
Pepin, Arthur D., 164
Performing arts, 153. *See also* Dance program; Theater
Perine, Gordie, 198, 339, 421(n115)
Perry, Ted, 383(n65)

Peskin, Bob, 421(n115)

Peters, Joan, 325

Petersen, Max, 290–91

Peterson, Bruce, 383(n65); and antiwar protests, 312; and college planning, 139, 159, 171, 176–77; and fraternities, 231, 342–43; and winter term controversy, 151

Peterson, Jon, 276

Pew Memorial Trust, 379(n14)

Phi Beta Phi, 400(n2)

Phi Kappa Tau (PKT), 221, 230

Philians, 393(n8)

Phillips, Harry, 285

Phillips, John, 285

Phi Mu, 219, 245, 400(n4)

Phi Sigma (Zeta Psi), 222

Physical education, 279–80, 407(n35)

Physical facilities, 2; and Armstrong presidency, 123–27, 133–34, 137–38; athletics, 104–6, 106(photo), 107, 109–10, 138, 164–65, 176, 280, 281–82, 293, 386(n122); at Bread Loaf, 65–66, 66–67; computers, 166, 384(n90); and fraternities, 229–30, 232, 236 (*see also* Fraternities); and Moody presidency, 27, 28–35, 45–46; and Robison presidency, 164–69, 386(n122); Snow Bowl, 286, 289, 290, 373(n24); during Stratton presidency, 104(photo), 104–13, 116, 372(n6), 373(nn 21, 22, 29), 373–74(n34), 374(n36); and Thomas presidency, 6–7, 20

Pi Beta Phi, 245, 400(n4)

Pickard, Robert, 71

Pitou, Penny, 287

Plante, Michelle, 281

Playhouse, 108, 108(photo)

Political activism: CIA recruitment and gay rights, 314–16; civil rights movement, 201–3, 305; at Middlebury, 295, 303–5, 320; South African apartheid, 313–14; Vietnam antiwar movement, 305–13

Pope, Phil, 276

Porter, Esther, 35

Porter, William H., 34–35

Porter Hospital, 34–35, 163, 361(nn 52, 57)

Porter Medical Center Corporation, 35

Pratt, Fletcher, 68

Proctor, Mrs. Fletcher D., 17

Proctor, Redfield, 71, 88, 110, 409(n75)

Proctor Hall, 106, 110, 110(photo), 235, 414(n95)

Protests, 412(n56); and CIA recruitment, 315; against college policies, 178, 179(photo), 213–14, 301–3, 411(n36); against South African apartheid, 314; tuition, 178, 179(photo), 213–14; Vietnam antiwar, 305–6, 309–13, 310(photo), 413(n76). *See also* Political activism

Prouty, David, 316

Publicity, 176, 272, 286

Punderson, Frank, 278, 407(n29)

Punderson, Ingred, 288

Radical Education Action Project (REAP), 313

Rafuse, Dorothy, 370(n8)

Rafuse, Robert, 88, 90, 370(n8)

Ransom, John Crowe, 68

Recitation Hall, burning of, 311, 311(photo)

Recruitment: and adequate athletic facilities, 105; alumni involvement in student, 201, 338, 418(n63); coeducational issue and student, 38; faculty, 127, 128–29, 157, 322; and maintaining socioeconomic diversity, 210–12; of minority faculty, 391(n90); and minority students, 204–7; of quality male students, 197–200

Reed, Pamela, 287

Reed, Paul "Rat," 289

Reichert, Rabbi Victor, 268(photo)

Reinertsen, Laura, 139

Religion: shifting importance on campus of, 263–69, 404(n99); and Stratton presidency, 98; student affiliation, 392(n106). *See also* Chapel, required attendance

Religious minorities, 208–9, 405(n116); and fraternities, 219–21

Report of the Admissions Long-Range Planning Committee, 205, 207

Report of the Visiting Committee on Literature, 322–23

Research and sabbaticals, 127, 128, 157, 160, 322–23, 325–26, 332, 382(n58), 416(nn 12, 14)

Research Corporation, 127, 376(n33)

Reserve Officers' Training Corps (ROTC), 305–6, 307–8, 309(photo), 412(nn 51, 57), 413(n64)

Reuman, Robert E., 220, 221
Reynolds, Thomas Hedley: career positions, 98, 132; and civil rights movement, 203; and college planning, 126, 127; and curriculum reform, 129; on faculty issues, 321; and fraternities, 215, 224, 225, 226, 227, 242; and Junior Fellows Program, 251-52; on parietal rules, 298-99
Rice, Margaret "Tib" Moody, 337-38
Riegelman, Herbert, 273
Righi, Paul, 277
Rikert, Carroll, Jr., 120, 132, 133(photo), 136, 162, 233-34
Rikert Ski Touring Center, 165, 289
Riley, David, 201, 389-90(n66)
Robison, Olin C., 82, 83, 147-50, 148(photo), 165(photo), 174-79; administration under, 160-64; and curriculum issues, 150-57; and development issues, 348-49; and faculty, 157-60, 322, 325-26, 415-16(n10); and fraternities, 234, 238, 239; fund-raising, 169-74; and gender issues, 319, 320; physical facilities under, 164-69; presidency position under, 337; and South African apartheid, 314; and student body diversity issues, 185-86, 201, 205, 206, 207, 210-14; student relations, 301-3
Robison, Sylvia, 338
Rockefeller, Steven, 161-62, 237, 259, 280
Rockefeller Foundation, 99, 169
Ross, Don, 290
Ross, Eleanor (Mrs. John Thomas), 21, 44-45, 91, 134, 256, 296, 318
Ross, James D., 350(photo)
Ross, Malcolm, 290
Ross, Stewart, 286, 373(n22), 409(n75)
ROTC. *See* Reserve Officers' Training Corps
Rowland, R. L., 284
Rubottom, George, 278
Russian School, 51, 80, 99, 154, 369(n46)
Russian Soviet studies, 379-80(n24)
Russian students, 207-8

Sage, Mrs. Russell, 15
Salinas, Pedro, 59
Sampson, Juliet, 268(photo)
Sanford, Myron, 251
Sargent, Tiffany Nourse, 345

Sass, Steve, 279
SATC, 11, 355(n26)
Saul, George, 383(n65)
Saunders, Richard, 154
Schine, Robert S., 268(photo)
Schlatter, Arthur, 286
Schmidt, Bruno, 54, 370-71(n22)
Scholarships. *See* Financial aid
Science Center, 125-27; library, 164, 384(n80)
SCIENS. *See* Departments/programs
Scott, Rev. Charles P., 98, 103, 117, 162, 267(photo), 267-68
Seixas, Vic, 275
Service Building, 373-74(n34)
Sharp, Dallas Lore, 64
Shattuck, Susan, 299
Sheehan, Robert "Bobo," 286, 287
Shelvey, Cy, 283
Shepley, Bulfinch, Richardson, and Abbott, 134
Shipler, David, xv
Sigma Kappa, 245, 247, 400(n4)
Sigma Phi Epsilon, 221, 238, 393(n1)
Sills, Beverly, 172(photo)
Simmons, Carleton, 291
Skiing, xvii, 282-90, 288(photo), 293, 408(n56), 409(nn 62, 75)
Ski jump, 283-84, 285(photo), 286, 409(n75)
Ski Touring Center, Carroll and Jane Rikert, 165, 289
Sloan (Alfred P.) Foundation, 126, 127, 376(n33)
Smith, Anne Freeman, 40
Smith, David K., 190, 193, 266
Smith, Leslie, 288
Smith, W. Wyman, 283
Sno' Time for Learning, 286
Snow Bowl, 282, 289-90, 409(n75); and Battell bequest, xiv; facilities, 109, 165, 286, 373(n24); 1950 hurricane, 108
Soccer, 278-79, 281, 407(n29)
Social-dining units (SDUs), 134, 227-29, 349. *See also* Housing/dining
Social life, xix-xx; and alcohol/drug abuse, 260-63; annual events for alumni, 339-40; and class traditions, 249-54; dances and annual events, 254-57, 257(photo), 401(n33); faculty, 326-28, 416(n20); and fraternities, 215, 216-17, 222, 225-26, 229, 237-38; and language schools, 61; and

parietal rules, 296–301; for women, 316–20; and World War II, 77. *See also* Extracurricular activities

Social sciences, 54, 98, 365(n29)

Socioeconomic diversity, 187–90, 194–200, 209–12

Sommers, Paul, 160

Sororities, xx, 182, 244–47, 400(nn 4, 7); community welfare projects, 344; and discriminatory clauses, 203, 219, 247

South African apartheid, 313–14, 413(nn 79, 81), 413–14(n83)

Spanish School, 58–60, 80, 99; and Graduate Schools Abroad Program, 101

Sparks, Kimberly, 129, 141

Special Committee on Attitudes toward Gender, 319–20, 415(n105)

Spencer, Fred, Jr., 312

Spencer, John, 161

Spooner, Esther, xv

Squash, 281

Staff Council, 335, 336

Stafford, Madelyn, 340(photo)

Stafford, Robert, 340(photo)

Starr, Cornelius V., 109, 373(n25)

Starr, M. Allen, 34, 361(n47)

Starr (C. V.) Foundation, 137, 152

Starr Hall, 107

Starr Library, 33(photo), 33–34, 112–13, 164, 361(n47), 374(nn 36, 37); adequacy of, 383–84(n78), 416(n12); computerizing, 168; holdings, 128, 376(n38)

STARTUP (Students Against the Rise in Tuition and Unjust Policies), 214

Steele, Harriet Hopkins, 40

Stegner, Wallace, 68

Stern, Claudia, 288

Stevens, James G., 13

Stewart Hall, 111–12

Stitt, Peter, 325

Stoddard Charitable Trust, 169

Stratton, Samuel S., 3, 75(photo), 82, 86, 112(photo), 116(photo); and faculty, 88–92, 97–98, 116, 322, 324, 370(nn 8, 9), 370–71(n22); and Faculty Advisory Council, 93(photo), 97; and fraternities/sororities, 230, 246; fund-raising campaigns, 109, 114–15; and Lee dispute, 94–97; and physical facilities, 103, 105, 289; presidency during World War II, 74–76, 79–80; and

publicity, 286; and required chapel, 267; retirement, 115–17, 374(n53); and ROTC, 306; and student politics, 305; on student quality and financial aid, 185, 194, 196, 197–99

Streeter, Les, 287

Stroebe, Lilian, xvi, 56

Student(s): alcohol/drugs and, 260–63; class traditions, 249–54, 256; clubs and organizations, 248–49, 254–56 (*see also* specific groups); and coeducational issue, 39–40, 362(n14); and curriculum issues, 51, 139–40, 151–52; employment for, 191–93 (*see also* Financial aid); foreign, 207–8; and gender ratio, 194–200, 200(table), 388(n34), 389(n59); geographic diversity, 200–201, 201(table); honor code for, 332, 417(n44); minority, 187, 201–7; and parietal rules, 296–301, 410(n5) (*see also* Parietal rules); political activism, 201–203, 303–16, 310(photo), 311(photo), 320, 412(nn 44, 57), 413(nn 76, 78, 81) (*see also* Protests); quality of, 186–90, 194–200, 209–12, 365(n19), 389(nn 52, 57); and religion, 208–9, 263–69, 392(n106); and student union, 166–67; and town relations, 341–47, 420(n91). *See also* Extracurricular activities; Fraternities; Sororities; Student-administration relations; Student-faculty relations; Student government; Women

Student Action Assembly, 304, 305

Student-administration relations, 301–3, 330, 412(n44); and fraternities, 223, 228, 232–33, 235, 238, 242

Student Association (SA), 299, 317

Student clubs and organizations, 10–11, 248–49, 256, 401(n28); community welfare projects by, 343–47; and dances, 254–56; sports, 279, 281, 407(n32). *See also* Fraternities; Social life; Sororities

Student Curriculum Committee, 51

Student-faculty relations, 328–33, 416(n26); and fraternities, 238–39

Student Forum, 314

Student government, 295–96, 299–300, 301–3, 411(nn 34, 40); and women, 245, 317

Student Investigating Committee (SIC), 132

Student Life Committee, 295, 298. *See also* Ad Hoc Committee on Student Life; Commission on Student Life
Student publications, 248, 317. *See also Middlebury Campus*
Students against Apartheid, 314
Students' Army Training Corps (SATC), 11, 355(n26)
Students Concerned about Middlebury (SCAM), 303, 398(n123)
Student Senate, 247, 299, 300, 419(n75)
Student services, 163–64, 300, 383(n72), 414–15(n102)
Student Sex Information Service, 300
Student union, 106, 110, 110(photo), 166–67
Summer Work Program, 333
Sunderland, Edwin S. S., 107, 109, 123, 373(n22), 374(n38)
Sunderland Language Center, 123–24, 167
Swallow, Peter, 289
Swett, Phelps, 370–71(n22)
Swift, Charles M., 12
Swift, Jessica Stewart, 165(photo)
Swimming, 279, 281
Swimming pool, 109–10

Talladega College, 202
Task Force on Student Social and Residential Life, 239–40
Tauber, Hank, 289
Tennis, 278, 281
Tenure/appointment issues, 142–44, 157–58, 160, 322, 323–25, 382(n59), 415(n9), 415–16(n10)
Terhune, Jim, 261
Theater, 99, 100(photo), 153
Theta Chi, 230, 342–43, 393(n1)
Thomas, Herb, 287
Thomas, John, 2, 6(photo), 20–21, 358(n77); and board of trustees, 71, 337; and coeducational issue, 17–20; and extracurricular activities, 243, 247–48, 406(n13); and faculty, 12–14, 322, 323, 324; fund-raising efforts, 7–9, 14–17, 26–27, 354(nn 12, 13); and language schools, 56, 59, 62; physical facilities under, 6–7; presidency position under, 336; on required chapel, 269; and student quality, 185, 186, 187–88; and student relations, 182, 330; and World War I, 9–12
Thompson, John, 277

Thomsen, Jeff, 279
Tillinghast, Pardon, 332(photo)
"To College with a Purpose," 55
Tolley, Howard B., Jr., 306
Tomas, Tomas Navarro, 59
Tower, Alice, 288
Town-gown relations, 341–50, 419(n75), 420(n91), 421(n115); and fraternities, 223; and Moody presidency, 71–72, 367(n13); and Porter Hospital, 35
Town's College: Middlebury College, 1800–1915, The (Stameshkin), xvii–xviii
Townsend, Ike, 286
Track, 278, 281
Trustee Committee on Conference, 88–92, 131, 325
Trustee Committee on Undergraduate Life, 315
Trustees. *See* Board of trustees
Tuition and fees: and Armstrong presidency, 127, 135, 136–37; in attracting quality students, 186, 187–90, 199; effect on socioeconomic diversity, 194 (*see also* Socioeconomic diversity); interwar years, 15, 17; during Moody presidency, 28, 387(n5); and Robison presidency, 158, 170–71, 178, 179(photo), 212–14, 213(table); and Stratton presidency, 114, 374(n44)
Turner, A. Richard, 129, 132, 139, 376(n40)
"21" Committee, 261
Twilight, Alexander, 165
Twilight Committee (Committee on Minority Concerns), 205
Twilight Hall, 165

Undergraduate Association, 14, 295
Undergraduate Life Committee (board of trustees), 302, 303, 314
Unsworth, Ray, 286
Untermeyer, Louis, 64, 68
Upson, Mrs. Marjory Wright, 363–64(n40)
Upson, William Hazlett, 68
Uyrus, Dave, 276

V-12 unit, 12, 76, 77, 79, 79(photo), 368(n29)
Vail, Theodore, 15
Valentine, Jack, 286
Valley Voice, 349
Van Winkle, A. Keith, 278

Van Winkle, W. Davis, 278
Vaughn, Paul, 348
Vermont, 19, 27–28
Vermont Volunteer Militia, 10, 10(photo)
Vietnam antiwar movement, 305–13, 310(photo), 412(n57), 413(n76)
Vigneron, Marcel, 59(photo)
Vins, Georgi, 176
Virtue, Ted, 276
Vocational education, 55–56, 366(n35)
Volkert, Erie, 52, 99
VonBerg, Karin, 281
Voter, Perley, 134, 283, 284, 370–71(n22), 409(n75)
Voter Hall, 134, 166

Walker, Henry Freeman, 15
Walsh, Chaplain John, 208, 392(n106)
Ward, Craig, 289
Warner Greenhouse, 110–11, 111(photo)
Warner Science, 126, 134, 167
Warren, Erwin, 387(n12)
War Service Committee, 11
Waterbury, Vermont, 347
Webb, J. Davis, 278
Wenthe, Marty, 279
Wheaton, Ruth R., 78(photo)
Wheeler, Joseph, 374(n36)
Whicher, George, 64
White, Raymond, 368(n29)
Whittemore, Fred, 256, 347
Whittemore, Hal, 291
Wiley, Edgar "Cap," 8, 339, 372(n5)
Wiley, Gordon, 251
Wiley, Pruda Harwood, 339
Wilks, Mrs. Hetty Sylvia Ann Howard Green, 114
Willard (Emma) Foundation, 15
Williams, Stanley, 62
Willis, Mrs. Hazel McLeod, 363–64(n40)
Wilson, James Southall, 64
Winter Carnival, 77, 254, 256, 283, 284, 284(photo), 288(photo), 331, 408(n57)
Wissler, Benjamin F., 54, 128(photo)
WMCR, 248–49
Women: applicant quality, 186, 194, 196,

198–200; and athletics, 280–82, 284, 286, 287–88, 288(photo), 293, 317, 319, 408(n46); campus life for, xix–xx, 182, 296–301, 316–20; class traditions for, 252–53, 253(photo); facilities for, 29–30, 38, 45–46, 106–7, 111, 318–19; faculty, 40–41, 318, 319, 319(photo), 415(n105), 416(n118); and fraternities, 225–26, 316–17, 398(n113); president's wife, 337–38; and World War II, 77, 78(photo), 80. *See also* Women's College of (at) Middlebury
Women's Advisory Committee, 44, 363–64(n40)
Women's Civics Club, 11
Women's College of (at) Middlebury: attempts for separate, 17–20, 26, 27, 37–46, 357(n68), 362(n2), 363(nn 20, 32, 33); establishment of, 43–46
Women's Forum, 344
Women's studies major, 379–80(n24)
Women's Union, 238
Womyn, 318
Wonnacott, Erica, 133, 162, 163(photo), 234, 257
Woodward, Dorothy Wunner, 328
World War I, 9–11, 56, 335(nn 18, 26)
World War II, 11–12, 70, 73–80, 304
Wright, Charles Baker, 14, 62, 109, 357(n58)
Wright, Mrs. Philip Anson, 107
Wright, Stanley, 197–98, 372(n5)
Wright Theater, 109, 373(n22)
WRMC, 248–49, 257

YMCA, 11
Youngman, Robert P., 122(photo)
Youngman, William, 386(n122)
Youths Opportunity for Understanding (Y.O.U.), 203, 204, 390(n78)
YWCA, 11, 263, 343

Zabriskie, John, 276
Zaccaro, John, 262
Zelermyer, Gerald B., 405(n116)
Zeta Psi, 237, 398(n123)

UNIVERSITY PRESS OF NEW ENGLAND publishes books under its own imprint
and is the publisher for Brandeis University Press, Dartmouth College, Middlebury College Press, University of New Hampshire, University of Rhode Island,
Tufts University, University of Vermont, Wesleyan University Press, and Salzburg
Seminar.

LIBRARY OF CONGRESS CATALOGING-IN-PUBLICATION DATA
Stameshkin, David M. (David Mitchell)
    The strength of the hills : Middlebury College, 1915-1990 / by
David M. Stameshkin.
        p.   cm.
    Includes bibliographical references (p.   ) and index.
    ISBN 0-87451-732-X (alk. paper)
        1. Middlebury College—History.   I. Title.
LD3311.M32S72   1995
378.743'5—dc20   95-4799